Advanced Topics in Term Rewriting

Springer
New York
Berlin
Heidelberg
Barcelona
Hong Kong
London
Milan
Paris
Singapore
Tokyo

Enno Ohlebusch

Advanced Topics in Term Rewriting

With 43 Figures

Springer

Enno Ohlebusch
Research Group in
Practical Computer Science
Faculty of Technology
University of Bielefeld
P.O. Box 10 01 31
D-33501 Bielefeld
Germany
enno@TechFak.Uni-Bielefeld.DE

Library of Congress Cataloging-in-Publication Data
Ohlebusch, Enno.
Advanced topics in term rewriting / Enno Ohlebusch.
p. cm.
Includes bibliographical references and index.

1. Rewriting systems (Computer science) I. Title.
QA267 .O36 2001
005.13'1—dc21 2001049270

Printed on acid-free paper.

ISBN 978-1-4419-2921-1

Production managed by Michael Koy; manufacturing supervised by Erica Bresler.
Photocomposed copy produced from the author's LaTeX files.

Printed in the United States of America.

9 8 7 6 5 4 3 2 1

Springer-Verlag New York Berlin Heidelberg
A member of BertelsmannSpringer Science+Business Media GmbH

To Imke, Miriam, and Silvia

Preface

Term rewriting techniques are applicable in various fields of computer science: in software engineering (e.g., equationally specified abstract data types), in programming languages (e.g., functional-logic programming), in computer algebra (e.g., symbolic computations, Gröbner bases), in program verification (e.g., automatically proving termination of programs), in automated theorem proving (e.g., equational unification), and in algebra (e.g., Boolean algebra, group theory). In other words, term rewriting has applications in practical computer science, theoretical computer science, and mathematics. Roughly speaking, term rewriting techniques can successfully be applied in areas that demand efficient methods for reasoning with equations.

One of the major problems one encounters in the theory of term rewriting is the characterization of classes of rewrite systems that have a desirable property like confluence or termination. If a term rewriting system is *confluent*, then the normal form of a given term is unique. A *terminating* rewrite system does not permit infinite computations, that is, every computation starting from a term must end in a normal form. Therefore, in a system that is both terminating and confluent every computation leads to a result that is unique, regardless of the order in which the rewrite rules are applied. This book provides a comprehensive study of termination and confluence as well as related properties.

Several survey articles about term rewriting have been available for quite a while, and more recently introductory textbooks on the subject have been published. However, only readers versed in the German language can appreciate the books of Avenhaus [Ave95] and Bündgen [Bün98]. The only

English language textbook is that of Baader and Nipkow [BN98]. In contrast to these three books, the book at hand deals with several important topics in term rewriting that go beyond the scope of an introductory textbook.

Overview

Chapter 1 provides some motivating examples.

In Chapter 2, the fundamental properties of rewrite systems are described on an abstract level. Abstract rewriting comprises several kinds of rewriting like term, string, graph, and conditional rewriting. Thus a repetition of similar definitions and concepts can be avoided by stating them once on an abstract level. The first three sections cover standard material. The last two sections deal with abstract reduction modulo an equivalence relation.

The basic notions of term rewriting that are needed in this book will be introduced in Chapter 3.

Chapter 4 is devoted to confluence and related properties. It reviews the two most important methods for proving confluence: (1) proving termination and the joinability of all critical pairs and (2) imposing syntactic restrictions like orthogonality.

Chapter 5 mainly deals with methods for proving termination of term rewriting systems. The first two sections cover well-known results and standard techniques like polynomial interpretations and recursive path orderings. The subsequent sections are devoted to newer techniques. First, the termination hierarchy is introduced, and then the dependency pair method is reviewed. After revisiting the semantic labeling technique, we review type introduction, which will be particularly useful in Chapter 6. The last section deals with innermost termination.

The problem of relative undecidability in the termination hierarchy will be addressed in Chapter 6. It will be shown that for all implications $X \Rightarrow Y$ in the termination and confluence hierarchies, except for one, the property X is undecidable for rewrite systems satisfying property Y. For example, it will be shown that termination is an undecidable property of innermost terminating term rewriting systems. For most of implications in the hierarchies, this is true, even for one-rule systems.

Conditional rewrite systems will be studied in Chapter 7. This chapter presents a mixture of known and new results in a unified theory. Conditional rewriting is inherently more complicated than unconditional rewriting. For example, termination of the rewrite relation is not enough to guarantee the absence of infinite computations because the evaluation of the conditions of a rewrite rule might not terminate. Thus, in order to ensure that every computation is finite, one has to replace termination with the stronger notion of effective termination. In Section 7.2, we will collect various methods for proving effective termination. First, systems without extra variables will be dealt with, then we will turn to systems with extra variables. The last two sections are devoted to confluence. Similar to unconditional term rewriting, there are in principle two methods for proving confluence of conditional rewrite systems: (1) either one first proves effective termination and then applies a suitable critical pair lemma or (2) one considers syntactically restricted classes of conditional rewrite systems.

Chapter 8 concerns modular aspects of term rewriting. Because modularity has been extensively studied in the last decade, it would be impossible to render a detailed account of all known modularity results. Instead, we will give an overview of the results obtained to date. Then the most important results will be treated in detail. Moreover, we will provide interesting new modularity results for unconditional and conditional rewrite systems. The material includes disjoint unions, constructor-sharing systems, and hierarchical combinations of term rewriting systems. First, we will provide a rather general theorem about the conditions under which termination is modular for disjoint unions, and we will discuss its consequences. Although for *finite* systems these results will be generalized to hierarchical combinations later, it is instructive to study this matter in detail. Second, we will characterize the conditions under which confluence is modular for term rewriting systems with shared constructors. As a corollary, a proof of the modularity of confluence for disjoint unions will be obtained. Third, we will shed light on the preservation of properties like (innermost) termination and confluence under hierarchical combinations. Fourth, the first modularity results for hierarchical combinations of conditional rewrite systems that have extra variables on the right-hand sides of the rewrite rules will be presented.

For reasons of efficiency, term rewriting is usually implemented by graph rewriting. This important issue will be addressed in Chapter 9. Although term rewriting and graph rewriting share many common features, neither is a special case of the other. A new uniform framework bridges this gap. In the last section, it will be shown that conditional graph rewriting is a sound and complete implementation of almost functional CTRSs. Furthermore, a kind of confluence theorem will be proven for the graph rewrite relations of these systems.

Termination is an equally important issue in logic programming as it is in term rewriting. In transformational approaches to proving termination of logic programs, one transforms well-moded logic programs into (conditional) term rewriting systems. If termination of the rewrite system implies termination of the logic program, then termination techniques for rewrite systems can be employed to show termination of logic programs. In Chapter 10 we will revisit three transformational approaches and show the surprising result that all three methods are equally powerful. Moreover, it will be shown that the methods are complete for the class of simply moded logic programs. Our implementation, the TALP system, uses the dependency pair method in combination with polynomial interpretations to automatically prove termination of the resulting rewrite system. The empirical results show that the system can compete with sophisticated norm-based approaches to proving termination of logic programs.

The concluding chapter contains a proof of Kruskal's theorem.

How to Use This Book

Parts of this book can be used as a textbook. The core material consists of the sections

$$1 \rightarrow 2.1\text{–}2.4 \rightarrow 3 \rightarrow 4 \rightarrow 5.1\text{–}5.2$$

If this material is used in an undergraduate course, it should be supplemented with course material on (syntactic) unification and Knuth-Bendix completion.

A more advanced introduction at the graduate level would include selected topics from Sections 5.3–5.6 and Chapters 7–8.

It might be helpful to the reader to know the dependencies between the sections of this book. Because Chapters 6–10 are more or less dependent on the core material and Sections 5.3–5.6, we recommend reading these sections first. It is also possible to skip Section 5.5 and look up the results when they are needed. Sections 2.5 –2.6 contain advanced material. Because only Chapter 9 uses a result from these sections, they can safely be skipped on first reading. Because subsequent chapters do not rely on Chapter 6, it is also possible to skip this chapter. For the most part, Chapters 7–9 can be read independently of each other. Only the last sections of Chapters 8 and 9 require some knowledge of Chapter 7. In contrast to that, Chapter 10 is heavily based on Chapter 7 (especially on Sections 7.2.5–7.2.8).

Acknowledgments

I am much indebted to Robert Giegerich for giving me the opportunity to write this book and for his constant support. I am also much obliged to Aart Middeldorp for the many beneficial discussions and whose many suggestions have improved previous papers. Furthermore, I would like to thank both of them and Jan Willem Klop for reviewing my third thesis, the "Habilitationsschrift." Thanks go also to Jürgen Giesl for his comments on a former version of this book.

I am grateful to my coauthors Mohamed Ibrahim Abouelhoda, Thomas Arts, Bernd Bütow, Jomuna Choudhuri, Claus Claves, Alfons Geser, Robert Giegerich, Jürgen Giesl, Frank Hischke, Michael Höhl, Stefan Kurtz, Claude

Marché, Aart Middeldorp, Chris Schleiermacher, Jens Stoye, Stephan Thesing, Esko Ukkonen, and Hans Zantema for working with me.

In addition to all those already mentioned, I would like to thank Michael Hanus, Masahito Kurihara, Tobias Nipkow, Hitoshi Ohsaki, Vincent van Oostrom, Fer-Jan de Vries, and everyone else who has given me feedback on my work.

Last but not least, I wish to thank my former and current colleagues in Bielefeld for creating a pleasant atmosphere.

Bielefeld, Germany — Enno Ohlebusch

Contents

1 Motivation

Equations were among the first mathematical achievements of mankind. For example, they appear in old Babylonian texts written in cuneiform characters that date back to the third millennium *B.C.* This is not surprising because equational reasoning (replacing equals with equals, that is) occurs frequently in day-to-day life. For example, in calculating a simple arithmetic expression like $(3+3)*6$, one first uses the equation $3+3=6$ to replace the expression or the *term* $(3+3)*6$ with $6*6$. In a second step this term further *rewrites* to 36, the result of the computation. In calculating the intuitively simplest term equal to $(3+3)*6$, no one would use the equation $3+3=6$ to replace the term $(3+3)*6$ with the term $(3+3)*(3+3)$. In other words, the equation $3+3=6$ is used as a *rewrite rule*: the left-hand side can be replaced with the right-hand side, but not vice versa. This one-directional replacement of equals with equals is what distinguishes *term rewriting* from equational logic.

From the viewpoint of modern computer science, term rewriting constitutes a Turing-complete computational model. Moreover, higher-order term rewriting generalizes functional programming. In a functional program for example, the definition of a function can only be based on constructor terms (patterns) whereas the left-hand side of the rewrite rule may contain defined functions. Both computational models concern the computation of normal forms, but in contrast to functional programming the result of a rewrite computation is not necessarily unique.

A rewrite (or reduction) step models a step in the transformation of terms with respect to some term rewriting system (program). From this point of view, term rewriting is the stepwise execution of some computation. Given a term, we are interested in its normal form—a final result of the computation (or transformation). The *termination* property guarantees that *every* computation ends in a normal form. Moreover, if the term rewriting system is *confluent*, then normal forms are unique. As a matter of fact, confluence is a stronger property than the unique normal form property. It ensures that whenever there are two "diverging" computations starting from the same term, a common term can be reached by "converging" computations. These two properties, termination and confluence, are of utmost importance and will be studied extensively in this book.

It is time for concrete examples. First, we consider two simple variants of the "coffee can problem" as described in [DJ90]. (These examples are string rewriting systems, but we shall see that every string rewriting system can be viewed as a term rewriting system.)

Imagine a can containing coffee beans of two varieties, black $\bullet$ and white $\circ$, arranged in some order. Thus, the contents of the can is a sequence such as $\circ\circ\circ\bullet\bullet\circ\bullet\circ\bullet$. The contents of the can may be modified according to the following rules:

$$
\begin{array}{lcl}
\bullet\circ & \to & \bullet \\
\circ\bullet & \to & \bullet \\
\bullet\bullet & \to & \circ \\
\circ\circ & \to & \circ
\end{array}
$$

The first two rules state that the white bean of any adjacent pair of different beans may be discarded. The last two rules state that two adjacent beans of the same color may be replaced with one white bean. Clearly, there are eight positions in the sequence $\circ\circ\circ\bullet\bullet\circ\bullet\circ\bullet$ at which a rule can be applied. If we always apply a rule at the leftmost (rightmost) position, then we obtain the rewrite sequence depicted on the left-hand (right-hand) side in Figure 1.1. It is obvious that the repeated application of the rules always ends in one bean because each application of a rule decreases the number of beans in the can by one. In other words, the "computation" terminates, no matter

$$
\begin{array}{llcll}
 & \underline{\circ\circ}\circ\bullet\bullet\circ\bullet\circ\bullet & \qquad & & \circ\circ\circ\bullet\bullet\circ\bullet\underline{\circ\bullet} \\
\to & \underline{\circ\circ}\bullet\bullet\circ\bullet\circ\bullet & & \to & \circ\circ\circ\bullet\bullet\circ\underline{\bullet\bullet} \\
\to & \underline{\circ\bullet}\bullet\circ\bullet\circ\bullet & & \to & \circ\circ\circ\bullet\bullet\underline{\circ\circ} \\
\to & \underline{\bullet\bullet}\circ\bullet\circ\bullet & & \to & \circ\circ\circ\bullet\underline{\bullet\circ} \\
\to & \underline{\circ\circ}\bullet\circ\bullet & & \to & \circ\circ\circ\underline{\bullet\bullet} \\
\to & \underline{\circ\bullet}\circ\bullet & & \to & \circ\circ\underline{\circ\circ} \\
\to & \underline{\bullet\circ}\bullet & & \to & \circ\underline{\circ\circ} \\
\to & \underline{\bullet\bullet} & & \to & \underline{\circ\circ} \\
\to & \circ & & \to & \circ
\end{array}
$$

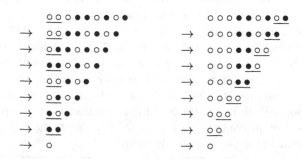

FIGURE 1.1. Different rewrite sequences.

at which positions rules are applied. In Figure 1.1 both computations end in one white bean. This is no coincidence because the result is uniquely determined (no matter where rules are applied). This can be seen as follows. For a can of beans w, let $|w|_\bullet$ denote the number of black beans in w. Then the number $|w|_\bullet \bmod 2$ is invariant under application of a rule. In other words, if w contains an even (odd) number of black beans, then every computation ends in one white (black) one.

A more difficult variant of the coffee can problem consists of the following rules:

$$\begin{array}{rcl} \bullet\circ & \to & \circ\circ\circ\bullet \\ \circ\bullet & \to & \bullet \\ \bullet\bullet & \to & \circ\circ\circ\circ \\ \circ\circ & \to & \circ \end{array}$$

It is not obvious whether or not this system terminates because some rules increase the number of coffee beans while others decrease it. The reader is invited to prove termination of this system. In Chapter 2, we will provide a formal termination proof using the lexicographic product of well-founded partial orderings. As a matter of fact, the system can automatically be proven to be terminating by means of recursive path orderings; see Chapter 5. Confluence—and hence uniqueness of normal forms—can be shown by analyzing overlapping rules. (Of course, the same is true for the first system.) For example, the first and second rules overlap. If we apply the first rule to the sequence $\bullet\circ\bullet$, we obtain the sequence $\circ\circ\circ\bullet\bullet$, and an application of the second rule to the same sequence yields $\bullet\bullet$. That is, there are two divergent computations starting from $\bullet\circ\bullet$. However, these computations converge by the following computation:

$$\circ\circ\underline{\circ\bullet}\bullet \to \circ\underline{\circ\bullet}\bullet \to \underline{\circ\bullet}\bullet \to \bullet\bullet$$

In term rewriting terminology, this overlap creates the critical pair $\langle \circ\circ\circ\bullet\bullet, \bullet\bullet\rangle$. This critical pair is joinable because converging computations starting from $\circ\circ\circ\bullet\bullet$ and $\bullet\bullet$ exist. We shall see in Chapter 4 that a terminating term rewriting system is confluent provided every critical pair is joinable. In the current example, it is easy to show that every critical pair is joinable; hence the system is confluent.

As another example, we consider the following rewrite rules:

$$\begin{array}{rcl} 0 - s(y) & \to & 0 \\ x - 0 & \to & x \\ s(x) - s(y) & \to & x - y \\ \mathit{quot}(0, s(y)) & \to & 0 \\ \mathit{quot}(s(x), s(y)) & \to & s(\mathit{quot}(x - y, s(y))) \end{array}$$

which compute (the ceiling of) the quotient of two natural numbers, where natural numbers are constructed by the constant 0 and the successor function s. There is no overlap between these rules. Furthermore, every rewrite rule is left-linear, that is, no variable occurs more than once on the left-hand side of a rewrite rule. It will be shown in Chapter 4 that these facts suffice to conclude confluence, even if the system is nonterminating. In other words, proving confluence is trivial in this example. Proving termination, however, is not so easy although it is intuitively clear that the system does terminate. For example, this system cannot be proven to be terminating by a recursive path ordering. However, in Chapter 5 the reader will become acquainted with the dependency pair method, which makes an automatic termination proof possible.

It is well known that confluence and termination are undecidable properties of term rewriting systems. It is even undecidable whether or not a term rewriting system consisting of a single rewrite rule is terminating. In Chapter 6 we will derive much stronger undecidability results.

It is quite customary to use guards and **where** clauses in functional programs. This can be seen, for example, in the following implementation of Hoare's [Hoa62] *quicksort* algorithm (written in Haskell):

```
split x []      = ([],[])
split x (y:ys) | x <= y       = (xs,y:zs)
               | otherwise    = (y:xs,zs)
                                where (xs,zs) = split x ys


qsort []        = []
qsort (x:xs)    = qsort ys ++ (x:qsort zs)
                  where (ys,zs) = split x xs
```

The natural counterpart of these concepts are conditions in term rewriting. The corresponding conditional term rewriting system consists of the following rewrite rules:

$$\begin{aligned}
split(x, nil) &\to \langle nil, nil\rangle \\
split(x, y : ys) &\to \langle xs, y : zs\rangle \Leftarrow x \le y \to true, split(x, ys) \to \langle xs, zs\rangle \\
split(x, y : ys) &\to \langle y : xs, zs\rangle \Leftarrow x \le y \to false, split(x, ys) \to \langle xs, zs\rangle \\
qsort(nil) &\to nil \\
qsort(x : xs) &\to qsort(ys) +\!\!+ (x : qsort(zs)) \Leftarrow split(x, xs) \to \langle ys, zs\rangle
\end{aligned}$$

In conditional term rewriting a rule is applicable only if its conditions are fulfilled. For example, $split(x, y : ys)$ matches the term $split(3, [8, 3, 2, 5, 1])$ and both the second and third conditional rewrite rules are potentially applicable. In order to determine which rule actually applies, one has to evaluate the conditions of the rewrite rules. In our example, the second rule will be used because $3 \le 8$ evaluates to *true*. Because $split(3, [3, 2, 5, 1])$ evaluates to $\langle [2, 1], [3, 5]\rangle$, the term $split(3, [8, 3, 2, 5, 1])$ rewrites to $\langle [2, 1], [8, 3, 5]\rangle$. As in unconditional term rewriting, it is desirable that every computation ends in a normal form and that this normal form is unique. Chapter 7 provides methods for proving effective termination and confluence of conditional term rewriting systems like the *quicksort* system. Here, effective termination means that every computation ends, including the evaluation of the conditions.

If we want a program that can compute the quotient of two natural numbers *and* sort a list of natural numbers, then we can simply combine the *quot* system and the *quicksort* system. Suppose confluence and effective termination of these systems have already been established. In Chapter 8, we will develop the theory of modularity. This theory characterizes classes of (conditional) term rewriting systems for which properties like confluence and termination are modular (preserved under combinations). In particular, we will derive methods that allow us to conclude that the combination of the *quot* system and *quicksort* system is indeed confluent and effectively terminating.

For reasons of efficiency, term rewriting is usually implemented by graph rewriting. In term rewriting, expressions are represented as terms, whereas in graph rewriting they are represented as directed graphs. In contrast to the former, the latter representation allows a sharing of common subexpressions. In graph rewriting, expressions are evaluated by rule-based graph transformations. Again, we encounter the problem of proving confluence and termination, this time for graph rewriting systems. Moreover, if one wants to implement term rewriting by graph rewriting, then one has to make sure that (1) the graph implementation cannot give incorrect results (soundness) and (2) the graph implementation gives all results (completeness). All these problems will be discussed in Chapter 9.

Another incarnation of declarative programming is logic programming. The following logic program implements the *quicksort* algorithm:

$$\begin{aligned}
&qsort([\,],[\,]) \leftarrow \\
&qsort(x:l,s) \leftarrow split(l,x,l_1,l_2), qsort(l_1,s_1), \\
&\qquad\qquad\qquad\quad qsort(l_2,s_2), app(s_1,x:s_2,s)
\end{aligned}$$

$$\begin{aligned}
&split([\,],x,[\,],[\,]) \leftarrow \\
&split(x:l,y,x:l_1,l_2) \leftarrow less(x,y), split(l,y,l_1,l_2) \\
&split(x:l,y,l_1,x:l_2) \leftarrow geq(x,y), split(l,y,l_1,l_2)
\end{aligned}$$

Again, we are faced with the problem of unique termination. That is, one has to prove that every SLD derivation—using Prolog's selection rule—starting from a goal is terminating and computes the same answer substitution. In Chapter 10, rewriting techniques will be used to achieve this goal.

2
Abstract Reduction Systems

We will introduce term rewriting by first abstracting from the term structure. In other words, to start, we will concentrate on the so-called abstract reduction systems (ARSs).

ARSs were first studied by Newman [New42]. The approach to term rewriting via ARSs was used in Rosen's and Huet's seminal papers [Ros73, Hue80] and has been propagated by Klop [Klo92], for example.

The abstract approach has two main advantages. First, it is instructive to see which definitions and properties depend on the term structure and which are more fundamental. Second, abstract rewriting comprises several kinds of rewriting including term, string, graph, and conditional rewriting. Thus a repetition of similar definitions and concepts can be avoided by stating them once and only on an abstract level.

A reduction step in an ARS models a step in the transformation of some object (for example, a term, string, or graph). Abstract reduction may also be viewed as a stepwise execution of some computation. Given an object, we are interested in a final result of the computation. If an ARS *terminates*, then *every* computation ends and one gets a result in finite time, no matter how the computation proceeded. Moreover, this result will be unique if the system is *confluent*. Confluence and termination, and variants thereof, will be studied extensively in this book.

Most of the material in Sections 2.1–2.3 is folklore. We start with a rather general definition of ARSs.

Definition 2.0.1 An *abstract reduction system* $\mathcal{A} = (A, \{\rightarrow_\alpha\}_{\alpha \in I}, \vdash\!\dashv)$ is a triple consisting of a set of objects A, a set of binary relations $\rightarrow_\alpha$ on A

(where I is an index set), and a symmetric relation $\vdash\!\dashv$ on A. A relation $\to_\alpha$ is said to be a *reduction* relation *labeled* by α. The reduction relation of $\mathcal{A}$ is defined by $\to_\mathcal{A} = \bigcup_{\alpha\in I} \to_\alpha$. Whenever the ARS $\mathcal{A}$ can be inferred from the context, it will be suppressed in the notation $\to_\mathcal{A}$, i.e., we will write $\to$ instead of $\to_\mathcal{A}$.

First, we only consider ARSs for which the symmetric relation is the identity on A. These ARSs will simply be denoted by $(A, \{\to_\alpha\}_{\alpha\in I})$ in the following. Furthermore, if there is only one reduction relation on A, then we write $(A, \to)$ instead of $(A, \{\to\})$. Later, we will see that $(A, \{\to_\alpha\}_{\alpha\in I})$ and $(A, \{\to_\alpha\}_{\alpha\in I}, \vdash\!\dashv)$ can be viewed as useful presentations of $(A, \to)$ and $(A, \to, \vdash\!\dashv)$, respectively (useful in the sense that they allow us to establish confluence of the system). In Sections 2.5 and 2.6 we will study abstract reduction modulo an equivalence relation generated by the symmetric relation $\vdash\!\dashv$.

Definition 2.0.2 Let $\mathcal{A} = (A, \to)$ be an ARS.

1. We write $a \to b$ for $(a, b) \in \to$ and we say that a *reduces to b in one step* and that b is a *one-step reduct* of a.

2. The relation $\to^0$ denotes the identity on A, i.e., $\to^0 = \{(a, a) \mid a \in A\}$.

3. If $\ell \in \mathbb{N}$, then $\to^{\ell+1}$ denotes the $(\ell + 1)$-fold composition of $\to$, i.e., $\to^{\ell+1} = \to^\ell \cdot \to$.

4. Let $\ell \in \mathbb{N}$. If $a \to^\ell b$, then there is a *reduction sequence* (or *derivation*) from a to b of *length* ℓ, i.e., a sequence $a = a_0 \to a_1 \to \cdots \to a_\ell = b$ consisting of ℓ reduction steps.

5. The relation $\to^{\leq\ell}$ is defined by $\to^{\leq\ell} = \bigcup_{i=0}^{\ell} \to^i$. Thus, $a \to^{\leq\ell} b$ denotes a reduction sequence of length $\leq \ell$.

6. The reflexive closure of $\to$ is the relation $\to^{\leq 1}$. In the following, it will also be denoted by $\to^=$.

7. The transitive closure of $\to$ is $\to^+ = \bigcup_{\ell\in\mathbb{N}_+} \to^\ell$.

8. The reflexive transitive closure of $\to$ is $\to^* = \to^+ \cup \to^0$. If $a \to^* b$, we say that a *reduces* or *rewrites* to b and we call b a *reduct* of a.

9. The inverse of $\to$ is $\leftarrow = \{(a, b) \mid b \to a\}$. In other words, we write $a \leftarrow b$ if $b \to a$ and analogously $a \,{}^*\!\!\leftarrow b$ if $b \to^* a$.

10. The symmetric closure of $\to$ is $\leftrightarrow = \to \cup \leftarrow$. The reflexive transitive closure of $\leftrightarrow$ is called *conversion* or *convertibility* and is denoted by $\leftrightarrow^*$.

11. Two elements $a, b \in A$ are *joinable*, written $a \downarrow b$, if there is a $c \in A$ such that $a \to^* c \,{}^*\!\!\leftarrow b$. We call c a *common reduct* of a and b.

2.1 Termination

The following definitions describe basic "termination" properties of ARSs. Other terminology that is also used in the literature is in parenthesis. The phrases "an ARS $\mathcal{A} = (A, \to)$ has a certain property" and "$\to$ has a certain property" will be used synonymously whenever the underlying set A can be inferred from the context.

Definition 2.1.1 Let $\mathcal{A} = (A, \to)$ be an ARS.

1. An element $a \in A$ is a *normal form w.r.t* $\to$ or is *irreducible w.r.t* $\to$ if there is no element $b \in A$ with $a \to b$. An element $a \in A$ *has a normal form w.r.t.* $\to$ if $a \xrightarrow{*} b$ for some normal form b. The phrase "w.r.t. $\to$" will be suppressed whenever $\to$ can be inferred from the context. The set of normal forms of $\mathcal{A}$ is denoted by NF($\mathcal{A}$) or NF($\to$) if there is no ambiguity about the set A.

2. $\mathcal{A}$ is *normalizing* (weakly normalizing) if every $a \in A$ has a normal form.

3. $\mathcal{A}$ is *terminating* (strongly normalizing, well-founded) if there is no infinite reduction sequence $a_1 \to a_2 \to a_3 \to \ldots$.

The terms weakly and strongly normalizing are usually used in λ-calculus. In the mathematical literature, a binary relation $\to$ on a set A is usually called well-founded if every subset B of A has a *minimal* element $b \in B$, that is, there is no $c \in B$ with $b \to c$. With the help of the axiom of choice, it is easy to show that this definition is equivalent to the preceding definition. We will use the term well-founded primarily if the relation under consideration is in fact a partial ordering $\succ$; see Section 2.3. So a partial ordering $\succ$ is well-founded if it admits no infinite *descending chain* $a_1 \succ a_2 \succ a_3 \succ \ldots$.[1]

Termination obviously implies normalization. Using the acronyms SN for termination and WN for normalization, this can be expressed as SN $\Rightarrow$ WN. The ARS in Figure 2.1 refutes the converse implication.

Normal forms are the results of computations. The normalization property is of interest because it ensures that there is at least one computation that terminates and yields a result. In some cases, it can replace the termination property, provided there is a strategy that avoids infinite computations. In contrast to normalization, however, termination admits induction.

---

[1] In the computer science literature, a relation without infinite descending chains (i.e., a terminating relation) is often called *Noetherian* (after the mathematician Emmy Noether, 1882–1935). However, in the mathematical literature, such a relation is usually called *Artinian* (after the mathematician Emil Artin, 1898–1962) and relations without infinite ascending chains are called Noetherian. In order to avoid confusion, we will not use Noetherian or Artinian notions in this book.

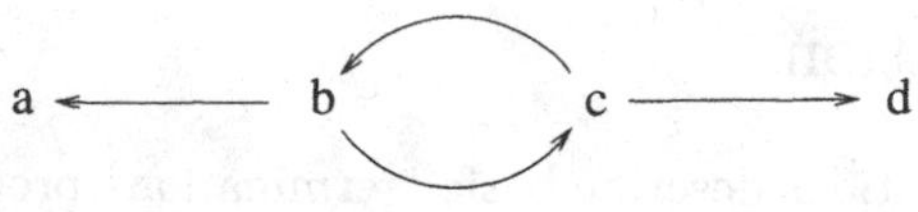

FIGURE 2.1. Hindley's [Hin74] counterexample to WCR ⇒ CR.

Definition 2.1.2 Let A be a set and $\mathcal{P}$ some property of elements of A. We write $\mathcal{P}(x)$ if $x \in A$ has the property $\mathcal{P}$. A relation $\to$ on A satisfies the *principle of well-founded induction* if

$$\frac{\forall x \in A\colon\ (\forall y \in A\colon\ x \to^+ y \Rightarrow \mathcal{P}(y)) \Rightarrow \mathcal{P}(x)}{\forall x \in A\colon\ \mathcal{P}(x)}$$

In words, if one can prove that an element x of A has the property $\mathcal{P}$ under the inductive hypothesis that all elements $y \in A$ with $x \to^+ y$ have property $\mathcal{P}$, then one may conclude that $\mathcal{P}$ holds for every element of A.

The base case of the induction is a little bit hidden: It consists of proving $\mathcal{P}$ for all irreducible (minimal) elements of A. If we consider the (well-founded) natural ordering $>$ on $\mathbb{N}$, then the principle of well-founded induction "degenerates" to induction over the natural numbers: A property $\mathcal{P}$ holds for all natural numbers n if we can show that n has property $\mathcal{P}$ under the inductive hypothesis that $\mathcal{P}$ holds for all natural numbers $m < n$.

Theorem 2.1.3 *Let $\to$ be a relation on a set A. If $\to$ terminates, then $\to$ satisfies the principle of well-founded induction.*

Proof For an indirect proof, suppose that $\to$ does not satisfy the principle of well-founded induction, that is, there is some property $\mathcal{P}$ that does not hold for all elements of A but nevertheless an element a of A has the property $\mathcal{P}$ whenever all elements $b \in A$ with $a \to^+ b$ have property $\mathcal{P}$. Say, $\mathcal{P}$ does not hold for a_0. If all elements $b \in A$ with $a_0 \to^+ b$ would have property $\mathcal{P}$, then a_0 would have property $\mathcal{P}$. Because this is not the case, there must be an element $a_1 \in A$ with $a_0 \to^+ a_1$ but without property $\mathcal{P}$. By continuing with this reasoning, we obtain an infinite sequence $a_0 \to^+ a_1 \to^+ a_2 \to^+ \ldots$. This contradicts the termination of $\to$. □

It is not difficult to see that the converse of the preceding theorem is also valid (let $\mathcal{P}(a)$ be true if and only if there is no infinite reduction sequence starting from a). We will exemplify the principle of well-founded induction by providing a proof of König's lemma that says that a finitely branching tree is infinite[2] if and only if it contains an infinite path.

[2] A tree is finite if it has a finite number of nodes; otherwise it is infinite.

Definition 2.1.4 Let $\mathcal{A} = (A, \rightarrow)$ be an ARS and $a \in A$. A *reduction tree* of a is a tree $T(a)$ whose nodes are labeled with elements from A and that satisfies the following conditions:

1. The root of $T(a)$ is labeled with a.

2. A node labeled with b has a child labeled with c if and only if $b \rightarrow c$.

3. No node has two distinct child nodes with the same label.

The reduction trees of $a \in A$ are equivalent under permutation of child nodes. By abuse of notation, we will speak of *the* reduction tree $T(a)$ of a if the ordering of the child nodes is irrelevant. (In fact, by Zermelo's theorem [KM68] there is a total well-founded ordering $\succ$ on A and if we assume that child nodes are ordered w.r.t. $\succ$, then the reduction tree is unique.)

Definition 2.1.5 An ARS $\mathcal{A} = (A, \rightarrow)$ is called *finitely branching* if for all $a \in A$ the set $\{b \in A \mid a \rightarrow b\}$ of one-step reducts of a is finite.

Apparently, an ARS is finitely branching if and only if every reduction tree is finitely branching. The next lemma is a reformulation of König's lemma.

Lemma 2.1.6 *Let $\mathcal{A} = (A, \rightarrow)$ be a finitely branching ARS. Then $T(a)$ is finite for each $a \in A$ if and only if $\mathcal{A}$ is terminating.*

Proof The only-if direction is straightforward: If $\rightarrow$ is nonterminating, then there exists an infinite reduction tree. For the if direction, let $\rightarrow$ be terminating and for $a \in A$ define $\mathcal{P}(a)$ to be true if and only if $T(a)$ is finite. We show that $\mathcal{P}(a)$ holds for all $a \in A$ by well-founded induction on the relation $\rightarrow$. Let $a \in A$ and suppose (the induction hypothesis) that $\mathcal{P}(b)$ holds for all $b \in A$ with $a \rightarrow^+ b$, i.e., $T(b)$ is finite for all $b \in A$ with $a \rightarrow^+ b$. Because $\mathcal{A}$ is finitely branching, the set $\{b \in A \mid a \rightarrow b\}$ of all one-step reducts of a is finite. Moreover, according to the inductive hypothesis, for all $b \in \{b \in A \mid a \rightarrow b\}$ the reduction tree $T(b)$ is finite. It follows that $T(a)$ is finite, i.e., $\mathcal{P}(a)$ holds. The if direction is a consequence of the principle of well-founded induction. □

2.2 Confluence

In this section we will treat the confluence hierarchy.

Definition 2.2.1 Let $\mathcal{A} = (A, \rightarrow)$ be an ARS.

1. $\mathcal{A}$ is *strongly confluent* if, for all $a, b, c \in A$ with $b \leftarrow a \rightarrow c$, there is a $d \in A$ such that $b \rightarrow^= d \; {}^*\!\!\leftarrow c$ (or more succinctly $\leftarrow \cdot \rightarrow \subseteq \rightarrow^= \cdot \; {}^*\!\!\leftarrow$). Note that this implies that there must also be an $e \in A$ such that $c \rightarrow^= e \; {}^*\!\!\leftarrow b$ because $c \leftarrow a \rightarrow b$.

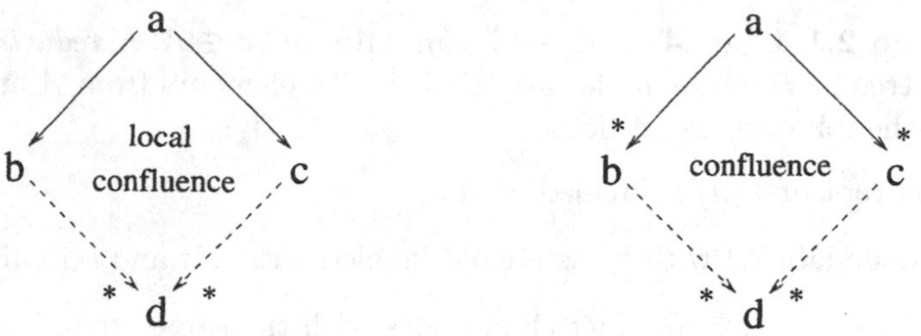

FIGURE 2.2. Local confluence and confluence. Solid arrows are universally quantified and dashed arrows are existentially quantified.

2. $\mathcal{A}$ is *Church-Rosser* if, for all $a, b \in A$ with $a \leftrightarrow^* b$, the elements a and b have a common reduct c (i.e., $\leftrightarrow^* \subseteq \rightarrow^* \cdot {}^*\!\leftarrow$).

3. $\mathcal{A}$ is *confluent* if, for all $a, b, c \in A$ with $b \; {}^*\!\leftarrow a \rightarrow^* c$, the elements b and c have a common reduct d (i.e., ${}^*\!\leftarrow \cdot \rightarrow^* \subseteq \rightarrow^* \cdot {}^*\!\leftarrow$); see Figure 2.2.

4. $\mathcal{A}$ is *locally confluent* (weakly Church-Rosser) if, for all $a, b, c \in A$ with $b \leftarrow a \rightarrow c$, the elements b and c have a common reduct d (i.e., $\leftarrow \cdot \rightarrow \subseteq \rightarrow^* \cdot {}^*\!\leftarrow$); see Figure 2.2.

5. $\mathcal{A}$ has *unique normal forms with respect to reduction* if no element of A reduces to different normal forms (i.e., $\forall a, b, c \in A$ if $a \rightarrow^* b$, $a \rightarrow^* c$ and $b, c \in NF(\rightarrow)$, then $b = c$).

6. $\mathcal{A}$ has *unique normal forms* if different normal forms are not convertible (i.e., $\forall a, b \in A$ if $a \leftrightarrow^* b$ and $a, b \in NF(\rightarrow)$, then $a = b$).

7. $\mathcal{A}$ has the *normal form property* if every element convertible to a normal form reduces to that normal form (i.e., $\forall a, b \in A$ if $a \leftrightarrow^* b$ and $b \in NF(\rightarrow)$, then $a \rightarrow^* b$).

If an ARS has unique normal forms with respect to reduction and there are different computations starting from the same object, then the result of these computations is unique (if it exists). Therefore, this property is very important. However, we will see that all the other properties, except for local confluence, imply this property and are often easier to establish. This is particularly true of the confluence property. We will treat this issue in more detail in Chapter 4.

First, it can be seen that confluence and the Church-Rosser property coincide.

Proposition 2.2.2 *An ARS is confluent if and only if it is Church-Rosser.*

Proof The if direction is trivial. Suppose that the ARS $\mathcal{A}$ is confluent and let $a, b \in A$ such that $a \leftrightarrow^* b$. In order to show that a and b have a common reduct, we proceed by induction on the number ℓ of reduction steps in $a \leftrightarrow^* b$. The case $\ell = 0$ holds vacuously. Consider $a \leftrightarrow^\ell c \leftrightarrow b$. By the inductive hypothesis, there is a $d \in A$ such that $a \to^* d \;{}^*\!\leftarrow c$. Now $c \leftarrow b$ immediately implies $a \downarrow b$. If $c \to b$, then confluence of $\to$ yields a common reduct e of d and b, which is also a common reduct of a and b. □

We use the acronyms SCR for strong confluence, CR for the Church-Rosser property (which is equivalent to confluence by Proposition 2.2.2), WCR for local confluence, NF for the normal form property, UN for unique normal forms, and $\text{UN}^\to$ for unique normal forms with respect to reduction.

Proposition 2.2.3 *The following implications hold:*

$$\begin{array}{ccccccccc} \text{SCR} & \Rightarrow & \text{CR} & \Rightarrow & \text{NF} & \Rightarrow & \text{UN} & \Rightarrow & \text{UN}^\to \\ & & \Downarrow & & & & & & \\ & & \text{WCR} & & & & & & \end{array}$$

Proof The implication SCR $\Rightarrow$ CR can be shown as follows; cf. [Hue80, lemma 2.5]:

- Prove that strong confluence of $\to$ implies that for all $a, b, c \in A$ with $b \;{}^*\!\leftarrow a \to c$ there is a $d \in A$ such that $b \to^= d \;{}^*\!\leftarrow c$ (use induction on the length of the derivation $b \;{}^*\!\leftarrow a$).
- Prove that if for all $a, b, c \in A$ with $b \;{}^*\!\leftarrow a \to c$ one has $b \downarrow c$, then $\to$ is confluent (again, use induction on the length of the derivation $b \;{}^*\!\leftarrow a$).

The other implications are straightforward. □

We call the preceding implications the *confluence hierarchy*. In general, none of the converse implications in the confluence hierarchy hold. The ARS defined by $b \leftarrow a \to c,\ b \to d \to e \leftarrow c$ shows that CR $\not\Rightarrow$ SCR. Figure 2.1 displays Hindley's famous counterexample to WCR $\Rightarrow$ CR. Consider the ARSs

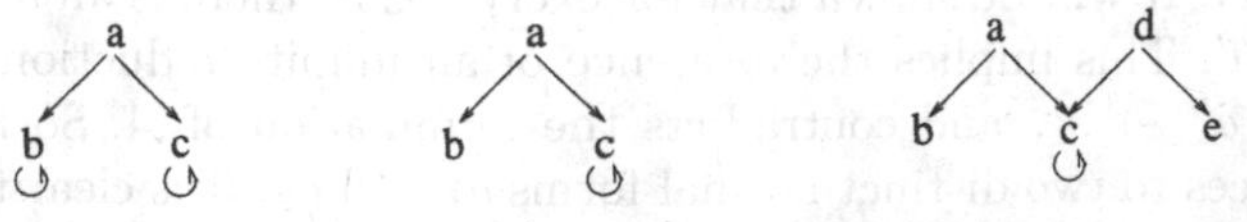

The left ARS refutes the implication NF $\Rightarrow$ CR, the ARS in the middle is a counterexample to UN $\Rightarrow$ NF, and the right one refutes $\text{UN}^\to \Rightarrow$ UN.

However, the following proposition shows that the properties CR, NF, UN, and $\text{UN}^\to$ coincide in the presence of normalization.

Proposition 2.2.4 *A normalizing ARS $\mathcal{A}$ with unique normal forms w.r.t. reduction is confluent.*

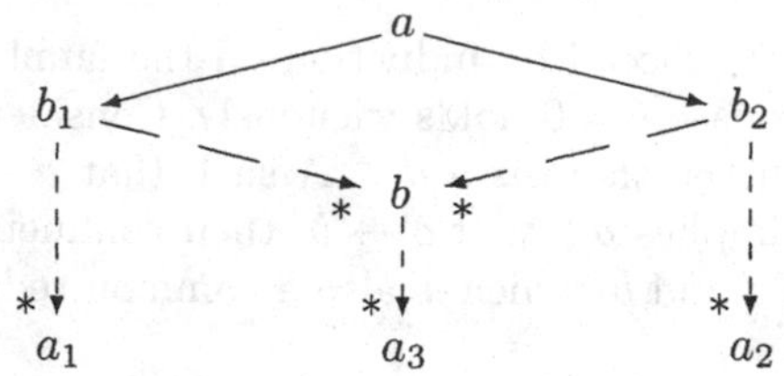

FIGURE 2.3. Proof of Newman's lemma.

Proof Let a, b, and c be elements of A such that $b \;{}^*\!\!\leftarrow a \rightarrow^* c$. It must be shown that $b \downarrow c$. Because $\mathcal{A}$ is normalizing, b and c reduce to normal forms b' and c', respectively. Hence $b' \;{}^*\!\!\leftarrow b \;{}^*\!\!\leftarrow a \rightarrow^* c \rightarrow^* c'$, where $b', c' \in NF(\mathcal{A})$. It follows that $b' = c'$ because $\mathcal{A}$ has unique normal forms w.r.t. reduction. $b' = c'$ is evidently a common reduct of b and c. □

Hindley's counterexample (Figure 2.1) shows that the combination of local confluence and normalization does not imply confluence. However, if we replace normalization with the stronger termination property, then CR and WCR are equivalent. This result was first proved by Newman [New42] and is thus referred to as Newman's lemma. Huet [Hue80] provided a very simple proof of Newman's lemma based on well-founded induction on the relation $\rightarrow$; cf. [BN98, lemma 2.7.2]. Instead of repeating this proof, we will follow the less-known elegant indirect proof of Barendregt [Bar84].

Lemma 2.2.5 *A terminating ARS is confluent if and only if it is locally confluent.*

Proof We have to prove that for a terminating ARS, local confluence implies confluence. According to Proposition 2.2.4, it suffices to show that $\mathcal{A}$ has unique normal forms w.r.t. reduction. For a proof by contradiction, suppose that $\mathcal{A}$ does not have unique normal forms w.r.t. reduction. Consequently, the set

$$S = \{a \in A \mid a_1 \;{}^*\!\!\leftarrow a \rightarrow^* a_2;\; a_1, a_2 \in NF(\mathcal{A});\; a_1 \neq a_2\}$$

is not empty. It will be shown that for every $a \in S$, there is an $a' \in S$ such that $a \rightarrow a'$. This implies the existence of an infinite reduction sequence $a \rightarrow a' \rightarrow a'' \rightarrow \ldots$ and contradicts the termination of $\mathcal{A}$. So let $a \in S$, i.e., a reduces to two distinct normal forms a_1 and a_2. It is clear that there are $b_1, b_2 \in A$ such that $a_1 \;{}^*\!\!\leftarrow b_1 \leftarrow a \rightarrow b_2 \rightarrow^* a_2$. Because $\mathcal{A}$ is locally confluent, b_1 and b_2 have a common reduct b. This reduct b reduces to some $a_3 \in NF(\mathcal{A})$ because $\mathcal{A}$ is terminating (see Figure 2.3). Now set $a' = b_1$ if $a_3 = a_2 \neq a_1$ and $a' = b_2$ otherwise. Evidently, $a' \in S$ and $a \rightarrow a'$. □

Newman's lemma is one of the most important results in term rewriting. This is because local confluence is decidable for finite term rewriting

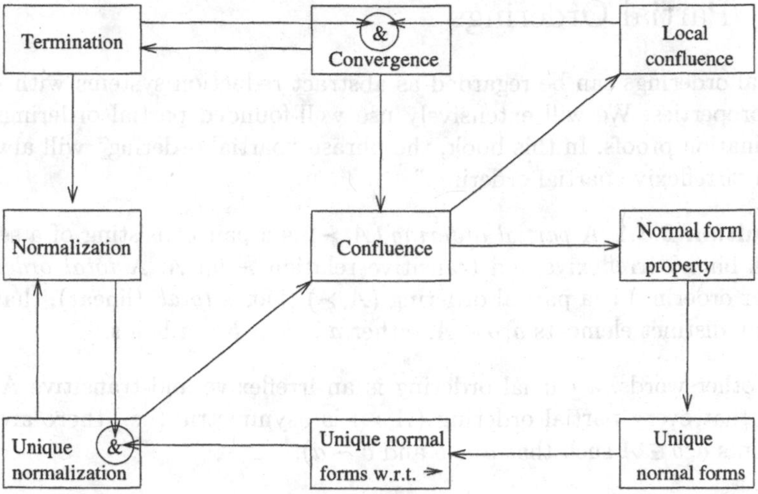

FIGURE 2.4. Relationships between the properties of ARSs.

systems and thus Newman's lemma implies that confluence is decidable for finite *terminating* term rewriting systems. This topic will be discussed in Chapter 4.

By combining confluence with normalization and termination, respectively, we obtain the following notions.

Definition 2.2.6 Let $\mathcal{A} = (A, \to)$ be an ARS.

1. $\mathcal{A}$ is said to be *uniquely normalizing* (semicomplete) if it is confluent and normalizing.

2. $\mathcal{A}$ is said to be *convergent* (complete) if it is confluent and terminating.

It is clear that convergence implies unique normalization. The removal of the arrow from b to a in Figure 2.1 yields an ARS that is uniquely normalizing but not convergent. Figure 2.4 summarizes the relationships between the various properties.

Given a uniquely normalizing ARS $\mathcal{A}$, we are faced with the problem of finding a normal form. If $\mathcal{A}$ is finitely branching, then the normal form of $a \in A$ can be found by a breadth-first traversal of the reduction tree $T(a)$. In other words, if there are only finitely many computations starting from each object, then a result can be obtained by first considering all one-step reducts, then all two-step reducts, etc.

2.3 Partial Orderings

Partial orderings can be regarded as abstract reduction systems with special properties. We will extensively use well-founded partial orderings in termination proofs. In this book, the phrase "partial ordering" will always mean "irreflexive partial ordering."

Definition 2.3.1 A *partial ordering* $(A, \succ)$ is a pair consisting of a set A and a binary irreflexive and transitive relation $\succ$ on A. A *total ordering* (linear ordering) is a partial ordering $(A, \succ)$ that is *total* (linear), that is, for any distinct elements $a, b \in A$, either $a \succ b$ or $b \succ a$ holds.

In other words, a partial ordering is an irreflexive and transitive ARS. Note that every partial ordering $(A, \succ)$ is asymmetric (i.e., there are no elements $a, b \in A$ such that $a \succ b$ and $b \succ a$).

Definition 2.3.2

1. A *quasi-ordering* $(A, \succsim)$ is a pair consisting of a set A and a binary reflexive and transitive relation $\succsim$ on A.

2. A *reflexive partial ordering* $(A, \succeq)$ is a quasi-ordering that is also antisymmetric.

Note that a quasi-ordering may fail to be a reflexive partial ordering because it is not antisymmetric, i.e., there may be two distinct elements $a, b \in A$ such that $a \succsim b$ and $b \succsim a$.

Example 2.3.3 Consider the set Σ^* of all finite sequences over the alphabet $\Sigma = \{\bullet, \circ\}$. For $w \in \Sigma^*$, let $|w|$ denote the length of w. If we define the binary relation $\succsim$ on Σ^* by $u \succsim v$ if $|u| \geq |v|$, then $\succsim$ is a quasi-ordering but not a reflexive partial ordering because it is not antisymmetric: $\bullet \succsim \circ$ and $\circ \succsim \bullet$.

With the help of the next lemma, we can alternate between reflexive and irreflexive partial orderings.

Lemma 2.3.4

1. *Given a partial ordering $(A, \succ)$, the definition $a \succeq b$ if $a \succ b$ or $a = b$ yields a reflexive partial ordering $(A, \succeq)$.*

2. *Given a reflexive partial ordering $(A, \succeq)$, the definition $a \succ b$ if $a \succeq b$ and $a \neq b$ yields a partial ordering $(A, \succ)$, which is called the* strict part *of $\succeq$.*

3. *Given a quasi-ordering $(A, \succsim)$, the definition $a \succ b$ if $a \succsim b$ but $b \not\succsim a$ yields a partial ordering $\succ$, which is also called the* strict part *of $\succsim$.*

Proof Routine. □

The reflexive or irreflexive partial ordering obtained by one of the preceding definitions is called the *associated* (or *corresponding*) *partial ordering*.

Given a quasi-ordering $\succsim$, the definition $a \succ b$ if $a \succsim b$ and $a \neq b$ does not in general yield a partial ordering. For example, consider the quasi-ordering $\succsim$ from Example 2.3.3. Let the binary relation $\succ$ on $\{\bullet, \circ\}^*$ be defined by $u \succ v$ if and only if $u \succsim v$ and $u \neq v$. That is, $u \succ v$ if and only if $|u| \geq |v|$ and $u \neq v$. Then $\bullet \succ \circ \succ \bullet$, hence $\succ$ is not irreflexive. If, however, the quasi-ordering is actually a reflexive partial ordering (i.e., it is also antisymmetric), then the definitions of the associated partial ordering coincide.

Note that every quasi-ordering $(A, \succsim)$ generates an equivalence relation, usually denoted by $\sim$ or $\approx$, on A that is defined by $a \sim b$ if $a \succsim b$ and $b \succsim a$. Furthermore, the definition $[a]_\sim \geq [b]_\sim$ if $a \succsim b$ yields a partial ordering $\geq$ on the quotient set $A/\sim = \{[a]_\sim \mid a \in A\}$, where $[a]_\sim = \{b \in A \mid a \sim b\}$ denotes the equivalence class of a.

Lexicographic Orderings

Lexicographic orderings are particularly useful in termination proofs, as we shall see shortly.

Definition 2.3.5 The *lexicographic product* of n partial orderings $(A_j, \succ_j)$, $j \in \{1, \ldots, n\}$, is the pair $(A_1 \times \cdots \times A_n, \succ_{lex})$, where $\succ_{lex}$ is defined by $(a_1, \ldots, a_n) \succ_{lex} (b_1, \ldots, b_n)$ if $a_j \succ_j b_j$ at the least $j \in \{1, \ldots, n\}$ for which $a_j \neq b_j$.

Proposition 2.3.6

1. *The lexicographic product of partial orderings is a partial ordering.*
2. *The lexicographic product of well-founded partial orderings is well-founded.*
3. *The lexicographic product of total orderings is total.*

Proof Routine. □

We exemplify the use of lexicographic orderings in termination proofs by means of the following example from Chapter 1.

Example 2.3.7 Consider the variant of the "coffee can problem" defined by the following set $\mathcal{S}$ of rules:

$$\begin{array}{lcl} \bullet\circ & \rightarrow & \circ\circ\circ\bullet \\ \circ\bullet & \rightarrow & \bullet \\ \bullet\bullet & \rightarrow & \circ\circ\circ\circ \\ \circ\circ & \rightarrow & \circ \end{array}$$

Formally, this is a *string rewriting system* (SRS) over the alphabet $\{\bullet, \circ\}$. In an SRS, the set of objects is the set Σ^* of all finite sequences over the alphabet Σ. Given a set of string rewriting rules $\mathcal{S} \subseteq \Sigma^* \times \Sigma^*$ the binary relation $\to_{\mathcal{S}}$ on Σ^* is defined by $u \to_{\mathcal{S}} v$ if there are $x, y \in \Sigma^*$ and a rule $l \to r \in \mathcal{S}$ such that $u = xly$ and $v = xry$.

In order to show that the system terminates, define the binary relation $\succ$ on $\{\bullet, \circ\}^*$ as follows: $u \succ v$ if and only if

1. $|u|_\bullet > |v|_\bullet$ or
2. $|u|_\bullet = |v|_\bullet = n$ and $(|u_0|, |u_1|, \ldots, |u_n|) >_{lex} (|v_0|, |v_1|, \ldots, |v_n|)$, where $>_{lex}$ is the n-fold product of the natural ordering on $\mathbb{N}$ and the sequences $u_i, v_i \in \{\circ\}^*$ are determined by $u = u_n \bullet u_{n-1} \bullet \cdots \bullet u_1 \bullet u_0$ and $v = v_n \bullet v_{n-1} \bullet \cdots \bullet v_1 \bullet v_0$.

In order to compare two sequences u and v w.r.t. $\succ$, one first compares the number of black beans in u and v. Only if the number of black beans in u equals that of v, one further lexicographically compares the lengths of the sequences of white beans between the black beans. Note that the comparison proceeds from right to left. It is not difficult to prove that $u \to_{\mathcal{S}} v$ implies $u \succ v$ for all $u, v \in \{\bullet, \circ\}^*$. Because $\succ$ is a well-founded partial ordering by Proposition 2.3.6, we conclude that $\mathcal{S}$ is terminating. This kind of reasoning will be treated in more detail in Chapter 5. Furthermore, it will be shown in Chapter 4 that the system $\mathcal{S}$ is also confluent.

Multiset Orderings

A multiset is a collection in which elements are allowed to occur more than once. Formally, it is defined as follows.

Definition 2.3.8 Let A be a set.

1. Let $\mathbb{N}_\infty$ be the set of natural numbers $\mathbb{N}$ extended with a new element ∞. The element ∞ is the maximal element of the natural ordering $>$ on $\mathbb{N}$ extended to $\mathbb{N}_\infty$. The operations minimum $(\wedge)$, maximum $(\vee)$, and addition $(+)$ are defined for $\mathbb{N}$ as usual. Cutoff subtraction $(\dot{-})$ is defined by

$$m \dot{-} n = \begin{cases} m - n & \text{if} \quad m \geq n \\ 0 & \text{if} \quad m < n \end{cases}$$

   The extended definition on $\mathbb{N}_\infty$ is specified in Table 2.1.

2.
   - A (*general*) *multiset* M over A is a map $M : A \to \mathbb{N}_\infty$.
   - A *finite* multiset F over A is a multiset with $\sum_{a \in A} F(a) < \infty$.
   - A *set* S over A is a multiset such that $\forall a \in A : S(a) \in \{0, \infty\}$.

$*$	$\infty * m$	$m * \infty$	$\infty * \infty$	$\circledast$
$\wedge$	m	m	∞	$\cap$
$\vee$	∞	∞	∞	$\cup$
$+$	∞	∞	∞	$\oplus$
$\dot{-}$	∞	0	0	$\setminus$

TABLE 2.1. Multiset operations

3. The *empty* multiset $\emptyset$ is the constant 0 function.

4. Multiset *membership* is defined by $a \in M$ if and only if $M(a) > 0$. Multiset *inclusion* is defined by $M \subseteq N$ if and only if $\forall a \in A$: $M(a) \leq N(a)$.

5. The classes of multisets, finite multisets, and sets over A are denoted by $\mathcal{M}(A)$, $\mathcal{FM}(A)$, and $\mathcal{S}(A)$, respectively.

6. To distinguish between set comprehension and finite multiset comprehension, braces will be used to denote the former and square brackets to denote the latter. For example, $[a]$ denotes the finite multiset with exactly one occurrence of a (i.e., it has the value 1 at a and 0 elsewhere), whereas $\{a\}$ denotes the set with infinitely many occurrences of a (i.e., it has value ∞ at a and 0 elsewhere).

7. The binary operations *intersection* ($\cap$), *union* ($\cup$), *sum* ($\oplus$) and *difference* ($\setminus$) are defined for $a \in A$ by: $(M \circledast N)(a) = M(a) * N(a)$ via the correspondence in Table 2.1.

Usually, a set S over A is defined to be a multiset such that for all $a \in A$ we have $S(a) \in \{0,1\}$. The reason why we use a different definition will become clear in Sections 2.5 and 2.6.

Example 2.3.9 The following (in)equalities illustrate the differences between finite and set multisets, as well as sum and union: $[a] \oplus [a] = [a,a] \neq [a] = [a] \cup [a]$, $\{a\} \oplus \{a\} = \{a,a\} = \{a\} = \{a\} \cup \{a\}$, $[a,a] \setminus [a] = [a]$, $\{a\} \setminus [a,a] = \{a\}$, and $[a,a] \setminus \{a\} = \emptyset$.

Definition 2.3.10 The *finite multiset extension* $(\mathcal{FM}(A), \succ_{mul})$ of a partial ordering $(A, \succ)$ is defined by:
$M_1 \succ_{mul} M_2$ if there exist finite multisets $X, Y \in \mathcal{FM}(A)$ such that

- $\emptyset \neq X \subseteq M_1$,
- $M_2 = (M_1 \setminus X) \oplus Y$,
- for all $y \in Y$ there exists an $x \in X$ such that $x \succ y$.

It is not difficult to prove that the finite multiset extension of a partial ordering is also a partial ordering.

Example 2.3.11 Let $>$ be the natural (well-founded total) ordering on $\mathbb{N}$. In its finite multiset extension $(\mathcal{FM}(\mathbb{N}), >_{mul})$, for example, we have

$$[3,3,4,0] >_{mul} [3,2,2,1,1,1,4,0] >_{mul} [3,4] >_{mul} [3,3,3,3,2,2] >_{mul} \emptyset$$

The following important theorem was first proved by Dershowitz and Manna [DM79].

Theorem 2.3.12 *The finite multiset extension of a partial ordering is well-founded if and only if the partial ordering is well-founded.*

Proof Let $(A, \succ)$ be a partial ordering. The only-if direction is straightforward: An infinite decreasing chain $a_0 \succ a_1 \succ a_2 \succ \ldots$ of elements from A gives rise to an infinite decreasing chain $[a_0] \succ_{mul} [a_1] \succ_{mul} [a_2] \succ_{mul} \cdots$. In order to show the if direction, let $\succ$ be well-founded. For an indirect proof, suppose that $\succ_{mul}$ is not well-founded, i.e., there is an infinite decreasing chain

$$M_0 \succ_{mul} M_1 \succ_{mul} M_2 \succ_{mul} \cdots$$

of finite multisets over A. Let $\bot$ be a new symbol, define $A_\bot = A \cup \{\bot\}$, and extend $\succ$ on $A_\bot$ by $a \succ \bot$ for all $a \in A$. Clearly, $(A_\bot, \succ)$ is a well-founded partial ordering. We iteratively construct trees $T_0, T_1, T_2, \ldots$ with the following properties:

1. The nodes of T_i, except the root, are labeled with elements from $A_\bot$.
2. The multiset of the labels $\neq \bot$ of the leaves of T_i coincides with M_i.
3. The labels along each path in T_i decrease w.r.t. $\succ$.

The initial tree T_0 has a nonlabeled root and, for every element a of M_0, a leaf labeled with a. Given T_i, we construct T_{i+1} as follows. Because $M_i \succ_{mul} M_{i+1}$, there are finite multisets $X, Y \in \mathcal{FM}(A)$ such that $\emptyset \neq X \subseteq M_i$, $M_{i+1} = (M_i \setminus X) \oplus Y$, and, for all $y \in Y$, there exists an $x \in X$ such that $x \succ y$. We fix $\sum_{x \in A} X(x)$ leaves in T_i, called X leaves, such that the multiset of their labels coincides with X. The existence of the X leaves is guaranteed by $X \subseteq M_i$ and property (2). For every $y \in Y$, we add a new leaf labeled y and make it the child of an X leaf labeled $x \succ y$. For all those X leaves that remain untouched in this process, we add a leaf labeled $\bot$. It is relatively easy to verify that T_{i+1} has properties (1)–(3) whenever T_i has. Moreover, the tree T_{i+1} has strictly more nodes than T_i (even if Y is empty) because $X \neq \emptyset$. Thus, the tree $T = \lim_{i \to \infty} T_i$ is infinite. According to König's lemma, T contains an infinite path because it is finitely branching. Because the labels along this path decrease w.r.t. $\succ$, there is an infinite decreasing chain $a_0 \succ a_1 \succ a_2 \succ \ldots$ of elements from A. This contradicts the well-foundedness of $\succ$. $\square$

2.4 Commutation

In this section we will briefly review sufficient conditions that do not rely on termination for establishing confluence. We first prove a useful lemma due to Rosen [Ros73].

Definition 2.4.1 A binary relation $\to$ on a set A has the *diamond property*—denoted by $\diamond(\to)$—if, for all $a, b, c \in A$ with $b \leftarrow a \to c$, there is a $d \in A$ such that $b \to d \leftarrow c$ (or more succinctly $\leftarrow \cdot \to \subseteq \to \cdot \leftarrow$).

Note that an ARS $\mathcal{A} = (A, \to)$ is confluent if and only if $\diamond(\to^*)$ holds. Furthermore, if $\to$ has the diamond property, then $\to$ is strongly confluent, hence confluent. In particular, $\diamond(\to)$ implies $\diamond(\to^*)$.

Lemma 2.4.2 *An ARS $\mathcal{A} = (A, \to)$ is confluent if there is a relation $\rightsquigarrow$ such that $\diamond(\rightsquigarrow)$ and $\to \subseteq \rightsquigarrow \subseteq \to^*$ hold.*

Proof We infer $\rightsquigarrow^* = \to^*$ from $\to \subseteq \rightsquigarrow \subseteq \to^*$. Because $\rightsquigarrow$ has the diamond property, so does $\rightsquigarrow^* = \to^*$. Therefore, $\to$ is confluent. □

The basic idea of the following results can be formulated as follows: If a reduction relation $\to$ can be divided into smaller relations $\to_\alpha$ that are confluent and interact "nicely," then $\to$ is confluent.

Definition 2.4.3 Let $\to_\alpha$ and $\to_\beta$ be relations on A. We say that $\to_\alpha$ *subcommutes* with $\to_\beta$ if ${}_\alpha\!\leftarrow \cdot \to_\beta \subseteq \to_\beta^= \cdot {}^=_\alpha\!\leftarrow$. If $\to_\alpha$ subcommutes with itself, then it is called *subcommutative*. Furthermore, $\to_\alpha$ *commutes* with $\to_\beta$ if ${}^*_\alpha\!\leftarrow \cdot \to_\beta^* \subseteq \to_\beta^* \cdot {}^*_\alpha\!\leftarrow$.

Clearly, if $\to_\alpha$ subcommutes with $\to_\beta$, then $\to_\alpha$ commutes with $\to_\beta$. Note that a relation commutes with itself if and only if it is confluent. Moreover, every subcommutative relation is strongly confluent. The following criterion can be taken from Hindley's work [Hin64]. It is called the lemma of Hindley-Rosen because it was rediscovered by Rosen [Ros73].

Lemma 2.4.4 *Let $\mathcal{A} = (A, \{\to_\alpha\}_{\alpha \in I})$ be an ARS. If for all $\alpha, \beta \in I$, $\to_\alpha$ commutes with $\to_\beta$, then $\mathcal{A}$ is confluent.*

Proof The idea of the proof is illustrated in Figure 2.5. Formally, let $\rightsquigarrow$ be $\bigcup_{\alpha \in I} \to_\alpha^*$ and apply Lemma 2.4.2. □

Corollary 2.4.5 *Let $\to_1$ and $\to_2$ be two relations on a set A. If $\to_1$ and $\to_2$ are confluent and commute, then $\to_1 \cup \to_2$ is also confluent.*

Proof This is a special case of Lemma 2.4.4, where the index set I has only the two elements 1 and 2. □

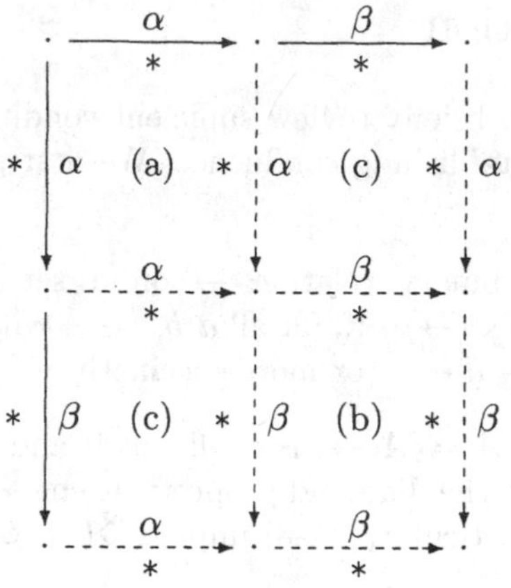

FIGURE 2.5. (a) α and α, (b) β and β, (c) α and β commute.

The problem of finding sufficient conditions that preserve confluence (or some other property) under union will also be addressed in Chapter 8.

The next lemma is called Rosen's request lemma; cf. [Ros73].

Definition 2.4.6 Let $\mathcal{A} = (A, \{\to_1, \to_2\})$ be an ARS. We say that $\to_2$ *requests* $\to_1$ if ${}_1^*\!\leftarrow \cdot \to_2^* \subseteq \to_2^* \cdot \to_1^* \cdot {}_1^*\!\leftarrow$.

Lemma 2.4.7 *Let* $\mathcal{A} = (A, \{\to_1, \to_2\})$. *If* $\to_1$ *and* $\to_2$ *are confluent and* $\to_2$ *requests* $\to_1$, *then* $\to_{\mathcal{A}} = \to_1 \cup \to_2$ *is confluent.*

Proof Let $\rightsquigarrow$ be $\to_2^* \cdot \to_1^*$. Figure 2.6 demonstrates that $\rightsquigarrow$ has the diamond property. Because $\to \subseteq \rightsquigarrow \subseteq \to^*$, an application of Lemma 2.4.2 yields confluence of $\to$. □

The following proposition shows that under a certain condition, we may conclude confluence of a relation $\to_1$ from confluence of another relation $\to_2 \subseteq \to_1^*$. It was first proved by Staples [Sta75].

Definition 2.4.8 Let $\to_1$ and $\to_2$ be relations on A. Relation $\to_1$ is called a *refinement* of $\to_2$ if $\to_2 \subseteq \to_1^*$; it is said to be a *compatible refinement* of $\to_2$ if it is a refinement of $\to_2$ and for all $a \to_1^* b$ there is a $c \in A$ such that $a \to_2^* c \; {}_2^*\!\leftarrow b$.

Proposition 2.4.9 *Let* $\to_1$ *be a compatible refinement of* $\to_2$ *on a set* A. *If* $\to_2$ *is confluent, then* $\to_1$ *is also confluent.*

Proof Consider a divergence $a \; {}_1^*\!\leftarrow \cdot \to_1^* b$, where $a, b \in A$. We have

$$a \to_2^* \cdot {}_2^*\!\leftarrow \cdot \to_2^* \cdot {}_2^*\!\leftarrow b \qquad \text{(compatibility)}$$
$$a \to_2^* \cdot \to_2^* \cdot {}_2^*\!\leftarrow \cdot {}_2^*\!\leftarrow b \qquad (\to_2 \text{ is CR})$$
$$a \to_1^* \cdot \to_1^* \cdot {}_1^*\!\leftarrow \cdot {}_1^*\!\leftarrow b \qquad \text{(refinement)}$$

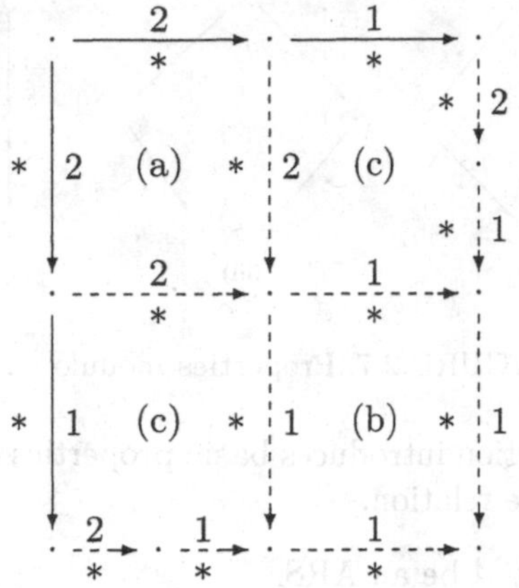

FIGURE 2.6. (a) $\rightarrow_2$ is CR, (b) $\rightarrow_1$ is CR, (c) $\rightarrow_2$ requests $\rightarrow_1$.

Therefore, $\rightarrow_1$ is confluent. □

The converse of the preceding proposition also holds; see [Sta75].

2.5 Reduction Modulo an Equivalence

The remainder of this chapter deals with abstract reduction modulo an equivalence relation. Part of the material appeared in [Ohl98a].

In what follows, $\mathcal{A}$ denotes an ARS $(A, \{\rightarrow_\alpha\}_{\alpha \in I}, \vdash\!\dashv)$[3] and $\sim$ always denotes the reflexive transitive closure of the symmetric relation $\vdash\!\dashv$. We write $(A, \{\rightarrow_\alpha\}_{\alpha \in I}, \sim)$ instead of $(A, \{\rightarrow_\alpha\}_{\alpha \in I}, \vdash\!\dashv)$ if the symmetric relation $\vdash\!\dashv$ is in fact an equivalence relation.

Definition 2.5.1 Let $\mathcal{A}$ be an ARS. We define the following relations:

- $\models\!\dashv \; = \rightarrow \cup \leftarrow \cup \sim$.
- The relation $\approx \; = \; \models\!\dashv^*$ is called *conversion modulo* $\sim$.
- The relation $\downarrow_\sim \; = \; \rightarrow^* \cdot \sim \cdot \, {}^*\!\!\leftarrow$ is called *joinability modulo* $\sim$.
- $\rightarrow_\sim \; = \; \sim \cdot \rightarrow \cdot \sim$.

$\mathcal{A}$ is *terminating modulo* $\sim$ (SN$\sim$) if there is no infinite reduction sequence w.r.t. $\rightarrow_\sim$.

---

[3]In term rewriting modulo an equational theory, $\vdash\!\dashv$ is the symmetric relation defined by a finite set of equations; see, e.g., [Ave95, Chapter 4].

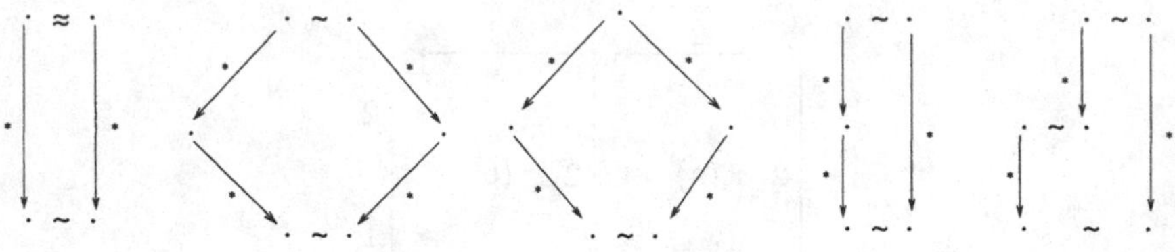

(i) (ii) (iii) (iv) (v)

FIGURE 2.7. Properties modulo $\sim$.

The following definition introduces basic properties of abstract reduction modulo an equivalence relation.

Definition 2.5.2 Let $\mathcal{A}$ be an ARS.

1. We write $\diamond(\rightarrow^* \cdot \sim)$ and say that the *diamond property* holds for $\rightarrow^* \cdot \sim$ if $\sim \cdot\, {}^*\!\leftarrow \cdot \rightarrow^* \cdot \sim\ \subseteq\ \downarrow_\sim$.
2. $\mathcal{A}$ is *Church-Rosser modulo* $\sim$ (CR$\sim$) if $\approx\ \subseteq\ \downarrow_\sim$.
3. $\mathcal{A}$ is *almost Church-Rosser modulo* $\sim$ (ACR$\sim$) if ${}^*\!\leftarrow \cdot \sim \cdot \rightarrow^*\ \subseteq\ \downarrow_\sim$.
4. $\mathcal{A}$ is *confluent modulo* $\sim$ (CON$\sim$) if ${}^*\!\leftarrow \cdot \rightarrow^*\ \subseteq\ \downarrow_\sim$.
5. $\mathcal{A}$ is *locally confluent modulo* $\sim$ (LCON$\sim$) if $\leftarrow \cdot \rightarrow\ \subseteq\ \downarrow_\sim$.
6. $\mathcal{A}$ is *strongly* LCON$\sim$ (SLCON$\sim$) if $\leftarrow \cdot \rightarrow\ \subseteq\ \rightarrow^= \cdot \sim \cdot\, {}^*\!\leftarrow$.
7. $\mathcal{A}$ is *coherent with* $\vdash\!\dashv$ (COH$\vdash\!\dashv$) if $\vdash\!\dashv \cdot \rightarrow^*\ \subseteq\ \downarrow_\sim$.
8. $\mathcal{A}$ is *locally coherent with* $\vdash\!\dashv$ (LCOH$\vdash\!\dashv$) if $\vdash\!\dashv \cdot \rightarrow\ \subseteq\ \downarrow_\sim$.
9. $\mathcal{A}$ is *strongly coherent with* $\vdash\!\dashv$ (SCOH$\vdash\!\dashv$) if $\vdash\!\dashv \cdot \rightarrow^* \cdot \sim\ \subseteq\ \downarrow_\sim$.
10. $\mathcal{A}$ is *compatible with* $\vdash\!\dashv$ (COM$\vdash\!\dashv$) if $\vdash\!\dashv \cdot \rightarrow^*\ \subseteq\ \rightarrow^* \cdot \sim$.
11. $\mathcal{A}$ is *strongly compatible with* $\vdash\!\dashv$ (SCOM$\vdash\!\dashv$) if $\vdash\!\dashv \cdot \rightarrow\ \subseteq\ \rightarrow^= \cdot \sim$.
12. $\mathcal{A}$ is *locally commuting with* $\vdash\!\dashv$ (LCMU$\vdash\!\dashv$) if $\vdash\!\dashv \cdot \rightarrow\ \subseteq\ \rightarrow^+ \cdot \sim$.

The term "confluent modulo $\sim$" for property CON$\sim$ stems from [Ave95]. Note that property ACR$\sim$ is also called "confluence modulo $\sim$" in [Hue80]. In order to avoid the same name for two different properties, we use the notion "almost Church-Rosser modulo $\sim$" for the latter. The term "locally commuting with $\vdash\!\dashv$" stems from [JM84].

Figure 2.7 illustrates the properties (i) CR$\sim$, (ii) ACR$\sim$, (iii) CON$\sim$, (iv) COH$\sim$, and (v) SCOH$\sim$. It is instructive to look at the special case in which $\vdash\!\dashv$ is the identity on A. In this case the first four properties of Definition 2.5.2 are equivalent to CR, the fifth coincides with WCR and the sixth is the same as SCR. In general, however, the Church-Rosser property

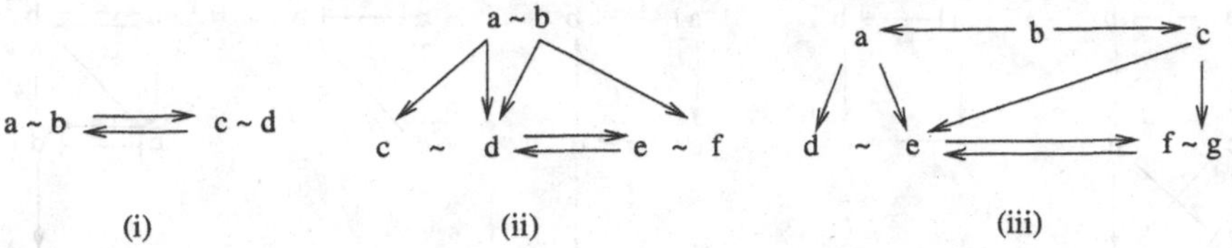

FIGURE 2.8. Counterexamples in the confluence modulo hierarchy.

modulo $\sim$ does not coincide with confluence modulo $\sim$. This well-known fact is one of the major differences from pure abstract reduction.

The first six and the last six properties from Definition 2.5.2 form hierarchies as we will show next.

Proposition 2.5.3 *The* confluence modulo hierarchy *reads as follows:*

$$\begin{array}{ccccccccc} & & & & & & & & \text{SLCON}\sim \\ & & & & & & & & \Downarrow \\ \Diamond(\rightarrow^* \cdot \sim) & \Leftrightarrow & \text{CR}\sim & \Rightarrow & \text{ACR}\sim & \Rightarrow & \text{CON}\sim & \Rightarrow & \text{LCON}\sim \end{array}$$

Proof The first equivalence is proven in Proposition 2.5.6. The other implications are trivial. □

None of the converse implications hold. LCON$\sim$ $\Rightarrow$ CON$\sim$ and LCON$\sim$ $\Rightarrow$ SLCON$\sim$ cannot hold because this would (if $\sim$ is the identity on A) imply WCR $\Rightarrow$ CR and WCR $\Rightarrow$ SCR, respectively. For the same reason, CR $\sim$ $\Rightarrow$ SLCON $\sim$ cannot be true because this would imply CR $\Rightarrow$ SCR. The other two implications are refuted by the ARSs in Figure 2.8. The ARS in Figure 2.8(i) is due to Aart Middeldorp and shows that ACR$\sim$ does not imply CR$\sim$ (the elements a and d are convertible modulo $\sim$ but not joinable modulo $\sim$). The ARS in Figure 2.8(ii) is CON$\sim$ (and COH$\sim$) but not ACR$\sim$. A simpler counterexample (which is not COH$\sim$) is $c \leftarrow a \sim b \rightarrow f$. Finally, SLCON$\sim$ does not imply CON$\sim$ (hence it does not imply ACR$\sim$ and CR$\sim$), as seen by the example in Figure 2.8(iii). That's why we call this property strong local confluence modulo $\sim$ instead of strong confluence modulo $\sim$.

It should be pointed out that ACR$\sim$ implies confluence of $\rightarrow/\sim$ in $A/\sim$ (as, for example, remarked in [PPE94]) but *not* vice versa. A simple counterexample is the ARS $a \sim b \rightarrow c$.

Proposition 2.5.4 *The* coherence hierarchy *reads as follows:*

$$\begin{array}{ccccccccc} & & & & & & & & \text{LCMU}\vdash\!\dashv \\ & & & & & & & & \Downarrow \\ \text{SCOM}\vdash\!\dashv & \Rightarrow & \text{COM}\vdash\!\dashv & \Rightarrow & \text{SCOH}\vdash\!\dashv & \Rightarrow & \text{COH}\vdash\!\dashv & \Rightarrow & \text{LCOH}\vdash\!\dashv \end{array}$$

Proof The first implication is proven in Lemma 2.5.5. The other implications are trivially true. □

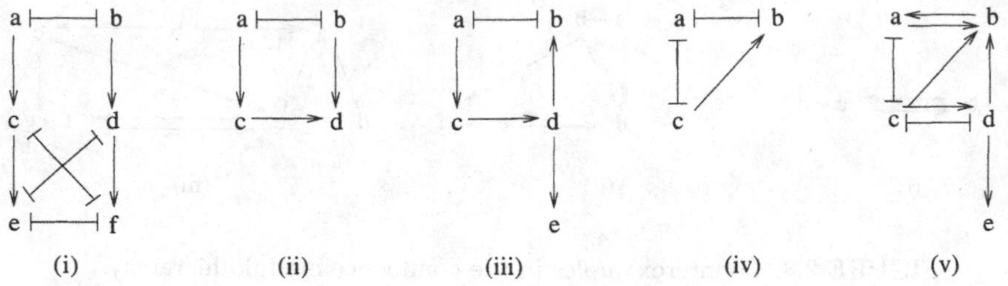

FIGURE 2.9. Counterexamples in the coherence hierarchy.

Again, none of the converse implications hold. Most of the counterexamples are depicted in Figure 2.9. The ARS in Figure 2.9(i) is COM$\vdash\!\dashv$ but not SCOM$\vdash\!\dashv$, while the ARS in Figure 2.9(ii) is SCOH$\vdash\!\dashv$ but not COM$\vdash\!\dashv$. We obtain a counterexample to SCOH$\vdash\!\dashv$ $\Rightarrow$ COH$\vdash\!\dashv$ by replacing the $\sim$-symbols with $\vdash\!\dashv$-symbols in Figure 2.8(i). The ARS depicted in Figure 2.9(iii) shows that LCOH$\vdash\!\dashv$ does not imply COH$\vdash\!\dashv$. The last two ARSs in Figure 2.9 deal with the relationship of LCMU$\vdash\!\dashv$ to the other properties in the coherence hierarchy. On the one hand, the ARS depicted in Figure 2.9(iv) shows that LCMU$\vdash\!\dashv$ is not a consequence of SCOM$\vdash\!\dashv$ (and hence of neither of the other properties). On the other hand, the ARS of Figure 2.9(v) is LCMU$\vdash\!\dashv$ but not COH$\vdash\!\dashv$. As a consequence, LCMU$\vdash\!\dashv$ does not imply any of the other properties apart from LCOH$\vdash\!\dashv$.

Lemma 2.5.5 *For every ARS $\mathcal{A}$ the following holds:*

1. COM$\vdash\!\dashv$ *is equivalent to* COM$\sim$.

2. SCOM$\vdash\!\dashv$ $\Rightarrow$ COM$\vdash\!\dashv$.

Proof (1) By induction on k one shows that $\vdash\!\dashv \cdot \rightarrow^* \subseteq \rightarrow^* \cdot \sim$ implies $\overset{k}{\vdash\!\dashv} \cdot \rightarrow^* \subseteq \rightarrow^* \cdot \sim$, where $\overset{k}{\vdash\!\dashv}$ denotes k $\vdash\!\dashv$ steps.
(2) We prove SCOM$\vdash\!\dashv$ $\Rightarrow$ COM$\sim$. To this end, we first show $a \sim b \rightarrow c \Rightarrow a \rightarrow^= d \sim c$ by induction on k in $a \overset{k}{\vdash\!\dashv} b$. The base case $k = 0$ clearly holds. Suppose $a \vdash\!\dashv b_1 \overset{k}{\vdash\!\dashv} b \rightarrow c$. According to the inductive hypothesis, we have $a \vdash\!\dashv b_1 \rightarrow^= b_2 \sim c$. Because $\mathcal{A}$ is SCOM$\vdash\!\dashv$, it follows $a \rightarrow^= b_3 \sim b_2 \sim c$. Hence $a \rightarrow^= b_3 \sim c$. We next show $a \sim b \rightarrow^* c \Rightarrow a \rightarrow^* d \sim c$ by induction on k in $b \rightarrow^k c$. Again, the base case $k = 0$ is true. So suppose $a \sim b \rightarrow b_1 \rightarrow^k c$. By this result, it follows $a \rightarrow^= b_2 \sim b_1 \rightarrow^k c$. Now the inductive hypothesis implies $a \rightarrow^= b_2 \rightarrow^* b_3 \sim c$. Thus, $a \rightarrow^* b_3 \sim c$. □

The combination of suitable confluence and coherence properties yields sufficient conditions for CR$\sim$. Figure 2.10 depicts some of the relationships between the properties defined earlier. The nontrivial implications will be proven in the remainder of this section.

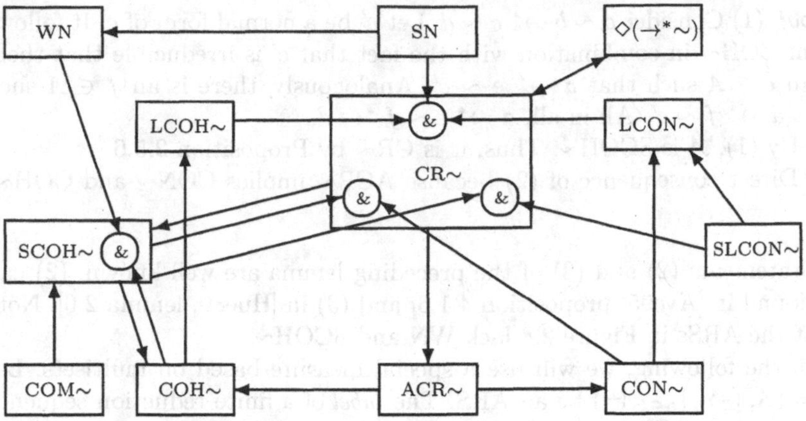

FIGURE 2.10. Connections between the properties.

Proposition 2.5.6 *Let $\mathcal{A}$ be an ARS. The following statements are equivalent:*

1. *$\mathcal{A}$ is* CR$\sim$.
2. *$\Diamond(\rightarrow^* \cdot \sim)$ holds.*
3. *$\mathcal{A}$ is* CON$\sim$ *and* SCOH$\sim$.

Proof Apparently, (1) implies (2) and (2) implies (3). We prove that (3) implies (1). Let $a \stackrel{k}{\models\!\mid} b$ be given, i.e., k is the number of $\models\!\mid$ steps in the conversion $a \approx b$. We show by induction on k that there are $c, d \in A$ such that $a \rightarrow^* c \sim d \;^*\!\leftarrow b$. If $k = 0$, then $a = b$ and the claim holds. Consider $a \stackrel{k}{\models\!\mid} b' \models\!\mid b$. According to the inductive hypothesis, there are $c, d \in A$ such that $a \rightarrow^* c \sim d \;^*\!\leftarrow b'$. We further proceed by case analysis.
(i) $b' \sim b$: Because $c \sim d \leftarrow b' \sim b$ and $\mathcal{A}$ is SCOH$\sim$, there exist $e, f \in A$ such that $c \rightarrow^* e \sim f \;^*\!\leftarrow b$. That is, $a \rightarrow^* e \sim f \;^*\!\leftarrow b$.
(ii) $b' \rightarrow b$: For $d \;^*\!\leftarrow b' \rightarrow b$ there are $e, f \in A$ such that $d \rightarrow^* e \sim f \;^*\!\leftarrow b$ because $\mathcal{A}$ is CON$\sim$. Because $\mathcal{A}$ is SCOH$\sim$, it follows from $c \sim d \rightarrow^* e \sim f$ that there are $g, h \in A$ with $a \rightarrow^* c \rightarrow^* g \sim h \;^*\!\leftarrow f \;^*\!\leftarrow b$.
(iii) $b' \leftarrow b$: Trivial. □

Lemma 2.5.7 *For every ARS $\mathcal{A}$ the following statements hold:*

1. *If $\mathcal{A}$ is* WN *and* COH$\sim$, *then it is* SCOH$\sim$.
2. *If $\mathcal{A}$ is* WN, CON$\sim$, *and* COH$\sim$, *then it is* CR$\sim$.
3. *If $\mathcal{A}$ is* WN *and* ACR$\sim$, *then it is* CR$\sim$.

Proof (1) Consider $a \sim b \to^* c \sim d$. Let c' be a normal form of c. It follows from COH$\sim$ in combination with the fact that c' is irreducible that there is an $e \in A$ such that $a \to^* e \sim c'$. Analogously, there is an $f \in A$ such that $d \to^* f \sim c'$. All in all, $a \to^* e \sim f \; {}^*\!\!\leftarrow d$.
(2) By (1), $\mathcal{A}$ is SCOH$\sim$. Thus, it is CR$\sim$ by Proposition 2.5.6.
(3) Direct consequence of (2) because ACR$\sim$ implies CON$\sim$ and COH$\sim$. □

Statements (2) and (3) of the preceding lemma are well known. (2) can be found in [Ave95, proposition 4.1.6] and (3) in [Hue80, lemma 2.6]. Note that the ARSs in Figure 2.8 lack WN and SCOH$\sim$.

In the following, we will use a special measure based on multisets. Let $\mathcal{A} = (A, \{\to_\alpha\}_{\alpha \in I}, \vdash\!\dashv)$ be an ARS. The *label* of a finite reduction sequence is the string of labels of its constituent reduction steps. For example, if $I = \{1, 2, 3, 4\}$, then the label of the reduction sequence $a \to_2 b \to_4 c \to_2 d$ is the string 242. The Greek letters σ, τ, μ, ν etc. will be used to denote strings. The concatenation of two strings σ and τ is denoted by $\sigma\tau$. Moreover, ε denotes the empty string. The multiset $[\sigma]$ of labels of a string σ is the sum of all label occurrences in it, so in particular we have $[\sigma\tau] = [\sigma] \uplus [\tau]$. For example, if $I = \{1, 2, 3, 4\}$, then $[132343] = [1, 3, 2, 3, 4, 3]$. In the next definition, we obtain a measure on strings over I (hence on labels of reduction sequences) from a given well-founded ordering on the index set I.

Definition 2.5.8 Let $\mathcal{A} = (A, \{\to_\alpha\}_{\alpha \in I}, \vdash\!\dashv)$ be an ARS and let $\succ$ be a well-founded partial ordering on the index set I.

1. The *down set* $\curlyvee\alpha$ of α is defined by $\curlyvee\alpha = \{\beta \mid \beta \prec \alpha\}$. This is extended to multisets and strings by defining $\curlyvee M = \bigcup_{\alpha \in M} \curlyvee\alpha$ and $\curlyvee\sigma = \curlyvee[\sigma]$.

2. The *lexicographic maximum measure* $\|\cdot\| : I^* \to \mathcal{FM}(I)$ is defined inductively by $\|\varepsilon\| = \emptyset$ and $\|\alpha\sigma\| = [\alpha] \oplus (\|\sigma\| \setminus \curlyvee\alpha)$.

For example, $\curlyvee 2 = \curlyvee[0, 2] = \curlyvee 221 = \{0, 1\}$, $\|211\| = [2]$, and $\|132343\| = [1, 3, 3, 4]$. Intuitively, the lexicographic maximum measure takes the multiset of elements that are maximal (in the $\succ$ ordering) with respect to the elements to their left in the string. Operationally, we obtain the lexicographic maximum measure of a given string $\alpha\sigma$ as follows. At first, we filter out all labels in σ that are strictly smaller than α. Let $\beta\tau$ be the string obtained in this fashion. Then we filter out all labels in τ that are strictly smaller than β and so on.

Two strings σ and τ are then compared by comparing $\|\sigma\|$ and $\|\tau\|$ with respect to the multiset extension $\succ_{mul}$ of the well-founded ordering $\succ$ on I. For example, if $I = \{1, 2, 3, 4\}$ and $>$ is the natural ordering on I, then $\|132343\| >_{mul} \|211\|$ because $[1, 3, 3, 4] >_{mul} [2]$.

In the following, $\succeq_{mul}$ denotes the reflexive closure of $\succ_{mul}$.

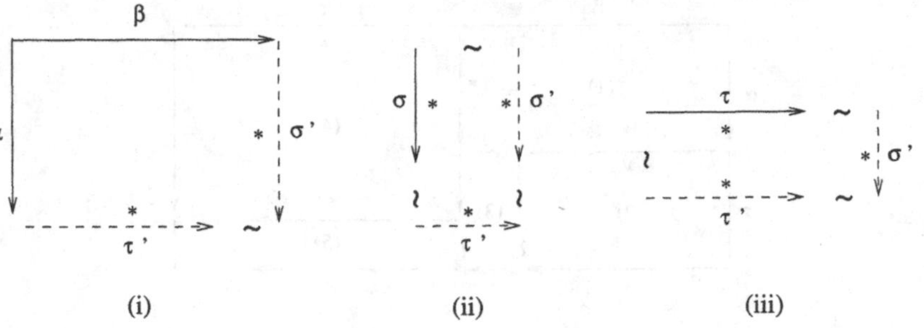

FIGURE 2.11. Assumptions of Theorem 2.5.10.

Definition 2.5.9 Let $\to_\alpha$ and $\to_\beta$ be two relations on A. We say that $\to_\alpha$ *subcommutes* with $\to_\beta$ modulo $\sim$ if ${}_\alpha\!\leftarrow \cdot \to_\beta \subseteq \to_{\beta}^{=} \cdot \sim \cdot {}_{\alpha}^{=}\!\leftarrow$. Moreover, $\to_\alpha$ *commutes* with $\to_\beta$ modulo $\sim$ if $\to_\alpha^*$ subcommutes with $\to_\beta^*$ modulo $\sim$.

Theorem 2.5.10 *Let $\mathcal{A} = (A, \{\to_\alpha\}_{\alpha\in I}, \sim)$ be an ARS and let $\succ$ be a well-founded partial ordering on I. Let $I_v, I_h \subseteq I$, $\to_v = \bigcup_{\alpha\in I_v} \to_\alpha$, and $\to_h = \bigcup_{\beta\in I_h} \to_\beta$.*

1. *If, $\forall \alpha \in I_v$, $\beta \in I_h$, $\sigma \in I_v^*$, $\tau \in I_h^*$ the diagrams in Figure 2.11 hold such that $\|\beta\| \succeq_{mul} \|\tau'\|$, $\sigma' \in I_v^*$, $\tau' \in I_h^*$, then $\to_v$ commutes with $\to_h$ modulo $\sim$.*

2. *If $\to_\mathcal{A} = \to_v = \to_h$, then $\mathcal{A}$ is* CR$\sim$.

Proof (1) Let $|\sigma|$ denote the length of σ, i.e., the number of labels in the string σ and let $>$ denote the natural ordering on $\mathbb{N}$. Let $>_{lex}$ be defined by $(\|\tau\|, |\sigma|) >_{lex} (\|\tau'\|, |\sigma'|)$ if $\|\tau\| \succ_{mul} \|\tau'\|$ or $\|\tau\| = \|\tau'\|$ and $|\sigma| > |\sigma'|$, where $\tau, \tau' \in I_h^*$ and $\sigma, \sigma' \in I_v^*$. First the horizontal labels are compared w.r.t. the lexicographic maximum measure and then the length of the vertical ones. Because $\succ$ is well-founded and $>_{lex}$ is the lexicographic product of $\succ_{mul}$ and $>$, $>_{lex}$ is well-founded by Proposition 2.3.6 and Theorem 2.3.12. Now we proceed by induction on $>_{lex}$. The proof is illustrated in Figure 2.12. The rectangle (1) exists by assumption; cf. Figure 2.11(i). Because $\|\beta\| \succeq_{mul} \|\nu\|$ and $|\alpha\sigma| > |\sigma|$, the inductive hypothesis is applicable in (2). (3) is true because of Figure 2.11(ii). Furthermore, one can apply the inductive hypothesis again in (4) because $\|\beta\tau\| \succ_{mul} \|\tau\|$. The proof of (1) is concluded by applying Figure 2.11(iii) in (5).
(2) Evidently, $\mathcal{A}$ is SCOH$\sim$. According to (1), $\to_\mathcal{A}$ is CON$\sim$, too. Hence $\mathcal{A}$ is CR$\sim$ by Proposition 2.5.6. □

Note that in this theorem, the ordering $\succ_{mul}$ can be replaced by any well-founded ordering $\gg$ on strings of labels satisfying the property $\beta\tau \gg \tau$.

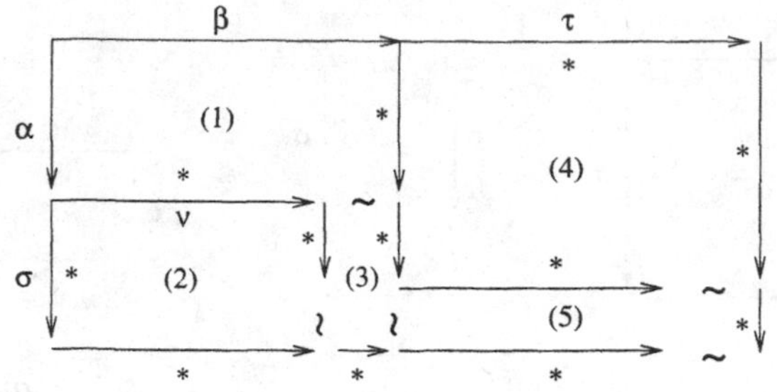

FIGURE 2.12. Proof of Theorem 2.5.10.

Because CON$\sim$ is not a consequence of SLCON$\sim$, the following result does not follow directly from Proposition 2.5.6.

Corollary 2.5.11 *If the ARS* $\mathcal{A} = (A, \rightarrow, \sim)$ *is* SLCON$\sim$ *and* SCOH$\sim$, *then it is* CR$\sim$.

Proof Define the ARS $\mathcal{B} = (A, \langle \rightarrow_h, \rightarrow_v \rangle, \sim)$ by $\rightarrow_h = \rightarrow_v = \rightarrow$ and note that $\rightarrow_{\mathcal{A}} = \rightarrow = \rightarrow_{\mathcal{B}}$. The idea is to simulate the "vertical" reduction steps in $\mathcal{A}$ by $\rightarrow_v$ in $\mathcal{B}$ and the "horizontal" reduction steps in $\mathcal{A}$ by $\rightarrow_h$ in $\mathcal{B}$. For example, every SLCON$\sim$ diagram in $\mathcal{A}$ translates to a diagram in $\mathcal{B}$ as depicted in Figure 2.13. Analogously, every SCOH$\sim$ diagram in $\mathcal{A}$ that is of the form as illustrated in Figure 2.11(ii) or (iii) translates to a respective diagram in $\mathcal{B}$. The claim follows by an application of Theorem 2.5.10 with ordering $h \succ v$. □

If $\sim$ is the identity on A, then Corollary 2.5.11 specializes to the statement SCR $\Rightarrow$ CR. The following proposition provided by Huet [Hue80] is the modulo analogue to Newman's lemma. It shows that in the presence of termination the combination of local confluence modulo $\sim$ and local coherence with $\sim$ is sufficient to infer CR$\sim$. If $\sim$ is the identity on A, then Proposition 2.5.12 specializes to Newman's lemma 2.2.5.

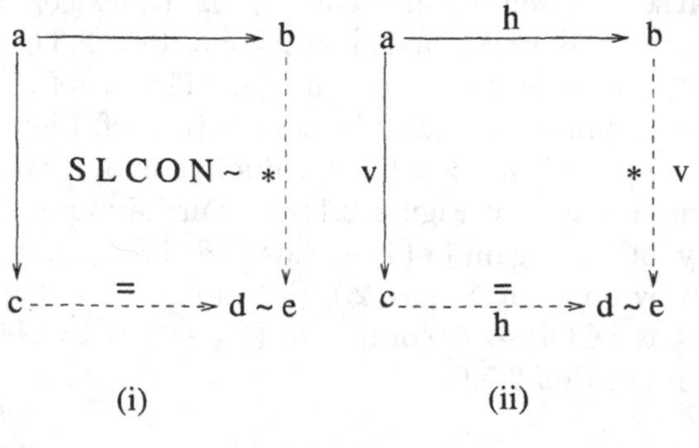

FIGURE 2.13. Proof of Corollary 2.5.11.

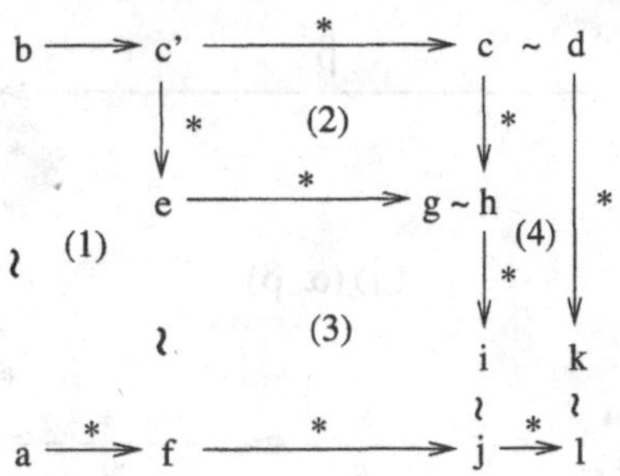

FIGURE 2.14. Proof of Proposition 2.5.12.

Proposition 2.5.12 *If $\mathcal{A}$ is* SN, LCON$\sim$, *and* LCOH$\sim$, *then it is* CR$\sim$.

Proof We show that $\mathcal{A}$ is CON$\sim$ and SCOH$\sim$. In order to show that if (i) $a \; {}^*\!\leftarrow b \rightarrow^* d$ or (ii) $a \sim b \rightarrow^* c \sim d$, then $a \downarrow_\sim d$, we use induction on the well-founded ordering $\rightarrow^+$, i.e., we assume that (i) and (ii) hold for all $e \in A$ with $b \rightarrow^+ e$. It is not difficult to verify (i) along the lines of the proof of Theorem 2.5.10. We then prove (ii). If $b = c$, then the claim holds vacuously. So suppose $b \rightarrow c' \rightarrow^* c$. Because $\mathcal{A}$ is LCOH$\sim$, there are $e, f \in A$ such that $a \rightarrow^* f \sim e \; {}^*\!\leftarrow c'$; see Figure 2.14(1). The proposition follows by applying the inductive hypothesis three times; see Figure 2.14(2)–(4). □

2.6 Local Decreasingness

The next result is due to van Oostrom [Oos94]. It shows how confluence can be derived from locally decreasing diagrams.

Definition 2.6.1 Let $\mathcal{A} = (A, \{\rightarrow_\alpha\}_{\alpha \in I})$ be an ARS and $\succ$ be a well-founded partial ordering on I. For every $\alpha \in I$, we define $\rightarrow_{\prec\alpha} = \bigcup_{\beta \prec \alpha} \rightarrow_\beta$. Furthermore, we write $LD(\alpha, \beta)$ if $b \;{}_\alpha\!\leftarrow a \rightarrow_\beta c$ implies the existence of a $d \in A$ such that $b \rightarrow^*_{\prec\alpha} \cdot \rightarrow^=_\beta \cdot \rightarrow^*_\gamma d$ and $c \rightarrow^*_{\prec\beta} \cdot \rightarrow^=_\alpha \cdot \rightarrow^*_\gamma d$, where $\rightarrow_\gamma = \rightarrow_{\prec\alpha} \cup \rightarrow_{\prec\beta}$; cf. Figure 2.15.

Theorem 2.6.2 *Let $\mathcal{A} = (A, \{\rightarrow_\alpha\}_{\alpha \in I})$ be an ARS. If there is a well-founded partial ordering $\succ$ on I such that $LD(\alpha, \beta)$ holds for all $\alpha, \beta \in I$, then $\mathcal{A}$ is confluent.*

Proof The proof is based on properties of the lexicographic maximum measure; see [Oos94] for details. □

As in Theorem 2.5.10, one can further distinguish between "vertical" and "horizontal" reductions in Theorem 2.6.2; see [Oos94]. Even without this distinction, this theorem has many consequences. Among them are:

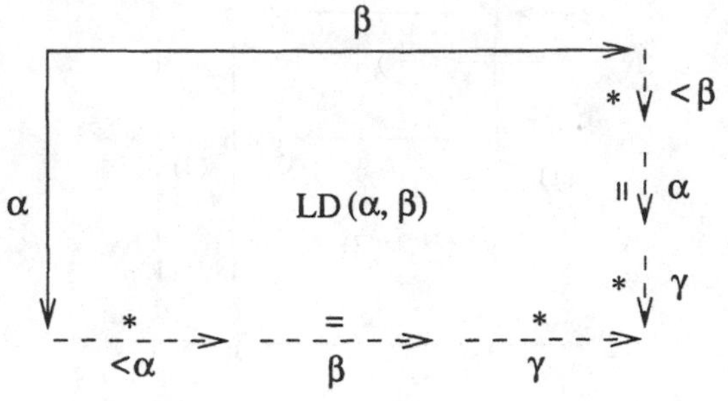

FIGURE 2.15. Locally decreasing diagram.

- Lemma 2.4.4 of Hindley-Rosen,
- Rosen's request lemma 2.4.7,
- Staples' result 2.4.9 about compatible refinements,
- Newman's lemma 2.2.5.

Generalizations of the aforementioned consequences to reduction modulo $\sim$ can also be useful. For example, we will use the generalization of Staples' result in Chapter 9. Therefore, will briefly review the generalization of Theorem 2.6.2 to reduction modulo $\sim$.

Definition 2.6.3 Let $\mathcal{A} = (A, \{\to_\alpha\}_{\alpha \in I}, \vdash\dashv)$ be an ARS and let $\succ$ be a well-founded partial ordering on I. We write $LD(\alpha, \beta)$ if $b \;{}_\alpha\!\leftarrow a \to_\beta c$ implies the existence of $d, e \in A$ such that $b \to^*_{\prec\alpha} \cdot \to^=_\beta \cdot \to^*_\gamma d$, $c \to^*_{\prec\beta} \cdot \to^=_\alpha \cdot \to^*_\gamma e$, and $d \sim e$, where $\to_\gamma = \to_{\prec\alpha} \cup \to_{\prec\beta}$. Furthermore, we write $LD(\alpha)$ if $b \;{}_\alpha\!\leftarrow a \vdash\dashv c$ implies the existence of $d, e \in A$ such that $b \to^*_{\prec\alpha} d$, $c \to^=_\alpha \cdot \to^*_{\prec\alpha} e$, and $d \sim e$; see Figure 2.16.

Theorem 2.6.4 *Let $\mathcal{A} = (A, \{\to_\alpha\}_{\alpha \in I}, \vdash\dashv)$ be an ARS. If there is a well-founded partial ordering $\succ$ on I such that for all $\alpha, \beta \in I$ properties $LD(\alpha, \beta)$ and $LD(\alpha)$ hold, then $\mathcal{A}$ is* CR$\sim$.

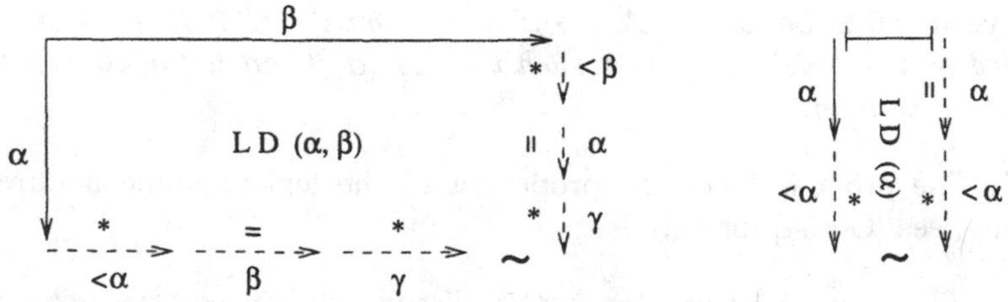

FIGURE 2.16. Locally decreasing diagrams.

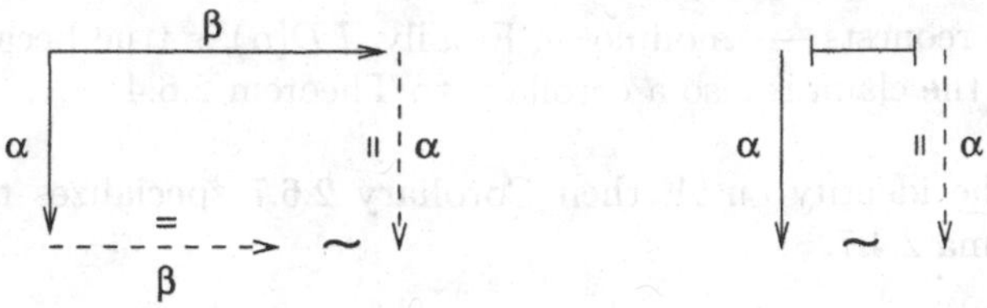

FIGURE 2.17. Subcommutation modulo ~ and SCOM⊢⊣.

Proof See [Ohl98a]. □

Next we will derive consequences of this theorem.

Corollary 2.6.5 *Let* $\mathcal{A} = (A, \{\to_\alpha\}_{\alpha \in I}, \vdash\dashv)$ *be an ARS. If, for all* $\alpha, \beta \in I$, $\to_\alpha$ *subcommutes with* $\to_\beta$ *modulo* $\sim$ *and* $\to_\alpha$ *is* SCOM⊢⊣, *then* $\mathcal{A}$ *is* CR~.

Proof Let $\succ$ be the empty ordering on I. Then we have $LD(\alpha, \beta)$ and $LD(\alpha)$ for all $\alpha, \beta \in I$; see Figure 2.17. Thus, the corollary follows from Theorem 2.6.4. □

If the constituent relations are transitive and reflexive, then subcommutation modulo ~ coincides with commutation modulo ~ and SCOM⊢⊣ coincides with COM⊢⊣. Note that the lemma of Hindley-Rosen is formulated in terms of commutation and in fact, if ⊢⊣ is the identity on A, then Corollary 2.6.5 specializes to Lemma 2.4.4.

Definition 2.6.6 Let $\mathcal{A} = (A, \{\to_1, \to_2\}, \vdash\dashv)$ be an ARS. We say that $\to_2$ *requests* $\to_1$ *modulo* $\sim$ if ${}_1^*\!\leftarrow \cdot \to_2^* \subseteq \to_2^* \cdot \to_1^* \cdot \sim \cdot {}_1^*\!\leftarrow$ and ${}_2^*\!\leftarrow \cdot \vdash\dashv \subseteq \to_1^* \cdot \sim \cdot {}_1^*\!\leftarrow \cdot {}_2^*\!\leftarrow$; see Figure 2.18.

Corollary 2.6.7 *Let* $\mathcal{A} = (A, \{\to_1, \to_2\}, \vdash\dashv)$. *If* $\to_1$ *and* $\to_2$ *are* CON~, $\to_2$ *requests* $\to_1$ *modulo* ~, *and* $\to_1$ *is* COM⊢⊣, *then* $\mathcal{A}$ *is* CR~.

Proof Define $\to_\alpha = \to_1^*$ and $\to_\beta = \to_2^*$. So $\to_\alpha$ and $\to_\beta$ are transitive and reflexive relations. Take as ordering $\alpha \prec \beta$. $LD(\alpha, \alpha)$ and $LD(\beta, \beta)$ hold because $\to_1$ and $\to_2$ are CON~. $LD(\alpha, \beta) = LD(\beta, \alpha)$ and $LD(\beta)$ hold

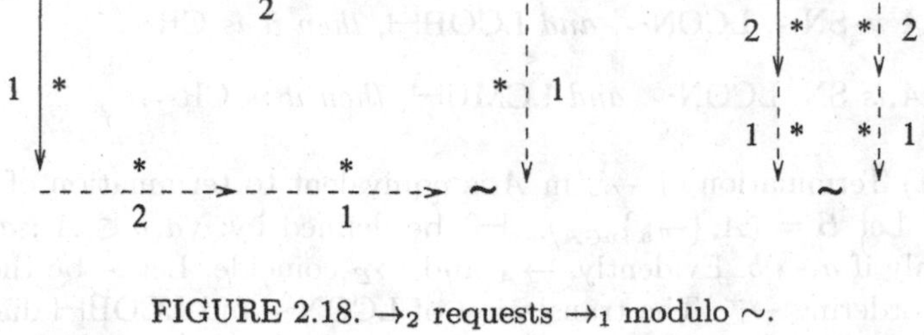

FIGURE 2.18. $\to_2$ requests $\to_1$ modulo ~.

because $\rightarrow_2$ requests $\rightarrow_1$ modulo $\sim$. Finally, $LD(\alpha)$ is true because $\rightarrow_1$ is COM$\vdash\dashv$. So the claim is also a corollary to Theorem 2.6.4. □

If $\vdash\dashv$ is the identity on A, then Corollary 2.6.7 specializes to Rosen's request lemma 2.4.7.

Definition 2.6.8 Let $\rightarrow_1$ and $\rightarrow_2$ be relations and $\sim$ an equivalence relation on A. Relation $\rightarrow_1$ is called a *refinement* of $\rightarrow_2$ if $\rightarrow_2 \subseteq \rightarrow_1^*$; it is said to be a *compatible refinement* of $\rightarrow_2$ *modulo* $\sim$ if it is a refinement of $\rightarrow_2$ and for all $a \rightarrow_1^* b$ there are $c, d \in A$ such that $a \rightarrow_2^* c \sim d\; {}_2^*\!\!\leftarrow b$.

Corollary 2.6.9 *Let $\mathcal{A}_1 = (A, \rightarrow_1, \vdash\dashv)$ be a compatible refinement of $\mathcal{A}_2 = (A, \rightarrow_2, \vdash\dashv)$ modulo $\sim$. If $\rightarrow_2$ is* CON$\sim$ *and $\rightarrow_1$ is* COM$\vdash\dashv$, *then $\rightarrow_1$ is* CR$\sim$.

Proof It is relatively simple to show that the corollary is also an immediate consequence of Theorem 2.6.4. We prefer to give the following direct proof (suggested by Vincent van Oostrom), however, because it is shorter.

Consider a divergence $a \sim \cdot\, {}_1^*\!\!\leftarrow \cdot \rightarrow_1^* \cdot \sim b$, where $a, b \in A$. We have

$$\begin{array}{rl}
a \sim \cdot \rightarrow_2^* \cdot \sim \cdot\, {}_2^*\!\!\leftarrow \cdot \rightarrow_2^* \cdot \sim \cdot\, {}_2^*\!\!\leftarrow \cdot \sim b & \text{(compatibility)}\\
a \sim \cdot \rightarrow_2^* \cdot \sim \cdot \rightarrow_2^* \cdot \sim \cdot\, {}_2^*\!\!\leftarrow \cdot \sim \cdot\, {}_2^*\!\!\leftarrow \cdot \sim b & (\rightarrow_2 \text{ is CON}\sim)\\
a \sim \cdot \rightarrow_1^* \cdot \sim \cdot \rightarrow_1^* \cdot \sim \cdot\, {}_1^*\!\!\leftarrow \cdot \sim \cdot\, {}_1^*\!\!\leftarrow \cdot \sim b & \text{(refinement)}\\
a \rightarrow_1^* \cdot \sim \cdot\, {}_1^*\!\!\leftarrow b & (\rightarrow_1 \text{ is COM}\sim)
\end{array}$$

Hence $\rightarrow_1$ is CR$\sim$. □

It is not difficult to prove the following converse of the preceding corollary. Let $\mathcal{A}_1 = (A, \rightarrow_1, \vdash\dashv)$ be a compatible refinement of $\mathcal{A}_2 = (A, \rightarrow_2, \vdash\dashv)$ modulo $\sim$. If $\rightarrow_1$ is CON$\sim$ and $\rightarrow_2$ is COM$\vdash\dashv$, then $\rightarrow_2$ is CR$\sim$. If $\vdash\dashv$ is the identity on A, then Corollary 2.6.9 specializes to Proposition 2.4.9.

Corollary 2.6.10 is closely related to Proposition 2.5.12. In its first statement (Huet [Hue80]), SN$\sim$ cannot be weakened to SN, as shown in Example 2.6.11 (see [Ave95, example 4.1.8]). However, if we replace LCOH$\vdash\dashv$ with the stronger property LCMU$\vdash\dashv$, then SN is sufficient. This fact is made precise in the second statement shown by Jouannaud and Munoz [JM84].

Corollary 2.6.10 *Let $\mathcal{A}$ be an ARS.*

1. *If $\mathcal{A}$ is* SN$\sim$, LCON$\sim$, *and* LCOH$\vdash\dashv$, *then it is* CR$\sim$.
2. *If $\mathcal{A}$ is* SN, LCON$\sim$, *and* LCMU$\vdash\dashv$, *then it is* CR$\sim$.

Proof (1) Termination of $\rightarrow_\sim$ in A is equivalent to termination of $\rightarrow/\sim$ in $A/\sim$. Let $\mathcal{B} = (A, \{\rightarrow_{\mathbf{a}}\}_{\mathbf{a} \in A/\sim}, \vdash\dashv)$ be defined by: $\forall a, b \in A : a \rightarrow_{\mathbf{a}} b$ if and only if $a \rightarrow b$. Evidently, $\rightarrow_{\mathcal{A}}$ and $\rightarrow_{\mathcal{B}}$ coincide. Let $\succ$ be the well-founded ordering $\rightarrow_\sim^+$. The translation of LCON$\sim$ and LCOH$\vdash\dashv$ diagrams

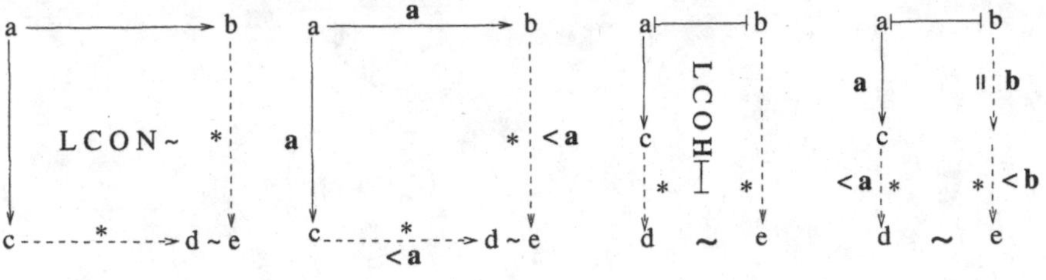

(i) (ii) (iii) (iv)

FIGURE 2.19. Translation of LCON$\sim$ and LCOH$\vdash\!\dashv$ diagrams.

is depicted in Figure 2.19. Note that a reduction sequence $a \to c \to^* d$ in $\mathcal{A}$ translates to a reduction sequence $a \to_{\mathbf{a}} c \to^*_{\prec \mathbf{a}} d$ in $\mathcal{B}$. Also note that in Figure 2.19(iv), we have $\mathbf{a} = \mathbf{b}$ because $a \sim b$. Thus (ii) and (iv) are locally decreasing diagrams and $\mathcal{B}$ is CR$\sim$ by Theorem 2.6.4. Because $\to_{\mathcal{A}} = \to_{\mathcal{B}}$, $\mathcal{A}$ is CR$\sim$.
(2) The combination of SN and LCMU$\vdash\!\dashv$ implies SN$\sim$; see [JM84, theorem 14]. The claim follows from (1) because LCMU$\vdash\!\dashv$ implies LCOH$\vdash\!\dashv$. □

Observe that if $\vdash\!\dashv$ is the identity on A, then both statements of Corollary 2.6.10 specialize to Newman's lemma 2.2.5.

Example 2.6.11 Let the ARS $\mathcal{A}$ be defined by $a \leftarrow b \overset{\vdash\!\dashv}{\leftarrow} c \overset{\vdash\!\dashv}{\rightarrow} d \to e$. $\mathcal{A}$ is SN, LCON$\sim$, and LCOH$\vdash\!\dashv$ but not CR$\sim$ (in fact, it lacks LCOH$\sim$).

For further details on the subject, see [Ohl98a].

3 Term Rewriting Systems

In this chapter we will present the basic concepts of term rewriting that are needed in this book. More details on term rewriting, its applications, and related subjects can be found in the textbook of Baader and Nipkow [BN98]. Readers versed in German are also referred to the textbooks of Avenhaus [Ave95], Bündgen [Bün98], and Drosten [Dro89]. Moreover, there are several survey articles [HO80, DJ90, Klo92, Pla93] that can also be consulted.

3.1 Terms and Substitutions

Definition 3.1.1 A *signature* is a countable set $\mathcal{F}$ of *function symbols* or *operators*, where every $f \in \mathcal{F}$ is associated with a natural number denoting its *arity* (the number of "arguments" it is supposed to have). $\mathcal{F}^{(n)}$ denotes the set of all function symbols of arity n, hence $\mathcal{F} = \bigcup_{n \in \mathbb{N}} \mathcal{F}^{(n)}$. Elements of $\mathcal{F}^{(0)}$ are called *constants*.

Other authors use the symbol Σ instead of $\mathcal{F}$ to denote signatures.

Definition 3.1.2 Let $\mathcal{F}$ be a signature and let $\mathcal{V}$ be a countable set of *variables* with $\mathcal{F} \cap \mathcal{V} = \emptyset$. The set of *terms* $\mathcal{T}(\mathcal{F}, \mathcal{V})$ is defined to be the smallest set such that

- $\mathcal{V} \subseteq \mathcal{T}(\mathcal{F}, \mathcal{V})$.
- If $f \in \mathcal{F}^{(n)}$ and $t_1, \ldots, t_n \in \mathcal{T}(\mathcal{F}, \mathcal{V})$, then $f(t_1, \ldots, t_n) \in \mathcal{T}(\mathcal{F}, \mathcal{V})$.

We write f instead of $f()$ for every constant f. The set of function symbols appearing in a term $t \in \mathcal{T}(\mathcal{F}, \mathcal{V})$ is denoted by $\mathcal{F}un(t)$, and the set of variables occurring in t is denoted by $\mathcal{V}ar(t)$. Terms without variables are called *ground* terms. The set of all ground terms is denoted by $\mathcal{T}(\mathcal{F})$. If a term t does not contain multiple occurrences of the same variable, it is said to be *linear*.

It is common to use the symbol $\mathcal{X}$ instead of $\mathcal{V}$ to denote a set of variables.

Definition 3.1.3 For $t \in \mathcal{T}(\mathcal{F}, \mathcal{V})$, $root(t)$ denotes the *root symbol* of t and is defined by:

$$root(t) = \begin{cases} t & \text{if} \quad t \in \mathcal{V} \\ f & \text{if} \quad t = f(t_1, \ldots, t_n) \end{cases}$$

Definition 3.1.4 Let $\Box \notin \mathcal{F} \cup \mathcal{V}$ be a special constant symbol. A *context* is a term in $\mathcal{T}(\mathcal{F} \cup \{\Box\}, \mathcal{V})$. If $C[, \ldots,]$ is a context with n occurrences of $\Box$ and $t_1, \ldots, t_n$ are terms, then $C[t_1, \ldots, t_n]$ is the result of replacing the occurrences of $\Box$ with $t_1, \ldots, t_n$ from left to right. A context containing precisely one occurrence of $\Box$ is denoted by $C[\,]$. A term t is a *subterm* of a term s if there exists a context $C[\,]$ such that $s = C[t]$. A subterm t of s is *proper*, which is denoted by $s \rhd t$, if $s \neq t$.

By abuse of notation we write $\mathcal{T}(\mathcal{F}, \mathcal{V})$ for $\mathcal{T}(\mathcal{F} \cup \{\Box\}, \mathcal{V})$, interpreting $\Box$ as a special constant that is always available but is used only for the aforementioned purpose. In those cases in which the notion of subterm is not precise enough, we will distinguish occurrences of subterms by means of positions.

Definition 3.1.5 The set $\mathcal{P}os(t)$ of *positions* in $t \in \mathcal{T}(\mathcal{F}, \mathcal{V})$ is defined by:

$$\mathcal{P}os(t) = \begin{cases} \{\varepsilon\} & \text{if} \quad t \in \mathcal{V} \\ \{\varepsilon\} \cup \{i.p \mid p \in \mathcal{P}os(t_i) \text{ and } 1 \leq i \leq n\} & \text{if} \quad t = f(t_1, \ldots, t_n) \end{cases}$$

A position p within a term t is thus a sequence of natural numbers (where ε denotes the empty sequence and the numbers are separated by dots) describing the path from the root of t to the root of the *subterm occurrence* $t|_p$, where

$$t|_p = \begin{cases} t & \text{if} \quad p = \varepsilon \\ t_i|_q & \text{if} \quad p = i.q,\ 1 \leq i \leq n, \text{ and } t = f(t_1, \ldots, t_n) \end{cases}$$

Furthermore, we define $\mathcal{VP}os(t) = \{p \in \mathcal{P}os(t) \mid t|_p \in \mathcal{V}\}$. That is, $\mathcal{VP}os(t)$ denotes the set of all *variable positions* in t.

Positions are partially ordered by the so-called *prefix ordering* $\geq$, i.e., $p \geq q$ if there is an o such that $p = q.o$. In this case we say that p is *below* q or q is *above* p. Moreover, if $p \neq q$, then we say that p is *strictly below* q

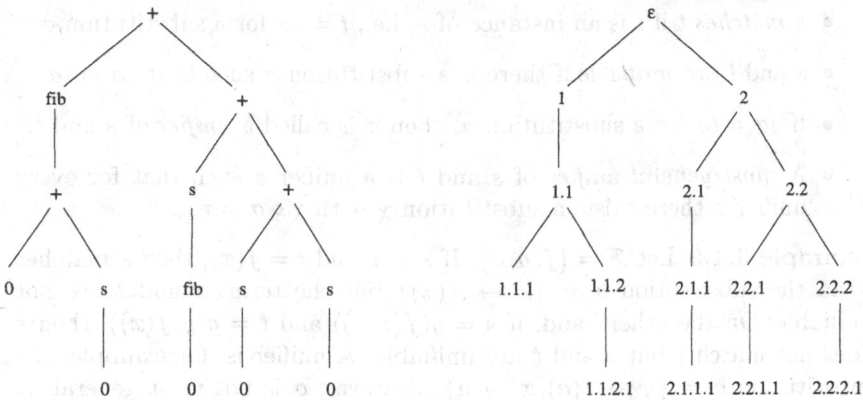

FIGURE 3.1. Positions in a term.

or q is *strictly above* p. Two positions p and q are *independent* or *disjoint*, denoted by $p \parallel q$, if neither is below the other.

Let $p \in \mathcal{P}os(t)$ and $s \in \mathcal{T}(\mathcal{F}, \mathcal{V})$. Then $t[p \leftarrow s]$ denotes the term obtained from t by replacing the subterm $t|_p$ of t at position p with s. Formally, it is defined as follows:

- $t[\varepsilon \leftarrow s] = s$.
- $f(t_1, \ldots, t_n)[i.q \leftarrow s] = f(t_1, \ldots, t_i[q \leftarrow s], \ldots, t_n)$.

The *size* $|t|$ of a term t is defined by $|t| = card(\mathcal{P}os(t))$, where $card(M)$ denotes the cardinality of a set M.

Example 3.1.6 Let the signature $\mathcal{F} = \{0, s, +, fib\}$ be given. Consider the ground term $t = fib(0 + s(0)) + (s(fib(0)) + (s(0) + s(0)))$, where $+$ is written in infix notation. Its root symbol is $+$ and its size is 15. The positions in t are depicted in Figure 3.1. There are three occurrences of the subterm $s(0)$ in t: at the positions 1.1.2, 2.2.1, and 2.2.2. Moreover, we have, for example, $t[2 \leftarrow s(0)] = fib(0 + s(0)) + s(0)$.

Definition 3.1.7 A *substitution* σ is a mapping from $\mathcal{V}$ to $\mathcal{T}(\mathcal{F}, \mathcal{V})$ such that the *domain* $\mathcal{D}om(\sigma) = \{x \in \mathcal{V} \mid \sigma(x) \neq x\}$ of σ is finite. Occasionally we present a substitution σ as $\{x \mapsto \sigma(x) \mid x \in \mathcal{D}om(\sigma)\}$. The substitution with empty domain will be denoted by ε. Every substitution σ extends uniquely to a morphism $\sigma : \mathcal{T}(\mathcal{F}, \mathcal{V}) \to \mathcal{T}(\mathcal{F}, \mathcal{V})$, where $\sigma(f(t_1, \ldots, t_n)) = f(\sigma(t_1), \ldots, \sigma(t_n))$ for each n-ary function symbol f and terms $t_1, \ldots, t_n$. $\sigma(t)$ is said to be an *instance* of t. We also use the notation $t\sigma$ for $\sigma(t)$. The *composition* $\tau \circ \sigma$ of two substitutions τ and σ is defined by $(\tau \circ \sigma)(x) = \tau(\sigma(x))$. A substitution σ is a *variable renaming* if there is a substitution τ such that $\tau \circ \sigma$ is the identity function on $\mathcal{V}$.

Definition 3.1.8 Let $s, t \in \mathcal{T}(\mathcal{F}, \mathcal{V})$:

- s *matches* t if t is an instance of s, i.e., $t = s\sigma$ for a substitution σ.
- s and t are *unifiable* if there is a substitution σ such that $s\sigma = t\sigma$.
- If $s\sigma = t\sigma$ for a substitution σ, then σ is called a *unifier* of s and t.
- A *most general unifier* of s and t is a unifier σ such that for every unifier τ there exists a substitution χ with $\chi \circ \sigma = \tau$.

Example 3.1.9 Let $\mathcal{F} = \{f, g, a\}$. If $s = x$ and $t = f(x)$, then s matches t via the substitution $\sigma = \{x \mapsto f(x)\}$ but the terms s and t are not unifiable. On the other hand, if $s = g(f(x), y)$ and $t = g(y, f(x))$, then s does not match t but s and t are unifiable. A unifier is, for example, the substitution $\sigma = \{y \mapsto f(a), x \mapsto a\}$. However, σ is not most general. A most general unifier of s and t is $\tau = \{y \mapsto f(x)\}$.

Matching and unifiability of two terms s and t are decidable. Furthermore, if two terms are unifiable, then they have a most general unifier that is unique except for variable renaming. For example, the algorithms of Robinson [Rob65] and Martelli and Montanari [MM82] construct a most general unifier of two terms.

3.2 Rewrite Systems

Definition 3.2.1 A *term rewriting system* (TRS) is a pair $(\mathcal{F}, \mathcal{R})$ consisting of a signature $\mathcal{F}$ and a set $\mathcal{R} \subset \mathcal{T}(\mathcal{F}, \mathcal{V}) \times \mathcal{T}(\mathcal{F}, \mathcal{V})$ of *rewrite rules* or *reduction rules*. A TRS $(\mathcal{F}, \mathcal{R})$ is *finite* if both $\mathcal{F}$ and $\mathcal{R}$ are finite. Every rewrite rule (l, r) must satisfy the following two constraints:

- $l \notin \mathcal{V}$, i.e., the left-hand side l is not a variable, and
- $\mathcal{V}ar(r) \subseteq \mathcal{V}ar(l)$, i.e., variables occurring on the right-hand side r also occur in l.

Rewrite rules (l, r) will be denoted by $l \to r$. The rewrite rules of a TRS $(\mathcal{F}, \mathcal{R})$ define a *rewrite relation* $\to_{\mathcal{R}}$ on $\mathcal{T}(\mathcal{F}, \mathcal{V})$ as follows: $s \to_{\mathcal{R}} t$ if there exists a rewrite rule $l \to r$ in $\mathcal{R}$, a substitution σ, and a context $C[\,]$ such that $s = C[l\sigma]$ and $t = C[r\sigma]$. We call $s \to_{\mathcal{R}} t$ a *rewrite step* or *reduction step*. We also say that s rewrites to t by *contracting* redex $l\sigma$, where an instance of a left-hand side of a rewrite rule is called a *redex* (reducible expression).

If $s \to_{\mathcal{R}} t$, then there is a position $p \in \mathcal{P}os(s)$ and a rewrite rule $l \to r \in \mathcal{R}$ such that $s = s[p \leftarrow l\sigma]$ and $t = t[p \leftarrow r\sigma]$. In order to make p and $l \to r$ explicit, we will sometimes use the notation $s \to_{p, l \to r} t$. Furthermore, we will often simply write $\mathcal{R}$ instead of $(\mathcal{F}, \mathcal{R})$ if the signature can be inferred from the context (by default we will assume that $\mathcal{F}$ consists of the function symbols occurring in $\mathcal{R}$).

All notions defined in Chapter 2 for abstract reduction systems carry over to term rewriting systems by associating the ARS $(\mathcal{T}(\mathcal{F},\mathcal{V}),\rightarrow_{\mathcal{R}})$ with the TRS $(\mathcal{F},\mathcal{R})$. We will also use "localized" versions of these notions. The phrase "a term t is terminating," for example, means that there is no infinite reduction sequence starting from t.

A substitution σ is *normalized* w.r.t. a TRS $\mathcal{R}$ if $x\sigma$ is a normal form w.r.t. $\mathcal{R}$ for every variable $x \in \mathcal{D}om(\sigma)$.

The following classification of operators will be of utmost importance. It separates functions from data.

Definition 3.2.2 The rules of a TRS $(\mathcal{F},\mathcal{R})$ partition $\mathcal{F}$ into two disjoint sets

- $\mathcal{D} = \{root(l) \mid l \rightarrow r \in \mathcal{R}\}$ of *defined symbols*, and
- $\mathcal{C} = \mathcal{F} \setminus \mathcal{D}$ of *constructors*.

A term $t \in \mathcal{T}(\mathcal{C},\mathcal{V})$ is called a *constructor term*. Furthermore, the TRS $(\mathcal{F},\mathcal{R})$ is a *constructor system* if every left-hand side $f(t_1,\dots,t_n)$ of a rewrite rule of $\mathcal{R}$ satisfies $t_1,\dots,t_n \in \mathcal{T}(\mathcal{C},\mathcal{V})$.

The phrase "defined function symbol" is justified by the existence of defining rules for that symbol.

Throughout this book, we will use the operator $\uplus$ to denote the *disjoint union* of sets. For example, to emphasize that $\mathcal{F}$ is the disjoint union of $\mathcal{D}$ and $\mathcal{C}$, we will often write $\mathcal{F} = \mathcal{D} \uplus \mathcal{C}$ instead of $\mathcal{F} = \mathcal{D} \cup \mathcal{C}$.

Example 3.2.3 The TRS $\mathcal{R}$ consisting of the following five rules computes the Fibonacci numbers:

$$
\begin{array}{rcl}
0 + y & \rightarrow & y \\
s(x) + y & \rightarrow & s(x+y) \\
fib(0) & \rightarrow & 0 \\
fib(s(0)) & \rightarrow & s(0) \\
fib(s(s(x))) & \rightarrow & fib(s(x)) + fib(x)
\end{array}
$$

We have $\mathcal{D} = \{+, fib\}$ and $\mathcal{C} = \{0, s\}$.

Next we introduce important (syntactic) properties of TRSs that rely on the structure of terms and thus cannot be expressed on the abstract level of ARSs.

Definition 3.2.4 Let $\mathcal{R}$ be a TRS. A rewrite rule $l \rightarrow r \in \mathcal{R}$ is called

1. *left-linear* if l is linear,
2. *right-linear* if r is linear,
3. *linear* if it is left- and right-linear,

4. *variable-preserving* (or nonerasing) if $\mathcal{V}ar(l) = \mathcal{V}ar(r)$,

5. *size-preserving* if $|l\sigma| = |r\sigma|$ holds for every substitution σ,

6. *nonsize-increasing* if $|l\sigma| \geq |r\sigma|$ holds for every substitution σ.

$\mathcal{R}$ has one of the properties if all of its rewrite rules have the property.

Clearly, if a rewrite rule $l \to r$ is size-preserving (nonsize-increasing), then $s \to_{l \to r} t$ implies that $|s| = |t|$ ($|s| \geq |t|$).

Definition 3.2.5 A rewrite rule $l \to r$ in a TRS $\mathcal{R}$ is called

1. *collapsing* if $r \in \mathcal{V}$,

2. *duplicating* if there is an $x \in \mathcal{V}$ that occurs more often in r than in l.

$\mathcal{R}$ has one of the properties if one of its rewrite rules has the property.

For example, the TRS in Example 3.2.3 is left-linear, variable-preserving, collapsing, and duplicating but not right-linear, size-preserving, or nonsize-increasing. The latter follows immediately from the following characterization of nonsize-increasingness.

Lemma 3.2.6 *A TRS $\mathcal{R}$ is nonsize-increasing if and only if*

1. $|l| \geq |r|$ for every rule $l \to r \in \mathcal{R}$ and

2. $\mathcal{R}$ is nonduplicating.

Proof It is fairly easy to verify that (1) and (2) imply that $\mathcal{R}$ is nonsize-increasing. Conversely, let $\mathcal{R}$ be nonsize-increasing and fix a rewrite rule $l \to r \in \mathcal{R}$. Then $|l\sigma| \geq |r\sigma|$ holds for every substitution σ. In particular, this inequality holds for the empty substitution, hence $|l| \geq |r|$. In order to show that the rule $l \to r$ is nonduplicating, let M_l and M_r denote the multisets of the variables occurring in l and r, respectively. We show that $M_l(x) \geq M_r(x)$ holds for every $x \in \mathcal{V}ar(l)$. For an indirect proof, suppose that there is a variable $x \in \mathcal{V}ar(r)$ with $M_r(x) > M_l(x)$. Note that $\mathcal{V}ar(r) \subseteq \mathcal{V}ar(l)$ implies $M_l(x) \geq 1$. With $\sigma = \{x \mapsto l\}$, it follows that

$$\begin{array}{rcl} |r\sigma| & = & |r| - M_r(x) + M_r(x) * |l| \\ & > & M_r(x) * |l| \\ & \geq & (M_l(x) + 1) * |l| \\ & = & |l| + M_l(x) * |l| \\ & > & |l| - M_l(x) + M_l(x) * |l| \\ & = & |l\sigma| \end{array}$$

This contradiction shows that $M_l(x) \geq M_r(x)$ holds for every $x \in \mathcal{V}ar(l)$. In other words, the rule $l \to r$ is nonduplicating. Because this rule was chosen arbitrarily, it follows (1) $|l| \geq |r|$ for every rule $l \to r \in \mathcal{R}$ and (2) $\mathcal{R}$ is nonduplicating. $\square$

A similar characterization exists for size-preservingness.

Lemma 3.2.7 *A TRS $\mathcal{R}$ is size-preserving if and only if*

1. $|l| = |r|$ *for every rule* $l \to r \in \mathcal{R}$ *and*
2. *the multiset of the variables in l coincides with the multiset of the variables in r.*

Proof Similar to the proof of Lemma 3.2.6. $\square$

We conclude this chapter by showing how every string rewriting system $\mathcal{S}$ over an alphabet Σ can be viewed as a term rewriting system. To this end, let the signature $\mathcal{F}$ contain a constant c and a unary function symbol for every letter $a \in \Sigma$. For example, if $\Sigma = \{\bullet, \circ\}$, then let $\mathcal{F} = \{b, w, c\}$, where b is associated with $\bullet$ and w with $\circ$. Then a word over Σ can be represented by a term over $\mathcal{F}$. For example, $w(w(w(b(c))))$ represents the word $\circ\circ\circ\bullet$. Furthermore, a string rewrite rule like $\bullet\circ \to \circ\circ\circ\bullet$ can be represented by the term rewrite rule $b(w(x)) \to w(w(w(b(x))))$. Thus, the SRS $\mathcal{S}$

$$\begin{array}{lcl} \bullet\circ & \to & \circ\circ\circ\bullet \\ \circ\bullet & \to & \bullet \\ \bullet\bullet & \to & \circ\circ\circ\circ \\ \circ\circ & \to & \circ \end{array}$$

from Example 2.3.7 corresponds to the TRS $\mathcal{R}$

$$\begin{array}{rcl} b(w(x)) & \to & w(w(w(b(x)))) \\ w(b(x)) & \to & b(x) \\ b(b(x)) & \to & w(w(w(w(x)))) \\ w(w(x)) & \to & w(x) \end{array}$$

and a reduction step like $\bullet\circ\circ \to \bullet\circ$ in $\mathcal{S}$ corresponds to the rewrite step $b(w(w(c))) \to_{\mathcal{R}} b(w(c))$.

A comprehensive study of SRSs (which are also called semi-Thue systems) can be found in [Jan88] and [BO93].

4
Confluence

In this chapter, we will recall several well-known results concerning confluence. First, it will be shown that confluence is in general an undecidable property of TRSs. Then we shall see that confluence is decidable for finite terminating systems. Moreover, two sufficient criteria for confluence of possibly nonterminating TRSs will be given.

4.1 Undecidability of Confluence

In this section we will show undecidability of confluence by using Post's correspondence problem (PCP). First, we recall PCP, which can be stated as follows:

> Given a finite alphabet Γ and a finite set $P \subset \Gamma^+ \times \Gamma^+$, is there some natural number $n > 0$ and $(\alpha_i, \beta_i) \in P$ for $i \in \{1, \ldots, n\}$ such that $\alpha_1\alpha_2 \cdots \alpha_n = \beta_1\beta_2 \cdots \beta_n$?

This problem is known to be undecidable even in the case of a two-letter alphabet; see Post [Pos46]. The set P is called an *instance* of PCP, the string $\alpha_1\alpha_2 \cdots \alpha_n = \beta_1\beta_2 \cdots \beta_n$ is a *solution* for P. Matiyasevich and Senizergues [MS96] showed that PCP is undecidable even when restricted to instances consisting of seven pairs. In the following, we assume that $\Gamma = \{0, 1\}$ and that P is nonempty. This entails no loss of generality.

As an example, consider the instance $\{(1, 111), (10111, 10), (10, 0)\}$. It has a solution $10111|1|1|10 = 10|111|111|0$. A negative example is the instance $\{(10,101),(011,11),(101,011)\}$, it has no solution. A more difficult instance is $\{(001,0),(01,011),(01,101),(10,001)\}$. It has solutions but these are quite long; see [Sch97].

In what follows, we represent words over $\Gamma = \{0,1\}$ by ground terms over the signature $\{0,1,c\}$, where c is a constant and $0,1$ are unary function symbols. For example, the word 011 will be represented by the ground term $0(1(1(c)))$. If, for example, $\alpha = 10$ and t is a term, then $\alpha(t)$ denotes the term $1(0(t))$.

In order to prove the undecidability of confluence, we associate with every PCP instance P the TRS

$$\mathcal{R}(P) = \begin{cases} A & \rightarrow & f(\alpha(c),\beta(c)) & \text{for all } (\alpha,\beta) \in P \\ f(x,y) & \rightarrow & f(\alpha(x),\beta(y)) & \text{for all } (\alpha,\beta) \in P \\ f(x,x) & \rightarrow & B \end{cases}$$

The next proposition plays a key role in the undecidability proof.

Proposition 4.1.1 *$A \rightarrow^*_{\mathcal{R}(P)} B$ if and only if P admits a solution.*

Proof Suppose $\gamma \in \Gamma^+$ is a solution of P. So $\gamma = \alpha_1 \cdots \alpha_n = \beta_1 \cdots \beta_n$ for some $n \geq 1$ with $(\alpha_i, \beta_i) \in P$ for $i \in \{1,\ldots,n\}$. We have the following reduction sequence in $\mathcal{R}(P)$:

$$A \rightarrow f(\alpha_n(c),\beta_n(c)) \rightarrow^* f(\alpha_1 \cdots \alpha_n(c), \beta_1 \cdots \beta_n(c)) = f(\gamma(c),\gamma(c)) \rightarrow B$$

Conversely, suppose that $A \rightarrow^*_{\mathcal{R}(P)} B$. The reduction sequence from A to B must be of the form

$$A \rightarrow_{\mathcal{R}(P)} f(\alpha_1(c),\beta_1(c)) \rightarrow^*_{\mathcal{R}(P)} f(\alpha_n \cdots \alpha_1(c), \beta_n \cdots \beta_1(c)) \rightarrow_{\mathcal{R}(P)} B$$

for some $n \geq 1$ with $(\alpha_i,\beta_i) \in P$ for $i \in \{1,\ldots,n\}$. The last step is only possible if $\alpha_n \cdots \alpha_1(c) = \beta_n \cdots \beta_1(c)$. Hence $\alpha_n \cdots \alpha_1$ is a solution of P. $\square$

As a matter of fact, in the undecidability proof we will work with $\mathcal{R}_0(P) = \mathcal{R}(P) \cup \{f(x,y) \rightarrow A\}$ instead of $\mathcal{R}(P)$.

Lemma 4.1.2 *$A \rightarrow^*_{\mathcal{R}_0(P)} B$ if and only if $A \rightarrow^*_{\mathcal{R}(P)} B$.*

Proof In a shortest $\mathcal{R}_0(P)$-reduction sequence from A to B the rewrite rule $f(x,y) \rightarrow A$ is not used. The other direction is trivial. $\square$

Proposition 4.1.3 *Confluence is an undecidable property of TRSs.*

Proof Let P be an instance of PCP. We will show that $\mathcal{R}_0(P)$ is confluent if and only if P admits a solution. The proposition then follows from the undecidability of PCP.

If P admits a solution, then $A \to^*_{\mathcal{R}_0(P)} B$ according to Proposition 4.1.1 and Lemma 4.1.2. With this observation it is fairly simple to prove by case analysis that every term is confluent. Suppose conversely that $\mathcal{R}_0(P)$ is confluent. The terms A and B are convertible in the system $\mathcal{R}_0(P)$ because $f(x,x) \to_{\mathcal{R}_0(P)} A$ and $f(x,x) \to_{\mathcal{R}_0(P)} B$. Because $\mathcal{R}_0(P)$ is confluent and B is a normal form, $A \to^*_{\mathcal{R}_0(P)} B$ must hold. Thus, P admits a solution by Proposition 4.1.1 and Lemma 4.1.2. □

Local confluence can be shown to be undecidable as in the previous proof.

4.2 Confluence of Terminating Systems

In this section we will see that local confluence is decidable for finite TRSs. In combination with Newman's lemma 2.2.5, this entails the decidability of confluence for terminating systems. First, we will state some prerequisites.

Definition 4.2.1 Let $\mathcal{R}$ be a TRS.

1. Let $l_1 \to r_1$ and $l_2 \to r_2$ be (variable) renamed versions of rewrite rules of $\mathcal{R}$ such that they have no variables in common. Suppose $l_1 = C[t]$ with $t \notin \mathcal{V}$ such that t and l_2 are unifiable. Let σ be a most general unifier of t and l_2. We call $\langle C[r_2]\sigma, r_1\sigma\rangle$ a *critical pair* of $\mathcal{R}$. If the two rules are renamed versions of the same rewrite rule of $\mathcal{R}$, we do not consider the case $C[\,] = \Box$.

2. $CP(\mathcal{R})$ denotes the set of all critical pairs between rules of $\mathcal{R}$.

3. A critical pair $\langle s,t\rangle \in CP(\mathcal{R})$ is called *joinable* if s and t are joinable.

4. A critical pair $\langle s,t\rangle \in CP(\mathcal{R})$ is called *trivial* if $s = t$.

Example 4.2.2 For

$$\mathcal{R} = \left\{ \begin{array}{rcl} b(w(x)) & \to & w(w(w(b(x)))) \\ w(b(x)) & \to & b(x) \\ b(b(x)) & \to & w(w(w(w(x)))) \\ w(w(x)) & \to & w(x) \end{array} \right.$$

the set $CP(\mathcal{R})$ consists of the critical pairs

$$\begin{array}{c} \langle b(b(x)),\ w(w(w(b(b(x)))))\rangle \\ \langle b(w(x)),\ w(w(w(b(w(x)))))\rangle \\ \langle w(w(w(w(b(x))))),\ b(w(x))\rangle \\ \langle w(w(w(w(w(x))))),\ b(b(x))\rangle \\ \langle b(w(w(w(b(x))))),\ w(w(w(w(w(x))))))\rangle \\ \langle b(w(w(w(w(x))))),\ w(w(w(w(b(x))))))\rangle \\ \langle w(b(x)),\ w(b(x))\rangle \\ \langle w(w(x)),\ w(w(x))\rangle \end{array}$$

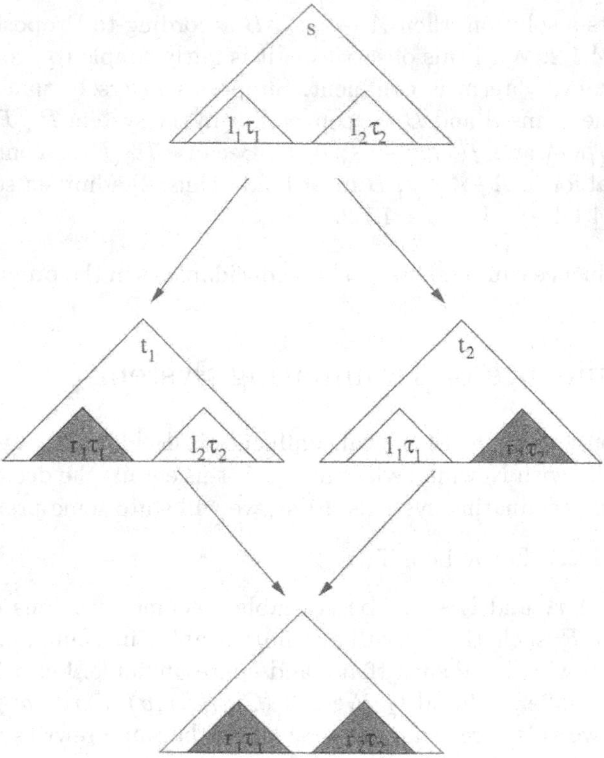

FIGURE 4.1. Contracting disjoint redexes.

Every critical pair in $CP(\mathcal{R})$ is joinable and, for example, the critical pair $\langle w(w(x)), w(w(x))\rangle$ arising from an overlap of the fourth rule with itself is trivial.

The next lemma, due to Huet [Hue80], is called the critical pair lemma.

Lemma 4.2.3 *A term rewriting system is locally confluent if and only if all its critical pairs are joinable.*

Proof Suppose that every critical pair in the TRS $\mathcal{R}$ is joinable and consider a "local divergence" $t_1 \;{}_{l_1\to r_1}\!\!\leftarrow s \to_{l_2\to r_2} t_2$. In order to show that $\mathcal{R}$ is locally confluent, we have to show that t_1 and t_2 have a common reduct. If the redexes contracted in $s \to_{l_1\to r_1} t_1$ and $s \to_{l_2\to r_2} t_2$ occur at independent positions, then we may write

$$t_1 = C[r_1\tau_1, l_2\tau_2] \leftarrow s = C[l_1\tau_1, l_2\tau_2] \to C[l_1\tau_1, r_2\tau_2] = t_2$$

In this case, $C[r_1\tau_1, r_2\tau_2]$ is a common reduct of t_1 and t_2; see Figure 4.1. Otherwise the redexes contracted in $s \to_{l_1\to r_1} t_1$ and $s \to_{l_2\to r_2} t_2$ do not

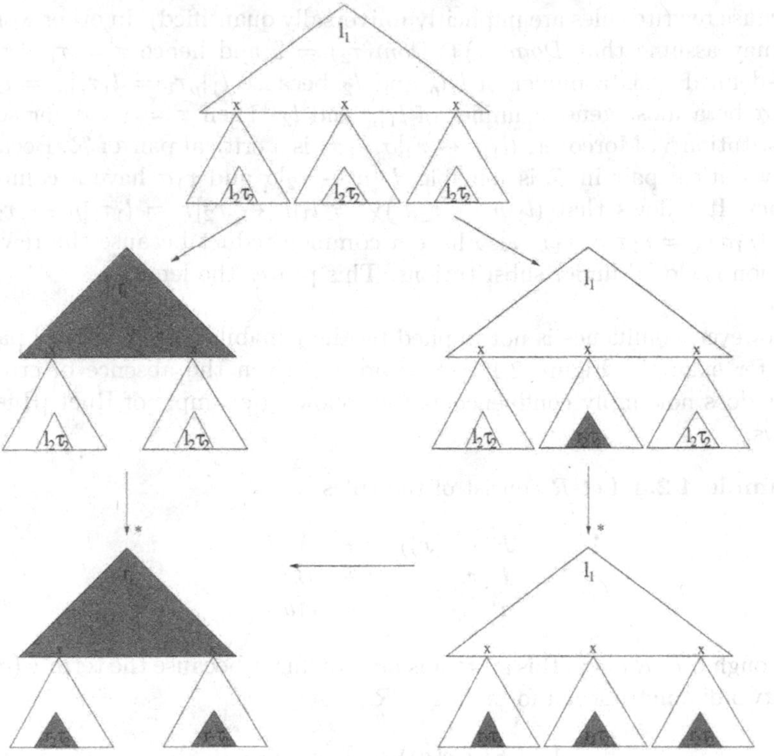

FIGURE 4.2. Noncritical overlap.

occur at independent positions. Without loss of generality, we may assume that the redex $l_2\tau_2$ is a subterm of $l_1\tau_1$, say, $l_1\tau_1|_p = l_2\tau_2$. In the following, we will show that $r_1\tau_1$ and $l_1\tau_1[p \leftarrow r_2\tau_2]$ have a common reduct. Clearly, this implies that t_1 and t_2 also have a common reduct.

Suppose first that p is either a variable position or not a position in l_1 at all. Then there is a variable $x \in \mathcal{V}ar(l_1)$ such that $l_2\tau_2$ is a subterm of $x\tau_1$ (this case is called a *variable-* or *noncritical overlap*). More precisely, $p = q_k.o$, where $l_1|_{q_k} = x$ and $x\tau_1|_o = l_2\tau_2$. Let $q_1, \ldots, q_m$ be all positions in l_1 such that $l_1|_{q_i} = x$ and note that q_k is one of them. Analogously, let $q'_1, \ldots, q'_n$ be all positions in r_1 such that $r_1|_{q'_j} = x$. The term $r_1\tau_1[q'_j.o \leftarrow r_2\tau_2 \mid 1 \leq j \leq n]$ can be obtained from $r_1\tau_1$ by contracting every redex $r_1\tau_1|_{q'_j.o} = l_2\tau_2$. Furthermore, it can be obtained from $l_1\tau_1[p \leftarrow r_2\tau_2]$ by contracting every redex $l_1\tau_1|_{q_i.o} = l_2\tau_2$, $1 \leq i \leq m$ and $i \neq k$, followed by an application of the rule $l_1 \rightarrow r_1$ to $l_1\tau_1[q_i.o \leftarrow r_2\tau_2 \mid 1 \leq i \leq m]$; see Figure 4.2. Thus $r_1\tau_1[q'_j.o \leftarrow r_2\tau_2 \mid 1 \leq j \leq n]$ is a common reduct of $r_1\tau_1$ and $l_1\tau_1[p \leftarrow r_2\tau_2]$. Finally, suppose that p is a nonvariable position in l_1 (this case is called a *critical overlap*). Without loss of generality, we may assume that l_1 and l_2 are renamed such that they have no variables in common (because rewrite rules are implicitly universally quantified). In other words, we may assume that $\mathcal{D}om(\tau_1) \cap \mathcal{D}om(\tau_2) = \emptyset$ and hence $\tau = \tau_1 \cup \tau_2$ is well-defined. τ is a unifier of $l_1|_p$ and l_2 because $l_1|_p\tau_1 = l_1\tau_1|_p = l_2\tau_2$. Let σ be a most general unifier of $l_1|_p$ and l_2. Then $\tau = \chi \circ \sigma$ for some substitution χ. Moreover, $\langle l_1[p \leftarrow r_2]\sigma, r_1\sigma\rangle$ is a critical pair of $\mathcal{R}$. Because every critical pair in $\mathcal{R}$ is joinable, $l_1[p \leftarrow r_2]\sigma$ and $r_1\sigma$ have a common reduct. It follows that $(l_1[p \leftarrow r_2]\sigma)\chi = l_1[p \leftarrow r_2]\tau = l_1\tau_1[p \leftarrow r_2\tau_2]$ and $(r_1\sigma)\chi = r_1\tau = r_1\tau_1$ also have a common reduct because the rewrite relation is closed under substitutions. This proves the lemma. □

However, confluence is not implied by the joinability of all critical pairs; see, for example, Figure 2.1 in Section 2.1. Even the absence of critical pairs does not imply confluence as the following example of Huet [Hue80] shows.

Example 4.2.4 Let $\mathcal{R}$ consist of the rules

$$\begin{array}{lcl} F(x, c(x)) & \to & A \\ F(x, x) & \to & B \\ a & \to & c(a) \end{array}$$

Although $CP(\mathcal{R}) = \emptyset$, this system is not confluent because the term $F(a, a)$ has two distinct normal forms w.r.t. $\mathcal{R}$:

$$A \leftarrow F(a, c(a)) \leftarrow F(a, a) \to B$$

By a combination of Newman's lemma and the critical pair lemma, we obtain the next important result. It was first shown by Knuth and Bendix [KB70].

Theorem 4.2.5 *A terminating term rewriting system is convergent if and only if all its critical pairs are joinable.*

Proof The assertion follows immediately from Lemma 4.2.3 in conjunction with Lemma 2.2.5. □

According to Theorem 4.2.5, the TRS from Example 4.2.2 is convergent because it is terminating (see Example 2.3.7) and all its critical pairs are joinable.

Corollary 4.2.6 *Confluence is a decidable property of terminating finite TRSs.*

Proof Let $\mathcal{R}$ be a finite terminating TRS. It is not difficult to show that the set $CP(\mathcal{R})$ is computable and finite. For every critical pair $\langle s, t\rangle \in CP(\mathcal{R})$, we reduce s and t to normal forms s' and t', respectively. If $s' = t'$ for every critical pair $\langle s, t\rangle \in CP(\mathcal{R})$, then $\mathcal{R}$ is confluent by Theorem 4.2.5.

Otherwise there is a critical pair $\langle s, t\rangle = \langle C[r_2]\sigma, r_1\sigma\rangle$ such that $s' \neq t'$. Therefore, $s' \;{}_{\mathcal{R}}^{*}\!\!\leftarrow s \;{}_{\mathcal{R}}\!\!\leftarrow l_1\sigma \rightarrow_{\mathcal{R}} t \rightarrow_{\mathcal{R}}^{*} t'$ in conjunction with the fact that s' and t' have no common reduct implies that $\mathcal{R}$ is not confluent. □

Theorem 4.2.5 is the basis of *Knuth-Bendix completion procedures.* A completion procedure tries to transform a finite set of equations E into an equivalent convergent TRS $\mathcal{R}$. If it succeeds, then the word problem for E is decidable by computing and comparing the unique normal forms of terms w.r.t. $\mathcal{R}$. Details can be found in [BN98, chapter 7].

4.3 Confluence of Nonterminating Systems

In this section we will review sufficient confluence conditions for possibly nonterminating TRSs. The first one is due to Huet [Hue80].

Definition 4.3.1 A TRS $\mathcal{R}$ is called *strongly closed* if for every critical pair $\langle s, t\rangle$ of $\mathcal{R}$ we have both $s \rightarrow_{\mathcal{R}}^{=} \cdot \;{}_{\mathcal{R}}^{*}\!\!\leftarrow t$ and $t \rightarrow_{\mathcal{R}}^{=} \cdot \;{}_{\mathcal{R}}^{*}\!\!\leftarrow s$.

Theorem 4.3.2 *A linear TRS is strongly closed if and only if it is strongly confluent.*

Proof A strongly confluent TRS is, of course, strongly closed. The other direction can be shown as in the proof of the critical pair lemma 4.2.3. □

We have seen that critical pairs arise from "overlaps" between rewrite rules. Let us specify this notion.

Definition 4.3.3 A term s *overlaps* a term t if s is unifiable with a nonvariable subterm of t. s and t are called *nonoverlapping* if neither s overlaps t nor t overlaps s. A term s *overlays* a term t if s and t are unifiable. We say that a rewrite rule $l_2 \rightarrow r_2$ *overlaps* (*overlays*) a rewrite rule $l_1 \rightarrow r_1$ if there are renamed versions $l_2' \rightarrow r_2'$ and $l_1' \rightarrow r_1'$ of $l_2 \rightarrow r_2$ and $l_1 \rightarrow r_1$, respectively, which have no variables in common and satisfy l_2' overlaps (overlays) l_1'. Again, we do not consider the trivial case in which a rewrite rule overlaps itself at the root (overlays itself, that is).

Definition 4.3.4 Let $\mathcal{R}$ be a TRS.

1. $\mathcal{R}$ is *nonoverlapping* (or nonambiguous) if $CP(\mathcal{R}) = \emptyset$, i.e., there is no overlap between rewrite rules of $\mathcal{R}$.
2. $\mathcal{R}$ is an *overlay* system if every critical pair of $CP(\mathcal{R})$ originates from an overlay of rewrite rules of $\mathcal{R}$.
3. $\mathcal{R}$ is *orthogonal* if it is left-linear and nonoverlapping.

4. $\mathcal{R}$ is *almost orthogonal* if it is a left-linear overlay system in which every critical pair is trivial.

5. $\mathcal{R}$ is *weakly orthogonal* if it is left-linear and every critical pair is trivial.

Clearly, every orthogonal TRS is almost orthogonal and every almost orthogonal TRS is weakly orthogonal. Furthermore, note that constructor systems are special overlay systems.

Example 4.3.5 A standard example of an orthogonal TRS is combinatory logic (CL), which is based on the constants S, K, and I with the following rewrite rules:

$$\begin{array}{ll} Ap(Ap(Ap(S,x),y),z) & \to Ap(Ap(x,z),Ap(y,z)) \\ Ap(Ap(K,x),y) & \to x \\ Ap(I,x) & \to x \end{array}$$

The binary operator *Ap* is called the *application* operator. Because there is only this binary operator, the following notational conventions are common:

- infix notation $s \cdot t$ is used instead of $Ap(s,t)$,
- then the dot is suppressed, and
- brackets are deleted in the convention of association to the left.

If one adopts these conventions, then the three rules of CL become

$$\begin{array}{ll} Sxyz & \to xz(yz) \\ Kxy & \to x \\ Ix & \to x \end{array}$$

CL was developed by Schönfinkel [Sch24] and rediscovered by Curry and Feys [CF58]. CL has "universal computational power": every (partial) recursive function on the natural numbers can be expressed in CL. This is one of the reasons variants of CL play an important role in the implementation of functional programming languages such as Haskell, ML, and Miranda;[1] see Turner [Tur79] and Peyton Jones [PJ87].

Our next goal is to show that every orthogonal TRS is confluent. As a matter of fact, we will show a little more than that.

Definition 4.3.6 Let $A : s \to_{p,l\to r} t$ be a rewrite step in a TRS $\mathcal{R}$ and let $q \in \mathcal{P}os(s)$. The set $q\backslash A$ of *descendants* of q in t is defined by:

$$q\backslash A = \begin{cases} \{q\} & \text{if } q < p \text{ or } q \parallel p, \\ \{p.p_3.p_2 \mid r|_{p_3} = l|_{p_1}\} & \text{if } q = p.p_1.p_2 \text{ with } p_1 \in \mathcal{VP}os(l) \\ \emptyset & \text{otherwise} \end{cases}$$

[1] Miranda is a trademark of Research Software Ltd.

If $Q \subseteq \mathcal{P}os(s)$, then $Q \backslash A$ denotes the set $\bigcup_{q \in Q} q \backslash A$.

Let $q \in \mathcal{P}os(s)$ such that $s|_q$ is a redex. Then every $t|_{q'}$ with $q' \in q \backslash A$ is called a *descendant* of $s|_q$. The notion of descendant is extended to rewrite sequences in the obvious way.

We will use CL to illustrate the notion of descendant. The following reduction sequence shows that CL is not terminating:

$$
\begin{array}{ll}
 & Ap(Ap(Ap(S,I),I),\underline{Ap}(Ap(S,I),I)) \\
\to & Ap(Ap(I,\underline{Ap}(Ap(S,I),I)),Ap(I,\underline{Ap}(Ap(S,I),I))) \\
\to & Ap(\underline{Ap}(Ap(S,I),I),Ap(I,\underline{Ap}(Ap(S,I),I))) \\
\to & Ap(\underline{Ap}(Ap(S,I),I),\underline{Ap}(Ap(S,I),I))
\end{array}
$$

In the starting term, one redex is marked by underlining its root symbol. The descendants of this marked redex can easily be traced in the reduction sequence by simply searching for the marked symbols. In the preceding reduction sequence, every descendant of the marked redex is again a redex. This is no coincidence, as the following lemma shows.

Lemma 4.3.7 *In an orthogonal TRS $\mathcal{R}$, every descendant of a redex is again a redex.*

Proof We will show the lemma by tracing the descendants of a redex in a reduction step as in the preceding example. Let $s \in \mathcal{T}(\mathcal{F}, \mathcal{V})$ and $q \in \mathcal{P}os(s)$ such that $v = s|_q$ is a redex, i.e., $v = l'\sigma'$ for some rule $l' \to r'$ in $\mathcal{R}$. Mark the root symbol of v by underlining it. So if $u = f(\dots)$, then it is marked as $\underline{f}(\dots)$. What happens to this redex in a rewrite step $s \to_{p,l \to r} t$ in which the redex $u = s|_p = l\sigma$ is contracted? We distinguish between the following cases:

Case $q < p$: If u is a proper subterm of v, then $root(t|_q)$ is underlined and $t|_q$ is the descendant of v. Because $\mathcal{R}$ is nonoverlapping, u must be a subterm of $x\sigma'$ for some $x \in \mathcal{V}ar(l')$. It follows that $t|_q$ is still a redex in t because the rule $l' \to r'$ is left-linear. It should be stressed that $t|_q$ need not necessarily be a redex if $\mathcal{R}$ is not orthogonal.

Case $q \parallel p$: If u and v occur at independent positions, then $root(t|_q)$ is underlined and $t|_q$, the descendant of v, is unaltered in t.

Case $q > p$: If v is a proper subterm of u, then it must be a subterm of $x\sigma$ for some $x \in \mathcal{V}ar(l)$ (again this is a consequence of nonoverlappingness). Now if the variable x appears m times in r, for some $m \geq 0$, then the marked redex appears m times in t, these copies of v are the descendants of v in t. If $m = 0$, then v has no descendant in t (v has been erased). Note that the descendants of v in t occur at pairwise disjoint positions.

Case $q = p$: If u and v coincide, then the marked redex has disappeared: t does not contain an underlined symbol. In other words, v has no descendant in t. □

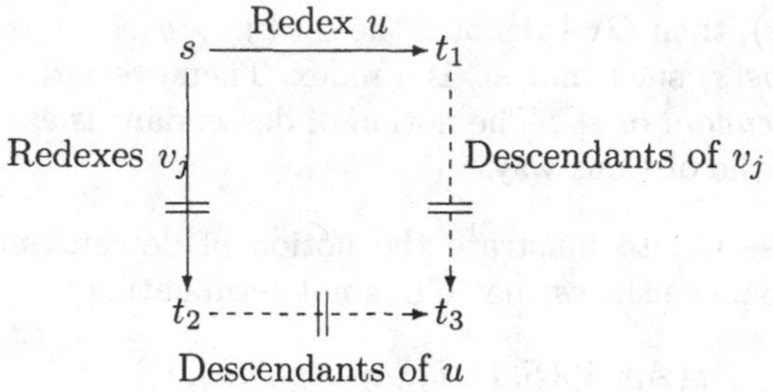

FIGURE 4.3. The parallel moves property.

The preceding lemma also holds for almost orthogonal systems but not for weakly orthogonal systems, as the following example shows. In the TRS $\{f(a) \to f(b), a \to b\}$, we have $\underline{f}(a) \to_{\mathcal{R}} \underline{f}(b)$ but $\underline{f}(b)$ is not a redex.

In order to show that every orthogonal TRS is confluent, we next introduce the parallel rewrite relation.

Definition 4.3.8 Let $\mathcal{R}$ be a TRS. We write $s \mathrel{+\!\!\!\!\!\rightarrow}_{\mathcal{R}} t$ if t can be obtained from s by contracting a (possibly empty) set of pairwise disjoint redexes in s by $\mathcal{R}$. The relation $\mathrel{+\!\!\!\!\!\rightarrow}$ is called the *parallel rewrite relation* w.r.t. $\mathcal{R}$. We sometimes also write $\mathrel{+\!\!\!\!\!\rightarrow}$ instead of $\mathrel{+\!\!\!\!\!\rightarrow}_{\mathcal{R}}$.

Lemma 4.3.9 *Let $\mathcal{R}$ be an orthogonal TRS. If $s \to_{\mathcal{R}} t_1$ by contracting redex u and $s \mathrel{+\!\!\!\!\!\rightarrow}_{\mathcal{R}} t_2$ by contracting the pairwise disjoint redexes $v_1, \ldots, v_n$, then there is a term t_3 such that $t_1 \mathrel{+\!\!\!\!\!\rightarrow}_{\mathcal{R}} t_3$ and $t_2 \mathrel{+\!\!\!\!\!\rightarrow}_{\mathcal{R}} t_3$. Moreover, the redexes contracted in $t_1 \mathrel{+\!\!\!\!\!\rightarrow}_{\mathcal{R}} t_3$ ($t_2 \mathrel{+\!\!\!\!\!\rightarrow}_{\mathcal{R}} t_3$) are the descendants of $v_1, \ldots, v_n$ (u) in t_1 (t_2); see Figure 4.3.*

Proof Let $s|_p = u = l\sigma$ for some rewrite rule $l \to r \in \mathcal{R}$ and $s|_{q_j} = v_j$ for $1 \le j \le n$. It is relatively simple to prove the lemma by case analysis as in Lemma 4.3.7. The only interesting case is that in which u contains several terms out of $v_1, \ldots, v_n$ as proper subterms. For simplicity, let us assume that u contains $v_1, \ldots, v_k$, $1 \le k \le n$, as proper subterms. That is, $p < q_j$ for $1 \le j \le k$ and $p \parallel q_i$ for $k+1 \le i \le n$. Because $\mathcal{R}$ is nonoverlapping, every v_j must be a subterm of $x\sigma$ for some $x \in \mathcal{V}ar(l)$. It follows that $t_1|_p$ is still a redex in t_1 because the rule $l \to r$ is left-linear. The rest of the proof is left to the reader. □

Now we can prove the parallel moves lemma for orthogonal TRS.

Lemma 4.3.10 *Let $\mathcal{R}$ be an orthogonal TRS. If $s \mathrel{+\!\!\!\!\!\rightarrow}_{\mathcal{R}} t_1$ and $s \mathrel{+\!\!\!\!\!\rightarrow}_{\mathcal{R}} t_2$, then there is a term t_3 such that $t_1 \mathrel{+\!\!\!\!\!\rightarrow}_{\mathcal{R}} t_3$ and $t_2 \mathrel{+\!\!\!\!\!\rightarrow}_{\mathcal{R}} t_3$. Moreover, the redexes contracted in $t_1 \mathrel{+\!\!\!\!\!\rightarrow}_{\mathcal{R}} t_3$ ($t_2 \mathrel{+\!\!\!\!\!\rightarrow}_{\mathcal{R}} t_3$) are the descendants in t_1 (t_2) of the redexes contracted in $s \mathrel{+\!\!\!\!\!\rightarrow}_{\mathcal{R}} t_2$ ($s \mathrel{+\!\!\!\!\!\rightarrow}_{\mathcal{R}} t_1$); see Figure 4.4.*

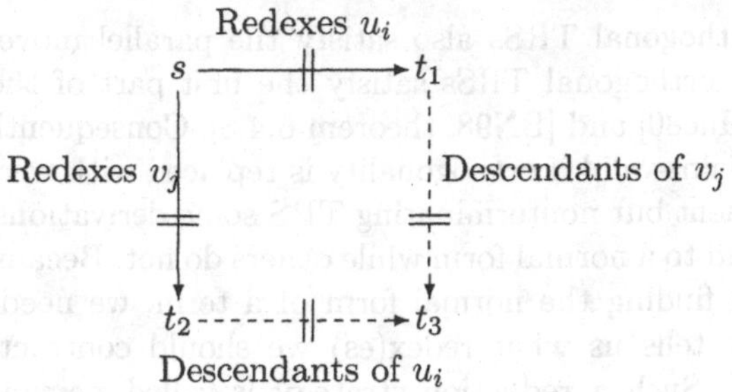

FIGURE 4.4. The parallel moves lemma.

Proof Let $u_1, \ldots, u_m$ be the redexes contracted in $s \mathrel{+\!\!\!\!\!\!\rightarrow}_{\mathcal{R}} t_1$ and let $v_1, \ldots, v_n$ be the redexes contracted in $s \mathrel{+\!\!\!\!\!\!\rightarrow}_{\mathcal{R}} t_2$. Let $s \to_{\mathcal{R}} \cdot \to_{\mathcal{R}} \ldots \to_{\mathcal{R}} \cdot \to_{\mathcal{R}} t_1$ be a reduction sequence in which the pairwise disjoint redexes are contracted in some order. According to Lemma 4.3.9, a common reduct t_3 of t_1 and t_2 can be obtained by contracting the descendants of $v_1, \ldots, v_n$ in t_1; see Figure 4.5, where $m = 3$. Moreover, the positions of the redexes contracted in the parallel reduction sequence $t_2 \mathrel{+\!\!\!\!\!\!\rightarrow}_{\mathcal{R}} \cdot \mathrel{+\!\!\!\!\!\!\rightarrow}_{\mathcal{R}} \ldots \mathrel{+\!\!\!\!\!\!\rightarrow}_{\mathcal{R}} \cdot \mathrel{+\!\!\!\!\!\!\rightarrow}_{\mathcal{R}} t_3$ are pairwise disjoint and coincide with the positions of the descendants of $u_1, \ldots, u_m$ in t_2. Therefore, $t_2 \mathrel{+\!\!\!\!\!\!\rightarrow}_{\mathcal{R}} t_3$ by contracting the descendants of $u_1, \ldots, u_m$. □

Finally, we are in a position to prove that orthogonal systems are confluent; this was first shown by Rosen [Ros73] but "earlier proofs of the confluence of CL (combinatory logic) work just as well for orthogonal TRSs" as Klop [Klo92] remarks.

Theorem 4.3.11 *Every orthogonal term rewriting system is confluent.*

Proof For every TRS $\mathcal{R}$ we clearly have $\to_{\mathcal{R}} \subseteq \mathrel{+\!\!\!\!\!\!\rightarrow}_{\mathcal{R}} \subseteq \to_{\mathcal{R}}^*$. Because $\mathrel{+\!\!\!\!\!\!\rightarrow}_{\mathcal{R}}$ has the diamond property according to the parallel moves lemma 4.3.10, it follows from Lemma 2.4.2 that $\mathcal{R}$ is confluent. □

Theorem 4.3.11 is of utmost importance for inferring confluence of nonterminating TRSs. For example, it allows us to conclude that CL is confluent.

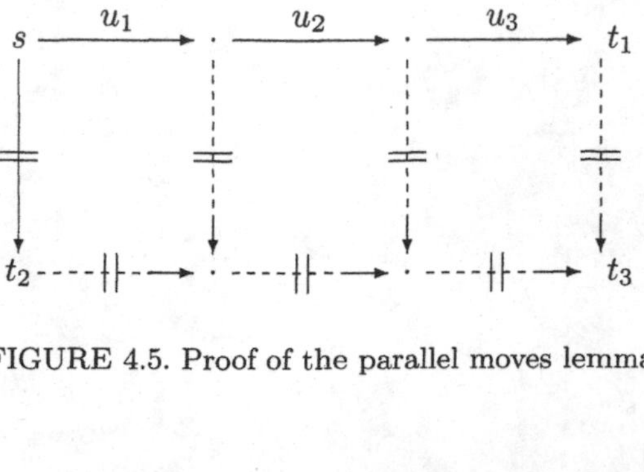

FIGURE 4.5. Proof of the parallel moves lemma.

Almost orthogonal TRSs also satisfy the parallel moves lemma. Moreover, weakly orthogonal TRSs satisfy the first part of the parallel moves lemma; cf. [Hue80] and [BN98, theorem 6.4.8]. Consequently, the preceding theorem remains valid if orthogonality is replaced with weak orthogonality.

In a confluent but nonterminating TRS some derivations starting from a term may lead to a normal form while others do not. Because we are usually interested in finding the normal form of a term, we need some *reduction strategy* that tells us what redex(es) we should contract to obtain that normal form. Such a reduction strategy is called *normalizing* if it finds the normal form whenever it exists. For orthogonal TRSs some "good" normalizing reduction strategies are known, and the notion of descendant plays a crucial role in this context. The reader is referred to Klop [Klo92, section 3.2] for details.

5 Termination

In this chapter we will first sketch a proof of the well-known fact that termination is undecidable. In Chapter 6 this result will be strengthened in several respects. In Section 5.2 standard methods for proving termination are reviewed: Polynomial interpretations yield polynomial termination, whereas recursive path orderings show simple termination. As a matter of fact, there are several other properties related to termination that form the so-called termination hierarchy. We will review this hierarchy in Section 5.3. After that, some newer techniques for proving termination will be treated: the dependency pair method, semantic labeling, and type introduction. Finally, we will study innermost termination.

5.1 Undecidability of Termination

Undecidability of termination was first shown by Huet and Lankford [HL78] by means of a reduction to the uniform halting problem for Turing machines. Similar proofs can be found in [BN98, Klo92, Der87]. Dauchet [Dau92] was the first to prove undecidability of termination for one-rule TRSs. He also used the uniform halting problem for Turing machines. Lescanne [Les94] showed that Dauchet's result can also be obtained by a reduction to Post's correspondence problem. We will obtain much stronger results in Chapter 6. To start, we sketch a simple proof of the undecidability of termination by using PCP. To this end, we associate the system

$$\mathcal{R}(P) = \begin{cases} F(c,c,a(z)) & \rightarrow & F(a(z),a(z),a(z)) & \text{for all } a \in \Gamma \\ F(\alpha(x),\beta(y),z) & \rightarrow & F(x,y,z) & \text{for all } (\alpha,\beta) \in P \end{cases}$$

with a PCP instance P. The system $\mathcal{R}(P)$ is a minor modification of the basic system from [Les94].

Proposition 5.1.1 *The following statements are equivalent:*

1. *The TRS $\mathcal{R}(P)$ is terminating.*

2. *The PCP instance P admits no solution.*

Proof We sketch the proof of the equivalence. Suppose $\gamma \in \Gamma^+$ is a solution for P. So $\gamma = \alpha_1 \cdots \alpha_n = \beta_1 \cdots \beta_n$ for some $n \geq 1$ with $(\alpha_i, \beta_i) \in P$ for $i \in \{1, \ldots, n\}$. We have the following cyclic derivation in $\mathcal{R}(P)$:

$$\begin{aligned} F(\gamma(c),\gamma(c),\gamma(c)) &\rightarrow F(\alpha_2 \cdots \alpha_n(c), \beta_2 \cdots \beta_n(c), \gamma(c)) \rightarrow^* F(c,c,\gamma(c)) \\ &\rightarrow F(\gamma(c),\gamma(c),\gamma(c)) \end{aligned}$$

Conversely, suppose that $\mathcal{R}(P)$ admits an infinite derivation. It is not difficult to see that there exists an infinite derivation in which all steps take place at the root position and both kinds of rewrite rules are used infinitely often. (This can be shown formally using type introduction; see Section 5.5.3.) Any such reduction sequence must contain a subsequence of the form

$$F(c,c,a(t)) \rightarrow F(a(t),a(t),a(t)) \rightarrow^+ F(c,c,a(t))$$

such that in $F(a(t),a(t),a(t)) \rightarrow^+ F(c,c,a(t))$ only rewrite rules of the form $F(\alpha(x),\beta(y),z) \rightarrow F(x,y,z)$ are used. Hence we have

$$a(t) = \alpha_1 \cdots \alpha_n(c) = \beta_1 \cdots \beta_n(c)$$

for some $n \geq 1$ with $(\alpha_i, \beta_i) \in P$ for $i \in \{1, \ldots, n\}$. Clearly, $a(t)$ is a solution for P. □

It should be pointed out that termination is decidable for certain restricted classes of TRSs. Huet and Lankford [HL78] showed that termination is decidable for *ground* TRSs (systems without variables) and Dershowitz [Der81] extended the result to *right-ground* TRSs (systems without variables on the right-hand sides of rules). Further progress on this subject is reported in [Sal91] and [NT99].

5.2 Standard Techniques

Because termination is an undecidable property of TRSs, several techniques for proving termination have been developed. The most important standard methods are the interpretation method and simplification orderings. Before introducing these concepts, let us review some well-known facts.

It is fairly easy to prove that a TRS $(\mathcal{F}, \mathcal{R})$ is terminating if and only if there is a well-founded partial ordering $\succ$ on $\mathcal{T}(\mathcal{F}, \mathcal{V})$ such that $\rightarrow_{\mathcal{R}} \subseteq \succ$. However, the relation $\rightarrow_{\mathcal{R}}$ is in general not finite, even if $\mathcal{R}$ is finite. It would be more convenient to have a finite test for termination. This is possible with reduction orderings.

Definition 5.2.1 Let $R \subseteq \mathcal{T}(\mathcal{F}, \mathcal{V}) \times \mathcal{T}(\mathcal{F}, \mathcal{V})$ be an arbitrary relation.

1. R is *closed under contexts* if $s \; R \; t$ implies $C[s] \; R \; C[t]$ for every context $C[\,]$.
2. R is *closed under substitutions* if $s \; R \; t$ implies $s\sigma \; R \; t\sigma$ for every substitution σ.
3. If R is closed under both contexts and substitutions, it is said to be a *rewrite relation*.
4. A *rewrite ordering* is a rewrite relation that is a partial ordering.
5. A *reduction ordering* is a well-founded rewrite ordering.

In the literature, closure under contexts is also called *monotonicity* or *replacement property*. Different phrases for closure under substitutions are *stability*, *compatibility*, or *full invariance property*. We will sometimes use the phrases "R is *monotone*" instead of "R is closed under contexts" and "R is *stable under substitutions*" instead of "R is closed under substitutions."

Definition 5.2.2 A TRS $(\mathcal{F}, \mathcal{R})$ and a partial ordering $\succ$ are *compatible* if $l \succ r$ holds for every rewrite rule $l \rightarrow r \in \mathcal{R}$.

For finite TRSs, reduction orderings indeed provide a finite test for termination, as the following proposition shows.

Proposition 5.2.3 *A TRS $(\mathcal{F}, \mathcal{R})$ is terminating if and only if it is compatible with a reduction ordering $\succ$ on $\mathcal{T}(\mathcal{F}, \mathcal{V})$.*

Proof If $\mathcal{R}$ is terminating, then $\rightarrow_{\mathcal{R}}^{+}$ is a reduction ordering that obviously satisfies $l \rightarrow_{\mathcal{R}}^{+} r$ for every $l \rightarrow r \in \mathcal{R}$. Suppose conversely that $\succ$ is a reduction ordering satisfying $l \succ r$ for all $l \rightarrow r \in \mathcal{R}$. Consider a rewrite step $s = C[l\sigma] \rightarrow C[r\sigma] = t$, where $l \rightarrow r \in \mathcal{R}$. Because $\succ$ is closed under contexts and under substitutions, $l \succ r$ implies $s \succ t$. Thus, if there were an infinite rewrite sequence $s_1 \rightarrow_{\mathcal{R}} s_2 \rightarrow_{\mathcal{R}} s_3 \rightarrow_{\mathcal{R}} \ldots$, then there would be an infinite descending chain $s_1 \succ s_2 \succ s_3 \succ \ldots$. This, however, contradicts the well-foundedness of $\succ$. □

5.2.1 The Interpretation Method

Our next goal is to construct reduction orderings. The method we will look at first is based on $\mathcal{F}$-algebras.

Definition 5.2.4 Let $\mathcal{F}$ be a signature. An *$\mathcal{F}$-algebra* $\mathcal{A}$ consists of a set A and *operations* $f_\mathcal{A} : A^n \to A$ for every $f \in \mathcal{F}^{(n)}$. The algebra operations are also called *interpretation functions*, and the set A is called the *carrier* (set) of $\mathcal{A}$.

In the following, we tacitly assume that the carrier of an $\mathcal{F}$-algebra is not empty.

A special algebra is the *term algebra* $\mathcal{T}(\mathcal{F}, \mathcal{V})$ consisting of the carrier $\mathcal{T}(\mathcal{F}, \mathcal{V})$ and the operations $f_{\mathcal{T}(\mathcal{F},\mathcal{V})}(t_1, \ldots, t_n) = f(t_1, \ldots, t_n)$. The *ground-term algebra* is defined analogously.

Given an $\mathcal{F}$-algebra $\mathcal{A}$, we assign to every ground term t its interpretation $[t]_\mathcal{A}$ in $\mathcal{A}$.

Definition 5.2.5 Let $\mathcal{A}$ be an $\mathcal{F}$-algebra. The mapping $[\cdot]_\mathcal{A}$ from $\mathcal{T}(\mathcal{F})$ to A is defined inductively by $[f(t_1, \ldots, t_n)]_\mathcal{A} = f_\mathcal{A}([t_1]_\mathcal{A}, \ldots, [t_n]_\mathcal{A})$. (In particular, if t is a constant, then $[t]_\mathcal{A} = t_\mathcal{A}$.)

If a term t contains variables, then its interpretation $[\cdot]_\mathcal{A}$ in $\mathcal{A}$ depends on the assignment of variables to elements of A.

Definition 5.2.6 Let $\mathcal{A}$ be an $\mathcal{F}$-algebra. A mapping $\alpha \colon \mathcal{V} \to A$ is called an *assignment*. For every assignment α, a mapping $[\alpha]_\mathcal{A} \colon \mathcal{T}(\mathcal{F}, \mathcal{V}) \to A$ is defined inductively by

$$[\alpha]_\mathcal{A}(t) = \begin{cases} \alpha(t) & \text{if } t \in \mathcal{V}, \\ f_\mathcal{A}([\alpha]_\mathcal{A}(t_1), \ldots, [\alpha]_\mathcal{A}(t_n)) & \text{if } t = f(t_1, \ldots, t_n) \end{cases}$$

Definition 5.2.7 Let $\mathcal{F}$ be a signature.

1. A *monotone* $\mathcal{F}$-algebra $(\mathcal{A}, \succ)$ is an $\mathcal{F}$-algebra $\mathcal{A}$ for which the carrier A is provided with a partial ordering $\succ$ such that every algebra operation is monotone in all of its arguments. More precisely, for all $f \in \mathcal{F}$ and $a, b \in A$ with $a \succ b$, we have $f_\mathcal{A}(\ldots, a, \ldots) \succ f_\mathcal{A}(\ldots, b, \ldots)$.

2. Every monotone $\mathcal{F}$-algebra $(\mathcal{A}, \succ)$ induces an ordering $\succ_\mathcal{A}$ on the set of terms $\mathcal{T}(\mathcal{F}, \mathcal{V})$ as follows: $t \succ_\mathcal{A} u$ if and only if $[\alpha]_\mathcal{A}(t) \succ [\alpha]_\mathcal{A}(u)$ for every assignment $\alpha \colon \mathcal{V} \to A$.

3. A monotone $\mathcal{F}$-algebra $(\mathcal{A}, \succ)$ is called *well-founded* if $\succ$ is a well-founded ordering.

By means of the next theorem, it is possible to use $\mathcal{F}$-algebras as a tool for proving termination.

Theorem 5.2.8 *If $(\mathcal{A}, \succ)$ is a well-founded monotone $\mathcal{F}$-algebra, then $\succ_{\mathcal{A}}$ is a reduction ordering on $\mathcal{T}(\mathcal{F}, \mathcal{V})$.*

Proof By definition, $\succ_{\mathcal{A}}$ is a well-founded ordering on $\mathcal{T}(\mathcal{F}, \mathcal{V})$. We have to show that $\succ_{\mathcal{A}}$ is also closed under contexts and substitutions. The former follows from the monotonicity of the algebra operations and the latter can be seen as follows. Let $s, t \in \mathcal{T}(\mathcal{F}, \mathcal{V})$ with $s \succ_{\mathcal{A}} t$ and let $\sigma : \mathcal{V} \to \mathcal{T}(\mathcal{F}, \mathcal{V})$ be an arbitrary substitution. We have $[\alpha]_{\mathcal{A}}(s\sigma) = [[\alpha]_{\mathcal{A}} \circ \sigma]_{\mathcal{A}}(s) \succ [[\alpha]_{\mathcal{A}} \circ \sigma]_{\mathcal{A}}(t) = [\alpha]_{\mathcal{A}}(t\sigma)$, where the equalities can easily be shown by structural induction. Thus, $s\sigma \succ_{\mathcal{A}} t\sigma$. □

We say that a TRS $(\mathcal{F}, \mathcal{R})$ is *compatible* with a well-founded monotone $\mathcal{F}$-algebra $(\mathcal{A}, \succ)$ if $(\mathcal{F}, \mathcal{R})$ is compatible with the reduction ordering $\succ_{\mathcal{A}}$.

Corollary 5.2.9 *A TRS $(\mathcal{F}, \mathcal{R})$ is terminating if and only if it is compatible with a well-founded monotone $\mathcal{F}$-algebra $(\mathcal{A}, \succ)$.*

Proof If $(\mathcal{F}, \mathcal{R})$ is terminating, then the term algebra $\mathcal{T}(\mathcal{F}, \mathcal{V})$ together with the reduction ordering $\to_{\mathcal{R}}^{+}$ is a well-founded monotone $\mathcal{F}$-algebra and $\to_{\mathcal{R}}^{+}$ is obviously compatible with $(\mathcal{F}, \mathcal{R})$. The converse direction is an immediate consequence of Theorem 5.2.8. □

Polynomial interpretations are special well-founded algebras. Lankford [Lan75, Lan79] first studied them in their final form but the ideas on which the polynomial interpretation method are based can be traced back to the work of Manna and Ness [MN70].

Definition 5.2.10 Let $\mathcal{F}$ be a signature. A *polynomial interpretation* is an $\mathcal{F}$-algebra $\mathcal{N}$ with carrier $N \subseteq \mathbb{N}$ and for every function symbol $f \in \mathcal{F}^{(n)}$ the interpretation function $f_{\mathcal{N}}$ is a polynomial[1] $P_f(x_1, \ldots, x_n) \in \mathbb{N}[x_1, \ldots, x_n]$ such that for all $a_1, \ldots, a_n \in N$ we have $P_f(a_1, \ldots, a_n) \in N$. A *monotone polynomial interpretation* is a polynomial interpretation in which every polynomial $P_f(x_1, \ldots, x_n)$ is monotone in all its arguments w.r.t. the natural ordering $>$ on $\mathbb{N}$ restricted to N.

According to Theorem 5.2.8, if $(\mathcal{N}, >)$ is a monotone polynomial interpretation, then it is a (well-founded) monotone $\mathcal{F}$-algebra and the induced ordering $>_{\mathcal{N}}$ is a reduction ordering on $\mathcal{T}(\mathcal{F}, \mathcal{V})$. Such a reduction ordering $>_{\mathcal{N}}$ is called a *polynomial ordering*. This motivates the following definition.

Definition 5.2.11 A TRS $(\mathcal{F}, \mathcal{R})$ is called *polynomially terminating* if it is compatible with a polynomial ordering.

---

[1] $P_f(x_1, \ldots, x_n)$ is a polynomial in n indeterminates $x_1, \ldots, x_n$ with coefficients in $\mathbb{N}$. In mathematical textbooks, the indeterminates $x_1, \ldots, x_n$ are often denoted by $X_1, \ldots, X_n$.

Therefore, in order to show (polynomial) termination of a given TRS, one must find monotone polynomials as interpretations of the function symbols. The following proposition states a sufficient criterion for that.

Proposition 5.2.12 *Let $(\mathcal{N}, >)$ be a polynomial interpretation of a signature $\mathcal{F}$ such that the carrier N is a subset of $\mathbb{N}_+$. Then $(\mathcal{N}, >)$ is a monotone polynomial interpretation if and only if every function symbol $f \in \mathcal{F}^{(n)}$, $n > 0$, is interpreted by a polynomial $P_f(x_1, \ldots, x_n) \in \mathbb{N}[x_1, \ldots, x_n]$ that for every $i \in \{1, \ldots, n\}$ contains a monomial $m\, x_1^{k_1} \cdots x_i^{k_i} \cdots x_n^{k_n}$ with $m, k_i \in \mathbb{N}_+$.*

Proof In order to show the if direction, i.e., that $(\mathcal{N}, >)$ is a monotone polynomial interpretation, one must show that every polynomial $P(x_1, \ldots, x_n)$ is monotone in all of its arguments. More precisely, it must be shown that $a, b \in N$ with $a > b$ and $a_1, \ldots, a_{i-1}, a_{i+1}, \ldots, a_n \in N$ imply that

$$P(a_1, \ldots, a_{i-1}, a, a_{i+1}, \ldots, a_n) > P(a_1, \ldots, a_{i-1}, b, a_{i+1}, \ldots, a_n)$$

For every i, $1 \le i \le n$, the polynomial $P(x_1, \ldots, x_n)$ can be viewed as a polynomial in the indeterminate x_i with coefficients $Q_0, Q_1, \ldots, Q_k$ in $\mathbb{N}[x_1, \ldots, x_{i-1}, x_{i+1}, \ldots, x_n]$:

$$P(x_1, \ldots, x_n) = Q_k x_i^k + Q_{k-1} x_i^{k-1} + \cdots + Q_1 x_i + Q_0$$

Apparently, we may assume $k > 0$ and $Q_k \neq 0$ because $P(x_1, \ldots, x_n)$ contains a monomial of the form $m\, x_1^{k_1} \cdots x_i^{k_i} \cdots x_n^{k_n}$, where $m, k_i \in \mathbb{N}_+$. Because $P(a_1, \ldots, a_{i-1}, x_i, a_{i+1}, \ldots, a_n)$ is a polynomial in the indeterminate x_i with coefficients in $\mathbb{N}$, $P(a_1, \ldots, a_{i-1}, a, a_{i+1}, \ldots, a_n) > P(a_1, \ldots, a_{i-1}, b, a_{i+1}, \ldots, a_n)$ is a consequence of $a > b$. Hence $(\mathcal{N}, >)$ is a monotone polynomial interpretation.

For the only-if direction suppose that an $f \in \mathcal{F}^{(n)}$, $n > 0$, is interpreted by a polynomial $P_f(x_1, \ldots, x_n) \in \mathbb{N}[x_1, \ldots, x_n]$ that for some $i \in \{1, \ldots, n\}$ does not contain a monomial $m\, x_1^{k_1} \cdots x_i^{k_i} \cdots x_n^{k_n}$ with $m, k_i \in \mathbb{N}_+$. That is, x_i does not occur at all in $P_f(x_1, \ldots, x_n)$. Let $a, b \in N$ with $a > b$ and $a_1, \ldots, a_{i-1}, a_{i+1}, \ldots, a_n \in N$. Then

$$P(a_1, \ldots, a_{i-1}, a, a_{i+1}, \ldots, a_n) = P(a_1, \ldots, a_{i-1}, b, a_{i+1}, \ldots, a_n)$$

In other words, $P_f(x_1, \ldots, x_n)$ is not monotone in the ith argument. This in turn implies that $(\mathcal{N}, >)$ is not a monotone polynomial interpretation.

□

We next show the use of polynomial orderings for termination proofs by means of an example taken from [BCL87].

Example 5.2.13 Consider the system $\mathcal{R}$ containing the rules

$$\begin{array}{rcl} f(x \circ y) & \to & f(x) \circ f(y) \\ (x \circ y) \circ z & \to & x \circ (y \circ z) \end{array}$$

We define a polynomial interpretation $\mathcal{N}$ as follows: The carrier set is $\mathbb{N}_+$ and the interpretation functions are the monotone polynomials

$$\begin{aligned} f_{\mathcal{N}}(x) &= x^2 \\ x \circ_{\mathcal{N}} y &= xy + x \end{aligned}$$

In order to show that $\mathcal{R}$ is (polynomially) terminating, one has to prove that $l >_{\mathcal{N}} r$ for every $l \to r \in \mathcal{R}$, that is,

$$\begin{aligned} f(x \circ y) &>_{\mathcal{N}} f(x) \circ f(y) \\ (x \circ y) \circ z &>_{\mathcal{N}} x \circ (y \circ z) \end{aligned}$$

These inequalities are indeed satisfied because

$$\begin{aligned} f_{\mathcal{N}}(x \circ_{\mathcal{N}} y) &= x^2y^2 + 2x^2y + x^2 > x^2y^2 + x^2 = f_{\mathcal{N}}(x) \circ_{\mathcal{N}} f_{\mathcal{N}}(y) \\ (x \circ_{\mathcal{N}} y) \circ_{\mathcal{N}} z &= xyz + xz + xy + x > xyz + xz + x = x \circ_{\mathcal{N}} (y \circ_{\mathcal{N}} z) \end{aligned}$$

for all $x, y, z \in \mathbb{N}_+$.

Given a polynomial ordering $>_{\mathcal{N}}$, it would be desirable to have a procedure that (for terms $l, r \in \mathcal{T}(\mathcal{F}, \mathcal{V})$) decides whether $l >_{\mathcal{N}} r$ holds, for then it would be decidable whether a finite TRS $\mathcal{R}$ is compatible with the ordering $>_{\mathcal{N}}$. According to the next proposition, however, such a decision procedure cannot exist.

Proposition 5.2.14 *Given a signature $\mathcal{F}$ and a monotone polynomial interpretation $(\mathcal{N}, >)$ of $\mathcal{F}$, it is undecidable whether $l >_{\mathcal{N}} r$ holds for two terms $l, r \in \mathcal{T}(\mathcal{F}, \mathcal{V})$.*

Proof Let $\mathcal{F} = \{add, times, succ, two\}$. We define a polynomial interpretation $(\mathcal{N}, >)$ of $\mathcal{F}$ as follows. The carrier set is $N = \mathbb{N} \setminus \{0, 1\}$ and the algebra operations $add_{\mathcal{N}} : N \times N \to N$, $times_{\mathcal{N}} : N \times N \to N$, $succ_{\mathcal{N}} : N \to N$, and $two_{\mathcal{N}} \in N$ are defined by

$$\begin{aligned} two_{\mathcal{N}} &= 2 \\ succ_{\mathcal{N}}(x_1) &= x_1 + 1 \\ add_{\mathcal{N}}(x_1, x_2) &= x_1 + x_2 \\ times_{\mathcal{N}}(x_1, x_2) &= x_1 x_2 \end{aligned}$$

According to Proposition 5.2.12, $(\mathcal{N}, >)$ is a monotone polynomial interpretation of $\mathcal{F}$. For $l, r \in \mathcal{T}(\mathcal{F}, \mathcal{V})$, we have

$$\begin{aligned} l >_{\mathcal{N}} r \quad &\Leftrightarrow \quad [\alpha]_{\mathcal{N}}(l) > [\alpha]_{\mathcal{N}}(r) \text{ for every assignment } \alpha \colon \mathcal{V} \to N \\ &\Leftrightarrow \quad [\alpha]_{\mathcal{N}}(l) - [\alpha]_{\mathcal{N}}(r) > 0 \text{ for every assignment } \alpha \colon \mathcal{V} \to N \end{aligned}$$

Now the proposition is a consequence of the fact that, for a polynomial $P \in \mathbb{Z}[x_1, \ldots, x_n]$, it is undecidable whether $P(a_1, \ldots, a_n) > 0$ holds for all $a_1, \ldots, a_n \in N$. The latter is a consequence of the undecidability of

Hilbert's tenth problem, which can be stated as follows: For a polynomial $P \in \mathbb{Z}[x_1, \ldots, x_n]$, are there $a_1, \ldots, a_n \in \mathbb{Z}$ such that $P(a_1, \ldots, a_n) = 0$? We refer to [Zan00, proposition 11] for details. □

Although polynomial orderings suffer from the severe drawback just discussed, useful heuristics for showing the compatibility of a polynomial ordering with a TRS are known; see [BCL87, Gie95a, Zan00].

5.2.2 Simplification Orderings

In the previous section we used a "semantic" method for proving termination. The semantics of a ground term t is the value of its interpretation $[t]_{\mathcal{A}}$ in the well-founded monotone algebra $(\mathcal{A}, \succ)$, and the interpretation must be chosen such that the value strictly decreases by a rewrite step. It is also possible to directly define rewrite orderings on $\mathcal{T}(\mathcal{F}, \mathcal{V})$ by induction on the structure of the terms. If one uses such a syntactic method, then one is faced with the problem of proving well-foundedness of the rewrite ordering. It is often much easier to show that the ordering has the subterm property than to prove that it is well-founded. With the help of Kruskal's theorem, one then gets the well-foundedness of such an ordering for free provided that the signature under consideration is finite. We need some prerequisites to show this.

Definition 5.2.15 A binary relation R on $\mathcal{T}(\mathcal{F}, \mathcal{V})$ has the *subterm property* if $\rhd \subseteq R$, i.e., $C[t]\, R\, t$ for all $C[\,] \neq \Box$ and $t \in \mathcal{T}(\mathcal{F}, \mathcal{V})$.

Definition 5.2.16 Let $\mathcal{F}$ be a signature. The TRS $\mathcal{E}mb(\mathcal{F})$ contains for every $f \in \mathcal{F}^{(n)}$, $n > 0$, the rewrite rules

$$f(x_1, \ldots, x_n) \to x_i \quad \text{for all } i \in \{1, \ldots, n\}$$

in which the variables $x_1, \ldots, x_n$ are pairwise distinct. These rewrite rules are called *embedding rules.* We abbreviate $\to^+_{\mathcal{E}mb(\mathcal{F})}$ to $\rhd_{\text{emb}}$. The relation $\unlhd_{\text{emb}}$ is called *embedding.*

Note that the proper subterm relation $\rhd$ is contained in $\rhd_{\text{emb}}$. Obviously, both relations are well-founded.

Lemma 5.2.17 *If R is a transitive rewrite relation on $\mathcal{T}(\mathcal{F}, \mathcal{V})$, then the following statements are equivalent:*

1. *R has the subterm property (i.e., $\rhd \subseteq R$).*
2. *$f(x_1, \ldots, x_n)\, R\, x_i$ for every $f \in \mathcal{F}^{(n)}$ and $i \in \{1, \ldots, n\}$.*
3. *$\rhd_{\text{emb}} \subseteq R$.*

Proof The implication (1) $\Rightarrow$ (2) is obvious. (2) implies (3) because R is a transitive rewrite relation. Finally, (3) $\Rightarrow$ (1) follows from $\rhd \subseteq \rhd_{\mathrm{emb}}$. □

Consequently, $\rhd_{\mathrm{emb}}$ is the smallest reduction ordering having the subterm property. Note that $\rhd$ is not a reduction ordering because it is not closed under contexts.

The definition of simplification orderings stems from Dershowitz [Der79].

Definition 5.2.18 A *simplification ordering* $\succ$ is a rewrite ordering possessing the subterm property, that is, $\rhd \subseteq \succ$.

It was first shown by Dershowitz [Der79] that every simplification ordering is well-founded provided that the signature under consideration is finite. The proof is based on the finite version of Kruskal's theorem. A proof of (the general version of) Kruskal's theorem can be found in Appendix A.

Theorem 5.2.19 *Let $\mathcal{F}$ be a finite signature. For every infinite sequence $t_1, t_2, t_3, \ldots$ of terms in $\mathcal{T}(\mathcal{F})$, there are indices $i < j$ such that $t_i \unlhd_{\mathrm{emb}} t_j$.*

Proof See Appendix A. □

With the help of Kruskal's theorem it is quite easy to prove that every simplification ordering on a set of terms over a finite signature is indeed well-founded.

Proposition 5.2.20 *Let $\mathcal{F}$ be a finite signature. Every simplification ordering $\succ$ on $\mathcal{T}(\mathcal{F}, \mathcal{V})$ is a reduction ordering.*

Proof We have to show that $\succ$ is well-founded. Suppose on the contrary that there is an infinite descending sequence

$$t_1 \succ t_2 \succ t_3 \succ \ldots$$

First, we show by contraction that $\mathcal{V}ar(t_{i+1}) \subseteq \mathcal{V}ar(t_i)$. That is, we assume that there is a variable $x \in \mathcal{V}ar(t_{i+1}) \setminus \mathcal{V}ar(t_i)$. Then $t_{i+1} = C[x]$ for some context $C[\;]$. With $\sigma = \{x \mapsto t_i\}$ it follows that $t_i = t_i\sigma \succ t_{i+1}\sigma = C[t_i]$, contradicting the subterm property or irreflexivity of $\succ$. Therefore, $\mathcal{V}ar(t_{i+1}) \subseteq \mathcal{V}ar(t_i)$ and $t_i \in \mathcal{T}(\mathcal{F}, \mathcal{V}ar(t_1))$ for every $i \in \mathbb{N}_+$. Let $\mathcal{V}ar(t_1) = \{x_1, \ldots, x_n\}$, let $c_1, \ldots, c_n$ be fresh constants, and define $\tau = \{x_1 \mapsto c_1, \ldots, x_n \mapsto c_n\}$. The infinite sequence $t_1\tau, t_2\tau, t_3\tau, \ldots$ consists of ground terms over $\mathcal{F} \cup \{c_1, \ldots, c_n\}$. According to Kruskal's Theorem 5.2.19, there are indices $i < j$ such that $t_j\tau \unrhd_{\mathrm{emb}} t_i\tau$. We obtain $t_j\tau \succeq t_i\tau$ because $\rhd_{\mathrm{emb}} \subset \succ$ by Lemma 5.2.17. On the other hand, $t_i \succ t_j$ implies $t_i\tau \succ t_j\tau$. The combination of these facts yields $t_i\tau \succ t_j\tau \succeq t_i\tau$ and thus $t_i\tau \succ t_i\tau$. This, however, contradicts the irreflexivity of $\succ$. □

If the signature $\mathcal{F}$ is infinite, then a simplification ordering on $\mathcal{T}(\mathcal{F}, \mathcal{V})$ need not be well-founded, as the following simple counterexample shows.

Let $\mathcal{F} = \{f_i \mid i \in \mathbb{N}\}$. Then the (rewrite) ordering defined by $f_i \succ f_{i+1}$ for all $i \in \mathbb{N}$ (vacuously) has the subterm property, but $\succ$ is obviously not well-founded. For this reason, Middeldorp and Zantema [MZ97] suggested that the definition of simplification ordering be brought into full accordance with the general version of Kruskal's theorem. In their definition, a simplification ordering is a rewrite ordering on $\mathcal{T}(\mathcal{F}, \mathcal{V})$ that contains the homeomorphic embedding relation for some partial well-ordering $\succ$ on $\mathcal{F}$; see Appendix A for a definition of these notions. For finite signatures, their definition coincides with that of Definition 5.2.18.

Next we will present two syntactically defined simplification orderings. Given such an ordering, it is decidable (in polynomial time) whether a finite TRSs is compatible with the ordering; a decision procedure can directly be derived from the definition of the ordering. This is in stark contrast to polynomial orderings. The question of whether there exists such an ordering, however, is an NP-complete problem; see [KN85].

In Dershowitz' [Der82] recursive path ordering, the multisets of the immediate subterms of two terms are compared. That's why it is now also called *multiset path ordering*.

Definition 5.2.21 Let $\succ_p$ be a partial ordering, called a *precedence* (ordering), on a given signature $\mathcal{F}$. The corresponding *recursive path ordering* $\succ_{rpo} \subseteq \mathcal{T}(\mathcal{F}, \mathcal{V}) \times \mathcal{T}(\mathcal{F}, \mathcal{V})$ is defined by:

$s = f(s_1, \ldots, s_m) \succ_{rpo} t$

1. if $s_i \succeq_{rpo} t$ for some $i \in \{1, \ldots, m\}$; or
2. $t = g(t_1, \ldots, t_n)$, $f \succ_p g$, and $s \succ_{rpo} t_j$ for every $j \in \{1, \ldots, n\}$; or
3. $t = f(t_1, \ldots, t_m)$ and $[s_1, \ldots, s_m] \succ_{rpo}^{mul} [t_1, \ldots, t_m]$.

Note that $\succ_{rpo}^{mul}$ denotes the finite multiset extension of $\succ_{rpo}$.

Theorem 5.2.22 *If $\mathcal{F}$ is finite, then every recursive path ordering (rpo) on $\mathcal{T}(\mathcal{F}, \mathcal{V})$ is a well-founded simplification ordering.*

Proof We refrain from giving a proof and refer to [Der82, theorem 3], [Ave95, proposition 3.7.24], and [Fer95, section 4.2] instead. Only the last reference contains a proof of the fact that the relation defined in Definition 5.2.21 is indeed well-defined. Note that condition (1) guarantees the subterm property. □

Example 5.2.23 Consider the one-rule TRS

$$\mathcal{R} = \{(x + y) * z \to (x * z) + (z * y)\}$$

and let the precedence ordering on $\mathcal{F} = \{+, *\}$ be defined by $* \succ_p +$. We have $(x + y) * z \succ_{rpo} (x * z) + (z * y)$ because $[x + y, z] \succ_{rpo}^{mul} [x, y, z]$.

Because $\mathcal{R}$ is compatible with the reduction ordering $\succ_{rpo}$, it is terminating by Proposition 5.2.3.

In order to appreciate the power of *rpo*, the reader is invited to prove termination of the system from Example 2.3.7 by means of *rpo* and to compare the two termination proofs.

The lexicographic path ordering was first introduced by Kamin and Lévy [KL80].

Definition 5.2.24 Given a precedence $\succ_p$ on a signature $\mathcal{F}$, the corresponding *lexicographic path ordering* $\succ_{lpo} \subseteq \mathcal{T}(\mathcal{F},\mathcal{V}) \times \mathcal{T}(\mathcal{F},\mathcal{V})$ is defined by:

$s = f(s_1, \ldots, s_m) \succ_{lpo} t$

1. if $s_i \succeq_{lpo} t$ for some $i \in \{1, \ldots, m\}$; or
2. $t = g(t_1, \ldots, t_n)$, $f \succ_p g$, and $s \succ_{lpo} t_i$ for all $i \in \{1, \ldots, n\}$; or
3. $t = f(t_1, \ldots, t_m)$ and there is an $i \in \{1, \ldots, m\}$ such that
   - $s_j = t_j$ for all $j \in \{1, \ldots, i-1\}$
   - $s_i \succ_{lpo} t_i$
   - $s \succ_{lpo} t_j$ for all $j \in \{i+1, \ldots, m\}$.

So in the lexicographic path ordering, the immediate subterms of two terms are compared from left to right. A different ordering of comparison is, of course, possible. More generally, one can associate every function symbol with a fixed permutation of its arguments and then compare the tuples of immediate subterms lexicographically along this permutation.

Theorem 5.2.25 *If $\mathcal{F}$ is finite, then every lexicographic path ordering (lpo) on $\mathcal{T}(\mathcal{F},\mathcal{V})$ is a well-founded simplification ordering.*

Proof See [BN98, theorem 5.4.14] and [Fer95, section 4.2]. □

Example 5.2.26 We consider Ackermann's function, which is known not to be primitive recursive:

$$\begin{array}{rcl} ack(0,y) & \to & s(y) \\ ack(s(x),0) & \to & ack(x,s(0)) \\ ack(s(x),s(y)) & \to & ack(x,ack(s(x),y)) \end{array}$$

Termination of Ackermann's function can easily be shown by the *lpo* with precedence $ack \succ_p s$.

There are TRSs that can be proven terminating with *rpo* but not with *lpo* (e.g., Example 5.2.23) and vice versa (e.g., Example 5.2.26). It is possible, however, to combine the two different kinds of path orderings by attaching a status to every function symbol $f \in \mathcal{F}$ that specifies how the tuples of immediate subterms should be compared. Furthermore, the two preceding theorems can be generalized to *infinite* signatures by demanding that the precedence ordering is a partial well-ordering; see [MZ97, theorem 7.4]. Moreover, both *rpo* and *lpo* are well-founded whenever the (possibly infinite) precedence is well-founded; see [MZ97, theorem 7.3]. Lastly, *lpo* is a total reduction ordering on $\mathcal{T}(\mathcal{F})$ whenever the precedence ordering is total on $\mathcal{F}$; see, e.g., [FZ96]. It is readily verified that *rpo* lacks this property.

We stress that many other recursively defined path orderings have been devised; see Rusinowitch [Rus87b] and Steinbach [Ste95] for an overview. Another kind of simplification orderings are Knuth-Bendix orderings. These will not be treated here; we refer readers to [KB70, DKM90, MZ97, BN98] for details on the subject.

We conclude this section with several useful characterizations of simply terminating TRSs, those systems that can be shown terminating by means of a well-founded simplification ordering.

Definition 5.2.27 A TRS $(\mathcal{F}, \mathcal{R})$ is called *simplifying* if it is compatible with a simplification ordering $\succ$ on $\mathcal{T}(\mathcal{F}, \mathcal{V})$. A TRS is called *simply terminating* if it is compatible with a well-founded simplification ordering.

Clearly, every simply terminating TRS is simplifying. The rewrite system $(\{f_i \mid i \in \mathbb{N}\}, \{f_i \to f_{i+1} \mid i \in \mathbb{N}\})$ refutes the converse statement. However, for finite signatures the notions coincide; this follows directly from Proposition 5.2.20. As a matter of fact, the two notions also coincide if the set of rewrite rules $\mathcal{R}$ is finite (even if the signature $\mathcal{F}$ is infinite). This is because every $\mathcal{R}$-derivation can contain only a finite number of function symbols; see, e.g., [Ohl92]. Consequently, a simplifying TRS that is not simply terminating must have an infinite signature *and* an infinite number of rewrite rules. One might be tempted to say that infinite rewrite systems over infinite signatures are uninteresting anyway, but this is not the case. Even if one is only interested in finite rewrite systems (over finite signatures), the infinite case is of interest: The method of semantic labeling (which will be studied later) often succeeds in proving termination of a given finite system by transforming it into an infinite system over an infinite signature to which *rpo* or *lpo* readily applies.

The following characterization of simplifyingness was first proven by Kurihara and Ohuchi [KO90, KO92].

Definition 5.2.28 A TRS $\mathcal{R}$ is *cyclic* if it admits a derivation $t \to_{\mathcal{R}}^{+} t$ for some term t. A TRS is called *acyclic* if it is not cyclic.

Lemma 5.2.29 *The following statements are equivalent:*

1. *The TRS $(\mathcal{F}, \mathcal{R})$ is simplifying.*
2. *The TRS $(\mathcal{F}, \mathcal{R} \cup \mathcal{E}mb(\mathcal{F}))$ is acyclic.*

Proof (1) $\Rightarrow$ (2): Let $(\mathcal{F}, \mathcal{R})$ be compatible with the simplification ordering $\succ$, i.e., $\rightarrow_{\mathcal{R}} \subseteq \succ$. According to Lemma 5.2.17, we also have $\rightarrow_{\mathcal{E}mb(\mathcal{F})} \subseteq \succ$. If $(\mathcal{F}, \mathcal{R} \cup \mathcal{E}mb(\mathcal{F}))$ were cyclic, i.e., there is a derivation $t \rightarrow^{+}_{\mathcal{R} \cup \mathcal{E}mb(\mathcal{F})} t$ for some term t, then it would follow from $\rightarrow_{\mathcal{R}} \subseteq \succ$ and $\rightarrow_{\mathcal{E}mb(\mathcal{F})} \subseteq \succ$ that $t \succ t$. This contradiction shows that $(\mathcal{F}, \mathcal{R} \cup \mathcal{E}mb(\mathcal{F}))$ is acyclic.

(2) $\Rightarrow$ (1): Let $\succ = \rightarrow^{+}_{\mathcal{R} \cup \mathcal{E}mb(\mathcal{F})}$. Because $(\mathcal{F}, \mathcal{R} \cup \mathcal{E}mb(\mathcal{F}))$ is acyclic, the relation $\succ$ is irreflexive and therefore a rewrite ordering. It follows from Lemma 5.2.17 that $\succ$ is even a simplification ordering because $\rhd_{\text{emb}} \subseteq \succ$. The TRS $(\mathcal{F}, \mathcal{R})$ is compatible with $\succ$ and hence is simplifying. $\Box$

Zantema [Zan94] gave a similar characterization of simple termination.

Lemma 5.2.30 *The following statements are equivalent.*

1. *The TRS $(\mathcal{F}, \mathcal{R})$ is simply terminating.*
2. *The TRS $(\mathcal{F}, \mathcal{R} \cup \mathcal{E}mb(\mathcal{F}))$ is simply terminating.*
3. *The TRS $(\mathcal{F}, \mathcal{R} \cup \mathcal{E}mb(\mathcal{F}))$ is terminating.*

Proof (1) $\Rightarrow$ (2): Let $(\mathcal{F}, \mathcal{R})$ be compatible with the well-founded simplification ordering $\succ$ on $\mathcal{T}(\mathcal{F}, \mathcal{V})$. According to Lemma 5.2.17, the TRS $(\mathcal{F}, \mathcal{E}mb(\mathcal{F}))$ is also compatible with $\succ$. Thus, $(\mathcal{F}, \mathcal{R} \cup \mathcal{E}mb(\mathcal{F}))$ is simply terminating.

(2) $\Rightarrow$ (3): Obvious.

(3) $\Rightarrow$ (1): Let $\succ = \rightarrow^{+}_{\mathcal{R} \cup \mathcal{E}mb(\mathcal{F})}$. Because $(\mathcal{F}, \mathcal{R} \cup \mathcal{E}mb(\mathcal{F}))$ is terminating, the relation $\succ$ is a reduction ordering. It follows from Lemma 5.2.17 that $\succ$ is even a simplification ordering because $\rhd_{\text{emb}} \subseteq \succ$. The TRS $(\mathcal{F}, \mathcal{R})$ is compatible with $\succ$ and hence is simply terminating. $\Box$

According to the preceding considerations, the statements in Lemma 5.2.29 and Lemma 5.2.30 are equivalent if $\mathcal{F}$ or $\mathcal{R}$ is finite. We would like to point out that Lemma 5.2.30 is particularly useful for showing that a TRS is *not* simply terminating.

Example 5.2.31 The TRS $\mathcal{R} = \{f(0,1,x) \rightarrow f(x,x,x)\}$ is not simply terminating because $\mathcal{R} \cup \mathcal{E}mb(\mathcal{F})$ admits the following cyclic derivation:

$$t = f(0,1,f(0,1,1)) \rightarrow_{\mathcal{R}} f(f(0,1,1), f(0,1,1), f(0,1,1)) \rightarrow^{+}_{\mathcal{E}mb(\mathcal{F})} t$$

Simple termination can also be characterized by $\mathcal{F}$-algebras, as was shown by Zantema [Zan94].

Definition 5.2.32 A monotone $\mathcal{F}$-algebra $(\mathcal{A}, \succ)$ is called *simple* if

$$f_{\mathcal{A}}(a_1, \ldots, a_n) \succeq a_i$$

is satisfied for all $f \in \mathcal{F}^{(n)}$, $a_1, \ldots, a_n \in A$, and $1 \leq i \leq n$.

Proposition 5.2.33 *A TRS $(\mathcal{F}, \mathcal{R})$ is simply terminating if and only if it is compatible with a well-founded simple $\mathcal{F}$-algebra $(\mathcal{A}, \succ)$.*

Proof Let $(\mathcal{F}, \mathcal{R})$ be simply terminating, i.e., the TRS $(\mathcal{F}, \mathcal{R} \cup \mathcal{E}mb(\mathcal{F}))$ is terminating by Lemma 5.2.30. Then the term algebra $\mathcal{T}(\mathcal{F}, \mathcal{V})$ together with the reduction ordering $\rightarrow^+_{\mathcal{R} \cup \mathcal{E}mb(\mathcal{F})}$ is a well-founded simple $\mathcal{F}$-algebra and $\rightarrow^+_{\mathcal{R} \cup \mathcal{E}mb(\mathcal{F})}$ is obviously compatible with $(\mathcal{F}, \mathcal{R})$. Suppose conversely that $(\mathcal{F}, \mathcal{R})$ is compatible with a well-founded simple $\mathcal{F}$-algebra $(\mathcal{A}, \succ)$. Because we allow syntactic equality in the definition of simple algebras but compatibility requires strict inequalities, the algebra has to be modified. We define a new $\mathcal{F}$-algebra $\mathcal{A}'$ by $A' = A \times \mathbb{N}$ and

$$f_{\mathcal{A}'}((a_1, m_1), \ldots, (a_n, m_n)) = (f_{\mathcal{A}}(a_1, \ldots, a_n), 1 + \sum_{i=1}^{n} m_i)$$

Furthermore, let $\succ_{lex}$ be the lexicographic product of $\succ$ and the natural ordering $>$ on $\mathbb{N}$. It is relatively easy to show that $(\mathcal{A}', \succ_{lex})$ is a well-founded simple $\mathcal{F}$-algebra that is compatible with both $\mathcal{R}$ and $\mathcal{E}mb(\mathcal{F})$. This means that $(\mathcal{F}, \mathcal{R} \cup \mathcal{E}mb(\mathcal{F}))$ is terminating (Corollary 5.2.9) and hence $(\mathcal{F}, \mathcal{R})$ is simply terminating (Lemma 5.2.30). □

Let $(\mathcal{N}, >)$ be a monotone polynomial interpretation of a signature $\mathcal{F}$ such that the carrier N is a subset of $\mathbb{N}_+$. It is not difficult to show that the induced reduction ordering $>_{\mathcal{N}}$ satisfies $C[t] \geq_{\mathcal{N}} t$ for every context $C[\,]$ and term t. Although $>_{\mathcal{N}}$ is not necessarily a simplification ordering (for example, if $\mathcal{F} = \{a, f\}$, $N = \mathbb{N}_+$, $a_{\mathcal{N}} = 1$, and $f_{\mathcal{N}}(x) = x$, then $[f(a)]_{\mathcal{N}} = 1 = a_{\mathcal{N}}$), it follows from Proposition 5.2.33 that every TRS $\mathcal{R}$ over $\mathcal{F}$ that is compatible with $>_{\mathcal{N}}$ is simply terminating (or rather the proof of Proposition 5.2.33 shows how $>_{\mathcal{N}}$ can be turned into a simplification ordering).

As a matter of fact, Zantema [Zan01] showed that the algebra operations $f_{\mathcal{A}}$ need only be weakly monotone in Proposition 5.2.33. That is, $a, b \in A$ with $a \succeq b$ must imply $f_{\mathcal{A}}(\ldots, a, \ldots) \succeq f_{\mathcal{A}}(\ldots, b, \ldots)$.

By similar reasoning as in Proposition 5.2.33, it can be shown that a TRS $(\mathcal{F}, \mathcal{R})$ is simplifying if and only if it is compatible with a simple $\mathcal{F}$-algebra $(\mathcal{A}, \succ)$.

As a consequence of the next lemma, simple termination and termination coincide for size-preserving systems. We will frequently use this observation later.

Lemma 5.2.34 *A nonsize-increasing TRS is simply terminating if and only if it is terminating.*

Proof Clearly, any simply terminating TRS is terminating. So let $(\mathcal{F}, \mathcal{R})$ be a nonsize-increasing and terminating TRS. In particular, $\succ = \rightarrow_{\mathcal{R}}^{+}$ is a reduction ordering on $\mathcal{T}(\mathcal{F}, \mathcal{V})$. We define an $\mathcal{F}$-algebra $\mathcal{A}$ as follows. The carrier is $A = \mathbb{N} \times \mathcal{T}(\mathcal{F}, \mathcal{V})$ and the operations are $f_{\mathcal{A}}((m_1, t_1), \ldots, (m_n, t_n)) = (1 + \sum_{i=1}^{n} m_i, f(t_1, \ldots, t_n))$. Furthermore, let $\succ_{lex}$ be the lexicographic product of the natural ordering $>$ on $\mathbb{N}$ and $\succ$. Apparently, $(\mathcal{A}, \succ_{lex})$ is a well-founded simple algebra. With the aid of Lemma 3.2.6, it is not difficult to prove that $(\mathcal{A}, \succ_{lex})$ is compatible with $\mathcal{R}$. Now it follows from Proposition 5.2.33 that $\mathcal{R}$ is simply terminating. □

5.3 The Termination Hierarchy

In previous sections we have seen that proving termination by means of polynomial interpretations yields polynomial termination, while recursive path orderings like *rpo* or *lpo* show simple termination. Polynomial and simple termination are part of the termination hierarchy, which we will review next. The termination hierarchy was introduced by Zantema [Zan94]; see also [Zan00, Zan01]. Throughout the following we assume that $\mathcal{F}$ is a finite signature containing at least one constant and that every $\mathcal{F}$-algebra is nonempty.

Definition 5.3.1 A TRS $(\mathcal{F}, \mathcal{R})$ is called *totally terminating* if it is compatible with a total reduction ordering $\succ$ on $\mathcal{T}(\mathcal{F})$.

Definition 5.3.1 requires some explanation. Clearly, we cannot directly compare two terms $l, r \in \mathcal{T}(\mathcal{F}, \mathcal{V})$ w.r.t. a reduction ordering on $\mathcal{T}(\mathcal{F})$ because l and r may (and usually do) contain variables. However, if we view $(\mathcal{T}(\mathcal{F}), \succ)$ as well-founded monotone $\mathcal{F}$-algebra, then $\mathcal{R}$ is compatible with $\succ$ if $l\sigma \succ r\sigma$ for every $l \rightarrow r \in \mathcal{R}$ and every ground substitution $\sigma : \mathcal{V} \rightarrow \mathcal{T}(\mathcal{F})$, and this is meant in Definition 5.3.1.

Ferreira and Zantema [FZ96] showed that total termination can also be characterized by $\mathcal{F}$-algebras.

Proposition 5.3.2 *A TRS $(\mathcal{F}, \mathcal{R})$ is totally terminating if and only if it is compatible with a well-founded monotone $\mathcal{F}$-algebra $(\mathcal{A}, \succ)$ in which the ordering $\succ$ is total on the carrier A.*

Proof If $(\mathcal{F}, \mathcal{R})$ is totally terminating, then it is compatible with a total reduction ordering $\succ$ on $\mathcal{T}(\mathcal{F})$. Clearly, the ground term algebra, together with $\succ$, has the desired properties. Suppose conversely that $(\mathcal{F}, \mathcal{R})$ is compatible with a well-founded monotone $\mathcal{F}$-algebra $(\mathcal{A}, \succ)$ in which the ordering $\succ$ is total on the carrier A. That is, $(\mathcal{F}, \mathcal{R})$ is compatible with the reduction ordering $\succ_{\mathcal{A}}$ on $\mathcal{T}(\mathcal{F},\mathcal{V})$. Because $\succ_{\mathcal{A}}$ is in general not total on $\mathcal{T}(\mathcal{F})$, we have to modify it. By Zermelo's theorem (see [KM68]) there is a total well-founded ordering on $\mathcal{F}$. According to the remarks at the end of Section 5.2, the corresponding lexicographic path ordering $\succ_{lpo}$ is a total reduction ordering on $\mathcal{T}(\mathcal{F})$. Let $\succ_{lex}$ be the lexicographic product of $\succ_{\mathcal{A}}$ and $\succ_{lpo}$. By Proposition 2.3.6, $\succ_{lex}$ is a well-founded ordering on $\mathcal{T}(\mathcal{F})$. Furthermore, because both $\succ_{\mathcal{A}}$ and $\succ_{lpo}$ are reduction orderings on $\mathcal{T}(\mathcal{F},\mathcal{V})$, so is $\succ_{lex}$. Clearly, $(\mathcal{F},\mathcal{R})$ is compatible with $\succ_{lex}$ because it is compatible with $\succ_{\mathcal{A}}$. In order to show that $\succ_{lex}$ is total on $\mathcal{T}(\mathcal{F})$, let $s,t \in \mathcal{T}(\mathcal{F})$ with $s \neq t$. We have $[s]_{\mathcal{A}} \succ [t]_{\mathcal{A}}$ or $[t]_{\mathcal{A}} \succ [s]_{\mathcal{A}}$ or $[s]_{\mathcal{A}} = [t]_{\mathcal{A}}$ because $\succ$ is total on A. In the latter case, we have either $s \succ_{lpo} t$ or $t \succ_{lpo} s$ as $\succ_{lpo}$ is total on $\mathcal{T}(\mathcal{F})$. This shows that $\succ_{lex}$ is total on $\mathcal{T}(\mathcal{F})$. All in all, $\succ_{lex}$ has the desired properties. □

If termination of a given rewrite system $\mathcal{R}$ can be shown by means of *rpo* or *lpo* (or a combination of both), then $\mathcal{R}$ is actually totally terminating; see [FZ94]. Hofbauer [Hof92] showed that $\mathcal{R}$ is even ω-terminating if its termination can be proven by *rpo*.

Definition 5.3.3 A TRS $(\mathcal{F},\mathcal{R})$ is called *ω-terminating* if it is compatible with a monotone $\mathcal{F}$-algebra $(\mathcal{N},>)$ in which the carrier N is a subset of $\mathbb{N}$ and $>$ is the restriction of the natural ordering on $\mathbb{N}$ to N.

Lastly, if a TRS is looping or cyclic, then it is obviously not terminating. Note that our definition of loopingness is slightly more general than the one in [Der87].

Definition 5.3.4 A TRS $\mathcal{R}$ is called *looping* if it admits a rewrite sequence $t \rightarrow^+_{\mathcal{R}} C[t\sigma]$ for some term t, some context $C[\;]$, and some substitution σ.

The *termination hierarchy* reads as follows:

$$\begin{array}{ccccccccccccc} \text{PT} & \Rightarrow & \omega\text{T} & \Rightarrow & \text{TT} & \Rightarrow & \text{ST} & \Rightarrow & \text{SN} & \Rightarrow & \text{NL} & \Rightarrow & \text{AC} \\ &&&&&&&& \Downarrow &&&& \\ &&&&&&&& \text{WN} &&&& \end{array}$$

The acronyms stand for polynomial termination (PT), ω-termination (ωT), total termination (TT), simple termination (ST), termination (strong normalization, SN), normalization (weak normalization, WN), nonloopingness (NL), and acyclicity (AC).

The validity of the implications in the termination hierarchy follows directly from the definitions, except for TT $\Rightarrow$ ST; that proof is given in Proposition 5.3.5. Apart from polynomial termination, all properties in the termination hierarchy are known to be undecidable ([HL78, Car91, MG95, Zan95b, Ges97]), sometimes even for single rules ([Dau92, MG95, Les94]). In Chapter 6, we will obtain much stronger results. There it will also be shown that none of the implications in the termination hierarchy are equivalences: For all implications $X \Rightarrow Y$ there is a TRS satisfying Y but not X. For the convenience of the reader, counterexamples to the converse implications in the termination hierarchy are also collected at the end of this section in Table 5.1. Clearly, one expects that polynomial termination is also undecidable; note that this does not follow from Proposition 5.2.14 because there the polynomial ordering is already fixed.

The following proof of the implication TT $\Rightarrow$ ST originates from [Zan94, proposition 7].

Proposition 5.3.5 *Every totally terminating TRS $\mathcal{R}$ is simply terminating.*

Proof Because $\mathcal{R}$ is totally terminating, there is a well-founded monotone $\mathcal{F}$-algebra $(\mathcal{A}, \succ)$ such that $\succ$ is total on the carrier A and $l \succ_{\mathcal{A}} r$ holds for every rewrite rule $l \to r \in \mathcal{R}$; see Proposition 5.3.2. We show that $(\mathcal{A}, \succ)$ is a simple monotone $\mathcal{F}$-algebra, the claim then follows from Proposition 5.2.33. Suppose that $(\mathcal{A}, \succ)$ is not simple. Then there are $a_1, \dots, a_n \in A$ and an $f \in \mathcal{F}^{(n)}$ such that $f_{\mathcal{A}}(a_1, \dots, a_n) \succeq a_i$ does not hold for some $i \in \{1, \dots, n\}$. Because $\succ$ is total, we infer

$$a_i \succ f_{\mathcal{A}}(a_1, \dots, a_n)$$

Let $g \colon A \to A$ be defined by $g(x) = f_{\mathcal{A}}(a_1, \dots, a_{i-1}, x, a_{i+1}, \dots, a_n)$. Because $a_i \succ g(a_i)$ and g is monotone, there is the infinite sequence

$$a_i \succ g(a_i) \succ g(g(a_i)) \succ g(g(g(a_i))) \succ \dots$$

This contradicts the well-foundedness of $\succ$. □

How can we prove that a TRS is *not* totally terminating? Clearly, we can use Lemma 5.2.30 to show that a TRS is *not* simply and hence not totally terminating (by Proposition 5.3.5). With this technique, however, one cannot deal with systems that are simply but not totally terminating. In contrast, the following characterization of total termination due to Zantema [Zan94] can deal with this situation.

Definition 5.3.6 Let $\mathcal{R}$ be a TRS. The *truncation closure* $TC(\mathcal{R})$ of $\mathcal{R}$ is the (infinite) TRS

$$TC(\mathcal{R}) = \{s \to t \mid C[s] \to_{\mathcal{R}}^{+} C[t] \text{ for some context } C[\,]\}$$

Proposition 5.3.7 *A TRS $\mathcal{R}$ is totally terminating if and only if $TC(\mathcal{R})$ is totally terminating.*

Proof The if direction is trivial. In order to show the only-if direction, let $\mathcal{R}$ be compatible with a total reduction ordering $\succ$ on $\mathcal{T}(\mathcal{F})$. We show that $\succ$ is also compatible with $TC(\mathcal{R})$. Let $s \to t \in TC(\mathcal{R})$, i.e., there is a context $C[\,]$ such that $C[s] \to_{\mathcal{R}}^{+} C[t]$. We have to show that $s\sigma \succ t\sigma$ for every ground substitution $\sigma : \mathcal{V} \to \mathcal{T}(\mathcal{F})$. Because $\to_{\mathcal{R}}$ is closed under substitutions, we have $C[s\sigma] \to_{\mathcal{R}}^{+} C[t\sigma]$. Moreover, $C[s\sigma] \succ C[t\sigma]$ because $\mathcal{R}$ is compatible with $\succ$. Now, for an indirect proof, suppose that $s\sigma \succ t\sigma$ is not valid. Then $t\sigma \succ s\sigma$ must hold because $\succ$ is total ($s = t$ would yield nontermination of $\mathcal{R}$). We further infer that $C[t\sigma] \succ C[s\sigma]$ because $\succ$ is closed under context. This contradiction proves that $s\sigma \succ t\sigma$, and we are done. □

Example 5.3.8 Let

$$\mathcal{R} = \left\{ \begin{array}{lcl} f(a) & \to & f(b) \\ g(b) & \to & g(a) \end{array} \right.$$

Apparently, $\mathcal{R}$ is terminating and size-preserving, hence simply terminating by Lemma 5.2.34. Because $TC(\mathcal{R})$ contains the rewrite rules $a \to b$ and $b \to a$, it is not (totally) terminating. Therefore, by Proposition 5.3.7, $\mathcal{R}$ is not totally terminating either.

The termination hierarchy can be refined in several ways; see [Zan00, Zan01]. As an example, we will prove that for TRSs over finite signatures, the notion of nonself-embeddingness (NSE) lies in between ST and SN. This was first shown by Dershowitz [Der82].

Definition 5.3.9 A TRS $(\mathcal{F}, \mathcal{R})$ is called *self-embedding* if it admits a rewrite sequence $t \to_{\mathcal{R}}^{+} u \to_{\mathcal{E}mb(\mathcal{F})}^{*} t$ for some terms t and u.

Lemma 5.3.10 *Every nonself-embedding TRS $\mathcal{R}$ over a finite signature $\mathcal{F}$ is terminating.*

Proof If $\mathcal{R}$ is not terminating, then there is an infinite derivation

$$t_1 \to_{\mathcal{R}} t_2 \to_{\mathcal{R}} t_3 \to_{\mathcal{R}} \cdots$$

of ground terms $t_i \in \mathcal{T}(\mathcal{F})$. According to Kruskal's theorem 5.2.19, there are indices i and j with $1 \le i < j$ such that $t_j \to_{\mathcal{E}mb(\mathcal{F})}^{*} t_i$. It follows

$$t_i \to_{\mathcal{R}}^{+} t_j \to_{\mathcal{E}mb(\mathcal{F})}^{*} t_i$$

which yields a contradiction to nonself-embeddingness of $\mathcal{R}$. □

The rewrite system $(\{f_i \mid i \in \mathbb{N}\}, \{f_i \to f_{i+1} \mid i \in \mathbb{N}\})$ shows that the finiteness requirement in Lemma 5.3.10 cannot be dropped. As most of the other properties in the termination hierarchy, nonself-embeddingness is also known to be undecidable; see [Pla85].

Lastly, we collect known counterexamples to the converse implications in the termination hierarchy. As a matter of fact, in all cases but one a string

SRS	Is	But not
$fgh \to gfhg$	ω-terminating	Polynomially terminating
$fg \to gff$	Totally terminating	ω-terminating
$fgh \to fhhgg$	Simply terminating	Totally terminating
$fg \to hggffh$	Nonself-embedding	Simply terminating
$ff \to fgf$	Terminating	Nonself-embedding
$fgfg \to gfgffg$	Normalizing	Terminating
?	Nonlooping	Terminating
$f \to fg$	Acyclic	Nonlooping

TABLE 5.1. Counterexamples in the termination hierarchy.

rewriting system refuting the converse implication is known; see Table 5.1 taken from [Zan01]. The corresponding proofs can be found in [Zan94] and [Zan01], except for WN $\not\Rightarrow$ SN: The SRS refuting this implication is due to Geser [Ges00]. It is an open problem whether a nonlooping nonterminating SRS exists. In contrast to that, the following one-rule *term rewriting system* from [ZG96] disproves NL $\Rightarrow$ SN:

$$f(d, b(x), y) \to g(f(d, x, b(y)), f(x, y, b(b(d)))))$$

5.4 The Dependency Pair Method

Polynomial interpretations and recursive path orderings are methods for automatically proving termination of rewrite systems, in the sense that these orderings can automatically be generated. A drawback of these orderings is that they cannot be used to show termination of nonsimply terminating TRSs. The dependency pair method of Arts and Giesl [AG00] remedies this situation because it allows us to prove termination of nonsimply terminating TRSs automatically.

In the dependency pair method a set IN of inequalities, each of the form $s \geq t$ or $s > t$, is generated and the existence of a reduction pair $(\succsim, \succ)$ satisfying these inequalities is sufficient for showing termination. The notion *reduction pair* was introduced by Kusakari et al. [KNT99] and is defined as follows.

Definition 5.4.1

1. A *quasi-rewrite ordering* is a quasi-ordering $\succsim$ that is closed under contexts and substitutions.

2. A *reduction pair* $(\succsim, \succ)$ consists of a quasi-rewrite ordering $\succsim$ and a partial ordering $\succ$ with the following properties:

   - $\succ$ is closed under substitutions and well-founded,

- $\succsim \circ \succ \subseteq \succ$ or $\succ \circ \succsim \subseteq \succ$.

Note that $\succ$ need not be closed under contexts.

Given a quasi-rewrite ordering $\succsim$, a natural candidate for the corresponding partial ordering $\succ$ is its strict part $\succ^s$ ($\succ^s$ is defined by $t \succ^s u$ if and only if $t \succsim u$ and $u \not\succsim t$). Unfortunately, the strict part $\succ^s$ is in general not closed under substitutions as the following example shows.

Example 5.4.2 Let $\mathcal{F} = \{a, f\}$, $\mathcal{R} = \{f(x) \to f(a)\}$, and $\succsim = \to^*_{\mathcal{R}}$. We have $f(x) \succsim f(a)$ and $f(a) \not\succsim f(x)$. Hence $f(x) \succ^s f(a)$. Because $f(a) \not\succ^s f(a)$, we conclude that $\succ^s$ is not closed under substitutions.

To overcome this obstacle, we define a corresponding stable-strict relation.

Definition 5.4.3 Let $\succsim$ be a quasi-ordering on $\mathcal{T}(\mathcal{F}, \mathcal{V})$. The corresponding *stable-strict* relation $\succ^{ss}$ is defined by $t \succ^{ss} u$ if and only if $t\sigma \succ^s u\sigma$ holds for all ground substitutions σ. In other words, for every ground substitution $\sigma\colon \mathcal{V} \to \mathcal{T}(\mathcal{F})$, we must have $t\sigma \succsim u\sigma$ and $u\sigma \not\succsim t\sigma$.

Let us briefly motivate the preceding definition. A polynomial interpretation $\mathcal{N}$ of a signature $\mathcal{F}$ induces a quasi-ordering $\geq_{\mathcal{N}}$ on $\mathcal{T}(\mathcal{F}, \mathcal{V})$ by defining $t \geq_{\mathcal{N}} u$ if and only if $[t\sigma]_{\mathcal{N}} \geq [u\sigma]_{\mathcal{N}}$ holds for all ground substitutions σ. A natural way to define a corresponding irreflexive ordering $>_{\mathcal{N}}$ is to let $t >_{\mathcal{N}} u$ hold if and only if $[t\sigma]_{\mathcal{N}} > [u\sigma]_{\mathcal{N}}$ for all ground substitutions σ. However, $>_{\mathcal{N}}$ is not the strict part of $\geq_{\mathcal{N}}$ but the stable-strict relation corresponding to $\geq_{\mathcal{N}}$. Thus, the irreflexive relation intuitively associated with a quasi-ordering is often the stable-strict one instead of the strict one.

If a quasi-ordering $\succsim$ is closed under substitutions, then the corresponding stable-strict relation $\succ^{ss}$ is also closed under substitutions, whereas this is not necessarily true for the strict relation $\succ^s$.

Example 5.4.2 also demonstrates that in general $\succ^s \subseteq \succ^{ss}$ is not true because we have $f(x) \not\succ^{ss} f(a)$ for the stable-strict relation $\succ^{ss}$. Moreover, in general $\succ^{ss} \subseteq \succsim$ does not hold either (hence $\succ^{ss} \subseteq \succ^s$ is false, too): If $\mathcal{R}$ is the TRS over the signature $\mathcal{F} = \{a, h\}$ containing only the rule $h(a) \to a$ and $\succsim$ is defined as $\to^*_{\mathcal{R}}$, then we have $h(x) \succ^{ss} x$, but $h(x) \not\succsim x$.

The following lemma states some straightforward properties of stable-strict relations.

Lemma 5.4.4 *Let $\succsim$ be a quasi-ordering on $\mathcal{T}(\mathcal{F}, \mathcal{V})$ that is closed under substitutions. Then we have*

1. *$\succ^{ss}$ is irreflexive.*
2. *$\succ^{ss}$ is transitive.*
3. *$\succ^{ss}$ is closed under substitutions.*
4. *If $\succ^s$ is closed under substitutions, then $\succ^s \subseteq \succ^{ss}$.*

5. *If* $\succ^s$ *is well founded, then* $\succ^{ss}$ *is also well founded.*

6. $s \succsim t \succ^{ss} u$ *implies* $s \succ^{ss} u$.

7. $s \succ^{ss} t \succsim u$ *implies* $s \succ^{ss} u$.

8. *If* $\succsim$ *is total, then* $\succ^{ss} \subseteq \succ^s$.

Proof Statements (1) and (2) follow from the irreflexivity and transitivity of $\succ^s$, respectively. Statements (3) and (4) are direct consequences of the definition. In (5), if there were an infinite descending sequence $t_0 \succ^{ss} t_1 \succ^{ss} \dots$, then there would be an infinite descending sequence $t_0\sigma \succ^s t_1\sigma \succ^s \dots$. Statements (6) and (7) follow from the transitivity of $\succsim$ in conjunction with the fact that $\succsim$ is closed under substitutions. Lastly, statement (8) is an immediate consequence of the definition. □

Thus, if $\succsim$ is a quasi-rewrite ordering, then $(\succsim, \succ^{ss})$ is a reduction pair by Lemma 5.4.4 provided that $\succ^{ss}$ is well-founded. Although the following results hold true for every reduction pair, we prefer to fix the reduction pair to $(\succsim, \succ^{ss})$. That is, we will always consider the stable-strict ordering corresponding to $\succsim$ in what follows. For the sake of brevity, we write $\succ$ instead of $\succ^{ss}$, i.e., $\succ$ always denotes the stable-strict ordering corresponding to $\succsim$. Consequently, we define the notion "quasi-reduction ordering" as follows.

Definition 5.4.5

1. A quasi-ordering on $\mathcal{T}(\mathcal{F}, \mathcal{V})$ is *well-founded* if the corresponding stable-strict ordering is well-founded.

2. A *quasi-reduction ordering* is a well-founded quasi-rewrite ordering.

We would like to remind the reader that in our considerations it will be taken for granted that every signature contains at least one constant and that every algebra is nonempty.

5.4.1 Dependency Pairs

In the dependency pair method, if $f(s_1, \dots, s_n) \to C[g(t_1, \dots, t_m)]$ and g is a defined symbol, then one has to compare the arguments $(s_1, \dots, s_n)$ and $(t_1, \dots, t_m)$. To avoid the handling of such tuples, a new *tuple symbol* $F \notin \mathcal{F}$ is introduced for every defined symbol f. Instead of comparing *tuples*, now the *terms* $F(s_1, \dots, s_n)$ and $G(t_1, \dots, t_m)$ are compared. Thus, to ease readability we assume that the signature $\mathcal{F}$ consists of lowercase symbols only and that tuple symbols are denoted by the corresponding uppercase symbols. In the following, we will sometimes denote a sequence of terms $s_1, \dots, s_n$ by $\vec{s}$. For example, $F(s_1, \dots, s_n)$ will also be denoted by $F(\vec{s})$.

Definition 5.4.6 If $f(s_1, \ldots, s_n) \to C[g(t_1, \ldots, t_m)]$ is a rewrite rule of a TRS $\mathcal{R}$ and g is a defined symbol, then $\langle F(s_1, \ldots, s_n), G(t_1, \ldots, t_m)\rangle$ is a *dependency pair* of $\mathcal{R}$.

Example 5.4.7 For the TRS

$$\begin{array}{rcl} f(x, c(y)) & \to & f(x, s(f(y, y))) \\ f(s(x), y) & \to & f(x, s(c(y))) \end{array}$$

we obtain the following dependency pairs:

$$\begin{array}{c} \langle F(x, c(y)), F(x, s(f(y, y)))\rangle \\ \langle F(x, c(y)), F(y, y)\rangle \\ \langle F(s(x), y), F(x, s(c(y)))\rangle \end{array}$$

To trace those subterms that may start new reductions, we examine special sequences of dependency pairs, so-called *chains*. In the following, we assume that different (occurrences of) dependency pairs have disjoint sets of variables. Furthermore, in order to ease readability, we will use substitutions whose domains may be infinite (this is just a notational convenience, as we shall see).

Definition 5.4.8 Let $\mathcal{R}$ be a TRS. A sequence of dependency pairs $\langle s_1, t_1\rangle\langle s_2, t_2\rangle \ldots$ of $\mathcal{R}$ is an *$\mathcal{R}$-chain* if there is a substitution σ such that $t_j\sigma \to^*_{\mathcal{R}} s_{j+1}\sigma$ holds for every two consecutive pairs $\langle s_j, t_j\rangle$ and $\langle s_{j+1}, t_{j+1}\rangle$ in the sequence. Furthermore, if every proper subterm of $s_j\sigma$ and $t_j\sigma$ is terminating (or equivalently, every $s_j\sigma$ and $t_j\sigma$ is terminating), then the $\mathcal{R}$-chain is said to be *minimal*.

For example, in Example 5.4.7 there is the chain

$$\langle F(x_1, c(y_1)), F(y_1, y_1)\rangle\ \langle F(x_2, c(y_2)), F(y_2, y_2)\rangle\ \langle F(x_3, c(y_3)), F(y_3, y_3)\rangle$$

because with $\sigma = \{x_2 \mapsto c(c(y_3)), x_3 \mapsto c(y_3), y_1 \mapsto c(c(y_3)), y_2 \mapsto c(y_3)\}$, we have $F(y_1, y_1)\sigma \to^*_{\mathcal{R}} F(x_2, c(y_2))\sigma$ and $F(y_2, y_2)\sigma \to^*_{\mathcal{R}} F(x_3, c(y_3))\sigma$. In fact, every finite sequence of the dependency pair $\langle F(x_2, c(y_2)), F(y_2, y_2)\rangle$ is a chain. Arts and Giesl [AG00] proved that the absence of *infinite* chains is a sufficient and necessary criterion for termination.

Theorem 5.4.9 *A TRS $\mathcal{R}$ is terminating if and only if there is no infinite $\mathcal{R}$-chain. In fact, if $\mathcal{R}$ is nonterminating, then there is a minimal infinite $\mathcal{R}$-chain.*

Proof First, we assume that $\mathcal{R}$ is nonterminating and we construct a minimal infinite $\mathcal{R}$-chain. Suppose that there is an infinite $\mathcal{R}$-derivation starting from s. The term s must contain a subterm $f(\vec{s}_1)$, i.e., $s = C[f_1(\vec{s}_1)]$, such that $f(\vec{s}_1)$ is nonterminating but every term in $\vec{s}_1$ is terminating. Let us consider an infinite $\mathcal{R}$-derivation starting from $f(\vec{s}_1)$. Because every term in $\vec{s}_1$ is terminating, it must be of the form

$$f_1(\vec{s}_1) \to^* f_1(\vec{t}_1) = l_1\sigma_1 \to r_1\sigma_1 \to \dots$$

where first the arguments $\vec{s}_1$ are reduced to $\vec{t}_1$ and then a rewrite rule $l_1 \to r_1 \in \mathcal{R}$ with $l_1 = f_1(\vec{u}_1)$ is applied to $f_1(\vec{t}_1)$. Because $\vec{t}_1 = \vec{u}_1\sigma_1$ and every term in $\vec{t}_1$ is terminating, it follows that $x\sigma_1$ is terminating for every $x \in \mathcal{V}ar(l_1)$. This again implies that r_1 can be written as $r_1 = C_1[f_2(\vec{s}_2)]$ such that $f_2(\vec{s}_2)\sigma_1$ is nonterminating but every term in $\vec{s}_2\sigma_1$ is terminating. As earlier there must be an infinite $\mathcal{R}$-derivation

$$f_2(\vec{s}_2\sigma_1) \to^* f_2(\vec{t}_2) = l_2\sigma_2 \to r_2\sigma_2 \to \dots$$

where first the arguments $\vec{s}_2\sigma_1$ are reduced to $\vec{t}_2$ and then a rewrite rule $l_2 = f_2(\vec{u}_2) \to C_2[f_3(\vec{s}_3)] = r_2 \in \mathcal{R}$ is applied to $f_2(\vec{t}_2)$ such that $f_3(\vec{s}_3)\sigma_2$ is nonterminating but every term in $\vec{s}_3\sigma_2$ is terminating. By continuing with this reasoning, we obtain an infinite $\mathcal{R}$-derivation

$$\begin{array}{llllll} f_1(\vec{s}_1) & \to^* & l_1\sigma_1 & \to & r_1\sigma_1 & = & C_1\sigma_1[f_2(\vec{s}_2\sigma_1)] \\ & \to^* & C_1\sigma_1[l_2\sigma_2] & \to & C_1\sigma_1[r_2\sigma_2] & = & C_1\sigma_1[C_2\sigma_2[f_3(\vec{s}_3\sigma_2)]] \\ & \to^* & \dots & & & & \end{array}$$

Let us consider the dependency pairs $\langle F_i(\vec{u}_i), F_{i+1}(\vec{s}_{i+1})\rangle$ corresponding to the rules $l_i = f_i(\vec{u}_i) \to C_i[f_{i+1}(\vec{s}_{i+1})] = r_i$ applied in the infinite $\mathcal{R}$-derivation. We claim that

$$\langle F_1(\vec{u}_1), F_2(\vec{s}_2)\rangle\ \langle F_2(\vec{u}_2), F_3(\vec{s}_3)\rangle\ \langle F_3(\vec{u}_3), F_4(\vec{s}_4)\rangle\ \dots$$

is a minimal infinite $\mathcal{R}$-chain. For all $i \in \mathbb{N}_+$, we have $F_{i+1}(\vec{s}_{i+1}\sigma_i) \to^* F_{i+1}(\vec{t}_{i+1})$ and $\vec{t}_{i+1} = \vec{u}_{i+1}\sigma_{i+1}$. Because we assume that the sets of variables of different occurrences of dependency pairs are disjoint, the substitution $\sigma = \sigma_1 \circ \sigma_2 \circ \sigma_3 \circ \dots$ satisfies $F_{i+1}(\vec{s}_{i+1}\sigma) \to^* F_{i+1}(\vec{u}_{i+1}\sigma)$ for all $i \in \mathbb{N}_+$. Moreover, every term in $\vec{u}_i\sigma$ and $\vec{s}_{i+1}\sigma$ is terminating. This proves the claim.

Next, we suppose that an infinite $\mathcal{R}$-chain exists and we construct an infinite $\mathcal{R}$-derivation. So let

$$\langle F_1(\vec{s}_1), F_2(\vec{t}_2)\rangle\ \langle F_2(\vec{s}_2), F_3(\vec{t}_3)\rangle\ \langle F_3(\vec{s}_3), F_4(\vec{t}_4)\rangle\ \dots$$

be an infinite $\mathcal{R}$-chain, that is, there is a substitution σ such that

$$F_2(\vec{t}_2)\sigma \to^* F_2(\vec{s}_2)\sigma,\ F_3(\vec{t}_3)\sigma \to^* F_3(\vec{s}_3)\sigma, \dots$$

Every dependency pair $\langle F_i(\vec{s}_i), F_{i+1}(\vec{t}_{i+1})\rangle$ originates from a rewrite rule $f_i(\vec{s}_i) \to C_i[f_{i+1}(\vec{t}_{i+1})]$. Because the tuple symbols $F_2, F_3, \dots$ are constructors, it follows that

$$f_2(\vec{t}_2)\sigma \to^* f_2(\vec{s}_2)\sigma,\ f_3(\vec{t}_3)\sigma \to^* f_3(\vec{s}_3)\sigma, \dots$$

This yields an infinite $\mathcal{R}$-derivation

$$\begin{array}{lllll} f_1(\vec{s}_1)\sigma & \to & C_1[f_2(\vec{t}_2)]\sigma & & \\ & & \downarrow_* & & \\ & & C_1[f_2(\vec{s}_2)]\sigma & \to & C_1[C_2[f_3(\vec{t}_3)]]\sigma \\ & & & & \downarrow_* \\ & & & & C_1[C_2[f_3(\vec{s}_3)]]\sigma \quad \to \quad \ldots \end{array}$$

and we are done. □

But how do we prove the absence of infinite chains? Theorem 5.4.9 can be used to obtain a termination criterion that can be automated. To this end, a set IN of inequalities, each of the form $s \gtrsim t$ or $s > t$, is generated and the existence of a quasi-reduction ordering $\succsim$ satisfying these inequalities is sufficient for showing termination.

Theorem 5.4.10 *Let $\mathcal{R}$ be a TRS over the signature $\mathcal{F} = \mathcal{D} \uplus \mathcal{C}$ and let $Tup_{\mathcal{F}} = \{F \mid f \in \mathcal{D}\}$ be the set of tuple symbols. $\mathcal{R}$ is terminating if and only there is a quasi-reduction ordering $\succsim$ on $\mathcal{T}(\mathcal{F} \cup Tup_{\mathcal{F}}, \mathcal{V})$ such that*

- *$l \succsim r$ for every rule $l \to r$ in $\mathcal{R}$ and*
- *$s \succ t$ for every dependency pair $\langle s, t\rangle$.*

Proof For an indirect proof of the if direction, suppose that $\mathcal{R}$ is non-terminating. Then, according to Theorem 5.4.9, there exists an infinite $\mathcal{R}$-chain $\langle s_1, t_1\rangle\langle s_2, t_2\rangle \ldots$ of dependency pairs from $\mathcal{R}$ and a substitution $\sigma : \mathcal{V} \to \mathcal{T}(\mathcal{F}, \mathcal{V})$ such that $t_j\sigma \to_{\mathcal{R}}^* s_{j+1}\sigma$ holds true for all consecutive pairs $\langle s_j, t_j\rangle$ and $\langle s_{j+1}, t_{j+1}\rangle$ in the sequence. Note that $C[l\tau] \to_{\mathcal{R}} C[r\tau]$ implies $C[l\tau] \succsim C[r\tau]$ because $l \succsim r$ and $\succsim$ is a quasi-reduction ordering. Consequently, $t_j\sigma \to_{\mathcal{R}}^* s_{j+1}\sigma$ implies $t_j\sigma \succsim s_{j+1}\sigma$. Moreover, because $s_j\sigma \succ t_j\sigma$ for each $j \in \mathbb{N}_+$, it follows from

$$s_1\sigma \succ t_1\sigma \succsim s_2\sigma \succ t_2\sigma \succsim s_3\sigma \succ \ldots$$

that there is an infinite sequence $s_1\sigma \succ s_2\sigma \succ s_3\sigma \succ \ldots$. This, however, contradicts the well-foundedness of $\succ$. Hence $\mathcal{R}$ is terminating.

Next, we turn to the only-if direction. It will be shown that termination of $\mathcal{R}$ implies termination of the TRS

$$\mathcal{R}' = \mathcal{R} \cup \{s \to t \mid \langle s, t\rangle \text{ is a dependency pair of } \mathcal{R}\}$$

This is a stronger result than the statement of the theorem because it shows that $\succ = \to_{\mathcal{R}'}^+$ is a reduction ordering satisfying $l \succ r$ for every rule $l \to r$ in $\mathcal{R}$ and $s \succ t$ for every dependency pair $\langle s, t\rangle$ of $\mathcal{R}$.

Suppose that $\mathcal{R}'$ is not terminating, i.e., there is an infinite $\mathcal{R}'$-derivation

$$s_1 \to_{\mathcal{R}'} s_2 \to_{\mathcal{R}'} s_3 \to_{\mathcal{R}'} \ldots$$

Because $\mathcal{R}$ is terminating, s_1 must contain tuple symbols. Moreover, we may assume that s_1 is minimal in the sense that all its proper subterms are terminating.

First, it will be shown that this implies that the root symbol of s_1 is a tuple symbol. Let z be a variable that does not occur in the infinite $\mathcal{R}'$-derivation. For every term s, let $[\![s]\!]$ denote the term obtained from s by replacing all subterms that have a tuple symbol at their root with the variable z. Let p_i be the position of the redex contracted in $s_i \rightarrow_{\mathcal{R}'} s_{i+1}$. On the one hand, $s_i \rightarrow_{\mathcal{R}'} s_{i+1}$ implies $[\![s_i]\!] \rightarrow_{\mathcal{R}} [\![s_{i+1}]\!]$ whenever there is no tuple symbol above p_i because tuple symbols do not occur in $\mathcal{R}$. On the other hand, if p_i is below a tuple symbol, then $s_i \rightarrow_{\mathcal{R}'} s_{i+1}$ implies $[\![s_i]\!] = [\![s_{i+1}]\!]$ (if there is a tuple symbol at p_i, then this follows from the fact that the root symbol of the right-hand side of a rule in $\mathcal{R}'$ is a tuple symbol whenever the root symbol of the left-hand side is a tuple symbol). Because $\mathcal{R}$ is terminating, there is no infinite $\mathcal{R}$-derivation starting from $[\![s_1]\!]$. As a consequence, there must be an index k such that every redex contracted in

$$s_k \rightarrow_{\mathcal{R}'} s_{k+1} \rightarrow_{\mathcal{R}'} s_{k+2} \rightarrow_{\mathcal{R}'} \cdots$$

is below a tuple symbol. We may write $s_k = C_k[t_1^k, \ldots, t_{n_k}^k]$, where $C_k[, \ldots,] \in \mathcal{T}(\mathcal{F}, \mathcal{V})$ and $root(t_j^k) \in Tup_{\mathcal{F}}$ for every $1 \leq j \leq n_k$. According to the preceding, there is an infinite $\mathcal{R}'$-derivation starting from some t_j^k, $1 \leq j \leq n_k$. Suppose that $root(s_1)$ is not a tuple symbol. That is, s_1 has the form $C_1[t_1^1, \ldots, t_{n_1}^1]$, where $C_1[, \ldots,] \in \mathcal{T}(\mathcal{F}, \mathcal{V})$ is nonempty and $root(t_j^1) \in Tup_{\mathcal{F}}$. It is not difficult to show by induction on k that for every t_j^k there is a t_i^1 such that $t_i^1 \rightarrow_{\mathcal{R}'}^* t_j^k$. This means that s_1 has a proper nonterminating subterm t_i^1 and yields a contradiction to our minimality assumption. Therefore, the root symbol of s_1 is a tuple symbol.

So s_1 can be written as $s_1 = F_1(\vec{s}_1)$, where every term in $\vec{s}_1$ is terminating. Thus, any derivation starting from s_1 must be of the form

$$F_1(\vec{s}_1) \rightarrow_{\mathcal{R}'}^* F_1(\vec{t}_1) = F_1(\vec{u}_1)\sigma_1 \rightarrow_{\mathcal{R}'} F_2(\vec{v}_2)\sigma_1 = F_2(\vec{s}_2) \rightarrow_{\mathcal{R}'} \cdots$$

where first the arguments $\vec{s}_1$ are reduced to $\vec{t}_1$ and then a rewrite rule $F_1(\vec{u}_1) \rightarrow F_2(\vec{v}_2) \in \mathcal{R}' \setminus \mathcal{R}$ is applied. That is, $\langle F_1(\vec{u}_1), F_2(\vec{v}_2) \rangle$ is a dependency pair of $\mathcal{R}$. Note that every subterm of a term in $\vec{s}_2$ with a tuple symbol at its root already appears in $\vec{t}_1$. Therefore, it follows from this considerations that every term in $\vec{s}_2$ is terminating. By the same reasoning, any derivation starting from $F_2(\vec{s}_2)$ must be of the form

$$F_2(\vec{s}_2) \rightarrow_{\mathcal{R}'}^* F_2(\vec{t}_2) = F_2(\vec{u}_2)\sigma_2 \rightarrow_{\mathcal{R}'} F_3(\vec{v}_3)\sigma_2 = F_3(\vec{s}_3) \rightarrow_{\mathcal{R}'} \cdots$$

where first the arguments $\vec{s}_2$ are reduced to $\vec{t}_2$ and then a rewrite rule $F_2(\vec{u}_2) \rightarrow F_3(\vec{v}_3) \in \mathcal{R}' \setminus \mathcal{R}$ is applied. By continuing along these lines, we obtain an infinite $\mathcal{R}'$-derivation

$$F_1(\vec{s}_1) \rightarrow_{\mathcal{R}'}^* F_1(\vec{t}_1) \rightarrow_{\mathcal{R}'} F_2(\vec{s}_2) \rightarrow_{\mathcal{R}'}^* F_2(\vec{t}_2) \rightarrow_{\mathcal{R}'} F_3(\vec{s}_3) \rightarrow_{\mathcal{R}'}^* \cdots$$

such that $\vec{s}_i \to^*_{\mathcal{R}'} \vec{t}_i$, $\vec{t}_i = \vec{u}_i\sigma_i$, $\vec{s}_{i+1} = \vec{v}_{i+1}\sigma_i$, and $\langle F_i(\vec{u}_i), F_{i+1}(\vec{v}_{i+1})\rangle$ is a dependency pair of $\mathcal{R}$.

We will show that the infinite sequence of dependency pairs

$$\langle F_1(\vec{u}_1), F_2(\vec{v}_2)\rangle\langle F_2(\vec{u}_2), F_3(\vec{v}_3)\rangle\langle F_3(\vec{u}_3), F_4(\vec{v}_4)\rangle \dots \tag{5.1}$$

is in fact an infinite $\mathcal{R}$-chain. To this end, we assume without loss of generality that the sets of variables used in the rewrite rules $F_i(\vec{u}_i) \to F_{i+1}(\vec{v}_{i+1})$ and $F_j(\vec{u}_j) \to F_{j+1}(\vec{v}_{j+1})$ are disjoint whenever $i \neq j$. If σ denotes the substitution $\sigma_1 \circ \sigma_2 \circ \sigma_3 \circ \dots$, then we have $\vec{s}_i = \vec{v}_i\sigma \to^*_{\mathcal{R}'} \vec{u}_i\sigma = \vec{t}_i$ for all $i \in \mathbb{N}_+$. Define the substitution $\sigma' : \mathcal{V} \to \mathcal{T}(\mathcal{F}, \mathcal{V})$ by

$$\sigma'(x) = [\![\sigma(x)]\!]$$

Because neither $\vec{u}_i$ nor $\vec{v}_i$ contains a tuple symbol (in a dependency pair, the root symbols are the only tuple symbols), it follows that $[\![\vec{s}_i]\!] = \vec{v}_i\sigma'$ and $[\![\vec{t}_i]\!] = \vec{u}_i\sigma'$. According to the preceding considerations, $\vec{s}_i \to^*_{\mathcal{R}'} \vec{t}_i$ implies $[\![\vec{s}_i]\!] \to^*_{\mathcal{R}} [\![\vec{t}_i]\!]$. In other words, $\vec{v}_i\sigma' \to^*_{\mathcal{R}} \vec{u}_i\sigma'$ and hence (5.1) is an infinite $\mathcal{R}$-chain. However, by Theorem 5.4.9, $\mathcal{R}$ does not admit infinite $\mathcal{R}$-chains because it is terminating. This contradiction shows that $\mathcal{R}'$ must be terminating. □

According to Theorem 5.4.10, in order to show termination of the TRS from Example 5.4.7, it suffices to find a quasi-reduction ordering satisfying the constraints

$$\begin{aligned}
f(x, c(y)) &\geq f(x, s(f(y, y))) \\
f(s(x), y) &\geq f(x, s(c(y))) \\
F(x, c(y)) &> F(x, s(f(y, y))) \\
F(x, c(y)) &> F(y, y) \\
F(s(x), y) &> F(x, s(c(y)))
\end{aligned}$$

In fact, for finite systems we can do even better. This is because some dependency pairs cannot occur twice in any chain and hence they need not be taken into account in a proof that no infinite chain exists. In order to identify these insignificant dependency pairs, the notion of dependency graph has been introduced by Arts and Giesl [AG00].

Definition 5.4.11 Let $\mathcal{R}$ be a TRS. The *dependency graph* of $\mathcal{R}$ is the directed graph whose nodes (vertices) are the dependency pairs of $\mathcal{R}$ and there is an arc (directed edge) from $\langle s, t\rangle$ to $\langle u, v\rangle$ if $\langle s, t\rangle\langle u, v\rangle$ is a chain.

The dependency graph for the system from Example 5.4.7 is given in Figure 5.1. If we restrict ourselves to *finite* TRSs, then every infinite chain corresponds to a cycle in the dependency graph. In other words, those dependency pairs not contained in a cycle need not be taken into account

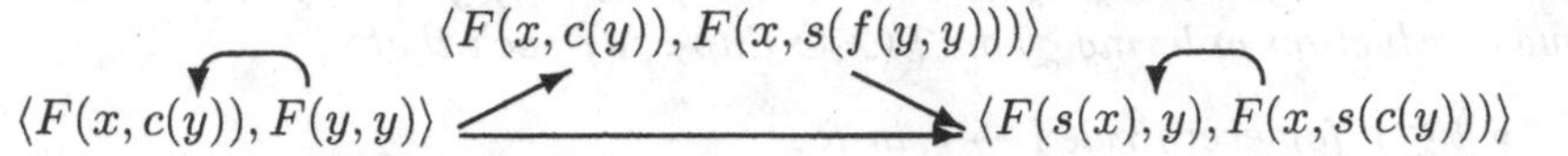

FIGURE 5.1. The dependency graph for the system from Example 5.4.7.

in a termination proof. It should be pointed out that for a finite TRS there is only a finite number of cycles because the number of dependency pairs is finite.

Definition 5.4.12 A nonempty set $\mathcal{P}$ of dependency pairs is called a *cycle* if, for any two dependency pairs $\langle s, t\rangle, \langle u, v\rangle \in \mathcal{P}$, there is a nonempty path from $\langle s, t\rangle$ to $\langle u, v\rangle$ and from $\langle u, v\rangle$ to $\langle s, t\rangle$ in the dependency graph that traverses dependency pairs from $\mathcal{P}$ only. (In particular, there must also be a path from $\langle s, t\rangle$ to itself.)

In the dependency graph of Figure 5.1, there are two cycles, namely, $\{\langle F(x, c(y)), F(y, y)\rangle\}$ and $\{\langle F(s(x), y), F(x, s(c(y)))\rangle\}$. It will be shown in Theorem 5.4.13 that the dependency pair $\langle F(x, c(y)), F(x, s(f(y, y)))\rangle$ is indeed irrelevant.

Note that in standard graph terminology, a path $v_0, v_1, \ldots, v_k$ in a directed graph forms a cycle if $v_0 = v_k$ and $k \geq 1$. In our context we identify cycles with the *set* of elements that occur in it, i.e., we call $\{v_0, v_1, \ldots, v_{k-1}\}$ a cycle. Because a set does not contain multiple occurrences of an element, it may happen that several cycling paths are identified with the same set.

Throughout the rest of this section, we consider only *finite* TRSs.

Theorem 5.4.13 *A finite TRS $\mathcal{R}$ is terminating if and only if for each cycle $\mathcal{P}$ in the dependency graph of $\mathcal{R}$ there exists no infinite $\mathcal{R}$-chain of dependency pairs from $\mathcal{P}$.*

Proof The only-if direction is a direct consequence of Theorem 5.4.9. For an indirect proof of the if direction, suppose that $\mathcal{R}$ is nonterminating. Then by Theorem 5.4.9 there exists an infinite $\mathcal{R}$-chain. As $\mathcal{R}$ is finite, there is only a finite number of dependency pairs and hence one dependency pair occurs infinitely many times in the chain (up to renaming the variables). Thus the infinite chain has the form $\ldots\langle s\rho_1, t\rho_1\rangle \ldots \langle s\rho_2, t\rho_2\rangle \ldots \langle s\rho_3, t\rho_3\rangle \ldots$, where $\rho_1, \rho_2, \rho_3, \ldots$ are renamings. Therefore, $\langle s\rho_1, t\rho_1\rangle \ldots \langle s\rho_2, t\rho_2\rangle \ldots$ is an infinite $\mathcal{R}$-chain consisting solely of dependency pairs from one cycle in the dependency graph. This contradiction shows that $\mathcal{R}$ is terminating. □

Similar to Theorem 5.4.9, Theorem 5.4.13 can be used to obtain a termination criterion that can be tested automatically.

Theorem 5.4.14 *Let $\mathcal{R}$ be a finite TRS over the signature $\mathcal{F} = \mathcal{D} \uplus \mathcal{C}$ and let $Tup_{\mathcal{F}} = \{F \mid f \in \mathcal{D}\}$ be the set of tuple symbols. $\mathcal{R}$ is terminating* *if and only if for every cycle $\mathcal{P}$ in the dependency graph of $\mathcal{R}$ there is a quasi-reduction ordering $\succsim$ on $\mathcal{T}(\mathcal{F} \cup Tup_{\mathcal{F}}, \mathcal{V})$ such that*

- *$l \succsim r$ for every rule $l \to r$ in $\mathcal{R}$,*
- *$s \succsim t$ for every dependency pair $\langle s, t\rangle$ in $\mathcal{P}$,*
- *$s \succ t$ for at least one dependency pair $\langle s, t\rangle$ in $\mathcal{P}$.*

Proof The only-if direction is a direct consequence of Theorem 5.4.10. For an indirect proof of the if direction, suppose that $\mathcal{R}$ is nonterminating. Then, according to Theorem 5.4.13 there is an infinite $\mathcal{R}$-chain of dependency pairs from a cycle $\mathcal{P}$ in the dependency graph of $\mathcal{R}$. W.l.o.g. we may assume that every dependency pair in $\mathcal{P}$ occurs infinitely many times in the chain (up to variable renaming). Let $\succsim$ be a quasi-reduction ordering satisfying the constraints. For at least one dependency pair $\langle s, t\rangle$ in $\mathcal{P}$ we have the strict inequality $s \succ t$. Because $\langle s, t\rangle$ occurs infinitely often in the chain, the chain has the form

$$\langle u_{1,1}, v_{1,1}\rangle \ldots \langle u_{1,n_1}, v_{1,n_1}\rangle \langle s\rho_1, t\rho_1\rangle \langle u_{2,1}, v_{2,1}\rangle \ldots \langle u_{2,n_2}, v_{2,n_2}\rangle \langle s\rho_2, t\rho_2\rangle \ldots$$

where $\rho_1, \rho_2, \ldots$ are renamings. Hence, there exists a substitution σ such that $v_{i,j}\sigma \to_{\mathcal{R}}^{*} u_{i,j+1}\sigma$, $v_{i,n_i}\sigma \to_{\mathcal{R}}^{*} s\rho_i\sigma$, and $t\rho_i\sigma \to_{\mathcal{R}}^{*} u_{i+1,1}\sigma$. We have $\to_{\mathcal{R}}^{*} \subseteq \succsim$ because $l \succsim r$ for every rule $l \to r \in \mathcal{R}$ and $\succsim$ is a quasi-reduction ordering. Moreover, every dependency pair $\langle s', t'\rangle$ from $\mathcal{P}$ satisfies $s' \succsim t'$. Thus, we obtain

$$\begin{aligned} &u_{1,1}\sigma \succsim v_{1,1}\sigma \succsim \cdots \succsim u_{1,n_1}\sigma \succsim v_{1,n_1}\sigma \succsim s\rho_1\sigma \succ t\rho_1\sigma \succsim \\ &u_{2,1}\sigma \succsim v_{2,1}\sigma \succsim \cdots \succsim u_{2,n_2}\sigma \succsim v_{2,n_2}\sigma \succsim s\rho_2\sigma \succ t\rho_2\sigma \succsim \ldots \end{aligned}$$

However, this is a contradiction to the well-foundedness of $\succ$. □

Theorems 5.4.10 and 5.4.14 originate from [AG00], but instead of the strict part of a quasi-ordering they use the corresponding stable-strict ordering; cf. [GAO02]. The present formulation with stable-strict relations has the following advantage over the formulation with strict relations: If one wants to show termination of a TRS $\mathcal{R}$ by means of one of the theorems, then one can also use quasi-orderings whose strict part is not closed under substitutions.

Note that Theorems 5.4.10 and 5.4.14 are *not* valid if one uses the strict part $\succ^{s}$ of $\succsim$ instead of $\succ^{ss}$ unless $\succ^{s}$ is closed under substitutions. Consider, for example, the TRS $\mathcal{R} = \{f(x) \to f(a)\}$ from Example 5.4.2. The only dependency pair $\langle F(x), F(a)\rangle$ forms a cycle in the dependency graph. Let $\succsim = \to_{\mathcal{R}'}^{*}$, where $\mathcal{R}' = \{f(x) \to f(a), F(x) \to F(a)\}$. We have $f(x) \succ^{s} f(a)$ and $F(x) \succ^{s} F(a)$; cf. Example 5.4.2. In other words, $\succsim$ and its strict part $\succ^{s}$ meet the requirements of Theorems 5.4.10 and 5.4.14, but $\mathcal{R}$ is obviously not terminating.

On the other hand, if the strict part $\succ^s$ of a quasi-ordering $\succsim$ is closed under substitutions, then $t \succ^s u$ implies $t \succ^{ss} u$ according to Lemma 5.4.4 (4). Hence every constraint satisfied by $\succ^s$ is also satisfied by the corresponding stable-strict ordering $\succ^{ss}$.

We stress that, according to Theorem 5.4.14, one may use different quasi-orderings for different cycles in a termination proof. This is in stark contrast to Theorem 5.4.10, where one quasi-ordering has to satisfy all the constraints simultaneously. For example, after computing the dependency graph of Figure 5.1, we must find two quasi-orderings $\succsim_1$ and $\succsim_2$ such that $\succsim_1$ satisfies the inequalities

$$\begin{aligned} f(x,c(y)) &\geq f(x,s(f(y,y))) && (5.2)\\ f(s(x),y) &\geq f(x,s(c(y))) && (5.3)\\ F(x,c(y)) &> F(y,y) && (5.4)\end{aligned}$$

and $\succsim_2$ satisfies the constraints

$$\begin{aligned} f(x,c(y)) &\geq f(x,s(f(y,y))) && (5.5)\\ f(s(x),y) &\geq f(x,s(c(y))) && (5.6)\\ F(s(x),y) &> F(x,s(c(y))) && (5.7)\end{aligned}$$

The primary goal of the dependency pair method is to use standard techniques to automatically generate a suitable quasi-reduction ordering satisfying the constraints of Theorem 5.4.14. In order to facilitate the synthesis of a suitable ordering, the following concept was introduced in [AG00].

Definition 5.4.15 An *argument filtering system* (AFS) over a signature $\mathcal{F}$ is a TRS whose rewrite rules are of the form

$$f(x_1,\ldots,x_n) \to r$$

with $f \in \mathcal{F}^{(n)}$ and there is at most one such rule for every $f \in \mathcal{F}$. In the rule $f(x_1,\ldots,x_n) \to r$, the variables $x_1,\ldots,x_n$ are pairwise distinct and r is either one of these variables or a term $f'(y_1,\ldots,y_m)$, where $f' \notin \mathcal{F}$ is a fresh function symbol of arity m occurring only once in the AFS and $y_1,\ldots,y_m$ are pairwise distinct variables out of $x_1,\ldots,x_n$.

Note that an AFS is a special form of a recursive program scheme; see [Cou90, Klo92]. It can readily be verified that every AFS is terminating. Every AFS is also confluent because it is orthogonal; see Theorem 4.3.11. Hence every AFS $\mathcal{A}$ is convergent and every term t has a unique normal form w.r.t. $\mathcal{A}$, which will be denoted by $t\downarrow_{\mathcal{A}}$.

In order to find a quasi-ordering satisfying a particular set of inequalities, one may first normalize the terms in the inequalities with respect to an AFS (where the AFS may also contain rules for the tuple symbols); see Lemma 5.4.16. Subsequently, one has to find a quasi-reduction ordering that satisfies these modified inequalities; see Corollary 5.4.17. For finite TRSs there are only finitely many AFSs (up to renaming of symbols). Thus, by combining the synthesis of a suitable AFS with well-known techniques for automatically generating simplification orderings, the search for a quasi-ordering satisfying the constraints can be automated.

Lemma 5.4.16 *Let $\mathcal{A}$ be an AFS and let* IN *be a set of inequalities. If the inequalities*

$$\mathrm{IN}{\downarrow_{\mathcal{A}}} = \{s\downarrow_{\mathcal{A}} > t\downarrow_{\mathcal{A}} \mid s > t \in \mathrm{IN}\} \cup \{s\downarrow_{\mathcal{A}} \geq t\downarrow_{\mathcal{A}} \mid s \geq t \in \mathrm{IN}\}$$

are satisfied by a quasi-reduction ordering, then there is also a quasi-reduction ordering satisfying the inequalities IN.

Proof Let $\succsim$ be a quasi-reduction ordering satisfying the inequalities $\mathrm{IN}{\downarrow_{\mathcal{A}}}$. We define the relation $\succsim'$ by $u \succsim' v$ if and only if $u\downarrow_{\mathcal{A}} \succsim v\downarrow_{\mathcal{A}}$. It is readily seen that $\succsim'$ is a well-founded quasi-ordering satisfying the inequalities IN. We will show that $\succsim'$ is in fact a quasi-reduction ordering, that is, it is closed under substitutions and contexts. Let $u \succsim' v$ be given. We have to show that $u\sigma \succsim' v\sigma$ and $C[u] \succsim' C[v]$ hold for every substitution σ and every context $C[\,]$.

For every term t and every substitution σ, one has $(t\sigma)\downarrow_{\mathcal{A}} = (t\downarrow_{\mathcal{A}})(\sigma\downarrow_{\mathcal{A}})$, where $\sigma\downarrow_{\mathcal{A}}$ is defined by $(\sigma\downarrow_{\mathcal{A}})(x) = \sigma(x)\downarrow_{\mathcal{A}}$. Hence $(u\sigma)\downarrow_{\mathcal{A}} \succsim (v\sigma)\downarrow_{\mathcal{A}}$ is a consequence of the fact that $\succsim$ is closed under substitutions. In other words, $u\sigma \succsim' v\sigma$ holds true. Similarly, for every term t and every context $C[\,]$, one has $C[t]\downarrow_{\mathcal{A}} = C{\downarrow_{\mathcal{A}}}[t\downarrow_{\mathcal{A}}]$. Because $\succsim$ is closed under contexts, it follows $C[u]\downarrow_{\mathcal{A}} \succsim C[v]\downarrow_{\mathcal{A}}$. That is, $C[u] \succsim' C[v]$ holds. □

The use of an appropriate AFS often facilitates a termination proof by either Theorem 5.4.10 or Theorem 5.4.14. The following result is a corollary to Theorem 5.4.14. A similar corollary can, of course, be derived from Theorem 5.4.10.

Corollary 5.4.17 *A finite TRS $\mathcal{R}$ is terminating if and only if for each cycle $\mathcal{P}$ in the dependency graph of $\mathcal{R}$ there is an AFS $\mathcal{A}$ and a quasi-reduction ordering $\succsim$ such that*

- *$l\downarrow_{\mathcal{A}} \succsim r\downarrow_{\mathcal{A}}$ for all rules $l \to r$ from $\mathcal{R}$,*
- *$s\downarrow_{\mathcal{A}} \succsim t\downarrow_{\mathcal{A}}$ for all dependency pairs $\langle s, t\rangle$ from $\mathcal{P}$,*
- *$s\downarrow_{\mathcal{A}} \succ t\downarrow_{\mathcal{A}}$ for at least one dependency pair $\langle s, t\rangle$ from $\mathcal{P}$.*

Proof The if direction is an immediate consequence of Theorem 5.4.14 in combination with Lemma 5.4.16. The converse direction follows from an application of Theorem 5.4.14 with the empty AFS. □

For example, in order to satisfy inequalities (5.2)–(5.4), we first apply the AFS $\{f(x,y) \to f'(x)\}$. This yields the modified constraints

$$\begin{array}{rcl} f'(x) & \geq & f'(x) \\ f'(s(x)) & \geq & f'(x) \\ F(x,c(y)) & > & F(y,y) \end{array}$$

These are satisfied by the lexicographic path ordering in which subterms are compared from right to left. For inequalities (5.5)–(5.7) we again use the AFS $\{f(x,y) \to f'(x)\}$. The resulting inequalities are also satisfied by the lexicographic path ordering with the precedence $F \succ_{\mathcal{P}} s$, $F \succ_{\mathcal{P}} c$, but this time subterms are compared from left to right. Hence, termination of the TRS under consideration is proven by Corollary 5.4.17. Note that this TRS is not simply terminating. So in the dependency pair method, simplification orderings like the *lpo* can be used to prove termination of TRSs for which their direct application would fail.

For an automatic approach the usage of dependency graphs is impractical because it is in general undecidable whether two dependency pairs form a chain. However, in order to obtain a sound technique for termination proofs, we can safely use any approximation of the dependency graph that preserves all its cycles. In case we use a rough approximation, we might not be able to determine all the insignificant dependency pairs that we could find with a more accurate approximation. Of course, one still has to prove that the remaining dependency pairs do not form an infinite chain. The stronger the method is for proving the latter, the less effort needs to be put in the approximation and vice versa.

To estimate which dependency pairs may occur consecutively in a chain, the estimated dependency graph has been introduced; cf. [AG00]. We first recall the needed notions. CAP(t) results from replacing all subterms of t that have a defined root symbol by different fresh variables and REN(t) results from replacing all variables in t by different fresh variables. Then, in order to determine whether $\langle u, v\rangle$ can follow $\langle s, t\rangle$ in a chain, one checks whether REN(CAP(t)) unifies with u. The function REN is needed to rename multiple occurrences of the same variable x in t because two different occurrences of $x\sigma$ in $t\sigma$ could reduce to different terms.

Definition 5.4.18 Let $\mathcal{R}$ be a TRS. The *estimated dependency graph* of $\mathcal{R}$, denoted by EDG($\mathcal{R}$), is the directed graph whose nodes are the dependency pairs of $\mathcal{R}$ and there is an arc from $\langle s, t\rangle$ to $\langle u, v\rangle$ if REN(CAP(t)) and u are unifiable.

In Example 5.4.7, the estimated dependency graph coincides with the dependency graph. If one uses the estimated dependency graph instead of the dependency graph, then, for example, Corollary 5.4.17 gets the following form.

Corollary 5.4.19 *A finite TRS $\mathcal{R}$ is terminating if and only if for each cycle $\mathcal{P}$ in* EDG($\mathcal{R}$) *there is an AFS $\mathcal{A}$ and a quasi-reduction ordering $\succsim$ such that*

- $l\downarrow_{\mathcal{A}} \succsim r\downarrow_{\mathcal{A}}$ *for all rules $l \to r$ from $\mathcal{R}$,*
- $s\downarrow_{\mathcal{A}} \succsim t\downarrow_{\mathcal{A}}$ *for all dependency pairs $\langle s,t\rangle$ from $\mathcal{P}$,*
- $s\downarrow_{\mathcal{A}} \succ t\downarrow_{\mathcal{A}}$ *for at least one dependency pair $\langle s,t\rangle$ from $\mathcal{P}$.*

Proof In order to show the if direction, we will show that the dependency graph is a subgraph of the estimated dependency graph. Clearly, both graphs have the same nodes. Thus, one must show that every arc in the dependency graph also appears in the estimated dependency graph. It is not difficult to prove (by induction on the structure of t) that $t\sigma \to_{\mathcal{R}}^* u\sigma$ implies that REN(CAP(t)) matches $u\sigma$. Because REN(CAP(t)) contains pairwise distinct fresh variables, this means that REN(CAP(t)) and u are unifiable. Now the corollary follows from Corollary 5.4.17 because every cycle in the dependency graph is also a cycle in the estimated dependency graph.

The only-if direction is a consequence of the fact that termination of $\mathcal{R}$ implies termination of the TRS (proof of Theorem 5.4.10)

$$\mathcal{R}' = \mathcal{R} \cup \{s \to t \mid \langle s,t\rangle \text{ is a dependency pair of } \mathcal{R}\}$$

More precisely, the empty AFS and the reduction ordering $\succ = \to_{\mathcal{R}'}^+$ satisfy $l \succ r$ for every rule $l \to r$ in $\mathcal{R}$ and $s \succ t$ for every dependency pair $\langle s,t\rangle$ of $\mathcal{R}$. □

For further refinements of the dependency pair method, like narrowing dependency pairs, we refer to [AG00]. Moreover, the reader is invited to prove termination of the *quot* system from Chapter 1 by means of the dependency pair method; see also [AG00].

5.4.2 Quasi-Simplification Orderings

How do we find suitable quasi-reduction orderings that satisfy a set of constraints? In the preceding example, we used the reflexive closure $\succeq_{lpo}$ of $\succ_{lpo}$. More generally, one may use the reflexive closure $\succeq$ of any simplification ordering $\succ$ because $\succeq$ is a quasi-reduction ordering (this is fairly easy to prove). By restricting ourselves to this class of quasi-reduction orderings, we obtain the notion of DP simple termination.

Definition 5.4.20 A finite TRS $\mathcal{R}$ is DP *simply terminating* (acronym: DP-ST) if for every cycle $\mathcal{P}$ in EDG($\mathcal{R}$) there is an AFS $\mathcal{A}$ and a simplification ordering $\succ$ such that

(a) $l\downarrow_{\mathcal{A}} \succeq r\downarrow_{\mathcal{A}}$ for every rule $l \to r$ in $\mathcal{R}$,

(b) $s\downarrow_{\mathcal{A}} \succeq t\downarrow_{\mathcal{A}}$ for every dependency pair $\langle s,t\rangle$ in $\mathcal{P}$,

(c) $s\downarrow_{\mathcal{A}} \succ t\downarrow_{\mathcal{A}}$ for at least one dependency pair $\langle s,t\rangle$ in $\mathcal{P}$.

Next the more general concept of quasi-simplification ordering is introduced.

Definition 5.4.21 A *quasi-simplification ordering* (QSO) $\succsim$ is a quasi-rewrite ordering possessing the subterm property, i.e., $\rhd \subseteq \succsim$.

It is not yet clear that QSOs are really useful for proving termination because they might lack well-foundedness. For finite signatures, however, they are well-founded.

Proposition 5.4.22 *If $\mathcal{F}$ is a finite signature, then every quasi-simplification ordering $\succsim$ on $\mathcal{T}(\mathcal{F},\mathcal{V})$ is well-founded.*

Proof The proof is quite similar to that of Proposition 5.2.20. Suppose that there is an infinite descending sequence

$$t_1 \succ t_2 \succ t_3 \succ \dots$$

First, we show by contraction that $\mathcal{V}ar(t_{i+1}) \subseteq \mathcal{V}ar(t_i)$. That is, we assume that there is a variable $x \in \mathcal{V}ar(t_{i+1}) \setminus \mathcal{V}ar(t_i)$. Let $\sigma = \{x \mapsto t_i\}$. Because $\succ$ is closed under substitutions by Lemma 5.4.4 (3), it follows $t_i = t_i\sigma \succ t_{i+1}\sigma$. Because t_i is a subterm of $t_{i+1}\sigma$ and $\succsim$ has the subterm property, we infer $t_{i+1}\sigma \succsim t_i$. According to Lemma 5.4.4 (7), it follows that $t_i \succ t_i$, which contradicts the irreflexivity of $\succ$. Therefore, $\mathcal{V}ar(t_{i+1}) \subseteq \mathcal{V}ar(t_i)$ and $t_j \in \mathcal{T}(\mathcal{F},\mathcal{V}ar(t_1))$ for every $j \in \mathbb{N}_+$. Let $\mathcal{V}ar(t_1) = \{x_1,\dots,x_n\}$, let $c_1,\dots,c_n$ be fresh constants, and define $\tau = \{x_1 \mapsto c_1,\dots,x_n \mapsto c_n\}$. The infinite sequence $t_1\tau, t_2\tau, t_3\tau,\dots$ consists of terms over $\mathcal{F} \cup \{c_1,\dots,c_n\}$. According to Kruskal's theorem 5.2.19, there are indices $i < j$ such that $t_j\tau \trianglerighteq_{\text{emb}} t_i\tau$. Hence we have either $t_j\tau = t_i\tau$ or, by Lemma 5.2.17, that $t_j\tau \succsim t_i\tau$. Because $\succsim$ is reflexive, we obtain $t_j\tau \succsim t_i\tau$ in both cases. Now $t_i\tau \succ t_j\tau$ in combination with $t_j\tau \succsim t_i\tau$ yields $t_i\tau \succ t_i\tau$ by Lemma 5.4.4 (7). This contradicts the irreflexivity of $\succ$ and concludes the proof. □

According to the previous proposition, every quasi-simplification ordering is indeed a quasi-reduction ordering, provided the signature is finite.

Definition 5.4.23 A finite TRS $\mathcal{R}$ is called DP *quasi-simply terminating* (acronym: DP-QST) if for every cycle $\mathcal{P}$ in EDG($\mathcal{R}$) there exists an AFS $\mathcal{A}$ and a QSO $\succsim$ such that $u \succsim v$ implies $\mathcal{V}ar(v) \subseteq \mathcal{V}ar(u)$ for all terms u and v, and

(a) $l\downarrow_{\mathcal{A}} \succsim r\downarrow_{\mathcal{A}}$ for every rule $l \to r$ in $\mathcal{R}$,

(b) $s\downarrow_{\mathcal{A}} \succsim t\downarrow_{\mathcal{A}}$ for every dependency pair $\langle s,t\rangle$ in $\mathcal{P}$,

(c) $s\downarrow_{\mathcal{A}} \succ t\downarrow_{\mathcal{A}}$ for at least one dependency pair $\langle s,t\rangle$ in $\mathcal{P}$.

The intention of Definition 5.4.23 is to cover most of the TRSs for which an automated termination proof using dependency pairs is potentially feasible. Because the dependency graph cannot be used in automated termination proofs (it is undecidable whether two dependency pairs form a chain), Definition 5.4.23 uses the estimated dependency graph instead of the dependency graph. Moreover, Definition 5.4.23 differs from the definition of DP quasi-simple termination in [GAO02] in that it allows only quasi-simplification orderings satisfying $u \succsim v \Rightarrow \mathcal{V}ar(v) \subseteq \mathcal{V}ar(u)$ instead of arbitrary quasi-simplification orderings. This is because all quasi-simplification orderings used in practice satisfy $u \succsim v \Rightarrow \mathcal{V}ar(v) \subseteq \mathcal{V}ar(u)$ anyway (see Theorems 5.4.25 and 5.4.27 and Lemma 5.4.37).

An example of a QSO violating $u \succsim v \Rightarrow \mathcal{V}ar(v) \subseteq \mathcal{V}ar(u)$ is the reduction ordering induced by the algebra $\mathcal{A}$ in Example 5.4.33: it satisfies, e.g., $f(x) \succsim_{\mathcal{A}} y$.

It is well known that recursive path orderings can be based on precedences that are quasi-orderings. These path orderings turn out to be QSOs.

Definition 5.4.24 Let $\succsim_p$ be a precedence (quasi-ordering) on a signature $\mathcal{F}$. We extend $\succsim_p$ to the set of variables $\mathcal{V}$ as follows: $x \approx_p x$ for every $x \in \mathcal{V}$ (i.e., variables and function symbols are incomparable under $\succsim_p$). The corresponding *recursive path ordering* is defined as follows; cf. [Der87, definition 18] and [Fer95, definition 4.33]. Let $s = f(s_1,\ldots,s_m)$ for some $f \in \mathcal{F} \cup \mathcal{V}$ and $m \in \mathbb{N}$ and $t = g(t_1,\ldots,t_n)$ or some $g \in \mathcal{F} \cup \mathcal{V}$ and $n \in \mathbb{N}$.

$s = f(s_1,\ldots,s_m) \succsim_{rpo} g(t_1,\ldots,t_n) = t$ if

1. $s_i \succsim_{rpo} t$ for some $i \in \{1,\ldots,m\}$; or
2. $f \succ_p g$, and $s \succ^s_{rpo} t_j$ for all $j \in \{1,\ldots,n\}$; or
3. $f \approx_p g$ and $[s_1,\ldots,s_m] \succsim^{mul}_{rpo} [t_1,\ldots,t_n]$.

Theorem 5.4.25 *Every recursive path ordering $\succsim_{rpo}$ is a QSO and its strict part $\succ^s_{rpo}$ is a simplification ordering. Furthermore, $u \succsim_{rpo} v$ implies $\mathcal{V}ar(v) \subseteq \mathcal{V}ar(u)$ for all $u,v \in \mathcal{T}(\mathcal{F},\mathcal{V})$.*

Proof The last statement is an easy consequence of the definition of $\succsim_{rpo}$. A proof of the other statements can be found in [Fer95, lemma 4.34]. □

Because $\succ^s_{rpo}$ is closed under substitutions, we infer $\succ^s_{rpo} \subseteq \succ^{ss}_{rpo}$ from Lemma 5.4.4 (4). As a consequence, whenever a recursive path ordering $\succsim_{rpo}$ and its strict part $\succ^s_{rpo}$ satisfy a set of inequalities IN, then $\succsim_{rpo}$ and its corresponding stable-strict ordering $\succ^{ss}_{rpo}$ satisfy IN as well.

Of course, lexicographic path orderings can also be based on precedences that are quasi-orderings.

Definition 5.4.26 Given a precedence $\succsim_p$ on a signature $\mathcal{F}$, we extend $\succsim_p$ to $\mathcal{V}$ as in Definition 5.4.24. The corresponding *lexicographic path ordering* $\succsim_{lpo} \subseteq \mathcal{T}(\mathcal{F},\mathcal{V}) \times \mathcal{T}(\mathcal{F},\mathcal{V})$ is defined as follows; cf. [KL80], [Der87, definition 19], and [Fer95, definition 4.33].

$s = f(s_1,\ldots,s_m) \succsim_{lpo} g(t_1,\ldots,t_n) = t$ if

1. $s_i \succsim_{lpo} t$ for some $i \in \{1,\ldots,m\}$; or
2. $f \succ_p g$ and $s \succ_{lpo}^s t_j$ for every $j \in \{1,\ldots,n\}$; or
3. $f \approx_p g$, $(s_1,\ldots,s_m) \succsim_{lpo}^{lex} (t_1,\ldots,t_n)$, and $s \succ_{lpo}^s t_j$ for every index $j \in \{1,\ldots,n\}$.

Theorem 5.4.27 *Every lexicographic path ordering $\succsim_{lpo}$ is a QSO and its strict part $\succ_{lpo}^s$ is a simplification ordering. Furthermore, $u \succsim_{lpo} v$ implies $\mathcal{V}ar(v) \subseteq \mathcal{V}ar(u)$ for all $u,v \in \mathcal{T}(\mathcal{F},\mathcal{V})$.*

Proof Again, the last statement follows directly from the definition of $\succsim_{lpo}$; a proof of the other statements can be found in [Fer95, lemma 4.34]. □

In order to clarify the connections between simple termination, DP simple termination, DP quasi-simple termination, and termination, we need the following lemma.

Lemma 5.4.28 *Let $\succ$ be a simplification ordering on $\mathcal{T}(\mathcal{F},\mathcal{V})$.*

1. *If $s \succ t$, then $\mathcal{V}ar(t) \subseteq \mathcal{V}ar(s)$ and $s \notin \mathcal{V}$.*
2. *If $s \succeq t$, then either $s = t$ or $\mathcal{V}ar(t) \subseteq \mathcal{V}ar(s)$ and $s \notin \mathcal{V}$.*

Proof (1) Assume that there is a variable $x \in \mathcal{V}ar(t) \setminus \mathcal{V}ar(s)$. Then $t = C[x]$ for some context $C[\,]$. With $\sigma = \{x \mapsto s\}$ it follows that $s = s\sigma \succ t\sigma = C[s]$. Because $C[s] \succeq s$ according to the subterm property, we obtain a contradiction to the irreflexivity of $\succ$. Thus $\mathcal{V}ar(t) \subseteq \mathcal{V}ar(s)$ holds. Now suppose that s is a variable, say x. If $x \in \mathcal{V}ar(t)$, then we obtain $x \succ t \succeq x$ by the subterm property, which is clearly impossible. Thus suppose $x \notin \mathcal{V}ar(t)$. Because $\succ$ is closed under substitutions, we infer $x\sigma = t \succ t\sigma = t$, where $\sigma = \{x \mapsto t\}$. This, however, contradicts the irreflexivity of $\succ$.

(2) Direct consequence of (1) because $s \succeq t$ means either $s = t$ or $s \succ t$. □

Lemma 5.4.29 *The following holds:* ST ⇒ DP-ST ⇒ DP-QST ⇒ SN.

Proof The second implication follows from Lemma 5.4.28 in conjunction with the fact that every simplification ordering $\succ$ is closed under substitutions and therefore $\succ$ is contained in the stable-strict ordering corresponding to $\succeq$; cf. Lemma 5.4.4 (4). The last implication follows from Corollary 5.4.19.

The first implication remains to be shown. Let $\mathcal{R}$ be a simply terminating TRS over the signature $\mathcal{F} = \mathcal{D} \uplus \mathcal{C}$ and let $Tup_{\mathcal{F}} = \{F \mid f \in \mathcal{D}\}$ be the set of tuple symbols. Because $\mathcal{R}$ is simply terminating, there exists a simplification ordering $\succ$ such that $l \succ r$ holds for all rules $l \to r$ of $\mathcal{R}$. Let Ω be the function that replaces every tuple symbol F in a term $s \in \mathcal{T}(\mathcal{F} \cup Tup_{\mathcal{F}}, \mathcal{V})$ with its corresponding function symbol $f \in \mathcal{F}$. Then $\succ$ can be extended to a simplification ordering $\succ'$ on $\mathcal{T}(\mathcal{F} \cup Tup_{\mathcal{F}}, \mathcal{V})$ by defining $t \succ' u$ if and only if $\Omega(t) \succ \Omega(u)$ holds. We claim that the simplification ordering $\succ'$ satisfies constraints (a)–(c) of Definition 5.4.20 without applying an AFS. Obviously, $l \succ' r$ holds for all rules $l \to r$ of $\mathcal{R}$. Thus $\succ'$ satisfies constraint (a). Moreover, for every dependency pair $\langle s, t\rangle$ we have $s \succ' t$. This is because every dependency pair $\langle F(s_1, \dots, s_n), G(t_1, \dots, t_m)\rangle$ originates from a rule $f(s_1, \dots, s_n) \to C[g(t_1, \dots, t_m)]$ in $\mathcal{R}$. Thus, $f(\dots) \succ C[g(\dots)]$ implies $f(\dots) \succ g(\dots)$ by the subterm property, which in turn implies $F(\dots) \succ' G(\dots)$. Hence, $\succ'$ also satisfies constraints (b) and (c) of Definition 5.4.20. □

The following examples show that none of the converse implications of Lemma 5.4.29 hold.

Example 5.4.30 The system $\mathcal{R} = \{f(f(x)) \to f(c(f(x)))\}$ is DP simply terminating because $\{\langle F(f(x)), F(x)\rangle\}$ is the only cycle in EDG($\mathcal{R}$) and the resulting constraints are satisfied by the recursive path ordering if one uses the AFS $\{c(x) \to x\}$. However, this TRS is obviously not simply terminating.

The TRS consisting of the rules

$$\begin{array}{rclcrcl} f(f(x)) & \to & f(c(f(x))) & \quad & g(c(0)) & \to & g(d(1)) \\ f(f(x)) & \to & f(d(f(x))) & & g(c(1)) & \to & g(d(0)) \\ g(c(x)) & \to & x & & g(d(x)) & \to & x \end{array}$$

is DP quasi-simply terminating. This can be proven in a similar fashion by using the AFS $\{c(x) \to x, d(x) \to x\}$ and the recursive path ordering in which 0 and 1 are equal in the precedence; see Definition 5.4.24. However, the system is not DP simply terminating because the AFS must reduce $c(x)$ and $d(x)$ to x because of the f rules and the collapsing g rules, and then $g(0) \geq g(1)$ and $g(1) \geq g(0)$ lead to a contradiction.

Finally, the system $\{f(0,1,x) \to f(x,x,x)\}$ is terminating but not DP quasi-simply terminating. Termination will be shown in Example 5.4.35. The fact that the system is not DP quasi-simply terminating follows from similar reasoning to Example 5.2.31. The dependency pair $\langle F(0,1,x), F(x,x,x)\rangle$ forms a cycle in the estimated dependency graph. If the system were DP quasi-simply terminating, then there would be an AFS $\mathcal{A}$ and a quasi-simplification ordering $\succsim$ satisfying $F(0,1,x){\downarrow_{\mathcal{A}}} \succ F(x,x,x){\downarrow_{\mathcal{A}}}$. If $\mathcal{A}$ is the empty AFS, then we obtain the following contradiction:

$$t = F(0,1,F(0,1,1)) \succ F(F(0,1,1),F(0,1,1),F(0,1,1)) \succsim t$$

It is not difficult to verify that the usage of a nonempty AFS $\mathcal{A}$ also yields a contradiction.

5.4.3 The Interpretation Method

We have seen that every quasi-simplification ordering on a set of terms over a finite signature is a quasi-reduction ordering. Representatives of such QSOs are path orderings like $\succsim_{rpo}$ and $\succsim_{lpo}$. Another method to construct quasi-reduction orderings on $\mathcal{T}(\mathcal{F},\mathcal{V})$ is based on $\mathcal{F}$-algebras. Polynomial quasi-orderings fall into this category.

Definition 5.4.31 Let $\mathcal{F}$ be a signature.

1. A *weakly monotone* $\mathcal{F}$-algebra $(\mathcal{A},\succsim)$ is an $\mathcal{F}$-algebra $\mathcal{A}$ for which the carrier set A is provided with a quasi-ordering $\succsim$ such that every algebra operation is *weakly monotone* in all of its arguments. More precisely, for all $f \in \mathcal{F}$ and $a,b \in A$ with $a \succsim b$ we have $f_\mathcal{A}(\dots,a,\dots) \succsim f_\mathcal{A}(\dots,b,\dots)$. An algebra operation $f_\mathcal{A}$ is called *strictly monotone* (or *strongly monotone*) if for all $a,b \in A$ with $a \succ b$ we have $f_\mathcal{A}(\dots,a,\dots) \succ f_\mathcal{A}(\dots,b,\dots)$. It should be pointed out that $\succ$ denotes the strict part of $\succsim$ as there is no stable-strict ordering corresponding to $\succsim$.

2. A weakly monotone $\mathcal{F}$-algebra $(\mathcal{A},\succsim)$ is called *well-founded* if $\succ$ is well-founded.

3. A weakly monotone $\mathcal{F}$-algebra $(\mathcal{A},\succsim)$ is *simple* if, for all $f \in \mathcal{F}^{(n)}$, $a_1,\dots,a_n \in A$, and $1 \le i \le n$, the inequality $f_\mathcal{A}(a_1,\dots,a_n) \succsim a_i$ holds.

4. Every weakly monotone $\mathcal{F}$-algebra $(\mathcal{A},\succsim)$ induces a quasi-ordering $\succsim_\mathcal{A}$ on $\mathcal{T}(\mathcal{F},\mathcal{V})$ as follows: $t \succsim_\mathcal{A} u$ if and only if $[\alpha]_\mathcal{A}(t) \succsim [\alpha]_\mathcal{A}(u)$ for all assignments $\alpha\colon \mathcal{V} \to A$.

As usual, the strict part $\succ^s_\mathcal{A}$ of $\succsim_\mathcal{A}$ is defined by $t \succ^s_\mathcal{A} u$ if and only if $t \succsim_\mathcal{A} u$ and $u \not\succsim_\mathcal{A} t$. The stable-strict ordering $\succ^{ss}_\mathcal{A}$ corresponding to $\succsim_\mathcal{A}$ is defined by $t \succ^{ss}_\mathcal{A} u$ if and only if $t\sigma \succ^s_\mathcal{A} u\sigma$ for all ground substitutions $\sigma : \mathcal{V} \to \mathcal{T}(\mathcal{F})$. In other words, for all ground substitutions σ we must have $[t\sigma]_\mathcal{A} \succ [u\sigma]_\mathcal{A}$, or equivalently, $[t\sigma]_\mathcal{A} \succsim [u\sigma]_\mathcal{A}$ and $[u\sigma]_\mathcal{A} \not\succsim [t\sigma]_\mathcal{A}$. In the following, $\succ_\mathcal{A}$ denotes the stable-strict ordering corresponding to $\succsim_\mathcal{A}$ unless stated otherwise.

Lemma 5.4.32 *Let* $(\mathcal{A},\succsim)$ *be a weakly monotone* $\mathcal{F}$*-algebra.*

1. *$\succsim_{\mathcal{A}}$ is a quasi-rewrite ordering.*

2. *If $(\mathcal{A}, \succsim)$ is well-founded, then $\succsim_{\mathcal{A}}$ is a quasi-reduction ordering.*

3. *If $(\mathcal{A}, \succsim)$ is simple, then $\succsim_{\mathcal{A}}$ is a quasi-simplification ordering.*

Proof (1) We have to show that the quasi-ordering $\succsim_{\mathcal{A}}$ is closed under contexts and substitutions. The former follows from weak monotonicity of the algebra operations and the latter follows as in Theorem 5.2.8.
(2) We have to show that $\succ_{\mathcal{A}}$ is well-founded. Suppose, on the contrary, that there is an infinite descending sequence $t_1 \succ_{\mathcal{A}} t_2 \succ_{\mathcal{A}} t_3 \succ_{\mathcal{A}} \dots$. Let σ be an arbitrary ground substitution. It follows that the descending sequence $[t_1\sigma]_{\mathcal{A}} \succ [t_2\sigma]_{\mathcal{A}} \succ [t_3\sigma]_{\mathcal{A}} \succ \dots$ is infinite, which contradicts the well-foundedness of $\succ$.
(3) Because $\succsim_{\mathcal{A}}$ is a quasi-rewrite ordering by (1), it remains to be shown that $\succsim_{\mathcal{A}}$ has the subterm property. By Lemma 5.2.17, it suffices to prove that $f(x_1, \dots, x_n) \succsim_{\mathcal{A}} x_i$ holds for every $f \in \mathcal{F}^{(n)}$ and every $i \in \{1, \dots, n\}$. This inequality holds true because $(\mathcal{A}, \succsim)$ is simple and thus $[\alpha]_{\mathcal{A}}(f(x_1, \dots, x_n)) = f_{\mathcal{A}}(\alpha(x_1), \dots, \alpha(x_n)) \succsim \alpha(x_i) = [\alpha]_{\mathcal{A}}(x_i)$ for any assignment $\alpha \colon \mathcal{V} \to A$. □

In general, neither $\succ_{\mathcal{A}}^{s}$ nor $\succ_{\mathcal{A}}^{ss}$ is closed under contexts, as seen in the next example.

Example 5.4.33 Let $\mathcal{F} = \{a, b, f\}$. As $\mathcal{F}$-algebra $\mathcal{A}$ we choose the carrier set $A = \{\circ, \bullet\}$ together with the interpretation functions $a_{\mathcal{A}} = \circ$, $b_{\mathcal{A}} = \bullet$, and $f_{\mathcal{A}}(x) = \circ$ for $x \in A$. Furthermore, we define a quasi-ordering $\succsim$ on A by $\circ \succsim \bullet$. Obviously, $(\mathcal{A}, \succsim)$ is a well-founded weakly monotone $\mathcal{F}$-algebra such that $a \succ_{\mathcal{A}}^{s} b$. On the other hand, we have $f(a) \not\succ_{\mathcal{A}}^{s} f(b)$. The same is true if $\succ_{\mathcal{A}}^{s}$ is replaced with $\succ_{\mathcal{A}}^{ss}$. Therefore, neither $\succ_{\mathcal{A}}^{s}$ nor $\succ_{\mathcal{A}}^{ss}$ is closed under contexts.

The usage of well-founded weakly monotone algebras yields the following variant of Corollary 5.4.19.

Corollary 5.4.34 *A finite TRS $\mathcal{R}$ is terminating if and only if for each cycle $\mathcal{P}$ in* EDG($\mathcal{R}$) *there exists an AFS $\mathcal{A}$ and a well-founded weakly monotone $\mathcal{F}'$-algebra $(\mathcal{B}, \succsim)$ such that*

- *$l \downarrow_{\mathcal{A}} \succsim_{\mathcal{B}} r \downarrow_{\mathcal{A}}$ for all rules $l \to r$ from $\mathcal{R}$,*
- *$s \downarrow_{\mathcal{A}} \succsim_{\mathcal{B}} t \downarrow_{\mathcal{A}}$ for all dependency pairs $\langle s, t \rangle$ from $\mathcal{P}$, and*
- *$s \downarrow_{\mathcal{A}} \succ_{\mathcal{B}} t \downarrow_{\mathcal{A}}$ for at least one dependency pair $\langle s, t \rangle$ from $\mathcal{P}$,*

where $\mathcal{F}'$ consists of all function symbols occurring in the inequalities.

Proof The corollary follows directly from Corollary 5.4.19 in combination with Lemma 5.4.32. □

Example 5.4.35 We prove termination of the TRS

$$\mathcal{R} = \{f(0,1,x) \to f(x,x,x)\}$$

by means of Corollary 5.4.34. There is only one dependency pair, namely: $\langle F(0,1,x), F(x,x,x)\rangle$. It is easy to see that $\mathcal{P} = \{\langle F(0,1,x), F(x,x,x)\rangle\}$ is a cycle in $\text{EDG}(\mathcal{R})$. After applying the AFS $\{f(x_1,x_2,x_3) \to f'\}$, we have to find a quasi-ordering $\succsim$ satisfying the inequality $F(0,1,x) > F(x,x,x)$. As $\mathcal{F}'$-algebra $\mathcal{A}$ we choose the carrier set $A = \{\circ, \bullet, \lozenge, \blacklozenge\}$ together with the interpretation functions $0_{\mathcal{A}} = \circ$, $1_{\mathcal{A}} = \bullet$, $f'_{\mathcal{A}} = \blacklozenge$, and

$$F_{\mathcal{A}}(a_1,a_2,a_3) = \begin{cases} \lozenge & \text{if } a_1 = \circ \text{ and } a_2 = \bullet \\ \blacklozenge & \text{otherwise} \end{cases}$$

Furthermore, we define a quasi-ordering $\succsim$ on A by $\lozenge \succsim \blacklozenge$. It is fairly simple to prove that $(\mathcal{A}, \succsim)$ is a well-founded weakly monotone $\mathcal{F}'$-algebra such that $F(0,1,x) \succ_{\mathcal{A}} F(x,x,x)$. Therefore, $\mathcal{R}$ is terminating by Corollary 5.4.34.

Clearly, every polynomial $P(x_1,\dots,x_n) \in \mathbb{N}[x_1,\dots,x_n]$ is weakly monotone on $\mathbb{N}$. That is, we have

$$P(a_1,\dots,a_{i-1},a,a_{i+1},\dots,a_n) \geq P(a_1,\dots,a_{i-1},b,a_{i+1},\dots,a_n)$$

for all $a,b,a_1,\dots,a_{i-1},a_{i+1},\dots,a_n \in \mathbb{N}$ with $a \geq b$ and $i \in \{1,\dots,n\}$. Consequently, every polynomial interpretation of $\mathcal{F}$ together with the natural ordering $\geq$ on $\mathbb{N}$ is a well-founded weakly monotone $\mathcal{F}$-algebra. The induced quasi-reduction ordering on $\mathcal{T}(\mathcal{F},\mathcal{V})$ is called a *polynomial quasi-ordering*.

In Section 7.2, we will learn how a conditional term rewriting system can be transformed into an unconditional TRS such that termination of the transformed TRS implies (effective) termination of the conditional term rewriting system. For example, if we transform the *quicksort* system from Chapter 1 into a TRS, then we get the system in Example 5.4.36; see Section 7.2.7 for details of the transformation. Termination of the transformed TRS can be shown automatically by using polynomial quasi-orderings, as we will show next.

Example 5.4.36 Let $\mathcal{R}$ have the rules

$$\begin{array}{rcl} 0 \le y & \to & true \\ s(x) \le 0 & \to & false \\ s(x) \le s(y) & \to & x \le y \\ nil +\!\!+\, ys & \to & ys \\ (x : xs) +\!\!+\, ys & \to & x : (xs +\!\!+\, ys) \\ split(x, nil) & \to & \langle nil, nil \rangle \\ split(x, y : ys) & \to & f(split(x, ys), x, y, ys) \\ f(\langle xs, zs \rangle, x, y, ys) & \to & g(x \le y, x, y, ys, xs, zs) \\ g(true, x, y, ys, xs, zs) & \to & \langle xs, y : zs \rangle \\ g(false, x, y, ys, xs, zs) & \to & \langle y : xs, zs \rangle \\ qsort(nil) & \to & nil \\ qsort(x : xs) & \to & h(split(x, xs), x, xs) \\ h(\langle ys, zs \rangle, x, xs) & \to & qsort(ys) +\!\!+\, (x : qsort(zs)) \end{array}$$

There are five cycles in EDG($\mathcal{R}$), viz.

$$\begin{array}{c} \{\langle \mathrm{LEQ}(s(x), s(y)), \mathrm{LEQ}(x, y) \rangle\} \\ \{\langle \mathrm{APP}(x : xs, ys), \mathrm{APP}(xs, ys) \rangle\} \\ \{\langle \mathrm{SPLIT}(x, y : ys), \mathrm{SPLIT}(x, ys) \rangle\} \\ \{\langle \mathrm{QSORT}(x : xs), \mathrm{H}(split(x, xs), x, xs) \rangle, \langle \mathrm{H}(\langle ys, zs \rangle, x, xs), \mathrm{QSORT}(ys) \rangle\} \\ \{\langle \mathrm{QSORT}(x : xs), \mathrm{H}(split(x, xs), x, xs) \rangle, \langle \mathrm{H}(\langle ys, zs \rangle, x, xs), \mathrm{QSORT}(zs) \rangle\} \end{array}$$

The polynomial quasi-ordering induced by the following polynomial interpretation with carrier $\mathbb{N}$ satisfies the relevant inequalities:

$$\begin{array}{rcl@{\qquad}rcl} 0_{\mathbb{N}} & = & 0 & s_{\mathbb{N}}(x) & = & x + 1 \\ x \le_{\mathbb{N}} y & = & 0 & true_{\mathbb{N}} & = & 0 \\ false_{\mathbb{N}} & = & 0 & nil_{\mathbb{N}} & = & 0 \\ x :_{\mathbb{N}} xs & = & xs + 1 & xs +\!\!+_{\mathbb{N}}\, ys & = & xs + ys \\ split_{\mathbb{N}}(x, ys) & = & ys + 1 & \langle xs, ys \rangle_{\mathbb{N}} & = & xs + ys + 1 \\ f_{\mathbb{N}}(z, x, y, ys) & = & z + 1 & g_{\mathbb{N}}(z, x, y, ys, xs, zs) & = & xs + zs + 2 \\ qsort_{\mathbb{N}}(xs) & = & xs & h_{\mathbb{N}}(z, x, xs) & = & z \\ \mathrm{LEQ}_{\mathbb{N}}(x, y) & = & x & \mathrm{APP}_{\mathbb{N}}(xs, ys) & = & xs \\ \mathrm{SPLIT}_{\mathbb{N}}(x, ys) & = & ys & \mathrm{QSORT}_{\mathbb{N}}(xs) & = & xs \\ \mathrm{H}_{\mathbb{N}}(z, x, xs) & = & z & & & \end{array}$$

Note that polynomial quasi-orderings are in general not QSOs. For example, in the preceding example we have $[0 \le s(0)]_{\mathbb{N}} = 0 \not\ge 1 = [s(0)]_{\mathbb{N}}$. However, the following lemma shows that if the polynomial quasi-ordering respects some restrictions, then it is indeed a QSO.

Lemma 5.4.37 *Let $(\mathcal{N}, \ge)$ be a polynomial interpretation of $\mathcal{F}$.*

1. *If the carrier N is an infinite subset of $\mathbb{N}_+$ and every function symbol $f \in \mathcal{F}^{(n)}$, $n > 0$, is associated with a strictly monotone polynomial, then $\ge_{\mathcal{N}}$ is a QSO satisfying $u \ge_{\mathcal{N}} v \Rightarrow \mathcal{V}ar(v) \subseteq \mathcal{V}ar(u)$.*

2. *If the carrier is infinite and every function symbol* $f \in \mathcal{F}^{(n)}$, $n > 0$, *is associated with a polynomial that, for all* $i \in \{1, \ldots, n\}$, *contains a (nonmixed) monomial of the form* $m_i\, x_i^{k_i}$ *with* $m_i, k_i \in \mathbb{N}_+$, *then* $\geq_{\mathcal{N}}$ *is a QSO satisfying* $u \geq_{\mathcal{N}} v \Rightarrow \mathcal{V}ar(v) \subseteq \mathcal{V}ar(u)$.

Proof (1) If the carrier N is a subset of $\mathbb{N}_+$ and every function symbol $f \in \mathcal{F}^{(n)}$, $n > 0$, is associated with a strictly monotone polynomial $P_f(x_1, \ldots, x_n) \in \mathbb{N}[x_1, \ldots, x_n]$, then $P_f(x_1, \ldots, x_n)$ contains a monomial $m\, x_1^{k_1} \cdots x_i^{k_i} \cdots x_n^{k_n}$ with $m, k_i \in \mathbb{N}_+$ for all $i \in \{1, \ldots, n\}$; see Proposition 5.2.12. Now the validity of $C[t] \geq_{\mathcal{N}} t$, for every context $C[\;]$ and term t, is easy to verify. Therefore, $\geq_{\mathcal{N}}$ is a QSO. Lastly, assume that $u \geq_{\mathcal{N}} v \Rightarrow \mathcal{V}ar(v) \subseteq \mathcal{V}ar(u)$ is not valid, i.e., there are terms $u, v \in \mathcal{T}(\mathcal{F}, \mathcal{V})$ with $u \geq_{\mathcal{N}} v$ but there is an $x \in \mathcal{V}ar(v) \setminus \mathcal{V}ar(u)$. Let $\alpha : \mathcal{V} \to N$ be an assignment and let $k = [\alpha]_{\mathcal{N}}(u)$. Because N is an infinite subset of $\mathbb{N}_+$, there is a $k' \in N$ with $k' > k$. Let $\alpha' : \mathcal{V} \to N$ be defined by $\alpha'(x) = k'$ and $\alpha'(y) = \alpha(y)$ for every $y \neq x$. It follows $[\alpha']_{\mathcal{N}}(u) = [\alpha]_{\mathcal{N}}(u) = k < k' = [\alpha']_{\mathcal{N}}(x) \leq [\alpha']_{\mathcal{N}}(v)$. This, however, contradicts $u \geq_{\mathcal{N}} v$.
(2) Similar to the proof of (1). □

By using a suitable AFS in combination with Lemma 5.4.37, it is often possible to show that a TRS is DP quasi-simply terminating. We exemplify this by the TRS from Example 5.4.36. If we simplify the constraints with the AFS $\mathcal{A}$ consisting of the rules

$$
\begin{array}{rclrcl}
x \leq y & \to & \leq' & x : xs & \to & :'(xs) \\
split(x, ys) & \to & split'(ys) & f(z, x, y, ys) & \to & f'(z) \\
g(z, x, y, ys, xs, zs) & \to & g'(xs, zs) & h(z, x, xs) & \to & z \\
\mathrm{LEQ}(x, y) & \to & \mathrm{LEQ}'(x) & \mathrm{APP}(xs, ys) & \to & \mathrm{APP}'(xs) \\
\mathrm{SPLIT}(x, ys) & \to & \mathrm{SPLIT}'(ys) & \mathrm{H}(z, x, xs) & \to & \mathrm{H}'(z)
\end{array}
$$

then the polynomial quasi-ordering induced by the following polynomial interpretation with carrier $\mathbb{N}$ satisfies the simplified inequalities.

$$
\begin{array}{rclrcl}
0_{\mathbb{N}} & = & 0 & s_{\mathbb{N}}(x) & = & x + 1 \\
\leq'\mathbb{N} & = & 0 & true_{\mathbb{N}} & = & 0 \\
false_{\mathbb{N}} & = & 0 & nil_{\mathbb{N}} & = & 0 \\
:'_{\mathbb{N}}(xs) & = & xs + 1 & xs +\!\!+_{\mathbb{N}}\, ys & = & xs + ys \\
split'\mathbb{N}(ys) & = & ys + 1 & \langle xs, ys \rangle_{\mathbb{N}} & = & xs + ys + 1 \\
f'_{\mathbb{N}}(z) & = & z + 1 & g'_{\mathbb{N}}(xs, zs) & = & xs + zs + 2 \\
qsort_{\mathbb{N}}(xs) & = & xs & \mathrm{LEQ}'_{\mathbb{N}}(x) & = & x \\
\mathrm{APP}'_{\mathbb{N}}(xs) & = & xs & \mathrm{SPLIT}'_{\mathbb{N}}(ys) & = & ys \\
\mathrm{QSORT}_{\mathbb{N}}(xs) & = & xs & \mathrm{H}'_{\mathbb{N}}(z) & = & z
\end{array}
$$

Because this polynomial quasi-ordering is a QSO satisfying $u \gtrsim v \Rightarrow \mathcal{V}ar(v) \subseteq \mathcal{V}ar(u)$ by Lemma 5.4.37(2), it follows that the system is DP quasi-simply terminating.

The considerations are not restricted to polynomial interpretations, as the following characterization of DP quasi-simple termination shows. Note that it bears a strong resemblance to Proposition 5.2.33.

Proposition 5.4.38 *A finite TRS $\mathcal{R}$ is DP quasi-simply terminating if and only if for every cycle $\mathcal{P}$ in* EDG($\mathcal{R}$) *there is an AFS $\mathcal{A}$ and a simple weakly monotone $\mathcal{F}'$-algebra $(\mathcal{B}, \succsim)$ such that $u \succsim_{\mathcal{B}} v \Rightarrow \mathcal{V}ar(v) \subseteq \mathcal{V}ar(u)$ and*

- $l \downarrow_{\mathcal{A}} \succsim_{\mathcal{B}} r \downarrow_{\mathcal{A}}$ *for every rule $l \to r$ in $\mathcal{R}$,*
- $s \downarrow_{\mathcal{A}} \succsim_{\mathcal{B}} t \downarrow_{\mathcal{A}}$ *for every dependency pair $\langle s, t\rangle$ in $\mathcal{P}$, and*
- $s \downarrow_{\mathcal{A}} \succ_{\mathcal{B}} t \downarrow_{\mathcal{A}}$ *for at least one dependency pair $\langle s, t\rangle$ in $\mathcal{P}$.*

where $\mathcal{F}'$ consists of all function symbols occurring in the inequalities.

Proof The if direction follows from the fact that $\succsim_{\mathcal{B}}$ is a QSO by Lemma 5.4.32. Conversely, if $\mathcal{R}$ is DP quasi-simply terminating, then the term algebra $\mathcal{T}(\mathcal{F}', \mathcal{V})$ together with the quasi-simplification ordering $\succsim$ is a simple $\mathcal{F}'$-algebra, which satisfies the inequalities. □

5.5 Transformational Methods

The methods discussed in this section are based on transformations between rewrite systems. If a TRS $(\mathcal{F}, \mathcal{R})$ can be transformed into a TRS $\Phi(\mathcal{F}, \mathcal{R})$ by a nontermination-preserving transformation Φ, then termination of $\Phi(\mathcal{F}, \mathcal{R})$ implies termination of $(\mathcal{F}, \mathcal{R})$. Such transformations are advantageous whenever it is easier to prove termination of the transformed system than to prove termination of the original system. This approach is not restricted to TRSs. In Section 7.2 and Chapter 10, we will use similar transformations for conditional term rewriting systems and logic programs.

5.5.1 Semantic Labeling

Zantema [Zan95a] devised the method of semantic labeling in which a given system $(\mathcal{F}, \mathcal{R})$ is transformed into a labeled system $(\mathcal{F}_{lab}, \mathcal{R}_{lab})$ by labeling the function symbols. The labeling is always based on a quasimodel of $\mathcal{R}$, and it turns out that $\mathcal{R}$ is terminating if and only if $\mathcal{R}_{lab}$ is terminating. Semantic labeling is an interesting technique for proving termination because termination of $\mathcal{R}_{lab}$ is often much easier to prove than termination of $\mathcal{R}$; for example, *rpo* might be applicable to $\mathcal{R}_{lab}$ but not to $\mathcal{R}$. However, Zantema remarks that "the technique of semantic labelling is hard to automate." In this section we will review his technique.

Definition 5.5.1 Let $\mathcal{F}$ be a signature and $\mathcal{A}$ an $\mathcal{F}$-algebra.

- A *labeling* for $\mathcal{F}$ consists of sets of labels L_f for every $f \in \mathcal{F}$. The *labeled signature* $\mathcal{F}_{lab}$ consists of n-ary function symbols f_ℓ for every $f \in \mathcal{F}^{(n)}$ and label $\ell \in L_f$ together with all function symbols $f \in \mathcal{F}$ where $L_f = \emptyset$.
- A *labeling* for $\mathcal{A}$ consists of a labeling L for the signature $\mathcal{F}$ together with mappings $lab_f : A^n \to L_f$ for every $f \in \mathcal{F}^{(n)}$ with $L_f \neq \emptyset$.
- Let (L, lab) be a labeling for $\mathcal{A}$. For every assignment $\alpha\colon \mathcal{V} \to A$, a mapping $lab_\alpha : \mathcal{T}(\mathcal{F}, \mathcal{V}) \to \mathcal{T}(\mathcal{F}_{lab}, \mathcal{V})$ is defined inductively by

$$lab_\alpha(t) = \begin{cases} t & \text{if } t \in \mathcal{V} \\ f(lab_\alpha(t_1), \ldots, lab_\alpha(t_n)) & \text{if } t = f(t_1, \ldots, t_n),\ L_f = \emptyset \\ f_\ell(lab_\alpha(t_1), \ldots, lab_\alpha(t_n)) & \text{if } t = f(t_1, \ldots, t_n),\ L_f \neq \emptyset \end{cases}$$

  where ℓ denotes the label $lab_f([\alpha]_{\mathcal{A}}(t_1), \ldots, [\alpha]_{\mathcal{A}}(t_n))$.

As an example, consider the signature $\mathcal{F} = \{0, 1, 2, f\}$, where 0, 1, and 2 are constants and f has arity 3. L, consisting of the sets $L_0 = L_1 = L_2 = \emptyset$, and $L_f = \{\circ, \bullet\}$, is a labeling for $\mathcal{F}$ and $\mathcal{F}_{lab} = \{0, 1, 2, f_\circ, f_\bullet\}$. Let $\mathcal{A}$ be the $\mathcal{F}$-algebra consisting of the carrier $A = \{a, b, c\}$ and the algebra operations $0_\mathcal{A} = a$, $1_\mathcal{A} = b$, $2_\mathcal{A} = c$, and $f_\mathcal{A}(x, y, z) = c$. Then L together with the mapping

$$lab_f(x, y, z) = \begin{cases} \circ & \text{if } x = a \text{ and } y = b \\ \bullet & \text{otherwise} \end{cases}$$

is a labeling for $\mathcal{A}$. If t is, for example, the term $f(x, 1, 1)$ and $\alpha\colon \mathcal{V} \to A$ satisfies $\alpha(x) = b$, then $lab_\alpha(t) = f_\bullet(x, 1, 1)$.

Definition 5.5.2 Let $(\mathcal{F}, \mathcal{R})$ be a TRS. Let $\mathcal{A}$ be an $\mathcal{F}$-algebra with labeling (L, lab). We define the *labeled* TRS $\mathcal{R}_{lab}$ over the signature $\mathcal{F}_{lab}$ as follows:

$$\mathcal{R}_{lab} = \{lab_\alpha(l) \to lab_\alpha(r) \mid l \to r \in \mathcal{R} \text{ and } \alpha\colon \mathcal{V} \to A\}$$

We continue our small example. If

$$\mathcal{R} = \begin{cases} f(0, 1, x) & \to & f(x, x, x) \\ f(x, y, z) & \to & 2 \\ 0 & \to & 2 \\ 1 & \to & 2 \end{cases}$$

and (L, lab) is the labeling defined earlier, then

$$\mathcal{R}_{lab} = \begin{cases} f_\circ(0, 1, x) & \to & f_\bullet(x, x, x) \\ f_\bullet(x, y, z) & \to & 2 \\ f_\circ(x, y, z) & \to & 2 \\ 0 & \to & 2 \\ 1 & \to & 2 \end{cases}$$

Definition 5.5.3 A *labeling for a weakly monotone $\mathcal{F}$-algebra* $(\mathcal{A}, \succsim)$ is a labeling (L, lab) such that for every $f \in \mathcal{F}^{(n)}$ the set L_f is equipped with a partial ordering $>_f$ and furthermore the mapping $lab_f : A^n \to L_f$ is weakly monotone in all its n arguments. That is, $a \succsim a'$ implies $lab_f(\ldots, a, \ldots) \geq_f lab_f(\ldots, a', \ldots)$, where $\geq_f$ is the reflexive closure of $>_f$.

In our example, let $\succsim$ be the quasi-ordering on $A = \{a, b, c\}$ defined by $a \succsim c$ and $b \succsim c$. It can readily be verified that $(\mathcal{A}, \succsim)$ is a weakly monotone $\mathcal{F}$-algebra. If we define $\geq_f$ on $L_f = \{\circ, \bullet\}$ by $\circ \geq_f \bullet$, then we obtain a labeling for $\mathcal{A}$ because lab_f is weakly monotone in all three arguments.

Definition 5.5.4 A weakly monotone $\mathcal{F}$-algebra $(\mathcal{M}, \succsim)$ is a *quasimodel* of the TRS $(\mathcal{F}, \mathcal{R})$ if $l \succsim_{\mathcal{M}} r$ holds for every $l \to r \in \mathcal{R}$.

In our current example, it is fairly easy to see that $(\mathcal{A}, \succsim)$ is a quasimodel of the TRS under consideration.

Theorem 5.5.5 *A TRS $(\mathcal{F}, \mathcal{R})$ is terminating if and only if there exists a nonempty quasimodel $(\mathcal{M}, \succsim)$ of $(\mathcal{F}, \mathcal{R})$ and a labeling (L, lab) for $\mathcal{M}$ such that the TRS $(\mathcal{F}_{lab}, \mathcal{R}_{lab} \cup dec(\mathcal{F}_{lab}))$ is terminating, where*

$$dec(\mathcal{F}_{lab}) = \bigcup_{f \in \mathcal{F}^{(n)}, n \in \mathbb{N}} \{f_a(x_1, \ldots, x_n) \to f_b(x_1, \ldots, x_n) \mid a >_f b\}$$

Proof In order to prove the only-if direction, let $\mathcal{M}$ be the trivial nonempty quasimodel of $(\mathcal{F}, \mathcal{R})$, that is, the carrier M of $\mathcal{M}$ has only one element, say m, and the quasi-ordering on M is empty. The only assignment $\alpha \colon \mathcal{V} \to M$ maps every variable to m. Furthermore, for every $f \in \mathcal{F}$, let $L_f = \{m\}$ and simply label f by m. Note that $dec(\mathcal{F}_{lab}) = \emptyset$. It can readily be verified that $(\mathcal{F}, \mathcal{R})$ is terminating if and only if $(\mathcal{F}_{lab}, \mathcal{R}_{lab} \cup dec(\mathcal{F}_{lab}))$ is terminating.

Suppose, conversely, that there exists a quasimodel $(\mathcal{M}, \succsim)$ of $(\mathcal{F}, \mathcal{R})$ and a labeling (L, lab) for $\mathcal{M}$ such that the TRS $(\mathcal{F}_{lab}, \mathcal{R}_{lab} \cup dec(\mathcal{F}_{lab}))$ is terminating. Let $\succ_{lab} = \to^+_{\mathcal{R}_{lab} \cup dec(\mathcal{F}_{lab})}$ and define an $\mathcal{F}$-algebra $\mathcal{A}$ by choosing carrier $A = M \times \mathcal{T}(\mathcal{F}_{lab}, \mathcal{V})$ and operations

$$f_{\mathcal{A}}(\langle m_1, t_1 \rangle, \ldots, \langle m_n, t_n \rangle) = \langle f_{\mathcal{M}}(m_1, \ldots, m_n), f_\ell(t_1, \ldots, t_n) \rangle$$

where $\ell = lab_f(m_1, \ldots, m_n)$. Let $\succ$ be the ordering on A defined by

$$\langle m, t \rangle \succ \langle m', t' \rangle \text{ if and only if } m \succsim m' \text{ and } t \succ_{lab} t'$$

Note that $\succ$ is well-founded because $\succ_{lab}$ is well-founded. Next we show that $(\mathcal{A}, \succ)$ is a monotone $\mathcal{F}$-algebra. Given $\langle m, t \rangle \succ \langle m', t' \rangle$, we have to show that

$$f_{\mathcal{A}}(\ldots, \langle m, t \rangle, \ldots) \succ f_{\mathcal{A}}(\ldots, \langle m', t' \rangle, \ldots)$$

Because $m \succsim m'$ and $(\mathcal{M}, \succsim)$ is a weakly monotone $\mathcal{F}$-algebra, it follows $f_{\mathcal{M}}(\ldots, m, \ldots) \succsim f_{\mathcal{M}}(\ldots, m', \ldots)$. Then $f_\ell(\ldots, t, \ldots) \succ_{lab} f_{\ell'}(\ldots, t', \ldots)$

remains to be shown. We have $\ell = lab_f(\ldots, m, \ldots) \geq_f lab_f(\ldots, m', \ldots) = \ell'$ because lab_f is weakly monotone in all its arguments. Moreover, because $\succ_{lab}$ is closed under contexts, it follows from $t \succ_{lab} t'$ that

$$f_\ell(\ldots, t, \ldots) \succ_{lab} f_\ell(\ldots, t', \ldots)$$

If $\ell = \ell'$, then we are done. Otherwise, $\ell >_f \ell'$, and it follows that

$$f_\ell(\ldots, t', \ldots) \succ_{lab} f_{\ell'}(\ldots, t', \ldots)$$

from $f_\ell(x_1, \ldots, x_n) \succ_{lab} f_{\ell'}(x_1, \ldots, x_n)$ in combination with the fact that $\succ_{lab}$ is closed under substitutions.

Because $(\mathcal{A}, \succ)$ is monotone and well-founded, $\succ_\mathcal{A}$ is a reduction ordering on $\mathcal{T}(\mathcal{F}, \mathcal{V})$ by Theorem 5.2.8. We finally have to show that $l \to r \in \mathcal{R}$ implies $l \succ_\mathcal{A} r$, that is, $[\alpha]_\mathcal{A}(l) \succ [\alpha]_\mathcal{A}(r)$ for every assignment $\alpha\colon \mathcal{V} \to A$. In other words, it must be shown that for every assignment $\mu\colon \mathcal{V} \to M$

$$\langle [\mu]_\mathcal{M}(l), lab_\mu(l)\rangle \succ \langle [\mu]_\mathcal{M}(r), lab_\mu(r)\rangle$$

holds. Clearly, $[\mu]_\mathcal{M}(l) \succsim [\mu]_\mathcal{M}(r)$ because $(\mathcal{M}, \succsim)$ is a quasimodel of $(\mathcal{F}, \mathcal{R})$. Moreover, $lab_\mu(l) \succ_{lab} lab_\mu(r)$ holds true because $lab_\mu(l) \to lab_\mu(r) \in \mathcal{R}_{lab}$. □

In the illustrating example, we have

$$dec(\mathcal{F}_{lab}) = \{f_\circ(x, y, z) \to f_\bullet(x, y, z)\}$$

Now *rpo* or *lpo* proves termination of $\mathcal{R}_{lab} \cup dec(\mathcal{F}_{lab})$. By Theorem 5.5.5, the original system $\mathcal{R}$ is also terminating.

In many cases the following special case is sufficient to prove termination by semantic labeling. Let $(\mathcal{M}, \succeq)$ be a nonempty quasimodel of $(\mathcal{F}, \mathcal{R})$, where $\succeq$ is the reflexive closure of a well-founded partial ordering $\succ$ on M. For every $f \in \mathcal{F}^{(n)}$, choose either $L_f = M$ or $L_f = \emptyset$. Furthermore, for $L_f = M$ define $lab_f(m_1, \ldots, m_n) = f_\mathcal{M}(m_1, \ldots, m_n)$. Thus, for every assignment $\mu\colon \mathcal{V} \to M$, the mapping $lab_\mu : \mathcal{T}(\mathcal{F}, \mathcal{V}) \to \mathcal{T}(\mathcal{F}_{lab}, \mathcal{V})$ is defined as

$$lab_\mu(t) = \begin{cases} t & \text{if } t \in \mathcal{V} \\ f(lab_\mu(t_1), \ldots, lab_\mu(t_n)) & \text{if } t = f(t_1, \ldots, t_n),\ L_f = \emptyset \\ f_{[\mu]_\mathcal{M}(t)}(lab_\mu(t_1), \ldots, lab_\mu(t_n)) & \text{if } t = f(t_1, \ldots, t_n),\ L_f \neq \emptyset \end{cases}$$

This means that the outermost function symbol f in a term $t = f(t_1, \ldots, t_n)$ is simply labeled (if at all) by the value of t in $\mathcal{M}$ under the assignment μ. In this case Theorem 5.5.5 specializes to the following corollary.

Corollary 5.5.6 *A TRS $(\mathcal{F}, \mathcal{R})$ is terminating if and only if there is a nonempty quasimodel $(\mathcal{M}, \succeq)$ of $(\mathcal{F}, \mathcal{R})$, where $\succeq$ is the reflexive closure of a partial ordering $\succ$ on M, such that $(\mathcal{F}_{lab}, \mathcal{R}_{lab} \cup dec(\mathcal{F}_{lab}))$ is terminating.*

Proof It is an immediate consequence of Theorem 5.5.5. □

Example 5.5.7 Let $\mathcal{R}$ be the TRS from Example 5.4.36. It is not difficult to check that the given polynomial interpretation of $\mathcal{R}$ is indeed a quasi-model of $\mathcal{R}$. In $\mathcal{R}$ we label only the function symbols *split*, *qsort*, and *h*. This yields the labeled system $\mathcal{R}_{lab}$ consisting of the rules

$$\begin{array}{rcll}
0 \leq y & \to & true & \\
s(x) \leq 0 & \to & false & \\
s(x) \leq s(y) & \to & x \leq y & \\
nil +\!\!+\ ys & \to & ys & \\
(x : xs) +\!\!+\ ys & \to & x : (xs +\!\!+\ ys) & \\
split_1(x, nil) & \to & \langle nil, nil \rangle & \\
split_{i+2}(x, y : ys) & \to & f(split_{i+1}(x, ys), x, y, ys) & \forall i \in \mathbb{N} \\
f(\langle xs, zs \rangle), x, y, ys) & \to & g(x \leq y, x, y, ys, xs, zs) & \\
g(true, x, y, ys, xs, zs) & \to & \langle xs, y : zs \rangle & \\
g(false, x, y, ys, xs, zs) & \to & \langle y : xs, zs \rangle & \\
qsort_0(nil) & \to & nil & \\
qsort_{i+1}(x : xs) & \to & h_{i+1}(split_{i+1}(x, xs), x, xs) & \forall i \in \mathbb{N} \\
h_{i+j+1}(\langle ys, zs \rangle, x, xs) & \to & qsort_i(ys) +\!\!+\ (x : qsort_j(zs)) & \forall i, j \in \mathbb{N}
\end{array}$$

Furthermore, the system $dec(\mathcal{F}_{lab})$ consists of the rules

$$\begin{array}{rcll}
split_i(x, ys) & \to & split_j(x, ys) & \forall i, j \in \mathbb{N} \text{ with } i > j \\
qsort_i(xs) & \to & qsort_j(xs) & \forall i, j \in \mathbb{N} \text{ with } i > j \\
h_i(z, x, xs) & \to & h_j(z, x, xs) & \forall i, j \in \mathbb{N} \text{ with } i > j
\end{array}$$

With the well-founded precedence

$$qsort_{i+1} \succ_p h_{i+1} \succ_p split_{i+1} \succ_p qsort_i \quad \text{for every } i \in \mathbb{N} \text{ and}$$

$$qsort_0 \succ_p h_0 \succ_p split_0 \succ_p f \succ_p g \succ_p \langle\rangle \succ_p +\!\!+ \succ_p : \succ_p \leq \succ_p true \succ_p false$$

termination of $\mathcal{R}_{lab} \cup dec(\mathcal{F}_{lab})$ is easily proved by *lpo*. Now Corollary 5.5.6 yields termination of $\mathcal{R}$.

The careful reader may have observed that in the preceding example both the labeled signature $\mathcal{F}_{lab}$ and the TRS $\mathcal{R}_{lab} \cup dec(\mathcal{F}_{lab})$ are infinite. This causes no problem: *lpo* is well-founded as long as the precedence is well-founded; see [MZ97, Theorem 7.3].

We give another application of Corollary 5.5.6, which originates from [Zan95a].

Example 5.5.8 Let $\circ$ and $\cdot$ be binary symbols, let λ be a unary symbol, and let 1, 2, and *id* be constants. Consider the TRS σ_0 consisting of the rules

$$\begin{array}{lcl}
\lambda(x) \circ y & \to & \lambda(x \circ (1 \cdot (y \circ 2))) \\
(x \cdot y) \circ z & \to & (x \circ z) \cdot (y \circ z) \\
(x \circ y) \circ z & \to & x \circ (y \circ z) \\
id \circ x & \to & x \\
1 \circ id & \to & 1 \\
2 \circ id & \to & 2 \\
1 \circ (x \cdot y) & \to & x \\
2 \circ (x \cdot y) & \to & y
\end{array}$$

taken from [CHR92], which is essentially the same as the system SUBST in [HL86]. The system σ_0 describes the process of substitution in combinatory categorical logic. Here "λ" corresponds to currying, "$\circ$" to composition, "*id*" to the identity, "$\cdot$" to pairing, and "1" and "2" to projections. Termination of σ_0 implies termination of the process of explicit substitutions in untyped λ-calculus. However, the termination proofs in [HL86, CHR92] are quite complicated. By means of semantic labeling, a simple termination proof can be given as follows. Define the TRS $\mathcal{R}$ to consist of the first three rules of σ_0 and the embedding rules

$$\lambda(x) \to x,\ x \circ y \to x,\ x \circ y \to y,\ x \cdot y \to x,\ x \cdot y \to y$$

It is easy to see that simple termination of σ_0 is equivalent to termination of $\mathcal{R}$. Termination of $\mathcal{R}$ can be proven with the help of Corollary 5.5.6 as follows. As algebra we choose $\mathbb{N}$ and the interpretation functions

$$\lambda_{\mathbb{N}}(x) = x + 1,\ x \circ_{\mathbb{N}} y = x + y,\ x \cdot_{\mathbb{N}} y = \max(x, y),\ 1_{\mathbb{N}} = 2_{\mathbb{N}} = 0$$

One easily verifies that $(\mathbb{N}, \geq)$ is a quasimodel for $\mathcal{R}$. We only label the symbol $\circ$ by the labeling function $lab_\circ(x, y) = x + y$. Now the system $\mathcal{R}_{lab} \cup dec(\mathcal{F}_{lab})$ reads as follows (where $i, j, k \in \mathbb{N}$)

$$\begin{array}{lcll}
\lambda(x) \circ_{i+1} y & \to & \lambda(x \circ_i (1 \cdot (y \circ_j 2))) & \text{with } i \geq j \\
(x \cdot y) \circ_i z & \to & (x \circ_j z) \cdot (y \circ_k z) & \text{with } i \geq j \text{ and } i \geq k \\
(x \circ_j y) \circ_i z & \to & x \circ_i (y \circ_k z) & \text{with } i \geq j \text{ and } i \geq k \\
\lambda(x) & \to & x & \\
x \circ_i y & \to & x & \\
x \circ_i y & \to & y & \\
x \cdot y & \to & x & \\
x \cdot y & \to & y & \\
x \circ_i y & \to & x \circ_j y & \text{with } i > j
\end{array}$$

With the well-founded precedence

$$\circ_i >_p \cdot,\ \circ_i >_p \lambda,\ \circ_i >_p 1,\ \circ_i >_p 2,\ \text{and } \circ_i >_p \circ_j \text{ for } i > j$$

termination is easily proven by *lpo*. Now Corollary 5.5.6 yields termination of $\mathcal{R}$, and hence simple termination of σ_0.

There are two other important special cases of Theorem 5.5.5 we would like to mention. The first is *self-labeling*, which uses the term algebra and thus labels function symbols with terms; see [MOZ96] for details. The second uses a model of a TRS instead of a quasimodel.

Definition 5.5.9 An $\mathcal{F}$-algebra $\mathcal{M}$ is a *model* of the TRS $(\mathcal{F}, \mathcal{R})$ if $[\mu]_{\mathcal{M}}(l) = [\mu]_{\mathcal{M}}(r)$ holds for every assignment $\mu\colon \mathcal{V} \to M$ and every rewrite rule $l \to r \in \mathcal{R}$.

Corollary 5.5.10 *The TRS $(\mathcal{F}, \mathcal{R})$ is terminating if and only if there is a nonempty model $\mathcal{M}$ of $(\mathcal{F}, \mathcal{R})$ and a labeling (L, lab) for $\mathcal{M}$ such that $(\mathcal{F}_{lab}, \mathcal{R}_{lab})$ is terminating.*

Proof The only-if direction can be proven as in the proof of Theorem 5.5.5. Suppose, conversely, that there is a nonempty model $\mathcal{M}$ of $(\mathcal{F}, \mathcal{R})$ and a labeling (L, lab) for $\mathcal{M}$ such that $(\mathcal{F}_{lab}, \mathcal{R}_{lab})$ is terminating. Let $\succsim$ be the discrete ordering on the carrier M, i.e., for all $m, n \in M$, we have $m \succsim n$ if and only $m = n$. Then $(\mathcal{M}, \succsim)$ is a nonempty quasimodel of $(\mathcal{F}, \mathcal{R})$. Furthermore, for every $f \in \mathcal{F}$ with $L_f \neq \emptyset$ let $\geq_f$ be the discrete ordering on L_f. Note that $dec(\mathcal{F}_{lab}) = \emptyset$. Because $(\mathcal{F}_{lab}, \mathcal{R}_{lab} \cup dec(\mathcal{F}_{lab}))$ is terminating, it follows from Theorem 5.5.5 that $(\mathcal{F}, \mathcal{R})$ is terminating. □

5.5.2 Semantic Labeling Meets Dependency Pairs

The dependency pair method and semantic labeling can quite naturally be combined, as we will show next. Given a finite TRS $\mathcal{R}$, we apply the dependency pair method to show termination. Suppose for a cycle $\mathcal{P}$ in EDG($\mathcal{R}$) we have found an AFS $\mathcal{A}$ and a well-founded weakly monotone $\mathcal{F}$-algebra $(\mathcal{M}, \succsim)$ such that

- $l \downarrow_{\mathcal{A}} \succsim_{\mathcal{M}} r \downarrow_{\mathcal{A}}$ for all rules $l \to r$ from $\mathcal{R}$,
- $s \downarrow_{\mathcal{A}} \succsim_{\mathcal{M}} t \downarrow_{\mathcal{A}}$ for all dependency pairs $\langle s, t \rangle$ from $\mathcal{P}$,

but there is no dependency pair $\langle s, t \rangle$ in $\mathcal{P}$ with $s \downarrow_{\mathcal{A}} \succ_{\mathcal{M}} t \downarrow_{\mathcal{A}}$ (if there were a dependency pair $\langle s, t \rangle \in \mathcal{P}$ with $s \downarrow_{\mathcal{A}} \succ_{\mathcal{M}} t \downarrow_{\mathcal{A}}$, then $\succsim_{\mathcal{M}}$ would be a quasi-reduction ordering satisfying the inequalities, and we are done).

In particular, for every dependency pair $\langle s, t \rangle \in \mathcal{P}$ and every ground substitution $\sigma\colon \mathcal{V} \to \mathcal{T}(\mathcal{F})$, we have $s \downarrow_{\mathcal{A}} \sigma \succsim_{\mathcal{M}} t \downarrow_{\mathcal{A}} \sigma$ because $\succsim_{\mathcal{M}}$ is closed under substitutions. Because $s \downarrow_{\mathcal{A}} \succ_{\mathcal{M}} t \downarrow_{\mathcal{A}}$ does not hold, it follows from the definition of the stable-strict relation $\succ_{\mathcal{M}}$ that there is a ground substitution $\sigma\colon \mathcal{V} \to \mathcal{T}(\mathcal{F})$ with $[t \downarrow_{\mathcal{A}} \sigma]_{\mathcal{M}} \succsim [s \downarrow_{\mathcal{A}} \sigma]_{\mathcal{M}}$. Therefore, we have to take care of all assignments $\mu\colon \mathcal{V} \to M$ with $[\mu]_{\mathcal{M}}(s \downarrow_{\mathcal{A}}) \approx [\mu]_{\mathcal{M}}(t \downarrow_{\mathcal{A}})$, where $\approx$ denotes the equivalence relation on M induced by $\succsim$. In this situation we try to use semantic labeling w.r.t. the labeling induced by the quasimodel $(\mathcal{M}, \succsim)$. In contrast to Theorem 5.5.5, $(\mathcal{M}, \succsim)$ is assumed to be well-founded. Moreover, because the quasimodel is fixed, the method is amenable to automation.

Definition 5.5.11 A weakly monotone $\mathcal{F}$-algebra $(\mathcal{M}, \succsim)$ is a *quasimodel* of a set of inequalities IN if $s \succsim_{\mathcal{M}} t$ for every $s > t$ and every $s \geq t$ in IN.

Given a quasimodel $(\mathcal{M}, \succsim)$, we label the function symbols as follows. For every $f \in \mathcal{F}^{(n)}$, choose either $L_f = M/{\approx}$ or $L_f = \emptyset$. That is, function symbols are labeled by equivalence classes from $M/{\approx}$. More precisely, in case $L_f \neq \emptyset$, define $lab_f(m_1, \ldots, m_n) = \mathbf{m}$, where $\mathbf{m}$ denotes the equivalence class of $f_{\mathcal{M}}(m_1, \ldots, m_n)$. Thus, for every assignment $\mu\colon \mathcal{V} \to M$, the mapping $lab_\mu : \mathcal{T}(\mathcal{F}, \mathcal{V}) \to \mathcal{T}(\mathcal{F}_{lab}, \mathcal{V})$ is defined as

$$lab_\mu(t) = \begin{cases} t & \text{if } t \in \mathcal{V} \\ f(lab_\mu(t_1), \ldots, lab_\mu(t_n)) & \text{if } t = f(t_1, \ldots, t_n) \text{ and } L_f = \emptyset \\ f_{\mathbf{m}}(lab_\mu(t_1), \ldots, lab_\mu(t_n)) & \text{if } t = f(t_1, \ldots, t_n) \text{ and } L_f \neq \emptyset \end{cases}$$

where $\mathbf{m}$ denotes the equivalence class of $[\mu]_{\mathcal{M}}(t)$.

If t is a ground term, then the labeling $lab_\mu(t)$ of t is independent of the assignment $\mu\colon \mathcal{V} \to M$ and will thus simply be denoted by $lab(t)$.

Theorem 5.5.12 *Let* IN *be a set of inequalities of the form $s > t$ or $s \geq t$, where $s, t \in \mathcal{T}(\mathcal{F}, \mathcal{V})$. There exists a quasi-reduction ordering on $\mathcal{T}(\mathcal{F}, \mathcal{V})$ satisfying the inequalities in* IN *if and only if there is a well-founded quasimodel $(\mathcal{M}, \succsim)$ of* IN *and a quasi-reduction ordering $\succsim_{lab}$ on $\mathcal{T}(\mathcal{F}_{lab}, \mathcal{V})$ satisfying the inequalities in* IN_{lab}*, where*

$$\begin{aligned} \mathrm{IN}_{lab} = {} & \{lab_\mu(s) > lab_\mu(t) \mid s > t \in \mathrm{IN}, \mu\colon \mathcal{V} \to M, [\mu]_{\mathcal{M}}(s) \approx [\mu]_{\mathcal{M}}(t)\} \\ \cup {} & \{lab_\mu(s) \geq lab_\mu(t) \mid s \geq t \in \mathrm{IN}, \mu\colon \mathcal{V} \to M, [\mu]_{\mathcal{M}}(s) \approx [\mu]_{\mathcal{M}}(t)\} \end{aligned}$$

Proof Suppose that there is a quasi-reduction ordering $\succsim$ that satisfies the inequalities in IN. Let $\mathcal{M}$ be the trivial nonempty quasimodel of IN (i.e., the carrier M of $\mathcal{M}$ has only one element, say m, and the quasi-ordering on M is empty). The only assignment $\mu\colon \mathcal{V} \to M$ maps every variable to m. Furthermore, label every $f \in \mathcal{F}$ by m and define $\succsim_{lab}$ by $lab_\mu(s) \succsim_{lab} lab_\mu(t)$ if and only if $s \succsim t$. Clearly, $\succsim_{lab}$ is a quasi-reduction ordering on $\mathcal{T}(\mathcal{F}_{lab}, \mathcal{V})$, which satisfies the inequalities in IN_{lab}.

In order to prove the converse direction, we define an $\mathcal{F}$-algebra $\mathcal{A}$ by choosing the carrier $A = M \times \mathcal{T}(\mathcal{F}_{lab}, \mathcal{V})$ and the algebra operations

$$f_{\mathcal{A}}(\langle m_1, t_1\rangle, \ldots, \langle m_n, t_n\rangle) = \langle f_{\mathcal{M}}(m_1, \ldots, m_n), f_{\mathbf{m}}(t_1, \ldots, t_n)\rangle$$

where $\mathbf{m}$ denotes the equivalence class of $f_{\mathcal{M}}(m_1, \ldots, m_n)$. Let $\succsim_{lex}$ be the lexicographic product of $\succsim$ and $\succsim_{lab}$, i.e.,

$$\langle m, t\rangle \succsim_{lex} \langle m', t'\rangle \text{ if } \quad \begin{array}{l} m \succ m' \\ \text{or } m \approx m' \text{ and } t \succsim_{lab} t' \end{array}$$

Note that $\succsim_{lex}$ is a well-founded quasi-ordering. We show that $(\mathcal{A}, \succsim_{lex})$ is a weakly monotone $\mathcal{F}$-algebra. Given $\langle m,t\rangle \succsim_{lex} \langle m',t'\rangle$, we have to show

$$f_{\mathcal{A}}(\ldots,\langle m,t\rangle,\ldots) \succsim_{lex} f_{\mathcal{A}}(\ldots,\langle m',t'\rangle,\ldots)$$

Because $m \succsim m'$ and $(\mathcal{M}, \succsim)$ is a weakly monotone $\mathcal{F}$-algebra, it follows $n = f_{\mathcal{M}}(\ldots,m,\ldots) \succsim f_{\mathcal{M}}(\ldots,m',\ldots) = n'$. If $n \succ n'$, then we are done. Otherwise $n \approx n'$ and it must be shown that $f_{\mathbf{n}}(\ldots,t,\ldots) \succsim_{lab} f_{\mathbf{n}}(\ldots,t',\ldots)$. This, however, is a consequence of $t \succsim_{lab} t'$ and the fact that $\succsim_{lab}$ is closed under contexts. So $(\mathcal{A}, \succsim_{lex})$ is a well-founded weakly monotone $\mathcal{F}$-algebra. Let $\succsim_{\mathcal{A}}$ be the induced quasi-ordering on the set of terms, i.e., for all $s,t \in \mathcal{T}(\mathcal{F},\mathcal{V})$ we have $s \succsim_{\mathcal{A}} t$ if and only if $[\alpha]_{\mathcal{A}}(s) \succsim_{lex} [\alpha]_{\mathcal{A}}(t)$ for every assignment $\alpha\colon \mathcal{V} \to A$. According to Lemma 5.4.32(2), $\succsim_{\mathcal{A}}$ is a quasi-reduction ordering on $\mathcal{T}(\mathcal{F},\mathcal{V})$. In order to show that $s \geq t \in \mathrm{IN}$ implies $s \succsim_{\mathcal{A}} t$, it must be shown that for every assignment $\alpha\colon \mathcal{V} \to A$ the inequality $[\alpha]_{\mathcal{A}}(s) \succsim_{lex} [\alpha]_{\mathcal{A}}(t)$ holds. In other words, for every assignment $\mu\colon \mathcal{V} \to M$ the inequality

$$\langle [\mu]_{\mathcal{M}}(s), lab_{\mu}(s)\rangle \succsim_{lex} \langle [\mu]_{\mathcal{M}}(t), lab_{\mu}(t)\rangle$$

must hold. Clearly, $[\mu]_{\mathcal{M}}(s) \succsim [\mu]_{\mathcal{M}}(t)$ because $(\mathcal{M}, \succsim)$ is a quasimodel of IN. So if $[\mu]_{\mathcal{M}}(s) \succ [\mu]_{\mathcal{M}}(t)$, then the assertion is true. Otherwise $[\mu]_{\mathcal{M}}(s) \approx [\mu]_{\mathcal{M}}(t)$. In this case $lab_{\mu}(s) \succsim_{lab} lab_{\mu}(t)$ holds true because $\succsim_{lab}$ satisfies the inequality $lab_{\mu}(s) \geq lab_{\mu}(t)$.

Finally, for $s > t \in \mathrm{IN}$, we have to show $s \succ_{\mathcal{A}} t$, i.e., for every ground substitution σ, one must have $[s\sigma]_{\mathcal{A}} \succsim_{lex} [t\sigma]_{\mathcal{A}}$ and $[t\sigma]_{\mathcal{A}} \not\succsim_{lex} [s\sigma]_{\mathcal{A}}$. So fix $\sigma : \mathcal{V} \to \mathcal{T}(\mathcal{F})$. Clearly, $[s\sigma]_{\mathcal{M}} \succsim [t\sigma]_{\mathcal{M}}$ because $(\mathcal{M}, \succsim)$ is a quasimodel of IN. For the same reason, $t\sigma \not\succ_{\mathcal{M}} s\sigma$. So if $[s\sigma]_{\mathcal{M}} \succ [t\sigma]_{\mathcal{M}}$ then $[s\sigma]_{\mathcal{A}} \succsim_{lex} [t\sigma]_{\mathcal{A}}$ and $[t\sigma]_{\mathcal{A}} \not\succsim_{lex} [s\sigma]_{\mathcal{A}}$. Otherwise $[s\sigma]_{\mathcal{M}} \approx [t\sigma]_{\mathcal{M}}$. In that case, one must show $lab(s\sigma) \succsim_{lab} lab(t\sigma)$ and $lab(t\sigma) \not\succsim_{lab} lab(s\sigma)$. Let $\mu\colon \mathcal{V} \to M$ be defined by $\mu(x) = [x\sigma]_{\mathcal{M}}$. We know that $lab_{\mu}(s) \succ_{lab} lab_{\mu}(t)$ because $\succ_{lab}$ satisfies the inequality $lab_{\mu}(s) > lab_{\mu}(t)$. In other words, for every ground substitution $\tau : \mathcal{V} \to \mathcal{T}(\mathcal{F}_{lab})$, we have $lab_{\mu}(s)\tau \succsim_{lab} lab_{\mu}(t)\tau$ and $lab_{\mu}(t)\tau \not\succsim_{lab} lab_{\mu}(s)\tau$. Define τ by $\tau(x) = lab(x\sigma)$. It is not difficult to show by structural induction on s that $lab_{\mu}(s)\tau = lab(s\sigma)$. It follows that

$$lab(s\sigma) = lab_{\mu}(s)\tau \succsim_{lab} lab_{\mu}(t)\tau = lab(t\sigma)$$

and $lab(t\sigma) = lab_{\mu}(t)\tau \not\succsim_{lab} lab_{\mu}(s)\tau = lab(s\sigma)$. □

Corollary 5.5.13 *A finite TRS $\mathcal{R}$ is terminating if for each cycle $\mathcal{P}$ in* EDG($\mathcal{R}$) *there is an AFS $\mathcal{A}$ and a well-founded weakly monotone $\mathcal{F}'$-algebra $(\mathcal{M}, \succsim)$ satisfying*

- $l \downarrow_{\mathcal{A}} \succsim_{\mathcal{M}} r \downarrow_{\mathcal{A}}$ *for all rules $l \to r$ from $\mathcal{R}$, and*
- $s \downarrow_{\mathcal{A}} \succsim_{\mathcal{M}} t \downarrow_{\mathcal{A}}$ *for all dependency pairs $\langle s,t\rangle$ from $\mathcal{P}$,*

where $\mathcal{F}'$ consists of all function symbols occurring in the inequalities, and a quasi-reduction ordering $\succsim_{lab}$ on $\mathcal{T}(\mathcal{F}'_{lab}, \mathcal{V})$ satisfying

- $lab_\mu(l \downarrow_\mathcal{A}) \succsim_{lab} lab_\mu(r \downarrow_\mathcal{A})$ *for every rule* $l \to r \in \mathcal{R}$ *and every assignment* $\mu \colon \mathcal{V} \to M$ *with* $[\mu]_\mathcal{M}(l \downarrow_\mathcal{A}) \approx [\mu]_\mathcal{M}(r \downarrow_\mathcal{A})$,
- $lab_\mu(s \downarrow_\mathcal{A}) \succsim_{lab} lab_\mu(t \downarrow_\mathcal{A})$ *for every dependency pair* $\langle s,t \rangle$ *from* $\mathcal{P}$ *and every assignment* $\mu \colon \mathcal{V} \to M$ *with* $[\mu]_\mathcal{M}(s \downarrow_\mathcal{A}) \approx [\mu]_\mathcal{M}(t \downarrow_\mathcal{A})$, *and*
- $lab_\mu(s \downarrow_\mathcal{A}) \succ_{lab} lab_\mu(t \downarrow_\mathcal{A})$ *for at least one dependency pair* $\langle s,t \rangle$ *from* $\mathcal{P}$ *and every assignment* $\mu \colon \mathcal{V} \to M$ *with* $[\mu]_\mathcal{M}(s \downarrow_\mathcal{A}) \approx [\mu]_\mathcal{M}(t \downarrow_\mathcal{A})$.

Proof It is a direct consequence of Corollary 5.4.19 and Theorem 5.5.12. □

Now we will show an application of the preceding corollary.

Example 5.5.14 Let $\mathcal{R}$ be the TRS

$$
\begin{array}{rcl}
f(\lambda(x), y) & \to & \lambda(f(x, g(1, f(y, 2)))) \\
f(g(x, y), z) & \to & g(f(x, z), f(y, z)) \\
f(\lambda(x), y) & \to & f(x, \lambda(c(y))) \\
f(x, c(y)) & \to & f(c(x), y)
\end{array}
$$

$\mathcal{R}$ contains the first two rules of the system σ_0 from Example 5.5.8 (in which the infix operators $\circ$ and $\cdot$ are replaced by the function symbols f and g, respectively) and two new rules. In EDG($\mathcal{R}$) the pair $\langle F(x, c(y)), F(c(x), y) \rangle$ forms a cycle and does not lie on any other cycle. For this cycle, there are the following inequalities:

$$
\begin{array}{rcl}
F(x, c(y)) & > & F(c(x), y) \\
f(\lambda(x), y) & \geq & \lambda(f(x, g(1, f(y, 2)))) \\
f(g(x, y), z) & \geq & g(f(x, z), f(y, z)) \\
f(\lambda(x), y) & \geq & f(x, \lambda(c(y))) \\
f(x, c(y)) & \geq & f(c(x), y)
\end{array}
$$

After using the AFS $\{f(x, y) \to f', g(x, y) \to g', \lambda(x) \to \lambda'\}$, the resulting constraints are satisfied by *lpo* (comparing arguments from right to left). Each of the dependency pairs

$$
\begin{array}{c}
\langle F(\lambda(x), y), F(x, g(1, f(y, 2))) \rangle \\
\langle F(\lambda(x), y), F(y, 2) \rangle \\
\langle F(g(x, y), z), F(x, z) \rangle \\
\langle F(g(x, y), z), F(y, z) \rangle \\
\langle F(\lambda(x), y), F(x, \lambda(c(y))) \rangle
\end{array}
$$

forms an individual cycle, and all of them lie on a big cycle. The inequalities of the big cycle, after normalization with the AFS $\{c(x) \to x\}$, are

$$F(\lambda(x), y) \geq F(x, g(1, f(y, 2))) \tag{5.8}$$
$$F(\lambda(x), y) \geq F(y, 2) \tag{5.9}$$
$$F(g(x, y), z) \geq F(x, z) \tag{5.10}$$
$$F(g(x, y), z) \geq F(y, z) \tag{5.11}$$
$$F(\lambda(x), y) \geq F(x, \lambda(y)) \tag{5.12}$$
$$f(\lambda(x), y) \geq \lambda(f(x, g(1, f(y, 2)))) \tag{5.13}$$
$$f(g(x, y), z) \geq g(f(x, z), f(y, z)) \tag{5.14}$$
$$f(\lambda(x), y) \geq f(x, \lambda(y)) \tag{5.15}$$
$$f(x, y) \geq f(x, y) \tag{5.16}$$

where one of the inequalities (5.8)–(5.12) must be strict. As algebra we choose the natural numbers $\mathbb{N}$ together with the interpretation functions $F_{\mathbb{N}}(x, y) = x + y$ and

$$\lambda_{\mathbb{N}}(x) = x + 1, \;\; f_{\mathbb{N}}(x, y) = x + y, \;\; g_{\mathbb{N}}(x, y) = \max(x, y), \;\; 1_{\mathbb{N}} = 2_{\mathbb{N}} = 0$$

The well-founded weakly monotone $\mathcal{F}$-algebra $(\mathbb{N}, \geq)$ satisfies the inequalities (5.8)–(5.16). In fact, it satisfies the constraints of every cycle in $\mathrm{EDG}(\mathcal{R})$ containing inequality (5.8) or (5.9). Finally, the cycle

$$\begin{gathered}\langle F(g(x, y), z), F(x, z)\rangle \\ \langle F(g(x, y), z), F(y, z)\rangle \\ \langle F(\lambda(x), y), F(x, \lambda(c(y)))\rangle\end{gathered}$$

yields—after normalization with the AFS $\{c(x) \to x\}$—the inequalities (5.10)–(5.16), where one of the inequalities (5.10)–(5.12) must be strict. Note that *lpo* (comparing arguments left to right) does not satisfy the constraints because of inequality (5.13). However, the algebra $(\mathbb{N}, \geq)$ with the preceding interpretation functions is a quasimodel of (5.10)–(5.16). In this situation, we use semantic labeling as suggested earlier. We only label the symbols f and F by the labeling functions $lab_f(x, y) = lab_F(x, y) = x + y$. The resulting set of inequalities IN_{lab} reads as follows (where $i, j, k \in \mathbb{N}$)

$$\begin{array}{lcll}
F_i(g(x, y), z) & \geq & F_j(x, z) & \text{with } i \geq j \\
F_i(g(x, y), z) & \geq & F_j(y, z) & \text{with } i \geq j \\
F_i(\lambda(x), y) & \geq & F_i(x, \lambda(y)) & \\
f_{i+j+1}(\lambda(x), y) & \geq & \lambda(f_{i+j}(x, g(1, f_j(y, 2)))) & \\
f_i(g(x, y), z) & \geq & g(f_j(x, z), f_k(y, z)) & \text{with } i = \max\{j, k\} \\
f_i(\lambda(x), y) & \geq & f_i(x, \lambda(y)) & \\
f_i(x, y) & \geq & f_i(x, y) &
\end{array}$$

where one of the first three inequalities must be strict. These constraints are satisfied by *lpo* (comparing arguments from left to right) based on the well-founded precedence

$$F_i \succ_p F_j,\ F_i \succ_p \lambda,\ f_i \succ_p f_j,\ \text{for all } i,j \in \mathbb{N} \text{ with } i > j \text{ and}$$
$$f_0 \succ_p g,\ f_0 \succ_p \lambda,\ f_0 \succ_p 1,\ f_0 \succ_p 2$$

As a matter of fact, this *lpo* satisfies the constraints of every cycle in EDG($\mathcal{R}$) containing one of the inequalities (5.10)–(5.12). Therefore, Corollary 5.5.13 yields termination of $\mathcal{R}$.

5.5.3 Type Introduction

Consider the algebraic specification (we refer to [EM85] for an introduction to algebraic specifications)

$$\begin{aligned} 0 + y &= y \\ s(x) + y &= s(x+y) \\ nil +\!\!+\, ys &= ys \\ (x : xs) +\!\!+\, ys &= x : (xs +\!\!+\, ys) \end{aligned}$$

which specifies *addition* on natural numbers and *concatenation* on lists. As usual, natural numbers are constructed by 0 and s and lists are built from *nil* and the *cons* operator ":". In our untyped (one-sorted) setting, $s(nil)$ is a legal but meaningless term. In order to forbid such terms, one usually introduces *types* or *sorts*. In the example, one would introduce the sorts NAT and LIST and type the operators as follows:

$$\begin{aligned} 0 &:: \text{NAT} \\ s &:: \text{NAT} \to \text{NAT} \\ nil &:: \text{LIST} \\ : &:: \text{NAT} \times \text{LIST} \to \text{LIST} \end{aligned}$$

The intuitive meaning of the typed *cons* operator ":" is: It takes two arguments, say x of type NAT and xs of type LIST, and it gives back the well-typed term $x : xs$ of type LIST. In this typed (many-sorted) framework, merely the well-typed terms are regarded as legal terms. For example, $s(nil)$ is not a legal term because it is ill-typed: s expects an argument of sort NAT but *nil* is a constructor of sort LIST.

This can be formalized as follows.

Definition 5.5.15 Let S be a finite nonempty set representing the set of types or sorts. An *S-sorted set* M is a family of sets $(M_s)_{s\in S}$. For S-sorted sets M and N, an *S-sorted mapping* $\phi : M \to N$ is a family of mappings $(\phi_s : M_s \to N_s)_{s\in S}$.

Let $\mathcal{F}$ be a set of *function symbols*. For every function symbol an *arity* and a *sort* are given, described by functions

$$ar : \mathcal{F} \to S^* \text{ and } st : \mathcal{F} \to S$$

$\mathcal{F}$ together with ar and st is called a *many-sorted* signature. If $f \in \mathcal{F}$ with $ar(f) = s_1, \ldots, s_n$ and $st(f) = s$, then we write $f :: s_1 \times \cdots \times s_n \to s$.

Let $\mathcal{V}$ be an S-sorted set of *variables*, where the sets $\mathcal{V}_s$, $s \in S$, are pairwise disjoint. The S-sorted set $\mathcal{T}(\mathcal{F}, \mathcal{V})$ of *well-typed* terms is defined by

- $\mathcal{V}_s \subseteq \mathcal{T}(\mathcal{F}, \mathcal{V})_s$ for $s \in S$
- $f(t_1, \ldots, t_n) \in \mathcal{T}(\mathcal{F}, \mathcal{V})_s$ for $f :: s_1 \times \cdots \times s_n \to s$ and $t_i \in \mathcal{T}(\mathcal{F}, \mathcal{V})_{s_i}$.

The set of *typed* terms is obtained by dropping the $t_i \in \mathcal{T}(\mathcal{F}, \mathcal{V})_{s_i}$ requirement in the preceding definition. A typed term that is not well-typed is called *ill-typed.* If $t \in \mathcal{T}(\mathcal{F}, \mathcal{V})_s$, then we say that t is of sort s and write $sort(t) = s$.

In order to define a typed context, we assume that for every $s \in S$ there is a special constant $\Box_s \notin \mathcal{F} \cup \bigcup_{s \in S} \mathcal{V}_s$ with $sort(\Box_s) = s$. An S-sorted *context* $C[\Box_{s_1}, \ldots, \Box_{s_n}]$ is a *well-typed term* that contains at least one of these special constants. As in the untyped case, $C[t_1, \ldots, t_n]$ denotes the result of replacing (from left to right) $\Box_{s_1}, \ldots, \Box_{s_n}$ with $t_1, \ldots, t_n$.

An S-sorted *substitution* σ is an S-sorted mapping $\sigma : \mathcal{V} \to \mathcal{T}(\mathcal{F}, \mathcal{V})$.

An S-sorted *term rewriting system* $\mathcal{R}$ is an S-sorted set of rewrite rules. A rewrite rule $l \to r$ of sort s is a pair of two *well-typed terms* l and r of sort s, where l is not a variable and r does not contain variables that do not occur in l. The corresponding rewrite relation on the set of *well-typed terms* is defined in the obvious way.

An S-sorted TRS $\mathcal{R}$ is also called a *many-sorted* TRS. If S has only one element, then $\mathcal{R}$ is called a *one-sorted* TRS.

In the rest of this section, Θ denotes the type elimination mapping. That is, if t is an S-sorted term, then $\Theta(t)$ denotes the term obtained from t by removing all type information. Analogously, $\Theta(\mathcal{R})$ denotes the TRS obtained from an S-sorted TRS $\mathcal{R}$ by removing all type information.

Zantema [Zan94] showed how typing can be used as a tool to prove termination of one-sorted TRSs. Middeldorp and Ohsaki [MO00] extended this technique to equational rewriting. In order to review the method of type introduction, we need the notion of persistence.

Definition 5.5.16 A property $\mathcal{P}$ is called *persistent* if, for every many-sorted TRS $\mathcal{R}$, the property $\mathcal{P}$ holds for $\mathcal{R}$ if and only if it holds for $\Theta(\mathcal{R})$.

We shall see in Chapter 8 that persistence is closely related to modularity. As a matter of fact, the proof of Proposition 5.5.24 goes back to a modularity proof [Ohl93b]. The following example shows that termination is not persistent. More precisely, termination of $\mathcal{R}$ does not imply termination of $\Theta(\mathcal{R})$. In contrast to that, the converse implication is true because $u \to_{\mathcal{R}} v$ implies $\Theta(u) \to_{\Theta(\mathcal{R})} \Theta(v)$.

Example 5.5.17 Let $S = \{s_1, s_2\}$, $x \in \mathcal{V}_{s_1}$, and $y, z \in \mathcal{V}_{s_2}$. Furthermore, let $\mathcal{F}$ be the many-sorted signature consisting of constants 0 and 1 of sort s_1, and the function symbols $f :: s_1 \times s_1 \times s_1 \to s_1$, and $g :: s_2 \times s_2 \to s_2$. On the one hand, the S-sorted TRS $\mathcal{R}$ consisting of the rules

$$\begin{array}{rcl} f(0,1,x) & \to & f(x,x,x) \\ g(y,z) & \to & y \\ g(y,z) & \to & z \end{array}$$

is terminating; see Example 5.4.35. On the other hand,

$$\begin{array}{rcl} \Theta(f(0,1,g(0,1))) & \to_{\Theta(\mathcal{R})} & \Theta(f(g(0,1),g(0,1),g(0,1))) \\ & \to_{\Theta(\mathcal{R})} & \Theta(f(0,g(0,1),g(0,1))) \\ & \to_{\Theta(\mathcal{R})} & \Theta(f(0,1,g(0,1))) \end{array}$$

is a cyclic (hence infinite) $\Theta(\mathcal{R})$-derivation. Therefore, termination is not persistent.

It is our next goal to show that termination is persistent for many-sorted TRSs that are noncollapsing or nonduplicating. In the rest of this section, $\mathcal{R}$ denotes an S-sorted TRS.

Definition 5.5.18 We define a relation $\to_{\Theta(\mathcal{R})}$ on the set of *typed terms* by $u \to_{\Theta(\mathcal{R})} v$ if and only if $\Theta(u) \to_{\Theta(\mathcal{R})} \Theta(v)$. Let t be a typed term of sort s. If t is ill-typed, then t has a unique representation $t = C[t_1, \ldots, t_n]$, where $C[\Box_{s_1}, \ldots, \Box_{s_n}]$ is a nonempty S-sorted context and $sort(t_i) \neq s_i$ for every $1 \leq i \leq n$. In other words, every t_i causes a type clash and there is no type clash strictly above the t_i. In this case, we write $t = C[\![t_1, \ldots, t_n]\!]$ and define $A(t) = [t_1, \ldots, t_n]$ to be the multiset of the *aliens* of t. If t is well-typed, then $A(t)$ is empty. A reduction step $u \to_{\Theta(\mathcal{R})} v$ is called *inner*, denoted by $u \to^i_{\Theta(\mathcal{R})} v$, if the reduction takes place in one of the aliens of u. Otherwise, we speak of an *outer* reduction step and and write $u \to^o_{\Theta(\mathcal{R})} v$.

The following lemma plays a key role in what follows.

Lemma 5.5.19 *Any $\Theta(\mathcal{R})$-reduction step of typed terms is either an inner or an outer step.*

Proof Consider a reduction step $u \to_{\Theta(\mathcal{R})} v$, i.e., $\Theta(u) \to_{\Theta(\mathcal{R})} \Theta(v)$ by some rewrite rule $\Theta(l) \to \Theta(r) \in \Theta(\mathcal{R})$. If u is well-typed, then $u \to_{\Theta(\mathcal{R})} v$ is an outer reduction step. Otherwise, u is ill-typed and can be written as $u = C[\![u_1, \ldots, u_n]\!]$. Suppose that the reduction step is neither inner nor outer. Then $\Theta(l)$ matches $\Theta(u)$ at a position p in $C[\Box_{s_1}, \ldots, \Box_{s_n}]$. Moreover, the root symbol of at least one u_j must be part of l, say, $root(u_j) = f$ with $st(f) = s_j$ occurs at position p' in l. That is, $l = C'[f(\ldots)]$ for some S-sorted context $C'[\Box_{s'}]$ with $l|_{p'} = f(\ldots)$. Because there is a type clash at position $p.p'$ in u, it follows that there is a type clash at position p' in l, i.e., $s_j \neq s'$. This means that l is ill-typed. However, every left-hand side of a rewrite rule in $\mathcal{R}$ must be well-typed. This contradiction shows that $u \rightarrow_{\Theta(\mathcal{R})} v$ is either an inner or an outer reduction step. □

Definition 5.5.20 The rank of a typed term t is defined by

$$rank(t) = \begin{cases} 1 & \text{, if } t \text{ is well-typed} \\ 1 + max\{rank(t_i) \mid 1 \leq i \leq n\}, & \text{if } t = C[\![t_1, \ldots, t_n]\!] \end{cases}$$

The *topmost well-typed part* of t, denoted by $top(t)$, is the well-typed term obtained from t by replacing all aliens with special constants $\Box_{s_i}$ of appropriate sort:

$$top(t) = \begin{cases} t & \text{if } \ rank(t) = 1 \\ C[\Box_{s_1}, \ldots, \Box_{s_n}] & \text{if } \ t = C[\![t_1, \ldots, t_n]\!] \end{cases}$$

An outer rewrite step $u \rightarrow_{\Theta(\mathcal{R})} v$ is called *destructive* if $sort(u) \neq sort(v)$, while an inner rewrite step $u \rightarrow_{\Theta(\mathcal{R})} v$ is called *destructive* if $top(u) \neq top(v)$.

Obviously, if a rewrite step is destructive, then the rewrite rule applied in that step is collapsing. The simple proofs of the following lemmas are omitted.

Lemma 5.5.21 *If $u \rightarrow_{\Theta(\mathcal{R})} v$, then $rank(u) \geq rank(v)$.*

Lemma 5.5.22 *If $u \rightarrow^{o}_{\Theta(\mathcal{R})} v$ is a nondestructive nonduplicating rewrite step, then the multiset inclusion $A(v) \subseteq A(u)$ holds.*

Lemma 5.5.23 *Consider an inner step $u = C[\![u_1, \ldots, u_j, \ldots, u_n]\!] \rightarrow^{i}_{\Theta(\mathcal{R})} C[u_1, \ldots, v_j, \ldots, u_n] = v$, where $u_j \rightarrow_{\Theta(\mathcal{R})} v_j$. If it is destructive, then $A(v) = (A(u) \setminus [u_j]) \oplus A(v_j)$; otherwise $A(v) = (A(u) \setminus [u_j]) \oplus [v_j]$.*

Proposition 5.5.24 *Let $\mathcal{R}$ be a terminating S-sorted TRS. If there is an infinite $\Theta(\mathcal{R})$-derivation of ill-typed terms, then there is also an infinite derivation*

$$D : u_1 \rightarrow_{\Theta(\mathcal{R})} u_2 \rightarrow_{\Theta(\mathcal{R})} u_3 \rightarrow_{\Theta(\mathcal{R})} \cdots$$

such that D contains

1. *an infinite number of outer steps,*

2. *an infinite number of destructive inner steps, and*

3. *an infinite number of duplicating outer steps.*

Proof For any derivation $D : u_1 \to_{\Theta(\mathcal{R})} u_2 \to_{\Theta(\mathcal{R})} u_3 \to_{\Theta(\mathcal{R})} \cdots$ we define the rank of D to be $rank(D) = rank(u_1)$. Now if there is an infinite $\Theta(\mathcal{R})$-derivation, then by Lemma 5.5.21 there is also an infinite $\Theta(\mathcal{R})$-derivation $D : u_1 \to_{\Theta(\mathcal{R})} u_2 \to_{\Theta(\mathcal{R})} u_3 \to_{\Theta(\mathcal{R})} \cdots$ of minimal rank. Notice that this implies $rank(u_j) = rank(D)$ for all indices j. In particular, there is no destructive outer reduction step. Let $sort(u_1) = s_1$. It follows that $sort(u_j) = s_1$ for any $j \in \mathbb{N}_+$.

(1) For an indirect proof, suppose that only a finite number of reduction steps in D are outer ones. Then there is an index $m \in \mathbb{N}$ such that the infinite $\Theta(\mathcal{R})$-derivation $u_m \to_{\Theta(\mathcal{R})} u_{m+1} \to_{\Theta(\mathcal{R})} u_{m+2} \to_{\Theta(\mathcal{R})} \cdots$ does not contain outer reduction step. In other words, without loss of generality we may assume that there is no outer reduction step in D. Thus, if $u_1 = C[\![v_1, \ldots, v_n]\!]$, then there must be an infinite rewrite derivation starting from some alien $v_\ell \in A(u_1)$. But this contradicts the minimality assumption on $rank(D)$ because $rank(v_\ell) < rank(u_1)$.

(2) For a proof by contradiction, suppose that only a finite number of inner reduction steps in D are destructive. Then we may further assume w.l.o.g. that none of the inner reduction steps in D are destructive. For any outer reduction step $u_j \to^{o}_{\Theta(\mathcal{R})} u_{j+1}$ in D it follows that $top(u_j) \to_{\mathcal{R}} top(u_{j+1})$ using the same rule from $\mathcal{R}$ and for every inner reduction step $u_j \to^{i}_{\Theta(\mathcal{R})} u_{j+1}$ we have $top(u_j) = top(u_{j+1})$. Hence, we conclude by (1) that $\mathcal{R}$ is nonterminating, which is a contradiction.

(3) Let $(\mathbb{N}, >)$ denote the usual well-founded ordering on natural numbers and $(\mathcal{M}(\mathbb{N}), >^{mul})$ its well-founded multiset extension. We define

$$K(u) = [rank(v) \mid v \in A(u)] \in \mathcal{M}(\mathbb{N})$$

i.e., $K(u)$ denotes the multiset of the ranks of the aliens of u.

For an indirect proof, suppose that there are only a finite number of duplicating outer rewrite steps in D. Again, we may assume that D does not contain duplicating outer rewrite steps. We distinguish between three cases:

- If $u_j \to^{o}_{\Theta(\mathcal{R})} u_{j+1}$, then, by Lemma 5.5.22, $A(u_{j+1}) \subseteq A(u_j)$ because the reduction step is nondestructive and nonduplicating. Clearly, this implies $K(u_j) \geq^{mul} K(u_{j+1})$.

- If $u_j = C[\![v_1, \ldots, v_k, \ldots, v_n]\!] \to^{i}_{\Theta(\mathcal{R})} C[\![v_1, \ldots, v'_k, \ldots, v_n]\!] = u_{j+1}$, where $v_k \to_{\Theta(\mathcal{R})} v'_k$, is nondestructive, then we have $A(u_{j+1}) = (A(u_j) \setminus [v_k]) \oplus [v'_k]$ according to Lemma 5.5.23. Consequently, $K(u_j) \geq^{mul} K(u_{j+1})$ because $rank(v_k) \geq rank(v'_k)$.

- If $u_j = C[\![v_1, \ldots, v_k, \ldots, v_n]\!] \to^{i}_{\Theta(\mathcal{R})} C[v_1, \ldots, v'_k, \ldots, v_n] = u_{j+1}$, where $v_k \to_{\Theta(\mathcal{R})} v'_k$, is destructive, then by Lemma 5.5.23 $A(u_{j+1}) = (A(u_j) \setminus [v_k]) \oplus A(v'_k)$. It follows from $rank(v_k) > rank(v'_k)$ in conjunction with $rank(v'_k) > rank(t)$ for any alien $t \in A(v'_k)$ that $K(u_j) >^{mul} K(u_{j+1})$.

We conclude from the well-foundedness of $(\mathcal{M}(\mathbb{N}), >^{mul})$ that D contains only a finite number of destructive inner reduction steps. This contradicts statement (2). □

Theorem 5.5.25 *Termination is persistent for the class of many-sorted TRSs that do not contain both collapsing and duplicating rules.*

Proof Let $\mathcal{R}$ be a terminating many-sorted TRS. For an indirect proof, assume that an infinite derivation

$$\Theta(u_1) \to_{\Theta(\mathcal{R})} \Theta(u_2) \to_{\Theta(\mathcal{R})} \Theta(u_3) \to_{\Theta(\mathcal{R})} \cdots$$

exists. Then

$$D : u_1 \to_{\Theta(\mathcal{R})} u_2 \to_{\Theta(\mathcal{R})} u_3 \to_{\Theta(\mathcal{R})} \cdots$$

is an infinite $\Theta(\mathcal{R})$-derivation of ill-typed terms. According to Proposition 5.5.24, D must contain destructive inner steps and duplicating outer steps. Thus $\mathcal{R}$ must contain both collapsing and duplicating rewrite rules. □

Theorem 5.5.25 can be used to prove termination of an untyped (one-sorted) TRS that is either noncollapsing or nonduplicating. As an example, we show termination of the rewrite system $f(0,1,x) \to f(x,x,x)$; cf. Example 5.4.35. Let s_1 and s_2 be distinct sorts. We type 0, 1, and x with sort s_1 and f by $f :: s_1 \times s_1 \times s_1 \to s_2$. The many-sorted TRS obtained in this way is obviously terminating and noncollapsing. Hence an application of Theorem 5.5.25 yields termination of the original system.

Some proofs can be considerably shortened by using type introduction. For example, undecidability of termination can easily be shown with type introduction; see Proposition 5.1.1. We will see more examples of this kind in Chapter 6. Another example is the proof of Theorem 10.3.3. Moreover, a short proof of Theorem 5.4.10 can be given with the help of type introduction; see [MO00].

We conclude this section with a summary of the properties that are known to be persistent:

- termination for noncollapsing TRSs and for nonduplicating TRSs; see Theorem 5.5.25.
- termination for TRSs in which all variables are of the same sort; see [Aot98].
- normalization; see [Zan94].
- nonloopingness for noncollapsing TRSs and for nonduplicating TRSs; see [MO00].

- acyclicity for noncollapsing TRSs and for nonduplicating TRSs; see [MO00].
- confluence; see [AT97b].
- local confluence; see [Zan94].

5.6 Innermost Termination

If a term t has a normal form w.r.t. a given TRS but there are also infinite derivations starting from t, then it is important to have a reduction strategy that avoids these infinite derivations. A reduction strategy selects the next redex(es) in a term that should be contracted. Innermost reduction strategies are of particular interest because they are used in the *call-by-value* parameter passing style in functional programming languages with *eager* semantics. Outermost reduction strategies play a crucial role in the evaluation mechanism of *lazy* functional programming languages.

Innermost termination is also important in other contexts. For example, in Chapter 10 we shall see that termination of a logic program can be proven by transforming it into an innermost terminating TRS. Moreover, it will be shown in Chapter 7 that the transformation of certain conditional term rewriting systems yields innermost terminating TRSs.

In this chapter we will prove some fundamental results about innermost termination. After that the dependency pair technique for innermost termination will briefly be reviewed. Furthermore, we will discuss the question of whether confluence might be decidable for innermost terminating TRSs. To start with, let us formally define what an innermost reduction step is.

Definition 5.6.1 Let $\mathcal{R}$ be a TRS. A reduction step $s \to_{\mathcal{R}} t$ is *innermost*, denoted by $s \xrightarrow{i}_{\mathcal{R}} t$, if no proper subterm of the contracted redex is itself a redex. An *innermost derivation* consists solely of innermost reduction steps. $\mathcal{R}$ is *innermost normalizing* (weakly innermost normalizing, WIN) if, for every term s, there is an innermost reduction sequence $s \to_{\mathcal{R}}^* t$ such that $t \in NF(\to_{\mathcal{R}})$. $\mathcal{R}$ is *innermost terminating* (strongly innermost normalizing, SIN) if there is no infinite innermost derivation. A reduction step $s \to_{\mathcal{R}} t$ is *outermost* if the contracted redex is not a proper subterm of another redex. The notions *outermost normalization* and *outermost termination* are defined analogously to these notions.

Lemma 5.6.2 *We have the following implications:*

$$\text{SN} \Rightarrow \text{SIN} \Rightarrow \text{WIN} \Rightarrow \text{WN}$$

An analogous statement holds if "innermost" is replaced with "outermost."

Proof The proof is routine. □

None of the reverse implications hold. The system $\{a \to f(a), f(x) \to b\}$ is normalizing but not innermost normalizing, while the reduction system $\{a \to a, a \to b\}$ is innermost normalizing but not innermost terminating. Finally, the system $\{a \to b, f(a) \to f(a)\}$ is innermost terminating but not terminating. However, we shall see in the next section that the notions coincide for some classes of TRSs.

5.6.1 Conditions for the Equivalence to Termination

Under what conditions are termination and innermost termination equivalent? For example, Gramlich [Gra95, theorem 3.23] showed that these notions coincide for locally confluent overlay systems. Thus, his theorem allows us to prove termination by proving innermost termination for this class of TRSs. It also has important applications in modularity because innermost termination has a much better modular behavior than termination; see Chapter 8. Because Gramlich's original proof was rather complicated, several authors have provided simpler proofs for this important theorem; see Middeldorp [Mid94b], Ohlebusch [Ohl94a], and Dershowitz and Hoot [DH95]. The proof presented here originates from Middeldorp [Mid94b].

In order to prove Gramlich's result, we need a few prerequisites. Until Theorem 5.6.8 we assume that $\mathcal{R}$ is a locally confluent TRS, and we will extensively use the localized variants of properties like termination and convergence. For example, a term t is called *convergent* if it is terminating and confluent, that is, every reduction sequence starting from t is finite and any two reducts of t are joinable. Every term t can uniquely be written as $C[t_1, \ldots, t_n]$ where $t_1, \ldots, t_n$ are the maximal convergent subterms of t. We define $\phi(t)$ as $C[t_1\downarrow, \ldots, t_n\downarrow]$, where $t_i\downarrow$ denotes the unique normal form of t_i. Obviously, $t \to_{\mathcal{R}}^{*} \phi(t)$. Because $\mathcal{R}$ is locally confluent, a term is convergent if and only if it is terminating (this follows from the localized variant of Newman's Lemma 2.2.5). Thus, a term is convergent if and only if all its subterms are convergent. Let $s \to_{\mathcal{R}} t$ be an arbitrary reduction step. We write $s \to_{\mathcal{R}}^{c} t$ if the contracted redex is convergent, and $s \to_{\mathcal{R}}^{nc} t$ if the contracted redex is not convergent. Clearly every reduction step can be written as either $\to_{\mathcal{R}}^{c}$ or $\to_{\mathcal{R}}^{nc}$.

Lemma 5.6.3

1. *The relation $\to_{\mathcal{R}}^{c}$ is terminating.*

2. *If $\mathcal{R}$ is nonterminating, then every infinite $\mathcal{R}$-derivation contains an infinite number of $\to_{\mathcal{R}}^{nc}$ steps.*

Proof (1) The proof is routine.

(2) The proof is an immediate consequence of (1). □

Lemma 5.6.4 *If $s \to_{\mathcal{R}}^{c} t$, then $\phi(s) \to_{\mathcal{R}}^{*} \phi(t)$.*

Proof Clearly, $t \to_{\mathcal{R}}^{*} \phi(s)$ by contracting only redexes in convergent subterms of t. Therefore, $\phi(s) \to_{\mathcal{R}}^{*} \phi(t)$. □

In Lemma 5.6.4, the equality $\phi(s) = \phi(t)$ is in general not valid; take, for example, $\mathcal{R}_1 = \{a \to b, f(a) \to f(a), f(b) \to c\}$ and consider the step $s = f(a) \to_{\mathcal{R}_1}^{c} f(b) = t$. The analogous statement of Lemma 5.6.4 for $\to_{\mathcal{R}}^{nc}$ does not hold either: In the TRS $\mathcal{R}_2 = \{a \to b, f(a) \to g(a), g(x) \to f(x)\}$ and the step $s = f(a) \to_{\mathcal{R}_2}^{nc} g(a) = t$ we have $\phi(s) = f(b)$ and $\phi(t) = g(b)$. Note that $\mathcal{R}_2$ is not an overlay system. Lemma 5.6.6 shows that this is essential.

Lemma 5.6.5 *Let $\mathcal{R}$ be a locally confluent overlay system. If $l \to r \in \mathcal{R}$ and σ is a substitution such that $l\sigma$ is not convergent, then $\phi(l\sigma) = l\tau$, where τ is defined by $\tau(x) = \phi(\sigma(x))$ for all $x \in \mathcal{V}ar(l)$.*

Proof If no subterm of $l\sigma$ is convergent, then $\phi(l\sigma) = l\sigma = l\tau$. Otherwise, we may write $l\sigma = C[t_1, \ldots, t_n]$, where $C[, \ldots,]$ is a nonempty context and $t_1, \ldots, t_n$ are the maximal convergent subterms of $l\sigma$. By definition, $\phi(l\sigma) = C[t_1\!\downarrow, \ldots, t_n\!\downarrow]$. Let p_i be the position in $l\sigma$ such that $l\sigma|_{p_i} = t_i$ and note that $p_i \neq \varepsilon$. We will show that $t_i\!\downarrow = l\tau|_{p_i}$. The lemma is an easy consequence of this fact. If p_i is below the position of a variable $x \in \mathcal{V}ar(l)$, then $t_i\!\downarrow = l\tau|_{p_i}$ because t_i is a convergent subterm of $x\sigma$. Otherwise, p_i is a nonvariable position in l. Because t_i is convergent, so is $x\sigma$ for all $x \in \mathcal{V}ar(l|_{p_i})$. Hence $t_i\!\downarrow = (l\sigma|_{p_i})\!\downarrow = (l\tau|_{p_i})\!\downarrow$. On the other hand, $l\tau|_{p_i}$ is a normal form because $\mathcal{R}$ is an overlay system and $x\tau$ is a normal form for all $x \in \mathcal{V}ar(l|_{p_i})$ (if $l\tau|_{p_i}$ were reducible, then there would be a critical pair in $\mathcal{R}$ that is not an overlay). All in all, $t_i\!\downarrow = (l\tau|_{p_i})\!\downarrow = l\tau|_{p_i}$ and we are done. □

Lemma 5.6.6 *If the TRS $\mathcal{R}$ is a locally confluent overlay system, then $s \to_{\mathcal{R}}^{nc} t$ implies $\phi(s) \to_{\mathcal{R}}^{+} \phi(t)$.*

Proof Let $s \to_{\mathcal{R}}^{nc} t$ by an application of the rewrite rule $l \to r$ at position p with substitution σ. That is, $s|_p = l\sigma$ and $t = s[p \leftarrow r\sigma]$. Because $s|_p$ is not convergent, p is a position in $\phi(s)$. According to Lemma 5.6.5, $\phi(s)|_p = l\tau$, where τ is defined by $\tau(x) = \phi(\sigma(x))$ for all $x \in \mathcal{V}ar(l)$. Therefore, $\phi(s) \to_{\mathcal{R}} \phi(s)[p \leftarrow r\tau]$. Because $t \to_{\mathcal{R}}^{*} \phi(s)[p \leftarrow r\tau]$ by contracting only redexes in convergent subterms of t, it follows that $\phi(s)[p \leftarrow r\tau] \to_{\mathcal{R}}^{*} \phi(t)$. We conclude that $\phi(s) \to_{\mathcal{R}}^{+} \phi(t)$. □

Lemma 5.6.7 *Let $\mathcal{R}$ be a locally confluent overlay system and t be a term. If $\phi(t)$ is terminating, then t is terminating.*

Proof For a proof by contradiction, we assume that t is not terminating, i.e., there is an infinite $\mathcal{R}$-derivation

$$D : t = t_0 \to_{\mathcal{R}} t_1 \to_{\mathcal{R}} t_2 \to_{\mathcal{R}} \cdots$$

According to Lemma 5.6.3(2), D contains an infinite number of $\to_{\mathcal{R}}^{nc}$ steps. Using Lemmas 5.6.4 and 5.6.6, we obtain an infinite $\mathcal{R}$-derivation

$$\phi(D) : \phi(t) = \phi(t_0) \to_{\mathcal{R}}^* \phi(t_1) \to_{\mathcal{R}}^* \phi(t_2) \to_{\mathcal{R}}^* \cdots$$

This contradicts the presupposition that $\phi(t)$ is terminating. □

Theorem 5.6.8 *Every locally confluent overlay system is innermost terminating if and only if it is terminating.*

Proof Let $\mathcal{R}$ be a locally confluent overlay system and t be a term. It will be shown that t is terminating whenever it is innermost terminating. For a proof by contradiction, suppose that t admits an infinite $\mathcal{R}$-derivation. Because t is innermost terminating, every infinite $\mathcal{R}$-derivation starting from t must contain a noninnermost step. We consider an infinite $\mathcal{R}$-derivation starting from t that has the property that the first noninnermost step is essential: Selecting any innermost redex at that point would result in a terminating term. Let

$$D : t = t_0 \to_{\mathcal{R}} t_1 \to_{\mathcal{R}} \cdots \to_{\mathcal{R}} t_n \to_{\mathcal{R}} t_{n+1} \to_{\mathcal{R}} \cdots$$

where $t_n \to_{\mathcal{R}} t_{n+1}$ is the first noninnermost step. By assumption, contracting an innermost redex in t_n yields a terminating term. This implies that every innermost redex in t_n is convergent. Because there is at least one innermost redex in t_n, we conclude that $\phi(t_n)$ is terminating. This, however, contradicts Lemma 5.6.7 because t is nonterminating. □

In view of Newman's lemma 2.2.5, Theorem 5.6.8 can be rephrased as follows: An overlay system is convergent if and only if it is locally confluent and innermost terminating.

Theorem 5.6.10 is also due to Gramlich [Gra95]. For *orthogonal* TRSs, statement (1) was proved by O'Donnell [O'D77], and the proof of statement (2) dates back to the work of Church [Chu41]. For the proof, we need the following auxiliary result.

Lemma 5.6.9 *Let $\mathcal{R}$ be a nonoverlapping TRS.*

1. *If $s \xrightarrow{i}_{\mathcal{R}} t_1$ and $s \xrightarrow{i}_{\mathcal{R}} t_2$, then either $t_1 = t_2$ or there is a term t_3 such that $t_1 \xrightarrow{i}_{\mathcal{R}} t_3$ and $t_2 \xrightarrow{i}_{\mathcal{R}} t_3$.*

2. *The relation $\xrightarrow{i}_{\mathcal{R}}$ is confluent.*

3. *If there is a derivation* $s \xrightarrow{i}_{\mathcal{R}}^{*} t \in NF(\mathcal{R})$ *of length* ℓ*, then every other innermost derivation from* s *to the normal form* t *has length* ℓ.

Proof (1) Let p and q be the positions of the redexes contracted in $s \xrightarrow{i}_{\mathcal{R}} t_1$ and $s \xrightarrow{i}_{\mathcal{R}} t_2$, respectively. If $p = q$, then the same rewrite rule was applied in both steps because $\mathcal{R}$ is nonoverlapping. In this case $t_1 = t_2$. Otherwise, p and q are independent positions in s. In this case, t_3 is obtained from t_1 (t_2) by contracting the redex at position q (p); cf. Figure 4.1.

(2) According to (1), $\xrightarrow{i}_{\mathcal{R}}$ is subcommutative, hence confluent.

(3) With the aid of (1), this follows by induction on ℓ. □

Theorem 5.6.10

1. *Every nonoverlapping TRS is innermost normalizing if and only if it is terminating (i.e., WIN* ⇔ *SIN* ⇔ *SN).*
2. *Every nonoverlapping and variable-preserving TRS is normalizing if and only if it is terminating (i.e., WN* ⇔ *WIN* ⇔ *SIN* ⇔ *SN).*

Proof (1) The equivalence SIN ⇔ SN is a special case of Theorem 5.6.8. In view of Lemma 5.6.2, we have to show WIN ⇒ SIN. If $\mathcal{R}$ is an innermost normalizing TRS, then every term s has a normal form t that can be reached by innermost reduction, that is, $s \xrightarrow{i}_{\mathcal{R}}^{*} t \in NF(\mathcal{R})$. Let the length of the derivation $s \xrightarrow{i}_{\mathcal{R}}^{*} t$ be ℓ. By Lemma 5.6.9(3), every other innermost derivation from s to the normal form t has the same length ℓ. Now suppose that $\mathcal{R}$ is not innermost terminating, i.e., there is an infinite innermost derivation

$$D : s = s_0 \xrightarrow{i}_{\mathcal{R}} s_1 \xrightarrow{i}_{\mathcal{R}} s_2 \xrightarrow{i}_{\mathcal{R}} \cdots$$

Because $\xrightarrow{i}_{\mathcal{R}}$ is confluent by Lemma 5.6.9(2), every term in D must also reduce to the normal form t. In particular, $s \xrightarrow{i}_{\mathcal{R}}^{*} s_\ell \xrightarrow{i}_{\mathcal{R}}^{+} t$ is an innermost derivation of length $> \ell$. This contradiction proves that $\mathcal{R}$ is innermost terminating.

(2) According to Lemma 5.6.2 and (1), it suffices to show the implication WN ⇒ WIN. Let $\mathcal{R}$ be a normalizing TRS. It will be shown that every term t is innermost normalizing. Because $\mathcal{R}$ is normalizing, there is an $\mathcal{R}$-derivation

$$D : t = t_0 \to_{\mathcal{R}} t_1 \to_{\mathcal{R}} t_2 \to_{\mathcal{R}} \cdots \to_{\mathcal{R}} t_n \in NF(\mathcal{R})$$

In particular, t_n is innermost normalizing. We will show by induction on the length n of the normalizing derivation D that every term t_i is innermost normalizing. If $n = 0$, then $t \in NF(\mathcal{R})$ and the claim follows. Suppose $n > 0$. According to the inductive hypothesis, the term t_1 is innermost normalizing and we have to show that t_0 is innermost normalizing as well. Let $t_0 = C[l\sigma] \to_{\mathcal{R}} C[r\sigma] = t_1$. Because t_1 is innermost normalizing, there is a substitution σ' and an innermost $\mathcal{R}$-derivation

$$t_1 = C[r\sigma] \xrightarrow{i}{}^{*}_{\mathcal{R}} C[r\sigma'] \xrightarrow{i}{}^{*}_{\mathcal{R}} u \in NF(\mathcal{R})$$

such that $x\sigma \xrightarrow{i}{}^{*}_{\mathcal{R}} x\sigma' \in NF(\mathcal{R})$ for every variable $x \in \mathcal{V}ar(r)$. We have $\mathcal{V}ar(r) = \mathcal{V}ar(l)$ because $\mathcal{R}$ is variable-preserving. It follows that $t_0 = C[l\sigma] \xrightarrow{i}{}^{*}_{\mathcal{R}} C[l\sigma']$. Furthermore, $C[l\sigma'] \xrightarrow{i}_{\mathcal{R}} C[r\sigma']$ because $\mathcal{R}$ is nonoverlapping. Altogether, this yields an innermost $\mathcal{R}$-derivation

$$t_0 = C[l\sigma] \xrightarrow{i}{}^{*}_{\mathcal{R}} C[l\sigma'] \xrightarrow{i}_{\mathcal{R}} C[r\sigma'] \xrightarrow{i}{}^{*}_{\mathcal{R}} u \in NF(\mathcal{R})$$

Therefore, t_0 is innermost normalizing. □

5.6.2 *Proving Innermost Termination*

Arts and Giesl [AG00] showed that the dependency pair method can be modified to prove innermost termination automatically. According to Theorem 5.6.8, their modified technique can also be used to prove termination of locally confluent overlay systems. For these systems, it is even advantageous to use the modified technique. This is because it is easier to prove innermost termination than to prove termination. More precisely, the constraints obtained from the innermost dependency pair technique are weaker than the constraints obtained from the dependency pair technique.

The new notions of this section will be illustrated by the TRS $\mathcal{R}$ consisting of the rewrite rules

$$\begin{aligned} f(x, c(x), c(y)) &\to f(y, y, f(y, x, y)) \\ f(s(x), y, z) &\to f(x, s(c(y)), c(z)) \\ f(c(x), x, y) &\to c(y) \\ g(x, y) &\to x \\ g(x, y) &\to y \end{aligned}$$

Let $t = g(x, c(x))$ and note that $t \to_{\mathcal{R}} x$ as well as $t \to_{\mathcal{R}} c(x)$. The TRS $\mathcal{R}$ is nonterminating because it admits the following cyclic derivation:

$$\begin{aligned} f(x, c(x), c(t)) &\to_{\mathcal{R}} f(t, t, f(t, x, t)) \\ &\to^{+}_{\mathcal{R}} f(x, c(x), f(c(x), x, t)) \\ &\to_{\mathcal{R}} f(x, c(x), c(t)) \end{aligned}$$

Note that this is not an innermost derivation because the term t itself is a redex. It will be shown that $\mathcal{R}$ is in fact innermost terminating.

In order to develop a criterion for innermost termination similar to Theorem 5.4.9, one has to restrict the notion of chains.

Definition 5.6.11 Let $\mathcal{R}$ be a TRS. A sequence of dependency pairs $\langle s_1, t_1\rangle \langle s_2, t_2\rangle \ldots$ of $\mathcal{R}$ is an *innermost $\mathcal{R}$-chain* if there is a substitution σ such that $s_j\sigma$ is in normal form and $t_j\sigma \xrightarrow{i}^*_{\mathcal{R}} s_{j+1}\sigma$ for every index j.

In innermost derivations, proper subterms of a redex must be in normal form before the redex is contracted. Therefore, in Definition 5.6.11, every $s_j\sigma$ has to be in normal form. Note that this implies that $x\sigma$ is a normal form for every $x \in \mathcal{V}ar(t_j) \subseteq \mathcal{V}ar(s_j)$. In other words, σ must be a normalized substitution.

Of course, every innermost chain is also a chain, but the converse does not hold. In our example, there are the following dependency pairs.

$$\langle F(x, c(x), c(y)), F(y, y, f(y, x, y))\rangle \tag{5.17}$$

$$\langle F(x, c(x), c(y)), F(y, x, y)\rangle \tag{5.18}$$

$$\langle F(s(x), y, z), F(x, s(c(y)), c(z))\rangle \tag{5.19}$$

The infinite sequence consisting of the dependency pair (5.17) is an infinite chain but not an innermost chain because $F(y_1, y_1, f(y_1, x_1, y_1))\sigma$ can only be reduced to $F(x_2, c(x_2), c(y_2))\sigma$ if $y_1\sigma$ is not a normal form.

The absence of infinite innermost chains proves to be a sufficient and necessary criterion for innermost termination.

Theorem 5.6.12 *A TRS $\mathcal{R}$ is innermost terminating if and only if there exists no infinite innermost $\mathcal{R}$-chain.*

Proof The proof of Theorem 5.4.9 applies, mutatis mutandis. □

In order to prove innermost termination (automatically), one proceeds as in Section 5.4. Again, a set of inequalities is generated and one searches for a quasi-reduction ordering $\gtrsim$ satisfying them. Again, one must guarantee $t\sigma \gtrsim u\sigma$ whenever $t\sigma$ reduces to $u\sigma$. However, demanding $l \gtrsim r$ for every rule of the TRS is no longer necessary because σ must be a normalized substitution, and hence not every rule is usable in a reduction of $t\sigma$. For example, no rule can be used to reduce a normalized instantiation of $F(y, x, y)$ because F is not a defined symbol. In general, if t contains a defined symbol f, then all f-rules are usable for t and every rule that is usable for the right-hand sides of the f-rules is also usable for t.

Definition 5.6.13 Let $(\mathcal{F}, \mathcal{R})$ be a TRS. For every function symbol $f \in \mathcal{F}$ let $\text{Rules}_{\mathcal{R}}(f) = \{l \to r \in \mathcal{R} \mid root(l) = f\}$. We define $\mathcal{U}_{\mathcal{R}}(x) = \emptyset$ and

$$\mathcal{U}_{\mathcal{R}}(f(t_1, \ldots, t_n)) = \text{Rules}_{\mathcal{R}}(f) \cup \bigcup_{l \to r \in \text{Rules}_{\mathcal{R}}(f)} \mathcal{U}_{\mathcal{R}'}(r) \cup \bigcup_{j=1}^{n} \mathcal{U}_{\mathcal{R}'}(t_j)$$

where $\mathcal{R}' = \mathcal{R} \setminus \text{Rules}_{\mathcal{R}}(f)$. For any term t, $\mathcal{U}_{\mathcal{R}}(t)$ is called the set of *usable rules* for t. Furthermore, for any set $\mathcal{P}$ of dependency pairs we define $\mathcal{U}_{\mathcal{R}}(\mathcal{P}) = \bigcup_{\langle s,t\rangle \in \mathcal{P}} \mathcal{U}_{\mathcal{R}}(t)$.

In our example, we have $\mathcal{U}_\mathcal{R}(\{(5.17)\}) = \text{Rules}_\mathcal{R}(f)$, $\mathcal{U}_\mathcal{R}(\{(5.18)\}) = \emptyset$, and $\mathcal{U}_\mathcal{R}(\{(5.19)\}) = \emptyset$ because $\text{Rules}_\mathcal{R}(c) = \emptyset$ for every constructor c.

Theorem 5.6.14 *A TRS $\mathcal{R}$ is innermost terminating if there exists a quasi-reduction ordering $\succsim$ such that for all dependency pairs $\langle s, t\rangle$ of $\mathcal{R}$*

- *$l \succsim r$ for all rules $l \to r$ in $\mathcal{U}_\mathcal{R}(t)$ and*
- *$s \succ t$.*

Proof The proof is similar to that of Theorem 5.4.10. □

Similar to Definition 5.4.11, the notion of a dependency graph is defined for innermost chains.

Definition 5.6.15 The *innermost dependency graph* of a TRS $\mathcal{R}$ is the directed graph whose nodes are the dependency pairs and there is an arc from $\langle s, t\rangle$ to $\langle u, v\rangle$ if and only if $\langle s, t\rangle\langle u, v\rangle$ is an innermost chain.

For the purpose of automation we again need an approximation, because in general it is undecidable whether two dependency pairs form an innermost chain. Analogous to Definition 5.4.18, one can define an estimated *innermost* dependency graph. In order to test whether a dependency pair $\langle u, v\rangle$ can follow another dependency pair $\langle s, t\rangle$ in an innermost chain, the subterms in t that have a defined root symbol are replaced with new variables and then it is checked whether this modification of t unifies with u. In contrast to Subsection 5.4.1, however, one does not have to rename multiple occurrences of the same variable. This is because for every variable $x \in \mathcal{V}ar(t)$ the term $x\sigma$ must be in normal form and hence it cannot be reduced (to different terms).

Definition 5.6.16 The *estimated innermost dependency graph* of a TRS $\mathcal{R}$ is the directed graph whose nodes are the dependency pairs and that has an arc from $\langle s, t\rangle$ to $\langle u, v\rangle$ if $\text{CAP}(t)$ and u are unifiable by a most general unifier σ such that $s\sigma$ and $u\sigma$ are normal forms.

In the innermost dependency graph of our example, there are arcs from dependency pair (5.18) to every dependency pair and there are arcs from dependency pair (5.17) to dependency pair (5.19) and from dependency pair (5.19) to itself. There is no arc from dependency pair (5.17) to itself, however, because the terms $\text{CAP}(F(y_1, y_1, f(y_1, x_1, y_1))) = F(y_1, y_1, z)$ and $F(x_2, c(x_2), c(y_2))$ are not unifiable. In this example, the estimated innermost dependency graph coincides with the innermost dependency graph. Analogous to Theorem 5.4.13, for finite systems it is sufficient to consider every cycle separately.

Theorem 5.6.17 *A finite TRS $\mathcal{R}$ is innermost terminating if and only if for every cycle $\mathcal{P}$ in the innermost dependency graph there is no infinite innermost $\mathcal{R}$-chain of dependency pairs from $\mathcal{P}$.*

Proof The proof is similar to the proof of Theorem 5.4.13. □

In our example, the cycles in the innermost dependency graph are $\{(5.18)\}$ and $\{(5.19)\}$. Note that there are no usable rules for the cycles.

Theorem 5.6.18 *A finite TRS $\mathcal{R}$ is innermost terminating if for every cycle $\mathcal{P}$ in the (estimated) innermost dependency graph of $\mathcal{R}$ there is a quasi-reduction ordering $\succsim$ such that*

- *$l \succsim r$ for every rule $l \to r$ in $\mathcal{U}_{\mathcal{R}}(\mathcal{P})$,*
- *$s \succsim t$ for every dependency pair $\langle s, t\rangle$ in $\mathcal{P}$, and*
- *$s \succ t$ for at least one dependency pair $\langle s, t\rangle$ in $\mathcal{P}$.*

Proof The proof is similar to that of Theorem 5.4.14 (and Corollary 5.4.19, respectively). □

In our example, we obtain the following constraints:

$$\begin{array}{rcll} F(x, c(x), c(y)) & \succ_1 & F(y, x, y) & \text{for the cycle } \{(5.18)\} \\ F(s(x), y, z) & \succ_2 & F(x, s(c(y)), c(z)) & \text{for the cycle } \{(5.19)\} \end{array}$$

Innermost termination of the TRS under consideration can easily be proven automatically: choose $\succ_1$ to be the *lpo* that compares immediate subterms from right to left and $\succ_2$ to be the *lpo* that compares immediate subterms from left to right.

The following example shows that in contrast to Theorems 5.4.10 and 5.4.14 the reverse direction of Theorems 5.6.14 and 5.6.18 does not hold true.

Example 5.6.19 Consider the TRS $\mathcal{R}$ consisting of the rules

$$\begin{array}{rcl} f(a(x), y) & \to & g(x, y) \\ g(x, y) & \to & h(x, y) \\ h(0, y) & \to & f(y, y) \\ a(0) & \to & 0 \end{array}$$

$\{\langle F(a(x), y), G(x, y)\rangle, \langle G(x, y), H(x, y)\rangle, \langle H(0, y), F(y, y)\rangle\}$ is the only cycle in the innermost dependency graph. In fact, this TRS is innermost terminating. However, the constraints of Theorem 5.6.18 imply

$$F(a(0), a(0)) \succsim G(0, a(0)) \succsim H(0, a(0)) \succsim F(a(0), a(0))$$

where one of these inequalities must be strict. Therefore, they cannot be satisfied by a quasi-reduction ordering.

In Theorems 5.6.14 and 5.6.18 one may also allow the use of AFSs.

Corollary 5.6.20 *A finite TRS $\mathcal{R}$ is terminating if for every cycle $\mathcal{P}$ in the (estimated) innermost dependency graph there is an AFS $\mathcal{A}$ and a quasi-reduction ordering $\succsim$ such that*

- $l\downarrow_{\mathcal{A}} \succsim r\downarrow_{\mathcal{A}}$ *for every rule* $l \to r$ *in* $\mathcal{U}_{\mathcal{R}}(\mathcal{P})$,
- $s\downarrow_{\mathcal{A}} \succsim t\downarrow_{\mathcal{A}}$ *for every dependency pair* $\langle s,t\rangle$ *in* $\mathcal{P}$, *and*
- $s\downarrow_{\mathcal{A}} \succ t\downarrow_{\mathcal{A}}$ *for at least one dependency pair* $\langle s,t\rangle$ *in* $\mathcal{P}$.

Proof This is an immediate consequence of Theorem 5.6.18 in conjunction with Lemma 5.4.16. □

Further refinements for automatically checking the innermost termination criterion can be found in [AG00].

5.6.3 Confluence and Innermost Termination

We saw in Chapter 4 that confluence is in general undecidable but decidable for terminating TRSs. It might happen that innermost termination of a TRS can be proven (automatically) by the dependency pair method but termination of the system cannot be proven (automatically). In this case one cannot apply the critical pair lemma 4.2.3 to decide confluence unless the system under consideration is an overlay system. It goes without saying that it would be nice to have a similar decision procedure for innermost terminating systems, too. Next we will discuss the question of whether confluence might be decidable for innermost terminating TRSs. (The TRS used in the undecidability proof in Section 4.1 is not innermost terminating.)

According to Theorem 4.2.5, a terminating TRS is convergent if and only if all its critical pairs are joinable. Hence the following question immediately arises: Does the theorem still hold if we weaken termination to innermost termination? The next example taken from [Gra95, example 3.15] shows that this approach is too simple-minded.

Example 5.6.21 Let $\mathcal{R}$ consist of the rules

$$
\begin{array}{rcl@{\qquad\qquad}rcl}
f(b) & \to & a & f(c) & \to & d \\
f(b) & \to & f(c) & f(c) & \to & f(b) \\
b & \to & e & c & \to & e' \\
f(e) & \to & a & f(e') & \to & d
\end{array}
$$

We have, for example, the following reductions:

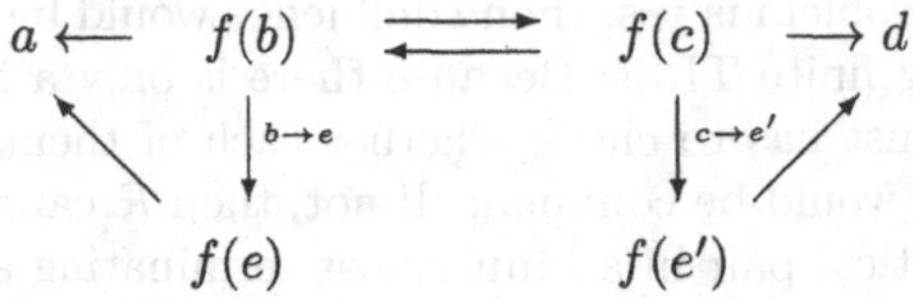

Obviously, $\mathcal{R}$ is not (outermost) terminating. We show that $\mathcal{R}$ is innermost terminating. The dependency pairs of $\mathcal{R}$ are $\langle F(b), F(c)\rangle$, $\langle F(b), C\rangle$, $\langle F(c), F(b)\rangle$, and $\langle F(c), B\rangle$. The estimated innermost dependency graph of $\mathcal{R}$ does not contain arcs because the terms $F(b)$ and $F(c)$ are not in normal form. Because there is no cycle in the estimated innermost dependency graph of $\mathcal{R}$, it (vacuously) follows from Theorem 5.6.18 that $\mathcal{R}$ is innermost terminating.

Observe that every critical pair is joinable, but $\mathcal{R}$ is obviously not confluent.

Therefore, a further restriction is necessary to obtain a critical pair lemma for innermost terminating TRSs. For example, one could demand that every critical pair be innermost joinable.

Definition 5.6.22 Let $\mathcal{R}$ be a TRS. Two terms s and t are *innermost joinable* if and only if they have a common reduct w.r.t. $\overset{i}{\to}_{\mathcal{R}}$.

As a matter of fact, for terminating systems joinability of all critical pairs is equivalent to innermost joinability of all critical pairs.

Lemma 5.6.23 *For a terminating TRS $\mathcal{R}$, the following statements are equivalent:*

1. *Every critical pair in $\mathcal{R}$ is joinable.*
2. *Every critical pair in $\mathcal{R}$ is innermost joinable.*

Proof The implication (2) $\Rightarrow$ (1) clearly holds. In order to show the converse direction, let $\langle s, t\rangle \in CP(\mathcal{R})$. Because every critical pair in $\mathcal{R}$ is joinable, $\mathcal{R}$ is convergent by Theorem 4.2.5. Therefore, $s \overset{i}{\to}{}^{*}_{\mathcal{R}} s\!\downarrow$ and $t \overset{i}{\to}{}^{*}_{\mathcal{R}} t\!\downarrow$, where $s\!\downarrow$ and $t\!\downarrow$ denote the unique normal forms of s and t, respectively. It follows $s\!\downarrow = t\!\downarrow$ because $\langle s, t\rangle \in CP(\mathcal{R})$. Hence s and t are innermost joinable. $\square$

Example 5.6.21 shows that the preceding lemma is not true for innermost terminating systems because the critical pair $\langle a, f(c)\rangle$ is joinable but not innermost joinable. Thus we pose the following open problem.

Open Problem: Suppose $\mathcal{R}$ is innermost terminating and every critical pair in $\mathcal{R}$ is innermost joinable. Does this imply that $\mathcal{R}$ is confluent?

If the answer to this problem is yes, then confluence would be decidable for innermost terminating finite TRSs: Because there is only a finite number of critical pairs, one just has to check whether each of them is innermost joinable. If so, then $\mathcal{R}$ would be confluent. If not, then $\mathcal{R}$ cannot be confluent (because every critical pair in an innermost terminating and confluent TRS is innermost joinable; cf. the proof of Lemma 5.6.23).

For overlay systems, the answer to this problem is yes. The major obstacle one encounters in attempts to prove that the same is true for nonoverlay systems is the fact that $\xrightarrow{i}_{\mathcal{R}}$ is not closed under substitutions.

6
Relative Undecidability

In order to motivate relative undecidability, let us consider the following scenario. All methods for proving termination of a TRS $\mathcal{R}$ fail but an implementation of the dependency pair method is able to prove innermost termination of $\mathcal{R}$ automatically. In view of the fact that nonterminating but innermost terminating systems hardly occur in practice, it is most likely that $\mathcal{R}$ is in fact terminating. But how can we prove this?

It would be very nice to have a decision procedure that takes an innermost terminating TRS $\mathcal{R}$ as input and decides whether $\mathcal{R}$ is terminating. However, we will prove that such a decision procedure cannot exist. In our terminology, we will show relative undecidability of the implication SN $\Rightarrow$ SIN.

The results in this chapter are not restricted to the implication SN $\Rightarrow$ SIN. We will systematically study relative undecidability in both the termination hierarchy and the confluence hierarchy. All undecidability results will be obtained by a reduction to Post's correspondence problem. The contents of this chapter cover most of the work published in Geser et al. [GMOZ97, GMOZ02a, GMOZ02b].

6.1 The Termination Hierarchy

In this section we will show *relative undecidability* of the following implications from the termination hierarchy

$$\omega\text{T} \;\Rightarrow\; \text{TT} \;\Rightarrow\; \text{ST} \;\Rightarrow\; \text{NSE} \;\Rightarrow\; \text{SN} \;\Rightarrow\; \text{NL} \;\Rightarrow\; \text{AC} \qquad (6.1)$$

for one-rule systems—TRSs consisting of a single rewrite rule. That is, we will show that for all implications $X \Rightarrow Y$ the property X is undecidable for one-rule TRSs satisfying property Y.

For many-rule systems, we will also show relative undecidability of the implications

$$\mathrm{SN} \Rightarrow \mathrm{SIN} \Rightarrow \mathrm{WIN} \Rightarrow \mathrm{WN} \tag{6.2}$$

We do not have such a result, however, for the implication PT $\Rightarrow$ ωT. This is not surprising because it is an open problem whether polynomial termination is undecidable.

Dauchet [Dau92] was the first to prove undecidability of termination for one-rule TRSs, by means of a reduction to the uniform halting problem for Turing machines. Middeldorp and Gramlich [MG95] reduced the undecidability of simple termination, nonself-embeddingness, and nonloopingness for one-rule TRSs to the uniform halting problem for linear bounded automata. Lescanne [Les94] showed that Dauchet's result can also be obtained by a reduction to Post's correspondence problem. The results presented in this section are stronger because (1) we obtain the same undecidability results for much smaller classes of one-rule TRSs, (2) we show the undecidability of total termination for one-rule (simply terminating) TRSs (so we solve problem 87 in [DJK95] and rectify a conjecture in [Zan95b]), and (3) we show the undecidability of ω-termination for one-rule totally terminating TRSs. The latter strengthens Geser's [Ges97] result that ω-termination is an undecidable property of totally terminating TRSs to the one-rule case.

We will obtain the relative undecidability results for one-rule systems by using PCP in the following uniform way: First we construct a TRS $\mathcal{U}(P,\mathcal{Q})$ parameterized by a PCP instance P and a TRS $\mathcal{Q}$. The TRS $\mathcal{U}(P,\mathcal{Q})$ has the following properties: (i) The left-hand sides of its rewrite rules are the same, (ii) if P admits no solution, then $\mathcal{U}(P,\mathcal{Q})$ is ω-terminating, and (iii) if P admits a solution, then $\mathcal{U}(P,\mathcal{Q})$ simulates $\mathcal{Q}$. Because of property (i) every $\mathcal{U}(P,\mathcal{Q})$ can be compressed into a one-rule TRS $\mathcal{S}(P,\mathcal{Q})$ without affecting (ii) and (iii). That is, if P admits no solution, then $\mathcal{S}(P,\mathcal{Q})$ is ω-terminating and if P admits a solution, then $\mathcal{S}(P,\mathcal{Q})$ simulates $\mathcal{Q}$. Finally, for all implications $X \Rightarrow Y$ in the hierarchy (6.1) we define a suitable TRS $\mathcal{Q}$ such that—by (ii) and (iii)—$\mathcal{S}(P,\mathcal{Q})$ satisfies Y and it satisfies X if and only if P admits no solution. The advantage of this approach is that the complicated part—the construction and properties of the TRS $\mathcal{U}(P,\mathcal{Q})$—is independent of the involved level in the termination hierarchy. The price to be paid is the complexity of the proof of property (ii). Nevertheless, it pays to take this uniform approach unless one is only interested in the lower implications of the hierarchy or in one special implication: in this case, an ad hoc proof might be easier to understand. Such ad hoc proofs can be found in [GMOZ97]. There, the relative undecidability results are obtained using PCP in the following way: For all implications $X \Rightarrow Y$ and for all PCP instances P a TRS is constructed that always satisfies Y and satisfies

X if and only if P admits no solution. In the same way, we will obtain the undecidability results for the implications in (6.2) and in the confluence hierarchy.

In this section, we proceed as follows. In Section 6.1.1 we define the TRS $\mathcal{U}(P, \mathcal{Q})$ and show that it simulates $\mathcal{Q}$ whenever P admits a solution. In Section 6.1.2 we present the difficult proof of ω-termination of $\mathcal{U}(P, \mathcal{Q})$ for PCP instances P that admit no solution. In Section 6.1.3 we transform $\mathcal{U}(P, \mathcal{Q})$ into a one-rule TRS $\mathcal{S}(P, \mathcal{Q})$. In the subsequent section, we instantiate $\mathcal{U}(P, \mathcal{Q})$ and $\mathcal{S}(P, \mathcal{Q})$ by suitable TRSs $\mathcal{Q}$ in order to conclude the desired relative undecidability results.

6.1.1 The TRS $\mathcal{U}(P, \mathcal{Q})$

We encode PCP instances P and, for each layer $X \Rightarrow Y$ of the hierarchy, a characteristic nonempty TRS $\mathcal{Q}$ into a TRS $\mathcal{U}(P, \mathcal{Q})$ such that $\mathcal{U}(P, \mathcal{Q})$ is in Y for all P and in X if and only if P has no solution. In order to facilitate the transformation (in Section 6.1.3) of $\mathcal{U}(P, \mathcal{Q})$ into a one-rule TRS $\mathcal{S}(P, \mathcal{Q})$, we require that all rewrite rules of $\mathcal{U}(P, \mathcal{Q})$ have the same left-hand side. It will inherit this property the TRS $\mathcal{Q}$.

The technical definition of $\mathcal{U}(P, \mathcal{Q})$ can be seen as an accumulation of a number of modifications of the following system from Zantema [Zan95b]:

$$\mathcal{S}_P = \begin{cases} F(w, \overline{a}(x), w, \overline{a}(x)) & \to & F(a(w), x, a(w), x) & \text{for all } a \in \Gamma \\ F(\alpha(w), x, \beta(y), z) & \to & F(w, \overline{\alpha}(x), y, \overline{\beta}(z)) & \text{for all } (\alpha, \beta) \in P \end{cases}$$

Here for every $a \in \Gamma$ two unary symbols a and $\overline{a}$ are defined, while

$$\alpha(t) = a_1(a_2(\cdots a_k(t)\cdots)) \quad \text{and} \quad \overline{\alpha}(t) = \overline{a}_k(\overline{a}_{k-1}(\cdots \overline{a}_1(t)\cdots))$$

for $\alpha = a_1 a_2 \ldots a_k$. The system $\mathcal{S}_P$ admits a cycle

$$F(\gamma(w), x, \gamma(w), x) \to^+ F(\gamma(w), x, \gamma(w), x)$$

if and only if γ is a solution of the PCP instance P. If P has no solution, then $\mathcal{S}_P$ is totally terminating. The use of barred symbols in the second and fourth argument of F is essential for the proof of total termination. It is now straightforward to change the cyclic behavior to any desired behavior that can be expressed by some nonempty TRS $\mathcal{Q}$. To this end F is equipped with an additional argument. This extra argument is left unchanged, except for the step that completes the cycle when it is rewritten by a rule in $\mathcal{Q}$. To avoid unintended rewrite steps, we refine control: We distinguish two states, exhibited by function symbols G and H, which enable only steps of the first and second shapes, respectively, in $\mathcal{S}_P$. A change from state G to state H is possible only if the second and fourth arguments are equal to ε. A change of state from H to G requires that the first and third arguments are equal to ε. This yields the TRS consisting of the rewrite rules

$$\begin{array}{rcll} G(w,\varepsilon,y,\varepsilon,\mathsf{LHS}) & \to & H(w,\varepsilon,y,\varepsilon,\mathsf{LHS}) & (1) \\ H(\alpha(w),x,\beta(y),z,\mathsf{LHS}) & \to & H(w,\overline{\alpha}(x),y,\overline{\beta}(z),\mathsf{LHS}) & (2) \\ H(\varepsilon,\overline{a}(x),\varepsilon,\overline{a}(z),\mathsf{LHS}) & \to & G(a(\varepsilon),x,a(\varepsilon),z,\mathsf{RHS}) & (3) \\ G(w,\overline{a}(x),y,\overline{a}(z),\mathsf{LHS}) & \to & G(a(w),x,a(y),z,\mathsf{LHS}) & (4) \end{array}$$

for every $(\alpha,\beta) \in P$, $a \in \Gamma$, and right-hand side RHS of the rewrite rules in $\mathcal{Q}$. Here LHS denotes the unique left-hand side of the rules in $\mathcal{Q}$. The TRS is linear whenever $\mathcal{Q}$ is linear.

Throughout the remainder of this section we assume that $\Gamma = \{0,1\}$. This entails no loss of generality. Writing n for the size of the PCP instance P and m for the number of rules of $\mathcal{Q}$, there is one rule of type (1), there are n rules of type (2), there are $2m$ rules of type (3), and there are two rules of type (4), hence there are $n + 2m + 3$ rules in total.

In view of the one-rule construction it is necessary to have equal left-hand sides. Subsequently we describe how to code the difference between G and H, the transfer of strings from one argument position to another argument position, and the treatment of the empty string. The accumulation of all of these modifications will yield the technical definition of the system $\mathcal{U}(P,\mathcal{Q})$ again consisting of $n+2m+3$ rules, in which the single left-hand side and all right-hand sides are of the shape $A(\cdots)$ for a symbol A of high arity. The encoding is highly inspired by Lescanne [Les94]. Basically, some of the matching is delayed and extra parameters serve for the delayed matching. Let us demonstrate the technique with a simple example. The TRS $\{f(a) \to f(a'), f(b) \to f(b')\}$ is translated into the TRS $\{f'(a,b,x) \to f'(x,b,a'), f'(a,b,x) \to f'(a,x,b')\}$. Rewrite steps $f(t) \to f(t')$ in the original system correspond to rewrite steps $f'(a,b,t) \to f'(a,b,t')$ in the translated system. Rewrite steps that have no counterpart in the original system, e.g., $f'(a,b,a) \to f'(a,a,b')$, produce an irreducible term.

For treating the difference between G and H we use four arguments of A. The system is transformed according to the following scheme:

Rule of shape	Is coded as
$G(\dots) \to H(\dots)$	$A(0,1,u,v,\dots) \to A(u,v,1,0,\dots)$
$H(\dots) \to H(\dots)$	$A(0,1,u,v,\dots) \to A(v,u,1,0,\dots)$
$H(\dots) \to G(\dots)$	$A(0,1,u,v,\dots) \to A(v,u,0,1,\dots)$
$G(\dots) \to G(\dots)$	$A(0,1,u,v,\dots) \to A(u,v,0,1,\dots)$

By coding $G(\dots)$ as $A(0,1,0,1,\dots)$ and $H(\dots)$ as $A(0,1,1,0,\dots)$ every rewrite step in the old system transforms to a rewrite step in the new system. Conversely, every rewrite step in the new system not corresponding to this coding of G and H will result in a term $A(1,0,\dots)$ not allowing further rewrite steps.

Next we describe the transfer of strings from one argument position to another argument position. In the system $\mathcal{S}_P$ string elements were coded by unary symbols. In order to allow variables as string elements we now choose another representation: Elements of Γ are represented by constants and combined into strings by a binary symbol cons. In order to distinguish between unbarred and barred strings as in $\mathcal{S}_P$ we introduce another binary symbol $\overline{\mathsf{cons}}$. For any term t and string $\alpha = t_1 t_2 \ldots t_n$ of terms we write

$$\alpha(t) = \mathsf{cons}(t_1, \mathsf{cons}(t_2, \ldots \mathsf{cons}(t_n, t) \ldots))$$

and

$$\overline{\alpha}(t) = \overline{\mathsf{cons}}(t_n, \overline{\mathsf{cons}}(t_{n-1}, \ldots \overline{\mathsf{cons}}(t_1, t) \ldots))$$

We introduce an extra constant \$ to mark the end of a string. The intention of the rules of type (2) is to enable a rewrite sequence

$$H(\gamma(\varepsilon), \varepsilon, \ldots) \to^+ H(\varepsilon, \overline{\gamma}(\varepsilon), \ldots)$$

for $\gamma = \alpha_{i_1} \alpha_{i_2} \ldots \alpha_{i_k}$ by means of rules of the shape

$$H(\alpha_i(x), y, \ldots) \to H(x, \overline{\alpha_i}(y), \ldots)$$

for $1 \leq i \leq n$. In the new notation the same can be achieved by a single left-hand side by adding $n+2$ arguments to the symbol A (the only $n+2$ arguments to be displayed for the moment) and choosing rules with left-hand side

$$A(\alpha_1(\varepsilon), \ldots, \alpha_n(\varepsilon), w_1 \ldots w_\mu(w), \overline{x_1}(x))$$

and right-hand sides

$$\begin{array}{l} A(\alpha_1(\varepsilon), \ldots, \alpha_{i-1}(\varepsilon), w_1 \ldots w_{|\alpha_i|}(\varepsilon), \alpha_{i+1}(\varepsilon), \ldots, \alpha_n(\varepsilon), \\ \quad w_{|\alpha_i|+1} \ldots w_\mu(w), \overline{x_1 \alpha_i}(x)) \end{array}$$

for $1 \leq i \leq n$. Here μ is a number satisfying $|\alpha_i| \leq \mu$ for all $1 \leq i \leq n$, and x, x_1, w, and $w_1, \ldots, w_\mu$ are fresh variables. The objective of $w_1 \ldots w_{|\alpha_i|}(\varepsilon)$ in the right-hand sides at the position of α_i is that rewriting can only be continued if the variables $w_1, \ldots, w_{|\alpha_i|}$ are instantiated by the successive elements of the string α_i. In this way we obtain the rewrite sequence

$$\begin{array}{ll} & A(\alpha_1(\varepsilon), \ldots, \alpha_n(\varepsilon), \gamma(t_1), \overline{\$}(x)) \\ \to & A(\alpha_1(\varepsilon), \ldots, \alpha_n(\varepsilon), \alpha_{i_2} \ldots \alpha_{i_k}(t_1), \overline{\$\alpha_{i_1}}(x)) \\ \to^* & A(\alpha_1(\varepsilon), \ldots, \alpha_n(\varepsilon), \alpha_{i_k}(t_1), \overline{\$\alpha_{i_1} \ldots \alpha_{i_{k-1}}}(x)) \\ \to & A(\alpha_1(\varepsilon), \ldots, \alpha_n(\varepsilon), t_1, \overline{\$\gamma}(x)) \end{array}$$

for $\gamma = \alpha_{i_1} \alpha_{i_2} \ldots \alpha_{i_k}$ and $t_1 = \$w_2 \ldots w_\mu(w)$. Here the variables after \$ in t_1 are needed to perform the last few steps in the rewrite sequence if the length of the remaining string to be transferred is less than μ. (Actually, any term t_1 of the form $s_1 \ldots s_\mu(s)$ will do here.)

The next thing to do is to represent the element-wise backward transfer of strings as is done by the rules of type (3) and (4). This is simpler than the forward transfer described earlier. We need three new arguments of A to code this; the arguments $w_1 \ldots w_\mu(w)$ and $\overline{x_1}(x)$, as they occur in the left-hand side, are also involved because the real string transfer has to take place here. For the moment we will only consider these five arguments of A. For transferring a "0" or "1" by rule (3) we provide rules

$$A(0, 1, \$, w_1 \ldots w_\mu(w), \overline{x_1}(x)) \to A(x_1, 1, w_1, 0\$w_2 \ldots w_\mu(w), x)$$

and

$$A(0, 1, \$, w_1 \ldots w_\mu(w), \overline{x_1}(x)) \to A(0, x_1, w_1, 1\$w_2 \ldots w_\mu(w), x)$$

For transferring a "0" or "1" by rule (4) we have rules

$$A(0, 1, \$, w_1 \ldots w_\mu(w), \overline{x_1}(x)) \to A(x_1, 1, \$, 0w_1 \ldots w_\mu(w), x)$$

and

$$A(0, 1, \$, w_1 \ldots w_\mu(w), \overline{x_1}(x)) \to A(0, x_1, \$, 1w_1 \ldots w_\mu(w), x)$$

These rules allow the full backward transfer

$$A(0, 1, \$, t_1, \overline{\$\gamma}(x)) \to^+ A(0, 1, \$, \gamma(t_1), \overline{\$}(x))$$

for $t_1 = \$w_2 \ldots w_\mu(w)$. Note that for continuation after the first step in this rewrite sequence it is essential that t_1 starts with \$.

Just like in the rules of type (2) the αs and βs are transferred simultaneously; in our system we will similarly add $n+2$ arguments again in order to simultaneously transfer βs, and another three arguments for elementwise backward transfer. In this way the arity of A becomes $2n + 15$: four arguments for coding the difference between G and H, $2(n + 2 + 3) = 2n + 10$ for transferring strings, and one final argument to contain LHS or RHS from $\mathcal{Q}$. In order to obtain rewrite sequences that have a consecutive group of nonchanging arguments (which will be very convenient when we present statements and proofs about the construction later), the arguments are not ordered in the way we just introduced them. Instead they are ordered as follows:

- arguments $1, 2, 2n + 9, 2n + 10$ are the four arguments for coding the difference between G and H;
- arguments $6, \ldots, n + 5$ are the n arguments for coding the matching with the αs;
- arguments $2n+11$ and $2n+12$ are the arguments in which the string transfer of the αs takes place as in the first two arguments of G and H;

- arguments 3, 4, and 5 are the three arguments for coding the elementwise backward transfer of the string consisting of αs;
- arguments $n+9, \dots, 2n+8$ are the n arguments for coding the matching with the βs;
- arguments $2n+13$ and $2n+14$ are the arguments in which the string transfer of the βs takes place as in the third and fourth argument of G and H;
- arguments $n+6$, $n+7$, and $n+8$ are the three arguments for coding the elementwise backward transfer of the string consisting of βs; and
- argument $2n+15$ contains LHS or RHS from $\mathcal{Q}$.

Combining all parts of the construction as described earlier in this order, we arrive at the following definition where (I), (II), (III), and (IV) refer to transformations of the rules of type (1), (2), (3), and (4), respectively.

Definition 6.1.1 Let $P = \{(\alpha_1, \beta_1), \dots, (\alpha_n, \beta_n)\}$ be an arbitrary PCP instance and let $\mathcal{Q} = \{\mathsf{LHS} \to \mathsf{RHS}_1, \dots, \mathsf{LHS} \to \mathsf{RHS}_m\}$ be a finite nonempty TRS with the property that all left-hand sides equal LHS. The maximum length of strings in P is denoted by μ: $\mu = \max\{|\alpha|, |\beta| \mid (\alpha, \beta) \in P\}$. We define the TRS $\mathcal{U}(P, \mathcal{Q})$ as follows. Its signature $\mathcal{F}_{\mathcal{U}}$ consists of the signature $\mathcal{F}_{\mathcal{Q}}$ of the TRS $\mathcal{Q}$ together with constants 0, 1, \$, and ε, binary function symbols cons and $\overline{\mathsf{cons}}$, and a function symbol A of arity $2n+15$. The TRS $\mathcal{U}(P, \mathcal{Q})$ consists of the rewrite rules $l \to r_i$, $1 \le i \le n+2m+3$, where l and r_i are defined as follows:

$$l = A(0, 1, 0, 1, \$, \alpha_1(\varepsilon), \dots, \alpha_n(\varepsilon), 0, 1, \$, \beta_1(\varepsilon), \dots, \beta_n(\varepsilon), u, v, w_1 \dots w_\mu(w), \overline{x_1}(x), y_1 \dots y_\mu(y), \overline{z_1}(z), \mathsf{LHS})$$

$$r_1 = A(u, v, 0, 1, x_1, \alpha_1(\varepsilon), \dots, \alpha_n(\varepsilon), 0, 1, z_1, \beta_1(\varepsilon), \dots, \beta_n(\varepsilon), 1, 0, w_1 \dots w_\mu(w), \overline{\$}(x), y_1 \dots y_\mu(y), \overline{\$}(z), \mathsf{LHS}) \quad \text{(I)}$$

$$r_{i+1} = A(v, u, 0, 1, \$, \alpha_1(\varepsilon), \dots, \alpha_{i-1}(\varepsilon), w_1 \dots w_{|\alpha_i|}(\varepsilon), \alpha_{i+1}(\varepsilon), \dots, \alpha_n(\varepsilon), 0, 1, \$, \beta_1(\varepsilon), \dots, \beta_{i-1}(\varepsilon), y_1 \dots y_{|\beta_i|}(\varepsilon), \beta_{i+1}(\varepsilon), \dots, \beta_n(\varepsilon), 1, 0, w_{|\alpha_i|+1} \dots w_\mu(w), \overline{x_1 \alpha_i}(x), y_{|\beta_i|+1} \dots y_\mu(y), \overline{z_1 \beta_i}(z), \mathsf{LHS}) \quad \text{(II)}$$

for all $1 \le i \le n$,

$$r_{n+1+j} = A(v, u, x_1, 1, w_1, \alpha_1(\varepsilon), \dots, \alpha_n(\varepsilon), z_1, 1, y_1, \beta_1(\varepsilon), \dots, \beta_n(\varepsilon), 0, 1, 0\$w_2 \dots w_\mu(w), x, 0\$y_2 \dots y_\mu(y), z, \mathsf{RHS}_j) \quad \text{(III)}$$

$$r_{n+1+m+j} = A(v, u, 0, x_1, w_1, \alpha_1(\varepsilon), \ldots, \alpha_n(\varepsilon), 0, z_1, y_1, \beta_1(\varepsilon), \ldots, \beta_n(\varepsilon), 0, 1, 1\$w_2 \ldots w_\mu(w), x, 1\$y_2 \ldots y_\mu(y), z, \mathsf{RHS}_j) \quad \text{(III)}$$

for all $1 \leq j \leq m$, and finally

$$r_{n+2m+2} = A(u, v, x_1, 1, \$, \alpha_1(\varepsilon), \ldots, \alpha_n(\varepsilon), z_1, 1, \$, \beta_1(\varepsilon), \ldots, \beta_n(\varepsilon), 0, 1, 0w_1 \ldots w_\mu(w), x, 0y_1 \ldots y_\mu(y), z, \mathsf{LHS}) \quad \text{(IV)}$$

$$r_{n+2m+3} = A(u, v, 0, x_1, \$, \alpha_1(\varepsilon), \ldots, \alpha_n(\varepsilon), 0, z_1, \$, \beta_1(\varepsilon), \ldots, \beta_n(\varepsilon), 0, 1, 1w_1 \ldots w_\mu(w), x, 1y_1 \ldots y_\mu(y), z, \mathsf{LHS}) \quad \text{(IV)}$$

Let $V = 0, 1, 0, 1, \$, \alpha_1(\varepsilon), \ldots, \alpha_n(\varepsilon), 0, 1, \$, \beta_1(\varepsilon), \ldots, \beta_n(\varepsilon)$ be the sequence of the first $2n + 8$ arguments of the left-hand side l and let $V_1, \ldots, V_{2n+8}$ denote its components.

The next lemma states that $\mathcal{U}(P, \mathcal{Q})$ can simulate root reductions in $\mathcal{Q}$ provided P admits a solution.

Lemma 6.1.2 *If the PCP instance P admits a solution, then there exist terms $W_1, \ldots, W_6$ such that for every rewrite rule* $\mathsf{LHS} \to \mathsf{RHS}$ *in $\mathcal{Q}$ there is a rewrite sequence*

$$A(V, W_1, \ldots, W_6, \mathsf{LHS}) \to^+_{\mathcal{U}(P,\mathcal{Q})} A(V, W_1, \ldots, W_6, \mathsf{RHS})$$

Proof Let $\gamma = \alpha_{i_1} \ldots \alpha_{i_k} = \beta_{i_1} \ldots \beta_{i_k} = \gamma' a$ be a solution of P. Define $t_1 = \$w_2 \ldots w_\mu(w)$, $t_2 = \$y_2 \ldots y_\mu(y)$, $W_1 = 0$, $W_2 = 1$, $W_3 = a(t_1)$, $W_4 = \overline{\$\gamma'}(x)$, $W_5 = a(t_2)$, and $W_6 = \overline{\$\gamma'}(z)$. It is easy to see that for every $\mathsf{LHS} \to \mathsf{RHS}$ in $\mathcal{Q}$ we have the following rewrite sequence in $\mathcal{U}(P, \mathcal{Q})$:

$$\begin{aligned}
& A(V, 0, 1, a(t_1), \overline{\$\gamma'}(x), a(t_2), \overline{\$\gamma'}(z), \mathsf{LHS}) \\
\to^*_{\text{(IV)}} \quad & A(V, 0, 1, \gamma(t_1), \overline{\$}(x), \gamma(t_2), \overline{\$}(z), \mathsf{LHS}) \\
\to_{\text{(I)}} \quad & A(V, 1, 0, \gamma(t_1), \overline{\$}(x), \gamma(t_2), \overline{\$}(z), \mathsf{LHS}) \\
\to_{\text{(II)}} \quad & A(V, 1, 0, \alpha_{i_2} \ldots \alpha_{i_k}(t_1), \overline{\$\alpha_{i_1}}(x), \beta_{i_2} \ldots \beta_{i_k}(t_2), \overline{\$\beta_{i_1}}(z), \mathsf{LHS}) \\
\to^*_{\text{(II)}} \quad & A(V, 1, 0, t_1, \overline{\$\gamma}(x), t_2, \overline{\$\gamma}(z), \mathsf{LHS}) \\
\to_{\text{(III)}} \quad & A(V, 0, 1, a(t_1), \overline{\$\gamma'}(x), a(t_2), \overline{\$\gamma'}(z), \mathsf{RHS})
\end{aligned}$$

□

Conversely, a rewrite sequence in $\mathcal{U}(P, \mathcal{Q})$ gives rise to either a rewrite sequence in $\mathcal{Q}$ or a rewrite sequence in $\mathcal{U}(P, \mathcal{Q})$ without the type (III) rules. We will denote the latter system by $\mathcal{U}_-(P, \mathcal{Q})$. From now on W and W' denote sequences of six arbitrary terms, and V' denotes a sequence of $2n+8$ arbitrary terms.

Lemma 6.1.3 *If W and the term t do not contain A symbols, then $A(V,W,t) \to_{\mathcal{U}(P,\mathcal{Q})} A(V',W',t')$ implies either $t \to_Q t'$ or both $t = t'$ and $A(V,W,t) \to_{\mathcal{U}_-(P,\mathcal{Q})} A(V',W',t)$.*

Proof Because there is only one A symbol in $A(V,W,t)$, the rewrite step must take place at the root position. If a rewrite rule of type (III) has been applied, then $t = \mathsf{LHS}\sigma \to_Q \mathsf{RHS}\sigma = t'$ for some rewrite rule $\mathsf{LHS} \to \mathsf{RHS}$ in $\mathcal{Q}$ and substitution σ. Otherwise, $A(V,W,t) \to_{\mathcal{U}_-(P,\mathcal{Q})} A(V',W',t')$, which obviously implies $t = t'$ by the form of the rules in $\mathcal{U}_-(P,\mathcal{Q})$. □

6.1.2 ω-Termination of $\mathcal{U}(P,\mathcal{Q})$

In this somewhat lengthy section we will show ω-termination of $\mathcal{U}(P,\mathcal{Q})$ for PCP instances P that do not have a solution and of $\mathcal{U}_-(P,\mathcal{Q})$ for arbitrary PCP instances P. Because we prefer not to treat the two cases separately, we write $\mathcal{U}'(P,\mathcal{Q})$ to denote either $\mathcal{U}(P,\mathcal{Q})$ under the assumption that P admits no solution or $\mathcal{U}_-(P,\mathcal{Q})$ without any assumptions on P.

The proof is quite complicated, so readers may want to skip it on first reading. The basic idea of the proof is similar to the one in Geser [Ges97], but the details are more intricate here.

First we will show that the length of rewrite sequences in $\mathcal{U}'(P,\mathcal{Q})$ is bounded. For a term t, let $\|t\|$ denote the maximal length of the "mixed" string $\zeta \in \{0,1,\overline{0},\overline{1}\}^*$ such that $t = \zeta(t')$ for some term t'.

Lemma 6.1.4 *No rewrite sequence in $\mathcal{U}'(P,\mathcal{Q})$ starting from a term $t = A(V,W,t')$ contains more than $1+4\|W_3\|+3\|W_4\|$ steps at the root position.*

Proof First we consider the case that $\mathcal{U}'(P,\mathcal{Q}) = \mathcal{U}(P,\mathcal{Q})$ and thus P lacks a solution. Consider a maximal rewrite sequence in $\mathcal{U}(P,\mathcal{Q})$ starting from t. Because rewrite steps that take place inside the first $2n+14$ arguments of t cannot create a redex at the root position, we may assume without loss of generality that there are no rewrite steps inside the first $2n+14$ arguments. This reasoning does not apply to the last argument of t because the left-hand side LHS of the rewrite rules in $\mathcal{Q}$ need not be linear. However, by taking $t' = \mathsf{LHS}\sigma = \mathsf{RHS}\sigma$ for some substitution σ, we are assured that there are no rewrite sequences starting from $A(V,W,t'')$ that have more steps at the root position than $A(V,W,t')$. (In other words, for the purpose of proving this lemma we may assume without loss of generality that $\mathcal{Q} = \{d \to d\}$.) So all steps in the maximal rewrite sequence starting from $t = A(V,W,t')$ take place at the root position.

We will write $\mathrm{root}'(s) = s'$ ($\mathrm{root}'(s) = \overline{s'}$) to indicate that $s = \mathsf{cons}(s',s'')$ ($s = \overline{\mathsf{cons}}(s',s'')$) for some term s''. For a proof by contradiction, consider a rewrite sequence starting from t that contains more than $1+4\|W_3\|+3\|W_4\|$ steps at the root position. We are going to show that P has a solution. We must have $(W_1,W_2) = (0,1)$ or $(W_1,W_2) = (1,0)$. First we consider the former.

All terms of the rewrite sequence, except possibly the last, are of the form $A(V, \ldots)$. Due to the fact that there must be changes in the state (W_1, W_2), the given rewrite sequence without its last step is a prefix of a rewrite sequence of the form

$$t \rightarrow^*_{(\mathrm{IV})} t^1 \rightarrow_{(\mathrm{I})} t^2 \rightarrow^*_{(\mathrm{II})} t^3 \rightarrow_{(\mathrm{III})} t^4 \rightarrow^*_{(\mathrm{IV})} t^5 \rightarrow_{(\mathrm{I})} t^6 \rightarrow \cdots \tag{6.3}$$

By the forms of the rules we can reason as follows.

In (6.3) we must have $t^1 = A(V, 0, 1, W_3^1, W_4^1, W_5^1, W_6^1, t')$ with

$$W_3^1 = \gamma(W_3) \qquad W_5^1 = \gamma(W_5)$$
$$\overline{\gamma}(W_4^1) = W_4 \qquad \overline{\gamma}(W_6^1) = W_6$$

for some $\gamma \in \{0,1\}^*$. Likewise, $t^2 = A(V, 1, 0, W_3^2, W_4^2, W_5^2, W_6^2, t')$ with $\mathrm{root}'(W_4^1) = \mathrm{root}'(W_6^1) = \$$ and

$$W_3^2 = W_3^1 \qquad W_5^2 = W_5^1$$
$$W_4^2 = W_4^1 \qquad W_6^2 = W_6^1$$

Furthermore, $t^3 = A(V, 1, 0, W_3^3, W_4^3, W_5^3, W_6^3, t')$ with

$$\alpha(W_3^3) = W_3^2 \qquad \beta(W_5^3) = W_5^2$$
$$W_4^3 = \overline{\alpha}(W_4^2) \qquad W_6^3 = \overline{\beta}(W_6^2)$$

and $\alpha = \alpha_{i_1} \ldots \alpha_{i_k}$ and $\beta = \beta_{i_1} \ldots \beta_{i_k}$ with $k \geq 0$ and $1 \leq i_j \leq n$ for all $1 \leq j \leq k$. Here k denotes the number of steps of type (II). Next, $t^4 = A(V, 0, 1, W_3^4, W_4^4, W_5^4, W_6^4, t')$ with $\mathrm{root}'(W_3^3) = \mathrm{root}'(W_5^3) = \$$ and

$$W_3^4 = i(W_3^3) \qquad W_5^4 = i(W_5^3)$$
$$\overline{i}(W_4^4) = W_4^3 \qquad \overline{i}(W_6^4) = W_6^3$$

for some $i \in \{0,1\}$. Next, $t^5 = A(V, 0, 1, W_3^5, W_4^5, W_5^5, W_6^5, t')$ with

$$W_3^5 = \delta(W_3^4) \qquad W_5^5 = \delta(W_5^4)$$
$$\overline{\delta}(W_4^5) = W_4^4 \qquad \overline{\delta}(W_6^5) = W_6^4$$

for some $\delta \in \{0,1\}^*$. Finally, $t^6 = A(V, 1, 0, \ldots)$ with $\mathrm{root}'(W_4^5) = \mathrm{root}'(W_6^5) = \$$. We have $\overline{i}(W_4^4) = \overline{\alpha}(W_4^2)$ and $\overline{i}(W_6^4) = \overline{\beta}(W_6^2)$. So there exist $\alpha', \beta' \in \{0,1\}^*$ such that $\alpha = \alpha' i$ and $\beta = \beta' i$. In particular, because $\alpha = \alpha_{i_1} \ldots \alpha_{i_k}$ (and $\beta = \beta_{i_1} \ldots \beta_{i_k}$), $k > 0$. We have $W_4^4 = \overline{\alpha'}(W_4^2) = \overline{\delta}(W_4^5)$ with $\mathrm{root}'(W_4^2) = \mathrm{root}'(W_4^5) = \$$. This implies that $\alpha' = \delta$. In the same way we obtain $\beta' = \delta$. Hence $\alpha = \beta$. In other words, P has a solution. Because this contradicts our assumption we conclude that rewrite sequence (6.3) cannot go beyond t^5. It still must be shown that there are at most $1 + 4\|W_3\| + 3\|W_4\|$ steps until t_5 is reached.

The sequence from t to t^1 contains $|\gamma|$ steps and clearly $|\gamma| \leq \|W_4\|$. Recall that $\alpha, \beta \in \{0,1\}^+$ for all $(\alpha, \beta) \in P$. So in every step in the sequence from t^2 to t^3 at least one symbol of W_3^2 is consumed. It follows that $k \leq \|W_3^2\|$. Because $W_3^2 = \gamma(W_3)$, we have $\|W_3^2\| = |\gamma| + \|W_3\| \leq \|W_3\| + \|W_4\|$. Next consider the sequence from t^4 to t^5. This part contains $|\delta|$ steps. Because $\delta i = \alpha$ and $|\alpha| \leq \|W_3^2\|$, we obtain $|\delta| \leq \|W_3\| + \|W_4\| - 1$. By putting everything together we obtain

$$\begin{aligned} &\|W_4\| + 1 + (\|W_3\| + \|W_4\|) + 1 + (\|W_3\| + \|W_4\| - 1) \\ &= 1 + 2\|W_3\| + 3\|W_4 \end{aligned}$$

as an upper bound for the maximum length of the sequence from t to t_5 in (6.3) and clearly $1 + 2\|W_3\| + 3\|W_4\| \leq 1 + 4\|W_3\| + 3\|W_4\|$.

In the other case we have $(W_1, W_2) = (1, 0)$. By using very similar arguments as earlier we obtain $4\|W_3\| + 2\|W_4\|$ as an upper bound on the maximum number of rewrite steps at the root position in a rewrite sequence starting from t. Because $4\|W_3\| + 2\|W_4\| < 1 + 4\|W_3\| + 3\|W_4\|$ this proves the lemma in the case that $\mathcal{U}'(P, \mathcal{Q}) = \mathcal{U}(P, \mathcal{Q})$ and P admits no solution.

Next we consider the case that $\mathcal{U}'(P, \mathcal{Q}) = \mathcal{U}_-(P, \mathcal{Q})$. If $(W_1, W_2) = (0, 1)$ then we obtain $1 + \|W_3\| + 2\|W_4\|$ as an upper bound on the maximum number of rewrite steps at the root position in a rewrite sequence starting from t; note that rewrite sequence (6.3) cannot go beyond t^3 because there are no rules of type (III) in $\mathcal{U}_-(P, \mathcal{Q})$. Similarly, if $(W_1, W_2) = (1, 0)$, then we obtain the upper bound $\|W_3\|$. Because both bounds do not exceed $1 + \|W_3\| + 2\|W_4\|$, the lemma also holds for $\mathcal{U}'(P, \mathcal{Q}) = \mathcal{U}_-(P, \mathcal{Q})$. □

Definition 6.1.5 Let $\mathsf{len}(W)$ denote the maximum number of root rewrite steps in any rewrite sequence in $\mathcal{U}'(P, \mathcal{Q})$ starting from a term of the form $A(V, W, t)$.

The following result is an immediate consequence of Lemma 6.1.4.

Corollary 6.1.6 *The function* len *satisfies* $\mathsf{len}(W) \leq 1 + 4\|W_3\| + 3\|W_4\|$.

We will define an interpretation [ ] into the positive integers that can orient all ground instances of the rewrite rules in $\mathcal{U}'(P, \mathcal{Q})$ from left to right.

We start by defining a few useful auxiliary functions on the positive integers $\mathbb{N}_+$. Let $\ell(x)$ denote the number of digits in the decimal representation of a positive integer x and let $\ell(0) = 0$. Define two binary operators $\circ$ and $\uparrow$ on nonnegative integers by

$$\begin{aligned} x \circ y &= 10^{\ell(y)} \cdot x + y \\ x \uparrow 0 &= 0 \\ x \uparrow (y + 1) &= x \uparrow y \circ x \end{aligned}$$

We will assume that $\circ$ binds more weakly than $+$ and $\uparrow$. Informally, $x \circ y$ yields the concatenation of the decimal representations of x and y without leading zeros and the expression $x \uparrow y$ denotes the y-fold repetition of x. Both functions are strictly monotone in all arguments, $\circ$ is associative, and the identities $\ell(x \circ y) = \ell(x) + \ell(y)$ and $\ell(x \uparrow y) = y \cdot \ell(x)$ hold. A function $\mathsf{code}\colon \mathbb{N}_+ \to \mathbb{N}_+$ is defined to take the octal representation of its argument and adds 2 to every digit greater than 4. The resulting digit sequence is the decimal representation of the result. For example, $\mathsf{code}(11209) = 27911$ as $(11209)_{10} = (25711)_8$. Note that code is strictly monotone. Note furthermore that $\mathsf{code}(x)$ does not contain the digits 5 and 6. It is not difficult to see that code is the smallest function with these two properties.

We will define the interpretation of all function symbols except A.

Definition 6.1.7 We interpret function symbols in $\{\varepsilon, \$, 0, 1, \mathsf{cons}, \overline{\mathsf{cons}}\}$ as follows:

$$\begin{aligned}
[\varepsilon] &= 1 \\
[\$] &= 2 \\
[0] &= 3 \\
[1] &= 4 \\
[\mathsf{cons}](x, y) &= y \circ 5 \circ x \circ 6 \\
[\overline{\mathsf{cons}}](x, y) &= 5 \circ x \circ 6 \circ y \circ 7 \uparrow (2 + \ell(x))
\end{aligned}$$

Every k-ary function symbol f in the signature of $\mathcal{Q}$ is interpreted as follows:

$$[f](x_1, \ldots, x_k) = \begin{cases} 10 \cdot \mathsf{code}(x_1 + \cdots + x_k) & \text{if } k > 0 \\ 10 & \text{if } k = 0 \end{cases}$$

Before we can extend the interpretation to A, we need a few more auxiliary functions, some of that depend on the interpretation of terms over $\mathcal{F}_{\mathcal{U}} \setminus \{A\}$.

For the treatment of the last argument of A we first define two unary functions $\phi_{\mathcal{Q}}$ and $\psi_{\mathcal{Q}}$ that depend on the TRS $\mathcal{Q}$. Function $\phi_{\mathcal{Q}}$ estimates the growth of the last argument of A caused by an application of a type (III) rewrite rule of $\mathcal{U}'(P, \mathcal{Q})$: For every upper bound x of the interpretations of LHS, $\phi_{\mathcal{Q}}(x)$ is an upper bound of the corresponding interpretations of RHS, for all $\mathsf{LHS} \to \mathsf{RHS} \in \mathcal{Q}$. Function $\phi_{\mathcal{Q}}\colon \mathbb{N}_+ \to \mathbb{N}_+$ is defined as follows:

$$\phi_{\mathcal{Q}}(x) = \max\ \{x\} \cup \{[\theta](\mathsf{RHS}) \mid \mathsf{LHS} \to \mathsf{RHS} \in \mathcal{Q} \text{ and } [\theta](\mathsf{LHS}) \le x\}$$

Because LHS and RHS only contain function symbols in the signature of $\mathcal{Q}$, we can compute $[\theta](\mathsf{LHS})$ and $[\theta](\mathsf{RHS})$ for every assignment θ of positive integers for the variables in $\mathsf{LHS} \to \mathsf{RHS}$. Here $[\theta](t)$ for $t \in \mathcal{T}(\mathcal{F}_{\mathcal{Q}}, \mathcal{V})$ is inductively defined as follows:

$$[\theta](t) = \begin{cases} [f]([\theta](t_1), \ldots, [\theta](t_k)) & \text{if } t = f(t_1, \ldots, t_k) \text{ with } k \geq 0 \\ \theta(t) & \text{if } t \in \mathcal{V} \end{cases}$$

Because the interpretation of every function symbol in $\mathcal{Q}$ is strictly monotone in all its arguments—an immediate consequence of the strict monotonicity of $\circ$ and code—there can only be a finite number of assignments θ such that $[\theta](\mathsf{LHS}) \leq x$ for a given $x \in \mathbb{N}_+$. Hence the maximum is formed over a finite computable set and thus the function $\phi_{\mathcal{Q}}$ is well-defined. Note that for every ground instance $t \to u$ of a rewrite rule in $\mathcal{Q}$, we have $\phi_{\mathcal{Q}}([t]) \geq [u]$. It is easy to check that $\phi_{\mathcal{Q}}$ is monotone and that $\phi_{\mathcal{Q}}(x) \geq x$ holds. Function $\psi_{\mathcal{Q}} \colon \mathbb{N} \times \mathbb{N}_+ \to \mathbb{N}_+$ is used to compensate a potential increase of the last argument of A along an application of a type (III) rewrite rule of $\mathcal{U}'(P, \mathcal{Q})$. It is defined inductively as follows:

$$\psi_{\mathcal{Q}}(0, y) = y + 1$$
$$\psi_{\mathcal{Q}}(x + 1, y) = y + \psi_{\mathcal{Q}}(x, \phi_{\mathcal{Q}}(y))$$

One easily verifies that $\psi_{\mathcal{Q}}$ is strictly monotone in both arguments.

One more auxiliary function is needed before we can define the interpretation of function symbol A. The interpretation defined earlier has the property that for a ground term t not containing any A symbol, the top part of t that consists of symbols in $\{\mathsf{cons}, \overline{\mathsf{cons}}, \varepsilon, \$, 0, 1\}$ can be extracted from $[t]$. A suitable extraction function π is defined next.

Definition 6.1.8 The function $\pi \colon \mathbb{N}_+ \to \mathcal{T}(\mathcal{F})$ from positive integers to ground terms is inductively defined as follows:

$$\pi(x) = \begin{cases} \varepsilon & \text{if } x = 1 \\ \$ & \text{if } x = 2 \\ 0 & \text{if } x = 3 \\ 1 & \text{if } x = 4 \\ \mathsf{cons}(\pi(y), \pi(z)) & \text{if } x = z \circ 5 \circ y \circ 6 \text{ with } y > 0 \text{ well-balanced} \\ \overline{\mathsf{cons}}(\pi(y), \pi(z)) & \text{if } x = 5 \circ y \circ 6 \circ z \circ 7 \uparrow (2 + \ell(y)) \text{ with} \\ & y > 0 \text{ well-balanced} \\ A(\varepsilon, \ldots, \varepsilon) & \text{otherwise} \end{cases}$$

Here for well-definedness we require that the digits 5 ("left parenthesis") and 6 ("right parenthesis") form a well-balanced sequence in the decimal representation of y in the fifth and sixth clauses of the definition. Formally, the decimal representation of a natural number is well-balanced if it is generated by the context-free grammar

$$\begin{aligned} S &\to 5S6 \mid SS \mid T \mid 56 \\ T &\to 0 \mid 1 \mid 2 \mid 3 \mid 4 \mid 7 \mid 8 \mid 9 \end{aligned}$$

with start symbol S. For example, 123 and 1556576236 are well-balanced numbers but 65 is not.

The premise on y in the fifth and sixth clauses of the definition ensures well-definedness of the definition of π.

Lemma 6.1.9 *The function π is well-defined.*

Proof First we show that there is no ambiguity in the fifth clause of the definition of π. Suppose, on the contrary, that there exists $x \in \mathbb{N}_+$ such that $x = z \circ 5 \circ y \circ 6 = z' \circ 5 \circ y' \circ 6$ with different well-balanced $y, y' > 0$. Without loss of generality, assume that $y > y'$. Then $y = z'' \circ 5 \circ y'$ for some $z'' \in \mathbb{N}$. However, because y' is well-balanced, y cannot be well-balanced (as there is no 6 in y' that corresponds to the displayed 5 in y). A similar argument shows that there is no ambiguity in the sixth clause of the definition of π. □

For example,

$$\begin{aligned}\pi(156655635626) &= \pi(1566 \circ 5 \circ 563562 \circ 6) = \mathsf{cons}(\pi(563562), \pi(1566)) \\ &= \mathsf{cons}(A(\varepsilon, \ldots, \varepsilon), A(\varepsilon, \ldots, \varepsilon))\end{aligned}$$

and $\pi(5462777536) = \mathsf{cons}(\pi(3), \pi(5462777)) = \mathsf{cons}(0, \overline{\mathsf{cons}}(1, \$))$.

We need two more definitions:

$$\begin{aligned}\mathsf{revc}(x, y) &= x \circ y \circ 7 \uparrow \ell(x) \\ \mathsf{bound}(x, y) &= 6\ell(x) + 3\ell(y)\end{aligned}$$

The function revc (for "reverse concatenation") is strictly monotone and bound is monotone in both arguments.

Definition 6.1.10 The interpretation $[A]$ is defined as follows:

$$[A](x_1, \ldots, x_{2n+15}) = \mathsf{code}(\psi_Q(D(x_1, \ldots, x_{2n+14}), x_{2n+15})) \circ 8$$

Here $D(x_1, \ldots, x_{2n+14})$ denotes the expression

$$\begin{aligned}&\left(\prod_{i=1}^{2n+8} \chi(x_i \geq [V_i])\right) \cdot E(x_1, \ldots, x_{2n+14}) \\ &+ \left(1 - \prod_{i=1}^{2n+8} \chi(x_i \geq [V_i])\right) \cdot \left(\sum_{i=1}^{2n+14} x_i\right)\end{aligned}$$

$\chi\colon \{\mathsf{false}, \mathsf{true}\} \to \{0, 1\}$ is defined by $\chi(\mathsf{false}) = 0$ and $\chi(\mathsf{true}) = 1$, and $E(x_1, \ldots, x_{2n+14})$ denotes the expression

$$\begin{aligned}&\mathsf{len}(\pi(x_{2n+9}), \ldots, \pi(x_{2n+14})) \\ &+ \mathsf{bound}(x_{2n+11}, x_{2n+12}) \cdot \mathsf{factor}(x_1, \ldots, x_{2n+14})\end{aligned}$$

where $\mathsf{factor}(x_1, \ldots, x_{2n+14})$ is an abbreviation for

$$2(x_{2n+9} + x_{2n+10}) + \mathsf{revc}(x_{2n+11}, x_{2n+12}) + \mathsf{revc}(x_{2n+13}, x_{2n+14}) + \sum_{i=1}^{2n+8} x_i$$

Note that $D(x_1, \ldots, x_{2n+14}) = E(x_1, \ldots, x_{2n+14})$ if $x_i \geq [V_i]$ for all $1 \leq i \leq 2n + 8$. If there is at least one $1 \leq i \leq 2n + 8$ such that $x_i < [V_i]$, then $D(x_1, \ldots, x_{2n+14}) = \sum_{i=1}^{2n+14} x_i$.

Lemma 6.1.11 *For every ground term t the decimal representation of its interpretation* $[t]$ *has a well-balanced sequence of* 5 *and* 6 *digits.*

Proof We use induction on the structure of t. If $t \in \{\varepsilon, \$, 0, 1\}$, then the decimal representation of $[t]$ does not contain any 5 or 6. If $t = \mathsf{cons}(t_1, t_2)$ or $t = \overline{\mathsf{cons}}(t_1, t_2)$, then the result follows from the induction hypothesis. If $t = A(t_1, \ldots, t_{2n+15})$ or $t = f(t_1, \ldots, t_k)$ with $f \in \mathcal{F}_{\mathcal{Q}}$, then the decimal representation of $[t]$ does not contain any 5 or 6 by the definition of the function code. □

The next lemma states that $\pi([t])$ is sufficiently close to t.

Definition 6.1.12 Let $\sim$ be the smallest congruence on ground terms such that $t \sim t'$ holds if $\mathrm{root}(t), \mathrm{root}(t') \in \{A\} \cup \mathcal{F}_{\mathcal{Q}}$. In other words, $t \sim t'$ if the top parts consisting of symbols in $\{\varepsilon, \$, 0, 1, \mathsf{cons}, \overline{\mathsf{cons}}\}$ in t and t' coincide. Let us call a term over the restricted signature $\{\varepsilon, \$, 0, 1, \mathsf{cons}, \overline{\mathsf{cons}}\}$ *pure*. We extend $\sim$ to sequences of terms componentwise.

If $f \in \mathcal{F}_{\mathcal{Q}}$, then $\mathsf{cons}(0, \mathsf{cons}(1, A(\ldots))) \sim \mathsf{cons}(0, \mathsf{cons}(1, f(\ldots)))$ for all sequences of arguments of A and f, for example. On the other hand, $\overline{\mathsf{cons}}(0, \varepsilon) \not\sim \overline{\mathsf{cons}}(1, \varepsilon)$.

Lemma 6.1.13 *If t is a ground term, then* $\pi([t]) \sim t$. *In addition, if t is pure, then* $\pi([t]) = t$.

Proof Let t be a ground term. We prove that $\pi([t]) \sim t$ by induction on the structure of t. The base case is an immediate consequence of the definitions of $[\,]$ and π. Suppose $t = \mathsf{cons}(t_1, t_2)$. We have $[t] = [t_2] \circ 5 \circ [t_1] \circ 6$. According to Lemma 6.1.11, the subsequence of the digits 5 and 6 in $[t_1]$ is well-balanced. Hence $\pi([t]) = \mathsf{cons}(\pi([t_1]), \pi([t_2])) \sim \mathsf{cons}(t_1, t_2)$ by the definition of π and the induction hypothesis. The case $t = \overline{\mathsf{cons}}(t_1, t_2)$ is just as easy. If $\mathrm{root}(t) = A$ or $\mathrm{root}(t) \in \mathcal{F}_{\mathcal{Q}}$, then the decimal representation of $[t]$ ends with the digit 8 or 0. Hence $\pi([t]) = A(\varepsilon, \ldots, \varepsilon)$ and thus $\pi([t]) \sim t$ by the definition of $\sim$.

To conclude the latter statement, according to the former statement and the definition of $\sim$, it is sufficient to show that $\pi([t])$ is pure whenever t is pure. This is easily proved by induction on the structure of t, similar to the preceding proof. □

Lemma 6.1.14 *If* $W \sim W'$, *then* $\mathsf{len}(W) = \mathsf{len}(W')$.

Proof Let $A(V, W, t) \to A(V_1, W_1, t_1)$ and $W \sim W'$. Due to the fact that the arguments of the left-hand side of the rewrite rules in $\mathcal{U}'(P, \mathcal{Q})$ are terms over the signature $\{\varepsilon, \$, 0, 1, \mathsf{cons}, \overline{\mathsf{cons}}\}$, it follows that $A(V, W', t)$ also matches the left-hand side. If we apply the same rewrite rule, we obtain $A(V, W', t) \rightarrow A(V_1', W_1', t_1)$ with $V_1 \sim V_1'$ and $W_1 \sim W_1'$. If one of V_1, V_1' equals V, then both are equal to V. From this observation we easily obtain $\mathsf{len}(W) = \mathsf{len}(W')$. □

Next we are going to show that the interpretation functions $[f]$ for $f \in \mathcal{F}_{\mathcal{U}}$ are strictly monotone in all arguments. The proof of this statement for function symbol A relies on the following lemma.

Lemma 6.1.15 *For all* $x_1, \ldots, x_6 \in \mathbb{N}_+$, *we have* $\mathsf{len}(\pi(x_1), \ldots, \pi(x_6)) < \mathsf{bound}(x_3, x_4)$.

Proof First we show that $\|\pi(x)\| \leq \ell(x)$ by induction on $x \in \mathbb{N}_+$ according to the definition of π. If $\pi(x) \in \{\varepsilon, \$, 0, 1, A(\varepsilon, \ldots, \varepsilon)\}$ then $\|\pi(x)\| = 0$. Suppose $x = z \circ 5 \circ y \circ 6$ with $y > 0$ being well-balanced, so $\pi(x) = \mathsf{cons}(\pi(y), \pi(z))$. We have $\|\pi(x)\| = 1 + \|\pi(z)\|$ if $\pi(y) \in \{0, 1\}$ and $\|\pi(x)\| = 0$ otherwise. (Here we exploit the fact that ζ in the definition of $\|t\|$ is a mixed string.) In the former case we obtain the desired $\|\pi(x)\| \leq \ell(x)$ from the induction hypothesis (applied to z). In the latter case the inequality $\|\pi(x)\| \leq \ell(x)$ is trivial. If $x = 5 \circ y \circ 6 \circ z \circ 7 \uparrow (2 + \ell(y))$ with $y > 0$ well-balanced, and thus $\pi(x) = \overline{\mathsf{cons}}(\pi(y), \pi(z))$, we obtain $\|\pi(x)\| \leq \ell(x)$ in exactly the same way. Using Corollary 6.1.6 we now obtain

$$
\begin{aligned}
\mathsf{len}(\pi(x_1), \ldots, \pi(x_6)) &\leq 1 + 4\|\pi(x_3)\| + 3\|\pi(x_4)\| \\
&\leq 1 + 4\ell(x_3) + 3\ell(x_4) \\
&< 6\ell(x_3) + 3\ell(x_4) \qquad (6.4) \\
&= \mathsf{bound}(x_3, x_4)
\end{aligned}
$$

Here (6.4) follows from the fact that $x_3 > 0$ and thus $\ell(x_3) > 0$. □

Proposition 6.1.16 *For every* $f \in \mathcal{F}_{\mathcal{U}}$, *the interpretation function* $[f]$ *is strictly monotone in all its arguments.*

Proof For constants in $\mathcal{F}_{\mathcal{U}}$ there is nothing to show. For $[\mathsf{cons}]$ and $[\overline{\mathsf{cons}}]$ the result follows directly from the strict monotonicity of $\circ$. We already observed that every $[f]$ with $f \in \mathcal{F}_{\mathcal{Q}}$ is strictly monotone. For function symbol A more effort is required. The strict monotonicity of $[A]$ in its last argument follows from the strict monotonicity of $\psi_{\mathcal{Q}}$, code, and $\circ$. For the other arguments we reason as follows. Let $x_i \geq y_i$ for $1 \leq i \leq 2n + 14$, where at least one of these inequalities is strict. We distinguish three cases. If

$$\prod_{i=1}^{2n+8} \chi(y_i \geq [V_i]) = 1$$

then also

$$\prod_{i=1}^{2n+8} \chi(x_i \geq [V_i]) = 1$$

because $x_i \geq y_i$. We have

$$\mathsf{factor}(x_1, \ldots x_{2n+14}) > \mathsf{factor}(y_1, \ldots, y_{2n+14})$$

by the strict monotonicity of revc and $+$, and

$$\mathsf{bound}(x_{2n+11}, x_{2n+12}) \geq \mathsf{bound}(y_{2n+11}, y_{2n+12})$$

by the monotonicity of bound. Using Lemma 6.1.15, it follows that

$$\begin{aligned}
&E(x_1, \ldots, x_{2n+14}) \\
&= \mathsf{len}(\pi(x_{2n+9}), \ldots, \pi(x_{2n+14})) \\
&\quad + \mathsf{bound}(x_{2n+11}, x_{2n+12}) \cdot \mathsf{factor}(x_1, \ldots, x_{2n+14}) \\
&\geq \mathsf{bound}(x_{2n+11}, x_{2n+12}) \cdot \mathsf{factor}(x_1, \ldots, x_{2n+14}) \\
&\geq \mathsf{bound}(y_{2n+11}, y_{2n+12}) \cdot \mathsf{factor}(x_1, \ldots, x_{2n+14}) \\
&\geq \mathsf{bound}(y_{2n+11}, y_{2n+12}) \cdot (1 + \mathsf{factor}(y_1, \ldots, y_{2n+14})) \\
&= \mathsf{bound}(y_{2n+11}, y_{2n+12}) + \mathsf{bound}(y_{2n+11}, y_{2n+12}) \cdot \mathsf{factor}(y_1, \ldots, y_{2n+14}) \\
&> \mathsf{len}(\pi(y_{2n+9}), \ldots, \pi(y_{2n+14})) \\
&\quad + \mathsf{bound}(y_{2n+11}, y_{2n+12}) \cdot \mathsf{factor}(y_1, \ldots, y_{2n+14}) \\
&= E(y_1, \ldots, y_{2n+14})
\end{aligned}$$

and so, by the strict monotonicity of ψ_Q, code, and $\circ$,

$$\begin{aligned}
[A](x_1, \ldots, x_{2n+14}, x_{2n+15}) &= \mathsf{code}(\psi_Q(E(x_1, \ldots, x_{2n+14}), x_{2n+15})) \circ 8 \\
&> \mathsf{code}(\psi_Q(E(y_1, \ldots, y_{2n+14}), x_{2n+15})) \circ 8 \\
&= [A](y_1, \ldots, y_{2n+14}, x_{2n+15})
\end{aligned}$$

Suppose

$$\prod_{i=1}^{2n+8} \chi(y_i \geq [V_i]) = \prod_{i=1}^{2n+8} \chi(x_i \geq [V_i]) = 0$$

We have

$$D(x_1, \ldots, x_{2n+14}) = \sum_{i=1}^{2n+14} x_i > \sum_{i=1}^{2n+14} y_i = D(y_1, \ldots, y_{2n+14})$$

and hence the assertion follows from the strict monotonicity of ψ_Q, code, and $\circ$. Finally, suppose

$$\prod_{i=1}^{2n+8} \chi(y_i \geq [V_i]) = 0$$

and

$$\prod_{i=1}^{2n+8} \chi(x_i \geq [V_i]) = 1$$

In this case, $D(x_1, \ldots, x_{2n+14})$ equals $\mathsf{len}(\pi(x_{2n+9}), \ldots, \pi(x_{2n+14})) + \mathsf{bound}(x_{2n+11}, x_{2n+12}) \cdot \mathsf{factor}(x_1, \ldots, x_{2n+14})$ and

$$D(y_1, \ldots, y_{2n+14}) = \sum_{i=1}^{2n+14} y_i.$$

Because $\mathsf{revc}(x_{2n+11}, x_{2n+12}) \geq x_{2n+11} + x_{2n+12}$ and $\mathsf{revc}(x_{2n+13}, x_{2n+14}) \geq x_{2n+13} + x_{2n+14}$, it follows that

$$\mathsf{factor}(x_1, \ldots, x_{2n+14}) \geq \sum_{i=1}^{2n+14} x_i$$

and thus $D(x_1, \ldots, x_{2n+14}) > D(y_1, \ldots, y_{2n+14})$. The desired result now follows from the strict monotonicity of ψ_Q, code, and $\circ$. □

In the final part of this section we will make good on our claim that the interpretation [ ] is capable of orienting all ground instances of the rewrite rules in $\mathcal{U}'(P, Q)$ from left to right. We need a few preliminary results concerning the interplay of revc and [ ].

Lemma 6.1.17 *Let α be a sequence of ground terms. For all ground terms s and t we have* $\mathsf{revc}([\alpha(s)], [t]) = \mathsf{revc}([s], [\overline{\alpha}(t)])$.

Proof We use induction on the length of α. If α is the empty sequence, then the lemma is trivially true. Let $\alpha = u\beta$. Then

$$\begin{aligned}
\mathsf{revc}([\alpha(s)], [t]) &= \mathsf{revc}([\mathsf{cons}(u, \beta(s))], [t]) \\
&= \mathsf{revc}([\mathsf{cons}]([u], [\beta(s)]), [t]) \\
&= \mathsf{revc}([\beta(s)] \circ 5 \circ [u] \circ 6, [t]) \\
&= [\beta(s)] \circ 5 \circ [u] \circ 6 \circ [t] \circ 7 \uparrow \ell([\beta(s)] \circ 5 \circ [u] \circ 6) \\
&= \mathsf{revc}([\beta(s)], 5 \circ [u] \circ 6 \circ [t] \circ 7 \uparrow \ell(5 \circ [u] \circ 6)) \\
&= \mathsf{revc}([\beta(s)], [\overline{\mathsf{cons}}]([u], [t])) \\
&= \mathsf{revc}([\beta(s)], [\overline{\mathsf{cons}}(u, t)]) \\
&= \mathsf{revc}([s], [\overline{\beta}(\overline{\mathsf{cons}}(u, t))]) \qquad (6.5) \\
&= \mathsf{revc}([s], [\overline{\beta}(\overline{u}(t))]) \\
&= \mathsf{revc}([s], [\overline{u\beta}(t)]) \\
&= \mathsf{revc}([s], [\overline{\alpha}(t)])
\end{aligned}$$

Here Eq. (6.5) follows from the induction hypothesis. □

Lemma 6.1.18 *Let s, t, and u be ground terms and x a positive integer. If $[s] \geq [t]$, then*

$$\mathsf{revc}([\mathsf{cons}(s,u)],x) + [t] \geq \mathsf{revc}([\mathsf{cons}(t,u)],x) + [s]$$
$$\mathsf{revc}(x,[\overline{\mathsf{cons}}(s,u)]) + [t] \geq \mathsf{revc}(x,[\overline{\mathsf{cons}}(t,u)]) + [s]$$

Moreover, if $[s] > [t]$, then both inequalities are strict.

Proof The first statement is obtained as follows:

$$\begin{aligned}
&\mathsf{revc}([\mathsf{cons}(s,u)],x) + [t] \\
&= [\mathsf{cons}(s,u)] \circ x \circ 7 \uparrow \ell([\mathsf{cons}(s,u)]) + [t] \\
&= [u] \circ 5 \circ [s] \circ 6 \circ x \circ 7 \uparrow \ell([\mathsf{cons}(s,u)]) + [t] \\
&\geq [u] \circ 5 \circ [t] \circ 6 \circ x \circ 7 \uparrow \ell([\mathsf{cons}(s,u)]) + [s] && (6.6)\\
&\geq [u] \circ 5 \circ [t] \circ 6 \circ x \circ 7 \uparrow \ell([\mathsf{cons}(t,u)]) + [s] && (6.7)\\
&= [\mathsf{cons}(t,u)] \circ x \circ 7 \uparrow \ell([\mathsf{cons}(t,u)]) + [s] \\
&= \mathsf{revc}([\mathsf{cons}(t,u)],x) + [s]
\end{aligned}$$

Here (6.6) follows from the fact that, for all $x, y, z \in \mathbb{N}_+$, $x \circ y \circ z + y' \geq x \circ y' \circ z + y$ whenever $y \geq y'$ and (6.7) follows from the monotonicity of ℓ, $\circ$, and $7^{\circ(\cdot)}$. If $[s] > [t]$, then (6.7) becomes strict, and so

$$\mathsf{revc}([\mathsf{cons}(s,u)],x) + [t] > \mathsf{revc}([\mathsf{cons}(t,u)],x) + [s]$$

The other two statements are obtained in a similar fashion. □

The last preliminary result is a variant of the previous lemma.

Lemma 6.1.19 *Let α and β be sequences of ground terms, t a ground term, and x a positive integer. If $[\alpha(\varepsilon)] \geq [\beta(\varepsilon)]$, then*

$$\mathsf{revc}([\alpha(t)],x) + [\beta(\varepsilon)] \geq \mathsf{revc}([\beta(t)],x) + [\alpha(\varepsilon)]$$

Moreover, if $[\alpha(\varepsilon)] > [\beta(\varepsilon)]$, then the inequality is strict.

Proof Write $\alpha = s_1 \dots s_k$ and $\beta = t_1 \dots t_l$. We have

$$\begin{aligned}
[\alpha(\varepsilon)] &= 1 \circ 5 \circ [s_k] \circ 6 \cdots \circ 5 \circ [s_1] \circ 6 \\
&\geq 1 \circ 5 \circ [t_l] \circ 6 \cdots \circ 5 \circ [t_1] \circ 6 = [\beta(\varepsilon)]
\end{aligned}$$

and thus

$$a = 5 \circ [s_k] \circ 6 \cdots \circ 5 \circ [s_1] \circ 6 \geq 5 \circ [t_l] \circ 6 \cdots \circ 5 \circ [t_1] \circ 6 = b$$

which implies $[\alpha(t)] = [t] \circ a \geq [t] \circ b = [\beta(t)]$. Now the desired inequality is obtained as in the proof of Lemma 6.1.18:

$$\begin{aligned}
\mathsf{revc}([\alpha(t)], x) + [\beta(\varepsilon)] &= [\alpha(t)] \circ x \circ 7 \uparrow \ell([\alpha(t)]) + [\beta(\varepsilon)] \\
&= [t] \circ a \circ x \circ 7 \uparrow \ell([\alpha(t)]) + 1 \circ b \\
&\geq [t] \circ b \circ x \circ 7 \uparrow \ell([\alpha(t)]) + 1 \circ a \qquad (6.8) \\
&\geq [t] \circ b \circ x \circ 7 \uparrow \ell([\beta(t)]) + 1 \circ a \\
&= [\beta(t)] \circ x \circ 7 \uparrow \ell([\beta(t)]) + [\alpha(\varepsilon)] \\
&= \mathsf{revc}([\beta(t)], x) + [\alpha(\varepsilon)]
\end{aligned}$$

Here (6.8) follows from the fact that, for all $x, y, z \in \mathbb{N}_+$, $x \circ y \circ z + 1 \circ y' \geq x \circ y' \circ z + 1 \circ y$ whenever $y \geq y'$. Note that the second inequality in the derivation becomes strict if $[\alpha(\varepsilon)] > [\beta(\varepsilon)]$. □

Theorem 6.1.20 *For every ground instance*

$$l\sigma = A(t_1, \ldots, t_{2n+15}) \to A(u_1, \ldots, u_{2n+15}) = r\sigma$$

of a rewrite rule $l \to r$ *in* $\mathcal{U}'(P, \mathcal{Q})$ *we have* $[l\sigma] > [r\sigma]$.

Proof First we consider the case that $[u_i] \geq [t_i]$ for all $1 \leq i \leq 2n + 8$. By definition of $\mathcal{U}'(P, \mathcal{Q})$ we have $t_1, \ldots, t_{2n+8} = V$, $t_{2n+15} = \mathsf{LHS}\sigma$, and either $u_{2n+15} = \mathsf{LHS}\sigma$ or $u_{2n+15} = \mathsf{RHS}_j\sigma$ for some $1 \leq j \leq m$. Positive integers E_1 and F_1 are defined as follows:

$$\begin{aligned}
E_1 &= [t_1] + [t_2] + 2([t_{2n+9}] + [t_{2n+10}]) \\
F_1 &= [u_1] + [u_2] + 2([u_{2n+9}] + [u_{2n+10}])
\end{aligned}$$

We claim that

$$E_1 \geq F_1 \tag{6.9}$$

We claim moreover that, if $[u_i] > [t_i]$ for some $i = 1, 2$, then $E_1 > F_1$. Inspection of the rewrite rules shows that $[t_1] + [t_2] = [u_{2n+9}] + [u_{2n+10}]$, and $[t_{2n+9}] + [t_{2n+10}] = [u_1] + [u_2]$. Hence $E_1 = [t_1] + [t_2] + 2([u_1] + [u_2])$ and $F_1 = [u_1] + [u_2] + 2([t_1] + [t_2])$. By assumption $[u_1] + [u_2] \geq [t_1] + [t_2]$ and thus $E_1 \geq F_1$. Clearly, either $[u_1] > [t_1]$ or $[u_2] > [t_2]$ is sufficient to conclude that $E_1 > F_1$.

Positive integers E_2 and F_2 are defined as follows:

$$\begin{aligned}
E_2 &= \mathsf{revc}([t_{2n+11}], [t_{2n+12}]) + \sum_{i=3}^{n+5} [t_i] \\
F_2 &= \mathsf{revc}([u_{2n+11}], [u_{2n+12}]) + \sum_{i=3}^{n+5} [u_i]
\end{aligned}$$

We claim that

$$E_2 \geq F_2. \tag{6.10}$$

Moreover we claim that, if $[u_i] > [t_i]$ for some $3 \leq i \leq n+5$, then $E_2 > F_2$. To prove this claim, we distinguish between the four types of rewrite rules.

Suppose a rule of type (I) is used. In this case the sequences of terms $t_3, \ldots, t_{n+5}$ and $u_3, \ldots, u_{n+5}$ differ only in their third terms: $t_5 = \$$ and $u_5 = x_1\sigma$. Hence $E_2 - F_2$ equals

$$\begin{aligned} E_2 - F_2 \quad = \quad & \mathsf{revc}([w_1 \ldots w_\mu(w)\sigma], [\overline{x_1}(x)\sigma]) + [\$] \\ & -(\mathsf{revc}([w_1 \ldots w_\mu(w)\sigma], [\overline{\$}(x)\sigma]) + [x_1\sigma]) \end{aligned}$$

which is nonnegative according to Lemma 6.1.18. Recall here that $[x_1\sigma] = [u_5] \geq [t_5] = [\$]$ as we are in the case that $[u_i] \geq [t_i]$ for all $1 \leq i \leq 2n+8$. In addition to that, if $[x_1\sigma] = [u_5] > [t_5] = [\$]$, then $E_2 - F_2 > 0$.

Next suppose that a rule of type (II) is used. More precisely, suppose rule $l \to r_{i+1}$ $(1 \leq i \leq n)$ is used. In this case the sequences of terms $t_3, \ldots, t_{n+5}$ and $u_3, \ldots, u_{n+5}$ differ only in their $i+3$th terms: $t_{i+5} = \alpha_i(\varepsilon)$ and $u_{i+5} = w_1 \ldots w_{|\alpha_i|}(\varepsilon)\sigma$. Hence

$$\begin{aligned} E_2 - F_2 = {} & \mathsf{revc}([w_1 \ldots w_\mu(w)\sigma], [\overline{x_1}(x)\sigma]) + [\alpha_i(\varepsilon)] - \\ & (\mathsf{revc}([w_{|\alpha_i|+1} \cdots w_\mu(w)\sigma], [\overline{x_1 \alpha_i}(x)\sigma]) + [w_1 \ldots w_{|\alpha_i|}(\varepsilon)\sigma]) \end{aligned}$$

From Lemmas 6.1.19 (with $\alpha = w_1 \ldots w_{|\alpha_i|}$, $\beta = \alpha_i$, and $t = w_{|\alpha_i|+1} \ldots w_\mu(w)$) and 6.1.17, it follows that

$$\begin{aligned} & \mathsf{revc}([w_1 \ldots w_\mu(w)\sigma], [\overline{x_1}(x)\sigma]) + [\alpha_i(\varepsilon)\sigma] \\ & \geq \mathsf{revc}([\alpha_i w_{|\alpha_i|+1} \cdots w_\mu(w)\sigma], [\overline{x_1}(x)\sigma]) + [w_1 \ldots w_{|\alpha_i|}(\varepsilon)\sigma] \\ & = \mathsf{revc}([w_{|\alpha_i|+1} \ldots w_\mu(w)\sigma], [\overline{\alpha_i}(\overline{x_1}(x))\sigma]) + [w_1 \ldots w_{|\alpha_i|}(\varepsilon)\sigma] \\ & = \mathsf{revc}([w_{|\alpha_i|+1} \cdots w_\mu(w)\sigma], [\overline{x_1 \alpha_i}(x)\sigma]) + [w_1 \ldots w_{|\alpha_i|}(\varepsilon)\sigma] \end{aligned}$$

and thus $E_2 - F_2 \geq 0$. We obtain $E_2 - F_2 > 0$ if $[u_{i+5}] > [t_{i+5}]$.

Suppose that a rule of type (III) is used. In this case the difference between the sequences of terms $t_3, \ldots, t_{n+5}$ and $u_3, \ldots, u_{n+5}$ is the third term and either the first or second term. Here we will consider the former (so a rule r_{n+1+j} with $1 \leq j \leq m$ is used); the latter is proved in exactly the same way. So $t_3 = 0$, $t_5 = \$$, $u_3 = x_1\sigma$, and $u_5 = w_1\sigma$. Hence

$$\begin{aligned} E_2 - F_2 = {} & \mathsf{revc}([w_1 \ldots w_\mu(w)\sigma], [\overline{x_1}(x)\sigma]) + [0] + [\$] - \\ & (\mathsf{revc}([0\$w_2 \ldots w_\mu(w)\sigma], [x\sigma]) + [x_1\sigma] + [w_1\sigma]) \end{aligned}$$

Two applications of Lemma 6.1.18 and a single application of Lemma 6.1.17 yield

$$\begin{aligned}
&\mathsf{revc}([w_1 \dots w_\mu(w)\sigma], [\overline{x_1}(x)\sigma]) + [0] + [\$] \\
&\geq \mathsf{revc}([\$w_2 \dots w_\mu(w)\sigma], [\overline{x_1}(x)\sigma]) + [0] + [w_1\sigma] \\
&\geq \mathsf{revc}([\$w_2 \dots w_\mu(w)\sigma], [\overline{0}(x)\sigma]) + [x_1\sigma] + [w_1\sigma] \\
&= \mathsf{revc}([0\$w_2 \dots w_\mu(w)\sigma], [x\sigma]) + [x_1\sigma] + [w_1\sigma]
\end{aligned}$$

and thus $E_2 - F_2 \geq 0$. Moreover, if $[u_3] > [t_3]$ or $[u_5] > [t_5]$, then $E_2 - F_2 > 0$.

Finally, suppose that a rule of type (IV) is used. In this case the difference between the sequences of terms $t_3, \dots, t_{n+5}$ and $u_3, \dots, u_{n+5}$ is either the first or the second term. We consider here the latter (so the rule r_{n+2m+3} is used); the former is proved in exactly the same way. So $t_4 = 1$ and $u_4 = x_1\sigma$. Hence

$$\begin{aligned}
E_2 - F_2 = \ &\mathsf{revc}([w_1 \dots w_\mu(w)\sigma], [\overline{x_1}(x)\sigma]) + [1] - \\
&(\mathsf{revc}([1w_1 \dots w_\mu(w)\sigma], [x\sigma]) + [x_1\sigma])
\end{aligned}$$

From Lemmata 6.1.18 (recall that $[x_1\sigma] = [u_4] \geq [t_4] = [1]$) and 6.1.17 we obtain

$$\begin{aligned}
&\mathsf{revc}([w_1 \dots w_\mu(w)\sigma], [\overline{x_1}(x)\sigma]) + [1] \\
&\geq \mathsf{revc}([w_1 \dots w_\mu(w)\sigma], [\overline{1}(x)\sigma]) + [x_1\sigma] \\
&= \mathsf{revc}([1w_1 \dots w_\mu(w)\sigma], [x\sigma]) + [x_1\sigma]
\end{aligned}$$

and thus $E_2 - F_2 \geq 0$. Moreover, if $[u_4] > [t_4]$, then $E_2 - F_2 > 0$.

This concludes the proof of claim (6.10). Positive integers E_3 and F_3 are defined as follows:

$$E_3 = \mathsf{revc}([t_{2n+13}], [t_{2n+14}]) + \sum_{i=n+6}^{2n+8} [t_i]$$

$$F_3 = \mathsf{revc}([u_{2n+13}], [u_{2n+14}]) + \sum_{i=n+6}^{2n+8} [u_i]$$

We claim that

$$E_3 \geq F_3 \tag{6.11}$$

Moreover, if $[u_i] > [t_i]$ for some $n+6 \leq i \leq 2n+8$, then $E_3 > F_3$. The proof of this claim is very similar to the proof of (6.10) and hence is omitted.

From (6.9), (6.10), and (6.11) we immediately obtain

$$\begin{aligned}
\mathsf{factor}([t_1], \dots, [t_{2n+14}]) &= E_1 + E_2 + E_3 \\
&\geq F_1 + F_2 + F_3 \qquad (6.12) \\
&= \mathsf{factor}([u_1], \dots, [u_{2n+14}])
\end{aligned}$$

and if $[u_i] > [t_i]$ for some $1 \le i \le 2n+8$, then

$$\mathsf{factor}([t_1], \ldots, [t_{2n+14}]) > \mathsf{factor}([u_1], \ldots, [u_{2n+14}]) \tag{6.13}$$

From (6.10) we easily obtain

$$\mathsf{revc}([t_{2n+11}], [t_{2n+12}]) \ge \mathsf{revc}([u_{2n+11}], [u_{2n+12}])$$

Hence

$$2\ell([t_{2n+11}]) + \ell([t_{2n+12}]) \ge 2\ell([u_{2n+11}]) + \ell([u_{2n+12}])$$

by the monotonicity of ℓ and the fact that $\ell(\mathsf{revc}(x, y)) = 2\ell(x) + \ell(y)$ for all $x, y \in \mathbb{N}_+$. Therefore

$$\mathsf{bound}([t_{2n+11}], [t_{2n+12}]) \ge \mathsf{bound}([u_{2n+11}], [u_{2n+12}]) \tag{6.14}$$

Now if $[u_i] > [t_i]$ for some $1 \le i \le 2n+8$, then the statement of the theorem follows from (6.13) and (6.14) as in the proof of Lemma 6.1.16. Otherwise, we have $[u_i] = [t_i]$ for all $1 \le i \le 2n+8$. From the first part of Lemma 6.1.13 we obtain $u_i \sim \pi([u_i]) = \pi([t_i]) \sim t_i = V_i$. Because V_i is a pure ground term, the second part yields $\pi([u_i]) = V_i$ and hence $u_i = V_i$ by the definition of $\sim$. Hence $r\sigma = A(V, u_{2n+9}, \ldots, u_{2n+15})$ and therefore

$$\mathsf{len}(t_{2n+9}, \ldots, t_{2n+14}) > \mathsf{len}(u_{2n+9}, \ldots, u_{2n+14}) \tag{6.15}$$

by the definition of **len**. From (6.12), (6.14), and (6.15) we obtain

$$\begin{aligned} D([t_1], \ldots, [t_{2n+14}]) &= E([t_1], \ldots, [t_{2n+14}]) \\ &> E([u_1], \ldots, [u_{2n+14}]) = D([u_1], \ldots, [u_{2n+14}]) \end{aligned}$$

With help of the strict monotonicity of the various functions, we now obtain

$$\begin{aligned} [l\sigma] &= \mathsf{code}(\psi_{\mathcal{Q}}(D([t_1], \ldots, [t_{2n+14}]), [t_{2n+15}])) \circ 8 \\ &\ge \mathsf{code}(\psi_{\mathcal{Q}}(D([u_1], \ldots, [u_{2n+14}]) + 1, [t_{2n+15}])) \circ 8 \\ &= \mathsf{code}([t_{2n+15}] + \psi_{\mathcal{Q}}(D([u_1], \ldots, [u_{2n+14}]), \phi_{\mathcal{Q}}([t_{2n+15}]))) \circ 8 \\ &> \mathsf{code}(\psi_{\mathcal{Q}}(D([u_1], \ldots, [u_{2n+14}]), \phi_{\mathcal{Q}}([t_{2n+15}]))) \circ 8 \\ &\ge \mathsf{code}(\psi_{\mathcal{Q}}(D([u_1], \ldots, [u_{2n+14}]), [u_{2n+15}])) \circ 8 \\ &= [r\sigma] \end{aligned}$$

Note that $\phi_{\mathcal{Q}}([t_{2n+15}]) \ge [u_{2n+15}]$ because either $t_{2n+15} \to u_{2n+15}$ is a ground instance of a rewrite rule in $\mathcal{Q}$, in which case the inequality follows from the definition of $\phi_{\mathcal{Q}}$, or $t_{2n+15} = u_{2n+15}$, in which case the inequality follows from $\phi_{\mathcal{Q}}(x) \ge x$.

In the second half of the proof we consider the case that $[u_i] < [t_i]$ for at least one $1 \le i \le 2n+8$. In this case $D([t_1], \ldots, [t_{2n+14}])$ equals

$$\begin{aligned} &\mathsf{len}(\pi([t_{2n+9}]), \ldots, \pi([t_{2n+14}])) \\ &\quad + \mathsf{bound}([t_{2n+11}], [t_{2n+12}]) \cdot \mathsf{factor}([t_1], \ldots, [t_{2n+14}]) \end{aligned}$$

and $D([u_1],\ldots,[u_{2n+14}])$ equals $\sum_{i=1}^{2n+14}[u_i]$. If we show that

$$\mathsf{factor}([t_1],\ldots,[t_{2n+14}]) \geq \sum_{i=1}^{2n+14}[u_i] \tag{6.16}$$

then $D([t_1],\ldots,[t_{2n+14}]) > D([u_1],\ldots,[u_{2n+14}])$ is a consequence of $\mathsf{bound}([t_{2n+11}],[t_{2n+12}]) > 0$ and thus we obtain the desired $[l\sigma] > [r\sigma]$ as in the preceding case. The proof of Eq. (6.16) has the same structure as the proof of Eq. (6.12). Positive integers are defined as follows:

$$\begin{aligned}
E_1 &= [t_1] + [t_2] + 2([t_{2n+9}] + [t_{2n+10}]) \\
F_1' &= [u_1] + [u_2] + [u_{2n+9}] + [u_{2n+10}] \\
E_2 &= \mathsf{revc}([t_{2n+11}],[t_{2n+12}]) + \sum_{i=3}^{n+5}[t_i] \\
F_2' &= [u_{2n+11}] + [u_{2n+12}] + \sum_{i=3}^{n+5}[u_i] \\
E_3 &= \mathsf{revc}([t_{2n+13}],[t_{2n+14}]) + \sum_{i=n+6}^{2n+8}[t_i] \\
F_3' &= [u_{2n+13}] + [u_{2n+14}] + \sum_{i=n+6}^{2n+8}[u_i]
\end{aligned}$$

Note that $\mathsf{factor}([t_1],\ldots,[t_{2n+14}]) = E_1 + E_2 + E_3$ and

$$\sum_{i=1}^{2n+14}[u_i] = F_1' + F_2' + F_3'.$$

In order to show Eq. (6.16), it is sufficient to show that $E_1 > F_1'$, $E_2 > F_2'$, and $E_3 > F_3'$. For every rewrite rule in $\mathcal{U}'(P,\mathcal{Q})$ we have

$$E_1 = [0] + [1] + 2([u\sigma] + [v\sigma]) > [u\sigma] + [v\sigma] + [0] + [1] = F_1'$$

We show $E_2 > F_2'$ and $E_3 > F_3'$ by distinguishing between the four types of rewrite rules. Actually, we only show $E_2 > F_2'$ for rules of type (II) and $E_3 > F_3'$ for rules of type (III). The other cases are very similar.

We start with $E_2 > F_2'$. Suppose that rule $l \to r_{i+1}$ $(1 \leq i \leq n)$ is used. In this case the only difference between the sequences of terms $t_3,\ldots,t_{n+5}$ and $u_3,\ldots,u_{n+5}$ is the $i+3$th term: $t_{i+5} = \alpha_i(\varepsilon)$ and $u_{i+5} = w_1\ldots w_{|\alpha_i|}(\varepsilon)\sigma$. Hence

$$\begin{aligned}
E_2 - F_2' = {} & \mathsf{revc}([w_1\ldots w_\mu(w)\sigma],[\overline{x_1}(x)\sigma]) + [\alpha_i(\varepsilon)] - \\
& ([w_{|\alpha_i|+1}\ldots w_\mu(w)\sigma] + [\overline{x_1\alpha_i}(x)\sigma] + [w_1\ldots w_{|\alpha_i|}(\varepsilon)\sigma])
\end{aligned}$$

If $[w_1 \dots w_{|\alpha_i|}(\varepsilon)\sigma] \geq [\alpha_i(\varepsilon)]$, then we obtain $E_2 - F_2 \geq 0$ from the first half of this proof (claim (6.10)) and therefore $E_2 - F_2' > 0$ as $\mathsf{revc}(a,b) > a+b$ for all positive integers a and b. So suppose that $[w_1 \dots w_{|\alpha_i|}(\varepsilon)\sigma] < [\alpha_i(\varepsilon)]$. Because the decimal representation of the interpretation of a term that is not a constant has at least two digits, this is possible only if $w_j\sigma$ is a constant for every $1 \leq j \leq |\alpha_i|$. This implies that the number of digits in $[w_1 \dots w_{|\alpha_i|}(\varepsilon)\sigma]$ and $[\alpha_i(\varepsilon)]$ coincides. We have

$$\begin{aligned} & E_2 - F_2' \\ & > \mathsf{revc}([w_1 \dots w_\mu(w)\sigma], [\overline{x_1}(x)\sigma]) - ([w_{|\alpha_i|+1} \dots w_\mu(w)\sigma] + [\overline{x_1 \alpha_i}(x)\sigma]) \end{aligned}$$

From Lemma 6.1.17 we obtain

$$\begin{aligned} & \mathsf{revc}([w_1 \dots w_\mu(w)\sigma], [\overline{x_1}(x)\sigma]) \\ & = \mathsf{revc}([w_{|\alpha_i|+1} \dots w_\mu(w)\sigma], [\overline{x_1 w_1 \dots w_{|\alpha_i|}}(x)\sigma]) \end{aligned}$$

Hence $\mathsf{revc}([w_1 \dots w_\mu(w)\sigma], [\overline{x_1}(x)\sigma])$ has

$$\ell_1 = 2 \cdot \ell([w_{|\alpha_i|+1} \dots w_\mu(w)\sigma]) + \ell([\overline{x_1 w_1 \dots w_{|\alpha_i|}}(x)\sigma])$$

digits. On the other hand, $[w_{|\alpha_i|+1} \dots w_\mu(w)\sigma] + [\overline{x_1 \alpha_i}(x)\sigma]$ has at most

$$\ell_2 = 1 + \max\{\ell([w_{|\alpha_i|+1} \dots w_\mu(w)\sigma]), \ell([\overline{x_1 \alpha_i}(x)\sigma])\}$$

digits. Because $\ell([\overline{x_1 w_1 \dots w_{|\alpha_i|}}(x)\sigma]) = \ell([\overline{x_1 \alpha_i}(x)\sigma])$, it follows that $\ell_1 > \ell_2$ and thus $E_2 > F_2'$.

Next we show that $E_3 > F_3'$ for rules of type (III). In this case the difference between the sequences of terms $t_{n+6}, \dots, t_{2n+8}$ and $u_{n+6}, \dots, u_{2n+8}$ is the third term and either the first or second term. We consider here the latter (so a rule $r_{n+1+m+j}$ with $1 \leq j \leq m$ is used); the former is proved in exactly the same way. So $t_{n+7} = 1$, $t_{n+8} = \$$, $u_{n+7} = z_1\sigma$, and $u_{n+8} = y_1\sigma$. Hence

$$\begin{aligned} E_3 - F_3' = \; & \mathsf{revc}([y_1 \dots y_\mu(y)\sigma], [\overline{z_1}(z)\sigma]) + [1] + [\$] - \\ & ([1\$y_2 \dots y_\mu(y)\sigma] + [z\sigma] + [z_1\sigma] + [y_1\sigma]) \end{aligned}$$

If both $[y_1\sigma] \geq [\$]$ and $[z_1\sigma] \geq [1]$ then we obtain

$$\begin{aligned} & \mathsf{revc}([y_1 \dots y_\mu(y)\sigma], [\overline{z_1}(z)\sigma]) + [1] + [\$] \\ & \geq \mathsf{revc}([\$y_2 \dots y_\mu(y)\sigma], [\overline{z_1}(z)\sigma]) + [1] + [y_1\sigma] \\ & \geq \mathsf{revc}([\$y_2 \dots y_\mu(y)\sigma], [\overline{1}(z)\sigma]) + [z_1\sigma] + [y_1\sigma] \\ & = \mathsf{revc}([1\$y_2 \dots y_\mu(y)\sigma], [z\sigma]) + [z_1\sigma] + [y_1\sigma] \\ & > [1\$y_2 \dots y_\mu(y)\sigma] + [z\sigma] + [z_1\sigma] + [y_1\sigma] \end{aligned}$$

by two applications of Lemma 6.1.18, a single application of Lemma 6.1.17, and the fact that $\mathsf{revc}(a,b) > a+b$ for all positive integers a and b. Consequently $E_3 - F_3' \geq 0$. If neither $[y_1\sigma] \geq [\$]$ nor $[z_1\sigma] \geq [1]$, then $y_1\sigma$ and $z_1\sigma$ are constants. From Lemma 6.1.17 we obtain

$$\mathsf{revc}([y_1 \dots y_\mu(y)\sigma], [\overline{z_1}(z)\sigma]) = \mathsf{revc}([z_1 y_1 \dots y_\mu(y)\sigma], [z\sigma])$$

Hence $\mathsf{revc}([y_1 \ldots y_\mu(y)\sigma], [\overline{z_1}(z)\sigma]) + [1] + [\$]$ has at least

$$\ell_1 = 2 \cdot \ell([z_1 y_1 \ldots y_\mu(y)\sigma]) + \ell([z\sigma])$$

digits. On the other hand, because $[z_1\sigma] + [y_1\sigma] \leq [1] + [\$] = 6$, we conclude that $[1\$y_2 \ldots y_\mu(y)\sigma] + [z\sigma] + [z_1\sigma] + [y_1\sigma]$ has at most

$$\ell_2 = 1 + \max\{\ell([1\$y_2 \ldots y_\mu(y)\sigma]), \ell([z\sigma])\}$$

digits. Because $\ell([z_1 y_1 \ldots y_\mu(y)\sigma]) = \ell([1\$y_2 \ldots y_\mu(y)\sigma])$, it follows $\ell_1 > \ell_2$ and thus $E_3 > F_3'$. If either $[y_1\sigma] \geq [\$]$ or $[z_1\sigma] \geq [1]$, then we obtain the desired $E_3 > F_3'$ by combining the argumentation for the preceding two cases. □

Theorem 6.1.21 *The TRS $\mathcal{U}'(P, \mathcal{Q})$ is ω-terminating.*

Proof Let $A = \{[t] \mid t \in \mathcal{T}(\mathcal{F}_\mathcal{U})\}$ be the set of all natural numbers that are the interpretation of some ground term. Note that the interpretation functions $[f]$ for $f \in \mathcal{F}_\mathcal{U}$ are well-defined on A. According to the preceding theorem, $\mathcal{U}'(P, \mathcal{Q})$ is compatible with $(A, >)$ and thus ω-terminating by definition. □

Corollary 6.1.22 *The TRS $\mathcal{U}(P, \mathcal{Q})$ is ω-terminating if P has no solution.*

Corollary 6.1.23 *The TRS $\mathcal{U}_-(P, \mathcal{Q})$ is ω-terminating for every PCP instance P.*

6.1.3 One-Rule Rewrite Systems

Transforming $\mathcal{U}(P, \mathcal{Q})$ into a one-rule TRS $\mathcal{S}(P, \mathcal{Q})$ is easy: We define $\mathcal{S}(P, \mathcal{Q})$ as the rule

$$l \to B(r_1, \ldots, r_{n+2m+3})$$

where B is a fresh function symbol of arity $n + 2m + 3$.

The transformation from $\mathcal{S}(P, \mathcal{Q})$ to $\mathcal{U}(P, \mathcal{Q})$ is an instance of the *distribution elimination* technique of Zantema [Zan94]. We will use the following results. (Actually, the right-linearity requirement can be dropped from the first [MOZ96] and third [Zan94] statements.)

Proposition 6.1.24 *Let $\mathcal{Q}$ be a right-linear TRS.*

1. *If $\mathcal{U}(P, \mathcal{Q})$ is terminating, then $\mathcal{S}(P, \mathcal{Q})$ is terminating.*

2. *$\mathcal{U}(P, \mathcal{Q})$ is simply terminating if and only if $\mathcal{S}(P, \mathcal{Q})$ is simply terminating.*

3. *$\mathcal{U}(P, \mathcal{Q})$ is totally terminating if and only if $\mathcal{S}(P, \mathcal{Q})$ is totally terminating.*

Proof Because $\mathcal{U}(P, \mathcal{Q})$ inherits right-linearity from $\mathcal{Q}$, this is an immediate consequence of [Zan94, theorem 12] (by noting that $\mathcal{U}(P, \mathcal{Q}) = E_B(\mathcal{S}(P, \mathcal{Q}))$). □

We would like to strengthen the last statement of the preceding lemma to ω-termination. One direction is easy.

Lemma 6.1.25 *If $\mathcal{S}(P, \mathcal{Q})$ is ω-terminating, then $\mathcal{U}(P, \mathcal{Q})$ is also ω-terminating.*

Proof By definition $l >_{\mathcal{N}} B(r_1, \ldots, r_{n+2m+3})$ for some monotone algebra $\mathcal{N} = (N, >)$ with $N \subseteq \mathbb{N}$. In Proposition 5.3.5 it is shown that every well-founded monotone algebra $\mathcal{N} = (N, >)$ with the property that the order $>$ is total on N is simple. Hence $B(r_1, \ldots, r_{n+2m+3}) \geq_{\mathcal{N}} r_i$ and thus $l >_{\mathcal{N}} r_i$ for every $1 \leq i \leq n + 2m + 3$. We conclude that $\mathcal{N}$ is compatible with $\mathcal{U}(P, \mathcal{Q})$. In other words, $\mathcal{U}(P, \mathcal{Q})$ is ω-terminating. □

We do not know whether the reverse direction holds for ω-termination. The following partial result, however, suffices for our purposes.

Proposition 6.1.26 *The TRS $\mathcal{S}(P, \mathcal{Q})$ is ω-terminating if P does not have a solution.*

Proof We refine the interpretation $[\,]$ that was used in the previous section to show ω-termination of $\mathcal{U}(P, \mathcal{Q})$ into an interpretation $[\![\,]\!]$ in the positive integers that orients $\mathcal{S}(P, \mathcal{Q})$. The interpretation of every k-ary function symbol $f \in \mathcal{F}_{\mathcal{U}} \setminus \{A\}$ is unchanged:

$$[\![f]\!](x_1, \ldots, x_k) = [f](x_1, \ldots, x_k)$$

The interpretation $[\![A]\!]$ of A is given by

$$[\![A]\!](x_1, \ldots, x_{2n+15}) = \lambda([A](x_1, \ldots, x_{2n+15}))$$

where $\lambda\colon \mathbb{N}_+ \to \mathbb{N}_+$ is the strictly monotone function inductively defined by

$$\lambda(x) = \begin{cases} 1 & \text{if } x = 1 \\ 10 \cdot (n + 2m + 3)^2 \cdot \lambda(x-1)^2 & \text{if } x > 1 \end{cases}$$

and the interpretation $[\![B]\!]$ of B is defined as

$$[\![B]\!](x_1, \ldots, x_{n+2m+3}) = 10 \cdot \mathsf{code}\left(\sum_{i=1}^{n+2m+3} x_i\right)$$

The interpretation of A is chosen in such a way that the inequality $[\![l\sigma]\!] > [\![r\sigma]\!]$ is easily proved for every ground substitution σ. The definition of $[\![B]\!]$ ensures that the interpretation $[\![t]\!]$ of every ground term t with root symbol B ends with a 0 and does not contain the digits 5 and 6. This is essential for the extension of Theorem 6.1.20 mentioned later. Using Lemma 6.1.16, we easily obtain the strict monotonicity of every interpretation function in all arguments. Let

$$l\sigma = A(t_1, \ldots, t_{2n+15}) \to B(r_1\sigma, \ldots, r_{n+2m+3}\sigma) = r\sigma$$

be a ground instance of the only rewrite rule of $\mathcal{S}(P, \mathcal{Q})$. We have to show that $[\![l\sigma]\!] > [\![r\sigma]\!]$. Write $r_i = A(u_1^i, \ldots, u_{2n+15}^i)$. By definition

$$[\![l\sigma]\!] = \lambda([A]([\![t_1]\!], \ldots, [\![t_{2n+15}]\!]))$$

and

$$[\![r\sigma]\!] = 10 \cdot \mathsf{code}\left(\sum_{i=1}^{n+2m+3} \lambda([A]([\![u_1^i]\!], \ldots, [\![u_{2n+15}^i]\!]))\right)$$

After extending the congruence relation $\sim$ of Definition 6.1.12 by defining $t \sim t'$ if $\mathrm{root}(t), \mathrm{root}(t') \in \{A, B\} \cup \mathcal{F}_{\mathcal{Q}}$, the proof of Theorem 6.1.20 can be reused to obtain

$$p = [A]([\![t_1]\!], \ldots, [\![t_{2n+15}]\!]) > [A]([\![u_1^i]\!], \ldots, [\![u_{2n+15}^i]\!]) = q_i$$

Hence

$$\sum_{i=1}^{n+2m+3} \lambda(q_i) \leq \sum_{i=1}^{n+2m+3} \lambda(p-1) = (n+2m+3) \cdot \lambda(p-1)$$

and thus

$$\begin{aligned} [\![r\sigma]\!] &\leq 10 \cdot \mathsf{code}((n+2m+3) \cdot \lambda(p-1)) \\ &< 10 \cdot (n+2m+3)^2 \cdot \lambda(p-1)^2 \\ &= \lambda(p) \\ &= [\![l\sigma]\!] \end{aligned}$$

because $\mathsf{code}(x) < x^2$ for every integer $x > 1$, which we show by induction on x as follows. For $x < 8$ one directly verifies that $\mathsf{code}(x) < x^2$. Suppose $x \geq 8$. Let y be the natural number uniquely determined by $8(y-1) \leq x < 8y$. We have $\mathsf{code}(x) < \mathsf{code}(8y)$ by the strict monotonicity of code. Because $(8y)_8 = 10(y)_8$, it follows that $\mathsf{code}(8y) = 10 \cdot \mathsf{code}(y)$ and hence $\mathsf{code}(x) < 10 \cdot y^2$ by the inductive hypothesis. From $y \geq 2$ we infer that $y/(y-1) \leq 2$ and thus $y^2/(y-1)^2 \leq 4 < 64/10$. Therefore, $\mathsf{code}(x) < 64 \cdot (y-1)^2 = (8 \cdot (y-1))^2 \leq x^2$ as desired. □

In the following we also need results about the relation between $\mathcal{U}(P,\mathcal{Q})$ and $\mathcal{S}(P,\mathcal{Q})$ for the other properties in the termination hierarchy. These results will be stated and proved in the respective sections.

The final result of this section will be used to transform rewrite sequences in $\mathcal{U}(P,\mathcal{Q})$ to rewrite sequences in $\mathcal{S}(P,\mathcal{Q})$ for PCP instances P that admit a solution.

Lemma 6.1.27 *If W and the term t do not contain A symbols and $A(V,W,t) \to^+_{\mathcal{U}(P,\mathcal{Q})} A(V',W',t')$, then $A(V,W,t) \to^+_{\mathcal{S}(P,\mathcal{Q})} C[A(V',W',t)]$ for some context $C[\,]$.*

Proof It is proven by straightforward induction on the length of $A(V,W,t) \to^+_{\mathcal{U}(P,\mathcal{Q})} A(V',W',t')$. □

6.1.4 Proving Relative Undecidability

In this section we will show relative undecidability of each of the implications in hierarchy (6.1). As already mentioned, we will achieve this by instantiating $\mathcal{U}(P,\mathcal{Q})$ and $\mathcal{S}(P,\mathcal{Q})$ with suitable TRSs $\mathcal{Q}$.

The Implication NL ⇒ AC

Let $\mathcal{Q}_1 = \{d \to d\}$.

Lemma 6.1.28 *The TRS $\mathcal{S}(P,\mathcal{Q}_1)$ is acyclic for every PCP instance P.*

Proof Because every rewrite step in $\mathcal{S}(P,\mathcal{Q}_1)$ increases the size of terms, acyclicity is obvious. □

Proposition 6.1.29 *The TRS $\mathcal{S}(P,\mathcal{Q}_1)$ is nonlooping if and only if P admits no solution.*

Proof If P admits a solution, then there exists a sextuple W such that $A(V,W,d) \to^+_{\mathcal{U}(P,\mathcal{Q}_1)} A(V,W,d)$ according to Lemma 6.1.2 and thus $A(V,W,d) \to^+_{\mathcal{S}(P,\mathcal{Q}_1)} C[A(V,W,d)]$ for some context $C[\,]$ by Lemma 6.1.27; hence $\mathcal{S}(P,\mathcal{Q}_1)$ is looping. On the other hand, if P has no solution, then $\mathcal{S}(P,\mathcal{Q}_1)$ is ω-terminating by Lemma 6.1.26 and thus also nonlooping. □

The Implication SN ⇒ NL

Before defining the TRS $\mathcal{Q}_2$ used for the relative undecidability of SN ⇒ NL, we will present two simple but useful facts about nonloopingness.

Lemma 6.1.30 *Every term in a loop is looping.*

Proof Let $t \to^* u \to^* C[t\sigma]$ be a nonempty rewrite sequence. Because rewriting is closed under substitution, we obtain $u \to^* C[t\sigma] \to^* C[u\sigma]$, which shows that u is looping. □

Lemma 6.1.31 *Every looping TRS admits a loop that starts with a root rewrite step.*

Proof Let $t \to^+ C[t\sigma]$ be any loop. We show by induction on the structure of t that there exists a loop (not necessarily starting at t) that contains a root rewrite step. In the base case (t is a constant) the first step of the given loop must take place at the root position. For the induction step, suppose $t = f(t_1, \ldots, t_k)$ with $k \geq 1$ and no step in $t \to^+ C[t\sigma]$ takes place at the root position. So $C[t\sigma] = f(u_1, \ldots, u_k)$ with $t_i \to^* u_i$ for all $1 \leq i \leq k$ and $t_j \to^+ u_j$ for at least one $1 \leq j \leq k$. If the context $C[\,]$ is empty, then $u_j = t_j\sigma$ and we obtain the desired loop from the induction hypothesis (applied to t_j). Otherwise there exist a context $C'[\,]$ and an index $1 \leq l \leq k$ such that $C[\,] = f(v_1, \ldots, v_{l-1}, C'[\,], v_{l+1}, \ldots, v_k)$ and $t_l \to^* C'[t\sigma] = C'[f(\ldots, t_l\sigma, \ldots)]$. Because $t_l \neq C'[f(\ldots, t_l\sigma, \ldots)]$ we can apply the induction hypothesis to t_l, yielding a loop that contains a root rewrite step. Now the result follows from the preceding lemma. □

Let

$$\mathcal{Q}_2 = \begin{cases} f(d, b(x), y) & \to & f(d, x, b(y)) \\ f(d, b(x), y) & \to & f(x, y, b(b(d))) \end{cases}$$

The following lemma stems from [ZG96].

Lemma 6.1.32 *The TRS $\mathcal{Q}_2$ is nonlooping and nonterminating.*

Proof First we show that $\mathcal{Q}_2$ is nonterminating. Define terms $t_i = f(d, b(d), b^i(d))$ for all $i \geq 1$. We have $t_i \to^+ t_{i+1}$ by one application of the second rewrite rule followed by $i - 1$ applications of the first rewrite rule. Hence $\mathcal{Q}_2$ admits the infinite rewrite sequence $t_1 \to^+ t_2 \to^+ t_3 \to^+ \cdots$. Next we show that $\mathcal{Q}_2$ is nonlooping. For a proof by contradiction suppose that $\mathcal{Q}_2$ is looping. According to Lemma 6.1.31, there must be a loop that starts with a root rewrite step, which is only possible if the loop is of the form

$$f(d, b(t_1), t_2) \to^+ C[f(d, b(t_1\sigma), t_2\sigma)] \tag{6.17}$$

Because rewrite steps do not change the number of f symbols, the context $C[\,]$ must be empty. Moreover, the substitution σ does not assign terms that contain any f symbols to the variables in t_1 and t_2. We may assume that t_1 and t_2 do not contain f symbols. (If they do, we replace their outermost f symbols with a fresh variable, resulting in a loop that has the desired property.) Consequently, all rewrite steps in (6.17) take place at the root position. We claim that t_1 and t_2 are ground terms. First note that the second rule of $\mathcal{Q}_2$ must be used in (6.17) as the first rule constitutes a terminating (and hence nonlooping) TRS. Hence we can render (6.17) as follows:

$$\begin{aligned} & f(d, b(t_1), t_2) \to^* f(d, b(u_1), u_2) \\ & \to f(u_1, u_2, b(b(d))) \to^* f(d, b(t_1\sigma), t_2\sigma) \end{aligned} \tag{6.18}$$

such that $t_1 = b^k(u_1)$ and $b^k(t_2) = u_2$ for some $k \geq 0$. Because of the form of the left-hand sides of the rules of $\mathcal{Q}_2$, we must have $u_1 = d$ and hence $t_1 = b^k(d)$ is a ground term. Repeating the same reasoning for the loop

$$f(d, u_2, b(b(d))) \to^+ f(d, u_2\sigma, b(b(d))) \tag{6.19}$$

whose existence is guaranteed by (the proof of) Lemma 6.1.30 shows that u_2, and thus also t_2, is a ground term. Hence $t_1\sigma = t_1$, $t_2\sigma = t_2$, and thus (6.17) is actually a cycle. Because applications of the second rewrite rule increase the size of terms whereas applications of the first rewrite rule do not change the size of terms, only the first rewrite rule can be used. However, we have already observed that the first rule constitutes a terminating (and thus acyclic) TRS. Therefore $\mathcal{Q}_2$ is nonlooping. □

We want to show that $\mathcal{S}(P, \mathcal{Q}_2)$ is nonlooping for every PCP instance P. Because it is easier to reason about $\mathcal{U}(P, \mathcal{Q}_2)$, we will show how to transform a loop in $\mathcal{S}(P, \mathcal{Q}_2)$ into a loop in $\mathcal{U}(P, \mathcal{Q}_2)$. Actually, we present a more general statement, which will also be used in Section 6.1.4.

Definition 6.1.33 We define two (partial) mappings ϕ and ψ as follows:

$$\begin{aligned} \phi(A(t_1, \ldots, t_{2n+15})) &= A(\psi(t_1), \ldots, \psi(t_{2n+15})), \\ \phi(B(t_1, \ldots, t_{n+2m+3})) &= B(\phi(t_1), \ldots, \phi(t_{n+2m+3})), \\ \psi(A(t_1, \ldots, t_{2n+15})) &= \psi(B(t_1, \ldots, t_{n+2m+3})) = z \end{aligned}$$

$\psi(g(t_1, \ldots, t_k)) = g(\psi(t_1), \ldots, \psi(t_k))$ for all function symbols g different from A and B, and $\psi(x) = x$ for all variables x. Here z is a distinguished fresh variable.

The purpose of these mappings is to simplify the structure of $\mathcal{S}(P, \mathcal{Q})$ rewrite sequences by replacing all descendants of nonoutermost A symbols by the variable z.

Lemma 6.1.34 *If $t \to^+_{\mathcal{S}(P,\mathcal{Q})} u$ with $\mathrm{root}(t) = A$ contains a root rewrite step, then $\phi(t) \to^+_{\mathcal{S}(P,\mathcal{Q})} \phi(u)$. Moreover, if v is a maximal subterm of u with root symbol A, then $\phi(v)$ is a subterm of $\phi(u)$ and $\phi(t) \to^+_{\mathcal{U}(P,\mathcal{Q})} \phi(v)$.*

Proof It is easy to see that for every step $t' \to_{\mathcal{S}(P,\mathcal{Q}_2)} u'$ in the given rewrite sequence we get $\phi(t') \to_{\mathcal{S}(P,\mathcal{Q}_2)} \phi(u')$ if the contracted redex is outermost and $\phi(t') = \phi(u')$ otherwise. Hence $\phi(t) \to^+_{\mathcal{S}(P,\mathcal{Q})} \phi(u)$. The term u can (uniquely) be written as $C[v_1, \ldots, v_k]$ such that $C[\,]$ is a context consisting of B symbols and every v_i starts with an A symbol. So v_1, $\ldots$, v_k are the maximal subterms of u with root symbol A. By definition $\phi(u) = C[\phi(v_1), \ldots, \phi(v_k)]$. A straightforward induction on the length of $t \to^*_{\mathcal{S}(P,\mathcal{Q})} u$ yields $\phi(t) \to^*_{\mathcal{U}(P,\mathcal{Q})} \phi(v_i)$ for every $1 \le i \le k$. □

Lemma 6.1.35 *If $\mathcal{U}(P, \mathcal{Q}_2)$ is nonlooping, then $\mathcal{S}(P, \mathcal{Q}_2)$ is nonlooping.*

Proof Suppose, on the contrary, that $\mathcal{S}(P, \mathcal{Q}_2)$ is looping. According to Lemma 6.1.31, there exists a loop $t \to^+_{\mathcal{S}(P,\mathcal{Q}_2)} C[t\sigma]$ that starts with a root rewrite step. This implies that $\text{root}(t) = A$. Because the maximum nesting of A symbols does not change by $\mathcal{S}(P, \mathcal{Q}_2)$ rewrite steps, there cannot be A symbols above the position of the hole in the context $C[\,]$. In other words, $t\sigma$ is a maximal subterm of $C[t\sigma]$ with root symbol A. Lemma 6.1.34 yields

$$\phi(t) \to^+_{\mathcal{U}(P,\mathcal{Q}_2)} \phi(t\sigma) \tag{6.20}$$

Note that $\phi(t\sigma) = \phi(t)\sigma'$ where the substitution σ' is defined as the composition of σ and ψ. Hence (6.20) is a loop, which contradicts the assumption. □

Lemma 6.1.36 *TRS $\mathcal{S}(P, \mathcal{Q}_2)$ is nonlooping for every PCP instance P.*

Proof Assume $\mathcal{S}(P, \mathcal{Q}_2)$ admits a loop. From Lemma 6.1.35 we obtain a loop, $t \to^+ C[t\sigma]$, in $\mathcal{U}(P, \mathcal{Q}_2)$. According to Lemma 6.1.31, we may assume that this loop starts with a root-rewrite step. This is only possible if t is a redex and hence we may write $t = A(V, W, t')$. The linear interpretation ϕ is defined by $\phi(b(t)) = \phi(t)$ and $\phi(g(t_1, \ldots, t_k)) = \phi(t_1) + \cdots + \phi(t_k) + 1$ for every other function symbol g of arity k. Clearly, $s \to_{\mathcal{U}(P,\mathcal{Q}_2)} s'$ implies $\phi(s) = \phi(s')$ for all terms s and s', hence $C[\,]$ consists of b symbols only. Another linear interpretation ψ is defined by $\psi(b(t)) = \psi(t) + 1$ and $\psi(g(t_1, \ldots, t_k)) = 0$ for every other function symbol g of arity k. For all terms s and s', if $s \to_{\mathcal{U}(P,\mathcal{Q}_2)} s'$, then $\psi(s) = \psi(s')$, hence $C[\,]$ is empty. We conclude that the loop must be of the form $A(V, W, t') \to^+ A(V, W\sigma, t'\sigma)$. Because $A(V, W, t') \to^+_{\mathcal{U}_-(P,\mathcal{Q})} A(V, W\sigma, t'\sigma)$ contradicts the (ω-)termination of $\mathcal{U}_-(P, \mathcal{Q})$ (Corollary 6.1.23), we obtain $t' \to^+_{\mathcal{Q}_2} t'\sigma$ from Lemma 6.1.3. This is impossible as $\mathcal{Q}_2$ is nonlooping (Lemma 6.1.32). □

Proposition 6.1.37 *TRS $\mathcal{S}(P, \mathcal{Q}_2)$ is terminating if and only if P admits no solution.*

Proof Suppose P has a solution. From (the proof of) Lemma 6.1.32 we know there exists an infinite rewrite sequence $t_1 \to_{\mathcal{Q}_2} t_2 \to_{\mathcal{Q}_2} t_3 \to_{\mathcal{Q}_2} \cdots$ in which all steps take place at the root position. According to Lemmas 6.1.2 and 6.1.27, this sequence can be transformed into an infinite rewrite sequence in $\mathcal{S}(P, \mathcal{Q}_2)$:

$$A(V, W, t_1) \to^+ C_1[A(V, W, t_2)] \to^+ C_1[C_2[A(V, W, t_3)]] \to \cdots$$

Note that for the applicability of Lemma 6.1.2 it is essential that all steps in the infinite $\mathcal{Q}_2$-rewrite sequence take place at the root position. Conversely, if P has no solution, then $\mathcal{S}(P, \mathcal{Q}_2)$ is ω-terminating by Lemma 6.1.26 and therefore also terminating. □

The Implication NSE ⇒ SN

Let $\mathcal{Q}_3 = \{f(d) \to f(g(d))\}$. This TRS is terminating and self-embedding.

Lemma 6.1.38 *TRS $\mathcal{S}(P, \mathcal{Q}_3)$ is terminating for every PCP instance P.*

Proof According to Lemma 6.1.24(1), it suffices to show that $\mathcal{U}(P, \mathcal{Q}_3)$ is terminating. There are several ways to achieve this. We use type introduction (Theorem 5.5.25), which is possible because $\mathcal{U}(P, \mathcal{Q}_3)$ lacks collapsing (and duplicating) rules. Hence we may assume that the function symbols come from a many-sorted signature such that the left- and right-hand sides of all rewrite rules are well-typed and of the same type. We use two sorts 1 and 2 with A of type $1 \times \cdots \times 1 \to 2$ and all other function symbols of type $1 \times \cdots \times 1 \to 1$. Terms of type 1 are in normal form. So if $\mathcal{U}(P, \mathcal{Q}_3)$ is not terminating, then there exists an infinite rewrite sequence consisting of terms of type 2. Hence all steps take place at the root position. Because terms of type 2 do not contain occurrences of A strictly below the root position, Lemma 6.1.3 applies. Because $\mathcal{U}_{-}(P, \mathcal{Q})$ is (simply) terminating (Lemma 6.1.23), we obtain an infinite rewrite sequence in $\mathcal{Q}_3$, contradicting its termination. □

Proposition 6.1.39 *The TRS $\mathcal{S}(P, \mathcal{Q}_3)$ is nonself-embedding if and only if P admits no solution.*

Proof If P admits a solution, then we obtain

$$A(V, W, f(d)) \to^+_{\mathcal{S}(P, \mathcal{Q}_3)} C[A(V, W, f(g(d)))]$$

from Lemmata 6.1.2 and 6.1.27. Because $A(V, W, f(d))$ is embedded in $C[A(V, W, f(g(d)))]$, this shows that $\mathcal{S}(P, \mathcal{Q}_3)$ is self-embedding. Conversely, if P has no solution then $\mathcal{S}(P, \mathcal{Q}_3)$ is ω-terminating by Lemma 6.1.26 and thus nonself-embedding. □

The Implication ST ⇒ NSE

Before defining the TRS $\mathcal{Q}_4$ used for the relative undecidability of ST ⇒ NSE, we present a simple fact about nonself-embeddingness.

Lemma 6.1.40 *If a TRS $\mathcal{R}$ is self-embedding, then it admits a rewrite sequence $t \to_{\mathcal{R}}^{+} u \to_{\mathcal{E}mb}^{*} t$ such that the subsequence from t to u contains a root rewrite step.*

Proof The proof is similar to the proof of Lemma 6.1.31, but note that we cannot prove that there exists a rewrite sequence $t \to_{\mathcal{R}}^{+} u \to_{\mathcal{E}mb}^{*} t$ that starts with root rewrite step: Consider $\{f(a) \to f(g(h(b))), g(b) \to a\}$. □

We define

$$\mathcal{Q}_4 = \left\{ \begin{array}{lcl} f(d,e,x) & \to & f(x,g(e),e) \\ f(d,e,x) & \to & f(g(d),x,d) \end{array} \right.$$

Lemma 6.1.41 *The TRS $\mathcal{Q}_4$ is nonself-embedding.*

Proof If $\mathcal{Q}_4$ is self-embedding, then by Lemma 6.1.40 there exists a rewrite sequence $t \to_{\mathcal{Q}_4}^{+} u \to_{\mathcal{E}mb}^{*} t$ such that the subsequence from t to u contains a root rewrite step. By the form of the rules in $\mathcal{Q}_4$, the latter condition requires that the first step in the subsequence from t to u is a root rewrite step. Moreover, later steps must take place strictly below the root. It follows that $t = f(d,e,s)$, $s \to_{\mathcal{Q}_4}^{*} s'$ and either $u = f(s', g(e), e)$ or $u = f(g(d), s', d)$. But then t can only be embedded in u if $s = e$ and $s' \to_{\mathcal{E}mb}^{*} d$ or $s = d$ and $s' \to_{\mathcal{E}mb}^{*} e$. Note that t cannot be embedded in s' as t contains one more f symbol than s'. However, both cases contradict $s \to_{\mathcal{Q}_4}^{*} s'$. Hence $\mathcal{Q}_4$ is nonself-embedding. □

Lemma 6.1.42 *The TRS $\mathcal{S}(P, \mathcal{Q}_4)$ is nonself-embedding for every PCP instance P.*

Proof Suppose, on the contrary, that $\mathcal{S}(P, \mathcal{Q}_4)$ is self-embedding. According to Lemma 6.1.40, there exists a rewrite sequence

$$t \to_{\mathcal{S}(P,\mathcal{Q}_4)}^{+} u \to_{\mathcal{E}mb}^{*} t \qquad (6.21)$$

such that its first part contains a step at the root position. By the form of the rules in $\mathcal{S}(P, \mathcal{Q}_4)$, this implies that t is a redex, so we may write $t = A(V, W, f(d, e, t'))$. The term u can be written (cf. the proof of Lemma 6.1.34) as $C[v_1, \ldots, v_k]$ such that $C[\ ]$ is a nonempty context consisting of B symbols and every v_i starts with an A symbol. We can rearrange the second part of (6.21) into $u \to_{\mathcal{E}mb}^{+} v_i \to_{\mathcal{E}mb}^{*} t$ for suitable $1 \leq i \leq k$. Lemma 6.1.34 yields $\phi(t) \to_{\mathcal{U}(P,\mathcal{Q}_4)}^{+} \phi(v_i)$. Because $\mathcal{Q}_4$ is nonduplicating and variable-preserving, v_i has the same number of A

symbols as t and hence no A symbol is erased in $v_i \to^*_{\mathcal{E}mb} t$. This implies that $\phi(v_i) \to^*_{\mathcal{E}mb} \phi(t)$. We have $\phi(t) = A(V, \phi(W), f(d, e, \phi(t')))$ and $\phi(v_i) = A(\phi(V'), \phi(W'), \phi(u'))$ for a certain $2n + 8$-tuple V', sextuple W', and term u'. We must have $\phi(V') \to^*_{\mathcal{E}mb} V$, $\phi(W') \to^*_{\mathcal{E}mb} \phi(W)$, and $\phi(u') \to^*_{\mathcal{E}mb} f(d, e, \phi(t'))$. From Lemma 6.1.3 we infer that either $f(d, e, \phi(t')) \to^+_{\mathcal{Q}_4} \phi(u')$ or $\phi(t) \to^+_{\mathcal{U}_-(P,\mathcal{Q})} \phi(v_i)$ (and $f(d, e, \phi(t')) = \phi(u')$). The former contradicts the fact that $\mathcal{Q}_4$ is nonself-embedding (Lemma 6.1.41), the latter the simple termination of $\mathcal{U}_-(P, \mathcal{Q})$ (which follows from Corollary 6.1.23). □

Proposition 6.1.43 *The TRS $\mathcal{S}(P, \mathcal{Q}_4)$ is simply terminating if and only if P admits no solution.*

Proof If P admits a solution, then with the help of Lemmas 6.1.2 and 6.1.27 we obtain the following cycle in $\mathcal{S}(P, \mathcal{Q}_4) \cup \mathcal{E}mb$:

$$\begin{aligned} A(V, W, f(d, e, d)) &\to^+ C_1[A(V, W, f(d, g(e), e))] \to^+ A(V, W, f(d, e, e)) \\ &\to^+ C_2[A(V, W, f(g(d), e, d))] \to^+ A(V, W, f(d, e, d)) \end{aligned}$$

So $\mathcal{S}(P, \mathcal{Q}_4)$ is not simply terminating. Conversely, if P has no solution, then $\mathcal{S}(P, \mathcal{Q}_4)$ is ω-terminating by Lemma 6.1.26 and thus simply terminating. □

The Implication $TT \Rightarrow ST$

Let

$$\mathcal{Q}_5 = \left\{ \begin{array}{lcl} f(d, e) & \to & f(e, e) \\ f(d, e) & \to & f(d, d) \end{array} \right.$$

Clearly, this TRS is terminating but not totally terminating (as d and e are incomparable). According to Lemma 5.2.34, it is even simply terminating because it is size-preserving.

Lemma 6.1.44 *The TRS $\mathcal{S}(P, \mathcal{Q}_5)$ is simply terminating for every PCP instance P.*

Proof According to Lemma 6.1.24(2), it is sufficient to show that $\mathcal{U}(P, \mathcal{Q}_5)$ is simply terminating. Because $\mathcal{U}(P, \mathcal{Q}_5)$ is size-preserving, simple termination follows from termination. By using typing, the termination of $\mathcal{U}(P, \mathcal{Q}_5)$ follows from the termination of $\mathcal{Q}_5$, just as in the proof of Lemma 6.1.38. □

Proposition 6.1.45 *The TRS $\mathcal{S}(P, \mathcal{Q}_5)$ is totally terminating if and only if P admits no solution.*

Proof If P has no solution, then ω-termination, and thus also total termination, of $\mathcal{S}(P, \mathcal{Q}_5)$ follows from Lemma 6.1.26. Let P have a solution. We show that $\mathcal{S}(P, \mathcal{Q}_5)$ is not totally terminating. According to Lemma 6.1.24(3), this is equivalent to showing that $\mathcal{U}(P, \mathcal{Q}_5)$ is not totally terminating. Suppose, on the contrary, that $\mathcal{U}(P, \mathcal{Q}_5)$ is totally terminating. So there exists a compatible total reduction order $>$. Because by Lemma 6.1.2 both $A(V, W, f(d, e)) \to^+ A(V, W, f(e, e))$ and $A(V, W, f(d, e)) \to^+ A(V, W, f(d, d))$, we have $A(V, W, f(d, e)) > A(V, W, f(e, e))$ and $A(V, W, f(d, e)) > A(V, W, f(d, d))$ by compatibility. According to the truncation rule for total reduction orders, one may remove a context $C[\,]$ from an inequality $C[t] > C[t']$; see Proposition 5.3.7. By removing $A(V, W, f(\ , e))$ and $A(V, W, f(d,\ ))$, respectively, we obtain the impossible $d > e$ and $e > d$. □

The Implication $\omega T \Rightarrow TT$

Geser [Ges97] showed the undecidability of ω-termination for totally terminating TRSs. In this section we will show that ω-termination is an undecidable property of one-rule totally terminating TRSs.

Let $\mathcal{Q}_6 = \{f(g(x)) \to g(f(f(x)))\}$. This TRS is totally terminating but not ω-terminating; see [Zan94, proposition 11] and cf. Table 5.1.

Lemma 6.1.46 *The TRS $\mathcal{S}(P, \mathcal{Q}_6)$ is totally terminating for every PCP instance P.*

Proof First we show that $\mathcal{U}(P, \mathcal{Q}_6)$ is totally terminating. Let the interpretation $[\,]'$ in $\mathbb{N}_+^2$ be defined by $[f]'(x, y) = (x, x+y)$, $[g]'(x, y) = (2x+1, y)$, and

$$[h]'((x_1, y_1), \dots, (x_n, y_n)) = (1 + \sum_{i=1}^{n} x_i, 1 + \sum_{i=1}^{n} y_i)$$

for every function symbol $h \in \mathcal{F}_{\mathcal{U}} \setminus \{f, g\}$. We claim that the interpretation $[\![\,]\!]$ in $\mathbb{N}_+^3$ (ordered lexicographically) defined by $[\![\,]\!] = ([\,]', [\,])$ proves total termination of $\mathcal{U}(P, \mathcal{Q}_6)$. For rules $l \to r$ of type (III) and ground substitutions σ we have $[l\sigma]' > [r\sigma]'$. For the rules in $\mathcal{U}_-(P, \mathcal{Q}_6)$ we have $[l\sigma]' = [r\sigma]'$ and $[l\sigma] > [r\sigma]$ by Theorem 6.1.20. From Lemma 6.1.24(3) it follows that $\mathcal{S}(P, \mathcal{Q}_6)$ is totally terminating. □

Proposition 6.1.47 *The TRS $\mathcal{S}(P, \mathcal{Q}_6)$ is ω-terminating if and only if P admits no solution.*

Proof If P has no solution, then ω-termination of $\mathcal{S}(P, \mathcal{Q}_6)$ follows from Lemma 6.1.26. Let P have a solution. We show that $\mathcal{S}(P, \mathcal{Q}_6)$ is not ω-terminating. According to Lemma 6.1.25, it is sufficient to show that

$\mathcal{U}(P, \mathcal{Q}_6)$ is not ω-terminating. Suppose, on the contrary, that $\mathcal{U}(P, \mathcal{Q}_6)$ is ω-terminating. So there exists a compatible well-founded monotone algebra $\mathcal{N} = (\mathbb{N}, >)$. According to Lemma 6.1.2, we have

$$A(V, W, f(g(t))) \to^+ A(V, W, g(f(f(t))))$$

and thus $A(V, W, f(g(t))) >_{\mathcal{N}} A(V, W, g(f(f(t))))$ for every ground term t. Because the interpretation of A is strictly monotone in its last argument, this is only possible if $f(g(t)) >_{\mathcal{N}} g(f(f(t)))$ for every ground term t, which contradicts the fact that $\mathcal{Q}_6$ is not ω-terminating. □

In this section we succeeded in proving relative undecidability of all the implications in hierarchy (6.1). What about the other implications in the extended termination hierarchy?

It is currently unknown whether polynomial termination is an undecidable property of (ω-terminating) TRSs. The TRS

$$f(g(h(x))) \quad \to \quad g(f(h(g(x))))$$

is ω-terminating but not polynomially terminating; see [Zan94, proposition 10] and cf. Table 5.1. So the polynomially terminating TRSs form a proper subclass of the ω-terminating TRSs. It has been conjectured in [GMOZ02a] that the implication PT $\Rightarrow$ ωT is relatively undecidable, even for one-rule TRSs.

A principle problem arises if we try to apply the preceding generic approach to the implications in hierarchy (6.2). This is due to the fact that the one-rule system $\mathcal{S}(P, \mathcal{Q})$ is nonoverlapping unless the TRS $\mathcal{Q}$ has the function symbol A at the root of the left-hand side LHS of its rules. And for nonoverlapping TRSs, we have WIN $\Leftrightarrow$ SIN $\Leftrightarrow$ SN according to Theorem 5.6.10(1). We will illustrate this problem by the implication SN $\Rightarrow$ SIN. It is known that the converse implication does not hold, even for one-rule TRSs. An example of an innermost terminating but nonterminating one-rule TRS (in fact SRS) is the system

$$\mathcal{Q}_8 = f(g(f(g(x)))) \to g(f(g(f(f(g(x))))))$$

from Geser [Ges00] (an innermost termination proof can also be found in [AG97b]). Note that this TRS is overlapping. Nevertheless, $\mathcal{S}(P, \mathcal{Q}_8)$ is nonoverlapping and thus it cannot be used to show relative undecidability of the implication SN $\Rightarrow$ SIN for one-rule TRSs.

Therefore, we will be content with showing relative undecidability of the implications in hierarchy (6.2) for many-rule systems. To this end, we use slight modifications of the system $\mathcal{R}(P)$ from Section 5.1.

The Implication SN ⇒ SIN

With every PCP instance P, we associate the TRS

$$\mathcal{S}_1(P) = \begin{cases} g(F(c,c,a(z))) & \rightarrow & g(F(a(z),a(z),a(z))) & \forall a \in \Gamma \\ g(F(\alpha(x),\beta(y),z)) & \rightarrow & g(F(x,y,z)) & \forall(\alpha,\beta) \in P \\ F(x,y,z) & \rightarrow & d \end{cases}$$

Lemma 6.1.48 *The TRS $\mathcal{S}_1(P)$ is innermost terminating for every PCP instance P.*

Proof The proof is straightforward by structural induction. (Alternatively, one may use Theorem 5.6.18.) □

Proposition 6.1.49 *The TRS $\mathcal{S}_1(P)$ is terminating if and only if P admits no solution.*

Proof The proof is similar to the proof of Proposition 5.1.1. □

The Implication SIN ⇒ WIN

Given PCP instance P, let

$$\mathcal{S}_2(P) = \begin{cases} F(c,c,a(z)) & \rightarrow & F(a(z),a(z),a(z)) & \forall a \in \Gamma \\ F(\alpha(x),\beta(y),z) & \rightarrow & F(x,y,z) & \forall(\alpha,\beta) \in P \\ F(x,y,z) & \rightarrow & d \end{cases}$$

Lemma 6.1.50 *The TRS $\mathcal{S}_2(P)$ is innermost normalizing for every PCP instance P.*

Proof The proof is straightforward by structural induction. □

Proposition 6.1.51 *The TRS $\mathcal{S}_2(P)$ is innermost terminating if and only if P admits no solution.*

Proof $\mathcal{S}_2(P)$ is terminating if and only if P admits no solution; cf. Proposition 5.1.1. By Theorem 5.6.8, $\mathcal{S}_2(P)$ is innermost terminating if and only if it is terminating because it is a locally confluent overlay system. □

The Implication WIN ⇒ WN

In order to prove relative undecidability of WIN ⇒ WN, we will use Theorem 5.6.10. This theorem is applicable to nonoverlapping systems only. Note that the system $\mathcal{R}(P)$ from Section 5.1—as well as $\mathcal{S}_1(P)$ and $\mathcal{S}_2(P)$—may be overlapping, consider, for example, $P = \{(100,10),(10,1)\}$. For this reason, we assume that PCP instances are presented as ordered lists (α_1,β_1), $(\alpha_2,\beta_2),\ldots,(\alpha_n,\beta_n)$ rather than sets. This entails no loss of generality. In this setting, Post's correspondence problem can be stated as follows:

Given a finite alphabet Γ and a finite list $P = (\alpha_1, \beta_1), \ldots, (\alpha_n, \beta_n)$ of pairs of nonempty strings over Γ, is there some natural number $m > 0$ and indices $1 \le i_1, \ldots, i_m \le n$ such that $\alpha_{i_1} \cdots \alpha_{i_m} = \beta_{i_1} \cdots \beta_{i_m}$?

With every PCP instance P, we associate the TRS $\mathcal{S}(P)$ consisting of the rewrite rules

$$
\begin{array}{rcll}
F(c, c, a(z), c, w) & \to & F(a(z), a(z), a(z), w, w) & \forall a \in \Gamma \\
F(\alpha_i(x), \beta_i(y), z, i(v), w) & \to & F(x, y, z, v, w) & \forall i \in \{1, \ldots, n\}
\end{array}
$$

The signature of $\mathcal{S}(P)$ consists of the function symbol F of arity 5, the constant c, and unary function symbols a and i for every element a and i from the alphabet Γ and the set $\{1, \ldots, n\}$, respectively. Note that $\mathcal{S}(P)$ is orthogonal for every PCP instance P. Apart from that, $\mathcal{S}(P)$ shares the following key property with $\mathcal{R}(P)$. The proof is essentially the same as that of Proposition 5.1.1.

Proposition 6.1.52 *The TRS $\mathcal{S}(P)$ is terminating if and only if the PCP instance P admits no solution.*

Proof Suppose $\gamma \in \Gamma^+$ is a solution for P. So $\gamma = \alpha_{i_1} \cdots \alpha_{i_m} = \beta_{i_1} \cdots \beta_{i_m}$ for some $m \ge 1$ and $1 \le i_1, \ldots, i_m \le n$. We have the following cyclic derivation in $\mathcal{S}(P)$:

$$
\begin{array}{rl}
 & F(\gamma(c), \gamma(c), \gamma(c), i_1 \cdots i_m(c), i_1 \cdots i_m(c)) \\
\to & F(\alpha_{i_2} \cdots \alpha_{i_{m-1}}(c), \beta_{i_2} \cdots \beta_{i_{m-1}}(c), \gamma(c), i_2 \cdots i_m(c), i_1 \cdots i_m(c)) \\
\to^* & F(c, c, \gamma(c), c, i_1 \cdots i_m(c)) \\
\to & F(\gamma(c), \gamma(c), \gamma(c), i_1 \cdots i_m(c), i_1 \cdots i_m(c))
\end{array}
$$

Conversely, suppose that $\mathcal{S}(P)$ admits an infinite derivation. Because $\mathcal{S}(P)$ is noncollapsing, we may use type introduction (Theorem 5.5.25). Hence we may assume that the function symbols come from a many-sorted signature such that the left- and right-hand sides of all rewrite rules are well-typed and of the same type. We use two sorts 1 and 2 with F of type $1 \times \cdots \times 1 \to 2$ and all other function symbols of type $1 \times \cdots \times 1 \to 1$. Terms of type 1 are in normal form. So if $\mathcal{S}(P)$ is nonterminating, then there exists an infinite derivation consisting of terms of type 2. Hence all steps take place at the root position. Obviously, in the infinite derivation both kinds of rewrite rules are used infinitely often. Any such reduction sequence must contain a cyclic subsequence of the form

$$F(c, c, a(t), c, t') \to F(a(t), a(t), a(t), t', t') \to^+ F(c, c, a(t), c, t')$$

such that in $F(a(t), a(t), a(t), t', t') \to^+ F(c, c, a(t), c, t')$ only rewrite rules of the form $F(\alpha_i(x), \beta_i(y), z, i(v), w) \to F(x, y, z, v, w)$ are used. Hence

$$a(t) = \alpha_{i_1} \cdots \alpha_{i_m} = \beta_{i_1} \cdots \beta_{i_m}$$

for some $m \geq 1$ and $1 \leq i_1, \ldots, i_m \leq n$. Clearly, $a(t)$ is a solution for P. □

Now let $\mathcal{S}_3(P)$ consist of the rewrite rules

$$\begin{array}{rcll} F(c,c,a(z),c,w) & \to & g(F(a(z),a(z),a(z),w,w)) & \forall a \in \Gamma \\ F(\alpha_i(x),\beta_i(y),z,i(v),w) & \to & F(x,y,z,v,w) & \forall i \in \{1,\ldots,n\} \\ g(x) & \to & d & \end{array}$$

Lemma 6.1.53 *The TRS $\mathcal{S}_3(P)$ is normalizing for all PCP instances P.*

Proof It is proven by induction on the structure of terms. □

Proposition 6.1.54 *The TRS $\mathcal{S}_3(P)$ is innermost normalizing if and only if P admits no solution.*

Proof Observe that $\mathcal{S}_3(P)$ is orthogonal. According to Theorem 5.6.10(1), it is thus sufficient to show that $\mathcal{S}_3(P)$ is terminating if and only if P admits no solution. It can be shown, as in the proof of Proposition 6.1.52, that this is indeed the case. □

The Properties WN and AC

We conclude this section by observing that the two properties in the termination hierarchy that do not appear in an X position of an implication $X \Rightarrow Y$ are also undecidable.

Corollary 6.1.55 *Normalization and acyclicity are undecidable properties of TRSs.*

Proof According to Proposition 6.1.52, the system $\mathcal{S}(P)$ is terminating if and only if P admits no solution. Because $\mathcal{S}(P)$ is nonoverlapping and variable-preserving, it is terminating if and only if it is normalizing; see Theorem 5.6.10(2). Therefore, normalization is undecidable. As a matter of fact, it can be seen from the proof of Proposition 6.1.52 that $\mathcal{S}(P)$ is acyclic if and only if P admits no solution. Hence acyclicity is also undecidable. □

6.2 The Confluence Hierarchy

Before we show relative undecidability of the implications in the confluence hierarchy, we augment it with the following three properties.

Definition 6.2.1 A TRS $\mathcal{R}$ is called *ground confluent* (or ground Church-Rosser, GCR) if all its ground terms are confluent.

TRS	Is	But not
$b \leftarrow a \rightarrow c, b \rightarrow d \rightarrow e \leftarrow c$	CR	SCR
$x \leftarrow f(x) \rightarrow a$, where $\mathcal{F} = \{a, f\}$	GCR	CR
$b \leftarrow a \rightarrow c,\ a \leftarrow c \rightarrow d$	WCR	CR
$b \leftarrow a \rightarrow c,\ b \rightarrow b,\ c \rightarrow c$	NF	CR
$b \leftarrow a \rightarrow c,\ c \rightarrow c$	UN	NF
$b \leftarrow a \rightarrow c \leftarrow d \rightarrow e,\ c \rightarrow c$	$\mathrm{UN}^{\rightarrow}$	UN
$b \leftarrow a \rightarrow c$	CON	UN
$b \leftarrow a \rightarrow c$	$\mathrm{CON}^{\rightarrow}$	$\mathrm{UN}^{\rightarrow}$
$x \leftarrow f(x) \rightarrow a$	$\mathrm{CON}^{\rightarrow}$	CON

TABLE 6.1. Counterexamples in the confluence hierarchy.

In many situations we do not need confluence—ground confluence suffices. Indeed, for most of the properties in the confluence hierarchy a "ground" version makes sense. A study of the resulting "ground confluence hierarchy," however, is beyond the scope of this book.

Definition 6.2.2 A TRS $\mathcal{R}$ is called *consistent* (CON) if, for all $x, y \in \mathcal{V}$, $x \leftrightarrow^*_{\mathcal{R}} y$ implies $x = y$ (so two distinct variables are not convertible). $\mathcal{R}$ is called *consistent w.r.t. reduction* ($\mathrm{CON}^{\rightarrow}$) if $x\ {}_{\mathcal{R}}^{*}\!\!\leftarrow t \rightarrow^*_{\mathcal{R}} y$ implies $x = y$ (so no term reduces to two distinct variables).

The notion of CON goes back to [SS89], and $\mathrm{CON}^{\rightarrow}$ plays a role in modularity issues; see Chapter 8.

The three properties fit into the confluence hierarchy as depicted here:

$$
\begin{array}{ccccccccc}
 & & \mathrm{GCR} & & & & & & \\
 & & \Uparrow & & & & & & \\
\mathrm{SCR} & \Rightarrow & \mathrm{CR} & \Rightarrow & \mathrm{NF} & \Rightarrow & \mathrm{UN} & \Rightarrow & \mathrm{UN}^{\rightarrow} \\
 & & \Downarrow & & & & \Downarrow & & \Downarrow \\
 & & \mathrm{WCR} & & & & \mathrm{CON} & \Rightarrow & \mathrm{CON}^{\rightarrow}
\end{array}
$$

None of the converse implications holds true. For most implications, this was shown in Section 2.2. For the convenience of the reader, all counterexamples are collected in Table 6.1. As already seen in Section 4.1, confluence is undecidable. Undecidability of the other properties in the confluence hierarchy can be shown in a similar fashion. Ground confluence is known to be undecidable for terminating systems; see Kapur et al. [KNO80]. In this section we will show the stronger result of relative undecidability: For all implications $X \Rightarrow Y$ in the confluence hierarchy we will prove that the property X is undecidable for TRSs satisfying Y. Most results are already contained in [GMOZ97]. For an even more detailed study of relative undecidability in the confluence hierarchy, we refer to [GMOZ02b].

In this section we assume that PCP instances are presented as ordered lists $(\alpha_1, \beta_1), (\alpha_2, \beta_2), \ldots, (\alpha_n, \beta_n)$ rather than sets. This entails no loss of generality.

We have seen that an arbitrary PCP instance P admits a solution if and only if $A \to^*_{\mathcal{R}(P)} B$ for the TRS $\mathcal{R}(P)$ from Section 4.1. To arrive at results for linear TRSs and for some technical convenience, this basic system is replaced with

$$\mathcal{R}_1(P) = \left\{ \begin{array}{rcll} A & \to & f(\alpha_i(c), \beta_i(c)) & \text{for all } i \in \{1, \ldots, n\} \\ f(x, y) & \to & f(\alpha_i(x), \beta_i(y)) & \text{for all } i \in \{1, \ldots, n\} \\ f(x, y) & \to & g(x, y) & \\ f(x, y) & \to & A & \\ g(x, y) & \to & A & \\ g(a(x), a(y)) & \to & g(x, y) & \text{for all } a \in \Gamma \\ g(c, c) & \to & B & \end{array} \right.$$

The TRS $\mathcal{R}_1(P)$ is the basis for many of our relative undecidability results in the confluence hierarchy. We show that it shares the desired key property with the TRS $\mathcal{R}(P)$ from Section 4.1.

Proposition 6.2.3 *$A \to^*_{\mathcal{R}_1(P)} B$ if and only if P admits a solution.*

Proof Suppose $\gamma \in \Gamma^+$ is a solution for P. So $\gamma = \alpha_{i_1} \cdots \alpha_{i_m} = \beta_{i_1} \cdots \beta_{i_m}$ for some $m \geq 1$ and $1 \leq i_1, \ldots, i_m \leq n$. We have the following rewrite sequence in $\mathcal{R}_1(P)$:

$$\begin{array}{l} A \to f(\alpha_{i_m}(c), \beta_{i_m}(c)) \to^* f(\alpha_{i_1} \cdots \alpha_{i_m}(c), \beta_{i_1} \cdots \beta_{i_m}(c)) = f(\gamma(c), \gamma(c)) \\ \quad \to g(\gamma(c), \gamma(c)) \to^+ g(c, c) \to B \end{array}$$

Conversely, suppose that $A \to^*_{\mathcal{R}_1(P)} B$. Beyond the last A occurring in this rewrite sequence, it is of the form

$$\begin{array}{l} A \to f(\alpha_{i_m}(c), \beta_{i_m}(c)) \to^* f(\alpha_{i_1} \cdots \alpha_{i_m}(c), \beta_{i_1} \cdots \beta_{i_m}(c)) \\ \quad \to \underbrace{g(\alpha_{i_1} \cdots \alpha_{i_m}(c), \beta_{i_1} \cdots \beta_{i_m}(c)) \to^* g(c, c)} \to B \end{array}$$

for some $m \geq 1$ with $1 \leq i_1, \ldots, i_m \leq n$. In the underbraced part only rewrite rules of the form $g(a(x), a(y)) \to g(x, y)$ are used. Hence $\alpha_{i_1} \cdots \alpha_{i_m}(c) = \beta_{i_1} \cdots \beta_{i_m}(c)$ is a solution for P. □

We use the preceding result to relate $\mathcal{R}_1(P)$ to some properties in the confluence hierarchy.

Lemma 6.2.4 *The following statements are equivalent:*

1. *The TRS $\mathcal{R}_1(P)$ has the normal form property.*
2. *The TRS $\mathcal{R}_1(P)$ is locally confluent.*

3. The TRS $\mathcal{R}_1(P)$ is ground confluent.

4. The TRS $\mathcal{R}_1(P)$ is confluent.

5. The PCP instance P admits a solution.

Proof Because confluence implies the normal form property, local confluence, and ground confluence, according to Proposition 6.2.3, it suffices to show that (i) $A \to^*_{\mathcal{R}_1(P)} B$ whenever $\mathcal{R}_1(P)$ has the normal form property, is locally confluent, or is ground confluent, and (ii) $\mathcal{R}_1(P)$ is confluent whenever $A \to^*_{\mathcal{R}_1(P)} B$. For (i) we note that $A \leftarrow g(c,c) \to B$ in $\mathcal{R}_1(P)$ with B a normal form, hence $A \to^*_{\mathcal{R}_1(P)} B$ by definition of the normal form property, local confluence, or ground confluence. For (ii) we consider the TRS $\mathcal{R}'_1(P) = \mathcal{R}_1(P) \cup \{A \to B, f(x,y) \to B, g(x,y) \to B\}$. Because $A \to^*_{\mathcal{R}_1(P)} B$, the relations $\leftrightarrow^*_{\mathcal{R}_1(P)}$ and $\leftrightarrow^*_{\mathcal{R}'_1(P)}$ coincide. The TRS $\mathcal{R}'_1(P)$ is linear and strongly closed and thus (strongly) confluent by Theorem 4.3.2. Hence $\mathcal{R}_1(P)$ is also confluent. □

To prove some of the relative undecidability results for properties dealing with conversion (UN and CON), we need to relate solvability of P to the existence of a *conversion* between A and B. TRS $\mathcal{R}_1(P)$ is not suitable for this purpose because in $\mathcal{R}_1(P)$ the terms A and B may be convertible even if P admits no solution. For example, in $\mathcal{R}_1(\{(100,10),(10,1)\})$ we have $A \to f(100(c),10(c)) \leftarrow f(0(c),0(c)) \to^* B$.

Let $\mathcal{R}_2(P) = \mathcal{R}^1_2(P) \cup \mathcal{R}^2_2(P)$, where

$$\mathcal{R}^1_2(P) = \left\{ \begin{array}{rcll} f(c,c,c,c) & \to & A & \\ f(c,c,c,i(w)) & \to & f(c,c,c,w) & \forall i \in \{1,\ldots,n\} \end{array} \right.$$

and

$$\mathcal{R}^2_2(P) = \left\{ \begin{array}{rcll} f(\alpha_i(x),\beta_i(y),i(z),w) & \to & f(x,y,z,i(w)) & \forall i \in \{1,\ldots,n\} \\ f(x,y,i(z),c) & \to & g(x,y,i(z)) & \forall i \in \{1,\ldots,n\} \\ g(a(x),a(y),z) & \to & g(x,y,z) & \forall a \in \Gamma \\ g(c,c,i(z)) & \to & g(c,c,z) & \forall i \in \{1,\ldots,n\} \\ g(c,c,c) & \to & B & \end{array} \right.$$

Note that $\mathcal{R}_2(P)$ is terminating for all PCP instances P.

Proposition 6.2.5 *$A \leftrightarrow^*_{\mathcal{R}_2(P)} B$ if and only if P admits a solution.*

Proof First suppose that P admits a solution $\gamma = \alpha_{i_1} \cdots \alpha_{i_m} = \beta_{i_1} \cdots \beta_{i_m}$ for some $m \geq 1$ and $1 \leq i_1, \ldots, i_m \leq n$. Then we have the following conversion between A and B:

$$\begin{array}{l} A \leftarrow f(c,c,c,c) \;{}^*\!\!\leftarrow f(c,c,c,i_m \cdots i_1(c)) \;{}^*\!\!\leftarrow f(\gamma(c),\gamma(c),i_1 \cdots i_m(c),c) \\ \quad \to g(\gamma(c),\gamma(c),i_1 \cdots i_m(c)) \to^* g(c,c,i_1 \cdots i_m(c)) \to^* g(c,c,c) \to B. \end{array}$$

Next suppose that A and B are convertible. Because $\mathcal{R}_2(P)$ is variable-preserving and noncollapsing, it follows that all steps in a conversion between A and B take place at the root position. It is also easy to see that any term of the form $f(t_1, t_2, t_3, t_4)$ in a conversion between A and B satisfies $t_4 = i_m \cdots i_1(c)$ with $1 \leq i_1, \ldots, i_m \leq n$ for some $m \geq 0$. Furthermore, there exists a conversion in $\mathcal{R}_2^1(P)$ between A and $f(c, c, c, i_m \cdots i_1(c))$ for all $m \geq 0$ and $1 \leq i_1, \ldots, i_m \leq n$. We claim that there exists a conversion

$$A \leftrightarrow^*_{\mathcal{R}_2^1(P)} t \leftrightarrow^*_{\mathcal{R}_2^2(P)} B$$

for some term $t = f(c, c, c, i_m \cdots i_1(c))$. This easily follows from the preceding observations by considering the last application of a rewrite rule of $\mathcal{R}_2^1(P)$ in a shortest conversion between A and B. Let $\mathcal{R}_2^3(P)$ be the TRS obtained from $\mathcal{R}_2^2(P)$ by orienting all

$$f(\alpha_i(x), \beta_i(y), i(z), w) \to f(x, y, z, i(w))$$

rules from right to left. Clearly, $\mathcal{R}_2^2(P)$ and $\mathcal{R}_2^3(P)$ generate the same conversion relation. The crucial observation is that $\mathcal{R}_2^1(P)$ and $\mathcal{R}_2^3(P)$ are orthogonal and thus confluent. Because A and B are normal forms, the conversion between A and B has the form

$$A \ {}_{\mathcal{R}_2^1(P)}^{\ \ *}\!\!\leftarrow t \to^*_{\mathcal{R}_2^3(P)} B$$

It follows that

$$\begin{aligned} A \leftarrow f(c,c,c,c) \ {}^*\!\!\leftarrow f(c,c,c,i_m \cdots i_1(c)) &\to^* f(\gamma_1(c), \gamma_2(c), i_1 \cdots i_m(c), c) \\ \to g(\gamma_1(c), \gamma_2(c), i_1 \cdots i_m(c)) &\to^* g(c, c, i_1 \cdots i_m(c)) \to^* g(c,c,c) \to B \end{aligned}$$

with $\gamma_1 = \alpha_{i_1} \cdots \alpha_{i_m}$ and $\gamma_2 = \beta_{i_1} \cdots \beta_{i_m}$. The step $f(\cdots) \to g(\cdots)$ is possible only if $m \geq 1$ and the sequence from $g(\gamma_1(c), \gamma_2(c), i_1 \cdots i_m(c))$ to $g(c, c, i_1 \cdots i_m(c))$ entails that $\gamma_1 = \gamma_2$. We conclude that P admits a solution. □

Now the approach to proving relative undecidability in the confluence hierarchy is as follows: For every implication $X \Rightarrow Y$ we construct a minor extension of $\mathcal{R}_1(P)$ or $\mathcal{R}_2(P)$ that always satisfies Y and that satisfies X if and only if P has a (or has no) solution.

The Implication SCR ⇒ CR

Let $\mathcal{R}_3(P) = \mathcal{R}_1(P) \cup \{B \to C, C \to A\}$.

Lemma 6.2.6 *The TRS $\mathcal{R}_3(P)$ is confluent for every PCP instance P.*

Proof One easily checks that the linear TRS $\mathcal{R}_3'(P) = \mathcal{R}_3(P) \cup \{B \to A\}$ is strongly closed, hence (strongly) confluent by Theorem 4.3.2. Because the relations $\to^*_{\mathcal{R}_3(P)}$ and $\to^*_{\mathcal{R}_3'(P)}$ coincide, $\mathcal{R}_3(P)$ is also confluent. □

Proposition 6.2.7 *The TRS $\mathcal{R}_3(P)$ is strongly confluent if and only if P admits a solution.*

Proof In a shortest $\mathcal{R}_3(P)$-reduction sequence from A to B the rewrite rules $B \to C$ and $C \to A$ are not used. Hence $A \to^*_{\mathcal{R}_3(P)} B$ if and only if $A \to^*_{\mathcal{R}_1(P)} B$. According to Proposition 6.2.3, we have to show that $\mathcal{R}_3(P)$ is strongly confluent if and only if $A \to^*_{\mathcal{R}_3(P)} B$. In $\mathcal{R}_3(P)$ we have $B \leftarrow g(c,c) \to A$. If $\mathcal{R}_3(P)$ is strongly confluent, then $B \to^= \cdot {}^*\!\leftarrow A$, so either $B\ {}^*\!\leftarrow A$ or $B \to C\ {}^*\!\leftarrow A$. Because any reduction sequence from A to C must pass through B, in both cases we have the desired $A \to^*_{\mathcal{R}_3(P)} B$. Conversely, if $A \to^*_{\mathcal{R}_3(P)} B$, then one easily checks that $\mathcal{R}_3(P)$ is strongly closed and therefore strongly confluent by Theorem 4.3.2. □

The Implication CR ⇒ WCR

Let $\mathcal{R}_4(P) = \mathcal{R}_1(P) \cup \{B \to f(c,c), B \to C\}$.

Lemma 6.2.8 *TRS $\mathcal{R}_4(P)$ is locally confluent for every PCP instance P.*

Proof One readily verifies that all critical pairs of $\mathcal{R}_4(P)$ are joinable. □

Proposition 6.2.9 *The TRS $\mathcal{R}_4(P)$ is confluent if and only if P admits a solution.*

Proof In a shortest $\mathcal{R}_4(P)$-reduction sequence from A to B the rewrite rules $B \to f(c,c)$ and $B \to C$ are not used. Hence $A \to^*_{\mathcal{R}_4(P)} B$ if and only if $A \to^*_{\mathcal{R}_1(P)} B$. According to Proposition 6.2.3, we have to show that $\mathcal{R}_4(P)$ is confluent if and only if $A \to^*_{\mathcal{R}_4(P)} B$. In $\mathcal{R}_4(P)$ we have $A \leftarrow f(c,c) \leftarrow B \to C$. If $\mathcal{R}_4(P)$ is confluent, then $A \to^*_{\mathcal{R}_4(P)} C$, which is equivalent to $A \to^*_{\mathcal{R}_4(P)} B$. Conversely, if $A \to^*_{\mathcal{R}_4(P)} B$, then we obtain confluence by considering the system $\mathcal{R}'_4(P) = \mathcal{R}_4(P) \cup \{A \to C, f(x,y) \to C, g(x,y) \to C\}$. It is not difficult to show that $\mathcal{R}'_4(P)$ is linear and strongly closed and thus (strongly) confluent by Theorem 4.3.2. Because the relations $\to^*_{\mathcal{R}_4(P)}$ and $\to^*_{\mathcal{R}'_4(P)}$ coincide, $\mathcal{R}_4(P)$ is confluent. □

The Implication CR ⇒ GCR

Let $\mathcal{R}_5(P)$ be the union of

$$\mathcal{R}^1_5(P) = \left\{ \begin{array}{rcll} A(z) & \to & f(\alpha_i(c), \beta_i(c), z) & \text{for all } i \in \{1,\ldots,n\} \\ f(x,y,z) & \to & f(\alpha_i(x), \beta_i(y), z) & \text{for all } i \in \{1,\ldots,n\} \\ f(x,y,z) & \to & g(x,y,z) & \\ f(x,y,z) & \to & A(z) & \\ g(x,y,z) & \to & A(z) & \\ g(a(x),a(y),z) & \to & g(x,y,z) & \text{for all } a \in \Gamma \\ g(c,c,z) & \to & B(z) & \end{array} \right.$$

and

$$\mathcal{R}_5^2(P) = \begin{cases} c & \to & D \\ a(D) & \to & D \quad \text{for all } a \in \Gamma \\ f(D,D,D) & \to & D \\ g(D,D,D) & \to & D \\ A(D) & \to & D \\ B(D) & \to & D \end{cases}$$

Note that the only difference between $\mathcal{R}_5^1(P)$ and $\mathcal{R}_1(P)$ is the addition of an extra argument that is simply propagated.

Lemma 6.2.10 *The TRS $\mathcal{R}_5(P)$ is ground confluent for every PCP instance P.*

Proof In $\mathcal{R}_5^2(P) \subseteq \mathcal{R}_5(P)$ every ground term rewrites to D. Hence $\mathcal{R}_5(P)$ is ground confluent. □

Proposition 6.2.11 *The TRS $\mathcal{R}_5(P)$ is confluent if and only if P admits a solution.*

Proof It is not difficult to see that the statements $A(z) \to^*_{\mathcal{R}_5(P)} B(z)$ and $A \to^*_{\mathcal{R}_1(P)} B$ are equivalent. According to Proposition 6.2.3, we have to show that $\mathcal{R}_5(P)$ is confluent if and only if $A(z) \to^*_{\mathcal{R}_5(P)} B(z)$. In $\mathcal{R}_5(P)$ we have $A(z) \leftarrow g(c,c,z) \to B(z)$ with $B(z)$ in normal form. So if $\mathcal{R}_5(P)$ is confluent, then necessarily $A(z) \to^*_{\mathcal{R}_5(P)} B(z)$. Conversely, if $A(z) \to^*_{\mathcal{R}_5(P)} B(z)$, then we obtain confluence by considering the linear and strongly closed TRS $\mathcal{R}_5'(P) = \mathcal{R}_5(P) \cup \{A(z) \to B(z), f(x,y,z) \to B(z), g(x,y,z) \to B(z)\}$. □

The Implication CR ⇒ NF

Let $\mathcal{R}_6(P) = \mathcal{R}_1(P) \cup \{B \to B\}$.

Lemma 6.2.12 *The TRS $\mathcal{R}_6(P)$ has the normal form property for every PCP instance P.*

Proof The set of normal forms of $\mathcal{R}_6(P)$ coincides with the set of normalizing terms. Hence the normal form property is trivially satisfied. □

Proposition 6.2.13 *The TRS $\mathcal{R}_6(P)$ is confluent if and only if P admits a solution.*

Proof Because the relations $\to^*_{\mathcal{R}_6(P)}$ and $\to^*_{\mathcal{R}_1(P)}$ coincide, $\mathcal{R}_6(P)$ is confluent if and only if $\mathcal{R}_1(P)$ is confluent. Hence the result follows from Lemma 6.2.4. □

The Implication NF ⇒ UN

Lemma 6.2.14 *The TRS $\mathcal{R}_1(P)$ has unique normal forms for every PCP instance P.*

Proof Consider the confluent TRS $\mathcal{R}'_1(P)$ defined in the proof of Lemma 6.2.4. The relations $\leftrightarrow^*_{\mathcal{R}_1(P)}$ and $\leftrightarrow^*_{\mathcal{R}'_1(P)}$ coincide and furthermore the normal forms of the two TRSs are the same. It follows that $\mathcal{R}_1(P)$ has unique normal forms. □

We already observed in Lemma 6.2.4 that the TRS $\mathcal{R}_1(P)$ has the normal form property if and only if P has a solution.

The Implication UN ⇒ CON

Let $\mathcal{R}_7(P)$ be the union of $\mathcal{R}_2(P)$ and the rules

$$
\begin{array}{rcll}
f(x,y,z,w) & \to & f(x,y,z,w) & \\
g(x,y,z) & \to & g(x,y,z) & \\
a(x) & \to & a(x) & \text{for all } a \in \Gamma \\
i(x) & \to & i(x) & \text{for all } i \in \{1,\ldots,n\} \\
c & \to & c &
\end{array}
$$

Lemma 6.2.15 *$A \leftrightarrow^*_{\mathcal{R}_7(P)} B$ if and only if P admits a solution.*

Proof The proof is a direct consequence of Proposition 6.2.5 as $\leftrightarrow^*_{\mathcal{R}_7(P)} = \leftrightarrow^*_{\mathcal{R}_2(P)}$. □

Lemma 6.2.16 *The TRS $\mathcal{R}_7(P)$ is consistent for every PCP instance P.*

Proof The proof is trivial, as $\mathcal{R}_7(P)$ lacks collapsing rules. □

Proposition 6.2.17 *The TRS $\mathcal{R}_7(P)$ has unique normal forms if and only if P does not have a solution.*

Proof According to Lemma 6.2.15, we have to show that $\mathcal{R}_7(P)$ admits two different convertible normal forms if and only if A and B are convertible. Because A and B are normal forms, the if direction is trivial. Conversely, suppose that $\mathcal{R}_7(P)$ admits two different convertible normal forms t_1 and t_2. The only normal forms of $\mathcal{R}_7(P)$ are A, B, and variables. Because $\mathcal{R}_7(P)$ is noncollapsing, variables are convertible only to themselves. Hence $t_1 = A$ and $t_2 = B$ or vice versa. □

The Implication CON ⇒ CON→

Let $\mathcal{R}_8(P) = \mathcal{R}_2(P) \cup \mathcal{R}_8^1$, where $\mathcal{R}_8^1$ consists of the two rules

$$e(A, x) \to C$$
$$e(B, x) \to x$$

Proposition 6.2.18 *$A \leftrightarrow^*_{\mathcal{R}_8(P)} B$ if and only if P admits a solution.*

Proof We show that in a shortest conversion between A and B, rules of $\mathcal{R}_8^1$ are not used. The desired result then follows from Proposition 6.2.5. Suppose, on the contrary, that in a shortest conversion between A and B rules of $\mathcal{R}_8^1$ are used. It is not difficult to see that this is only possible if the conversion contains an outermost e symbol that is introduced and eliminated by a rule of $\mathcal{R}_8^1$. In other words, there exists a fragment

$$C[t] \leftarrow \underbrace{C[e(t_1, t_2)] \leftrightarrow^* C'[e(t_1', t_2')]}\to C'[t'] \tag{6.22}$$

such that every step in the underbraced part is of the form $C_1[e(s_1, s_2)] \leftrightarrow C_2[e(s_1', s_2')]$ with no occurrences of e strictly above the displayed ones and (i) a rewrite rule of $\mathcal{R}_2(P)$ is applied strictly above the displayed occurrences of e, (ii) a rewrite rule is applied to a subterm of $C_1[e(s_1, s_2)]$ ($C_2[e(s_1', s_2')]$) disjoint from $e(s_1, s_2)$ ($e(s_1', s_2')$), or (iii) a rewrite rule is applied to one of the arguments of the displayed occurrences of e. Because $\mathcal{R}_2(P)$ is linear and variable-preserving, we can shift all (i) steps in the underbraced part in front of $C[t]$. We do the same with all (ii) steps. The result is a new fragment

$$C[t] \leftrightarrow^* C'[t] \leftarrow \underbrace{C'[e(t_1, t_2)] \leftrightarrow^* C'[e(t_1', t_2')]} \to C'[t'] \tag{6.23}$$

of the same length as conversion (6.22) such that all steps in the underbraced part take place strictly below the displayed occurrences of e. So $t_1 \leftrightarrow^* t_1'$ and $t_2 \leftrightarrow^* t_2'$. There are four possibilities:

1. $t_1 = t_1' = B$, $t = t_2$, and $t' = t_2'$,
2. $t_1 = t_1' = A$ and $t = t' = C$,
3. $t_1 = B$, $t_1' = A$, $t = t_2$, and $t' = C$,
4. $t_1 = A$, $t_1' = B$, $t = C$, and $t' = t_2'$.

In the first case we obtain the shorter fragment

$$C[t] \leftrightarrow^* C'[t] = C'[t_2] \leftrightarrow^* C'[t_2'] = C'[t']$$

contradicting the fact that the given conversion between A and B is shortest. In the second case we obtain the shorter fragment

$$C[t] \leftrightarrow^* C'[t] = C'[C] = C'[t']$$

In the third case we have the shorter conversion $B = t_1 \leftrightarrow^* t_1' = A$ between A and B, again contradicting the fact that the given conversion between A and B is shortest. Finally, in the fourth case we obtain a contradiction in the same way. □

Lemma 6.2.19 *The TRS $\mathcal{R}_8(P)$ is consistent with respect to reduction.*

Proof If $\mathcal{R}_8(P)$ is inconsistent with respect to reduction, then there must be different variables x and y and a term t such that

$$x \leftarrow e(B,x) \;{}^*\!\!\leftarrow t \rightarrow^* e(B,y) \rightarrow y$$

because $e(B,x) \rightarrow x$ is the only collapsing rule in $\mathcal{R}_8(P)$. Only terms in the set

$$S_x = \{e(t_1,x), e(t_1,e(t_2,x)), e(t_1,e(t_2,e(t_3,x))), \cdots \mid t_i \rightarrow^* B\}$$

rewrite to $e(B,x)$. Similarly, only terms in the set

$$S_y = \{e(t_1,y), e(t_1,e(t_2,y)), e(t_1,e(t_2,e(t_3,y))), \cdots \mid t_i \rightarrow^* B\}$$

rewrite to $e(B,y)$. However, as $S_x \cap S_y = \emptyset$, term t does not exist. □

Proposition 6.2.20 *The TRS $\mathcal{R}_8(P)$ is consistent if and only if P does not have a solution.*

Proof According to Proposition 6.2.18, we have to show that $\mathcal{R}_8(P)$ is inconsistent if and only if A and B are convertible. If $A \leftrightarrow^*_{\mathcal{R}_8(P)} B$, then $\mathcal{R}_8(P)$ is inconsistent as

$$x \leftarrow e(B,x) \leftrightarrow^* e(A,x) \rightarrow C \leftarrow e(A,y) \leftrightarrow^* e(B,y) \rightarrow y$$

for different variables x and y. If $\mathcal{R}_8(P)$ is inconsistent, then all terms are convertible. In particular, $A \leftrightarrow^*_{\mathcal{R}_8(P)} B$. □

The Implication $UN \Rightarrow UN^{\rightarrow}$

Let $\mathcal{R}_9(P) = \mathcal{R}_7(P) \cup \mathcal{R}_8^1 \cup \{e(x,y) \rightarrow e(x,y), C \rightarrow C\}$.

Lemma 6.2.21 *$A \leftrightarrow^*_{\mathcal{R}_9(P)} B$ if and only if P admits a solution.*

Proof The proof is a direct consequence of Proposition 6.2.18 as $\leftrightarrow^*_{\mathcal{R}_9(P)} = \leftrightarrow^*_{\mathcal{R}_8(P)}$. □

Lemma 6.2.22 *The TRS $\mathcal{R}_9(P)$ has unique normal forms with respect to reduction for every PCP instance P.*

Proof By induction on the structure of terms we can easily prove that every term has at most one normal form. □

Proposition 6.2.23 *The TRS $\mathcal{R}_9(P)$ has unique normal forms if and only if P does not have a solution.*

Proof Because the normal forms of $\mathcal{R}_9(P)$ and $\mathcal{R}_7(P)$ coincide, the if direction follows from Lemma 6.2.17. Suppose that $\mathcal{R}_9(P)$ admits two different convertible normal forms t_1 and t_2. According to Lemma 6.2.21, it suffices to show that A and B are convertible. The only normal forms of $\mathcal{R}_9(P)$ are A, B, and variables. If t_1 and t_2 are different variables, then we obtain a conversion between A and B by substituting A for all occurrences of t_1 and B for all occurrences of A in the conversion $t_1 \leftrightarrow^* t_2$. If one of the normal forms t_1 or t_2 is a variable and the other is A (B), then we obtain a conversion between A and B by substituting B (A) for all occurrences of the variable in the conversion $t_1 \leftrightarrow^* t_2$. □

The Implication $UN^{\rightarrow} \Rightarrow CON^{\rightarrow}$

Let $\mathcal{R}_{10}(P) = \mathcal{R}_1(P) \cup \{A \to C\}$.

Lemma 6.2.24 *The TRS $\mathcal{R}_{10}(P)$ is consistent with respect to reduction for every PCP instance P.*

Proof The proof is trivial because $\mathcal{R}_{10}(P)$ is noncollapsing. □

Proposition 6.2.25 *The TRS $\mathcal{R}_{10}(P)$ has unique normal forms with respect to reduction if and only if P does not have a solution.*

Proof If P admits a solution, then $A \to^*_{\mathcal{R}_1(P)} B$ and thus $A \to^*_{\mathcal{R}_{10}(P)} B$ by Proposition 6.2.3. Because $A \to_{\mathcal{R}_{10}(P)} C$ and both B and C are normal forms, $\mathcal{R}_{10}(P)$ does not have unique normal forms with respect to reduction. Conversely, suppose that P does not have a solution. Then, by Proposition 6.2.3, $A \to^*_{\mathcal{R}_1(P)} B$ does not hold. This immediately implies that $A \to^*_{\mathcal{R}_{10}(P)} B$ does not hold. Now one easily shows by structural induction that every term has at most one normal form. Hence $\mathcal{R}_{10}(P)$ has unique normal forms with respect to reduction. □

The Properties WCR, GCR, and $CON^{\rightarrow}$

Finally, we investigate decidability issues for the three properties in the confluence hierarchy that do not appear in an X position of an implication $X \Rightarrow Y$. We start with local confluence and ground confluence.

Corollary 6.2.26 *Local confluence and ground confluence are undecidable for linear TRSs.*

Proof The proof is an immediate consequence of Lemma 6.2.4. □

In order to show undecidability of consistency with respect to reduction, we consider the TRS

$$\mathcal{R}_{11}(P) = \begin{cases} f(\alpha_i(x), \beta_i(y), z) & \to & f(x, y, z) & \text{for all } i \in \{1, \ldots, n\} \\ f(c, c, z) & \to & z & \\ h(x, y, z, w) & \to & f(x, y, z) & \\ h(a(x), a(y), z, w) & \to & g(x, y, w) & \text{for all } a \in \Gamma \\ g(a(x), a(y), z) & \to & g(x, y, z) & \text{for all } a \in \Gamma \\ g(c, c, z) & \to & z & \end{cases}$$

Note that $\mathcal{R}_{11}(P)$ is terminating for every PCP instance P.

Proposition 6.2.27 *The TRS $\mathcal{R}_{11}(P)$ is consistent with respect to reduction if and only P admits a solution.*

Proof If P admits a solution $\gamma = \alpha_{i_1} \cdots \alpha_{i_m} = \beta_{i_1} \cdots \beta_{i_m}$ for some $m \geq 1$ and $1 \leq i_1, \ldots, i_m \leq n$, then we have the following diverging reductions in $\mathcal{R}_{11}(P)$ starting from the term $t = h(\gamma(c), \gamma(c), x, y)$:

$$x \leftarrow f(c, c, x) \;{}^*\!\!\leftarrow f(\gamma(c), \gamma(c), x) \leftarrow t \to g(\gamma'(c), \gamma'(c), y) \to^* g(c, c, y) \to y$$

Here γ' is the string γ minus its first symbol. Hence $\mathcal{R}_{11}(P)$ is inconsistent with respect to reduction. Conversely, assume that $\mathcal{R}_{11}(P)$ is inconsistent with respect to reduction. Then $x \;{}^*\!\!\leftarrow t \to^* y$ for some term t and distinct variables x and y. Without loss of generality we assume that the size of t is minimal. This immediately implies that the root symbol of t must be f, g, or h. We show that it must be h. If $t = f(t_1, t_2, t_3)$, then the reduction from t to x must be of the form $t \to^* f(c, c, t_3') \to t_3' \to^* x$ with $t_3 \to^* t_3'$. Hence $t_3 \to^* x$. The same reasoning yields $t_3 \to^* y$, contradicting the minimality of t. A similar argument reveals that the root symbol of t cannot be g. Hence $t = h(t_1, t_2, t_3, t_4)$. We must have

$$x \;{}^*\!\!\leftarrow u \;{}^*\!\!\leftarrow h(t_1, t_2, t_3, t_4) \to^* u' \to^* y \tag{6.24}$$

with $t_3 \to^* u$ or $t_4 \to^* u$ and $t_3 \to^* u'$ or $t_4 \to^* u'$. If $t_3 \to^* u$ and $t_3 \to^* u'$, then t is not minimal because $x \;{}^*\!\!\leftarrow u \;{}^*\!\!\leftarrow t_3 \to^* u' \to y$. Likewise, t is not minimal if $t_4 \to^* u$ and $t_4 \to^* u'$. Now suppose that $t_3 \to^* u$ and $t_4 \to^* u'$. (In the remaining case $t_4 \to^* u$ and $t_3 \to^* u'$ we obtain a PCP solution in exactly the same way.) Then we obtain the divergence

$$x \;{}^*\!\!\leftarrow h(t_1, t_2, x, y) \to^* y \tag{6.25}$$

from conversion (6.24) by replacing t_3 by x and t_4 by y. We claim that t_1 and t_2 contain no occurrences of f, g, and h. The reason is that any subterm in t_1 or t_2 with one of these function symbols at its root position can be replaced with a fresh variable without affecting the possibility of performing the preceding diverging reductions; just drop all rewrite steps that took place (at or) below the replaced subterm. It follows that all steps in (6.25) take place at the root position. We may therefore write conversion (6.25) as

$$x \leftarrow f(c,c,x) \;{}^*\!\!\leftarrow f(t_1,t_2,x) \leftarrow h(t_1,t_2,x,y) \rightarrow g(t_1',t_2',y) \rightarrow^* g(c,c,y) \rightarrow y$$

with $t_1 = a(t_1')$ and $t_2 = a(t_2')$ for some $a \in \Gamma$. Now $\alpha_{i_1} \cdots \alpha_{i_m}(c) = t_1 = t_2 = \beta_{i_1} \cdots \beta_{i_m}(c)$ for some $m \geq 1$ and $1 \leq i_1, \ldots, i_m \leq n$. Hence P admits a solution. □

6.3 Summary

The results proved in this chapter can be summarized as follows.

For the following implications $X \Rightarrow Y$ from the termination hierarchy, X is an undecidable property of one-rule TRSs that satisfy property Y:

$$\omega\text{T} \Rightarrow \text{TT} \Rightarrow \text{ST} \Rightarrow \text{NSE} \Rightarrow \text{SN} \Rightarrow \text{NL} \Rightarrow \text{AC}$$

For many-rule systems, we also showed relative undecidability of the implications

$$\text{SN} \Rightarrow \text{SIN} \Rightarrow \text{WIN} \Rightarrow \text{WN}$$

and the following implications from the confluence hierarchy:

$$\begin{array}{ccccccccc} & & \text{GCR} & & & & & & \\ & & \Uparrow & & & & & & \\ \text{SCR} & \Rightarrow & \text{CR} & \Rightarrow & \text{NF} & \Rightarrow & \text{UN} & \Rightarrow & \text{UN}^{\rightarrow} \\ & & \Downarrow & & & & \Downarrow & & \Downarrow \\ & & \text{WCR} & & & & \text{CON} & \Rightarrow & \text{CON}^{\rightarrow} \end{array}$$

Furthermore, the properties in the hierarchies that do not appear in an X position of an implication $X \Rightarrow Y$ were also shown undecidable. The following problems remain open: Which of the relative undecidability results for many-rule TRSs can be strengthened to one-rule TRSs? Is the implication PT $\Rightarrow \omega$T relative undecidable? Finally, can the results obtained in this chapter be strengthened to string rewriting systems?

7

Conditional Rewrite Systems

Conditional term rewriting systems naturally come into play in the algebraic specification of abstract data types. The specification by positive conditional equations is not only more natural but also more expressive; see [BM84, BN98]. Papers like Kaplan [Kap84] and Bergstra and Klop [BK86] are mainly motivated by this point of view. Now, conditional term rewriting plays a fundamental role in the integration of functional and logic programming; see Hanus [Han94] for an overview of this field. Moreover, it should not be forgotten that conditional systems have been used as a proof-theoretic tool for establishing properties of unconditional term rewriting systems as well as λ-calculus extensions; for an overview, see Klop and de Vrijer [KV90].

For conditional rewrite systems, the same questions arise as for unconditional rewrite systems: How can we check whether a system has a desirable property like termination or confluence? Conditional rewriting, however, is inherently (much) more complicated than unconditional rewriting. For example, termination of a conditional rewrite relation is not enough to guarantee the absence of infinite computations because the evaluation of the conditions of a rewrite rule might not terminate. Thus, in order to ensure that every computation is finite, one has to replace the notion of "termination" with a stronger notion, called "effective termination". In Section 7.2, we will collect various (known and new) methods for proving effective termination. First, we will deal with systems without extra variables and then we will turn to systems with extra variables. Similar to unconditional term rewriting systems, in principle there are two methods for proving confluence of conditional rewrite systems: Either one first proves effective termination and then applies a suitable critical pair lemma (Section 7.3) or one considers syntactically restricted classes of conditional rewrite systems (Section 7.4).

7.1 Basic Notions

To start, conditional term rewriting systems are formally defined as follows.

Definition 7.1.1 A *conditional term rewriting system* (abbreviated CTRS) is a pair $(\mathcal{F}, \mathcal{R})$ consisting of a signature $\mathcal{F}$ and a set $\mathcal{R}$ of *conditional rewrite rules.* Each of these rewrite rules is of the form $l \to r \Leftarrow s_1 = t_1, \ldots, s_k = t_k$ with $l, r, s_1, \ldots, s_k, t_1, \ldots, t_k \in \mathcal{T}(\mathcal{F}, \mathcal{V})$. The term l may not be a variable. We frequently abbreviate the conditional part of the rule—the sequence $s_1 = t_1, \ldots, s_k = t_k$—by c. If a rewrite rule has no conditions, we write $l \to r$, demand that $\mathcal{V}ar(r) \subseteq \mathcal{V}ar(l)$, and call $l \to r$ an unconditional rule.

As in [MH94], rewrite rules $l \to r \Leftarrow c$ will be classified according to the distribution of variables among l, r, and c, as follows:

Type	Requirement
1	$\mathcal{V}ar(r) \cup \mathcal{V}ar(c) \subseteq \mathcal{V}ar(l)$
2	$\mathcal{V}ar(r) \subseteq \mathcal{V}ar(l)$
3	$\mathcal{V}ar(r) \subseteq \mathcal{V}ar(l) \cup \mathcal{V}ar(c)$
4	No restrictions

An n-CTRS contains only rewrite rules of type n. For every rule $l \to r \Leftarrow c$, we define the set of *extra variables* by

$$\mathcal{EV}ar(l \to r \Leftarrow c) = (\mathcal{V}ar(r) \cup \mathcal{V}ar(c)) \setminus \mathcal{V}ar(l)$$

Thus a 1-CTRS has no extra variables, a 2-CTRS has no extra variables on the right-hand sides of the rules, and a 3-CTRS may contain extra variables on the right-hand sides of the rules provided that these also occur in the conditions.

Definition 7.1.2 With every CTRS $(\mathcal{F}, \mathcal{R})$ we associate the system $(\mathcal{F}, \mathcal{R}_u)$, where

$$\mathcal{R}_u = \{l \to r \mid l \to r \Leftarrow s_1 = t_1, \ldots, s_k = t_k \in \mathcal{R}\}$$

Note that $(\mathcal{F}, \mathcal{R}_u)$ is an unconditional TRS in the usual sense provided that $(\mathcal{F}, \mathcal{R})$ is a 2-CTRS. This is not true for 3-CTRSs because a rule of type 3 may contain variables on the right-hand side of the rule that do not occur on the left-hand side.

The $=$ symbol in the conditions can be interpreted in different ways, which leads to different rewrite relations.

Definition 7.1.3

1. In an *oriented* CTRS $(\mathcal{F}, \mathcal{R})$ the $=$ symbol in the conditions of the rewrite rules is interpreted as *reachability* ($\rightarrow_{\mathcal{R}}^*$). From now on, rewrite rules of an oriented CTRS will be written as $l \rightarrow r \Leftarrow s_1 \rightarrow t_1, \ldots, s_k \rightarrow t_k$.

2. A *normal* CTRS $(\mathcal{F}, \mathcal{R})$ is an oriented CTRS in which the rewrite rules are subject to the additional constraint that every t_j is a ground normal form with respect to $\mathcal{R}_u$. Rewrite rules of a normal CTRS will also be written as $l \rightarrow r \Leftarrow s_1 \rightarrow t_1, \ldots, s_k \rightarrow t_k$.

3. In a *join* CTRS $(\mathcal{F}, \mathcal{R})$ the $=$ symbol in the conditions of the rewrite rules is interpreted as *joinability* ($\downarrow_{\mathcal{R}}$). Rewrite rules of a join CTRS will be written as $l \rightarrow r \Leftarrow s_1 \downarrow t_1, \ldots, s_k \downarrow t_k$. Join CTRSs are sometimes called *standard* CTRSs.

4. Interpreting the $=$ symbol in the conditions as *conversion* ($\leftrightarrow_{\mathcal{R}}^*$) leads to *semiequational* CTRSs.

These are the most common interpretations. In the seminal paper of Bergstra and Klop [BK86] semiequational, join, oriented, and normal systems were called type I, II, III, and III_n systems, respectively. Our terminology stems from [DOS88]; the reader is referred to that paper for other interpretations of the $=$ symbol.

In the following, we will focus on oriented systems and variants thereof (normal systems, almost normal systems, and systems with strict equality). We will sometimes comment on differences to join systems, but we will not consider semiequational systems at all. Thus the term *conditional system* stands for *oriented conditional system* unless stated otherwise. Consequently, the following definitions deal only with oriented CTRSs. It is obvious, however, how the definitions have to be modified for other kinds of CTRSs.

Let us formally define the rewrite relation associated with a CTRS.

Definition 7.1.4 Let $\mathcal{R}$ be a CTRS. We inductively define *unconditional* TRSs $\mathcal{R}_n$ for $n \in \mathbb{N}$ by:

$$\begin{aligned} \mathcal{R}_0 &= \emptyset \\ \mathcal{R}_{n+1} &= \{l\sigma \rightarrow r\sigma \mid l \rightarrow r \Leftarrow s_1 \rightarrow t_1, \ldots, s_k \rightarrow t_k \in \mathcal{R} \text{ and} \\ &\qquad s_j\sigma \rightarrow_{\mathcal{R}_n}^* t_j\sigma \text{ for all } j \in \{1, \ldots, k\}\} \end{aligned}$$

The rewrite relation $\rightarrow_{\mathcal{R}}$ associated with a CTRS $\mathcal{R}$ is defined by $\rightarrow_{\mathcal{R}} = \bigcup_{n \in \mathbb{N}} \rightarrow_{\mathcal{R}_n}$. In other words, $s \rightarrow_{\mathcal{R}_{n+1}} t$ if and only if there exists a rewrite rule $\rho : l \rightarrow r \Leftarrow s_1 \rightarrow t_1, \ldots, s_k \rightarrow t_k$ in $\mathcal{R}$, a substitution $\sigma : \mathcal{V}ar(\rho) \rightarrow \mathcal{T}(\mathcal{F}, \mathcal{V})$, and a context $C[\,]$ such that $s = C[l\sigma], t = C[r\sigma]$, and $s_j\sigma \rightarrow_{\mathcal{R}_n}^* t_j\sigma$ for all $1 \leq j \leq k$. We say that $s \rightarrow_{\mathcal{R}} t$ is a *rewrite step* or *reduction* *step* at *redex* $l\sigma$. The *depth* of a rewrite step $s \to_{\mathcal{R}} t$ is defined to be the minimum n such that $s \to_{\mathcal{R}_n} t$. Depths of reduction sequences $s \to^*_{\mathcal{R}} t$, conversions $s \leftrightarrow^*_{\mathcal{R}} t$, and valleys $s \downarrow_{\mathcal{R}} t$ are defined analogously.

Let us illustrate these concepts with some examples.

Example 7.1.5 Let $\mathcal{F} = \{0, s, false, true, <, -, gcd\}$, and let

$$\mathcal{R} = \begin{cases} x < 0 & \to false & & 0 - s(y) & \to 0 \\ 0 < s(x) & \to true & & x - 0 & \to x \\ s(x) < s(y) & \to x < y & & s(x) - s(y) & \to x - y \\ gcd(x, x) & \to x & & & \\ gcd(s(x), 0) & \to s(x) & & & \\ gcd(0, s(y)) & \to s(y) & & & \\ gcd(s(x), s(y)) & \to gcd(x - y, s(y)) & \Leftarrow & y < x \to true & \\ gcd(s(x), s(y)) & \to gcd(s(x), y - x) & \Leftarrow & x < y \to true & \end{cases}$$

The system $(\mathcal{F}, \mathcal{R})$ computes the greatest common divisor of two natural numbers. It is a normal 1-CTRS. The depth of the reduction step $gcd(s(s(0)), s(s(0))) \to_{\mathcal{R}} s(s(0))$ is 1 and the depth of the reduction sequence $gcd(s(s(s(s(0)))), s(s(0))) \to^+_{\mathcal{R}} s(s(0))$ is 2.

By replacing the last five rules with

$$\begin{array}{llll} quorem(0, s(y)) & \to \langle 0, 0 \rangle & & \\ quorem(s(x), s(y)) & \to \langle 0, s(x) \rangle & \Leftarrow & x < y \to true \\ quorem(s(x), s(y)) & \to \langle s(q), r \rangle & \Leftarrow & x < y \to false, \\ & & & quorem(x - y, s(y)) \to \langle q, r \rangle \end{array}$$

we obtain a CTRS that computes the quotient and the remainder of two natural numbers. It is an oriented 3-CTRS because the variables q and r occur on the right-hand side of the last rule but not on its left-hand side. It makes perfect sense to allow extra variables on the right-hand sides whenever it is guaranteed that these variables are "bound" during the evaluation of the conditions. Finally, the rule

$$p(x, z) \to true \Leftarrow p(x, y) \to true, p(y, z) \to true$$

constitutes a normal 2-CTRS.

It should be pointed out that every normal CTRS can be viewed as a join CTRS. On the other hand, every join system can be simulated by a (nonleft-linear) normal system, as was first shown by Dershowitz and Okada [DO90].

Definition 7.1.6 Let $(\mathcal{F}, \mathcal{R})$ be a join CTRS. We assume that *eq* and *true* are function symbols that do not occur in $\mathcal{F}$. For every rewrite rule

$$\rho : l \to r \Leftarrow s_1 \downarrow t_1, \ldots, s_k \downarrow t_k$$

in $\mathcal{R}$, we define:

$$n(\rho) = l \to r \Leftarrow eq(s_1, t_1) \to true, \ldots, eq(s_k, t_k) \to true$$

Then $n(\mathcal{R}) = \{eq(x, x) \to true\} \cup \bigcup_{\rho \in \mathcal{R}} \{n(\rho)\}$ is a normal CTRS.

Proposition 7.1.7 *For all terms $s, t \in \mathcal{T}(\mathcal{F}, \mathcal{V})$, we have $s \to_{\mathcal{R}} t$ if and only if $s \to_{n(\mathcal{R})} t$.*

Proof The proposition can be proven by simple induction on the depth of $s \to_{\mathcal{R}} t$ and $s \to_{n(\mathcal{R})} t$, respectively; cf. the proofs of theorems 2.4 and 2.5 in [DO90]. □

The preceding proposition states that the expressive power of the class of (nonleft-linear) normal CTRSs is the same as that of join systems; see Marchiori [Mar97b] for more details on this subject.

All notions defined in Chapter 2 carry over to CTRSs by associating $(\mathcal{F}, \mathcal{R})$ with the ARS $(\mathcal{T}(\mathcal{F}, \mathcal{V}), \to_{\mathcal{R}})$. Furthermore, for a CTRS $\mathcal{R}$, notions like left-linearity, defined symbol, constructor, and constructor term are defined via the system $\mathcal{R}_u$. As in the unconditional case, the definition of orthogonality is based on the absence of (conditional) critical pairs.

Definition 7.1.8 Let $\mathcal{R}$ be a CTRS.

1. Let $l_1 \to r_1 \Leftarrow c_1$ and $l_2 \to r_2 \Leftarrow c_2$ be renamed versions of rewrite rules of $\mathcal{R}$ such that they have no variables in common. Suppose $l_1 = C[t]$ with $t \notin \mathcal{V}$ such that $t\sigma = l_2\sigma$ for a most general unifier σ. We call

$$\langle C[r_2]\sigma, r_1\sigma \rangle \Leftarrow c_1\sigma, c_2\sigma$$

   a *conditional critical pair* (CCP) of $\mathcal{R}$. If the two rules are renamed versions of the same rewrite rule of $\mathcal{R}$, we do not consider the case $C[\,] = \Box$.

2. A conditional critical pair $\langle s, t \rangle \Leftarrow s_1 \to t_1, \ldots, s_n \to t_n$ of $\mathcal{R}$ is *joinable* if $s\sigma \downarrow_{\mathcal{R}} t\sigma$ for every substitution σ that satisfies $s_j\sigma \to_{\mathcal{R}}^* t_j\sigma$ for all $j \in \{1, \ldots, n\}$.

3. A conditional critical pair $\langle s, t \rangle \Leftarrow s_1 \to t_1, \ldots, s_n \to t_n$ is *feasible* if there is a substitution σ that satisfies $s_j\sigma \to_{\mathcal{R}}^* t_j\sigma$ for all $j \in \{1, \ldots, n\}$. Otherwise it is called *infeasible*.

4. A conditional critical pair $\langle t, t \rangle \Leftarrow s_1 \to t_1, \ldots, s_n \to t_n$ is called *trivial*.

Note that an infeasible conditional critical pair is (vacuously) joinable.

Example 7.1.9 Consider the *gcd* system from Example 7.1.5. There is, for example, the conditional critical pair

$$\langle gcd(x - y, s(y)), gcd(s(x), y - x)\rangle \Leftarrow y < x \to true,\ x < y \to true$$

It is infeasible because there is no substitution σ such that $y\sigma < x\sigma \to^*_{\mathcal{R}} true$ and $x\sigma < y\sigma \to^*_{\mathcal{R}} true$.

Definition 7.1.10 Let $\mathcal{R}$ be a left-linear CTRS.

1. $\mathcal{R}$ is *orthogonal* if it has no conditional critical pair.
2. $\mathcal{R}$ is *almost orthogonal* if every conditional critical pair is trivial and results from an overlay (i.e., an overlap at root positions).
3. $\mathcal{R}$ is *weakly orthogonal* if every conditional critical pair is trivial.

In a weakly orthogonal 3-CTRS none of the type 3 rules may overlap another rule. This is because whenever two rules $l_1 \to r_1 \Leftarrow c_1$ and $l_2 \to r_2 \Leftarrow c_2$ overlap and one of the rules, say $l_1 \to r_1 \Leftarrow c_1$, has an extra variable z on its right-hand side (so $z \in \mathcal{V}ar(r_1) \setminus \mathcal{V}ar(l_1)$), then the resulting critical pair $\langle s, t\rangle$ cannot be trivial because z occurs in t but not in s. By the same reasoning, none of the type 3 rules may overlay another rule in an almost orthogonal 3-CTRS.

We shall see later that orthogonal CTRSs are level-confluent. The notion of level-confluence plays a key role in the integration of the functional and logic programming paradigms because—in contrast to confluence—it guarantees the completeness of *narrowing* in the presence of extra variables. (The operational semantics of most functional-logic programming languages is based on conditional narrowing.)

Definition 7.1.11 A CTRS $\mathcal{R}$ is called *level-confluent* if, for every $n \in \mathbb{N}$, the TRS $\mathcal{R}_n$ is confluent.

The following lemma is sometimes useful for proving termination of CTRSs.

Lemma 7.1.12 *A 2-CTRS $\mathcal{R}$ is terminating if $\mathcal{R}_u$ is terminating.*

Proof The proof is straightforward because $s \to_{\mathcal{R}} t$ implies $s \to_{\mathcal{R}_u} t$. □

If $\mathcal{R}$ is, for example, the *gcd* system from Example 7.1.5, then termination of $\mathcal{R}_u$ can be shown by the dependency pair method (for example, if $\mathcal{P}$ is the cycle $\{\langle \mathrm{GCD}(s(x), s(y)), \mathrm{GCD}(x - y, s(y))\rangle\}$, then we can use the interpretation $0_{\mathbb{N}} = 0$, $s_{\mathbb{N}}(x) = x+1$, $true_{\mathbb{N}} = 0$, $false_{\mathbb{N}} = 0$, $x <_{\mathbb{N}} y = x+y$, $x -_{\mathbb{N}} y = x$, and $gcd_{\mathbb{N}}(x, y) = \mathrm{GCD}_{\mathbb{N}}(x, y) = x + y$).

Conditional rewriting is inherently more complicated than unconditional rewriting. We have seen that for a finite TRS $\mathcal{R}$ it is decidable whether a term s is reducible w.r.t. $\mathcal{R}$. In the case of conditional rewriting, however, this is no longer true. If the left-hand side l of a conditional rewrite rule matches a subterm of s via substitution σ (so $s = C[l\sigma]$), then we call $l\sigma$ a *preredex*. In order to determine whether the preredex is really a redex, one has to check whether the conditions are satisfied. Kaplan [Kap84] showed that this question is undecidable for finite convergent 1-CTRSs. We use PCP to prove this fact. The construction is inspired by a similar construction in [ALS93]. Let $\Gamma = \{a, b\}$. We represent words over Γ by ground terms over the signature $\{a, b, \varepsilon\}$, where ε is a constant and a, b are unary function symbols. For example, the word *abb* will be represented by the ground term $a(b(b(\varepsilon)))$. Moreover, if, for example, $\alpha_i = bb$ and t is a term, then $\alpha_i(t)$ denotes the term $b(b(t))$.

With every PCP instance $P = \{(\alpha_1, \beta_1), (\alpha_2, \beta_2), \ldots, (\alpha_n, \beta_n)\}$ we associate the CTRS $\mathcal{R}(P)$ consisting of the rules

$$
\begin{array}{lll}
true \vee x & \to true & \\
false \vee x & \to x & \\
f(nil) & \to \varepsilon & \\
f(i : is) & \to \alpha_i(f(is)) & \text{for all } 1 \le i \le n \\
g(nil) & \to \varepsilon & \\
g(i : is) & \to \beta_i(g(is)) & \text{for all } 1 \le i \le n \\
h(is) & \to true \quad \Leftarrow \quad c & \\
eq(\varepsilon, \varepsilon) & \to true & \\
eq(a(x), a(y)) & \to eq(x, y) & \\
eq(b(x), b(y)) & \to eq(x, y) & \\
eq(a(x), b(y)) & \to false & \\
eq(b(x), a(y)) & \to false & \\
eq(a(x), \varepsilon) & \to false & \\
eq(b(x), \varepsilon) & \to false & \\
eq(\varepsilon, a(y)) & \to false & \\
eq(\varepsilon, b(y)) & \to false &
\end{array}
$$

over the signature $\mathcal{F} = \{a, b, \varepsilon, 1, \ldots, n, nil, :, f, g, h, eq, \vee, true, false\}$, where c stands for the condition

$$\bigvee_{i=1}^{n} eq(f(i : is), g(i : is)) \vee \bigvee_{i=1}^{n} h(i : is) \to true$$

and $\vee$ is assumed to be right-associative. The normal 1-CTRS $\mathcal{R}(P)$ is level-confluent (because it is orthogonal; see Corollary 7.4.6) and terminating because $\mathcal{R}_u(P)$ is terminating.

If one wants to know whether $h(nil)$ is a normal form, then one has to check (according to the condition c) whether P has a solution. To show this, we need a simple lemma.

Lemma 7.1.13 *For every PCP instance P and $i_1, \ldots, i_m \in \{1, \ldots, n\}$: $\alpha_{i_1}\alpha_{i_2}\ldots\alpha_{i_m} = \beta_{i_1}\beta_{i_2}\ldots\beta_{i_m}$ is (not) a solution of P if and only if in $\mathcal{R}(P)$ the term $eq(f([i_1, i_2, \ldots, i_m]), g([i_1, i_2, \ldots, i_m]))$ can be reduced to $true$ ($false$).*

Proof The proof is routine. □

Proposition 7.1.14 *The following statements are equivalent:*

1. *$h(nil) \to_{\mathcal{R}(P)} true$.*
2. *The PCP instance P has a solution.*

Proof On the one hand, if the PCP instance P has a solution $\gamma = \alpha_{i_1}\alpha_{i_2}\ldots\alpha_{i_m}$, then $eq(f([i_1, \ldots, i_m]), g([i_1, \ldots, i_m])) \to^+_{\mathcal{R}(P)} true$ by Lemma 7.1.13 and it readily follows that $h(nil) \to_{\mathcal{R}(P)} true$. On the other hand, if $h(nil) \to_{\mathcal{R}(P)} true$, then there must be a list $[i_1, i_2, \ldots, i_m]$ such that $eq(f([i_1, i_2, \ldots, i_m]), g([i_1, i_2, \ldots, i_m])) \to^+_{\mathcal{R}(P)} true$. According to Lemma 7.1.13, $\alpha_{i_1}\alpha_{i_2}\ldots\alpha_{i_m} = \beta_{i_1}\beta_{i_2}\ldots\beta_{i_m}$ is a solution of P. □

Thus it is in general undecidable whether a preredex is a redex. Consequently, it is in general undecidable whether a term t is in normal form w.r.t. a CTRS $\mathcal{R}$. For this reason, in a normal CTRS $\mathcal{R}$, every t_i in a rule $l \to r \Leftarrow s_1 \to t_1, \ldots, s_k \to t_k \in \mathcal{R}$ must be a normal form w.r.t. $\mathcal{R}_u$.

Proposition 7.1.14 gives a negative answer to the following question from [BK86, remark 4.9.1]: Does termination of $\mathcal{R}_u$ imply decidability of normal forms w.r.t. an orthogonal normal CTRS $\mathcal{R}$?

7.2 Effective Termination

In order to determine whether a term $s = C[l\sigma]$ reduces to $t = C[r\sigma]$ by the rule $l \to r \Leftarrow s_1 \to t_1, \ldots, s_k \to t_k \in \mathcal{R}$, one has to reduce the terms $s_1\sigma, \ldots, s_k\sigma$. Because this recursive reduction might not terminate even though the rewrite relation $\to_{\mathcal{R}}$ is terminating, the word "terminating" may lead to misunderstandings in the context of CTRSs. The phrase "$\mathcal{R}$ is terminating" means, as usual, that there are no infinite reduction sequences w.r.t. $\to_{\mathcal{R}}$. A terminating CTRS $\mathcal{R}$ is called effectively terminating[1] if the recursive reduction of the instantiated conditions also terminates. The formal definition reads as follows.

Definition 7.2.1 A CTRS $\mathcal{R}$ is called *effectively terminating* if

1. $\mathcal{R}$ is terminating, and

[1] This notion was coined by Marchiori [Mar96b].

2. the set $\Delta^*(s) = \{t \in \mathcal{T}(\mathcal{F}, \mathcal{V}) \mid s \to_{\mathcal{R}}^* t\}$ of all $\mathcal{R}$-reducts of a term $s \in \mathcal{T}(\mathcal{F}, \mathcal{V})$ is finite and computable.

In this section we will state several sufficient criteria that ensure effective termination. The first four subsections deal with 1-CTRSs. Because these systems do not have extra variables, the conditions of a rewrite rule can be evaluated in parallel. In the presence of extra-variables, however, a conditional rewrite system can only be effectively terminating if every extra-variable gets a binding during the evaluation of the conditions. For this reason, the conditions of a rewrite rule of type 3 have be evaluated sequentially (say, from left to right). The last six parts of the section are devoted to 3-CTRSs.

7.2.1 Systems without Extra Variables

The first sufficient criterion was introduced by Kaplan [Kap87].

Definition 7.2.2 A CTRS $(\mathcal{F}, \mathcal{R})$ is *simplifying* if there exists a simplification ordering $\succ$ on $\mathcal{T}(\mathcal{F}, \mathcal{V})$ satisfying $l \succ r$ and[2] $l \succ s_j$ for each rewrite rule $l \to r \Leftarrow s_1 \to t_1, \ldots, s_k \to t_k$ and every index $j \in \{1, \ldots, k\}$.

Of course, we are only interested in well-founded simplification orderings. To avoid confusion, we will consider only *finite* CTRSs (a finite CTRS consists of a finite number of rules over a finite signature) unless stated otherwise. Recall that a finite TRS (a CTRS without conditions) is simplifying if and only if it is simply terminating; cf. Section 5.2.2.

Subsequently, Jouannaud and Waldmann [JW86] and Dershowitz et al. [DOS88] refined the notion of simplifyingness.

Definition 7.2.3 Let $\mathcal{R}$ be a CTRS and let $\succ$ be a partial ordering such that (1) $\succ$ is well-founded, (2) $\to_{\mathcal{R}} \subseteq \succ$, and (3) for every rule $l \to r \Leftarrow s_1 \to t_1, \ldots, s_k \to t_k$ of $\mathcal{R}$ and every substitution σ we have[3] $l\sigma \succ s_j\sigma$ for all $j \in \{1, \ldots, k\}$. $\mathcal{R}$ is called *reductive* [JW86] if (4) $\succ$ is closed under contexts. $\mathcal{R}$ is said to be *decreasing* [DOS88] if $\succ$ has properties (1)–(3) and the subterm property.

Observe that every terminating TRS can be viewed as a reductive CTRS. Furthermore, note that if a CTRS $\mathcal{R}$ is simplifying, reductive, or decreasing, then the variables appearing in the conditions of a rule must also appear on the left-hand side of that rule. In other words, such a CTRS does not permit extra variables in its conditions.

Similar to the termination hierarchy of unconditional TRSs, the following implications hold:

simplifyingness $\Rightarrow$ reductivity $\Rightarrow$ decreasingness $\Rightarrow$ effective termination

[2] For join systems, $l \succ t_j$ must also hold.
[3] For join systems, $l\sigma \succ t_j\sigma$ must also hold.

And as in the unconditional case, it is worthwhile to study all of these properties. For example, we shall see in Chapter 8 that only simplifyingness is modular. To prove the implications, we need two auxiliary results, the first of which is folklore.

Lemma 7.2.4 *Let $\succ$ be a binary relation on $T \subseteq \mathcal{T}(\mathcal{F},\mathcal{V})$. If $\succ$ is closed under contexts and well-founded on T, then $\succ_{st} = (\succ \cup \rhd)^+$ is a well-founded partial ordering on T.*[4]

Proof $\succ_{st}$ is transitive by definition. We show that $\succ_{st}$ is well-founded. This implies that $\succ_{st}$ is also irreflexive. Suppose that $\succ_{st}$ is not well-founded, that is, there exists an infinite derivation

$$D: \; s_1 \; (\succ \cup \rhd) \; s_2 \; (\succ \cup \rhd) \; s_3 \; (\succ \cup \rhd) \; \ldots$$

If there were only a finite number of $\succ$ steps in D, then there would be an infinite $\rhd$ derivation, which contradicts the well-foundedness of $\rhd$. So D contains infinitely many $\succ$ steps. All $\succ$ steps can be pushed back to the beginning of D because $C[s] \rhd s \succ t$ implies $C[s] \succ C[t] \rhd t$ (because $\succ$ is closed under contexts). Hence there is an infinite $\succ$ derivation that contradicts the well-foundedness of $\succ$. It should be pointed out that $\succ_{st}$ is in general not closed under contexts. □

Definition 7.2.5 With every 1-CTRS $(\mathcal{F},\mathcal{R})$ we associate the unconditional TRS $(\mathcal{F},\mathcal{R}_s)$, where[5]

$$\mathcal{R}_s = \mathcal{R}_u \cup \{l \to s_j \mid l \to r \Leftarrow s_1 \to t_1, \ldots, s_k \to t_k \in \mathcal{R}; 1 \le j \le k\}$$

Lemma 7.2.6 *A 1-CTRS $(\mathcal{F},\mathcal{R})$ is simplifying if and only if $(\mathcal{F},\mathcal{R}_s)$ is simply terminating.*

Proof We have the following equivalences:

$\mathcal{R}$ is simplifying.
$\Leftrightarrow$ There is a simplification ordering $\succ$ such that $l \succ r$ and $l \succ s_j$ for every $l \to r \Leftarrow s_1 \to t_1, \ldots, s_k \to t_k \in \mathcal{R}$ and $j \in \{1, \ldots, k\}$.
$\Leftrightarrow$ $\mathcal{R}_s$ is simply terminating.

Thus, the lemma holds true. □

Now we can prove the implications.

Proposition 7.2.7 *Every simplifying 1-CTRS $(\mathcal{F},\mathcal{R})$ is reductive.*

---

[4]The subscript *st* in $\succ_{st}$ indicates that $\succ$ is extended with the *s*ub*t*erm relation.
[5]For join systems, $\mathcal{R}_s$ must also contain $l \to t_j$.

Proof Because $\mathcal{R}$ is simplifying, the TRS $\mathcal{R}_s$ is simply terminating. We claim that the well-founded partial ordering $\to_{\mathcal{R}_s}^+$ meets requirements (1)–(4) of Definition 7.2.3. It is obvious that $\to_{\mathcal{R}} \subseteq \to_{\mathcal{R}_s}^+$ and that $\to_{\mathcal{R}_s}^+$ is closed under contexts. The remaining property can be verified just as easily. □

Proposition 7.2.8 *Every reductive 1-CTRS is decreasing.*

Proof If $(\mathcal{F}, \mathcal{R})$ is reductive, then there is a partial ordering $\succ$ on $\mathcal{T}(\mathcal{F}, \mathcal{V})$ satisfying properties (1)–(4) of Definition 7.2.3. Recall that $\succ_{st} = (\succ \cup \rhd)^+$. We claim that $(\mathcal{F}, \mathcal{R})$ is decreasing w.r.t. $\succ_{st}$. (1) $\succ_{st}$ is well-founded according to Lemma 7.2.4 because $\succ$ is well-founded and closed under contexts, (2) $\to_{\mathcal{R}} \subseteq \succ_{st}$ because $\to_{\mathcal{R}} \subseteq \succ$, and (3) if $l \to r \Leftarrow s_1 \to t_1, \ldots, s_k \to t_k$ is a rewrite rule of $\mathcal{R}$ and σ is a substitution, then $l\sigma \succ_{st} s_j\sigma$ for all $j \in \{1, \ldots, k\}$ because $l\sigma \succ s_j\sigma$ for all $j \in \{1, \ldots, k\}$. Moreover, $\succ_{st}$ has the subterm property by definition. □

The next proposition has been proven in [Kap87], [JW86], and [DOS88] for simplifying, reductive, and decreasing join CTRSs, respectively. It explains why those systems have been extensively studied by several authors.

Theorem 7.2.9 *Every decreasing 1-CTRS $\mathcal{R}$ is effectively terminating.*

Proof Termination of $\mathcal{R}$ is obvious. Let $\mathcal{R}$ be decreasing w.r.t. $\succ$. We proceed by induction on the well-founded ordering $\succ$. If no subterm of a term s is an instance of a left-hand side of a rule from $\mathcal{R}$, then $\Delta^*(s) = \{s\}$. Otherwise, suppose $s = C[l\sigma]$ for some rule $l \to r \Leftarrow s_1 \to t_1, \ldots, s_k \to t_k$. Because $\mathcal{R}$ is decreasing, we have $s = C[l\sigma] \succeq l\sigma$ and $l\sigma \succ s_j\sigma$ for every $j \in \{1, \ldots, k\}$. It follows from the inductive hypothesis that the sets $\Delta^*(s_j\sigma)$ are finite and computable. If, for every $j \in \{1, \ldots, k\}$, $t_j\sigma \in \Delta^*(s_j\sigma)$, then the conditions are satisfied and hence $s \to_{\mathcal{R}} C[r\sigma]$. If not, then s does not reduce to $C[r\sigma]$. Because s has only finitely many preredexes and $\mathcal{R}$ has only finitely many rewrite rules, we can compute the finite set $\Delta(s) = \{t \in \mathcal{T}(\mathcal{F}, \mathcal{V}) \mid s \to_{\mathcal{R}} t\}$ of all one step reducts of s. Let $t \in \Delta(s)$. It follows from a renewed application of the inductive hypothesis that the set $\Delta^*(t)$ is finite and computable. Hence $\Delta^*(s) = \{s\} \cup \bigcup_{\{t \mid s \to_{\mathcal{R}} t\}} \Delta^*(t)$ is also finite and computable. □

Next we give counterexamples to the converse implications. The TRS $\{f(0, 1, x) \to f(x, x, x)\}$ is terminating (see Example 5.4.35), hence reductive. On the other hand, it is not simply terminating (see Example 5.2.31), hence not simplifying. Thus it exemplifies that a reductive CTRS need not be simplifying. The next example taken from [DOS88] shows that a decreasing CTRS need not be reductive.

Example 7.2.10 Let $\mathcal{F} = \{a, b, c, f\}$ and

$$\mathcal{R} = \begin{cases} b & \to c \\ f(b) & \to f(a) \\ a & \to c & \Leftarrow b \to c \end{cases}$$

If $\mathcal{R}$ were reductive, then there would be a partial ordering $\succ$ closed under contexts with $a \succ b$ and $f(b) \succ f(a)$. This is clearly impossible. It will be shown later that the system is indeed decreasing.

Lastly, the CTRS $\{a \to b \Leftarrow f(a) \to b\}$ is effectively terminating but not decreasing. If it were decreasing w.r.t. $\succ$, then we would infer $a \succ f(a) \succ a$, where the first inequality is due to $l\sigma \succ s_1\sigma$ and the second follows from the subterm property.

7.2.2 Transforming 1-CTRSs

Lemma 7.2.6 provides a method of showing simplifyingness. Next we will address the problem of proving decreasingness. The technique is based on a transformation that originated from [BK86, definition 2.5.1]. For normal 1-CTRSs, Marchiori [Mar96b, Mar95] studied the properties of this transformation (which he denoted by U_n) in detail.[6] We will review his results in the following.

Definition 7.2.11 Let $(\mathcal{F}, \mathcal{R})$ be a 1-CTRS. For every conditional rewrite rule $\rho : l \to r \Leftarrow s_1 \to t_1, \ldots, s_k \to t_k \in \mathcal{R}$, we need a fresh function symbol U^ρ. Moreover, by abuse of notation, $\mathcal{V}ar$ denotes a function that assigns the sequence of the variables (in some fixed ordering) in the set $\mathcal{V}ar(t)$ to a term t. Then $U_n(\rho)$ is the set consisting of the two rules

$$l \to U^\rho(s_1, \ldots, s_k, \mathcal{V}ar(l)) \text{ and } U^\rho(t_1, \ldots, t_k, \mathcal{V}ar(l)) \to r$$

The system $U_n(\mathcal{R}) = \bigcup_{\rho \in \mathcal{R}} U(\rho)$ is an unconditional TRS over the extended signature $\mathcal{F}' = \mathcal{F} \cup \bigcup_{\rho \in \mathcal{R}} \{U^\rho\}$. In the following, the symbols from $\mathcal{F}' \setminus \mathcal{F}$ are called U *symbols*.

If one uses the preceding transformation, then conditions can be evaluated in parallel. In Definition 7.2.48 we will encounter a transformation in which the evaluation of the conditions proceeds from left to right.

In subsequent examples, if a CTRS $\mathcal{R}$ contains just one conditional rewrite rule ρ, we will omit the superscript ρ in U^ρ. Furthermore, we will often just use dashes or numbers to distinguish different U symbols instead of labeling them with the different conditional rewrite rules.

[6] The transformation U_n was called *unraveling* in [Mar96b, Mar95]. The subscript n in U_n indicates that this transformation was (originally) applied to *n*ormal CTRSs.

Example 7.2.12 Let $\mathcal{R}$ be the normal 1-CTRS from Example 7.1.5. The transformed system $U_n(\mathcal{R})$ is the system obtained from $\mathcal{R}$ by replacing the two conditional rules with

$$
\begin{array}{rcl}
gcd(s(x), s(y)) & \to & U'(y < x, x, y) \\
U'(true, x, y) & \to & gcd(x - y, s(y)) \\
gcd(s(x), s(y)) & \to & U''(x < y, x, y) \\
U''(true, x, y) & \to & gcd(s(x), y - x)
\end{array}
$$

We shall see that termination of $U_n(\mathcal{R})$ is a sufficient but not a necessary condition for decreasingness of $\mathcal{R}$.

Lemma 7.2.13 *If* $s \to_{\mathcal{R}} t$, *then* $s \to^{+}_{U_n(\mathcal{R})} t$.

Proof We proceed by induction on the depth n of the rewrite step $s = C[l\sigma] \to_{\mathcal{R}} C[r\sigma] = t$, where the rule $\rho : l \to r \Leftarrow s_1 \to t_1, \ldots, s_k \to t_k$ is used. Because $s_j\sigma \to^{*}_{\mathcal{R}} t_j\sigma = t_j$ for every $1 \leq j \leq k$, it follows $s_j\sigma \to^{*}_{U_n(\mathcal{R})} t_j$ for every $1 \leq j \leq k$ by the inductive hypothesis. Hence the reduction sequence

$$
\begin{array}{rl}
l\sigma & \to_{U_n(\mathcal{R})} \; U^{\rho}(s_1, \ldots, s_k, \mathcal{V}ar(l))\sigma \\
& \to^{*}_{U_n(\mathcal{R})} \; U^{\rho}(t_1, \ldots, t_k, \mathcal{V}ar(l))\sigma \\
& \to_{U_n(\mathcal{R})} \; r\sigma
\end{array}
$$

shows the assertion. □

It is a bit surprising that the converse of the preceding lemma is not true. This was first shown by Marchiori [Mar95].

Example 7.2.14 Let the normal 1-CTRS $\mathcal{R}$ consist of the rules

$$
\begin{array}{rclcrcl}
a & \to & c & \quad & a & \to & d \\
b & \to & c & & b & \to & d \\
c & \to & e & & c & \to & l \\
k & \to & l & & k & \to & m \\
d & \to & m & & & & \\
A & \to & h(f(a), f(b)) & & & & \\
h(x, x) & \to & g(x, x, f(k)) & & & & \\
g(d, x, x) & \to & A & & & & \\
f(x) & \to & x & & \Leftarrow x \to e & &
\end{array}
$$

The relationship between the first nine rules of $\mathcal{R}$ is depicted in Figure 7.1.

The transformed system $U_n(\mathcal{R})$ is the system obtained from $\mathcal{R}$ by replacing the last rule with

$$
\begin{array}{rcl}
f(x) & \to & U(x, x) \\
U(e, x) & \to & x
\end{array}
$$

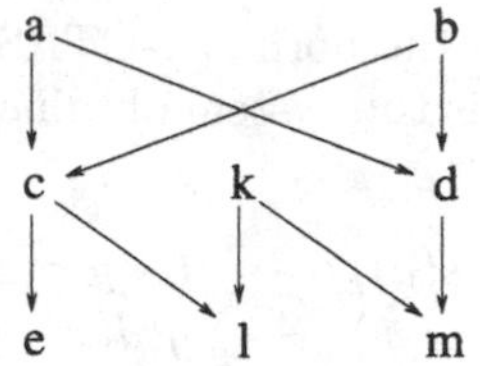

FIGURE 7.1. The first nine rules of $\mathcal{R}$.

As in [Mar95], we show that $h(f(a), f(b)) \to^+_{U_n(\mathcal{R})} A$ but $h(f(a), f(b)) \not\to^+_{\mathcal{R}} A$. The former is true because of the following $U_n(\mathcal{R})$ derivation

$$\begin{aligned}
&h(f(a), f(b)) \to^+_{U_n(\mathcal{R})} h(U(c,d), f(b)) \to^+_{U_n(\mathcal{R})} h(U(c,d), U(c,d)) \\
&\to_{U_n(\mathcal{R})} g(U(c,d), U(c,d), f(k)) \to_{U_n(\mathcal{R})} g(U(e,d), U(c,d), f(k)) \\
&\to_{U_n(\mathcal{R})} g(d, U(c,d), f(k)) \to^+_{U_n(\mathcal{R})} g(d, U(l,m), f(k)) \\
&\to^+_{U_n(\mathcal{R})} g(d, U(l,m), U(l,m)) \to_{U_n(\mathcal{R})} A
\end{aligned}$$

For an indirect proof of the latter claim, suppose $h(f(a), f(b)) \to^+_{\mathcal{R}} A$. Then there must be terms s and t such that

$$h(f(a), f(b)) \to^+_{\mathcal{R}} h(s,s) \to_{\mathcal{R}} g(s,s,f(k)) \to^*_{\mathcal{R}} g(d,t,t) \to_{\mathcal{R}} A$$

So s must be a common reduct of $f(a)$ and $f(b)$ and s must rewrite to d and t. Moreover, t must be a reduct of $f(k)$. The common reducts of $f(a)$ and $f(b)$ are $f(c), f(d), f(e), f(l), f(m), c, d, e, l, m$. It is easy to see that none of the terms $f(c), f(d), f(e), f(l), f(m), c, e, l$, or m rewrite to d. We infer $s = d$ and thus t must be a common reduct of d and $f(k)$. However, d can only be rewritten to m and the only reducts of $f(k)$ are $f(m)$ and $f(l)$. This contradiction proves that $h(f(a), f(b)) \not\to^+_{\mathcal{R}} A$

The preceding counterexample is rather complicated. In fact, Marchiori [Mar95] conjectured that no simpler counterexample exists for normal 1-CTRSs. For 1-CTRSs that are not necessarily normal, a simpler example can be found in [GA01].

Proposition 7.2.15 *Let $(\mathcal{F}, \mathcal{R})$ be a 1-CTRS. If $(\mathcal{F}', U_n(\mathcal{R}))$ is terminating, then $(\mathcal{F}, \mathcal{R})$ is decreasing.*

Proof Let $> = \to^+_{U_n(\mathcal{R})}$ and note that $>$ is a reduction ordering on $\mathcal{T}(\mathcal{F}', \mathcal{V})$. Thus $>_{st}$ is a well-founded ordering on $\mathcal{T}(\mathcal{F}', \mathcal{V})$ by Lemma 7.2.4. Let $\succ$ be the restriction of $>_{st}$ to $\mathcal{T}(\mathcal{F}, \mathcal{V})$. It will be shown that $\mathcal{R}$ is decreasing w.r.t. $\succ$. The partial ordering $\succ$ is obviously well-founded. According to Lemma 7.2.13, we have $\to_{\mathcal{R}} \subseteq \succ$. Moreover, $\rhd \subseteq \succ$ by definition. It still must be shown that for every rule $l \to r \Leftarrow s_1 \to t_1, \ldots, s_k \to t_k$ in $\mathcal{R}$, the inequality $l\sigma \succ s_j\sigma$ holds. This is true because $l\sigma \to_{U_n(\mathcal{R})} U^\rho(s_1, \ldots, s_k, \mathcal{V}ar(l))\sigma$ implies $l\sigma >_{st} s_j\sigma$. □

Again, Example 7.2.14 shows that the converse of Proposition 7.2.15 does not hold. It is relatively easy to show that the system $\mathcal{R}$ is terminating because $h(f(a), f(b)) \not\to_{\mathcal{R}}^{+} A$. This implies that $\succ = \to_{\mathcal{R}}^{+}$ is a reduction ordering and it is not difficult to verify that $\mathcal{R}$ is decreasing w.r.t. the ordering $\succ_{st}$ because $f(x\sigma) \rhd x\sigma$. The TRS $U_n(\mathcal{R})$, however, is nonterminating. It should be pointed out that $\mathcal{R}$ is not reductive. If it were reductive w.r.t. a reduction ordering $\succ$, then it would follow from Definition 7.2.3(3) that $f(x)\sigma \succ x\sigma$ for every substitution σ. Hence

$$\begin{aligned} A &\succ h(f(a), f(b)) \succ h(a, f(b)) \succ h(a, b) \succ h(d, b) \succ h(d, d) \\ &\succ g(d, d, f(k)) \succ g(d, d, k) \succ g(d, m, k) \succ g(d, m, m) \succ A \end{aligned}$$

which is impossible.

According to Proposition 7.2.15, in order to show decreasingness of a CTRS, we can use standard methods for proving termination of unconditional systems. Consider, for example, the CTRS $\mathcal{R}$ from Example 7.2.10. Termination of the TRS

$$U_n(\mathcal{R}) = \begin{cases} b & \to c \\ f(b) & \to f(a) \\ a & \to U(b) \\ U(c) & \to c \end{cases}$$

can be shown by the dependency pair method. Thus $\mathcal{R}$ is decreasing by Proposition 7.2.15. This example also shows that termination of $U_n(\mathcal{R})$ does not imply reductivity of $\mathcal{R}$.

Decreasingness of the *gcd* system from Example 7.1.5 can also be shown by Proposition 7.2.15 in conjunction with the dependency pair method. For the cycle

$$\{\langle \mathrm{GCD}(s(x), s(y)), \mathbf{U}'(y < x, x, y)\rangle, \langle \mathbf{U}'(true, x, y), \mathrm{GCD}(x - y, s(y))\rangle\}$$

we can use, for example, the interpretation $0_{\mathbb{N}} = 0$, $s_{\mathbb{N}}(x) = x+1$, $true_{\mathbb{N}} = 0$, $false_{\mathbb{N}} = 0$, $x <_{\mathbb{N}} y = x + y$, $x -_{\mathbb{N}} y = x$, $gcd_{\mathbb{N}}(x, y) = \mathrm{GCD}_{\mathbb{N}}(x, y) = x + y$, and $U'_{\mathbb{N}}(z, x, y) = \mathbf{U}'_{\mathbb{N}}(z, x, y) = x + y + 1$.

The following two examples show that simple termination of $U_n(\mathcal{R})$ does not imply simplifyingness of $\mathcal{R}$ and vice versa. The first example is taken from [Mar95].

Example 7.2.16 The transformed system $U_n(\mathcal{R})$ of the normal 1-CTRS $\mathcal{R} = \{a \to b, b \to a \Leftarrow c \to d\}$ is the TRS $\{a \to b, b \to U(c), U(d) \to a\}$. The *lpo* with precedence $d \succ_p a \succ_p b \succ_p c \succ_p U$ shows that $U_n(\mathcal{R})$ is simply terminating, but $\mathcal{R}$ is apparently not simplifying.

Example 7.2.17 Consider the normal 1-CTRS $(\mathcal{F}, \mathcal{R})$ consisting of the rules

$$\begin{array}{rcl@{\qquad\qquad}rcl} a & \to & d & a & \to & e \\ b & \to & d & b & \to & e \\ A & \to & h(f(a), f(b)) \\ h(x,x) & \to & g(x,x) \\ g(d,e) & \to & A \\ f(x) & \to & x & \Leftarrow & x \to d \end{array}$$

We claim that $\mathcal{R}$ is simplifying. By Lemmas 5.2.30 and 7.2.6, it suffices to show that $\mathcal{R}_s \cup \mathcal{E}mb(\mathcal{F})$ is terminating. For an indirect proof of the claim, suppose that there is an infinite $\mathcal{R}_s \cup \mathcal{E}mb(\mathcal{F})$ reduction sequence. It is not difficult to see that this implies that there is a cycle $A \to_{\mathcal{R}_s \cup \mathcal{E}mb(\mathcal{F})} h(f(a), f(b)) \to^+_{\mathcal{R}_s \cup \mathcal{E}mb(\mathcal{F})} A$. If $h(f(a), f(b)) \to^+_{\mathcal{R}_s \cup \mathcal{E}mb(\mathcal{F})} A$, then there must be a term t such that

$$h(f(a), f(b)) \to^+_{\mathcal{R}_s \cup \mathcal{E}mb(\mathcal{F})} g(t,t) \to^+_{\mathcal{R}_s \cup \mathcal{E}mb(\mathcal{F})} g(d,e) \to_{\mathcal{R}_s \cup \mathcal{E}mb(\mathcal{F})} A$$

So t must be a common reduct of $f(a)$ and $f(b)$ and t must rewrite to d and e. The common reducts of $f(a)$ and $f(b)$ are $f(d)$, $f(e)$, d, and e. None of them reduces to both d and e. We conclude that $\mathcal{R}_s \cup \mathcal{E}mb(\mathcal{F})$ is terminating. Thus, $\mathcal{R}$ is simplifying.

$U_n(\mathcal{R})$ is obtained from $\mathcal{R}$ by replacing the conditional rewrite rule with the unconditional rewrite rules $f(x) \to U(x,x)$ and $U(d,x) \to x$. The following cyclic derivation shows that $U_n(\mathcal{R})$ is not simply terminating.

$$\begin{array}{rll} A & \to_{U_n(\mathcal{R})} & h(f(a), f(b)) \to^+_{U_n(\mathcal{R})} h(U(a,a), U(b,b)) \\ & \to^+_{U_n(\mathcal{R})} & h(U(d,e), U(d,e)) \to_{U_n(\mathcal{R})} g(U(d,e), U(d,e)) \\ & \to^+_{\mathcal{E}mb(\mathcal{F}')} & g(d,e) \to_{U_n(\mathcal{R})} A. \end{array}$$

The preceding example is also interesting because it refutes the following claim, which is a reformulation of [Mar96b, lemma 5.6]. Let us first review the definition of the transformation $\mathbb{U}$ as given in [Mar96b, definition 4.1]. Given a join 1-CTRS $\mathcal{R}$ and a rule $\rho : l \to r \Leftarrow s_1 \downarrow t_1, \ldots, s_k \downarrow t_k \in \mathcal{R}$, the transformation $\mathbb{U}(\rho)$ yields the two unconditional rules

$$\begin{array}{l} l \to U^\rho(s_1, t_1, \ldots, s_k, t_k, \mathcal{V}ar(l)) \\ U^\rho(x_1, x_1, \ldots, x_k, x_k, \mathcal{V}ar(l)) \to r \end{array}$$

where $x_1, \ldots, x_k$ are fresh and pairwise distinct variables. Moreover, $\mathbb{U}(\mathcal{R})$ is defined as usual: $\mathbb{U}(\mathcal{R}) = \bigcup_{\rho \in \mathcal{R}} \mathbb{U}(\rho)$.

Claim: If a join 1-CTRS $\mathcal{R}$ is simplifying, then the transformed TRS $\mathbb{U}(\mathcal{R})$ is simply terminating.

If we view the system $\mathcal{R}$ from Example 7.2.17 as a join CTRS, then $\mathbb{U}(\mathcal{R}) = \mathcal{R}' \cup \{f(x) \to U(x,d,x), U(x_1,x_1,x) \to x\}$, where $\mathcal{R}'$ consists of the unconditional rules of $\mathcal{R}$. As in Example 7.2.17, it can be shown that the system $\mathcal{R}' \cup \{f(x) \to x, f(x) \to d\}$ is simply terminating. Thus the join 1-CTRS $\mathcal{R}$ is simplifying according to Lemma 7.2.6. On the other hand, the transformed system $\mathbb{U}(\mathcal{R})$ is not simply terminating because there is a cyclic derivation as in Example 7.2.17.

7.2.3 Left-Linear Normal 1-CTRSs

In this section it will be shown that the converse of Proposition 7.2.15 is true if the system under consideration is a left-linear normal 1-CTRS. This result is due to Marchiori [Mar96b]; however, the proof in [Mar95] is incomplete.[7] Here we will provide a rigorous proof that is different from the one in [Mar95] although it uses the same proof structure. The new idea is to postpone the introduction of U symbols until they are actually eliminated.

The proof consists of proving the following statements:

1. Every unbalanced $U_n(\mathcal{R})$ derivation starting from a term $s \in \mathcal{T}(\mathcal{F},\mathcal{V})$ can be transformed into a balanced derivation.
2. There is a function $\nabla : \mathcal{T}(\mathcal{F}',\mathcal{V}) \to \mathcal{T}(\mathcal{F},\mathcal{V})$ such that a balanced $U_n(\mathcal{R})$ derivation $s \to^*_{U_n(\mathcal{R})} t$ with $s \in \mathcal{T}(\mathcal{F},\mathcal{V})$ can be transformed into a derivation $s \to^*_{\mathcal{R}} \nabla(t) \to^*_{U_n(\mathcal{R})} t$ in which $\nabla(t) \to^*_{U_n(\mathcal{R})} t$ is balanced.
3. There is no infinite $U_n(\mathcal{R})$ derivation starting from $s \in \mathcal{T}(\mathcal{F},\mathcal{V})$.
4. There is no infinite $U_n(\mathcal{R})$ derivation starting from $s \in \mathcal{T}(\mathcal{F}',\mathcal{V})$.

Throughout this section, $\mathcal{R}$ denotes a left-linear normal 1-CTRS unless stated otherwise. Observe that the transformed system $U_n(\mathcal{R})$ of such a system $\mathcal{R}$ is also left-linear. First, we refine the usual notion of descendant.

Definition 7.2.18 Let $A : s \to_{p,l\to r} t$ be a rewrite step in a left-linear TRS $U_n(\mathcal{R})$ and let $q \in \mathcal{P}os(s)$. The set $q\backslash A$ of *descendants* of q in t is defined by:

$$q\backslash A = \begin{cases} \{q\} & \text{if } q < p \text{ or } q \parallel p, \\ \{q\} & \text{if } q = p \text{ and } root(t|_q) \text{ is a } U \text{ symbol}, \\ \{p.p_3.p_2 \mid r|_{p_3} = l|_{p_1}\} & \text{if } q = p.p_1.p_2 \text{ with } p_1 \in \mathcal{VP}os(l) \\ \emptyset & \text{otherwise} \end{cases}$$

[7] In [Mar95, lemma 6.11], the case in which a U term has a descendant that is eliminated and another one that cannot be eliminated is not taken into account. It is unclear whether the proof can be rectified. Furthermore, in [Mar95, theorem 6.18] it is not shown that there is no infinite $U_n(\mathcal{R})$ derivation starting from a term that already contains U symbols.

If $q' \in q\backslash A$ is a descendant of q in t, then q is called the *antecedent* of q' (because $U_n(\mathcal{R})$ is left-linear, every position q' in t has at most one antecedent q in s). If $Q \subseteq \mathcal{P}os(s)$, then $Q\backslash A$ denotes the set $\bigcup_{q \in Q} q\backslash A$. The notion of descendant and antecedent, respectively, is extended to rewrite sequences in the obvious way.

In the following, a U *term* is a term with a U symbol at its root. Analogously, a subterm of a term s with a U symbol at its root is called a U *subterm* of s.

Definition 7.2.19 Consider a $U_n(\mathcal{R})$ derivation

$$u_1 \to_{U_n(\mathcal{R})} u_2 \to_{U_n(\mathcal{R})} \cdots \to_{U_n(\mathcal{R})} u_m$$

where $u_1 \in \mathcal{T}(\mathcal{F}, \mathcal{V})$. If $q' \in \mathcal{P}os(u_j)$ for some $1 < j \le m$ such that $u_j|_{q'}$ is a U subterm of u_j, i.e., $root(u_j|_{q'}) = U^\rho$, then the *antecedent* $\nabla_a(u_j|_{q'})$ of the U term $u_j|_{q'}$ is the redex $l\sigma$, which introduced the symbol U^ρ. Formally, it is the term $u_\ell|_q$, where q is the first antecedent of q' (from right to left) with $root(u_\ell|_q) \in \mathcal{F}$; that is, $u_\ell|_q = l\sigma \to_{U_n(\mathcal{R})} U^\rho(s_1, \ldots, s_k, \mathcal{V}ar(l))\sigma = u_{\ell+1}|_q$. Furthermore, the U term $u_j|_{q'}$ is called a U *descendant* of $u_\ell|_q$.

As an example, consider the system $\mathcal{R}$

$$\begin{array}{rll} f(x) & \to x & \Leftarrow x \to c \\ g(x) & \to x & \Leftarrow x \to c \\ a & \to b & \\ a & \to c & \end{array}$$

The transformed system $U_n(\mathcal{R})$ consists of the rewrite rules

$$\begin{array}{rl} f(x) & \to U^1(x, x) \\ U^1(c, x) & \to x \\ g(x) & \to U^2(x, x) \\ U^2(c, x) & \to x \\ a & \to b \\ a & \to c \end{array}$$

In the $U_n(\mathcal{R})$ derivation

$$\begin{array}{rll} u_1 = g(f(a)) & \to_{U_n(\mathcal{R})} & u_2 = g(U^1(a, a)) \\ & \to_{U_n(\mathcal{R})} & u_3 = U^2(U^1(a, a), U^1(a, a)) \\ & \to^+_{U_n(\mathcal{R})} & u_4 = U^2(a, U^1(a, a)) \\ & \to^+_{U_n(\mathcal{R})} & u_5 = U^2(c, U^1(b, a)) \\ & \to_{U_n(\mathcal{R})} & u_6 = U^1(b, a) \end{array}$$

the antecedent of $U^1(b, a) = u_6|_\varepsilon$ is the term $f(a) = u_1|_1$, while the antecedent of $U^2(c, U^1(b, a)) = u_5|_\varepsilon$ is the term $g(U^1(a, a)) = u_2|_\varepsilon$.

Definition 7.2.20 A $U_n(\mathcal{R})$ derivation is called *balanced* if for every rewrite step of the form $s = C[l\sigma] \to_{U_n(\mathcal{R})} C[U^\rho(s_1, \ldots, s_k, \mathcal{V}ar(l))\sigma] = t$ none of the terms $x\sigma$, $x \in \mathcal{V}ar(l)$, contains a U symbol. In other words, whenever a U symbol is *introduced*, there can only be other U symbols above it.

Our first goal is to show that every unbalanced $U_n(\mathcal{R})$ derivation starting from a term $s \in \mathcal{T}(\mathcal{F}, \mathcal{V})$ can be transformed into a balanced derivation. As already mentioned, the idea of the proof is to postpone the introduction of U symbols until they are actually eliminated. To illustrate this idea, consider the unbalanced derivation. It can be transformed into the balanced derivation

$$\begin{aligned} g(f(a)) &\to_{U_n(\mathcal{R})} U^2(f(a), f(a)) \to_{U_n(\mathcal{R})} U^2(U^1(a,a), f(a)) \\ &\to_{U_n(\mathcal{R})} U^2(U^1(c,a), f(a)) \to_{U_n(\mathcal{R})} U^2(a, f(a)) \\ &\to_{U_n(\mathcal{R})} U^2(c, f(a)) \to_{U_n(\mathcal{R})} f(a) \end{aligned}$$

We need the following lemmas.

Lemma 7.2.21 *If $s \to^*_{U_n(\mathcal{R})} t$ and $t \to^*_{U_n(\mathcal{R})} u$ are balanced derivations, then the derivation $s \to^*_{U_n(\mathcal{R})} t \to^*_{U_n(\mathcal{R})} u$ is also balanced.*

Proof The proof is obvious. □

Lemma 7.2.22 *Let $s \in \mathcal{T}(\mathcal{F}, \mathcal{V})$ and $D : s \to^*_{U_n(\mathcal{R})} t$ be a balanced derivation. If t' is a U subterm of t, then the antecedent $\nabla_a(t') = l\sigma$ does not contain U symbols, that is, $l\sigma \in \mathcal{T}(\mathcal{F}, \mathcal{V})$.*

Proof If $l\sigma$ contains a U symbol, then the reduction step $l\sigma \to_{U_n(\mathcal{R})} U^\rho(s_1, \ldots, s_k, \mathcal{V}ar(l))\sigma$ would not be balanced. This, however, is impossible because D is balanced. □

Lemma 7.2.23 *Let the $U_n(\mathcal{R})$ derivation D starting from $u_1 \in \mathcal{T}(\mathcal{F}, \mathcal{V})$*

$$D : u_1 \to_{U_n(\mathcal{R})} u_2 \to_{U_n(\mathcal{R})} \cdots \to_{U_n(\mathcal{R})} u_m$$

be balanced. Suppose, furthermore, that in the rewrite step $u_i \to_{U_n(\mathcal{R})} u_{i+1}$ a U symbol is introduced, i.e.,

$$u_i = u_i[p \leftarrow l\sigma] \to_{U_n(\mathcal{R})} u_i[p \leftarrow U^\rho(s_1, \ldots, s_k, \mathcal{V}ar(l))\sigma] = u_{i+1}$$

For every $j \in \{i+1, \ldots, m\}$, let $Q_j = p\backslash(u_i \to^*_{U_n(\mathcal{R})} u_j)$ be the set of descendants of p in u_j and define $\Delta(u_j) = u_j[q \leftarrow l\sigma \mid q \in Q_j]$. Note that $\Delta(u_j)$ is obtained from u_j by replacing every U descendant of $l\sigma$ with $l\sigma$. Then for every $j \in \{i+1, \ldots, m\}$ there are balanced derivations

$$D' : u_1 \to_{U_n(\mathcal{R})} \cdots \to_{U_n(\mathcal{R})} u_i = \Delta(u_{i+1}) \to^*_{U_n(\mathcal{R})} \cdots \to^*_{U_n(\mathcal{R})} \Delta(u_j)$$

and $\Delta(u_j) \to^*_{U_n(\mathcal{R})} u_j$.

Proof The derivations $u_1 \to_{U_n(\mathcal{R})} \cdots \to_{U_n(\mathcal{R})} u_i = \Delta(u_{i+1})$ and $\Delta(u_{i+1}) = u_i \to_{U_n(\mathcal{R})} u_{i+1}$ are balanced because D is balanced. Let $j \in \{i+1, \ldots, m-1\}$. By an inductive argument, there are balanced derivations

$$u_1 \to_{U_n(\mathcal{R})} \cdots \to_{U_n(\mathcal{R})} u_i = \Delta(u_{i+1}) \to^*_{U_n(\mathcal{R})} \cdots \to^*_{U_n(\mathcal{R})} \Delta(u_j)$$

and $\Delta(u_j) \to^*_{U_n(\mathcal{R})} u_j$, and it is sufficient to show that there are balanced derivations $\Delta(u_j) \to^*_{U_n(\mathcal{R})} \Delta(u_{j+1})$ and $\Delta(u_{j+1}) \to^*_{U_n(\mathcal{R})} u_{j+1}$. Suppose $u_j \to_{U_n(\mathcal{R})} u_{j+1}$ by contracting a redex $l'\sigma'$ at position p' to $r'\sigma'$. We proceed by case analysis.

(a) p' and q are disjoint for every $q \in Q_j$. Then u_j can be written as $u_j = C[U^\rho(\ldots), \ldots, U^\rho(\ldots), l'\sigma', U^\rho(\ldots), \ldots, U^\rho(\ldots)]$ in which every U descendant $U^\rho(\ldots)$ of $l\sigma$ is displayed. Then $\Delta(u_j) = C[l\sigma, \ldots, l\sigma, l'\sigma', l\sigma, \ldots, l\sigma] \to_{U_n(\mathcal{R})} C[l\sigma, \ldots, l\sigma, r'\sigma', l\sigma, \ldots, l\sigma] = \Delta(u_{j+1})$. This reduction step is balanced because the reduction step $u_j \to_{U_n(\mathcal{R})} u_{j+1}$ is balanced. Moreover, because $\Delta(u_j) \to^*_{U_n(\mathcal{R})} u_j$ is balanced, the derivation $\Delta(u_{j+1}) \to^*_{U_n(\mathcal{R})} u_{j+1}$ in which exactly the same redexes are contracted is balanced as well.

(b) There is a $q \in Q_j$ such that $q < p'$, that is, the rewrite step $u_j \to_{U_n(\mathcal{R})} u_{j+1}$ takes place within a U descendant of $l\sigma$. Then we have $\Delta(u_j) = \Delta(u_{j+1})$ and $\Delta(u_j) \to^*_{U_n(\mathcal{R})} u_j \to_{U_n(\mathcal{R})} u_{j+1}$. This reduction sequence is balanced because both $\Delta(u_j) \to^*_{U_n(\mathcal{R})} u_j$ and $u_j \to_{U_n(\mathcal{R})} u_{j+1}$ are balanced.

(c) There is a position $q \in Q_j$ such that $q = p'$. In this case, u_j has the form

$$C[U^\rho(\ldots), \ldots, U^\rho(\ldots), U^\rho(t_1, \ldots, t_k, \mathcal{V}ar(l))\sigma', U^\rho(\ldots), \ldots, U^\rho(\ldots)]$$

in which every U descendant $U^\rho(\ldots)$ of $l\sigma$ is displayed. Furthermore, we obtain u_{j+1} by contracting the redex $U^\rho(t_1, \ldots, t_k, \mathcal{V}ar(l))\sigma'$ to $r\sigma'$. Clearly, the derivation D must contain a subsequence D'

$$\begin{array}{rl} l\sigma & \to_{U_n(\mathcal{R})} \ U^\rho(s_1, \ldots, s_k, \mathcal{V}ar(l))\sigma \\ & \to^*_{U_n(\mathcal{R})} \ U^\rho(t_1, \ldots, t_k, \mathcal{V}ar(l))\sigma' \\ & \to_{U_n(\mathcal{R})} \ r\sigma' \end{array}$$

This derivation is balanced because D is balanced. It follows that $\Delta(u_j) = C[l\sigma, \ldots, l\sigma, l\sigma, l\sigma, \ldots, l\sigma] \to^*_{U_n(\mathcal{R})} C[l\sigma, \ldots, l\sigma, r\sigma', l\sigma, \ldots, l\sigma] = \Delta(u_{j+1})$. This derivation is balanced because D' is balanced. Moreover, because $\Delta(u_j) = C[l\sigma, \ldots, l\sigma] \to^*_{U_n(\mathcal{R})} u_j$ is balanced, so is the derivation $\Delta(u_{j+1}) = C[l\sigma, \ldots, l\sigma, r\sigma', l\sigma, \ldots, l\sigma] \to^*_{U_n(\mathcal{R})} u_{j+1}$ in which the same redexes are contracted, except for those at positions $\geq p'$.

(d) There is a $q \in Q_j$ such that $q > p'$. Let σ'_Δ be the substitution obtained from σ' by replacing every U descendant of $l\sigma$ in $x\sigma'$ with $l\sigma$. Then $u_j = C[U^\rho(\ldots), \ldots, U^\rho(\ldots), l'\sigma', U^\rho(\ldots), \ldots, U^\rho(\ldots)]$ and $\Delta(u_j) = C[l\sigma, \ldots, l\sigma, l'\sigma'_\Delta, l\sigma, \ldots, l\sigma]$. Because $u_j \to_{U_n(\mathcal{R})} u_{j+1}$ is balanced, the same is true for $\Delta(u_j) = C[l\sigma, \ldots, l\sigma, l'\sigma'_\Delta, l\sigma, \ldots, l\sigma] \to_{U_n(\mathcal{R})}$

$C[l\sigma,\ldots,l\sigma,r'\sigma'_\Delta,l\sigma,\ldots,l\sigma] = \Delta(u_{j+1})$. Moreover, because $\Delta(u_j) = C[l\sigma,\ldots,l\sigma,l'\sigma'_\Delta,l\sigma,\ldots,l\sigma] \to^*_{U_n(\mathcal{R})} C[U^\rho(\ldots),\ldots,U^\rho(\ldots),l'\sigma',U^\rho(\ldots),\ldots,U^\rho(\ldots)] = u_j$ is a balanced derivation, we conclude that the derivations $C[\ldots,l\sigma,l'\sigma'_\Delta,l\sigma,\ldots] \to^*_{U_n(\mathcal{R})} C[\ldots,U^\rho(\ldots),l'\sigma'_\Delta,U^\rho(\ldots),\ldots]$ and $x\sigma'_\Delta \to^*_{U_n(\mathcal{R})} x\sigma'$ (for all $x \in \mathcal{V}ar(l')$) are balanced, too. Hence there is also a balanced derivation $\Delta(u_{j+1}) = C[l\sigma,\ldots,l\sigma,r'\sigma'_\Delta,l\sigma,\ldots,l\sigma] \to^*_{U_n(\mathcal{R})} C[U^\rho(\ldots),\ldots,U^\rho(\ldots),r'\sigma',U^\rho(\ldots),\ldots,U^\rho(\ldots)] = u_{j+1}$. □

Lemma 7.2.24 *For every $U_n(\mathcal{R})$ derivation $D : u_1 \to_{U_n(\mathcal{R})} \cdots \to_{U_n(\mathcal{R})} u_m$ with $u_1 \in \mathcal{T}(\mathcal{F},\mathcal{V})$, there exists a balanced $U_n(\mathcal{R})$ derivation D' starting at u_1 and ending at u_m.*

Proof If D is balanced, then there is nothing to show. If D is not balanced, then there is at least one clash, that is, a rewrite step $u_i \to_{U_n(\mathcal{R})} u_{i+1}$ in which a U symbol is introduced but there is another U symbol below it. Suppose that there are ℓ clashes in D. We show that D can be transformed into a derivation D' with only $\ell-1$ clashes. If we apply this transformation ℓ times, then we obviously get a balanced derivation.

Let $u_i = u_i[p \leftarrow l\sigma] \to_{U_n(\mathcal{R})} u_i[p \leftarrow U^\rho(s_1,\ldots,s_k,\mathcal{V}ar(l))\sigma] = u_{i+1}$ be the first clash (from left to right) in D. That is, the derivation

$$u_1 \to_{U_n(\mathcal{R})} \cdots \to_{U_n(\mathcal{R})} u_i$$

is balanced. Let p_j, $j \in \{1,\ldots,n\}$, be the smallest positions in u_i such that $p_j > p$ and $root(u_i|_{p_j})$ is a U symbol. Let $l'\sigma'$ be the antecedent of $u_i|_{p_1}$ and suppose $u_{i'} = u_{i'}[p' \leftarrow l'\sigma'] \to_{U_n(\mathcal{R})} u_{i'}[p' \leftarrow U^{\rho'}(s'_1,\ldots,s'_k,\mathcal{V}ar(l'))\sigma'] = u_{i'+1}$, i.e., in this rewrite step the symbol $root(u_i|_{p_1}) = U^{\rho'}$ was introduced. Because the rewrite step $u_{i'} \to_{U_n(\mathcal{R})} u_{i'+1}$ is balanced, $l'\sigma'$ does not contain U symbols. For $j' \in \{i'+1,\ldots,i\}$, define $\Delta(u_{j'}) = u_{j'}[q \leftarrow l'\sigma' \mid q \in p'\backslash(u_{i'} \to^*_{U_n(\mathcal{R})} u_{j'})]$. By Lemma 7.2.23, there are balanced derivations

$$u_1 \to_{U_n(\mathcal{R})} \cdots \to_{U_n(\mathcal{R})} u_{i'} \to_{U_n(\mathcal{R})} \Delta(u_{i'+1}) \to^*_{U_n(\mathcal{R})} \cdots \to^*_{U_n(\mathcal{R})} \Delta(u_i)$$

and $\Delta(u_i) \to^*_{U_n(\mathcal{R})} u_i$. If p_j, $j \in \{2,\ldots,n\}$ is a descendant of p' in u_i, then $u_i|_{p_j}$ is a U descendant of $l'\sigma'$. Because every U descendant of $l'\sigma'$ is replaced with $l'\sigma'$ in $\Delta(u_i)$, it follows that $\Delta(u_i)|_{p_j}$ does not contain U symbols. If there is still a position p_j, $j \in \{2,\ldots,n\}$ such that $root(\Delta(u_i)|_{p_j})$ is a U symbol, then we repeat the same process with p_j. After at most n repetitions, we obtain a term u'_i that differs from u_i in that every U descendant of the antecedent of every $u_i|_{p_j}$, $j \in \{1,\ldots,n\}$, is replaced with its antecedent. Hence $u'_i|_{p_j}$ does not contain U symbols. Moreover, there are balanced derivations

$$u_1 \to_{U_n(\mathcal{R})} \cdots \to_{U_n(\mathcal{R})} u'_i$$

and $u'_i \rightarrow^*_{U_n(\mathcal{R})} u_i$. Now we have $u'_i = u'_i[p \leftarrow l\tau]$ for the substitution τ obtained from σ by replacing every maximal U term in $x\sigma$ with its antecedent. Note that there is a balanced derivation $x\tau \rightarrow^*_{U_n(\mathcal{R})} x\sigma$ for every $x \in \mathcal{V}ar(l)$. The rewrite step

$$u'_i = u'_i[p \leftarrow l\tau] \rightarrow_{U_n(\mathcal{R})} u'_i[p \leftarrow U^\rho(s_1, \ldots, s_k, \mathcal{V}ar(l))\tau] = u'_{i+1}$$

is balanced because $x\tau$ does not contain U symbols for every $x \in \mathcal{V}ar(l)$. Altogether, we obtain a balanced derivation

$$\begin{array}{rcl} u'_{i+1} & = & u'_i[p \leftarrow U^\rho(s_1, \ldots, s_k, \mathcal{V}ar(l))\tau] \\ & \rightarrow^*_{U_n(\mathcal{R})} & u_i[p \leftarrow U^\rho(s_1, \ldots, s_k, \mathcal{V}ar(l))\tau] \\ & \rightarrow^*_{U_n(\mathcal{R})} & u_i[p \leftarrow U^\rho(s_1, \ldots, s_k, \mathcal{V}ar(l))\sigma] \\ & = u_{i+1} & \end{array}$$

Therefore, there is a balanced derivation

$$u_1 \rightarrow_{U_n(\mathcal{R})} \cdots \rightarrow_{U_n(\mathcal{R})} u'_i \rightarrow_{U_n(\mathcal{R})} u'_{i+1} \rightarrow^*_{U_n(\mathcal{R})} u_{i+1}$$

This means that the derivation

$$D' : u_1 \rightarrow_{U_n(\mathcal{R})} \cdots \rightarrow_{U_n(\mathcal{R})} u'_{i+1} \rightarrow^*_{U_n(\mathcal{R})} u_{i+1} \rightarrow_{U_n(\mathcal{R})} \cdots \rightarrow_{U_n(\mathcal{R})} u_m$$

contains only $\ell - 1$ clashes. □

We have achieved our first goal: Every unbalanced $U_n(\mathcal{R})$ derivation starting from a term $s \in \mathcal{T}(\mathcal{F}, \mathcal{V})$ can indeed be transformed into a balanced derivation. The second goal is to show the existence of a function $\nabla : \mathcal{T}(\mathcal{F}', \mathcal{V}) \rightarrow \mathcal{T}(\mathcal{F}, \mathcal{V})$ such that every balanced $U_n(\mathcal{R})$ derivation $s \rightarrow^*_{U_n(\mathcal{R})} t$ with $s \in \mathcal{T}(\mathcal{F}, \mathcal{V})$ can be transformed into a derivation $s \rightarrow^*_{\mathcal{R}} \nabla(t) \rightarrow^*_{U_n(\mathcal{R})} t$.

Definition 7.2.25 For every balanced $U_n(\mathcal{R})$ derivation D, we define a transformation $\nabla\colon \mathcal{T}(\mathcal{F}', \mathcal{V}) \rightarrow \mathcal{T}(\mathcal{F}, \mathcal{V})$ by

$$\nabla(t) = \begin{cases} t & \text{if } t \in \mathcal{V} \cup \mathcal{F}^{(0)} \\ f(\nabla(t_1), \ldots, \nabla(t_n)) & \text{if } t = f(t_1, \ldots, t_n), f \in \mathcal{F}^{(n)} \\ l\sigma & \text{if } t = U^\rho(\ldots) \text{ and } \nabla_a(t) = l\sigma \end{cases}$$

Note that $l\sigma$ does not contain U symbols according to Lemma 7.2.22.

Lemma 7.2.26 *Let $s \in \mathcal{T}(\mathcal{F}, \mathcal{V})$ and $D : s \rightarrow^*_{U_n(\mathcal{R})} t$ be a balanced derivation. Then $s \rightarrow^*_{\mathcal{R}} \nabla(t) \rightarrow^*_{U_n(\mathcal{R})} t$.*

Proof The lemma is shown by induction on the length ℓ of the derivation $D : s \rightarrow^*_{U_n(\mathcal{R})} t$. The base case $\ell = 0$ is obviously true. Suppose

$$D\colon s \rightarrow^{\ell}_{U_n(\mathcal{R})} t' \rightarrow_{U_n(\mathcal{R})} t$$

By the inductive hypothesis, we have

$$s \to_{\mathcal{R}}^* \nabla(t') \to_{U_n(\mathcal{R})}^* t'$$

We show $\nabla(t') \to_{\mathcal{R}}^* \nabla(t) \to_{U_n(\mathcal{R})}^* t$ by case analysis. Suppose first that the redex contracted in the reduction step $t' \to_{U_n(\mathcal{R})} t$ is below a U symbol. Then

$$\nabla(t) = \nabla(t') \to_{U_n(\mathcal{R})}^* t' \to_{U_n(\mathcal{R})} t$$

Next we assume that there is no U symbol above the contracted redex. If $t = C[l'\tau] \in \mathcal{T}(\mathcal{F}', \mathcal{V})$ with $l' \to r' \in U_n(\mathcal{R})$ and there is no U symbol above $l'\tau$ in C, then $\nabla(t) = \nabla(C)[\nabla(l'\tau)]$, and hence it suffices to show the claim for the following cases:

1. $t' = l\tau \to_{U_n(\mathcal{R})} r\tau = t$, where $l \to r \in \mathcal{R}$.
2. $t' = l\tau \to_{U_n(\mathcal{R})} U^\rho(s_1, \ldots, s_k, \mathcal{V}ar(l))\tau = t$.
3. $t' = U^\rho(t_1, \ldots, t_k, \mathcal{V}ar(l))\tau \to_{U_n(\mathcal{R})} r\tau = t$.

The first two cases are easy to prove. In case (3), we have to show that $\nabla(t') = l\sigma \to_{\mathcal{R}}^* \nabla(t) = \nabla(r\tau) \to_{U_n(\mathcal{R})}^* r\tau = t$. The derivation D must contain a balanced subsequence

$$\begin{aligned} D' : l\sigma &\to_{U_n(\mathcal{R})} U^\rho(s_1, \ldots, s_k, \mathcal{V}ar(l))\sigma \\ &\to_{U_n(\mathcal{R})}^* U^\rho(t_1, \ldots, t_k, \mathcal{V}ar(l))\tau \to_{U_n(\mathcal{R})} r\tau \end{aligned}$$

Because D' is balanced, it follows that $l\sigma$ does not contain a U symbol. So if $length(D') < length(D)$, then the claim follows from the inductive hypothesis. We have to treat the case $D' = D$. Consider the proper subderivation $s_j\sigma \to_{U_n(\mathcal{R})}^* t_j$. By the inductive hypothesis, we have $s_j\sigma \to_{\mathcal{R}}^* \nabla(t_j) = t_j$ (the equality holds because t_j is a ground term without U symbols). Therefore, $l\sigma \to_{\mathcal{R}} r\sigma$. Furthermore, because $x\sigma \to_{U_n(\mathcal{R})}^* x\tau$ for every $x \in \mathcal{V}ar(l)$, renewed applications of the inductive hypothesis yield $x\sigma \to_{\mathcal{R}}^* \nabla(x\tau) \to_{U_n(\mathcal{R})}^* x\tau$. All in all, $l\sigma \to_{\mathcal{R}} r\sigma \to_{\mathcal{R}}^* r\tau_\nabla = \nabla(r\tau) \to_{U_n(\mathcal{R})}^* r\tau$. □

Corollary 7.2.27 *If* $s, t \in \mathcal{T}(\mathcal{F}, \mathcal{V})$ *and* $s \to_{U_n(\mathcal{R})}^* t$, *then* $s \to_{\mathcal{R}}^* t$.

Proof By Lemma 7.2.24, there is a balanced derivation $D : s \to_{U_n(\mathcal{R})}^* t$. Then it follows from Lemma 7.2.26 that $s \to_{\mathcal{R}}^* \nabla(t) = t$. □

Lemma 7.2.28 *If* $\mathcal{R}$ *is a decreasing left-linear normal 1-CTRS, then there is no infinite* $U_n(\mathcal{R})$ *derivation starting from a term* $s \in \mathcal{T}(\mathcal{F}, \mathcal{V})$.

Proof Let $\mathcal{R}$ be decreasing w.r.t. the ordering $\succ$. The proof uses well-founded induction on $\succ$. First, we show that there is no infinite $U_n(\mathcal{R})$ derivation of the form

$$D\colon l\sigma \rightarrow_{U_n(\mathcal{R})} U^\rho(s_1,\ldots,s_k,\mathcal{V}ar(l))\sigma \rightarrow_{U_n(\mathcal{R})} \cdots$$

where $l\sigma \in \mathcal{T}(\mathcal{F},\mathcal{V})$. Because $l\sigma \succ s_j\sigma$ for every $j \in \{1,\ldots,k\}$ and $l\sigma \succ x\sigma$ for every $x \in \mathcal{V}ar(l)$, every $U_n(\mathcal{R})$ derivation starting from one of these terms is finite. Hence D must be of the form

$$\begin{array}{ll} l\sigma & \rightarrow_{U_n(\mathcal{R})} U^\rho(s_1,\ldots,s_k,\mathcal{V}ar(l))\sigma \\ & \rightarrow^*_{U_n(\mathcal{R})} U^\rho(t_1,\ldots,t_k,\mathcal{V}ar(l))\tau \rightarrow_{U_n(\mathcal{R})} r\tau \rightarrow_{U_n(\mathcal{R})} \cdots \end{array}$$

In other words, there is an infinite derivation starting from $r\tau$. Because $r\sigma \rightarrow^*_{U_n(\mathcal{R})} r\tau$, there is also an infinite $U_n(\mathcal{R})$ derivation starting from $r\sigma$. On the other hand, because $\mathcal{R}$ is decreasing, we have $l\sigma \succ r\sigma$ and this implies that every $U_n(\mathcal{R})$ derivation starting from $r\sigma$ is finite.

Now we suppose that there exists an infinite $U_n(\mathcal{R})$ derivation starting from a term $u_1 \in \mathcal{T}(\mathcal{F},\mathcal{V})$, say

$$u_1 \rightarrow_{U_n(\mathcal{R})} u_2 \rightarrow_{U_n(\mathcal{R})} \cdots$$

Because $u_1 \rightarrow_{U_n(\mathcal{R})} u_2$ is balanced, it is a consequence of Lemma 7.2.26 that $u_1 \rightarrow^*_{\mathcal{R}} \nabla(u_2) \rightarrow^*_{U_n(\mathcal{R})} u_2$. Now consider the derivation $\nabla(u_2) \rightarrow^*_{U_n(\mathcal{R})} u_2 \rightarrow_{U_n(\mathcal{R})} u_3$ starting from $u'_2 = \nabla(u_2) \in \mathcal{T}(\mathcal{F},\mathcal{V})$. By Lemma 7.2.24, there is a balanced derivation $u'_2 \rightarrow^*_{U_n(\mathcal{R})} u_3$. Therefore, it follows from Lemma 7.2.26 that $u'_2 \rightarrow^*_{\mathcal{R}} u'_3 = \nabla(u_3) \rightarrow^*_{U_n(\mathcal{R})} u_3$. By continuing along these lines, we obtain an $\mathcal{R}$ derivation

$$D'\colon u_1 \rightarrow^*_{\mathcal{R}} u'_2 \rightarrow^*_{\mathcal{R}} u'_3 \rightarrow^*_{\mathcal{R}} \cdots$$

D' must be finite because $\mathcal{R}$ is decreasing. So there is an index j such that $u'_i = u'_j$ for all $i \geq j$. Therefore, there must be an infinite $U_n(\mathcal{R})$ derivation starting from a U subterm v of u_j. Let $l\sigma$ be the antecedent of v. Then $l\sigma \rightarrow^+_{U_n(\mathcal{R})} v$ implies that there is an infinite $U_n(\mathcal{R})$ derivation starting from $l\sigma$, which is impossible as we have shown. □

It remains to be shown that there is no $U_n(\mathcal{R})$ derivation starting from a term s that contains U symbols. In order to distinguish the U subterms that have an antecedent in s from those created in a derivation, we mark every U subterm in s by underlining the U symbol at its root.

Definition 7.2.29 The *marked U depth* of a term $t \in \mathcal{T}(\mathcal{F},\mathcal{V})$ is defined as follows.

$$\mathrm{depth}_{\underline{U}}(t) = \begin{cases} 0 & \text{if } t \in \mathcal{V} \cup \mathcal{F}^{(0)} \\ \max\{\mathrm{depth}_{\underline{U}}(t_j) \mid 1 \leq j \leq n\} & \text{if } t = f(t_1,\ldots,t_n) \\ 1 + \max\{\mathrm{depth}_{\underline{U}}(t_j) \mid 1 \leq j \leq n\} & \text{if } t = \underline{U}^\rho(t_1,\ldots,t_n) \end{cases}$$

Note that reduction steps do not increase the marked U depth. More precisely, if $s \to_{U(\mathcal{R})} t$, then $\text{depth}_{\underline{U}}(s) \geq \text{depth}_{\underline{U}}(t)$ because marked U symbols may disappear but are not introduced.

Definition 7.2.30 We define a transformation $\Psi\colon \mathcal{T}(\mathcal{F}', \mathcal{V}) \to \mathcal{T}(\mathcal{F}, \mathcal{V})$ by

$$\Psi(t) = \begin{cases} t & \text{if } t \in \mathcal{V} \cup \mathcal{F}^{(0)} \\ f(\Psi(t_1), \ldots, \Psi(t_n)) & \text{if } t = f(t_1, \ldots, t_n), f \in \mathcal{F}^{(n)} \\ r\tau & \text{if } t = \underline{U}^{\rho}(u_1, \ldots, u_k, v_1, \ldots, v_n) \end{cases}$$

where r is the right-hand side of the rule ρ, $\mathcal{V}ar(l) = x_1, \ldots, x_n$ (that is, $U^{\rho}(s_1, \ldots, s_k, \mathcal{V}ar(l)) = U^{\rho}(s_1, \ldots, s_k, x_1, \ldots, x_n)$), and $\tau\colon \mathcal{V}ar(l) \to \mathcal{T}(\mathcal{F}, \mathcal{V})$ is defined by $\tau(x_j) = \Psi(v_j)$. Furthermore, for any substitution σ, we define σ_Ψ by $x\sigma_\Psi = \Psi(x\sigma)$.

Theorem 7.2.31 *If $\mathcal{R}$ is a decreasing left-linear normal 1-CTRS, then $U_n(\mathcal{R})$ is terminating.*

Proof For a proof by contradiction, suppose that there exists an infinite $U_n(\mathcal{R})$ derivation $D : u_1 \to_{U(\mathcal{R})} u_2 \to_{U(\mathcal{R})} u_3 \to_{U(\mathcal{R})} \cdots$ starting from a term $u_1 \in \mathcal{T}(\mathcal{F}', \mathcal{V})$. We mark every U symbol in u_1. If $\text{depth}_{\underline{U}}(u_1) = 0$, then $u_1 \in \mathcal{T}(\mathcal{F}, \mathcal{V})$ but according to Lemma 7.2.28, there is no infinite $U_n(\mathcal{R})$ derivation starting from a term without U symbols. So $\text{depth}_{\underline{U}}(u_1) = m > 0$ and we may write u_1 as $u_1 = C[v_1, \ldots, v_n]$, where the v_j are the maximal marked U subterms of u_1, i.e., the context C does not contain marked U symbols and the root of every v_j is a marked U symbol. Suppose that there is an infinite $U_n(\mathcal{R})$ derivation starting from some v_j. Let $v_j = \underline{U}^{\rho}(w_1, \ldots, w_\ell)$. Because $\text{depth}_{\underline{U}}(w_p) < m$ for every $1 \leq p \leq \ell$, it follows from the inductive hypothesis that there is no infinite $U_n(\mathcal{R})$ derivation starting from w_p. Hence the derivation must have the form

$$v_j = \underline{U}^{\rho}(w_1, \ldots, w_\ell) \to^*_{U(\mathcal{R})} \underline{U}^{\rho}(w'_1, \ldots, w'_\ell) \to_{U(\mathcal{R})} r\sigma \to_{U(\mathcal{R})} \cdots$$

but this is impossible because $\text{depth}_{\underline{U}}(r\sigma) < m$.

We write $u_i \to_m u_{i+1}$ if the contracted redex is a subterm of a marked U subterms of u_i and $u_i \to_{nm} u_{i+1}$ otherwise. It is not difficult to show that for every marked U subterm t of u_{i+1} there is a marked U subterm s of u_1 such that $s \to^*_{U(\mathcal{R})} t$. Because every $U_n(\mathcal{R})$ derivation starting from s is finite, the relation $\to_m$ is terminating. Consequently, D must contain infinitely many $\to_{nm}$ steps.

It will be shown (i) that $u_i \to_m u_{i+1}$ implies $\Psi(u_i) \to^*_{U(\mathcal{R})} \Psi(u_{i+1})$ and (ii) that $u_i \to_{nm} u_{i+1}$ implies $\Psi(u_i) \to_{U(\mathcal{R})} \Psi(u_{i+1})$. It then follows that the derivation $\Psi(D)$ starting from $\Psi(u_1) \in \mathcal{T}(\mathcal{F}, \mathcal{V})$ is infinite. This yields the desired contradiction to Lemma 7.2.28.

(i) To show that $u_i \to_m u_{i+1}$ implies $\Psi(u_i) \to^*_{U(\mathcal{R})} \Psi(u_{i+1})$, we write u_i as $u_i = C[v_1, \ldots, v_n]$, where the v_j are the maximal marked

U subterms of u_i, i.e., the context C does not contain marked U symbols and the root of every v_j is a marked U symbol. If (a) the contracted redex is a proper subterm of some v_j, then $v_j \to_{U(\mathcal{R})} v'_j$ implies $\Psi(v_j) \to^*_{U(\mathcal{R})} \Psi(v'_j)$ according to the inductive hypothesis and the assertion easily follows. If (b), the contracted redex coincides with some v_j, then $v_j = \underline{U}^\rho(\ldots, w_1, \ldots, w_\ell) \to_{U(\mathcal{R})} r\sigma$, where $\sigma : \mathcal{V}ar(l) \to \mathcal{T}(\mathcal{F}', \mathcal{V})$ is defined by $\sigma(x_p) = w_p$ for $p \in \{1, \ldots, \ell\}$. Consequently, $\Psi(v_j) = r\sigma_\Psi = \Psi(r\sigma)$ and again the assertion immediately follows.

(ii) If $u_i \to_{nm} u_{i+1}$, then $u_i = C[v_1, \ldots, v_n] \to_{U(\mathcal{R})} C'[v_{i_1}, \ldots, v_{i_q}] = u_{i+1}$ for some context C' without marked U symbols and $\{v_{i_1}, \ldots, v_{i_q}\} \subseteq \{v_1, \ldots, v_n\}$ because none of the left-hand sides l' of the rules $l' \to r' \in U_n(\mathcal{R})$ have a U symbol strictly below the root. In this case,

$$\Psi(u_i) = C[\Psi(v_1), \ldots, \Psi(v_n)] \to_{U(\mathcal{R})} C'[\Psi(v_{i_1}), \ldots, \Psi(v_{i_q})] = \Psi(u_{i+1})$$

by an application of the same rule as in the reduction step $u_i \to_{U(\mathcal{R})} u_{i+1}$.
□

Corollary 7.2.32 *A left-linear normal 1-CTRS $\mathcal{R}$ is decreasing if and only if $U_n(\mathcal{R})$ is terminating.*

Proof Combine Proposition 7.2.15 with Theorem 7.2.31. □

7.2.4 Summary: Methods for 1-CTRSs

Let us briefly summarize what has been achieved so far. In order to show effective termination of a 1-CTRS $\mathcal{R}$, one has to prove simplifyingness or reductivity or decreasingness. And $\mathcal{R}$ can be shown decreasing by showing termination of the TRS $U_n(\mathcal{R})$; see Proposition 7.2.15. This approach is particularly fruitful in combination with the dependency pair method. For example, we proved decreasingness of the CTRS from Example 7.1.5 in this fashion. Giesl and Arts elaborate on this issue in [GA01] (using the technique of narrowing dependency pairs). It should be pointed out that decreasingness of $\mathcal{R}$ does not imply termination of $U_n(\mathcal{R})$ unless $\mathcal{R}$ is a left-linear normal 1-CTRS.

Simplifyingness of $\mathcal{R}$ is equivalent to simple termination of the TRS $\mathcal{R}_s$; see Lemma 7.2.6. We would like to stress that simple termination of the TRS $U_n(\mathcal{R})$ neither proves simplifyingness of $\mathcal{R}$ or vice versa.

7.2.5 Extra Variables on Right-Hand Sides

Variables on the right-hand side of a rewrite rule that do not occur on the left-hand side are often forbidden because it is in general not clear how to instantiate them. On the other hand, restricted use of these extra variables enables a more natural and efficient way of writing programs. For example, the functional program *quicksort* (written in Haskell) from Chapter 1

```
split x []           = ([],[])
split x (y:ys) | x <= y      = (xs,y:zs)
               | otherwise   = (y:xs,zs)
                               where (xs,zs) = split x ys

qsort []        = []
qsort (x:xs)    = qsort ys ++ (x:qsort zs)
                  where (ys,zs) = split x xs
```

corresponds to the CTRS

$$\begin{array}{rl} split(x, nil) & \to \langle nil, nil\rangle \\ split(x, y : ys) & \to \langle xs, y : zs\rangle \Leftarrow split(x, ys) \to \langle xs, zs\rangle, x \le y \to true \\ split(x, y : ys) & \to \langle y : xs, zs\rangle \Leftarrow split(x, ys) \to \langle xs, zs\rangle, x \le y \to false \\ qsort(nil) & \to nil \\ qsort(x : xs) & \to qsort(ys) +\!\!+ (x : qsort(zs)) \Leftarrow split(x, xs) \to \langle ys, zs\rangle \end{array}$$

which has extra variables on the right-hand side of every conditional rule. Note that the order of the conditions in the *split* rules differs from the *quicksort* CTRS of Chapter 1. In fact, the order of the conditions in the *split* rules does not matter because both versions of the *quicksort* system are deterministic. Let us recall the definition of this notion from [Gan91].

Definition 7.2.33 An oriented 3-CTRS $\mathcal{R}$ is called *deterministic* if for every $l \to r \Leftarrow s_1 \to t_1, \ldots, s_k \to t_k$ in $\mathcal{R}$ and every $1 \le i \le k$, we have $\mathcal{V}ar(s_i) \subseteq \mathcal{V}ar(l) \cup \bigcup_{j=1}^{i-1} \mathcal{V}ar(t_j)$. In what follows, we will frequently use the notation $\mathcal{EV}ar(t_i) = \mathcal{V}ar(t_i) \setminus (\mathcal{V}ar(l) \cup \bigcup_{j=1}^{i-1} \mathcal{V}ar(t_j))$.

Recall that the rewrite relation $\to_\mathcal{R}$ associated with an oriented deterministic 3-CTRS $\mathcal{R}$ is defined by $\to_\mathcal{R} = \bigcup_{n \ge 0} \to_{\mathcal{R}_n}$, where $\to_{\mathcal{R}_0} = \emptyset$ and $s \to_{\mathcal{R}_{n+1}} t$ if and only if there exists a rewrite rule $\rho : l \to r \Leftarrow s_1 \to t_1, \ldots, s_k \to t_k$ in $\mathcal{R}$, a substitution $\sigma : \mathcal{V}ar(\rho) \to \mathcal{T}(\mathcal{F}, \mathcal{V})$, and a context $C[\,]$ such that $s = C[l\sigma], t = C[r\sigma]$, and $s_i\sigma \to_{\mathcal{R}_n}^* t_i\sigma$ for all $1 \le i \le k$. We would like to stress the fact that σ instantiates every variable in ρ and not only those variables occurring in l; for an extra variable x, $x\sigma$ is determined as follows. The conditions are evaluated from left to right. Because s_1 contains only variables from $\mathcal{V}ar(l)$, the variables in $\mathcal{V}ar(s_1)$ have a binding. Then $s_1\sigma$ is rewritten until $t_1\sigma$ matches a reduct. The term $t_1\sigma$ may contain extra variables but all of these are bound during the match. Now s_2 contains only variables that already occurred to its left (in l and t_1) and are thus bound. The instantiated term s_2 is then reduced until the (partially) instantiated term t_2 matches a reduct and so on. If all conditions are satisfied, then all variables in the conditions are bound in the process of evaluating the conditions. Hence the reduct of $l\sigma$ is well-defined (but in general not unique) because r contains only variables that also appear in the conditions or in l.

Example 7.2.34 As another example, consider the deterministic 3-CTRS $\mathcal{R}$ consisting of the rules

$$\begin{array}{lll} 0+y & \to y & \\ s(x)+y & \to x+s(y) & \\ f(x,y) & \to y+z & \Leftarrow \quad x+y \to z+z \end{array}$$

We have, for example, $f(s^5(0), s(0)) \to_{\mathcal{R}} s(0) + s^3(0)$ because $s^5(0) + s(0) \to_{\mathcal{R}}^* s^3(0) + s^3(0)$ (here s^n denotes the n fold application of s).

There is a fundamental difference between the system $\mathcal{R}$ of Example 7.2.34 and the *quicksort* system. In the *quicksort* system, it is always possible to first reduce the instantiated left-hand side of a condition to normal form and then to check whether the right-hand side of the condition matches the normal form. This is, of course, not true for $\mathcal{R}$: If we are interested in the reducts of $f(s^5(0), s(0))$ and we first reduce $s^5(0) + s(0)$ to its normal form $s^6(0)$, then we find that $z+z$ does not match $s^6(0)$. This phenomenon arises because the right-hand side $z+z$ of the condition contains a defined symbol (and consequently, even for normalized substitutions τ, the term $z\tau + z\tau$ is not necessarily a normal form). In order to exclude such a behavior, Avenhaus and Loría-Sáenz [ALS94] introduced the class of strongly deterministic 3-CTRSs.

Definition 7.2.35 Let $\mathcal{R}$ be a deterministic 3-CTRS.

1. A term t is called *strongly irreducible* w.r.t. $\mathcal{R}$ if $t\sigma$ is a normal form for every normalized substitution σ.

2. $\mathcal{R}$ is called *strongly deterministic* if, for every rule $l \to r \Leftarrow s_1 \to t_1, \ldots, s_k \to t_k$ in $\mathcal{R}$, every term t_i is strongly irreducible.

3. $\mathcal{R}$ is called *syntactically deterministic* if, for every rule $l \to r \Leftarrow s_1 \to t_1, \ldots, s_k \to t_k$ in $\mathcal{R}$, every term t_i is a constructor term or a ground $\mathcal{R}_u$ normal form.

Note that it is undecidable whether a term t is strongly irreducible w.r.t. $\mathcal{R}$; see Proposition 7.1.14. But there is an important decidable syntactic criterion: If t_i is a constructor term or a ground $\mathcal{R}_u$ normal form, then it is strongly irreducible. Thus every syntactically deterministic CTRS is strongly deterministic. Syntactically deterministic CTRSs are a natural generalization of normal CTRSs and the *quicksort* system shows that these systems arise quite naturally.

7.2.6 Quasi-Reductive Deterministic 3-CTRSs

In the next definition, the ordering $\succ_{st}$ is well-founded because $\succ$ is well-founded; cf. Lemma 7.2.4.

Definition 7.2.36 A deterministic 3-CTRS $(\mathcal{F}, \mathcal{R})$ is called *quasi-reductive* if there is an extension $\mathcal{F}'$ of the signature $\mathcal{F}$ (so $\mathcal{F} \subseteq \mathcal{F}'$) and a well-founded partial ordering $\succ$ on $\mathcal{T}(\mathcal{F}', \mathcal{V})$ that is closed under contexts and that satisfies the following conditions for every rule $l \to r \Leftarrow s_1 \to t_1, \ldots, s_k \to t_k \in \mathcal{R}$, every substitution $\sigma\colon \mathcal{V} \to \mathcal{T}(\mathcal{F}', \mathcal{V})$, and every $0 \leq i < k$:

1. if $s_j\sigma \succeq t_j\sigma$ for every $1 \leq j \leq i$, then $l\sigma \succ_{st} s_{i+1}\sigma$,
2. if $s_j\sigma \succeq t_j\sigma$ for every $1 \leq j \leq k$, then $l\sigma \succ r\sigma$.

Quasi-reductive deterministic 3-CTRSs were introduced by Ganzinger [Gan91, definition 4.2] without mentioning that the original signature can be extended. This, however, is crucial because otherwise propositions 4.3 and 4.4 in [Gan91] would be incorrect. If signature extensions are permitted, then these propositions are valid. That is why we decided to define quasi-reductivity as stated in Definition 7.2.36. The original definition of quasi-reductivity [Gan91, definition 4.2] is additionally based on reduction orderings. However, it is unnecessary to insist that $\succ$ must be closed under substitutions because conditions (1) and (2) in Definition 7.2.36 must hold for every substitution σ. Therefore, the following lemma from [Gan91, lemma 4.5] holds independently of whether $\succ$ is closed under substitutions or not.

Lemma 7.2.37 *If $\mathcal{R}$ is a deterministic 3-CTRS that is quasi-reductive w.r.t. the ordering $\succ$, then $\to_{\mathcal{R}} \subseteq \succ$.*

Proof The proof is routine. □

In view of Section 7.2.1, it is quite natural to introduce the new notions of quasi-simplifyingness and quasi-decreasingness.

Definition 7.2.38 We call $\mathcal{R}$ *quasi-simplifying* if it is quasi-reductive w.r.t. a simplification ordering $\succ$ (note that in this case $\succ = \succ_{st}$).

As a consequence of the definition, every quasi-simplifying CTRS is quasi-reductive. We shall see later that the converse is not true. In contrast to quasi-reductivity, quasi-simplifyingness is independent of signature extensions in the following sense: If a deterministic 3-CTRS $(\mathcal{F}, \mathcal{R})$ is quasi-simplifying w.r.t. a simplification ordering $\succ$ on $\mathcal{T}(\mathcal{F}', \mathcal{V})$, where $\mathcal{F} \subseteq \mathcal{F}'$, then $(\mathcal{F}, \mathcal{R})$ is quasi-simplifying w.r.t. to the restriction of $\succ$ to $\mathcal{T}(\mathcal{F}, \mathcal{V})$. The simple proof of this fact is left to the reader.

Definition 7.2.39 A deterministic 3-CTRS $(\mathcal{F}, \mathcal{R})$ is said to be *quasi-decreasing* if there is a well-founded partial ordering $\succ$ on $\mathcal{T}(\mathcal{F}, \mathcal{V})$ satisfying:

1. $\to_{\mathcal{R}} \subseteq \succ$,

2. $\succ$ has the subterm property (hence $\succ = \succ_{st}$), and

3. for every rule $l \to r \Leftarrow s_1 \to t_1, \ldots, s_k \to t_k \in \mathcal{R}$, every substitution σ, and $0 \leq i < k$: if $s_j\sigma \to_{\mathcal{R}}^* t_j\sigma$ for every $1 \leq j \leq i$, then $l\sigma \succ s_{i+1}\sigma$.

The next lemma clarifies the relationship between the different notions.

Lemma 7.2.40 *The following implications hold true:*

$$\begin{array}{ccccc} \textit{simplifyingness} & \Rightarrow & \textit{reductivity} & \Rightarrow & \textit{decreasingness} \\ \Downarrow & & \Downarrow & & \Downarrow \\ \textit{quasi-simplifyingness} & \Rightarrow & \textit{quasi-reductivity} & \Rightarrow & \textit{quasi-decreasingness} \end{array}$$

Proof It was already shown in Section 7.2.1 that the first three horizontal implications hold and that none of them can be reversed. It is easy to verify that the three vertical implications hold. Furthermore, it has already been observed that quasi-simplifyingness implies quasi-reductivity.

It remains to be shown that every quasi-reductive deterministic 3-CTRS is quasi-decreasing. If $(\mathcal{F}, \mathcal{R})$ is quasi-reductive, then there is an extension $\mathcal{F}'$ of the signature $\mathcal{F}$ and a reduction order $>$ on $\mathcal{T}(\mathcal{F}', \mathcal{V})$ that satisfies the requirements of Definition 7.2.36. According to Lemma 7.2.37, the relation $\to_{\mathcal{R}}$ on $\mathcal{T}(\mathcal{F}', \mathcal{V})$ is a subset of $>$. Let $\succ$ denote the restriction of $>_{st}$ on $\mathcal{T}(\mathcal{F}, \mathcal{V})$. Clearly, $\succ$ is a well-founded ordering on $\mathcal{T}(\mathcal{F}, \mathcal{V})$ such that $\to_{\mathcal{R}} \subseteq \succ$ and $\rhd \subseteq \succ$. Thus $\mathcal{R}$ is quasi-decreasing w.r.t. $\succ$ provided that for every rule $l \to r \Leftarrow s_1 \to t_1, \ldots, s_k \to t_k \in \mathcal{R}$, every substitution $\sigma\colon \mathcal{V} \to \mathcal{T}(\mathcal{F}, \mathcal{V})$, and $0 \leq i < k$ we have: $s_j\sigma \to_{\mathcal{R}}^* t_j\sigma$ for every $1 \leq j \leq i$ implies $l\sigma \succ s_{i+1}\sigma$. Obviously, $s_j\sigma \geq t_j\sigma$ is a consequence of $s_j\sigma \to_{\mathcal{R}}^* t_j\sigma$, where $1 \leq j \leq i$. Because $(\mathcal{F}, \mathcal{R})$ is quasi-reductive, it follows $l\sigma >_{st} s_{i+1}\sigma$. Finally, we obtain $l\sigma \succ s_{i+1}\sigma$ from $l\sigma, s_{i+1}\sigma \in \mathcal{T}(\mathcal{F}, \mathcal{V})$. □

The following examples show that even for 1-CTRSs none of the vertical implications in Lemma 7.2.40 can be reversed. In essence, this is because the conditions are evaluated from left to right in the "quasi-case."

Example 7.2.41 Let $\mathcal{R}_1 = \{a \to a \Leftarrow b \to c\}$. On the one hand, the system is definitely not simplifying because no simplification ordering $\succ$ can satisfy $a \succ a$. On the other hand, the simplification ordering $\succ$ defined by $a \succ b$ shows that $\mathcal{R}_1$ is quasi-simplifying (note that $\to_{\mathcal{R}_1} = \emptyset$ and $b \not\to_{\mathcal{R}_1} c$). In fact, this ordering also shows that $\mathcal{R}_1$ is reductive.

The CTRS $\mathcal{R}_2 = \{a \to d \Leftarrow b \to c, a \to c\}$ is neither reductive nor decreasing because no partial ordering $\succ$ can satisfy $a \succ a$. On the other hand, the partial ordering $\succ$ defined by $a \succ b$ shows that $\mathcal{R}_2$ is quasi-reductive and hence quasi-decreasing (again, $\to_{\mathcal{R}_2} = \emptyset$ and $b \not\to_{\mathcal{R}_2} c$).

Examples 7.2.10 and 7.2.14 shed more light on the difference between reductivity and quasi-reductivity. Consider the nonreductive 1-CTRS from

Example 7.2.10:

$$\mathcal{R} = \begin{cases} b & \to c \\ f(b) & \to f(a) \\ a & \to c \quad \Leftarrow b \to c \end{cases}$$

over the signature $\mathcal{F} = \{a, b, c, f\}$. If we extend $\mathcal{F}$ by a unary symbol U (so $\mathcal{F}' = \mathcal{F} \cup \{U\}$), then $\mathcal{R}$ is quasi-reductive w.r.t. the reduction ordering $\succ = \to^+_{\mathcal{R}'}$ on $\mathcal{T}(\mathcal{F}', \mathcal{V})$, where $\mathcal{R}'$ is the terminating TRS

$$\mathcal{R}' = \begin{cases} b & \to c \\ f(b) & \to f(a) \\ a & \to U(b) \\ U(c) & \to c \end{cases}$$

Thus $\mathcal{R}$ is *not* reductive but is quasi-reductive. This is due to the fact that we may extend the signature to show quasi-reductivity. Note that no reduction ordering on $\mathcal{T}(\mathcal{F}, \mathcal{V})$ can prove quasi-reductivity of $\mathcal{R}$ because no partial ordering $\succ$ on $\mathcal{T}(\mathcal{F}, \mathcal{V})$ that is closed under contexts and has $f(b) \succ f(a)$ can have $a \succ b$.

Now consider the 1-CTRS from Example 7.2.14. It has already been shown that this CTRS is *not* reductive because it was impossible to satisfy the constraint $l\sigma = f(x)\sigma \succ x\sigma = s_1\sigma$ originating from the conditional rewrite rule $f(x) \to x \Leftarrow x \to e$. Quasi-reductivity, however, only demands $l\sigma = f(x)\sigma \succ_{st} x\sigma = s_1\sigma$, which is always satisfied because x is a subterm of $f(x)$. Therefore, $\mathcal{R}$ is quasi-reductive w.r.t. the reduction ordering $\to^+_{\mathcal{R}}$ (recall that $\mathcal{R}$ is terminating).

We will see later that the 1-CTRS from Example 7.2.14 is not quasi-simplifying. Consequently, quasi-simplifyingness is not implied by quasi-reductivity. We do not know whether quasi-decreasingness implies quasi-reductivity. It is favorable, however, to handle quasi-decreasingness because it has two advantages over quasi-reductivity: (i) It does not depend on signature extensions and (ii) in requirement (3) of Definition 7.2.39, $l\sigma \succ_{st} s_{i+1}\sigma$ must hold only if $s_j\sigma \to^*_{\mathcal{R}} t_j\sigma$ whereas it must hold for all $s_j\sigma \succeq t_j\sigma$ according to Definition 7.2.36(1).

The following theorem was proven for quasi-reductive systems in [Gan91, lemma 4.5] and [ALS94, theorem 3.1], and the proof also applies to quasi-decreasing systems. It is a generalization of Theorem 7.2.9.

Theorem 7.2.42 *Every quasi-decreasing deterministic 3-CTRS $\mathcal{R}$ is effectively terminating.*

Proof Termination of $\mathcal{R}$ is obvious. Let $\mathcal{R}$ be quasi-decreasing w.r.t. $\succ$ and let $s \in \mathcal{T}(\mathcal{F}, \mathcal{V})$. In order to show that $\Delta^*(s) = \{t \in \mathcal{T}(\mathcal{F}, \mathcal{V}) \mid s \to^*_{\mathcal{R}} t\}$ is finite and computable, we proceed by induction on the well-founded ordering $\succ$. If no subterm of s is an instance of a left-hand side of a rule from $\mathcal{R}$, then $\Delta^*(s) = \{s\}$. Otherwise, suppose $s = C[l\sigma]$ for a rewrite rule $l \to r \Leftarrow s_1 \to t_1, \ldots, s_k \to t_k$ and a substitution σ with $\mathcal{D}om(\sigma) = \mathcal{V}ar(l)$. Because $\mathcal{R}$ is deterministic, we have $\mathcal{V}ar(s_1) \subseteq \mathcal{V}ar(l)$. Furthermore, quasi-decreasingness implies $s = C[l\sigma] \succeq l\sigma$ and $l\sigma \succ s_1\sigma$. It follows from the inductive hypothesis that the set $\Delta^*(s_1\sigma)$ is finite and computable. Thus there are only finitely many extensions σ' of σ to $\mathcal{V}ar(l) \cup \mathcal{V}ar(t_1)$ such that $t_1\sigma' = u$ for some $u \in \Delta^*(s_1\sigma)$ and we can compute all of them. Let σ_1 be such an extension. Now $s_1\sigma \to_{\mathcal{R}}^* t_1\sigma_1$ implies $l\sigma = l\sigma_1 \succ s_2\sigma_1$ by quasi-decreasingness. In this way, we can compute every extension σ_i of σ to $\mathcal{V}ar(l) \cup \bigcup_{j=1}^{i} \mathcal{V}ar(t_j)$ such that $s_j\sigma_i \to_{\mathcal{R}}^* t_j\sigma_i$ for all $1 \le j \le i$. If there is an extension σ_k of σ to $\mathcal{V}ar(l) \cup \bigcup_{j=1}^{k} \mathcal{V}ar(t_j)$ such that $s_j\sigma_k \to_{\mathcal{R}}^* t_j\sigma_k$ for all $1 \le j \le k$, then the conditions are satisfied and hence $s \to_{\mathcal{R}} C[r\sigma]$. If not, then s does not reduce to $C[r\sigma]$. Because s has only finitely many preredexes and $\mathcal{R}$ has only a finite number of rules, we can compute the finite set $\Delta(s) = \{t \in \mathcal{T}(\mathcal{F}, \mathcal{V}) \mid s \to_{\mathcal{R}} t\}$ of all one step reducts of s. Let $t \in \Delta(s)$. We have $s \succ t$ because $\mathcal{R}$ is quasi-decreasing. It follows from a renewed application of the inductive hypothesis that the set $\Delta^*(t)$ is finite and computable. Thus $\Delta^*(s) = \{s\} \cup \bigcup_{\{t \mid s \to_{\mathcal{R}} t\}} \Delta^*(t)$ is also finite and computable. □

The system $\{a \to b \Leftarrow f(a) \to b\}$ shows that an effectively terminating CTRS need not be quasi-decreasing.

Next we will show that every join 1-CTRS can be simulated by a syntactically deterministic 3-CTRS. Let us first recall a definition from Ganzinger [Gan91, proposition 4.4].

Definition 7.2.43 Let $\rho : l \to r \Leftarrow s_1 \downarrow t_1, \ldots, s_k \downarrow t_k$ be a conditional rewrite rule in a join 1-CTRS $\mathcal{R}$. We define a transformation o by $o(\rho) = l \to r \Leftarrow s_1 \to x_1, t_1 \to x_1, \ldots, s_k \to x_k, t_k \to x_k$, where the x_i are fresh and pairwise distinct variables. Moreover, $o(\mathcal{R}) = \bigcup_{\rho \in \mathcal{R}} \{o(\rho)\}$.

Lemma 7.2.44 *For every join 1-CTRS $\mathcal{R}$ the following statements hold:*

1. *$o(\mathcal{R})$ is a syntactically deterministic 3-CTRS.*
2. *The rewrite relations $\to_{\mathcal{R}}$ and $\to_{o(\mathcal{R})}$ coincide.*
3. *If $\mathcal{R}$ is simplifying, then $o(\mathcal{R})$ is quasi-simplifying.*
4. *If $\mathcal{R}$ is decreasing, then $o(\mathcal{R})$ is quasi-decreasing.*

Proof (1) This part of the proof is obvious.

(2) One shows that $s \to_{\mathcal{R}} t$ implies $s \to_{o(\mathcal{R})} t$ by induction on the depth of the rewrite step $s \to_{\mathcal{R}} t$. The converse statement can be shown similarly.

(3) If $\mathcal{R}$ is simplifying, then there is a simplification ordering $\succ$ on $\mathcal{T}(\mathcal{F}, \mathcal{V})$ satisfying $l \succ r$, $l \succ s_j$, and $l \succ t_j$ for every rewrite rule

$l \to r \Leftarrow s_1 \downarrow t_1, \ldots, s_k \downarrow t_k$ and every index $j \in \{1, \ldots, k\}$. This directly shows that $o(\mathcal{R})$ is also quasi-simplifying w.r.t. $\succ$.

(4) This part of the proof is analogous to (3). □

In [Gan91, proposition 4.4], it is stated without proof that reductivity of $\mathcal{R}$ implies quasi-reductivity of $o(\mathcal{R})$. A proof of this fact seems to be nontrivial because it must be based on the possibility of extending the original signature. This can be seen in the following example.

Example 7.2.45 The join 1-CTRS

$$\mathcal{R} = \begin{cases} a \to a \Leftarrow b \downarrow c \\ b \to d \Leftarrow d \downarrow e \\ c \to d \Leftarrow d \downarrow e \end{cases}$$

over the signature $\mathcal{F} = \{a, b, c, d, e\}$ is reductive w.r.t. the ordering $\succ$ on $\mathcal{T}(\mathcal{F}, \mathcal{V})$ defined by $a \succ b$, $a \succ c$, $b \succ d$, $b \succ e$, $c \succ d$, and $c \succ e$. Note that $\succ = \succ_{st}$ because $\mathcal{F}$ contains only constants. The system

$$o(\mathcal{R}) = \begin{cases} a \to a \Leftarrow b \to x,\ c \to x \\ b \to d \Leftarrow d \to x,\ e \to x \\ c \to d \Leftarrow d \to x,\ e \to x \end{cases}$$

however, is *not* quasi-reductive w.r.t. $\succ$ on $\mathcal{T}(\mathcal{F}, \mathcal{V})$. If it were quasi-reductive w.r.t. $\succ$, then we would have $b \succ_{st} d$ and $c \succ_{st} d$, which would further imply $a \succ a$, but this contradicts the irreflexivity of $\succ$.

7.2.7 *Transforming 3-CTRSs*

In this section we will give sufficient criteria for quasi-reductivity of deterministic 3-CTRSs. The first criterion is based on the following transformation.

Definition 7.2.46 For a deterministic 3-CTRS $\mathcal{R}$, define $\mathcal{R}_q = \bigcup_{\rho \in \mathcal{R}} q(\rho)$, where the transformation q of a rule $\rho : l \to r \Leftarrow s_1 \to t_1, \ldots, s_k \to t_k$ is defined to be the set of conditional rewrite rules

$$\begin{aligned} q(\rho) = \{\ & l \to s_1 \\ & l \to s_2 \quad \Leftarrow s_1 \to t_1 \\ & \ldots \\ & l \to s_k \quad \Leftarrow s_1 \to t_1, \ldots, s_{k-1} \to t_{k-1} \\ & l \to r \quad \Leftarrow s_1 \to t_1, \ldots, s_{k-1} \to t_{k-1}, s_k \to t_k\} \end{aligned}$$

Note that $\mathcal{R} \subseteq \mathcal{R}_q$. Termination of $\mathcal{R}_q$ proves to be a sufficient but not a necessary condition for quasi-reductivity of $\mathcal{R}$.

Proposition 7.2.47 *A deterministic 3-CTRS $\mathcal{R}$ is quasi-reductive if the deterministic 3-CTRS $\mathcal{R}_q$ is terminating.*

Proof Because $\mathcal{R}_q$ is terminating, the relation $\rightarrow^+_{\mathcal{R}_q}$ is a reduction ordering and it is easy to see that $\mathcal{R}$ is quasi-reductive w.r.t. this ordering. □

The quasi-reductive CTRS $\mathcal{R}$ from Example 7.2.14 shows that the converse of Proposition 7.2.47 does not hold: The system $\mathcal{R}_q = \mathcal{R} \cup \{f(x) \rightarrow x\}$ is not terminating because there is the following cyclic derivation:

$$\begin{array}{ll} A & \rightarrow_{\mathcal{R}_q} h(f(a), f(b)) \rightarrow_{\mathcal{R}_q} h(a, f(b)) \rightarrow_{\mathcal{R}_q} h(a, b) \rightarrow_{\mathcal{R}_q} h(d, b) \\ & \rightarrow_{\mathcal{R}_q} h(d, d) \rightarrow_{\mathcal{R}_q} g(d, d, f(k)) \rightarrow_{\mathcal{R}_q} g(d, d, k) \\ & \rightarrow_{\mathcal{R}_q} g(d, m, k) \rightarrow_{\mathcal{R}_q} g(d, m, m) \rightarrow_{\mathcal{R}_q} A \end{array}$$

Ganzinger [Gan91, proposition 4.3] provided the following sufficient condition for quasi-reductivity (cf. [BG89]): Let $\mathcal{F}'$ be an enrichment of the original signature $\mathcal{F}$ such that the ordering $\succ$ can be extended to a reduction ordering over $\mathcal{T}(\mathcal{F}', \mathcal{V})$. A deterministic rule $l \rightarrow r \Leftarrow s_1 \rightarrow t_1, \ldots, s_k \rightarrow t_k$ is quasi-reductive if there exists a sequence $h_i(x)$ of terms in $\mathcal{T}(\mathcal{F}', \mathcal{V})$, $x \in \mathcal{V}$, such that $l \succ h_1(s_1), h_i(t_i) \succeq h_{i+1}(s_{i+1})$, $1 \leq i < k$, and $h_k(t_k) \succeq r$.

This criterion, however, does not tell us how the terms $h_i(x)$ should be chosen. Our next goal is to provide a systematic way of showing quasi-reductivity (hence quasi-decreasingness). To this end, we transform every deterministic 3-CTRS $\mathcal{R}$ into an unconditional TRS $U(\mathcal{R})$.

Definition 7.2.48 Let $\mathcal{R}$ be a deterministic 3-CTRS over the signature $\mathcal{F}$. For every rewrite rule $\rho : l \rightarrow r \Leftarrow c \in \mathcal{R}$, let $|\rho|$ denote the number of conditions in ρ. For every conditional rule $\rho \in \mathcal{R}$, we need $|\rho|$ fresh function symbols $U_1^\rho, \ldots, U_{|\rho|}^\rho$ in the transformation. Moreover, by abuse of notation, $\mathcal{V}ar$ (resp. $\mathcal{EV}ar$) denotes a function that assigns the sequence of the variables (in some fixed order) in the set $\mathcal{V}ar(t)$ (resp. $\mathcal{EV}ar(t)$; cf. Definition 7.2.33) to a term t. We transform $\rho : l \rightarrow r \Leftarrow s_1 \rightarrow t_1, \ldots, s_{|\rho|} \rightarrow t_{|\rho|}$ into a set $U(\rho)$ of $|\rho| + 1$ unconditional rewrite rules as follows:

$$\begin{array}{rl} l & \rightarrow U_1^\rho(s_1, \mathcal{V}ar(l)) \\ U_1^\rho(t_1, \mathcal{V}ar(l)) & \rightarrow U_2^\rho(s_2, \mathcal{V}ar(l), \mathcal{EV}ar(t_1)) \\ U_2^\rho(t_2, \mathcal{V}ar(l), \mathcal{EV}ar(t_1)) & \rightarrow U_3^\rho(s_3, \mathcal{V}ar(l), \mathcal{EV}ar(t_1), \mathcal{EV}ar(t_2)) \\ & \ldots \\ U_{|\rho|}^\rho(t_{|\rho|}, \mathcal{V}ar(l), \ldots, \mathcal{EV}ar(t_{|\rho|-1})) & \rightarrow r \end{array}$$

Because $\mathcal{R}$ is deterministic, the system $U(\mathcal{R}) = \bigcup_{\rho \in \mathcal{R}} U(\rho)$ is an unconditional TRS over the extended signature $\mathcal{F}' = \mathcal{F} \cup \bigcup_{\rho \in \mathcal{R}, 1 \leq i \leq |\rho|} \{U_i^\rho\}$; that is, $\mathcal{V}ar(r') \subseteq \mathcal{V}ar(l')$ holds for every rewrite rule $l' \rightarrow r' \in U(\mathcal{R})$. Again, the symbols from $\mathcal{F}' \setminus \mathcal{F}$ are called U symbols.

Similar transformations were (independently) obtained by several other authors. An early forerunner was Giovannetti and Moiso [GM87], which is restricted to a rather small class of convergent CTRSs. In an unpublished manuscript [CR93], Chtourou and Rusinowitch state a similar transformation for the particular case in which $\mathcal{R}$ is the result of a transformation of a logic program $\mathcal{P}$ into a deterministic 3-CTRS; see Chapter 10. Moreover, our transformation differs only slightly from Marchiori's [Mar97a, definition 4.1]: In the sequence $\mathcal{V}ar(l), \mathcal{EV}ar(t_1), \ldots, \mathcal{EV}ar(t_i)$ every variable occurs exactly once which is not the case in the sequence $\mathrm{VAR}(l, t_1, \ldots, t_i)$ from [Mar97a, definition 4.1]. The results of this book, however, are completely different from the ones reported in the technical report [Mar97a], except for one: Proposition 7.2.50 is akin to [Mar97a, lemma 4.6]. Lastly, Giesl and Arts [GA01] studied such a transformation for 1-CTRSs.

Example 7.2.49 If ρ is the last rule of the system $\mathcal{R}$ from Example 7.2.34, then $U(\rho) = \{f(x,y) \to U_1^\rho(x+y,x,y), U_1^\rho(z+z,x,y) \to y+z\}$. In the following, if a CTRS $\mathcal{R}$ contains just one conditional rewrite rule ρ, we omit the superscript ρ in U_i^ρ. If $|\rho| = 1$, then we further suppress the subscript 1 in U_1. In our example this gives $U(\rho) = \{f(x,y) \to U(x+y,x,y), U(z+z,x,y) \to y+z\}$. The transformation of the *quicksort* system is

$$
\begin{array}{rcl}
split(x, nil) & \to & \langle nil, nil\rangle \\
split(x, y : ys) & \to & U_1'(split(x, ys), x, y, ys) \\
U_1'(\langle xs, zs\rangle, x, y, ys) & \to & U_2'(x \le y, x, y, ys, xs, zs) \\
U_2'(true, x, y, ys, xs, zs) & \to & \langle xs, y : zs\rangle \\
split(x, y : ys) & \to & U_1''(split(x, ys), x, y, ys) \\
U_1''(\langle xs, zs\rangle, x, y, ys) & \to & U_2''(x \le y, x, y, ys, xs, zs) \\
U_2''(false, x, y, ys, xs, zs) & \to & \langle y : xs, zs\rangle \\
qsort(nil) & \to & nil \\
qsort(x : xs) & \to & U_1'''(split(x, xs), x, xs) \\
U_1'''(\langle ys, zs\rangle, x, xs) & \to & qsort(ys) +\!\!+ (x : qsort(zs))
\end{array}
$$

If functions are specified via distinct cases as in the *split* function (that is, the left-hand sides of two or more rules and a prefix of the sequences of their conditions coincide), then the transformation can be "optimized" as follows:

$$
\begin{array}{rcl}
split(x, y : ys) & \to & U_1'(split(x, ys), x, y, ys) \\
U_1'(\langle xs, zs\rangle, x, y, ys) & \to & U_2'(x \le y, x, y, ys, xs, zs) \\
U_2'(true, x, y, ys, xs, zs) & \to & \langle xs, y : zs\rangle \\
U_2'(false, x, y, ys, xs, zs) & \to & \langle y : xs, zs\rangle
\end{array}
$$

In this way, a nonoverlapping TRS is obtained. We omit the formal definition of this obvious optimization of the transformation U.

Termination of $U(\mathcal{R})$ is a sufficient but not a necessary condition for quasi-reductivity of $\mathcal{R}$, as we will show. Consequently, it is advantageous if the transformation yields a nonoverlapping TRS. Then innermost termination of $U(\mathcal{R})$ yields quasi-reductivity of $\mathcal{R}$; cf. Theorem 5.6.10(1). On the other hand, even the "optimized" transformation will often yield an overlapping TRS. This is exemplified by the *gcd* system from Example 7.1.5.

Proposition 7.2.50 *If $U(\mathcal{R})$ is terminating, then $\mathcal{R}$ is quasi-reductive.*

Proof Let $\succ = \rightarrow^+_{U(\mathcal{R})}$ and note that $\succ$ is a reduction ordering on $\mathcal{T}(\mathcal{F}', \mathcal{V})$. For every rewrite rule $l \to r \Leftarrow s_1 \to t_1, \ldots, s_k \to t_k$ in $\mathcal{R}$, we show that $s_j\sigma \succeq t_j\sigma$ for every $1 \le j \le i < k$ implies $l\sigma \succ_{st} s_{i+1}\sigma$. We have the following reduction sequence

$$\begin{array}{ll} l\sigma & \rightarrow_{U(\mathcal{R})} U_1^\rho(s_1, \mathcal{V}ar(l))\sigma \\ & \rightarrow^*_{U(\mathcal{R})} U_1^\rho(t_1, \mathcal{V}ar(l))\sigma \\ & \rightarrow_{U(\mathcal{R})} U_2^\rho(s_2, \mathcal{V}ar(l), \mathcal{E}\mathcal{V}ar(t_1))\sigma \\ & \ldots \\ & \rightarrow^*_{U(\mathcal{R})} U_i^\rho(t_i, \mathcal{V}ar(l), \mathcal{E}\mathcal{V}ar(t_1), \ldots, \mathcal{E}\mathcal{V}ar(t_{i-1}))\sigma \\ & \rightarrow_{U(\mathcal{R})} U_{i+1}^\rho(s_{i+1}, \mathcal{V}ar(l), \mathcal{E}\mathcal{V}ar(t_1), \ldots, \mathcal{E}\mathcal{V}ar(t_i))\sigma \end{array}$$

because $s_j\sigma \rightarrow^*_{U(\mathcal{R})} t_j\sigma$. Thus $l\sigma \succ_{st} s_{i+1}\sigma$. Requirement (2) of Definition 7.2.36 can be shown similarly. □

Once again, Example 7.2.14 shows that the converse of Proposition 7.2.50 does not hold.

Termination of the transformed system of the *quicksort* system (including the missing rewrite rules for $+\!\!+$ and $\le$) can be shown automatically by the dependency pair technique; see Example 5.4.36. Thus the system is quasi-reductive.

Let $\mathcal{R}$ be the 3-CTRS from Example 7.2.34. The lexicographic path order, where the precedence ordering $\succ_p$ on $\mathcal{F}'$ is defined by $f \succ_p U \succ_p + \succ_p s$, shows that $U(\mathcal{R})$ is (simply) terminating. Hence $\mathcal{R}$ is also quasi-reductive.

According to Corollary 7.2.32, a left-linear normal 1-CTRS $\mathcal{R}$ is decreasing if and only if its transformed TRS $U_n(\mathcal{R})$ is terminating. It is thus tempting to conjecture that a left-linear syntactically deterministic 3-CTRS $\mathcal{R}$ is quasi-decreasing if and only if the TRS $U(\mathcal{R})$ is terminating. The following example shows that this is not the case.

Example 7.2.51 Let $\mathcal{R}$ contain the rules

$$\begin{array}{rcll} g(x) & \to & k(y) & \Leftarrow h(x) \to d, h(x) \to c(y) \\ h(d) & \to & c(a) & \\ h(d) & \to & c(b) & \\ f(k(a), k(b), x) & \to & f(x, x, x) & \end{array}$$

We have $\mathcal{R}_q = \mathcal{R} \cup \{g(x) \to h(x), g(x) \to h(x) \Leftarrow h(x) \to d\}$. Let $\mathcal{R}'$ contain the rule $g(x) \to h(x)$ and the unconditional rules of $\mathcal{R}$. The rewrite relations $\rightarrow_{\mathcal{R}'}$ and $\rightarrow_{\mathcal{R}_q}$ coincide because the rule $g(x) \to k(y) \Leftarrow h(x) \to d, h(x) \to c(y)$ is never applicable (there is no term t such that $h(t) \rightarrow^*_{\mathcal{R}} d$). It can be shown that $\mathcal{R}'$ is terminating (by semantic labeling, for example;

cf. Section 5.5.1). Hence $\mathcal{R}$ is quasi-reductive by Proposition 7.2.47. The transformed system $U(\mathcal{R})$ contains the rules

$$\begin{array}{rcl} g(x) & \to & U_1(h(x), x) \\ U_1(d, x) & \to & U_2(h(x), x) \\ U_2(c(y), x) & \to & k(y) \end{array}$$

and the last three rules of $\mathcal{R}$. $U(\mathcal{R})$ is not terminating because of the following cyclic derivation:

$$\begin{array}{rl} f(k(a), k(b), U_2(h(d), d)) & \to_{U(\mathcal{R})} f(U_2(h(d), d), U_2(h(d), d), U_2(h(d), d)) \\ & \to^+_{U(\mathcal{R})} f(U_2(c(a), d), U_2(c(b), d), U_2(h(d), d)) \\ & \to^+_{U(\mathcal{R})} f(k(a), k(b), U_2(h(d), d)) \end{array}$$

The fact that $\mathcal{R}$ is not confluent is not essential in this counterexample. If we add the rules

$$a \to e, \; b \to e, \; f(x, y, z) \to e$$

then the whole system is confluent because every (unconditional) critical pair is joinable.

To sum up, one can say that left-linearity and confluence of a quasi-reductive 3-CTRS $\mathcal{R}$ are not sufficient to guarantee termination of $U(\mathcal{R})$. Note that the cyclic derivation in the preceding example is not innermost. This will prove to be essential.

7.2.8 Innermost Termination of $U(\mathcal{R})$

We have seen that quasi-decreasingness of a deterministic 3-CTRS $\mathcal{R}$ does not imply termination of its transformed system $U(\mathcal{R})$. It does, however, imply innermost termination of $U(\mathcal{R})$. Our next goal is to show this fact. The following two definitions are crucial to the proof of Theorem 7.2.58.

Definition 7.2.52 Let $\mathcal{R}$ be a TRS. We write $s \;{}^{i}\!\!\twoheadrightarrow\!\!\!\!\!\!\!\parallel_{\mathcal{R}} t$ if t can be obtained from s by contracting a set of pairwise disjoint innermost redexes in s by $\to_{\mathcal{R}}$. The relation ${}^{i}\!\!\twoheadrightarrow\!\!\!\!\!\!\!\parallel_{\mathcal{R}}$ is called *parallel innermost rewrite relation* w.r.t. $\mathcal{R}$.

It should be pointed out that in a parallel innermost rewrite step not necessarily all innermost redexes are contracted.

Definition 7.2.53 Let $\mathcal{R}$ be a deterministic 3-CTRS and $U(\mathcal{R})$ its transformed TRS. We define a transformation $\nabla\colon \mathcal{T}(\mathcal{F}', \mathcal{V}) \to \mathcal{T}(\mathcal{F}, \mathcal{V})$ by

$$\nabla(t) = \begin{cases} t & \text{if } t \in \mathcal{V} \cup \mathcal{F}^{(0)} \\ f(\nabla(t_1), \ldots, \nabla(t_n)) & \text{if } t = f(t_1, \ldots, t_n), f \in \mathcal{F}^{(n)} \\ l_T & \text{if } t = U_i^\rho(u, t_1, \ldots, t_n, \ldots) \end{cases}$$

where l is the left-hand side of the rule ρ, $\mathcal{V}ar(l) = x_1, \dots, x_n$ (that is, $U_i^\rho(u, \mathcal{V}ar(l), \dots) = U_i^\rho(u, x_1, \dots, x_n, \dots)$), and $\tau\colon \mathcal{V}ar(l) \to \mathcal{T}(\mathcal{F}, \mathcal{V})$ is defined by $\tau(x_j) = \nabla(t_j)$. For any substitution σ, we define σ_∇ by $x\sigma_\nabla = \nabla(x\sigma)$.

Note that the preceding definition implies $\nabla(s) = s$ for every term $s \in \mathcal{T}(\mathcal{F}, \mathcal{V})$. Furthermore, if $t = U_i^\rho(u, x_1, \dots, x_n, \dots)\sigma$, then $\nabla(t) = l\sigma_\nabla$.

Informally, in an innermost derivation $D : s \xrightarrow{i\,*}_{U(\mathcal{R})} t$, where $s \in \mathcal{T}(\mathcal{F}, \mathcal{V})$, the transformation ∇ applied to t undoes all "unfinished" U reductions. That is, it (recursively) replaces every maximal U subterm u (a U *subterm* is a subterm with a U symbol at the root) in t by the term $\nabla(u) \in \mathcal{T}(\mathcal{F}, \mathcal{V})$—the term that, roughly speaking, created u in D. The next example illustrates this.

Example 7.2.54 Let $\mathcal{R}$ contain the rules

$$\begin{array}{rrcll} \rho_1: & f(x,y) & \to & z & \Leftarrow \quad x \to z \\ \rho_2: & g(x) & \to & b & \Leftarrow \quad h(x) \to d \\ \rho_3: & h(c) & \to & d & \end{array}$$

Its transformed system $U(\mathcal{R})$ has the rules

$$\begin{array}{rcl@{\qquad\qquad}rcl} f(x,y) & \to & U_1^{\rho_1}(x,x,y) & U_1^{\rho_1}(z,x,y) & \to & z \\ g(x) & \to & U_1^{\rho_2}(h(x),x) & U_1^{\rho_2}(d,x) & \to & b \\ h(c) & \to & d & & & \end{array}$$

Consider the innermost derivation

$$\begin{array}{rcl} f(g(c),g(d)) & \to^+_{U(\mathcal{R})} & f(U_1^{\rho_2}(h(c),c), U_1^{\rho_2}(h(d),d)) \\ & \to_{U(\mathcal{R})} & f(U_1^{\rho_2}(d,c), U_1^{\rho_2}(h(d),d)) \\ & \to_{U(\mathcal{R})} & f(b, U_1^{\rho_2}(h(d),d)) \\ & \to_{U(\mathcal{R})} & U_1^{\rho_1}(b,b,U_1^{\rho_2}(h(d),d)) = t \end{array}$$

Then $\nabla(t) = f(\nabla(b), \nabla(U_1^{\rho_2}(h(d),d))) = f(b, g(\nabla(d))) = f(b, g(d))$.

Note, however, that the transformation ∇ is defined independently of a particular innermost derivation. As an example, consider the term $t' = U_1^{\rho_2}(c, U_1^{\rho_1}(U_1^{\rho_2}(d, g(b)), b, h(d)))$. We have $\nabla(t') = g(\nabla(U_1^{\rho_1}(U_1^{\rho_2}(d,g(b)), b, h(d)))) = g(f(\nabla(b), \nabla(h(d))) = g(f(b, h(d)))$.

Lemma 7.2.55 *Let $s \in \mathcal{T}(\mathcal{F}, \mathcal{V})$. If $s \mathrel{\overset{i}{+\!\!\!\!+\!\!\!\!\!\to}}^*_{U(\mathcal{R})} t' = U(\dots) \mathrel{\overset{i}{+\!\!\!\!+\!\!\!\!\!\to}}_{U(\mathcal{R})} t$ and the redexes contracted in the last parallel rewrite step are strictly below the root, then $\nabla(t') = \nabla(t)$.*

Proof Because $s \in \mathcal{T}(\mathcal{F}, \mathcal{V})$, the outermost U symbol in t' must have been introduced in $s \mathrel{\overset{i}{+\!\!\!\!+\!\!\!\!\!\to}}^*_{U(\mathcal{R})} t'$. Note that $l\sigma \xrightarrow{i}_{U(\mathcal{R})} U_1^\rho(s_1, \mathcal{V}ar(l))\sigma$ or $U_i^\rho(t_i, \mathcal{V}ar(l), \dots)\sigma \xrightarrow{i}_{U(\mathcal{R})} U_{i+1}^\rho(s_{i+1}, \mathcal{V}ar(l), \dots)\sigma$ imply that every argument in the terms $U_1^\rho(s_1, \mathcal{V}ar(l))\sigma$ and $U_{i+1}^\rho(s_{i+1}, \mathcal{V}ar(l), \dots)\sigma$ is in normal form except for (possibly) the first one. This means that the redexes contracted in $t' \xrightarrow{i}\!\!\!\!\!\!\Vdash_{U(\mathcal{R})} t$ are subterms of the first argument of $t' = U(\dots)$. It follows that $\nabla(t) = \nabla(t')$ because (by definition) $\nabla(U(\dots))$ is independent of the first argument of $U(\dots)$. □

Lemma 7.2.56 *Let $s \in \mathcal{T}(\mathcal{F}, \mathcal{V})$. If $s \;{}^{i}\!\!\Vdash^{\ell}_{U(\mathcal{R})} t$, then we have $s \to^*_{\mathcal{R}} \nabla(t) \;{}^{i}\!\!\Vdash^{\leq \ell}_{U(\mathcal{R})} t$. Moreover, if $q_1, \dots, q_m$ are the positions of the outermost U symbols in t, then every redex contracted in $\nabla(t) \;{}^{i}\!\!\Vdash^{\leq \ell}_{U(\mathcal{R})} t$ is below a q_i, $1 \leq i \leq m$.*

Proof The lemma is proved by induction on the number ℓ of parallel innermost rewrite steps. The base case $\ell = 0$ is obviously true. Suppose $s \;{}^{i}\!\!\Vdash^{\ell}_{U(\mathcal{R})} t' \;{}^{i}\!\!\Vdash_{U(\mathcal{R})} t$. According to the inductive hypothesis, we have $s \to^*_{\mathcal{R}} \nabla(t') \;{}^{i}\!\!\Vdash^{\leq \ell}_{U(\mathcal{R})} t'$ and thus $\nabla(t') \;{}^{i}\!\!\Vdash^{\leq \ell}_{U(\mathcal{R})} t' \;{}^{i}\!\!\Vdash_{U(\mathcal{R})} t$. Let $q'_1, \dots, q'_{m'}$ be the positions of the outermost U symbols in t'. Note that these positions are pairwise independent. By the definition of ∇, we have $\nabla(t') = t'[q'_i \leftarrow \nabla(t'|_{q'_i}) | 1 \leq i \leq m']$. Moreover, we may assume by the inductive hypothesis that every redex contracted in $\nabla(t') \;{}^{i}\!\!\Vdash^{\leq \ell}_{U(\mathcal{R})} t'$ is below a q'_i, $1 \leq i \leq m'$. In particular, we may assume that $\nabla(t'|_{q'_i}) \;{}^{i}\!\!\Vdash^{\leq \ell}_{U(\mathcal{R})} t'|_{q'_i}$ for every $1 \leq i \leq m'$.

Let $p_1, \dots, p_n$ be the positions of the innermost redexes in t' that are contracted in $t' \;{}^{i}\!\!\Vdash_{U(\mathcal{R})} t$. Again, these positions are pairwise independent. Consider the set of positions $P \subset \mathcal{P}os(t')$ defined by

$$\begin{aligned} P \;=\; & \{q'_i \mid 1 \leq i \leq m' \text{ and } q'_i \text{ is not strictly below a } p_j, 1 \leq j \leq n\} \\ \cup\; & \{p_j \mid 1 \leq j \leq n \text{ and } p_j \text{ is not strictly below a } q'_i, 1 \leq i \leq m'\} \end{aligned}$$

Obviously, the positions in P are pairwise independent. For example, if t' is the term depicted in Figure 7.2, then $P = \{q'_1, p_3, p_4, p_5, p_6\} = \{q'_1, p_3, q'_4, q'_5, p_6\}$. By the definition of ∇, the symbols of $\nabla(t')$ and $\nabla(t)$ coincide at every position which is either strictly above some position from P or independent of every position in P (simply because all these symbols are from $\mathcal{F} \cup \mathcal{V}$). This common upper part is denoted by C in Figures 7.2 and 7.3.

The idea of the proof is to show for every position $o \in P$ that there is a rewrite sequence $\nabla(t'|_o) \to^*_{\mathcal{R}} \nabla(t|_o) \;{}^{i}\!\!\Vdash^{\leq \ell+1}_{U(\mathcal{R})} t|_o$ such that every redex contracted in $\nabla(t|_o) \;{}^{i}\!\!\Vdash^{\leq \ell+1}_{U(\mathcal{R})} t|_o$ is below the position of an outermost U symbol in $t|_o$. The rewrite sequences $\nabla(t'|_o) \to^*_{\mathcal{R}} \nabla(t|_o)$ and $\nabla(t|_o) \;{}^{i}\!\!\Vdash^{\leq \ell+1}_{U(\mathcal{R})} t|_o$, respectively, can then be combined into one rewrite sequence $\nabla(t') \to^*_{\mathcal{R}} \nabla(t)$ and $\nabla(t) \;{}^{i}\!\!\Vdash^{\leq \ell+1}_{U(\mathcal{R})} t$, respectively, because the positions in P are pairwise independent. Moreover, because every position q_i of an outermost U symbol in t is below a position in P, it follows that every redex contracted in the constructed rewrite sequence $\nabla(t) \;{}^{i}\!\!\Vdash^{\leq \ell+1}_{U(\mathcal{R})} t$ is below a q_i, $1 \leq i \leq m$.

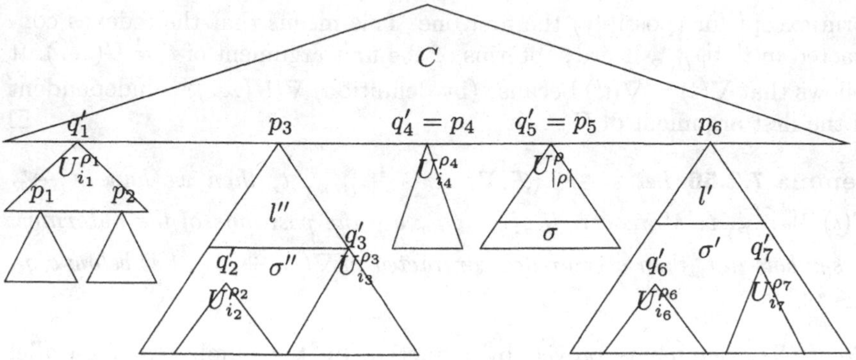

FIGURE 7.2. The term t'.

In order to show this claim, we further proceed by case analysis on the positions in P. For simplicity, we will assume that the situation depicted in Figures 7.2 and 7.3 holds. The general case can be shown similarly.

Suppose that q'_i is a position in P with at least one redex position p_j, $1 \leq j \leq n$, strictly below it. This case is illustrated in Figures 7.2 and 7.3 by the subterms $t'|_{q'_1}$ and $t|_{q'_1}$, respectively. An application of Lemma 7.2.55 to $\nabla(t'|_{q'_1}) \overset{i}{\Vdash}\!\!\rightarrow^{\leq \ell}_{U(\mathcal{R})} t'|_{q'_1} \overset{i}{\Vdash}\!\!\rightarrow_{U(\mathcal{R})} t|_{q'_1}$ yields $\nabla(t'|_{q'_1}) = \nabla(t|_{q'_1})$. Hence the claim follows by taking the reduction sequence $\nabla(t|_{q'_1}) = \nabla(t'|_{q'_1}) \overset{i}{\Vdash}\!\!\rightarrow^{\leq \ell}_{U(\mathcal{R})} t'|_{q'_1} \overset{i}{\Vdash}\!\!\rightarrow_{U(\mathcal{R})} t|_{q'_1}$.

If q'_i is a position in P that is independent of every p_j, $1 \leq j \leq n$, then $t'|_{q'_i} = t|_{q'_i}$ and $\nabla(t'|_{q'_i}) = \nabla(t|_{q'_i})$. Thus the claim follows by taking the reduction sequence $\nabla(t|_{q'_i}) = \nabla(t'|_{q'_i}) \overset{i}{\Vdash}\!\!\rightarrow^{\leq \ell}_{U(\mathcal{R})} t'|_{q'_i} = t|_{q'_i}$ (this case is not depicted in Figures 7.2 and 7.3).

Next, we assume that p_j is in P. In other words, there is no q'_i, $1 \leq i \leq m'$, strictly above p_j. By the form of the rewrite rules, the innermost reduction step $t'|_{p_j} \rightarrow_{U(\mathcal{R})} t|_{p_j}$ must have one of the following forms:

1. $t'|_{p_j} = l\sigma \overset{i}{\rightarrow}_{U(\mathcal{R})} U^{\rho}_1(s_1, \mathcal{V}ar(l))\sigma = t|_{p_j}$.

2. $t'|_{p_j} = U^{\rho}_i(t_i, \mathcal{V}ar(l), \dots)\sigma \overset{i}{\rightarrow}_{U(\mathcal{R})} U^{\rho}_{i+1}(s_{i+1}, \mathcal{V}ar(l), \dots)\sigma = t|_{p_j}$.

3. $t'|_{p_j} = U^{\rho}_{|\rho|}(t_{|\rho|}, \mathcal{V}ar(l), \dots)\sigma \overset{i}{\rightarrow}_{U(\mathcal{R})} r\sigma = t|_{p_j}$.

4. $t'|_{p_j} = l\sigma \overset{i}{\rightarrow}_{U(\mathcal{R})} r\sigma = t|_{p_j}$, where $l \rightarrow r \in \mathcal{R}$.

We further distinguish between these cases. An innermost reduction step of type (1) is illustrated in Figures 7.2 and 7.3 by the reduction step $t'|_{p_3} = l''\sigma'' \overset{i}{\rightarrow}_{U(\mathcal{R})} U^{\rho''}_1(s''_1, \mathcal{V}ar(l''))\sigma'' = t|_{p_3}$ at position p_3. It follows from $\nabla(t'|_{q'_2}) \overset{i}{\Vdash}\!\!\rightarrow^{\leq \ell}_{U(\mathcal{R})} t'|_{q'_2}$ and $\nabla(t'|_{q'_3}) \overset{i}{\Vdash}\!\!\rightarrow^{\leq \ell}_{U(\mathcal{R})} t'|_{q'_3}$ that $\nabla(t'|_{p_3}) \overset{i}{\Vdash}\!\!\rightarrow^{\leq \ell}_{U(\mathcal{R})} t'|_{p_3}$ because q'_2 and q'_3 are independent (and there are only symbols from $\mathcal{F} \cup \mathcal{V}$

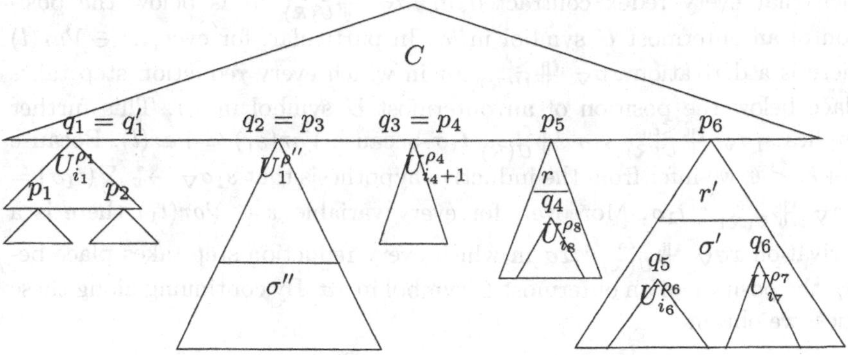

FIGURE 7.3. The term t.

at each position in $\mathcal{P}os(t|_{p_3})$, which is either above q'_2 or q'_3 or independent of both q'_2 and q'_3). Furthermore, by the definition of ∇, we infer $\nabla(t'|_{p_3}) = l''\sigma''_{\nabla} = \nabla(t|_{p_3})$. Consequently, the claim follows by taking the derivation $\nabla(t|_{p_3}) = \nabla(t'|_{p_3}) \;{}^{i}\!\!\Downarrow^{\le \ell}_{U(\mathcal{R})}\; t'|_{p_3} \overset{i}{\rightarrow}_{U(\mathcal{R})} t|_{p_3}$.

The innermost reduction step at position p_4 in Figures 7.2 and 7.3 is of type (2). Again, by the definition of ∇, we obtain $\nabla(t'|_{p_4}) = \nabla(t|_{p_4})$. This implies that the reduction sequence $\nabla(t|_{p_4}) = \nabla(t'|_{p_4}) \;{}^{i}\!\!\Downarrow^{\le \ell}_{U(\mathcal{R})}\; t'|_{p_4} \overset{i}{\rightarrow}_{U(\mathcal{R})} t|_{p_4}$ meets the requirements.

Now let the innermost reduction step be of type (3). This case is illustrated in Figures 7.2 and 7.3 by the reduction step $t'|_{p_5} = U^{\rho}_{|\rho|}(t_{|\rho|}, \mathcal{V}ar(l), \dots)\sigma \overset{i}{\rightarrow}_{U(\mathcal{R})} r\sigma = t|_{p_5}$ at position p_5. Let ρ be the rule $l \rightarrow r \Leftarrow s_1 \rightarrow t_1, \dots, s_k \rightarrow t_k$. According to the inductive hypothesis, we have $\nabla(t'|_{p_5}) \;{}^{i}\!\!\Downarrow^{\le \ell}_{U(\mathcal{R})}\; t'|_{p_5}$. Therefore, there is a derivation

$$\nabla(t'|_{p_5}) = l\sigma_{\nabla} \;{}^{i}\!\!\Downarrow^{\le \ell}_{U(\mathcal{R})}\; t'|_{p_5} = U^{\rho}_{|\rho|}(t_{|\rho|}, \mathcal{V}ar(l), \dots)\sigma \overset{i}{\rightarrow}_{U(\mathcal{R})} r\sigma \qquad (7.1)$$

where $r\sigma = t|_{p_5}$. This derivation must contain a reduction step $l\tau \overset{i}{\rightarrow}_{U(\mathcal{R})} U^{\rho}_1(s_1, \mathcal{V}ar(l))\tau$, which introduces the U^{ρ}_1 symbol. That τ coincides with σ on every $x \in \mathcal{V}ar(l)$ can be seen as follows. For every variable $x \in \mathcal{V}ar(l)$, $x\tau$ is in normal form because the reduction step is innermost. Because $l\tau \overset{i}{\rightarrow}_{U(\mathcal{R})} U^{\rho}_1(s_1, \mathcal{V}ar(l))\tau \;{}^{i}\!\!\Downarrow^{*}_{U(\mathcal{R})}\; U^{\rho}_{|\rho|}(t_{|\rho|}, \mathcal{V}ar(l), \dots)\sigma \overset{i}{\rightarrow}_{U(\mathcal{R})} r\sigma$ and $x\tau$ is in normal form for every variable $x \in \mathcal{V}ar(l)$, it follows that $x\tau = x\sigma$ for every variable $x \in \mathcal{V}ar(l)$. Hence, derivation (7.1) must be of the form

$$\begin{aligned} l\sigma_{\nabla} \;& {}^{i}\!\!\Downarrow^{\ell_0}_{U(\mathcal{R})}\; l\sigma \overset{i}{\rightarrow}_{U(\mathcal{R})} U^{\rho}_1(s_1, \mathcal{V}ar(l))\sigma \;{}^{i}\!\!\Downarrow^{\ell_1}_{U(\mathcal{R})}\; U^{\rho}_1(t_1, \mathcal{V}ar(l))\sigma \\ & \overset{i}{\rightarrow}_{U(\mathcal{R})} U^{\rho}_2(s_2, \mathcal{V}ar(l), \mathcal{E}\mathcal{V}ar(t_1))\sigma \;{}^{i}\!\!\Downarrow^{\ell_2}_{U(\mathcal{R})}\; \cdots \\ & {}^{i}\!\!\Downarrow^{\ell_{|\rho|}}_{U(\mathcal{R})}\; U^{\rho}_{|\rho|}(t_{|\rho|}, \mathcal{V}ar(l), \dots)\sigma \overset{i}{\rightarrow}_{U(\mathcal{R})} r\sigma \end{aligned}$$

where $\sum_{j=0}^{|\rho|} \ell_j < \ell$. An application of the inductive hypothesis to $l\sigma_{\nabla} \;{}^{i}\!\!\Downarrow^{\ell_0}_{U(\mathcal{R})}\; l\sigma$ yields a derivation $l\sigma_{\nabla} \rightarrow^{*}_{\mathcal{R}} \nabla(l\sigma_{\nabla}) = l\sigma_{\nabla} \;{}^{i}\!\!\Downarrow^{\le \ell_0}_{U(\mathcal{R})}\; l\sigma$

such that every redex contracted in $l\sigma_\nabla \overset{i}{\twoheadrightarrow}{}^{\le \ell_0}_{U(\mathcal{R})} l\sigma$ is below the position of an outermost U symbol in $l\sigma$. In particular, for every $x \in \mathcal{V}ar(l)$ there is a derivation $x\sigma_\nabla \overset{i}{\twoheadrightarrow}{}^{\le \ell_0}_{U(\mathcal{R})} x\sigma$ in which every reduction step takes place below the position of an outermost U symbol in $x\sigma$. This further implies $s_1\sigma_\nabla \overset{i}{\twoheadrightarrow}{}^{\le \ell_0}_{U(\mathcal{R})} s_1\sigma \overset{i}{\twoheadrightarrow}{}^{\ell_1}_{U(\mathcal{R})} t_1\sigma$ because $\mathcal{V}ar(s_1) \subseteq \mathcal{V}ar(l)$. Because $\ell_0 + \ell_1 < \ell$, we infer from the inductive hypothesis that $s_1\sigma_\nabla \to^*_{\mathcal{R}} \nabla(t_1\sigma) = t_1\sigma_\nabla \overset{i}{\twoheadrightarrow}{}^{\le \ell_0+\ell_1}_{U(\mathcal{R})} t_1\sigma$. Moreover, for every variable $x \in \mathcal{V}ar(t_1)$ there is a derivation $x\sigma_\nabla \overset{i}{\twoheadrightarrow}{}^{\le \ell_0+\ell_1}_{U(\mathcal{R})} x\sigma$ in which every reduction step takes place below the position of an outermost U symbol in $x\sigma$. By continuing along these lines, we obtain

$$s_j\sigma_\nabla \to^*_{\mathcal{R}} t_j\sigma_\nabla \overset{i}{\twoheadrightarrow}{}^{\le \ell_0+\cdots+\ell_j}_{U(\mathcal{R})} t_j\sigma$$

for all $j \in \{1, \ldots, |\rho|\}$ and, moreover, for every variable $x \in \mathcal{V}ar(l) \cup \bigcup_{j=1}^{|\rho|} \mathcal{V}ar(t_j)$ there is a derivation $x\sigma_\nabla \overset{i}{\twoheadrightarrow}{}^{<\ell}_{U(\mathcal{R})} x\sigma$ in which every reduction step takes place below the position of an outermost U symbol in $x\sigma$. It is a consequence of $s_j\sigma_\nabla \to^*_{\mathcal{R}} t_j\sigma_\nabla$ for all $j \in \{1, \ldots, |\rho|\}$ that $l\sigma_\nabla \to_{\mathcal{R}} r\sigma_\nabla$. Furthermore, by combining the derivations $x\sigma_\nabla \overset{i}{\twoheadrightarrow}{}^{<\ell}_{U(\mathcal{R})} x\sigma$ for every $x \in \mathcal{V}ar(r) \subseteq \mathcal{V}ar(l) \cup \bigcup_{j=1}^{|\rho|} \mathcal{V}ar(t_j)$, we obtain a reduction sequence $r\sigma_\nabla \overset{i}{\twoheadrightarrow}{}^{<\ell}_{U(\mathcal{R})} r\sigma$ in which every reduction step takes place below the position of an outermost U symbol in $r\sigma$. This concludes the case of reduction steps of type (3).

The reduction step $t'|_{p_6} = l'\sigma' \overset{i}{\to}_{U(\mathcal{R})} r'\sigma' = t|_{p_6}$ at position p_6 in Figures 7.2 and 7.3 is of type (4). In this case, we have $\nabla(t'|_{p_6}) = \nabla(l'\sigma') = l'\sigma'_\nabla$ and $\nabla(t|_{p_6}) = \nabla(r'\sigma') = r'\sigma'_\nabla$. Because $l' \to r'$ is an unconditional rule in $\mathcal{R}$, it is immediately clear that $l'\sigma'_\nabla \to_{\mathcal{R}} r'\sigma'_\nabla$. Because neither l' nor r' contains a U symbol, there must exist positions o_1, o_2, o_3, and o_4 such that $q_5 = p_6.o_1.o_2$, $q_6 = p_6.o_3.o_4$, $r'|_{o_1} = x \in \mathcal{V}$, and $r'|_{o_3} = y \in \mathcal{V}$. In the following, we assume that $x \neq y$; the case $x = y$ can be shown in a similar fashion. According to the inductive hypothesis, $\nabla(t'|_{q'_6}) \overset{i}{\twoheadrightarrow}{}^{\le \ell}_{U(\mathcal{R})} t'|_{q'_6} = t|_{q_5}$ and $\nabla(t'|_{q'_7}) \overset{i}{\twoheadrightarrow}{}^{\le \ell}_{U(\mathcal{R})} t'|_{q'_7} = t|_{q_6}$. It follows that every redex contracted in $x\sigma'_\nabla \overset{i}{\twoheadrightarrow}{}^{\le \ell}_{U(\mathcal{R})} x\sigma'$ is below o_2 and every redex contracted in $y\sigma'_\nabla \overset{i}{\twoheadrightarrow}{}^{\le \ell}_{U(\mathcal{R})} y\sigma'$ is below o_4. Hence, every redex contracted in $r'\sigma'_\nabla \overset{i}{\twoheadrightarrow}{}^{\le \ell}_{U(\mathcal{R})} r'\sigma'$ is either below $o_1.o_2$ or below $o_3.o_4$. In summary, we have shown that the rewrite sequence $\nabla(t'|_{p_6}) = l'\sigma'_\nabla \to_{\mathcal{R}} r'\sigma'_\nabla = \nabla(t|_{p_6}) \overset{i}{\twoheadrightarrow}{}^{\le \ell}_{U(\mathcal{R})} r'\sigma' = t|_{p_6}$ meets the requirements. This concludes the proof. □

Lemma 7.2.57 *If $\mathcal{R}$ is a quasi-decreasing deterministic 3-CTRS, then there is no infinite innermost $U(\mathcal{R})$ derivation starting from a term $s \in \mathcal{T}(\mathcal{F}, \mathcal{V})$.*

Proof Let $\mathcal{R}$ be quasi-decreasing w.r.t. $\succ$. We show by well-founded induction on $\succ$ that every innermost $U(\mathcal{R})$ derivation starting from $s \in \mathcal{T}(\mathcal{F}, \mathcal{V})$

is finite. If $s \to_{\mathcal{R}}^{+} u \in \mathcal{T}(\mathcal{F},\mathcal{V})$, then $s \succ u$ because $\to_{\mathcal{R}} \subseteq \succ$, and it follows from the inductive hypothesis that every innermost $U(\mathcal{R})$ derivation starting from $u \in \mathcal{T}(\mathcal{F},\mathcal{V})$ is finite. Moreover, if t is a proper subterm of s and $t \to_{\mathcal{R}}^{*} u \in \mathcal{T}(\mathcal{F},\mathcal{V})$, then we infer $s \succ t \succeq u$ because $\succ$ has the subterm property and $\to_{\mathcal{R}} \subseteq \succ$. Hence every innermost $U(\mathcal{R})$ derivation starting from t or u is also finite.

For a proof by contradiction, suppose that there is an infinite innermost $U(\mathcal{R})$ derivation D starting from $s = f(u_1,\dots,u_m)$. According to the preceding, D must be of the form

$$\begin{aligned} D : s = f(u_1,\dots,u_m) &\xrightarrow{i\ *}_{U(\mathcal{R})} f(v_1,\dots,v_m) = l\sigma \\ &\xrightarrow{i}_{U(\mathcal{R})} U_1^{\rho}(s_1, \mathcal{V}ar(l))\sigma \xrightarrow{i}_{U(\mathcal{R})} \cdots \end{aligned}$$

where every $v_j \in NF(U(\mathcal{R}))$, i.e., every v_j is a normal form w.r.t. $U(\mathcal{R})$. Let ρ (which appears in U_1^{ρ}) be the rule $l \to r \Leftarrow s_1 \to t_1,\dots,s_{|\rho|} \to t_{|\rho|}$. Because $u_j \xrightarrow{i\ *}_{U(\mathcal{R})} v_j$, we derive from Lemma 7.2.56 that $u_j \to_{\mathcal{R}}^{*} \nabla(v_j) \xrightarrow{i\ *}_{U(\mathcal{R})} v_j$. If $u_j \to_{\mathcal{R}}^{+} \nabla(v_j)$, then the derivation

$$\begin{aligned} s &\to_{\mathcal{R}}^{+} f(u_1,\dots,u_{j-1},\nabla(v_j),u_{j+1},\dots u_m) = t \\ &\xrightarrow{i\ *}_{U(\mathcal{R})} f(v_1,\dots,v_m) \xrightarrow{i}_{U(\mathcal{R})} \cdots \end{aligned}$$

would be infinite. This is impossible because $\to_{\mathcal{R}}^{+} \subseteq \succ$ and hence there is no infinite innermost $U(\mathcal{R})$ derivation starting from t. Thus $u_j = \nabla(v_j)$ for every $j \in \mathbb{N}$. It is not difficult to check that $s = l\sigma_{\nabla}$ and $x\sigma_{\nabla} \xrightarrow{i\ *}_{U(\mathcal{R})} x\sigma$ for every $x \in \mathcal{V}ar(l)$ follows as a consequence (if a redex $l'\sigma_{\nabla}$, where $l' \notin \mathcal{V}$ is a proper subterm of l, were reduced in $l\sigma_{\nabla} \xrightarrow{i\ *}_{U(\mathcal{R})} l\sigma$, then its reduct would have the form $U_{j'}^{\rho'}(\dots)$ in $l\sigma$, which is clearly impossible). Therefore, D has the form

$$D : s = l\sigma_{\nabla} \xrightarrow{i\ *}_{U(\mathcal{R})} l\sigma \xrightarrow{i}_{U(\mathcal{R})} U_1^{\rho}(s_1, \mathcal{V}ar(l))\sigma \xrightarrow{i}_{U(\mathcal{R})} \cdots$$

The validity of the inequality $l\sigma_{\nabla} \succ s_1\sigma_{\nabla}$ is a consequence of the fact that $\mathcal{R}$ is quasi-decreasing. Hence there is no infinite innermost $U(\mathcal{R})$ derivation starting from $s_1\sigma_{\nabla}$. Because $x\sigma_{\nabla} \xrightarrow{i\ *}_{U(\mathcal{R})} x\sigma$ for every $x \in \mathcal{V}ar(l)$ and $\mathcal{V}ar(s_1) \subseteq \mathcal{V}ar(l)$, it follows that $s_1\sigma_{\nabla} \xrightarrow{i\ *}_{U(\mathcal{R})} s_1\sigma$. Therefore, every infinite innermost $U(\mathcal{R})$ derivation starting from $s_1\sigma$ must be finite. The derivation D thus looks like[8]

$$\begin{aligned} s = l\sigma_{\nabla} &\xrightarrow{i\ *}_{U(\mathcal{R})} l\sigma \xrightarrow{i}_{U(\mathcal{R})} U_1^{\rho}(s_1, \mathcal{V}ar(l))\sigma \\ &\xrightarrow{i\ *}_{U(\mathcal{R})} U_1^{\rho}(t_1, \mathcal{V}ar(l))\sigma \xrightarrow{i}_{U(\mathcal{R})} \cdots \end{aligned}$$

---

[8] According to the remark after Definition 7.2.33, we may assume that σ instantiates every variable in ρ.

Now $s_1\sigma_\nabla \xrightarrow{i\ *}_{U(\mathcal{R})} s_1\sigma \xrightarrow{i\ *}_{U(\mathcal{R})} t_1\sigma$ yields $s_1\sigma_\nabla \to^*_{\mathcal{R}} t_1\sigma_\nabla \xrightarrow{i\ *}_{U(\mathcal{R})} t_1\sigma$ by Lemma 7.2.56. It follows $l\sigma_\nabla \succ s_2\sigma_\nabla$ because $\mathcal{R}$ is quasi-decreasing w.r.t. $\succ$ and we may continue with our line of reasoning. All in all, D must have the form

$$\begin{aligned} l\sigma_\nabla &\xrightarrow{i\ +}_{U(\mathcal{R})} U_1^\rho(s_1, \mathcal{V}ar(l))\sigma \\ &\xrightarrow{i\ *}_{U(\mathcal{R})} U_{|\rho|}^\rho(t_{|\rho|}, \mathcal{V}ar(l), \dots)\sigma \\ &\xrightarrow{i}_{U(\mathcal{R})} r\sigma \xrightarrow{i}_{U(\mathcal{R})} \cdots \end{aligned}$$

Hence $l\sigma_\nabla \to_{\mathcal{R}} r\sigma_\nabla \xrightarrow{i\ *}_{U(\mathcal{R})} r\sigma$ according to Lemma 7.2.56 (note that σ_∇ satisfies the conditions of ρ because $s_j\sigma_\nabla \xrightarrow{i\ *}_{U(\mathcal{R})} t_j\sigma_\nabla$ for $1 \le j \le |\rho|$). We conclude that there is an infinite innermost $U(\mathcal{R})$ derivation starting from $r\sigma_\nabla$, which is impossible because $s = l\sigma_\nabla \succ r\sigma_\nabla$. □

Theorem 7.2.58 *If $\mathcal{R}$ is a quasi-decreasing deterministic 3-CTRS, then $U(\mathcal{R})$ is innermost terminating.*

Proof Clearly, every variable is an element of $NF(U(\mathcal{R}))$. Furthermore, a constant from $\mathcal{F}$ cannot start an infinite innermost $U(\mathcal{R})$ derivation according to Lemma 7.2.57. First, we show that there is no infinite innermost $U(\mathcal{R})$ derivation starting from a term of the form

(a) $f(u_1, \dots, u_m)$, where $f \in \mathcal{F}$
(b) $C[u_1, \dots, u_m]$, where $C[, \dots,] \in \mathcal{T}(\mathcal{F}, \mathcal{V})$
(c) $U_i^\rho(u_1, \dots, u_m)$

under the assumption that none of the subterms $u_j \in \mathcal{T}(\mathcal{F}', \mathcal{V})$, $1 \le j \le m$, starts an infinite innermost $U(\mathcal{R})$ derivation.

(a) For an indirect proof, suppose that $s = f(u_1, \dots, u_m)$ starts an infinite innermost $U(\mathcal{R})$ derivation. Because every innermost $U(\mathcal{R})$ derivation starting from u_j, $1 \le j \le m$, is finite, there is an infinite innermost $U(\mathcal{R})$ derivation

$$D : s = f(u_1, \dots, u_m) \xrightarrow{i\ *}_{U(\mathcal{R})} f(v_1, \dots, v_m) = t \xrightarrow{i}_{U(\mathcal{R})} \cdots$$

where $v_j \in NF(U(\mathcal{R}))$. If $t \in \mathcal{T}(\mathcal{F}, \mathcal{V})$, then we obtain a contradiction by Lemma 7.2.57. Otherwise, t contains U subterms, but all of them are in normal form. We may write $t = C[w_1, \dots, w_n]$, where $C \in \mathcal{T}(\mathcal{F}, \mathcal{V})$ and every term w_i is a (maximal) U subterm of t. In order to cope with nonleft-linear rules, we have to distinguish between those U subterms of t that can be created by a term without U symbols and those that cannot. For the sake of simplicity, let us assume that for every $1 \le j \le i$ there is a term $w'_j \in \mathcal{T}(\mathcal{F}, \mathcal{V})$ such that $w'_j \xrightarrow{i\ +}_{U(\mathcal{R})} w_j$ but for every $i < j \le n$ no such term exists. Then there is an infinite innermost $U(\mathcal{R})$ derivation

$$D' : s' = C[w'_1, \dots, w'_i, w_{i+1}, \dots, w_n] \xrightarrow{i\ *}_{U(\mathcal{R})} f(v_1, \dots, v_m) = t \xrightarrow{i}_{U(\mathcal{R})} \cdots$$

In order to get rid of the remaining U subterms $w_{i+1}, \dots, w_n$, we mark[9] every w_j, $i < j \le n$, and choose fresh variables $x_{i+1}, \dots, x_n$ with the property that $x_j = x_k$ if and only if $w_j = w_k$ for $i < j < k \le n$. Let Ψ be the transformation that replaces every marked occurrence of w_j in a term with x_j. We claim that the transformed derivation $\Psi(D')$

$$\begin{aligned}\Psi(s') &= C[w'_1, \dots, w'_i, x_{i+1}, \dots, x_n] \xrightarrow{i\,*}_{U(\mathcal{R})} \Psi(f(v_1, \dots, v_m)) \\ &= \Psi(t) \xrightarrow{i}_{U(\mathcal{R})} \cdots\end{aligned}$$

is an infinite innermost $U(\mathcal{R})$ derivation. Because $\Psi(s') \in \mathcal{T}(\mathcal{F}, \mathcal{V})$, this yields the desired contradiction to Lemma 7.2.57. Let $C[l\sigma] \xrightarrow{i}_{U(\mathcal{R})} C[r\sigma]$ be a reduction step in D', where $l \to r \in U(\mathcal{R})$. The reduction step cannot take place in a marked subterm because every marked subterm is in normal form, so $\Psi(C[l\sigma]) = \Psi(C)[\Psi(l\sigma)]$. Moreover, we have $\Psi(l\sigma) = l\sigma_\Psi$, where σ_Ψ is defined by $x\sigma_\Psi = \Psi(x\sigma)$, because no proper subterm of l contains a U symbol. It is thus sufficient to show $l\sigma_\Psi \xrightarrow{i}_{U(\mathcal{R})} r\sigma_\Psi$ because this yields

$$\Psi(C[l\sigma]) = \Psi(C)[l\sigma_\Psi] \xrightarrow{i}_{U(\mathcal{R})} \Psi(C)[r\sigma_\Psi] = \Psi(C[r\sigma])$$

We first show $l\sigma_\Psi \to_{U(\mathcal{R})} r\sigma_\Psi$. Because l may be nonleft-linear, we have to show that $x\sigma = y\sigma$ implies $x\sigma_\Psi = y\sigma_\Psi$ for every pair x, y of variables from $\mathcal{V}ar(l)$. Suppose that $x\sigma$ contains a marked U subterm, say at position p. Then $y\sigma$ contains the same subterm u at position p. Because u has not been created in the derivation $\Psi(D')$—there is no $u' \in \mathcal{T}(\mathcal{F}, \mathcal{V})$ with $u' \xrightarrow{i\,+}_{U(\mathcal{R})} u$—it is also marked. Therefore, $l\sigma_\Psi \to_{U(\mathcal{R})} r\sigma_\Psi$. Furthermore, by the choice of fresh variables $x_{i+1}, \dots, x_n$, the equality $x\sigma_\Psi = y\sigma_\Psi$ implies $x\sigma = y\sigma$. Consequently, $l\sigma_\Psi \to_{U(\mathcal{R})} r\sigma_\Psi$ is an innermost reduction step (otherwise $l\sigma \to_{U(\mathcal{R})} r\sigma$ would not be innermost). This concludes the proof of (a).

(b) Let $s = C[u_1, \dots, u_m]$, where $C[, \dots,] \in \mathcal{T}(\mathcal{F}, \mathcal{V})$. With the aid of (a), a simple proof by structural induction on $C[, \dots,]$ shows that every innermost $U(\mathcal{R})$ derivation starting from s is finite.

(c) Suppose that $s = U_i^\rho(u_1, \dots, u_m)$ starts an infinite innermost $U(\mathcal{R})$ derivation. Because every innermost $U(\mathcal{R})$ derivation starting from u_j, $1 \le j \le m$, is finite, any infinite innermost $U(\mathcal{R})$ derivation starting from s must have the form

$$\begin{aligned}D: s = U_i^\rho(u_1, \dots, u_m) &\xrightarrow{i\,*}_{U(\mathcal{R})} U_i^\rho(v_1, \dots, v_m) = U_i^\rho(t_i, \mathcal{V}ar(l), \dots)\sigma \\ &\xrightarrow{i}_{U(\mathcal{R})} U_{i+1}^\rho(s_{i+1}, \mathcal{V}ar(l), \dots)\sigma \xrightarrow{i}_{U(\mathcal{R})} \cdots\end{aligned}$$

where $v_j \in NF(U(\mathcal{R}))$ for every $1 \le j \le m$. Note that $x\sigma \in NF(U(\mathcal{R}))$ for every $x \in \mathcal{V}ar(s_{i+1})$. We may write $s_{i+1} = C_{i+1}[x_1, \dots, x_n]$ for some

[9] For example, by underlining the root symbol.

context $C_{i+1}[,\dots,] \in \mathcal{T}(\mathcal{F},\mathcal{V})$ such that all variables from $\mathcal{V}ar(s_{i+1})$ are displayed. We infer from case (b) that there is no infinite innermost $U(\mathcal{R})$ derivation starting from $s_{i+1}\sigma = C_{i+1}[x_1\sigma,\dots,x_n\sigma]$ because $x_j\sigma \in NF(U(\mathcal{R}))$ for $1 \le j \le n$. A repetition of these arguments shows that D has the form

$$D : s = U_i^\rho(u_1,\dots,u_m) \xrightarrow{i\,*}_{U(\mathcal{R})} U_{|\rho|}^\rho(t_{|\rho|}, \mathcal{V}ar(l),\dots)\sigma \xrightarrow{i}_{U(\mathcal{R})} r\sigma \xrightarrow{i}_{U(\mathcal{R})} \cdots$$

By the same reasoning as earlier, it follows from case (b) that there is no infinite innermost $U(\mathcal{R})$ derivation starting from $r\sigma$. This yields the desired contradiction and proves (c).

Now we are ready to prove the theorem. For a proof by contradiction, suppose that there is an infinite innermost $U(\mathcal{R})$ derivation starting from a term $s \in \mathcal{T}(\mathcal{F}',\mathcal{V})$. Without loss of generality, we may assume that every innermost $U(\mathcal{R})$ derivation starting from a proper subterm of s is finite (if there were a subterm t of s starting an infinite innermost $U(\mathcal{R})$ derivation, then we would simply take t instead of s). However, according to the previous considerations, every innermost $U(\mathcal{R})$ derivation starting from s must be finite because every innermost $U(\mathcal{R})$ derivation starting from its proper subterms is finite. □

Corollary 7.2.59 *If $\mathcal{R}$ is a deterministic 3-CTRS, then the following implications hold:*

$$\begin{aligned} U(\mathcal{R}) \textit{ is terminating } &\Rightarrow \mathcal{R} \textit{ is quasi-reductive } \Rightarrow \mathcal{R} \textit{ is quasi-decreasing} \\ &\Rightarrow U(\mathcal{R}) \textit{ is innermost terminating.} \end{aligned}$$

Proof Combine Proposition 7.2.50 and Theorem 7.2.58. □

According to Theorem 5.6.10(1), if $U(\mathcal{R})$ is nonoverlapping, then all properties in Corollary 7.2.59 are equivalent. It should be pointed out, however, that even for strongly deterministic 3-CTRSs nonoverlappingness of $U(\mathcal{R})$ is not implied by nonoverlappingness of $\mathcal{R}$. Consider, for example, the system $\mathcal{R} = \{a \to b \Leftarrow b \to a\}$ and its transformed system $U(\mathcal{R}) = \{a \to U(b), U(a) \to b\}$. The situation is different for syntactically deterministic 3-CTRSs, which will be considered next.

Lemma 7.2.60 *The transformed system $U(\mathcal{R})$ of a syntactically deterministic 3-CTRS $\mathcal{R}$ is nonoverlapping if $\mathcal{R}$ is nonoverlapping.*

Proof Let $l_1 \to r_1$ and $l_2 \to r_2$ be renamed versions of rewrite rules from $U(\mathcal{R})$ such that they do not have variables in common. If l_1 and l_2 are left-hand sides of rules from $\mathcal{R}$, then they cannot overlap because $\mathcal{R}$ is nonoverlapping. If both l_1 and l_2 have a U symbol at their root, then they cannot overlap either because of the shape of the U rules (U symbols only occur at root positions and the root symbols of two different U rules cannot be the same). Thus let l_1 be a left-hand side of a rule from $\mathcal{R}$ and $l_2 = U_i^\rho(t_i, \mathcal{V}ar(l), \dots)$. For an indirect proof, suppose that l_1 and l_2 do overlap. Obviously, l_1 must overlap with a subterm of t_i. This, however, is impossible because t_i is either a constructor term or a ground $\mathcal{R}_u$ normal form. □

On the one hand, nonoverlappingness of $\mathcal{R}$ can be slightly weakened in the preceding lemma. For example, we may allow infeasible critical pairs as in the *quicksort* system by using the "optimized" U transformation explained in Example 7.2.49. On the other hand, the next example shows that we cannot replace "nonoverlappingness" with "locally confluent overlay system."

Example 7.2.61 Let $\mathcal{R} = \{a \to b, a \to c \Leftarrow b \to c\}$. Because the second rule of $\mathcal{R}$ can never be applied, $\mathcal{R}$ is a (locally) confluent overlay system. But its transformed unconditional system $U(\mathcal{R}) = \{a \to b, a \to U(b), U(c) \to c\}$ is not locally confluent.

Corollary 7.2.62 *If $\mathcal{R}$ is a nonoverlapping syntactically deterministic 3-CTRS, then all properties in Corollary 7.2.59 are equivalent. In particular, a nonoverlapping syntactically deterministic 3-CTRS $\mathcal{R}$ is quasi-reductive if and only if $U(\mathcal{R})$ is terminating.*

Proof In order to show that all properties in Corollary 7.2.59 are equivalent, it is sufficient to prove that $U(\mathcal{R})$ is innermost terminating $\Rightarrow$ $U(\mathcal{R})$ is terminating. Because $\mathcal{R}$ is nonoverlapping, the same is true for $U(\mathcal{R})$ by Lemma 7.2.60. Hence $U(\mathcal{R})$ is terminating according to Theorem 5.6.10(1). □

7.2.9 Quasi-Simplifying Deterministic 3-CTRSs

In this section, we will provide several criteria that guarantee quasi-simplifyingness. The first uses the system $\mathcal{R}_q$ from Definition 7.2.46.

Proposition 7.2.63 *A deterministic 3-CTRS $\mathcal{R}$ over a signature $\mathcal{F}$ is quasi-simplifying if and only if the deterministic 3-CTRS $\mathcal{R}_q \cup \mathcal{E}mb(\mathcal{F})$ is terminating.*

Proof If the deterministic 3-CTRS $\mathcal{R}_q \cup \mathcal{E}mb(\mathcal{F})$ is terminating, then it is not difficult to prove that $\to^+_{\mathcal{R}_q \cup \mathcal{E}mb(\mathcal{F})}$ is a simplification ordering[10] and that $\mathcal{R}$ is quasi-simplifying w.r.t. that ordering. Suppose, conversely, that $\mathcal{R}$ is quasi-simplifying w.r.t. the simplification ordering $\succ$. We will show that $\to^+_{\mathcal{R}_q \cup \mathcal{E}mb(\mathcal{F})} \subseteq \succ$. Clearly, it is sufficient to show that $s \to_{\mathcal{R}_q \cup \mathcal{E}mb(\mathcal{F})} t$

[10] Recall that we only consider finite signatures.

implies $s \succ t$. If $s \rightarrow_{\mathcal{E}mb(\mathcal{F})} t$, that is, $s = C[f(u_1, \ldots, u_n)]$ and $t = C[u_j]$ for some $f \in \mathcal{F}$, then the assertion follows from the fact that $\succ$ has the subterm property and is closed under contexts. We prove by induction on the depth of the rewrite step that $s \rightarrow_{\mathcal{R}_q \cup \mathcal{E}mb(\mathcal{F})} t$ also implies $s \succ t$. Consider the reduction step $s = C[l\sigma] \rightarrow_{\mathcal{R}_q \cup \mathcal{E}mb(\mathcal{F})} C[s_{i+1}\sigma] = t$, where the rewrite rule $l \rightarrow s_{i+1} \Leftarrow s_1 \rightarrow t_1, \ldots, s_i \rightarrow t_i$ is used, so $s_j\sigma \rightarrow^*_{\mathcal{R}_q \cup \mathcal{E}mb(\mathcal{F})} t_j\sigma$ for $1 \leq j \leq i$. (The case where $l \rightarrow r \Leftarrow s_1 \rightarrow t_1, \ldots, s_k \rightarrow t_k$ is used can be proven similarly.) One has $s_j\sigma \succeq t_j\sigma$ by the inductive hypothesis. It then follows from quasi-simplifyingness that $l\sigma \succ s_{i+1}\sigma$. We eventually infer that $s \succ t$ because $\succ$ is closed under contexts. □

Proposition 7.2.63 can, of course, also be used to show that a CTRS is *not* quasi-simplifying. Consider, for example, the quasi-reductive CTRS $\mathcal{R}$ from Example 7.2.14. We have already seen that the transformed system $\mathcal{R}_q = \mathcal{R} \cup \{f(x) \rightarrow x\}$ is not terminating. Hence, $\mathcal{R}$ is not quasi-simplifying by Proposition 7.2.63.

Next we will show that simple termination of $U(\mathcal{R})$ implies not only quasi-reductivity of $\mathcal{R}$ but also quasi-simplifyingness.

Proposition 7.2.64 *If $(\mathcal{F}', U(\mathcal{R}))$ is simply terminating, then $(\mathcal{F}, \mathcal{R})$ is quasi-simplifying.*

Proof By Lemma 5.2.30, $U(\mathcal{R}) \cup \mathcal{E}mb(\mathcal{F}')$ is terminating. We will show that $\rightarrow_{\mathcal{R}_q \cup \mathcal{E}mb(\mathcal{F})} \subseteq \rightarrow^+_{U(\mathcal{R}) \cup \mathcal{E}mb(\mathcal{F}')}$. The proposition then follows from Proposition 7.2.63.

If $s \rightarrow_{\mathcal{E}mb(\mathcal{F})} t$, then $s \rightarrow_{\mathcal{E}mb(\mathcal{F}')} t$ because $\mathcal{F} \subseteq \mathcal{F}'$. We prove by induction on the depth of the rewrite step that $s \rightarrow_{\mathcal{R}_q \cup \mathcal{E}mb(\mathcal{F})} t$ implies $s \rightarrow^+_{U(\mathcal{R}) \cup \mathcal{E}mb(\mathcal{F}')} t$. Consider the reduction step $s = C[l\sigma] \rightarrow_{\mathcal{R}_q \cup \mathcal{E}mb(\mathcal{F})} C[s_{i+1}\sigma] = t$, where the rewrite rule $l \rightarrow s_{i+1} \Leftarrow s_1 \rightarrow t_1, \ldots, s_i \rightarrow t_i$ is used, so $s_j\sigma \rightarrow^*_{\mathcal{R}_q \cup \mathcal{E}mb(\mathcal{F})} t_j\sigma$ for $1 \leq j \leq i$. One has $s_j\sigma \rightarrow^*_{U(\mathcal{R}) \cup \mathcal{E}mb(\mathcal{F}')} t_j\sigma$ by the inductive hypothesis. Therefore,

$$
\begin{array}{lll}
l\sigma & \rightarrow_{U(\mathcal{R})} & U_1^\rho(s_1, \mathcal{V}ar(l))\sigma \\
 & \rightarrow^*_{U(\mathcal{R}) \cup \mathcal{E}mb(\mathcal{F}')} & U_1^\rho(t_1, \mathcal{V}ar(l))\sigma \\
 & \rightarrow_{U(\mathcal{R})} & U_2^\rho(s_2, \mathcal{V}ar(l), \mathcal{EV}ar(t_1))\sigma \\
 & \cdots & \\
 & \rightarrow^*_{U(\mathcal{R}) \cup \mathcal{E}mb(\mathcal{F}')} & U_i^\rho(t_i, \mathcal{V}ar(l), \mathcal{EV}ar(t_1), \ldots, \mathcal{EV}ar(t_{i-1}))\sigma \\
 & \rightarrow_{U(\mathcal{R})} & U_{i+1}^\rho(s_{i+1}, \mathcal{V}ar(l), \mathcal{EV}ar(t_1), \ldots, \mathcal{EV}ar(t_i))\sigma \\
 & \rightarrow_{\mathcal{E}mb(\mathcal{F}')} & s_{i+1}\sigma
\end{array}
$$

and hence $s \rightarrow^+_{U(\mathcal{R}) \cup \mathcal{E}mb(\mathcal{F}')} t$. □

The converse of Proposition 7.2.64 does not hold; see Example 7.2.70.

Example 7.2.65 Consider the system $\mathcal{R}_{fib}$, which computes the Fibonacci numbers (cf. [Klo92]):

$$\begin{array}{rcll} 0+y & \rightarrow & y & \\ s(x)+y & \rightarrow & s(x+y) & \\ fib(0) & \rightarrow & \langle 0, s(0)\rangle & \\ fib(s(x)) & \rightarrow & \langle z, y+z\rangle & \Leftarrow fib(x) \rightarrow \langle y, z\rangle \end{array}$$

The transformation of the system $\mathcal{R}_{fib}$ yields the TRS $U(\mathcal{R}_{fib})$

$$\begin{array}{rcl} 0+y & \rightarrow & y \\ s(x)+y & \rightarrow & s(x+y) \\ fib(0) & \rightarrow & \langle 0, s(0)\rangle \\ fib(s(x)) & \rightarrow & U_1(fib(x), x) \\ U_1(\langle y, z\rangle, x) & \rightarrow & \langle z, y+z\rangle \end{array}$$

Termination of the transformed system $U(\mathcal{R}_{fib})$ can be shown by *rpo*. Thus the system $\mathcal{R}_{fib}$ is quasi-simplifying by Proposition 7.2.64.

Another sufficient criterion for quasi-simplifyingness is given in [ALS94, lemma 3.1]. As a matter of fact, it is claimed in [ALS94, lemma 3.1] that the criterion shows quasi-reductivity (see the following claim) but this is not the case.

Definition 7.2.66 Let $\rho : l \rightarrow r \Leftarrow s_1 \rightarrow t_1, \ldots, s_k \rightarrow t_k$ be a conditional rule of the deterministic 3-CTRS $\mathcal{R}$. The transformed rule $\overline{\rho}$ is defined as follows. For $x \in \mathcal{EV}ar(\rho)$ let $\alpha(x)$ be the smallest i, $1 \leq i \leq k$, such that $x \in \mathcal{V}ar(t_i)$ and define

$$\begin{array}{rcl} \varphi_1 & = & id \\ \varphi_{i+1} & = & \{x \leftarrow \overline{s}_{\alpha(x)} \mid x \in \mathcal{V}ar(t_1, \ldots, t_i) \cap \mathcal{EV}ar(\rho)\} \text{ for } 1 \leq i \leq k \\ \overline{s}_i & = & \varphi_i(s_i) \end{array}$$

Then the *backward substituted rule* $\overline{\rho}$ is $l \rightarrow \overline{r} \Leftarrow \overline{s}_1 \rightarrow c, \ldots, \overline{s}_k \rightarrow c$, where c is a new constant and $\overline{r} = \varphi_{k+1}(r)$. Furthermore, the *backward substituted system* $\overline{\mathcal{R}}$ is defined by $\overline{\mathcal{R}} = \bigcup_{\rho \in \mathcal{R}} \{\overline{\rho}\}$.

Claim: Let $\succ$ be a reduction ordering and let $\mathcal{R}$ be a deterministic 3-CTRS. If, for every rule ρ in $\mathcal{R}$, the backward substituted rule $\overline{\rho}$ satisfies $l \succ_{st} \overline{s}_i$ for $1 \leq i \leq k$ and $l \succ \overline{r}$, then $\mathcal{R}$ is quasi-reductive w.r.t. $\succ$.

The next example, however, refutes this claim.

Example 7.2.67 Consider $\mathcal{R}$ and its backward substituted system $\overline{\mathcal{R}}$:

$$\mathcal{R} = \begin{cases} b & \rightarrow & g(d) \\ f(d) & \rightarrow & f(a) \\ a & \rightarrow & y & \Leftarrow b \rightarrow g(y) \end{cases}$$

$$\overline{\mathcal{R}} = \begin{cases} b & \rightarrow & g(d) \\ f(d) & \rightarrow & f(a) \\ a & \rightarrow & b & \Leftarrow b \rightarrow c \end{cases}$$

The unconditional TRS $\overline{\mathcal{R}}_u$ obtained from $\overline{\mathcal{R}}$ by dropping the conditions is terminating. Hence the ordering $\succ = \rightarrow^+_{\overline{\mathcal{R}}_u}$ is a reduction ordering that satisfies the claim. The original system $\mathcal{R}$, however, is not even terminating because there is the infinite rewrite sequence $f(d) \rightarrow_{\mathcal{R}} f(a) \rightarrow_{\mathcal{R}} f(d) \rightarrow_{\mathcal{R}} \ldots$.

The mistake in the claim is the following: One needs $l\sigma \succ \overline{r}\sigma \succ_{st} r\sigma$ (hence $l\sigma \succ_{st} r\sigma$) but in contrast to $\succ$, $\succ_{st}$ is not closed under contexts. Thus the claim is true if we replace "reduction ordering" by "simplification ordering."

Proposition 7.2.68 *Let $(\mathcal{F}, \mathcal{R})$ be a deterministic 3-CTRS. If its backward substituted system $(\mathcal{F} \cup \{c\}, \overline{\mathcal{R}})$ is simplifying, then $(\mathcal{F}, \mathcal{R})$ is quasi-simplifying.*

Proof If $(\mathcal{F} \cup \{c\}, \overline{\mathcal{R}})$ is simplifying, then there is a simplification ordering $\succ$ such that $l \succ \overline{r}$ and $l \succ \overline{s}_i$ for $1 \leq i \leq k$ for every backward substituted rule $\overline{\rho}$ of a rule $\rho = l \rightarrow r \Leftarrow s_1 \rightarrow t_1, \ldots, s_k \rightarrow t_k$ from $\mathcal{R}$.

We will only show that the first condition of Definition 7.2.38 (if $s_j\sigma \succeq t_j\sigma$ for every $1 \leq j \leq i$, then $l\sigma \succ s_{i+1}\sigma$) is satisfied. The second condition (if $s_j\sigma \succeq t_j\sigma$ for every $1 \leq j \leq k$, then $l\sigma \succ r\sigma$) follows by similar reasoning. It will be shown by induction on i that $s_j\sigma \succeq t_j\sigma$ for every $1 \leq j \leq i$ implies $\overline{s}_{i+1}\sigma \succeq s_{i+1}\sigma$. This is sufficient because $l \succ \overline{s}_{i+1}$ further implies $l\sigma \succ \overline{s}_{i+1}\sigma \succeq s_{i+1}\sigma$. The base case $i = 0$ holds as $\overline{s}_1 = s_1$. In order to show the inductive step, note that $\overline{s}_{i+1}\sigma = \varphi_{i+1}(s_{i+1})\sigma$. Let $y \in \mathcal{V}ar(t_1, \ldots, t_i) \cap \mathcal{EV}ar(\rho)$. According to the inductive hypothesis, $\overline{s}_{\alpha(y)}\sigma \succeq s_{\alpha(y)}\sigma$. Therefore, $\overline{s}_{\alpha(y)}\sigma \succeq s_{\alpha(y)}\sigma \succeq t_{\alpha(y)}\sigma \succeq y\sigma$ and hence $\varphi_{i+1}(y)\sigma = \overline{s}_{\alpha(y)}\sigma \succeq y\sigma$. Now $\overline{s}_{i+1}\sigma \succeq s_{i+1}\sigma$ is a consequence of the following observation: If $u_1 \succeq v_1, \ldots, u_n \succeq v_n$, then $C[u_1, u_2, \ldots, u_n] \succeq C[v_1, u_2, \ldots, u_n] \succeq \cdots \succeq C[v_1, \ldots, v_n]$ because $\succ$ is closed under contexts. □

Proposition 7.2.68 can also be used to show quasi-simplifyingness of the system $\mathcal{R}_{fib}$ from Example 7.2.65. This can be seen as follows. $\overline{\mathcal{R}}_{fib}$ consists of the rules

$$\begin{array}{rcll} 0+y & \to & y & \\ s(x)+y & \to & s(x+y) & \\ fib(0) & \to & \langle 0, s(0)\rangle & \\ fib(s(x)) & \to & \langle fib(x), fib(x)+fib(x)\rangle & \Leftarrow fib(x) \to c \end{array}$$

According to Lemma 7.2.6, simplifyingness of $\overline{\mathcal{R}}_{fib}$ is equivalent to simple termination of the TRS $(\overline{\mathcal{R}}_{fib})_s$ and simple termination of this TRS can easily be shown by *rpo*.

Because both Propositions 7.2.64 and 7.2.68 are sufficient conditions for proving quasi-simplifyingness, it is natural to ask whether one is subsumed by the other. This is not the case, as the following examples show.

Example 7.2.69 Let $\mathcal{R} = \{f(s(x)) \to f(s(y)) \Leftarrow f(x) \to f(s(y))\}$. It is fairly simple to show that $U(\mathcal{R})$ is simply terminating. To verify that Proposition 7.2.68 is not applicable is equally simple; see [ALS94].

Example 7.2.70 Let $(\mathcal{F}, \mathcal{R})$ be the 1-CTRS from Example 7.2.17 and let $(\mathcal{F} \cup \{c\}, \overline{\mathcal{R}})$ be its backward substituted system. $\overline{\mathcal{R}}$ is obtained from $\mathcal{R}$ by replacing the rule $f(x) \to x \Leftarrow x \to d$ with $f(x) \to x \Leftarrow x \to c$. It can be shown as in Example 7.2.17 that $\overline{\mathcal{R}}$ is simplifying. Hence $\mathcal{R}$ is quasi-simplifying according to Proposition 7.2.68. However, $U(\mathcal{R}) = U_n(\mathcal{R})$ is not simply terminating.

The following question is still open: Does quasi-simplifyingness of $\mathcal{R}$ imply that $U(\mathcal{R})$ is terminating? If so, then one can show quasi-reductivity of $\mathcal{R}$ by means of Proposition 7.2.50 whenever Proposition 7.2.68 proves quasi-simplifyingness of $\mathcal{R}$ (hence Proposition 7.2.68 is somewhat superfluous if one is only interested in quasi-reductivity).

7.2.10 Summary: Methods for 3-CTRSs

Next we will briefly summarize the methods for showing effective termination of 3-CTRSs. In order to show effective termination of a 3-CTRS $\mathcal{R}$, one has to prove quasi-simplifyingness or quasi-reductivity or quasi-decreasingness. $\mathcal{R}$ can be shown to be quasi-reductive by showing termination of the 3-CTRS $\mathcal{R}_q$ (Proposition 7.2.47). A more promising method originates from [Ohl99b]. It consists of proving termination of the transformed unconditional TRS $U(\mathcal{R})$ (Proposition 7.2.50). This method is advantageous because many sophisticated techniques for proving termination of unconditional TRSs are known; see Chapter 5. Quasi-reductivity of $\mathcal{R}$ implies innermost termination but not termination of $U(\mathcal{R})$; see Theorem 7.2.58. In the special case where $\mathcal{R}$ is a syntactically deterministic nonoverlapping system, however, quasi-reductivity of $\mathcal{R}$ and termination of $U(\mathcal{R})$ are equivalent; see Corollary 7.2.62.

Quasi-simplifyingness of $\mathcal{R}$ is equivalent to termination of the 3-CTRS $\mathcal{R}_q \cup \mathcal{E}mb(\mathcal{F})$ (Proposition 7.2.63). The following two methods, however, are more relevant in practice because they can be used in combination with well-known standard techniques like recursive path orderings: In order to show quasi-simplifyingness, it is sufficient to prove simple termination of the TRS $U(\mathcal{R})$ (Proposition 7.2.64) or of the TRS $(\overline{\mathcal{R}})_s$ (Proposition 7.2.68 in conjunction with Lemma 7.2.6). The results on quasi-simplifyingness were first reported in [Ohl99a].

7.3 Confluence of Terminating Systems

In this section we will address the problem of proving confluence of effectively terminating CTRSs. As in the unconditional case, (conditional) critical pairs play a crucial role in this context.

The critical pair lemma (Lemma 4.2.3) does not hold for normal 1-CTRSs, as the following example taken from [Mid90, example 1.3.13] shows.

Example 7.3.1 In the normal 1-CTRS

$$\mathcal{R} = \begin{cases} a & \rightarrow & b \\ c & \rightarrow & f(a) \\ f(a) & \rightarrow & c \\ c & \rightarrow & g(b) \\ f(x) & \rightarrow & g(x) & \Leftarrow f(x) \rightarrow g(b) \end{cases}$$

every conditional critical pair is joinable but $\mathcal{R}$ is not locally confluent. This is because $f(a) \rightarrow_{\mathcal{R}} f(b)$ and $f(a) \rightarrow_{\mathcal{R}} g(a)$ but $f(b)$ and $g(a)$ are not joinable.

Nonetheless, a kind of critical pair lemma holds for quasi-decreasing strongly deterministic 3-CTRSs.

Theorem 7.3.2 *Every quasi-decreasing strongly deterministic 3-CTRS with joinable conditional critical pairs is confluent.*

Proof The theorem has been proven for quasi-reductive systems in [ALS94, Theorem 4.1], and the proof applies to quasi-decreasing systems. □

Because every decreasing normal 1-CTRS can be viewed as a quasi-decreasing strongly deterministic 3-CTRS, it directly follows that every decreasing normal 1-CTRS with joinable conditional critical pairs is confluent.[11]

---

[11] This criterion, however, does not guarantee level-confluence; see [SMI95] for a counterexample.

The preceding theorem does not hold for CTRSs that are not strongly deterministic as the next example taken from [SMI95, counterexample 3.3] shows.

Example 7.3.3

$$\mathcal{R} = \left\{ \begin{array}{lll} a & \to b & \\ f(x) & \to c & \Leftarrow x \to a \end{array} \right.$$

The system $\mathcal{R}$ is a 1-CTRS and thus is deterministic. It is (quasi-)decreasing and there are no critical pairs at all. The term $f(a)$ rewrites to $f(b)$ and c but these terms do not have a common reduct because they are normal forms.

Dershowitz et al. [DOS88, theorem 3.8] first showed the next result, which turns out to be a corollary to Theorem 7.3.2.

Corollary 7.3.4 *A decreasing join 1-CTRS is convergent if and only if all its conditional critical pairs are joinable.*

Proof It is sufficient to show that a decreasing join 1-CTRS $\mathcal{R}$ with joinable conditional critical pairs is confluent. Let $o(\mathcal{R})$ be the transformed 3-CTRS according to Definition 7.2.43. According to Lemma 7.2.44, $o(\mathcal{R})$ is a syntactically deterministic quasi-decreasing system. We will show that every conditional critical pair in $o(\mathcal{R})$ is joinable. It then follows from Theorem 7.3.2 that $\mathcal{R}$ is confluent because $\to_{\mathcal{R}} = \to_{o(\mathcal{R})}$ according to Lemma 7.2.44. Let $\rho : l \to r \Leftarrow s_1 \downarrow t_1, \ldots, s_k \downarrow t_k$ and $\rho' : l' \to r' \Leftarrow s'_1 \downarrow t'_1, \ldots, s'_{k'} \downarrow t'_{k'}$ be renamed versions of rewrite rules of $\mathcal{R}$ such that they have no variables in common. Suppose $o(\rho) = l \to r \Leftarrow s_1 \to x_1, t_1 \to x_1, \ldots, s_k \to x_k, t_k \to x_k$ and $o(\rho') = l' \to r' \Leftarrow s'_1 \to x'_1, t'_1 \to x'_1, \ldots, s'_{k'} \to x'_{k'}, t'_{k'} \to x'_{k'}$ give rise to the conditional critical pair

$$\begin{array}{rl} \langle s, t \rangle \Leftarrow & s_1\sigma \to x_1, t_1\sigma \to x_1, \ldots, s_k\sigma \to x_k, t_k\sigma \to x_k, \\ & s'_1\sigma \to x'_1, t'_1\sigma \to x'_1, \ldots, s'_{k'}\sigma \to x'_{k'}, t'_{k'}\sigma \to x'_{k'} \end{array}$$

Let τ be a substitution such that $s_1\sigma\tau \to^*_{o(\mathcal{R})} x_1\tau$, $t_1\sigma\tau \to^*_{o(\mathcal{R})} x_1\tau$, $\ldots$, $s_k\sigma\tau \to^*_{o(\mathcal{R})} x_k\tau$, $t_k\sigma\tau \to^*_{o(\mathcal{R})} x_k\tau$, $s'_1\sigma\tau \to^*_{o(\mathcal{R})} x'_1\tau$, $t'_1\sigma\tau \to^*_{o(\mathcal{R})} x'_1\tau$, $\ldots$, $s'_{k'}\sigma\tau \to^*_{o(\mathcal{R})} x'_{k'}\tau$, $t'_{k'}\sigma\tau \to^*_{o(\mathcal{R})} x'_{k'}\tau$. It must be shown that $s\tau \downarrow_{o(\mathcal{R})} t\tau$. It is not difficult to see that $\langle s, t \rangle \Leftarrow s_1\sigma \downarrow t_1\sigma$, $\ldots$, $s_k\sigma \downarrow t_k\sigma$, $s'_1\sigma \downarrow t'_1\sigma$, $\ldots$, $s'_{k'}\sigma \downarrow t'_{k'}\sigma$ is also a conditional critical pair in $\mathcal{R}$. Moreover, for the substitution τ we have $s_1\sigma\tau \downarrow_{\mathcal{R}} t_1\sigma\tau, \ldots, s_k\sigma\tau \downarrow_{\mathcal{R}} t_k\sigma\tau, s'_1\sigma\tau \downarrow_{\mathcal{R}} t'_1\sigma\tau, \ldots$, $s'_{k'}\sigma\tau \downarrow_{\mathcal{R}} t'_{k'}\sigma\tau$, because $\to_{\mathcal{R}}$ and $\to_{o(\mathcal{R})}$ coincide by Lemma 7.2.44. Because every conditional critical pair in $\mathcal{R}$ is joinable, it follows that $s\tau \downarrow_{\mathcal{R}} t\tau$. Hence $s\tau \downarrow_{o(\mathcal{R})} t\tau$. □

However, it is known that infeasibility (hence joinability) of conditional critical pairs is in general undecidable; cf. [ALS94]. This is true even for very special simplifying normal 1-CTRSs, as we show by a small modification of Proposition 7.1.14.

With every PCP instance $P = \{(\alpha_1, \beta_1), (\alpha_2, \beta_2), \ldots, (\alpha_n, \beta_n)\}$ we associate the following CTRS

$$\mathcal{R}(P) = \begin{cases} f(nil) & \to \varepsilon & \\ f(i : is) & \to \alpha_i(f(is)) & \text{for all } 1 \le i \le n \\ g(nil) & \to \varepsilon & \\ g(i : is) & \to \beta_i(g(is)) & \text{for all } 1 \le i \le n \\ h(i : is) & \to \varepsilon & \\ h(i : is) & \to nil & \Leftarrow eq(f(i : is), g(i : is)) \to true \\ eq(\varepsilon, \varepsilon) & \to true & \\ eq(a(x), a(y)) & \to eq(x, y) & \\ eq(b(x), b(y)) & \to eq(x, y) & \end{cases}$$

over the signature $\mathcal{F} = \{a, b, \varepsilon, 1, \ldots, n, nil, :, f, g, h, eq, true\}$. The normal 1-CTRS $\mathcal{R}(P)$ is a left-linear and simplifying constructor system (apply *rpo* with precedence $h \succ_p eq \succ_p f \succ_p g \succ_p a \succ_p b \succ_p \varepsilon \succ_p true \succ_p nil$).

Proposition 7.3.5 *The following statements are equivalent:*

1. *The CCP* $\langle nil, \varepsilon\rangle \Leftarrow eq(f(i : is), g(i : is)) \to true$ *is infeasible.*
2. *The PCP instance P has no solution.*

Proof If the PCP instance P has a solution $\gamma = \alpha_{i_1}\alpha_{i_2}\ldots\alpha_{i_m}$, then $eq(f([i_1, \ldots, i_m]), g([i_1, \ldots, i_m])) \to^+_{\mathcal{R}(P)} true$ and hence the CCP is feasible. On the other hand, if the CCP is feasible, then there exists a substitution σ such that $eq(f(i : is), g(i : is))\sigma \to^+_{\mathcal{R}(P)} true$. It is easy to see that $\sigma(i : is)$ must have the form $[i_1, i_2, \ldots, i_m]$, where $1 \le i_j \le n$ and $m \ge 1$ is the length of the list $\sigma(i : is)$. Thus, $\alpha_{i_1}\alpha_{i_2}\ldots\alpha_{i_m} = \beta_{i_1}\beta_{i_2}\ldots\beta_{i_m}$ is a solution of P. □

In view of this undecidability result, one has to resort to sufficient conditions that ensure that CCPs are joinable or infeasible. We refer to Gonzáles-Moreno et al. [GMHGRA92] and to Avenhaus and Loría-Sáenz [ALS94] for such criteria, but apart from these papers very little is known about this topic. For example, none of the aforementioned criteria can prove infeasibility of the CCP from Example 7.1.9.

7.4 Orthogonal Systems

In this section we will study CTRSs, which are confluent independently of (effective) termination. Throughout the section, every CTRS is assumed to be orthogonal unless stated otherwise. To show that every orthogonal

CTRS is level-confluent, it suffices to show that these systems satisfy the parallel moves property. This notion was coined by Yamada [Yam01]. As a matter of fact, we will follow his presentation.

Definition 7.4.1 Let $\mathcal{R}$ be a CTRS. We write $s \twoheadrightarrow\!\!\!\!\!\shortmid\,_{\mathcal{R}_n} t$ if t can be obtained from s by contracting a (possibly empty) set of pairwise disjoint redexes in s by $\mathcal{R}_n$. We write $s \twoheadrightarrow\!\!\!\!\!\shortmid\, t$ if $s \twoheadrightarrow\!\!\!\!\!\shortmid\,_{\mathcal{R}_n} t$ for some $n \in \mathbb{N}$. The minimum such n is called the depth of $s \twoheadrightarrow\!\!\!\!\!\shortmid\, t$. The relation $\twoheadrightarrow\!\!\!\!\!\shortmid$ is called *parallel rewrite relation.*

Definition 7.4.2 Let $\mathcal{R}$ be a CTRS. We say that $\mathcal{R}_m$ and $\mathcal{R}_n$ satisfy the *parallel moves property* if $u = l\sigma \rightarrow_{\mathcal{R}_m} r\sigma = u_1$ and $u \twoheadrightarrow\!\!\!\!\!\shortmid\,_{\mathcal{R}_n} u_2$ imply the existence of a term u_3 such that $u_1 \twoheadrightarrow\!\!\!\!\!\shortmid\,_{\mathcal{R}_n} u_3$ and $u_2 \twoheadrightarrow\!\!\!\!\!\shortmid\,_{\mathcal{R}_m} u_3$.

Proposition 7.4.3 *For all $\ell \in \mathbb{N}$, the following statements are equivalent:*

1. *For all m, n with $m + n \leq \ell$, $\mathcal{R}_m$ and $\mathcal{R}_n$ satisfy the parallel moves property.*
2. *For all m, n with $m + n \leq \ell$, $\twoheadrightarrow\!\!\!\!\!\shortmid\,_{\mathcal{R}_m}$ subcommutes with $\twoheadrightarrow\!\!\!\!\!\shortmid\,_{\mathcal{R}_n}$.*

Proof The implication (2) $\Rightarrow$ (1) is obvious. In order to prove the converse implication, we have to show for all m, n with $m + n \leq \ell$: If $u \twoheadrightarrow\!\!\!\!\!\shortmid\,_{\mathcal{R}_m} u_1$ and $u \twoheadrightarrow\!\!\!\!\!\shortmid\,_{\mathcal{R}_n} u_2$, then there is a term u_3 such that $u_1 \twoheadrightarrow\!\!\!\!\!\shortmid\,_{\mathcal{R}_n} u_3$ and $u_2 \twoheadrightarrow\!\!\!\!\!\shortmid\,_{\mathcal{R}_m} u_3$. The proof proceeds by induction on the structure of u and case analysis. If $u = u_1$, then take $u_3 = u_2$. (Analogously, if $u = u_2$, then take $u_3 = u_1$.) If $u = l\sigma \rightarrow_{\mathcal{R}_m} r\sigma = u_1$ or $u = l'\sigma' \rightarrow_{\mathcal{R}_n} r'\sigma' = u_2$, then the claim follows from (1) because $m + n \leq \ell$. If the redexes contracted in both $u \twoheadrightarrow\!\!\!\!\!\shortmid\,_{\mathcal{R}_m} u_1$ and $u \twoheadrightarrow\!\!\!\!\!\shortmid\,_{\mathcal{R}_n} u_2$ are strictly below the root position, then we may write $u = f(s_1, \ldots, s_j)$, $u_1 = f(t_1, \ldots, t_j)$, and $u_2 = f(v_1, \ldots, v_j)$ for some $j \geq 1$, where s_i reduces to t_i (v_i) in one parallel $\mathcal{R}_{m_i}$ step ($\mathcal{R}_{n_i}$ step) with $m_i \leq m$ ($n_i \leq n$). Because $m_i + n_i \leq m + n \leq \ell$, we infer from the inductive hypothesis that there are terms $w_1, \ldots, w_j$ such that t_i (v_i) reduces to w_i in one parallel $\mathcal{R}_{n_i}$ step ($\mathcal{R}_{m_i}$ step). Let $u_3 = f(w_1, \ldots, w_j)$. Then $u_1 \twoheadrightarrow\!\!\!\!\!\shortmid\,_{\mathcal{R}_n} u_3$ and $u_2 \twoheadrightarrow\!\!\!\!\!\shortmid\,_{\mathcal{R}_m} u_3$. □

Corollary 7.4.4 *Let $\mathcal{R}$ be a CTRS. If, for all $m, n \in \mathbb{N}$, the systems $\mathcal{R}_m$ and $\mathcal{R}_n$ satisfy the parallel moves property, then $\mathcal{R}$ is level-confluent.*

Proof According to Proposition 7.4.3, $\twoheadrightarrow\!\!\!\!\!\shortmid\,_{\mathcal{R}_m}$ subcommutes with $\twoheadrightarrow\!\!\!\!\!\shortmid\,_{\mathcal{R}_n}$ for all $m, n \in \mathbb{N}$. In particular, $\twoheadrightarrow\!\!\!\!\!\shortmid\,_{\mathcal{R}_m}$ is subcommutative for all $m \in \mathbb{N}$. This means that $\twoheadrightarrow\!\!\!\!\!\shortmid\,_{\mathcal{R}_m}$ has the diamond property because it is reflexive. Because $\rightarrow_{\mathcal{R}_m} \subseteq \twoheadrightarrow\!\!\!\!\!\shortmid\,_{\mathcal{R}_m} \subseteq \rightarrow^*_{\mathcal{R}_m}$, it follows from Lemma 2.4.2 that $\mathcal{R}_m$ is confluent. Hence $\mathcal{R}$ is level-confluent. □

7.4.1 Normal 2-CTRSs

We start with a result from Bergstra and Klop [BK86]. They have shown that orthogonal normal 2-CTRSs satisfy the parallel moves lemma. Hence these systems are confluent. In fact, they are level-confluent as was first observed by Giovannetti and Moiso [GM86]. The "normal" requirement cannot be dropped, as Example 7.3.3 shows.

Lemma 7.4.5 *If $\mathcal{R}$ is an almost orthogonal normal 2-CTRS, then $\mathcal{R}_m$ and $\mathcal{R}_n$ satisfy the parallel moves property for all $m, n \in \mathbb{N}$.*

Proof It must be shown that $u = l\sigma \rightarrow_{\mathcal{R}_m} r\sigma = u_1$ and $u \mathrel{+\!\!\!\!\!\!\rightarrow}_{\mathcal{R}_n} u_2$ imply the existence of a term u_3 such that $u_1 \mathrel{+\!\!\!\!\!\!\rightarrow}_{\mathcal{R}_n} u_3$ and $u_2 \mathrel{+\!\!\!\!\!\!\rightarrow}_{\mathcal{R}_m} u_3$.

Let $u = l\sigma \rightarrow_{\mathcal{R}_m} r\sigma = u_1$ by the conditional rewrite rule $\rho : l \rightarrow r \Leftarrow s_1 \rightarrow t_1, \ldots, s_k \rightarrow t_k \in \mathcal{R}$, that is, $s_i\sigma \mathrel{+\!\!\!\!\!\!\rightarrow}^*_{\mathcal{R}_{m-1}} t_i$ for all $1 \leq i \leq k$. The proof proceeds by induction on $\ell = m + n$. The base case $m + n = 0$ holds vacuously. Suppose the lemma holds for all m' and n' with $m' + n' < \ell$. In the induction step, we have to prove that the lemma holds for all m and n with $m + n = \ell$. If $u = l'\sigma' \rightarrow_{\mathcal{R}_n} r'\sigma' = u_2$ is also a rewrite step at the root of u, then we infer $u_1 = r\sigma = r'\sigma' = u_2$ because $\mathcal{R}$ is an almost orthogonal normal 2-CTRS. Otherwise u does not rewrite to u_2 by a root rewrite step. Let $v_1, \ldots, v_j$ be the redexes contracted in $u \mathrel{+\!\!\!\!\!\!\rightarrow}_{\mathcal{R}_n} u_2$ to the terms $v'_1, \ldots, v'_j$. For every v_i, $1 \leq i \leq j$, there is a variable $x \in \mathcal{V}ar(l)$ such that v_i is a subterm of $x\sigma$ because $\mathcal{R}$ is almost orthogonal. So $x\sigma = C[v_{i_1}, \ldots, v_{i_p}]$ for some context $C[\,]$ and indices $i_1, \ldots, i_p \in \{1, \ldots, j\}$. We define a substitution σ' by $x\sigma' = C[v'_{i_1}, \ldots, v'_{i_p}]$ whenever $x \in \mathcal{V}ar(l)$ and $y\sigma' = y\sigma$ for all extra variables $y \in (\bigcup_{i=1}^k \mathcal{V}ar(s_i)) \setminus \mathcal{V}ar(l)$ of the rule ρ. Note that $u_2 = l\sigma'$ because ρ is left-linear, and $u_1 = r\sigma \mathrel{+\!\!\!\!\!\!\rightarrow}_{\mathcal{R}_n} r\sigma'$ because $\mathcal{V}ar(r) \subseteq \mathcal{V}ar(l)$.

Next we show that $u_2 = l\sigma' \mathrel{+\!\!\!\!\!\!\rightarrow}_{\mathcal{R}_m} r\sigma'$, i.e., $u_3 = r\sigma'$ is the term we are looking for. To this end, we have to prove that $s_i\sigma' \mathrel{+\!\!\!\!\!\!\rightarrow}^*_{\mathcal{R}_{m-1}} t_i$ for all $1 \leq i \leq k$. Because $s_i\sigma \mathrel{+\!\!\!\!\!\!\rightarrow}^*_{\mathcal{R}_n} s_i\sigma'$ and $s_i\sigma \mathrel{+\!\!\!\!\!\!\rightarrow}^*_{\mathcal{R}_{m-1}} t_i$ for all $1 \leq i \leq k$, we conclude from the inductive hypothesis that $s_i\sigma' \mathrel{+\!\!\!\!\!\!\rightarrow}^*_{\mathcal{R}_{m-1}} t_i$ (note that t_i is a ground $\mathcal{R}_u$ normal form). □

It can readily be seen that we may also allow infeasible conditional critical pairs in the preceding lemma.

Corollary 7.4.6 *Every almost orthogonal normal 2-CTRS $\mathcal{R}$ is level-confluent.*

Proof This is a consequence of Corollary 7.4.4 and Lemma 7.4.5. □

It is a bit surprising that a similar statement does not hold for join systems. This can be seen in the following example taken from [BK86, example 3.6].

Example 7.4.7

$$\mathcal{R} = \left\{ \begin{array}{lll} a & \rightarrow f(a) & \\ f(x) & \rightarrow b & \Leftarrow x \downarrow f(x) \end{array} \right.$$

The system $\mathcal{R}$ is obviously orthogonal. The term $f(a)$ rewrites to b because a and $f(a)$ are joinable. This implies $f(f(a)) \to_{\mathcal{R}} f(b)$. Apparently, we also have $f(f(a)) \to_{\mathcal{R}} b$. But the terms $f(b)$ and b do not have a common reduct.

7.4.2 Almost Normal 2-CTRSs

We have seen that almost orthogonal normal 2-CTRSs satisfy the parallel moves lemma. Next we will generalize this result by relaxing the ground normal form requirement for every t_i.

Definition 7.4.8 A CTRS $\mathcal{R}$ is called

- *right-stable* if every rewrite rule $l \to r \Leftarrow s_1 = t_1, \ldots, s_k = t_k$ in $\mathcal{R}$ satisfies the following conditions for all $i \in \{1, \ldots, k\}$:

$$(\mathcal{V}ar(l) \cup \bigcup_{j=1}^{i-1} \mathcal{V}ar(s_j = t_j) \cup \mathcal{V}ar(s_i)) \cap \mathcal{V}ar(t_i) = \emptyset$$

  and t_i is either a linear constructor term or a ground $\mathcal{R}_u$ normal form (note that every variable $y \in \bigcup_{i=1}^{k} \mathcal{V}ar(t_i)$ is an extra variable, i.e., y does not occur in l); and

- *almost normal* if it is right-stable and oriented.

Note that every normal CTRS is almost normal.

The following example shows that almost normal 2-CTRSs occur naturally.

Example 7.4.9 We define a function $filter$ that filters all elements out of a list of natural numbers that have remainder r when divided by n:

$$\begin{array}{rcll}
eq(0,0) & \to & true & \\
eq(s(x),0) & \to & false & \\
eq(0,s(y)) & \to & false & \\
eq(s(x),s(y)) & \to & eq(x,y) & \\
0 \leq y & \to & true & \\
s(x) \leq 0 & \to & false & \\
s(x) \leq s(y) & \to & x \leq y & \\
0 - s(y) & \to & 0 & \\
x - 0 & \to & x & \\
s(x) - s(y) & \to & x - y & \\
mod(0,y) & \to & 0 & \\
mod(s(x),0) & \to & 0 & \\
mod(s(x),s(y)) & \to & mod(x-y,s(y)) & \Leftarrow y \leq x \to true \\
mod(s(x),s(y)) & \to & s(x) & \Leftarrow y \leq x \to false
\end{array}$$

$$\begin{array}{rcl} filter(n,r,nil) & \to & nil \\ filter(n,r,x:xs) & \to & x:filter(n,r,xs) \\ & & \Leftarrow mod(x,n) \to r', eq(r,r') \to true \\ filter(n,r,x:xs) & \to & filter(n,r,xs) \\ & & \Leftarrow mod(x,n) \to r', eq(r,r') \to false \end{array}$$

These rules constitute a left-linear almost normal 2-CTRS. It has two overlays, but each creates an infeasible critical pair.

Lemma 7.4.10 *If $\mathcal{R}$ is an almost orthogonal almost normal 2-CTRS, then $\mathcal{R}_m$ and $\mathcal{R}_n$ satisfy the parallel moves property for all $m, n \in \mathbb{N}$.*

Proof The beginning of the proof is the same as that of Lemma 7.4.5. Only the definition of σ' on the extra variables $y \in \bigcup_{i=1}^{k} \mathcal{V}ar(t_i)$ of the rule ρ needs some modifications. So let the substitution σ_1' be defined on $(\mathcal{V}ar(l) \cup \bigcup_{i=1}^{k} \mathcal{V}ar(s_i)) \setminus \bigcup_{i=1}^{k} \mathcal{V}ar(t_i)$ as the substitution σ' in Lemma 7.4.5. Note that $u_2 = l\sigma_1'$ because ρ is left-linear and $u_1 = r\sigma \mathrel{+\!\!\!\!\!\!\;+\!\!\!\!\!\to}_{\mathcal{R}_n} r\sigma_1' = u_3$ because $\mathcal{V}ar(r) \subseteq \mathcal{V}ar(l)$.

In order to show that $u_2 \mathrel{+\!\!\!\!\!\!\;+\!\!\!\!\!\to}_{\mathcal{R}_m} u_3$, we show how σ_1' can be extended to a substitution σ' with $\mathcal{D}om(\sigma') = \mathcal{V}ar(\rho)$ such that $s_i\sigma' \mathrel{+\!\!\!\!\!\!\;+\!\!\!\!\!\to}^*_{\mathcal{R}_{m-1}} t_i\sigma'$ for all $1 \le i \le k$. (It then follows that $u_2 = l\sigma' \to_{\mathcal{R}_m} r\sigma' = u_3$.) According to the inductive hypothesis on ℓ in combination with $s_1\sigma \mathrel{+\!\!\!\!\!\!\;+\!\!\!\!\!\to}^*_{\mathcal{R}_{m-1}} t_1\sigma$ and $s_1\sigma \mathrel{+\!\!\!\!\!\!\;+\!\!\!\!\!\to}_{\mathcal{R}_n} s_1\sigma_1'$, there is a term w such that $s_1\sigma_1' \mathrel{+\!\!\!\!\!\!\;+\!\!\!\!\!\to}^*_{\mathcal{R}_{m-1}} w$ and $t_1\sigma \mathrel{+\!\!\!\!\!\!\;+\!\!\!\!\!\to}_{\mathcal{R}_n} w$.

Because t_1 is a linear constructor term and $(\mathcal{V}ar(l) \cup \mathcal{V}ar(s_1)) \cap \mathcal{V}ar(t_1) = \emptyset$, it follows that $w = t_1\tau$ for some substitution τ with $\mathcal{D}om(\tau) = \mathcal{V}ar(t_1)$. Note that $z\sigma \mathrel{+\!\!\!\!\!\!\;+\!\!\!\!\!\to}_{\mathcal{R}_n} z\tau$ for all $z \in \mathcal{V}ar(t_1)$. We define σ_2' by

$$x\sigma_2' = \begin{cases} x\sigma_1' & \text{if } x \in (\mathcal{V}ar(l) \cup \bigcup_{i=1}^{k} \mathcal{V}ar(s_i)) \setminus \bigcup_{i=1}^{k} \mathcal{V}ar(t_i) \\ x\tau & \text{if } x \in \mathcal{V}ar(t_1) \end{cases}$$

Notice that we now have $s_2\sigma \mathrel{+\!\!\!\!\!\!\;+\!\!\!\!\!\to}_{\mathcal{R}_n} s_2\sigma_2'$. By continuing with the preceding reasoning, we can successively extend σ_i' to σ_{i+1}' for $1 \le i < k$ such that eventually $s_i\sigma' \mathrel{+\!\!\!\!\!\!\;+\!\!\!\!\!\to}^*_{\mathcal{R}_{m-1}} t_i\sigma'$ for all $1 \le i \le k$, where $\sigma' = \sigma_k'$. All in all, $u_2 = l\sigma' \to_{\mathcal{R}_m} r\sigma' = u_3$. □

Analogous to Lemma 7.4.5, one may allow infeasible conditional critical pairs in the preceding lemma.

Corollary 7.4.11 *Every almost orthogonal almost normal 2-CTRS $\mathcal{R}$ is level-confluent.*

Proof The corollary is an immediate consequence of Corollary 7.4.4 in conjunction with Lemma 7.4.10. □

Because Corollary 7.4.11 also holds true in the presence of infeasible conditional critical pairs, it follows that the CTRS from Example 7.4.9 is level-confluent.

7.4.3 Level-Confluence for 3-CTRSs

Orthogonal almost normal 3-CTRSs do not satisfy the parallel moves lemma, as the following simple example taken from [SMI95, example 4.4] shows.

Example 7.4.12 Let

$$\mathcal{R} = \begin{cases} f(x) \to y & \Leftarrow x \to y \\ a \to b \\ b \to c \end{cases}$$

Then $f(a) \mathrel{+\!\!\!\!\!\!\twoheadrightarrow}_{\mathcal{R}_1} a$ and $f(a) \mathrel{+\!\!\!\!\!\!\twoheadrightarrow}_{\mathcal{R}_2} c$ but not $a \mathrel{+\!\!\!\!\!\!\twoheadrightarrow}_{\mathcal{R}_2} c$.

Note that $\mathcal{R}$ is a quasi-decreasing strongly deterministic 3-CTRS. Thus it is confluent by Theorem 7.3.2. Next we will review a criterion that shows level-confluence of 3-CTRSs like $\mathcal{R}$. Of course, one has to make sure that the extra variables on the right-hand sides of the rules are bound during the evaluation of the conditions.

Definition 7.4.13 An arbitrary 3-CTRS $\mathcal{R}$ is called *properly oriented* if every rule $l \to r \Leftarrow s_1 = t_1, \ldots, s_k = t_k$ in $\mathcal{R}$ satisfies: If $\mathcal{V}ar(r) \not\subseteq \mathcal{V}ar(l)$, then $\mathcal{V}ar(s_i) \subseteq \mathcal{V}ar(l) \cup \bigcup_{j=1}^{i-1} \mathcal{V}ar(t_j)$ for all $1 \le i \le k$.

In contrast to deterministic 3-CTRSs, it is not required that $\mathcal{V}ar(s_i) \subseteq \mathcal{V}ar(l) \cup \bigcup_{j=1}^{i-1} \mathcal{V}ar(t_j)$ holds for all $1 \le i \le k$ when the right-hand side r of a rule $l \to r \Leftarrow s_1 \to t_1, \ldots, s_k \to t_k$ does not contain extra variables. Therefore, every deterministic 3-CTRS is properly oriented but not vice versa.

By using an extended parallel rewrite relation, Suzuki et al. [SMI95] showed the following theorem.

Theorem 7.4.14 *Every orthogonal properly oriented right-stable 3-CTRS is level-confluent.*

Proof See [SMI95, theorem 4.6]. □

The theorem also holds for join systems and it can be extended in several ways. First, it can be generalized to almost orthogonal systems (note, however, that at most rules of type 2 may overlay). Second, one may allow infeasible critical pairs. Third, the theorem holds true for *extended properly oriented* systems; see [SMI95, definition 7.1].

Note that Corollary 7.4.11 is also a corollary to (the extended version of) Theorem 7.4.14.

7.4.4 CTRSs with Strict Equality

In this section we are interested in CTRSs in which the conditions of a rule are interpreted as "being terms that are reducible to a common ground constructor term." These systems play a fundamental role in functional-logic programming.

Definition 7.4.15 In a 3-CTRS $(\mathcal{F}, \mathcal{R})$ *with strict equality* the $=$ symbol in the conditions of the rewrite rules is interpreted as: the terms in the conditions are reducible to a common ground constructor term in $\mathcal{R}$. That is, the rewrite relation $\rightarrow_{\mathcal{R}}$ associated with $\mathcal{R}$ is defined by $\rightarrow_{\mathcal{R}} = \bigcup_{n \geq 0} \rightarrow_{\mathcal{R}_n}$, where $\rightarrow_{\mathcal{R}_0} = \emptyset$ and $s \rightarrow_{\mathcal{R}_{n+1}} t$ if and only if there exists a rewrite rule $\rho : l \rightarrow r \Leftarrow s_1 = t_1, \ldots, s_k = t_k$ in $\mathcal{R}$, a substitution $\sigma : \mathcal{V} \rightarrow \mathcal{T}(\mathcal{F}, \mathcal{V})$ with $\mathcal{D}om(\sigma) = \mathcal{V}ar(\rho)$, a context $C[\,]$, and ground constructor terms $u_1, \ldots, u_k$ such that $s = C[l\sigma]$, $t = C[r\sigma]$, $s_i\sigma \rightarrow^*_{\mathcal{R}_n} u_i$, and $t_i\sigma \rightarrow^*_{\mathcal{R}_n} u_i$ for all $1 \leq i \leq k$.

Proposition 7.4.16 *Let $(\mathcal{F}, \mathcal{R})$ be a CTRS with strict equality. The following statements are equivalent for all terms s and t in $\mathcal{T}(\mathcal{F}, \mathcal{V})$:*

a. *s and t are reducible to a common ground constructor term in $(\mathcal{F}, \mathcal{R})$,*

b. *$s == t$ is reducible to true in the normal CTRS $(\mathcal{F} \uplus \mathcal{F}_{eq}, \mathcal{R}' \uplus \mathcal{R}_{eq})$, where $\mathcal{F}_{eq}$, $\mathcal{R}_{eq}$, and $\mathcal{R}'$ are defined as follows:*

   1. *$\mathcal{F}_{eq} = \{==, \wedge, true, false\}$, and $\wedge$ is assumed to be right-associative.*

   2. *The TRS $\mathcal{R}_{eq}$ consists of the rules (where $c, d \in \mathcal{C}$ are distinct constructors of $\mathcal{R}$)*

$$\begin{array}{rcl} c == c & \rightarrow & true \\ c == d & \rightarrow & false \\ c(x_1, \ldots, x_n) == c(y_1, \ldots, y_n) & \rightarrow & \bigwedge_{i=1}^{n} (x_i == y_i) \\ c(x_1, \ldots, x_n) == d(y_1, \ldots, y_m) & \rightarrow & false \\ true \wedge x & \rightarrow & x \\ false \wedge x & \rightarrow & false \end{array}$$

   3. $\mathcal{R}' = \{l \rightarrow r \Leftarrow s_1 == t_1 \rightarrow true, \ldots, s_k == t_k \rightarrow true \mid l \rightarrow r \Leftarrow s_1 = t_1, \ldots, s_k = t_k \in \mathcal{R}\}$.

Proof The proof is similar to the proof for unconditional TRSs; see [AEH94]. □

According to the preceding proposition, every CTRS with strict equality can be viewed as a normal CTRS. From now on, rewrite rules of a CTRS with strict equality will be written as $l \rightarrow r \Leftarrow s_1 == t_1, \ldots, s_k == t_k$.

Definition 7.4.17 A 3-CTRS $\mathcal{R}$ with strict equality is called *almost functional* if it is orthogonal and every rule $l \rightarrow r \Leftarrow s_1 == t_1, \ldots, s_k == t_k$ in $\mathcal{R}$ satisfies:

1. If $\mathcal{V}ar(r) \not\subseteq \mathcal{V}ar(l)$, then $\mathcal{V}ar(s_i) \subseteq \mathcal{V}ar(l) \cup \bigcup_{j=1}^{i-1} \mathcal{V}ar(t_j)$ for all $1 \leq i \leq k$.

2. Every t_j, $1 \leq j \leq k$, is a constructor term.

The reader may wonder why the term "almost functional" is used for the preceding class of CTRSs. We have chosen this name because in our opinion the following CTRSs should be called "functional."

An almost functional 3-CTRS $\mathcal{R}$ is called *functional* if every rule $l \to r \Leftarrow s_1 == t_1, \ldots, s_k == t_k$ in $\mathcal{R}$ satisfies:

1. $(\mathcal{V}ar(l) \cup \bigcup_{j=1}^{i-1} \mathcal{V}ar(s_j = t_j) \cup \mathcal{V}ar(s_i)) \cap \mathcal{V}ar(t_i) = \emptyset$ for all $1 \leq i \leq k$.

2. Every t_j, $1 \leq j \leq k$, is a *linear* constructor term.

For example, the Fibonacci system $\mathcal{R}_{fib}$ from Example 7.2.65 regarded as a 3-CTRS with strict equality is a functional system.

Note that a functional system must satisfy almost the same conditions as an orthogonal properly oriented right-stable 3-CTRS. Therefore, it is not surprising that functional CTRSs do not satisfy the parallel moves lemma. This can be seen in the following variant of Example 7.4.12:

$$\mathcal{R} = \begin{cases} f(x) \to y \Leftarrow x == y \\ a \to b \\ b \to c \end{cases}$$

Here $f(a) \Downarrow\!\!\!\!\!\!\not\;\;\; _{\mathcal{R}_2} a$ and $f(a) \Downarrow\!\!\!\!\!\!\not\;\;\; _{\mathcal{R}_2} c$ but not $a \Downarrow\!\!\!\!\!\!\not\;\;\; _{\mathcal{R}_2} c$.

Next we introduce a special "deterministic" rewrite relation $\to_{\mathcal{R}^d}$ that is closely related to $\to_{\mathcal{R}}$ (the only difference is that in $\to_{\mathcal{R}^d}$ extra variables on right-hand sides must be instantiated by ground constructor terms).

Definition 7.4.18 Let $\mathcal{R}$ be an almost functional CTRS. Let $\to_{\mathcal{R}^d_0} = \emptyset$ and for $n > 0$ define $s \to_{\mathcal{R}^d_n} t$ if there exists a rewrite rule $\rho : l \to r \Leftarrow s_1 == t_1, \ldots, s_k == t_k$ in $\mathcal{R}$, a substitution $\sigma : \mathcal{V} \to \mathcal{T}(\mathcal{F}, \mathcal{V})$ with $\mathcal{D}om(\sigma) = \mathcal{V}ar(\rho)$, a context $C[\,]$, and ground constructor terms $u_1, \ldots, u_k$ such that $s = C[l\sigma]$, $t = C[r\sigma]$, $s_i\sigma \to^*_{\mathcal{R}^d_{n-1}} u_i$ and $t_i\sigma \to^*_{\mathcal{R}^d_{n-1}} u_i$ for all $1 \leq i \leq k$, and $x\sigma$ must be a ground constructor term for every $x \in \mathcal{EV}ar(\rho)$. Finally, define $\to_{\mathcal{R}^d} = \bigcup_{n \geq 0} \to_{\mathcal{R}^d_n}$.

For example, in the CTRS $\mathcal{R}$ defined earlier we have $f(a) \to_{\mathcal{R}^d} c$, but neither $f(a) \to_{\mathcal{R}^d} a$ nor $f(a) \to_{\mathcal{R}^d} b$.

It is easy to prove (by induction on the depth n) that $s \to_{\mathcal{R}^d_n} t$ implies $s \to_{\mathcal{R}_n} t$ but not vice versa. The first statement of the next lemma shows that $\to_{\mathcal{R}^d}$ is deterministic in the sense that the contractum of a redex is uniquely determined. Furthermore, in contrast to $\to_{\mathcal{R}}$, the relation $\to_{\mathcal{R}^d}$ satisfies the parallel moves lemma. Due to the first statement of Lemma 7.4.19, there is a strong resemblance between the proof of the second statement and that of Lemma 7.4.5.

Lemma 7.4.19 *Let $\mathcal{R}$ be almost functional. For all $m, n \in \mathbb{N}$, the following holds:*

1. *If $s = l_1\sigma_1 \rightarrow_{\mathcal{R}^d_m} r_1\sigma_1$ and $s = l_2\sigma_2 \rightarrow_{\mathcal{R}^d_n} r_2\sigma_2$, then $r_1\sigma_1 = r_2\sigma_2$.*

2. *If $u \mathrel{\|\!\!\!\rightarrow}_{\mathcal{R}^d_m} u_1$ and $u \mathrel{\|\!\!\!\rightarrow}_{\mathcal{R}^d_n} u_2$, then there is a term u_3 such that $u_1 \mathrel{\|\!\!\!\rightarrow}_{\mathcal{R}^d_n} u_3$ and $u_2 \mathrel{\|\!\!\!\rightarrow}_{\mathcal{R}^d_m} u_3$.*

Proof The proof proceeds by induction on $m+n$. The base case $m+n=0$ holds vacuously. Suppose the lemma holds for all m' and n' with $m'+n' < \ell$. In the induction step, we have to prove that the lemma holds for all m and n with $m+n=\ell$.

(1) Suppose $s = l_1\sigma_1 \rightarrow_{\mathcal{R}^d_m} r_1\sigma_1$ and $s = l_2\sigma_2 \rightarrow_{\mathcal{R}^d_n} r_2\sigma_2$. Because $\mathcal{R}$ is orthogonal, the rewrite rules coincide and will be denoted by $\rho : l \rightarrow r \Leftarrow s_1 == t_1, \ldots, s_k == t_k$ in what follows. Obviously, $\sigma_1 = \sigma_2\ [\mathcal{V}ar(l)]$, i.e., the restrictions of σ_1 and σ_2 to $\mathcal{V}ar(l)$ coincide. So if $\mathcal{V}ar(r) \subseteq \mathcal{V}ar(l)$, then $r_1\sigma_1 = r_2\sigma_2$. Suppose otherwise that $\mathcal{V}ar(r) \not\subseteq \mathcal{V}ar(l)$. We show by induction on i that $\sigma_1 = \sigma_2\ [\mathcal{V}ar(l) \cup \bigcup_{j=1}^{i} \mathcal{V}ar(t_j)]$. It then follows $\sigma_1 = \sigma_2\ [\mathcal{V}ar(\rho)]$ and hence $r_1\sigma_1 = r_2\sigma_2$. If $i = 0$, then $\sigma_1 = \sigma_2\ [\mathcal{V}ar(l)]$. Let $i > 0$. According to the inductive hypothesis, $\sigma_1 = \sigma_2\ [\mathcal{V}ar(l) \cup \bigcup_{j=1}^{i-1} \mathcal{V}ar(t_j)]$. Because $\mathcal{V}ar(s_i) \subseteq \mathcal{V}ar(l) \cup \bigcup_{j=1}^{i-1} \mathcal{V}ar(t_j)$, it is sufficient to show that $\sigma_1 = \sigma_2\ [\mathcal{V}ar(t_i)]$. By definition of $\mathrel{\|\!\!\!\rightarrow}_{\mathcal{R}^d_m}$ and $\mathrel{\|\!\!\!\rightarrow}_{\mathcal{R}^d_n}$, there exist ground constructor terms v_1 and v_2 such that $s_i\sigma_1 \rightarrow^*_{\mathcal{R}^d_{m-1}} v_1 \;{}^*_{\mathcal{R}^d_{m-1}}\!\leftarrow t_i\sigma_1$ and $s_i\sigma_2 \rightarrow^*_{\mathcal{R}^d_{n-1}} v_2 \;{}^*_{\mathcal{R}^d_{n-1}}\!\leftarrow t_i\sigma_2$. It is an immediate consequence of $s_i\sigma_1 = s_i\sigma_2$, $s_i\sigma_1 \mathrel{\|\!\!\!\rightarrow}^*_{\mathcal{R}^d_{m-1}} v_1$, $s_i\sigma_2 \mathrel{\|\!\!\!\rightarrow}^*_{\mathcal{R}^d_{n-1}} v_2$, and the inductive hypothesis on ℓ that the two ground normal forms v_1 and v_2 coincide. Hence $t_i\sigma_1 \rightarrow^*_{\mathcal{R}^d_{m-1}} v_1 \;{}^*_{\mathcal{R}^d_{n-1}}\!\leftarrow t_i\sigma_2$. Observe that for every variable $x \in \mathcal{V}ar(t_i) \setminus (\mathcal{V}ar(l) \cup \bigcup_{j=1}^{i-1} \mathcal{V}ar(t_j))$, it follows from the definition of $\rightarrow^*_{\mathcal{R}^d_{m-1}}$ and $\rightarrow^*_{\mathcal{R}^d_{n-1}}$ that $x\sigma_1$ and $x\sigma_2$ are ground constructor terms because $x \in \mathcal{EV}ar(\rho)$. Therefore, the fact that t_i is a constructor term implies $x\sigma_1 = x\sigma_2$.

(2) By Proposition 7.4.3, it is sufficient to show that $u = l\sigma \rightarrow_{\mathcal{R}^d_m} r\sigma = u_1$ and $u \mathrel{\|\!\!\!\rightarrow}_{\mathcal{R}^d_n} u_2$ imply the existence of a term u_3 such that $u_1 \mathrel{\|\!\!\!\rightarrow}_{\mathcal{R}^d_n} u_3$ and $u_2 \mathrel{\|\!\!\!\rightarrow}_{\mathcal{R}^d_m} u_3$. We proceed as in Lemma 7.4.5. Let $u = l\sigma \rightarrow_{\mathcal{R}^d_m} r\sigma = u_1$ by the conditional rewrite rule $\rho : l \rightarrow r \Leftarrow s_1 == t_1, \ldots, s_k == t_k \in \mathcal{R}$, that is, there exist ground constructor terms w_i such that $s_i\sigma \mathrel{\|\!\!\!\rightarrow}^*_{\mathcal{R}^d_{m-1}} w_i$ and $t_i\sigma \mathrel{\|\!\!\!\rightarrow}^*_{\mathcal{R}^d_{m-1}} w_i$ for all $s_i == t_i$. If $u = l'\sigma' \rightarrow_{\mathcal{R}_n} r'\sigma' = u_2$ is also a rewrite step at the root of u, then we infer from (1) that $u_1 = r\sigma = r'\sigma' = u_2$. Otherwise u does not rewrite to u_2 by a root rewrite step. Let $v_1, \ldots, v_j$ be the redexes contracted in $u \mathrel{\|\!\!\!\rightarrow}_{\mathcal{R}^d_n} u_2$ to the terms $v'_1, \ldots, v'_j$. For every v_i, $1 \le i \le j$, there is a variable $x \in \mathcal{V}ar(l)$ such that v_i is a subterm of $x\sigma$ because $\mathcal{R}$ is orthogonal. So $x\sigma = C[v_{i_1}, \ldots, v_{i_p}]$ for some context $C[\,]$ and indices $i_1, \ldots, i_p \in \{1, \ldots, j\}$. We define a substitution σ' by $x\sigma' = C[v'_{i_1}, \ldots, v'_{i_p}]$ whenever $x \in \mathcal{V}ar(l)$ and $y\sigma' = y\sigma$ for all extra variables $y \in \mathcal{EV}ar(\rho)$.

Note that $u_2 = l\sigma'$ because ρ is left-linear, and $u_1 = r\sigma \mathrel{+\!\!\!\!\!\!\;\Vdash}_{\mathcal{R}_n} r\sigma' = u_3$. In order to show that $u_2 \mathrel{+\!\!\!\!\!\!\;\Vdash}_{\mathcal{R}^d_m} u_3$, we show $s_i\sigma' \mathrel{+\!\!\!\!\!\!\;\Vdash}^*_{\mathcal{R}^d_{m-1}} w_i$ and $t_i\sigma' \mathrel{+\!\!\!\!\!\!\;\Vdash}^*_{\mathcal{R}^d_{m-1}} w_i$. Because $s_i\sigma \mathrel{+\!\!\!\!\!\!\;\Vdash}^*_{\mathcal{R}^d_n} s_i\sigma'$, $s_i\sigma \mathrel{+\!\!\!\!\!\!\;\Vdash}^*_{\mathcal{R}^d_{m-1}} w_i$, and w_i is a normal form, it follows from the inductive hypothesis that $s_i\sigma' \mathrel{+\!\!\!\!\!\!\;\Vdash}^*_{\mathcal{R}^d_{m-1}} w_i$. Analogously, we obtain $t_i\sigma' \mathrel{+\!\!\!\!\!\!\;\Vdash}^*_{\mathcal{R}^d_{m-1}} w_i$. Hence $u_2 = l\sigma' \rightarrow_{\mathcal{R}^d_m} r\sigma' = u_3$. □

Corollary 7.4.20 *The relation $\rightarrow_{\mathcal{R}^d}$ is level-confluent (i.e., for every $n \in \mathbb{N}$, $\rightarrow_{\mathcal{R}^d_n}$ is confluent).*

Proof The proof is an immediate consequence of Lemma 7.4.19. □

In order to show that every almost functional CTRS $\mathcal{R}$ is level-confluent, we need one more proposition.

Proposition 7.4.21 *If $s \rightarrow^*_{\mathcal{R}_n} t$, then there is a term u such that $s \rightarrow^*_{\mathcal{R}^d_n} u$ and $t \rightarrow^*_{\mathcal{R}^d_n} u$.*

Proof We proceed by induction on the depth n of $s \rightarrow^*_{\mathcal{R}} t$. The proposition holds vacuously for $n = 0$. So let $n > 0$. We proceed further by induction on the length ℓ of the reduction sequence $s \rightarrow^*_{\mathcal{R}_n} t$. Again, the case $\ell = 0$ holds vacuously. Suppose the claim is true for ℓ. In order to show it for $\ell + 1$, we consider $s = C[l\sigma] \rightarrow_{\mathcal{R}_n} C[r\sigma] = t' \rightarrow^{\ell}_{\mathcal{R}_n} t$, where $s \rightarrow_{\mathcal{R}_n} t'$ by the rule $\rho : l \rightarrow r \Leftarrow s_1 == t_1, \ldots, s_k == t_k$. It follows from the inductive hypothesis on ℓ that there is a term u' such that $t' \rightarrow^*_{\mathcal{R}^d_n} u'$ and $t \rightarrow^*_{\mathcal{R}^d_n} u'$. Because $s \rightarrow_{\mathcal{R}_n} t'$, there are ground constructor terms u_i such that $s_i\sigma \rightarrow^*_{\mathcal{R}_{n-1}} u_i \;{}^*_{\mathcal{R}_{n-1}}\!\!\leftarrow t_i\sigma$. By the inductive hypothesis on n and the fact that u_i is a normal form, we conclude $s_i\sigma \rightarrow^*_{\mathcal{R}^d_{n-1}} u_i \;{}^*_{\mathcal{R}^d_{n-1}}\!\!\leftarrow t_i\sigma$. Now if $\mathcal{V}ar(r) \subseteq \mathcal{V}ar(l)$, then $s \rightarrow_{\mathcal{R}^d_n} t'$ and the claim follows. Suppose otherwise that $\mathcal{V}ar(r) \not\subseteq \mathcal{V}ar(l)$ and let $x \in \mathcal{EV}ar(\rho)$. Then $x \in \mathcal{V}ar(t_j)$ for some $s_j == t_j$. Because $t_j\sigma \rightarrow^*_{\mathcal{R}^d_{n-1}} u_j$, t_j is a constructor term, and u_j is a ground constructor term, it follows that $x\sigma \rightarrow^*_{\mathcal{R}^d_{n-1}} u_x$ for some ground constructor subterm u_x of u_j. Note that u_x is unique because $\rightarrow_{\mathcal{R}^d_{n-1}}$ is confluent ($\rightarrow_{\mathcal{R}^d}$ is level-confluent by Corollary 7.4.20). Define σ' by $x\sigma' = u_x$ for every $x \in \mathcal{EV}ar(\rho)$ and $y\sigma' = y\sigma$ otherwise. Observe that $z\sigma \rightarrow^*_{\mathcal{R}^d_{n-1}} z\sigma'$ for every variable $z \in \mathcal{D}om(\sigma)$. Let $s' = C[r\sigma']$. According to the preceding, $t' \rightarrow^*_{\mathcal{R}^d_{n-1}} s'$. Observe that also $s \rightarrow_{\mathcal{R}^d_n} s'$ because $s_j\sigma' \rightarrow^*_{\mathcal{R}^d_{n-1}} u_j \;{}^*_{\mathcal{R}^d_{n-1}}\!\!\leftarrow t_j\sigma'$ for every $s_j == t_j$ (it is a consequence of $s_j\sigma \rightarrow^*_{\mathcal{R}^d_{n-1}} u_j$, $s_j\sigma \rightarrow^*_{\mathcal{R}^d_{n-1}} s_j\sigma'$ and confluence of $\rightarrow_{\mathcal{R}^d_{n-1}}$ that $s_j\sigma' \rightarrow^*_{\mathcal{R}^d_{n-1}} u_j$). It now follows from confluence of $\rightarrow_{\mathcal{R}^d_n}$ in conjunction with $t' \rightarrow^*_{\mathcal{R}^d_{n-1}} s'$ and $t' \rightarrow^*_{\mathcal{R}^d_n} u'$ that s' and u' have a common reduct u w.r.t. $\rightarrow_{\mathcal{R}^d_n}$. Clearly, u is a common reduct of s and t w.r.t. $\rightarrow_{\mathcal{R}^d_n}$ as well. □

Theorem 7.4.22 *Every almost functional CTRS $\mathcal{R}$ is level-confluent.*

Proof It follows from $\rightarrow_{\mathcal{R}^d_n} \subseteq \rightarrow_{\mathcal{R}_n}$ and Proposition 7.4.21 that $\rightarrow_{\mathcal{R}_n}$ is a compatible refinement of $\rightarrow_{\mathcal{R}^d_n}$. According to Proposition 2.4.9, $\rightarrow_{\mathcal{R}_n}$ is confluent if $\rightarrow_{\mathcal{R}^d_n}$ is confluent. Hence the theorem follows from Corollary 7.4.20. $\square$

As a matter of fact, by carefully checking the proof of Theorem 7.4.14 (given in [SMI95]) one finds that Theorem 7.4.22 is a special case of that theorem. The proof techniques, however, are totally different. Our proof depends heavily on the parallel moves lemma for $\rightarrow_{\mathcal{R}^d}$, which will also be very useful in proving that graph rewriting is an adequate implementation of almost functional CTRSs; see Section 9.4.

Because term rewriting is mainly concerned with computing normal forms, it is worthwhile to investigate whether the deterministic conditional rewrite relation has the same normal forms as the ordinary conditional rewrite relation.

Lemma 7.4.23 *Let $\mathcal{R}$ be an almost functional CTRS. Then, for every $n \geq 0$, the sets of normal forms $NF(\rightarrow_{\mathcal{R}_n})$ and $NF(\rightarrow_{\mathcal{R}^d_n})$ coincide.*

Proof Obviously, $NF(\rightarrow_{\mathcal{R}_n}) \subseteq NF(\rightarrow_{\mathcal{R}^d_n})$ because $\rightarrow_{\mathcal{R}^d_n} \subseteq \rightarrow_{\mathcal{R}_n}$. We prove $NF(\rightarrow_{\mathcal{R}^d_n}) \subseteq NF(\rightarrow_{\mathcal{R}_n})$ indirectly. To this end, suppose there is a term $s \in NF(\rightarrow_{\mathcal{R}^d_n})$ but $s \notin NF(\rightarrow_{\mathcal{R}_n})$. Because s is not a normal form w.r.t. $\rightarrow_{\mathcal{R}_n}$, there is a rule $\rho : l \rightarrow r \Leftarrow c \in \mathcal{R}$, a context $C[\,]$, and a substitution σ such that $s = C[l\sigma] \rightarrow_{\mathcal{R}_n} C[r\sigma]$. In particular, for every $s_j == t_j$ in c, there is a ground constructor term u_j such that $s_j\sigma \rightarrow^*_{\mathcal{R}_{n-1}} u_j \;{}_{\mathcal{R}_{n-1}}^{*}\!\!\leftarrow t_j\sigma$. It follows as in the proof of Proposition 7.4.21 that $s_j\sigma' \rightarrow^*_{\mathcal{R}^d_{n-1}} u_j \;{}_{\mathcal{R}^d_{n-1}}^{*}\!\!\leftarrow t_j\sigma'$. Hence $s = C[l\sigma] = C[l\sigma'] \rightarrow_{\mathcal{R}^d_n} C[r\sigma']$. This is a contradiction to $s \in NF(\rightarrow_{\mathcal{R}^d_n})$. $\square$

Similar to Theorem 7.4.14, the orthogonality requirement can be weakened, that is, the preceding results remain valid if we replace orthogonality with almost orthogonality and furthermore allow infeasible CCPs.

8 Modularity

Modularity is a well-known programming paradigm in computer science. Programmers should design their programs in a modular way, that is, as a combination of small programs. These so-called modules are implemented separately and are then integrated to form the program as a whole. Because TRSs have many important applications in computer science, it is important (not only from a theoretical viewpoint but also from a practical point of view) to know under which conditions a combined system inherits desirable properties from its constituent systems. For this reason modular aspects of term rewriting have been extensively studied in the past decade. To render a detailed account of all known modularity results goes beyond the scope of this book. Instead, we will give an overview of the most important results for TRSs (Section 8.2) and CTRSs (Section 8.7). We will also present selected results in detail.

8.1 Different Kinds of Combinations

Definition 8.1.1 A property $\mathcal{P}$ is *modular* for TRSs if, for all TRSs $(\mathcal{F}_1, \mathcal{R}_1)$ and $(\mathcal{F}_2, \mathcal{R}_2)$ having property $\mathcal{P}$, their *combination* (union) $(\mathcal{F}, \mathcal{R}) = (\mathcal{F}_1 \cup \mathcal{F}_2, \mathcal{R}_1 \cup \mathcal{R}_2)$ also has the property $\mathcal{P}$.

The knowledge that (perhaps under certain conditions) a property $\mathcal{P}$ is modular allows an incremental development of programs. On the other hand, it provides a divide-and-conquer approach to establishing properties of TRSs. If one wants to know whether a large TRS has a certain modular property $\mathcal{P}$, then this system can be decomposed into small subsystems and one merely has to check whether each of these subsystems has property $\mathcal{P}$.

First, we will show that all interesting properties are in general not modular.

Example 8.1.2 Let $\mathcal{R}_1 = \{a \to b\}$ and $\mathcal{R}_2 = \{f(b) \to f(a)\}$. Both systems are terminating and hence normalizing. Their combined system $\mathcal{R}$, however, is not normalizing because $f(a)$ has no normal form. The only reduction sequence starting from $f(a)$ is:

$$f(a) \to_{\mathcal{R}} f(b) \to_{\mathcal{R}} f(a) \to_{\mathcal{R}} f(b) \to_{\mathcal{R}} \cdots$$

Example 8.1.3 Let $\mathcal{R}_1 = \{a \to b\}$ and $\mathcal{R}_2 = \{f(a) \to c\}$. Both systems are confluent and hence locally confluent. Their combined system $\mathcal{R}$, however, is not even locally confluent: $f(a) \to_{\mathcal{R}} f(b)$ and $f(a) \to_{\mathcal{R}} c$ but $f(b)$ and c are two distinct normal forms.

As all interesting properties are in general not modular, the starting-point of research was *disjoint unions*, i.e., combinations of TRSs having no function symbols in common. In his seminal paper [Toy87b], Toyama proved that confluence is modular for disjoint systems. In contrast to that, termination and convergence lack a modular behavior; see [Toy87a]. Kurihara and Ohuchi [KO92] were the first to investigate *constructor-sharing systems*—systems that have constructors in common. Middeldorp and Toyama [MT93] introduced *composable systems*, which have to contain all rewrite rules that define a defined symbol whenever that symbol is shared. The authors, however, restricted their investigations to constructor systems. In [Ohl95a], the constructor system requirement is dropped, so the composable systems considered there are a proper generalization of constructor-sharing systems. *Hierarchical combinations* of TRSs also generalize constructor-sharing systems and allow a certain sharing of defined symbols; they were first studied by Krishna Rao [KR94, KR95a, KR95b] and Dershowitz [Der95]. In practice, *hierarchical combinations with a common subsystem* [KR95a, KR95b] are most important because they generalize both composable systems and hierarchical combinations.

Definition 8.1.4 Let $(\mathcal{F}, \mathcal{R})$ be the union of $(\mathcal{F}_1, \mathcal{R}_1)$ and $(\mathcal{F}_2, \mathcal{R}_2)$. It is easy to see that the set of defined symbols in $(\mathcal{F}, \mathcal{R})$ is $\mathcal{D} = \mathcal{D}_1 \cup \mathcal{D}_2$ and the set of constructors is $\mathcal{C} = \mathcal{F} \setminus \mathcal{D}$, where $\mathcal{D}_i$ ($\mathcal{C}_i$) denotes the set of defined symbols (constructors) in $(\mathcal{F}_i, \mathcal{R}_i)$, $i \in \{1, 2\}$.

1. $(\mathcal{F}_1, \mathcal{R}_1)$ and $(\mathcal{F}_2, \mathcal{R}_2)$ are *disjoint* if they do not share function symbols, that is, $\mathcal{F}_1 \cap \mathcal{F}_2 = \emptyset$ (or equivalently $\mathcal{C}_1 \cap \mathcal{C}_2 = \mathcal{C}_1 \cap \mathcal{D}_2 = \mathcal{D}_1 \cap \mathcal{C}_2 = \mathcal{D}_1 \cap \mathcal{D}_2 = \emptyset$). The disjoint union $(\mathcal{F}, \mathcal{R}) = (\mathcal{F}_1 \uplus \mathcal{F}_2, \mathcal{R}_1 \uplus \mathcal{R}_2)$ is sometimes also called the *direct sum* of $(\mathcal{F}_1, \mathcal{R}_1)$ and $(\mathcal{F}_2, \mathcal{R}_2)$.

2. $(\mathcal{F}_1, \mathcal{R}_1)$ and $(\mathcal{F}_2, \mathcal{R}_2)$ are *constructor-sharing* if they share at most constructors, i.e., $\mathcal{F}_1 \cap \mathcal{F}_2 \subseteq \mathcal{C}$ (or equivalently $\mathcal{C}_1 \cap \mathcal{D}_2 = \mathcal{D}_1 \cap \mathcal{C}_2 = \mathcal{D}_1 \cap \mathcal{D}_2 = \emptyset$).

3. $(\mathcal{F}_1, \mathcal{R}_1)$ and $(\mathcal{F}_2, \mathcal{R}_2)$ are *composable* if $\mathcal{C}_1 \cap \mathcal{D}_2 = \mathcal{D}_1 \cap \mathcal{C}_2 = \emptyset$ and both systems contain all rewrite rules that define a defined symbol whenever that symbol is shared; more precisely, the following inclusion holds: $\{l \to r \in \mathcal{R} \mid root(l) \in \mathcal{D}_1 \cap \mathcal{D}_2\} \subseteq \mathcal{R}_1 \cap \mathcal{R}_2$.

4. $(\mathcal{F}, \mathcal{R})$ is a *hierarchical combination* of the *base system* $(\mathcal{F}_1, \mathcal{R}_1)$ and the *extension* $(\mathcal{F}_2, \mathcal{R}_2)$ if $\mathcal{F}_1 \cap \mathcal{D}_2 = \emptyset$ (or equivalently $\mathcal{C}_1 \cap \mathcal{D}_2 = \mathcal{D}_1 \cap \mathcal{D}_2 = \emptyset$). That is, defined symbols of $\mathcal{R}_1$ may occur as constructors in $\mathcal{R}_2$ but not vice versa.

5. $(\mathcal{F}, \mathcal{R})$ is a *hierarchical combination* of the *base system* $(\mathcal{F}_1, \mathcal{R}_1)$ and the *extension* $(\mathcal{F}_2, \mathcal{R}_2)$ with common subsystem $(\mathcal{F}_0, \mathcal{R}_0)$, where $\mathcal{R}_0 = \{l \to r \in \mathcal{R} \mid root(l) \in \mathcal{D}_1 \cap \mathcal{D}_2\}$, and $\mathcal{F}_0 = \{f \mid f \text{ occurs in } \mathcal{R}_0\}$, if $\mathcal{R}_0 = \mathcal{R}_1 \cap \mathcal{R}_2$ and $\mathcal{F}_1 \cap (\mathcal{D}_2 \setminus \mathcal{D}_1) = \emptyset$.

Definition 8.1.5 A property $\mathcal{P}$ is *modular for disjoint TRSs* if, for all disjoint TRSs $(\mathcal{F}_1, \mathcal{R}_1)$ and $(\mathcal{F}_2, \mathcal{R}_2)$ that have the property $\mathcal{P}$, their union $(\mathcal{F}_1 \uplus \mathcal{F}_2, \mathcal{R}_1 \uplus \mathcal{R}_2)$ also has the property $\mathcal{P}$.

In many papers a property $\mathcal{P}$ is called modular for disjoint TRSs if, for all disjoint TRSs $(\mathcal{F}_1, \mathcal{R}_1)$ and $(\mathcal{F}_2, \mathcal{R}_2)$, their union $(\mathcal{F}_1 \uplus \mathcal{F}_2, \mathcal{R}_1 \uplus \mathcal{R}_2)$ has the property $\mathcal{P}$ if and only if both $(\mathcal{F}_1, \mathcal{R}_1)$ and $(\mathcal{F}_2, \mathcal{R}_2)$ have the property $\mathcal{P}$. We will focus only on the important if direction and will neglect the less important only-if direction (which in most cases is very easy to prove anyway). We will also use the phrases *modular for constructor-sharing TRSs*, *modular for composable TRSs*, etc.

The first four kinds of combination are illustrated in Figure 8.1. The relationships between them is depicted in Figure 8.2 (where the arrows symbolize inclusion). It should be pointed out that composable systems are neither a generalization of hierarchical systems or vice versa. However, hierarchical combinations with a common subsystem comprise both kinds of combinations.

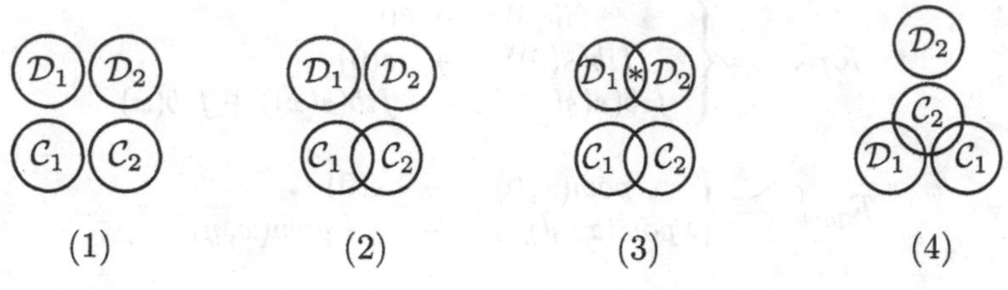

FIGURE 8.1. Different combinations.

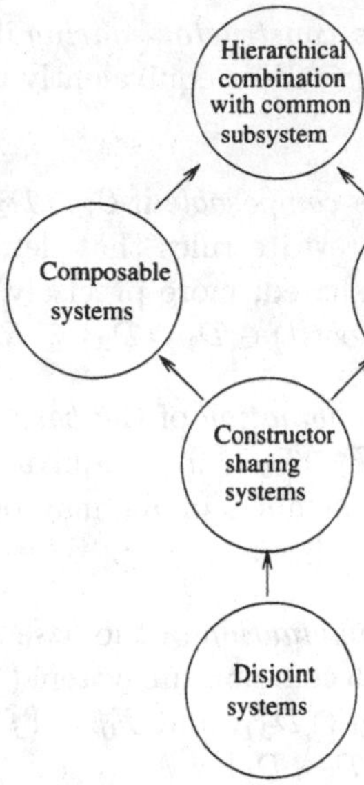

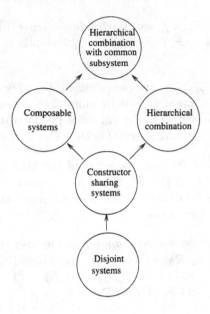

FIGURE 8.2. Relating the different combinations.

Example 8.1.6 Consider the TRSs

$$\mathcal{R}_+ = \begin{cases} 0+y \to y \\ s(x)+y \to s(x+y) \end{cases}$$

$$\mathcal{R}_{app} = \begin{cases} nil +\!\!+\, ys \to ys \\ (x:xs) +\!\!+\, ys \to x:(xs +\!\!+\, ys) \end{cases}$$

$$\mathcal{R}_- = \begin{cases} 0 - s(y) \to 0 \\ x - 0 \to x \\ s(x) - s(y) \to x - y \end{cases}$$

$$\mathcal{R}_* = \begin{cases} 0 * y \to 0 \\ s(x) * y \to (x*y)+y \end{cases}$$

$$\mathcal{R}_{fib} = \begin{cases} fib(0) \to 0 \\ fib(s(0)) \to s(0) \\ fib(s(s(x)) \to fib(s(x)) + fib(x) \end{cases}$$

$$\mathcal{R}_{pow} = \begin{cases} pow(x,0) \to s(0) \\ pow(x,s(y)) \to x * pow(x,y) \end{cases}$$

The TRSs $\mathcal{R}_+$ and $\mathcal{R}_{app}$ are disjoint, $\mathcal{R}_+$ and $\mathcal{R}_-$ are constructor-sharing, while $\mathcal{R}_+ \cup \mathcal{R}_*$ and $\mathcal{R}_+ \cup \mathcal{R}_{fib}$ are composable. Both systems $\mathcal{R}_*$ and $\mathcal{R}_{fib}$

are extensions of the base system $\mathcal{R}_+$. Lastly, $\mathcal{R}_+ \cup \mathcal{R}_{pow}$ is an extension of the base system $\mathcal{R}_+ \cup \mathcal{R}_*$ with common subsystem $\mathcal{R}_+$.

Of course, we are not only interested in the combination of two TRSs. It should also be possible to deal with situations in which more than two systems are combined. The next proposition shows that the combination of n composable TRSs, $n \geq 2$, can be reduced to the case $n = 2$ by successive combinations of two systems.

Proposition 8.1.7 *Let $(\mathcal{F}_1, \mathcal{R}_1), \ldots, (\mathcal{F}_n, \mathcal{R}_n)$ be n, $n \geq 2$, pairwise composable TRSs. Then the term rewriting systems $(\bigcup_{j=1}^{n-1} \mathcal{F}_j, \bigcup_{j=1}^{n-1} \mathcal{R}_j)$ and $(\mathcal{F}_n, \mathcal{R}_n)$ are composable.*

Proof We have

$$\bigcup_{j=1}^{n-1} \mathcal{C}_j \cap \mathcal{D}_n = \bigcup_{j=1}^{n-1} (\mathcal{C}_j \cap \mathcal{D}_n) = \bigcup_{j=1}^{n-1} \emptyset = \emptyset$$

$$\bigcup_{j=1}^{n-1} \mathcal{D}_j \cap \mathcal{C}_n = \bigcup_{j=1}^{n-1} (\mathcal{D}_j \cap \mathcal{C}_n) = \bigcup_{j=1}^{n-1} \emptyset = \emptyset$$

and

$$\begin{aligned}
&\{l \to r \in \textstyle\bigcup_{j=1}^{n-1} \mathcal{R}_j \cup \mathcal{R}_n \mid root(l) \in \bigcup_{j=1}^{n-1} \mathcal{D}_j \cap \mathcal{D}_n\} \\
=\ &\{l \to r \in \textstyle\bigcup_{j=1}^{n-1} (\mathcal{R}_j \cup \mathcal{R}_n) \mid root(l) \in \bigcup_{j=1}^{n-1} (\mathcal{D}_j \cap \mathcal{D}_n)\} \\
=\ &\textstyle\bigcup_{j=1}^{n-1} \{l \to r \in \mathcal{R}_j \cup \mathcal{R}_n \mid root(l) \in \mathcal{D}_j \cap \mathcal{D}_n\} \\
&\subseteq \textstyle\bigcup_{j=1}^{n-1} (\mathcal{R}_j \cap \mathcal{R}_n) = \bigcup_{j=1}^{n-1} \mathcal{R}_j \cap \mathcal{R}_n
\end{aligned}$$

These equalities prove the proposition. □

For hierarchical combinations the situation is different because its definition is asymmetric. Here a base system defining some functions is given, and one proceeds by defining new functions using the given ones in an auxiliary manner. In an iteration of this process, the extended system will act as a base system, which is further extended by new functions and so on. Note that Examples 8.1.2 and 8.1.3 show that neither termination nor confluence are modular for hierarchical combinations. That is, further restrictions are needed to obtain modularity results for hierarchical combinations; see Section 8.6.

Property	Disjoint union	Shared cons.	Composable
Strong confluence	No	No	No
+ linearity	Yes [Hue80]	Yes [Hue80]	Yes [Hue80]
Ground confluence	No	No	No
Confluence	Yes [Toy87b]	No [KO92]	No
+ left-linearity	Yes [RV80]	Yes [RV80]	?
+ layer-preservation	Yes [Toy87b]	Yes [Ohl94b]	Yes [Ohl94a]
Local confluence	Yes [Mid90]	Yes [Mid90]	Yes [Mid90]
Normal form property	No [Mid89a]	No	No
+ left-linearity	Yes [Mid90]	No [Ohl94a]	No
Unique normal forms	Yes [Mid89a]	No [Ohl94a]	No
$UN^{\rightarrow}$	No [Mid89a]	No	No
+ left-linearity	Yes [Mar96a]	No [Ohl94a]	No
Consistency	Yes [SS89]	No [Gra96b]	No
Consistency w.r.t. $\rightarrow$	No [Mar96a]	No	No
+ left-linearity	Yes [Mar96a]	No [Mar96a]	No

TABLE 8.1. Modularity in the confluence hierarchy.

8.2 A Short History of Modularity Results

Because many modularity results have been published in the last decade, it would be impossible to render a detailed account of all of them here. Instead, the main results are summarized in Tables 8.1–8.3, and we will briefly comment on the tables. We would like to emphasize that the tables are not exhaustive. The results are tagged with a reference to the article in which they appear (note that some of them first appeared in preliminary versions of the cited articles). Selected results will be treated in subsequent sections of this chapter. Details on many more results can be found in the dissertations of Middeldorp [Mid90], Ohlebusch [Ohl94a], and Gramlich [Gra96b], for example.

8.2.1 The Confluence Hierarchy

Let us start with the confluence hierarchy in Table 8.1. The research on modularity started with the seminal work of Toyama [Toy87b], who showed that confluence is modular for disjoint unions. A simpler proof of his theorem can be found in [KMTV94]. The situation changes, however, if one considers TRSs with shared constructors. The following example originates from Huet [Hue80] and was first used by Kurihara and Ohuchi [KO92] as a counterexample to the modularity of confluence for constructor-sharing TRSs.

Example 8.2.1 Let

$$\mathcal{R}_1 = \left\{ \begin{array}{lll} F(x, c(x)) & \rightarrow & A \\ F(x, x) & \rightarrow & B \end{array} \right.$$

and $\mathcal{R}_2 = \{a \rightarrow c(a)\}$. Both $\mathcal{R}_1$ and $\mathcal{R}_2$ are confluent and share the constructor c. We have

$$A\ {}_{\mathcal{R}_1}\!\leftarrow F(a, c(a))\ {}_{\mathcal{R}_2}\!\leftarrow F(a, a) \rightarrow_{\mathcal{R}_1} B$$

that is, the term $F(a, a)$ has two different normal forms with respect to the combined system $\mathcal{R} = \mathcal{R}_1 \cup \mathcal{R}_2$. Thus $\mathcal{R}$ is not confluent.

Sufficient conditions for the modularity of confluence in the presence of shared constructors can be found in Section 8.5; cf. [Ohl94b]. The material includes a proof of Toyama's theorem.

Confluence is also modular for layer-preserving composable TRSs; see [Ohl94a]. The union of composable TRSs $(\mathcal{F}_1, \mathcal{R}_1)$ and $(\mathcal{F}_2, \mathcal{R}_2)$ is *layer-preserving* if, for all rules $l \rightarrow r \in \mathcal{R}_d$, $d \in \{1, 2\}$, we have $root(r) \in \mathcal{F}_d \setminus \mathcal{F}_{3-d}$ whenever $root(l) \in \mathcal{F}_d \setminus \mathcal{F}_{3-d}$; see [Ohl95a] for more details. Disjoint TRSs are layer-preserving if and only if they are noncollapsing, whereas constructor-sharing TRSs are layer-preserving if and only if they contain neither collapsing nor *constructor-lifting* rules (rules with a shared constructor at the root of the right-hand side of a rule). The constructor-sharing case will be treated in Section 8.5.

In a different context, Raoult and Vuillemin [RV80] showed that confluence is preserved under the combination of left-linear TRSs which are *orthogonal to each other* (systems in which there is no overlap between a rule from $\mathcal{R}_1$ and one from $\mathcal{R}_2$). Consequently, confluence is modular for left-linear constructor-sharing TRSs and certain hierarchical combinations; see Section 8.6.3 for details. It is an open problem as to whether confluence is also modular for left-linear composable systems.

The modularity of local confluence for composable TRSs is ascribed to Middeldorp because it follows from the same principle as the respective results in [Mid90]. As a matter of fact, it is easy to see that the union of two locally confluent TRSs $\mathcal{R}_1$ and $\mathcal{R}_2$ is also locally confluent provided that the equality $CP(\mathcal{R}_1 \cup \mathcal{R}_2) = CP(\mathcal{R}_1) \cup CP(\mathcal{R}_2)$ holds. Note that composable TRSs and certain hierarchical combinations satisfy this equality; see Section 8.6.3.

Modularity of strong confluence has not yet been examined. The following example shows that this property is not modular for disjoint systems.[1]

[1]The example was obtained by Aart Middeldorp by simplifying a similar counter-example for the constructor-sharing case given by the author.

Example 8.2.2 The system $\mathcal{R}_1$ consisting of the rules

$$\begin{array}{lcl} F(x,x) & \to & A \\ F(A,x) & \to & A \\ F(x,A) & \to & A \end{array} \qquad \begin{array}{lcl} F(F(x,y),z) & \to & A \\ F(x,F(y,z)) & \to & A \end{array}$$

is strongly confluent because every term over the signature $\mathcal{F}_1 = \{A, F\}$ can be reduced to A in at most one step.

Let $\mathcal{R}_2 = \{g(x) \to x\}$. The disjoint union $\mathcal{R}_1 \uplus \mathcal{R}_2$ is not strongly confluent, because $F(g(x), x) \;{}_{\mathcal{R}_2}\!\leftarrow F(g(x), g(x)) \to_{\mathcal{R}_1} A$ and two rewrite steps are needed to reduce $F(g(x), x)$ to the normal form A.

On the other hand, modularity of strong confluence for *linear* composable rewrite systems is a direct consequence of Theorem 4.3.2 because the equality $CP(\mathcal{R}_1 \cup \mathcal{R}_2) = CP(\mathcal{R}_1) \cup CP(\mathcal{R}_2)$ holds for composable TRSs $\mathcal{R}_1$ and $\mathcal{R}_2$ and certain hierarchical combinations; cf. Section 8.6.3.

Ground confluence is not modular because it is not preserved under signature extensions. For example, the system $(\{a, f\}, \{f(x) \to x, f(x) \to a\})$ is ground confluent. However, if we add a new constant b to the signature, then the divergence $a \leftarrow f(b) \to b$ shows that the obtained system is no longer ground confluent.

The normal form property is not modular for disjoint unions, as the next example from [Mid89a, example 3.1] shows.

Example 8.2.3 Let $\mathcal{R}_1 = \{F(x,x) \to G\}$ and let $\mathcal{R}_2$ contain the rules

$$\begin{array}{lcl} a & \to & b \\ a & \to & c \end{array} \qquad \begin{array}{lcl} b & \to & b \\ c & \to & c \end{array}$$

The term $F(b, c)$ and the normal form G are convertible in $\mathcal{R}_1 \uplus \mathcal{R}_2$ because

$$F(b,c) \;{}_{\mathcal{R}_2}\!\leftarrow F(a,c) \;{}_{\mathcal{R}_2}\!\leftarrow F(a,a) \to_{\mathcal{R}_1} G$$

but $F(b, c)$ does not reduce to G. Thus the disjoint union $\mathcal{R}_1 \uplus \mathcal{R}_2$ does not have the normal form property.

In the preceding example, the system $\mathcal{R}_1$ is not left-linear, and Middeldorp [Mid90, theorem 5.2.13] has shown that this is essential. This modular behavior for left-linear systems is destroyed in the presence of shared constructors. The counterexample stems from [Ohl94a, example 9.1.2].

Example 8.2.4 Let

$$\mathcal{R}_1 = \left\{ \begin{array}{lcl} F(c(x)) & \to & A \\ F(d(x)) & \to & B \end{array} \right.$$

and

$$\mathcal{R}_2 = \left\{ \begin{array}{lcl} a & \to & c(a) \\ a & \to & d(a) \end{array} \right.$$

Both systems are left-linear and have the normal form property but their combined system does not have the normal form property:

$$A \;{}_{\mathcal{R}_1}\!\leftarrow F(c(a)) \;{}_{\mathcal{R}_2}\!\leftarrow F(a) \rightarrow_{\mathcal{R}_2} F(d(a)) \rightarrow_{\mathcal{R}_1} B$$

Middeldorp [Mid89a, theorem 2.21] showed that the unique normal form property is modular for disjoint TRSs, but this result does not extend to shared constructors, as Example 8.2.4 shows.

The modular behavior of the property $\mathrm{UN}^{\rightarrow}$ bears a strong resemblance to the normal form property. The following example taken from [Mid90, example 5.2.14] shows that $\mathrm{UN}^{\rightarrow}$ is not modular for disjoint unions.

Example 8.2.5 Let $\mathcal{R}_1 = \{F(x,x) \rightarrow G\}$ and let $\mathcal{R}_2$ consist of the rules

$$\begin{array}{lllcll} a & \rightarrow & b & \quad & d & \rightarrow & e \\ a & \rightarrow & c & & d & \rightarrow & c \\ c & \rightarrow & c & & & & \end{array}$$

Both systems have the property $\mathrm{UN}^{\rightarrow}$, but in $\mathcal{R}_1 \uplus \mathcal{R}_2$ the term $F(a,d)$ can be reduced to two distinct normal forms:

$$F(b,e) \;{}_{\mathcal{R}_2}\!\leftarrow F(b,d) \;{}_{\mathcal{R}_2}\!\leftarrow F(a,d) \rightarrow_{\mathcal{R}_2} F(c,d) \rightarrow_{\mathcal{R}_2} F(c,c) \rightarrow_{\mathcal{R}_1} G$$

Marchiori [Mar96a] showed that $\mathrm{UN}^{\rightarrow}$ is modular for left-linear disjoint TRSs. Again, the modular behavior is destroyed in the presence of shared constructors, as Example 8.2.4 shows.

Schmidt-Schauß [SS89] proved that consistency is modular for disjoint unions but again shared constructors make a difference, as seen in Example 8.2.6, which originates from [Gra96b, example 4.3.6].

Example 8.2.6 The left-linear and consistent TRSs

$$\mathcal{R}_1 = \left\{ \begin{array}{lll} F(b,x,y) & \rightarrow & x \\ F(c,x,y) & \rightarrow & y \end{array} \right.$$

and $\mathcal{R}_2 = \{a \rightarrow b, a \rightarrow c\}$ share the constructors b and c. Their union $\mathcal{R}_1 \cup \mathcal{R}_2$ is inconsistent because the term $F(a,x,y)$ can be reduced to two distinct variables:

$$x \;{}_{\mathcal{R}_1}\!\leftarrow F(b,x,y) \;{}_{\mathcal{R}_2}\!\leftarrow F(a,x,y) \rightarrow_{\mathcal{R}_2} F(c,x,y) \rightarrow_{\mathcal{R}_1} y$$

The following example, taken from Marchiori [Mar96a], shows that consistency w.r.t. reduction is not modular for disjoint unions.

Example 8.2.7 The disjoint TRSs

$$\mathcal{R}_1 = \left\{ \begin{array}{lll} F(x,y,y) & \rightarrow & x \\ F(x,x,y) & \rightarrow & y \end{array} \right.$$

and $\mathcal{R}_2 = \{g(x) \to x, g(x) \to c\}$ are both consistent w.r.t. reduction. In their union $\mathcal{R}_1 \uplus \mathcal{R}_2$, however, the term $F(g(x), c, g(y))$ can be reduced to two distinct variables:

$$x\ {}_{\mathcal{R}_1}\!\leftarrow F(x,c,c)\ {}^{+}_{\mathcal{R}_2}\!\leftarrow F(g(x),c,g(y)) \to^{+}_{\mathcal{R}_2} F(c,c,y) \to_{\mathcal{R}_1} y$$

In contrast to that, it has been shown by Marchiori [Mar96a] that consistency w.r.t. reduction is modular for *left-linear* disjoint unions. This result cannot be generalized for constructor-sharing systems, as Example 8.2.6 shows. A similar counterexample in which both systems have unique normal forms w.r.t. reduction can be found in [Mar96a].

Because hierarchical combinations subsume TRSs with shared constructors, every property that is not modular for constructor-sharing systems is also not modular for hierarchical combinations. Example 8.1.3 shows that the properties in the confluence hierarchy that are modular for constructor-sharing systems are not modular for hierarchical combinations. Therefore, further restrictions are needed to obtain modularity results for hierarchical combinations; see Section 8.6.3.

8.2.2 The Termination Hierarchy

The modularity results of properties in the termination hierarchy are summarized in Table 8.2. In contrast to confluence, termination is not modular for disjoint TRSs. Let us review Toyama's famous counterexample [Toy87a].

Example 8.2.8 The TRS $\mathcal{R}_1 = \{F(0,1,x) \to F(x,x,x)\}$ was shown terminating in Example 5.4.35. Its combination with the terminating TRS $\mathcal{R}_2 = \{g(x,y) \to x,\ g(x,y) \to y\}$ yields a nonterminating system because there is the cyclic derivation

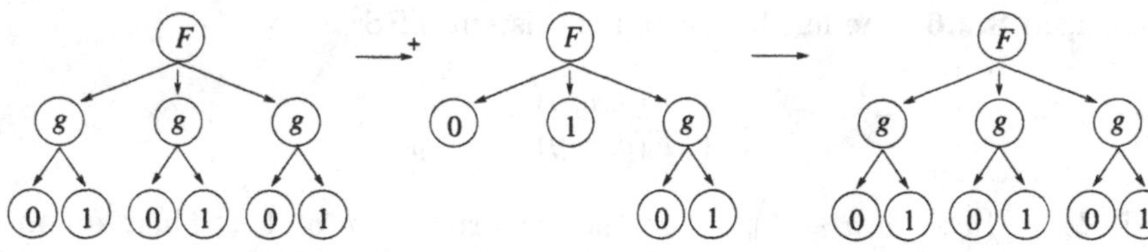

Naturally, the question arises as to what restrictions have to be imposed on the constituent TRSs so that their disjoint union is again terminating. The first results were obtained by investigating the distribution of collapsing and duplicating rules among the TRSs (in Example 8.2.8, $\mathcal{R}_1$ consists of a duplicating rule, whereas $\mathcal{R}_2$ contains two collapsing rules). Rusinowitch [Rus87a] first showed that termination is modular for nonduplicating and for noncollapsing disjoint TRSs. (Drosten [Dro89] obtained parts of these results independently.) Later, Middeldorp [Mid89b] proved that termination is preserved under the combination of disjoint systems provided that one of the systems contains neither collapsing nor duplicating rules. One

Property	Disjoint union	Shared cons.	Composable
Polynomial termination	?	No [MZ97]	No
ω-termination	Yes [MZ97]	No [MZ97]	No
Total termination	?	No [MZ97]	No
+ nonduplication	Yes [FZ96]	No [MZ97]	No
Simplifyingness	Yes [KO90]	Yes [KO92]	Yes [Ohl95a]
Simple termination	Yes [Ohl94c]	No [Ohl94c]	No
+ finitely branching	Yes [Gra94]	Yes [Gra94]	Yes [Gra96b]
revised definition	Yes [MZ97]	Yes [MZ97]	Yes [MZ97]
DP simple termination	No [GAO02]	No	No
restricted	Yes [GAO02]	No [GAO02]	No
$\mathcal{G}$-restricted	Yes [GAO02]	Yes [GAO02]	Yes [GAO02]
DP quasi-simple term.	Yes [GAO02]	No [GAO02]	No
$\mathcal{C}_{\mathcal{E}}$-termination	Yes [Ohl94c]	No [Ohl94c]	No
+ finitely branching	Yes [Gra94]	Yes [Gra94]	Yes [KO95a]
Nonself-embeddingness	No [Gra94]	No	No
Termination	No [Toy87a]	No	No
+ nonduplication	Yes [Rus87a]	Yes [Ohl94c]	Yes [Ohl95a]
+ layer-preservation	Yes [Rus87a]	Yes [Gra94]	Yes [Ohl95a]
+ nonoverlappingness	Yes [Gra95]	Yes [Der95]	Yes [Ohl95a]
+ variable-preservation	No [Ohl95c]	No	No
Innermost termination	Yes [TKB95]	Yes [Gra95]	Yes [Ohl95a]
Innermost normalization	Yes [Mid90]	Yes [Ohl95a]	Yes [Ohl95a]
Normalization	Yes [Mid90]	Yes [Ohl95a]	Yes [Ohl95a]
Nonloopingness	No [Toy87a]	No	No
+ nonduplication	Yes [MO00]	?	?
+ layer-preservation	Yes [MO00]	?	?
Acyclicity	No [Toy87a]	No	No
+ nonduplication	Yes [MO00]	No	No
+ layer-preservation	Yes [MO00]	?	?

TABLE 8.2. Modularity in the termination hierarchy.

simple proof for all three results can be found in [Ohl93b]. In Section 8.4 an alternative proof will by obtained as a by-product. Furthermore, the aforementioned results can be extended to composable systems; see [Ohl95a] for details.

In contrast to term rewriting, termination is modular for graph rewriting. Because nonduplicating term rewriting is closely related to graph rewriting, one proof for both modularity results will be given in Chapter 9.

Termination is also modular for nonoverlapping composable TRSs. Because terminating nonoverlapping TRSs can be regarded as convergent overlay systems, they will be treated later; see Table 8.3.

It is a bit surprising that termination is not modular for variable-preserving disjoint systems. The counterexample is taken from [Ohl95c].

Example 8.2.9 Let $\mathcal{R}_1$ consist of the rewrite rules

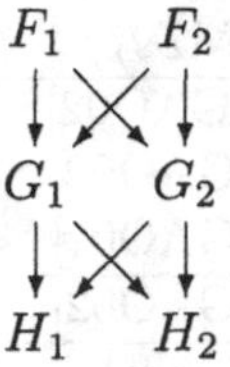

$$
\begin{aligned}
&E_1(H_1, H_2, x, y, z) \to E_2(x, x, y, z, z)\\
&E_2(F_1, x, y, z, F_2) \to E_3(x, y, x, y, y, z, y, z, x, y, z)\\
&E_3(x_1, x_1, x_2, x_2, x_3, x_3, x_4, x_4, x, y, z) \to\\
&\qquad\qquad E_4(x_1, x_1, x_2, x_2, x_3, x_3, x_4, x_4, x, y, z)\\
&E_4(G_1, x_1, G_2, x_1, G_1, x_1, G_2, x_1, x, y, z) \to E_1(x_1, x_1, x, y, z)
\end{aligned}
$$

and let

$$
\mathcal{R}_2 = \left\{ \begin{array}{lcl} f(x,y) & \to & h(x,y) \\ f(x,y) & \to & h(y,x) \\ h(x,x) & \to & x \end{array} \right.
$$

Both TRSs are variable-preserving and terminating. (A termination proof of $\mathcal{R}_1$ can be found in [Ohl95c].) Their disjoint union $\mathcal{R} = \mathcal{R}_1 \uplus \mathcal{R}_2$ is not terminating because there is the following cyclic derivation

$$
\begin{aligned}
&E_1(H_1, H_2, s_1, s_2, s_3)\\
&\to_{\mathcal{R}_1} E_2(s_1, s_1, s_2, s_3, s_3)\\
&\to^*_{\mathcal{R}} E_2(F_1, s_1, s_2, s_3, F_2)\\
&\to_{\mathcal{R}_1} E_3(s_1, s_2, s_1, s_2, s_2, s_3, s_2, s_3, s_1, s_2, s_3)\\
&\to^*_{\mathcal{R}} E_3(t_1, t_1, t_2, t_2, t_3, t_3, t_4, t_4, s_1, s_2, s_3)\\
&\to_{\mathcal{R}_1} E_4(t_1, t_1, t_2, t_2, t_3, t_3, t_4, t_4, s_1, s_2, s_3)\\
&\to^*_{\mathcal{R}} E_4(G_1, u, G_2, u, G_1, u, G_2, u, s_1, s_2, s_3)\\
&\to_{\mathcal{R}_1} E_1(u, u, s_1, s_2, s_3)\\
&\to^*_{\mathcal{R}} E_1(H_1, H_2, s_1, s_2, s_3)
\end{aligned}
$$

where $s_1 = f(F_1, F_1)$, $s_2 = f(F_1, F_2)$, $s_3 = f(F_2, F_2)$, $t_1 = h(G_1, F_1)$, $t_2 = h(F_1, G_2)$, $t_3 = h(G_1, F_2)$, $t_4 = h(F_2, G_2)$, $u = h(G_1, G_2)$.

It is easy to see that polynomial termination and ω-termination are modular for disjoint unions provided the carrier sets of the interpretations coincide. This, however, cannot be generalized for constructor-sharing systems. For example, the constructor-sharing TRSs $F(a) \to F(b)$ and $g(b) \to g(a)$ are polynomially terminating but their union is not totally terminating; see Example 5.3.8 and [Zan94]. These observations appeared in [MZ97] but other authors may have made the same observations earlier. Note that our definitions of polynomial termination and ω-termination allow an arbitrary subset N of $\mathbb{N}$ as a carrier set of the compatible algebra. ω-termination is nevertheless modular for disjoint TRSs because an ω-terminating TRS always has a compatible algebra with carrier $\mathbb{N}$ as the following lemma from [GMOZ02a] shows.

Lemma 8.2.10 *Every ω-terminating TRS $(\mathcal{F}, \mathcal{R})$ is compatible with a monotone $\mathcal{F}$-algebra with carrier set $\mathbb{N}$.*

Proof Let $(\mathcal{F}, \mathcal{R})$ be compatible with the monotone $\mathcal{F}$-algebra $(\mathcal{N}, >)$ with carrier $N \subset \mathbb{N}$. Without loss of generality, we may assume that N is infinite. There exists exactly one monotone bijection $\phi\colon N \to \mathbb{N}$. Let ψ be its (monotone) inverse and define $f_{\mathbb{N}}(x_1, \ldots, x_n) = \phi(f_{\mathcal{N}}(\psi(x_1), \ldots, \psi(x_n)))$ for every $f \in \mathcal{F}$. The carrier set $\mathbb{N}$, together with the interpretation functions $f_{\mathbb{N}}$, forms a monotone $\mathcal{F}$-algebra and it is not difficult to show that $(\mathcal{F}, \mathcal{R})$ is also compatible with this algebra. □

It is unclear whether a similar lemma holds for polynomially terminating TRSs. Therefore, the question of whether polynomial termination is modular for disjoint TRSs remains open.

Total termination is known to be modular for nonduplicating disjoint systems. This result was first shown by Ferreira and Zantema [FZ96], and a totally different proof was provided by Rubio [Rub95]. However, it is unknown whether the nonduplication requirement can be dropped.

Modularity of simplifyingness for disjoint unions was first shown by Kurihara and Ohuchi [KO90] and then extended to constructor-sharing and composable systems in [KO92, Ohl95a]. The proofs of these results are based on Lemma 5.2.29. As a consequence, for finite signatures or a finite number of rewrite rules, simple termination is also modular. Gramlich [Gra94] showed that simple termination is also modular for finitely branching disjoint TRSs and conjectured that the finitely branching requirement is superfluous. The proof in Section 8.4.1 shows that he was right; the proof originally appeared in [Ohl94c]. In Section 8.4.1 it will also be shown that simple termination is *not* modular for constructor-sharing systems. Nevertheless, simple termination is modular for finitely branching constructor-sharing systems [Gra94], composable systems [Gra96b], and certain hierarchical combinations [KR94]. All these results will be reviewed in Section 8.6.1.

In fact, Gramlich's approach is based on the modularity of $\mathcal{C}_\mathcal{E}$-termination. The notion of $\mathcal{C}_\mathcal{E}$-termination was originally called "termination preserving under nondeterministic collapses" in [Gra94]. We prefer to use the shorter phrase $\mathcal{C}_\mathcal{E}$-termination, which is formally defined as follows.

Definition 8.2.11 A TRS $\mathcal{R}$ is called *$\mathcal{C}_\mathcal{E}$-terminating* if the *collapsing extended* term rewriting system $\mathcal{R} \uplus \{Cons(x,y) \to x, Cons(x,y) \to y\}$ is terminating, where *Cons* is some binary function symbol that does not occur in the signature of $\mathcal{R}$.

$\mathcal{C}_\mathcal{E}$-termination plays a crucial role in proving termination in a modular way. It has almost the same modular behavior as simple termination (see Sections 8.4.1 and 8.6.1), but it is by far less restrictive than simple termination. As a matter of fact, in Section 8.3 it will be shown that DP quasi-simple termination implies $\mathcal{C}_\mathcal{E}$-termination.

It was shown in [GAO02] that (under a minor restriction) DP quasi-simple termination is modular for disjoint TRSs but not for constructor-sharing systems. The proofs of these facts can be found in Section 8.4.2. There it will also be shown that DP simple termination is not modular for disjoint systems. However, under certain natural conditions it is modular even for composable systems.

Nonself-embeddingness is not modular, as the following example from [Gra94, example 5] shows.

Example 8.2.12 Consider the TRSs

$$\mathcal{R}_1 = \left\{ \begin{array}{lcl} F(0,1,x) & \to & H(x,x,x) \\ H(0,1,x) & \to & F(x,x,x) \end{array} \right.$$

and $\mathcal{R}_2 = \{g(x,y) \to x, g(x,y) \to y\}$. Both are nonself-embedding but their disjoint union $\mathcal{R} = \mathcal{R}_1 \uplus \mathcal{R}_2$ admits a (self-embedding) cyclic derivation

$$F(0,1,t) \to_{\mathcal{R}_1} H(t,t,t) \to^+_{\mathcal{R}_2} H(0,1,t) \to_{\mathcal{R}_1} F(t,t,t) \to^+_{\mathcal{R}} F(0,1,t)$$

where $t = g(0,1)$.

In contrast to termination, innermost termination has a nice modular behavior. This was proven for disjoint unions in [TKB95], for constructor-sharing systems in [Gra95], for composable systems in [Ohl95a], and for certain hierarchical combinations (with common subsystem) in [KR95a, GAO02]. We will review these results in Section 8.6.2.

Several authors (Bergstra et al. [BKM89], Drosten [Dro89], Kurihara and Kaji [KK90]) have independently observed that normalization is a modular property of disjoint TRSs, and the same proofs show that innermost normalization is also modular; see [Mid90] for details. We will show in

Property	Disjoint union	Shared cons.	Composable
Convergence	No [Toy87a]	No	No
+ left-linearity	Yes [TKB95]	No [Ohl94a]	No
+ nonoverlappingness	Yes [Gra95]	Yes [Der95]	Yes [Ohl95a]
+ constructor systems	Yes [MT93]	Yes [MT93]	Yes [MT93]
+ overlay systems	Yes [Gra95]	Yes [Der95]	Yes [Ohl95a]
+ variable-preservation	No [Ohl95c]	No	No
Termination + left-lin.	No [Toy87a]	No	No
+ consistency	Yes [SSMP95]	No [Ohl94a]	No
+ consistency w.r.t. $\rightarrow$	Yes [SSMP95]	No [Ohl94a]	No
+ variable-preservation	Yes [SSMP95]	No [Ohl94a]	No
Unique normalization	Yes [Mid90]	Yes [Ohl94b]	Yes [Ohl95a]

TABLE 8.3. Modularity of combined properties.

Section 8.5.2 that both properties are modular for constructor-sharing systems. Even better, they are modular for composable systems and certain hierarchical combinations; we refer to [Ohl95a, KR95b] for details.

Toyama's counterexample also shows that neither nonloopingness nor acyclicity are modular for disjoint systems. Middeldorp and Ohsaki [MO00] have proven that both properties are modular for nonduplicating and for noncollapsing disjoint TRSs. The example $\mathcal{R}_1 = \{F(x, c(x)) \rightarrow F(x, x)\}$ and $\mathcal{R}_2 = \{a \rightarrow c(a)\}$ shows that acyclicity is not modular for nonduplicating TRSs with shared constructors, but the remaining cases are open; see Table 8.2.

8.2.3 Combined Properties

Finally, let us consider the combination of properties from the confluence hierarchy with properties from the termination hierarchy; see Table 8.3. First, because local confluence is modular for composable TRSs, it follows that convergence is modular for composable TRSs whenever termination is. For example, convergence is modular for $\mathcal{C}_\mathcal{E}$-terminating composable TRSs. All those modularity results that can be obtained in the same fashion are not listed in Table 8.3.

In Toyama's counterexample 8.2.8 to the modularity of termination for disjoint unions, the system $(\mathcal{F}_2, \mathcal{R}_2)$ lacks confluence. Therefore, Toyama [Toy87b] conjectured that convergence is modular for disjoint unions. Because confluence is modular for disjoint systems, this is equivalent to the statement that the disjoint union of two convergent TRSs is terminating. But Barendregt and Klop disproved this conjecture. Their example appeared in [Toy87a]. Independently, Drosten [Dro89] gave the following simpler counterexample to the modularity of convergence.

Example 8.2.13 Let

$$\mathcal{R}_1 = \left\{ \begin{array}{lcl} F(0,1,x) & \to & F(x,x,x) \\ F(x,y,z) & \to & 2 \\ 0 & \to & 2 \\ 1 & \to & 2 \end{array} \right.$$

and

$$\mathcal{R}_2 = \left\{ \begin{array}{lcl} g(x,y,y) & \to & x \\ g(y,y,x) & \to & x \end{array} \right.$$

Termination of $\mathcal{R}_1$ was shown in Section 5.5.1 and $\mathcal{R}_2$ is apparently terminating. Because all critical pairs are joinable, both systems are convergent. But as in Example 8.2.8, there is a cyclic $\mathcal{R}$ derivation starting from $F(g(0,1,1), g(0,1,1), g(0,1,1))$.

In contrast to the negative result, Toyama et al. [TKB95] showed that convergence is modular for left-linear disjoint TRSs. It is natural to address the question of whether their deep result can be extended to constructor-sharing or even composable systems. The next example, which is taken from [Ohl94a, example 6.2.1], shows that this is not the case.

Example 8.2.14 Consider

$$\mathcal{R}_1 = \left\{ \begin{array}{lcl} F(0,1,x) & \to & F(x,x,x) \\ F(x,y,z) & \to & 2 \\ 0 & \to & 2 \\ 1 & \to & 2 \\ G(0) & \to & c(1) \\ G(x) & \to & c(x) \end{array} \right.$$

and $\mathcal{R}_2 = \{f(c(x)) \to x\}$. Both systems are convergent and left-linear. They share the constructor c. Again, there is a cyclic reduction derivation

$$\begin{array}{rll} F(0,1,f(G(0))) & \to_{\mathcal{R}_1} & F(f(G(0)), f(G(0)), f(G(0))) \\ & \to^{+}_{\mathcal{R}_1} & F(f(c(0)), f(c(1)), f(G(0))) \\ & \to^{+}_{\mathcal{R}_2} & F(0,1,f(G(0))) \end{array}$$

Nice modularity results can be obtained by combining the modularity of innermost termination and local confluence with the fact that termination and innermost termination are equivalent in locally confluent overlay systems; cf. Theorem 5.6.8. An immediate consequence is that convergence is modular for composable overlay systems because the combination of two composable convergent overlay systems yields an innermost terminating and locally confluent overlay system. Because constructor systems and nonoverlapping systems are special overlay systems, convergence is modular for these systems as well. These results can be extended to certain hierarchical combinations; see Section 8.6.3.

It is surprising that convergence is not modular for variable-preserving disjoint systems. The counterexample is a modification of Example 8.2.9. It is too complex to be repeated here; interested readers are referred to [Ohl95c].

It has been shown in [SSMP95] that termination is modular for the following classes of *left-linear* TRSs: consistent systems, systems that are consistent w.r.t. reduction, and variable-preserving TRSs. None of these results extend to the constructor-sharing case, as Example 8.2.14 shows (in order to get a variable-preserving system, one may drop the rule $F(x, y, z) \to 2$). The main result in [SSMP95] also proves the fact that convergence is modular for left-linear disjoint TRSs: Because local confluence is modular and termination is modular for left-linear TRSs that are consistent w.r.t. reduction, it follows that the combined system of two convergent TRSs is locally confluent and terminating (hence convergent).

Because both confluence and normalization are modular for disjoint systems, their combination "unique normalization" is modular for those systems as well. The same argument does not apply, however, to TRSs with shared constructors because confluence is not modular in this case. Nevertheless, unique normalization is modular for this kind of combination, as we will show in Section 8.5.2. It is even modular for composable TRSs and certain hierarchical combinations; see [Ohl95a, KR95b].

A glance at Tables 8.1–8.3 reveals that they do not contain a property that is modular for constructor-sharing systems but not modular for composable systems. In fact, no natural property with such a modular behavior is known.

It has already been mentioned that the abundance of modularity results cannot be reviewed in every facet. Apart from those results that have already been mentioned, recent papers on modularity include [Pre94, FJ95, AT97a, Der97, Mar98].

8.3 $\mathcal{C}_\mathcal{E}$-Termination and the Termination Hierarchy

We saw in Section 8.2 that $\mathcal{C}_\mathcal{E}$-termination plays a crucial role if one is concerned with the modularity of termination. How can we test whether a TRS is $\mathcal{C}_\mathcal{E}$-terminating? The next proposition states some sufficient conditions that can easily be checked; it is due to Gramlich [Gra94].

Proposition 8.3.1 *Let $(\mathcal{F}, \mathcal{R})$ be a terminating TRS.*

1. *If $\mathcal{R}$ is nonduplicating, then it is $\mathcal{C}_\mathcal{E}$-terminating.*

2. *If $\mathcal{R}$ is inconsistent w.r.t. reduction, then it is $\mathcal{C}_\mathcal{E}$-terminating.*

Proof We have to prove that $\mathcal{R} \uplus \mathcal{C}_\mathcal{E}$ is terminating.

(1) Let $|s|_{Cons}$ denote the number of $Cons$ symbols in a term s. Because both $\mathcal{R}$ and $\mathcal{C}_\mathcal{E}$ are nonduplicating and $Cons$ symbols do not occur on right-hand sides of rewrite rules, it follows from $s \to_{\mathcal{R}\uplus\mathcal{C}_\mathcal{E}} t$ that $|s|_{Cons} \geq |t|_{Cons}$. We proceed by induction on $m = |s|_{Cons}$. If there is no $Cons$ symbol in a rewrite derivation, then the derivation must be finite. The inductive hypothesis states that any $\mathcal{R} \uplus \mathcal{C}_\mathcal{E}$ rewrite derivation starting from a term t with $|t|_{Cons} < m$ is finite. Suppose there exists an infinite derivation $D : s_1 \to_{\mathcal{R}\uplus\mathcal{C}_\mathcal{E}} s_2 \to_{\mathcal{R}\uplus\mathcal{C}_\mathcal{E}} s_3 \to_{\mathcal{R}\uplus\mathcal{C}_\mathcal{E}} \cdots$ with $|s_1|_{Cons} = m$. Obviously, this implies that $|s_j|_{Cons} = m$ for any index j. Now if $s_1 = Cons(t_1, t_2)$, then we derive a contradiction because any rewrite derivation starting from t_1 or t_2 must terminate. Hence $root(s_1)$ is an element of $\mathcal{F}$. The application of a rule from $\mathcal{C}_\mathcal{E}$ would decrease the number of occurrences of $Cons$ symbols, hence there is no application of such a rule in the whole derivation D. For any term t, let $top(t)$ be the term obtained from t by replacing each of its subterm with a $Cons$ symbol at the root with the special constant $\Box$. For every reduction step $s_j \to_\mathcal{R} s_{j+1}$, there are two possibilities:

(a) The contracted redex is a proper subterm of a subterm of s_j with a $Cons$ symbol at the root. In this case $top(s_j) = top(s_{j+1})$.

(b) The contracted redex is not contained in a subterm with a $Cons$ symbol at the root. In this case it is relatively simple to prove that $top(s_j) \to_\mathcal{R} top(s_{j+1})$.

It follows from these considerations that there is only a finite number of reduction steps of type (a) in D. Hence D contains infinitely many reduction steps of type (b). This yields an infinite $\mathcal{R}$-derivation, contradicting the termination of $\mathcal{R}$.

(2) If $\mathcal{R}$ is inconsistent w.r.t. reduction, then there is a term $C[x, y]$ with $C[x, y] \to_\mathcal{R}^+ x$ and $C[x, y] \to_\mathcal{R}^+ y$. Suppose that there exists an infinite derivation $D : s_1 \to_{\mathcal{R}\uplus\mathcal{C}_\mathcal{E}} s_2 \to_{\mathcal{R}\uplus\mathcal{C}_\mathcal{E}} s_3 \to_{\mathcal{R}\uplus\mathcal{C}_\mathcal{E}} \cdots$. In every s_j replace each $Cons(t_1, t_2)$ with $C[t_1, t_2]$ and denote this term by s'_j. Note that $Cons$ does not occur in any rule of $\mathcal{R}$. Then $D' : s'_1 \to_\mathcal{R}^+ s'_2 \to_\mathcal{R}^+ s'_3 \to_\mathcal{R}^+ \cdots$ is an infinite rewrite derivation of terms $s'_j \in \mathcal{T}(\mathcal{F}, \mathcal{V})$, where s'_j is rewritten to s'_{j+1} by $C[x, y] \to_\mathcal{R}^+ x$ ($C[x, y] \to_\mathcal{R}^+ y$, respectively) if s_j is reduced to s_{j+1} using the rule $Cons(x, y) \to x$ ($Cons(x, y) \to y$, respectively). $\Box$

Proposition 8.3.2 *If $(\mathcal{F}, \mathcal{R})$ is simply terminating, then $\mathcal{R} \cup \mathcal{E}mb(\mathcal{F})$ is $\mathcal{C}_\mathcal{E}$-terminating.*

Proof If $\mathcal{F}$ contains at most constants and unary function symbols, then $\mathcal{R} \cup \mathcal{E}mb(\mathcal{F})$ is nonduplicating and the assertion follows from statement (1) of Proposition 8.3.1. Otherwise, if $\mathcal{F}$ contains at least one function symbol f of arity $n \geq 2$, then $\mathcal{R} \cup \mathcal{E}mb(\mathcal{F})$ is inconsistent w.r.t. reduction and the assertion follows from statement (2) of Proposition 8.3.1. $\Box$

Lemma 8.3.3 *A TRS $\mathcal{R}$ is $\mathcal{C}_\mathcal{E}$-terminating if and only if $\mathcal{R} \uplus \mathcal{C}_\mathcal{E}$ is $\mathcal{C}_\mathcal{E}$-terminating.*

Proof If $\mathcal{R}$ is $\mathcal{C}_\mathcal{E}$-terminating, then $\mathcal{R} \uplus \mathcal{C}_\mathcal{E}$ is inconsistent w.r.t. reduction and terminating. By statement (2) of Proposition 8.3.1, it is $\mathcal{C}_\mathcal{E}$-terminating. The if direction is trivial. □

How does $\mathcal{C}_\mathcal{E}$-termination fit into the termination hierarchy? Proposition 8.3.2 yields the implications

$$\text{ST} \Rightarrow \mathcal{C}_\mathcal{E}\text{T} \Rightarrow \text{SN}$$

where $\mathcal{C}_\mathcal{E}$T stands for $\mathcal{C}_\mathcal{E}$-termination. For finite TRSs we even have

$$\text{ST} \Rightarrow \text{DP-ST} \Rightarrow \text{DP-QST} \Rightarrow \mathcal{C}_\mathcal{E}\text{T} \Rightarrow \text{SN}$$

This will be shown next.

Lemma 8.3.4 *A finite TRS $\mathcal{R}$ is DP quasi-simply terminating if and only if $\mathcal{R} \uplus \mathcal{C}_\mathcal{E}$ is DP quasi-simply terminating. In particular, DP quasi-simple termination implies $\mathcal{C}_\mathcal{E}$-termination.*

Proof The if direction is obviously true. For the other direction, let $\mathcal{R}$ be a DP quasi-simply terminating TRS. That is, for every cycle $\mathcal{P}$ in EDG($\mathcal{R}$) there exists an AFS $\mathcal{A}$ and a QSO $\succsim$ on $\mathcal{T}(\mathcal{F}', \mathcal{V})$ such that $u \succsim v$ implies $\mathcal{V}ar(v) \subseteq \mathcal{V}ar(u)$, and $\succsim$ satisfies the constraints

(a) $l \downarrow_\mathcal{A} \geq r \downarrow_\mathcal{A}$ for each rule $l \to r$ from $\mathcal{R}$,

(b) $s \downarrow_\mathcal{A} \geq t \downarrow_\mathcal{A}$ for each dependency pair $\langle s, t\rangle$ from $\mathcal{P}$,

(c) $s \downarrow_\mathcal{A} > t \downarrow_\mathcal{A}$ for at least one dependency pair $\langle s, t\rangle$ from $\mathcal{P}$,

where $\mathcal{F}'$ consists of all function symbols occurring in the constraints. We have to show that $\mathcal{R} \uplus \mathcal{C}_\mathcal{E}$ is DP quasi-simply terminating. First, note that every cycle $\mathcal{P}$ in EDG($\mathcal{R} \uplus \mathcal{C}_\mathcal{E}$) is also a cycle in EDG($\mathcal{R}$).[2]

Let Ω be the function that replaces every subterm $Cons(u_1, u_2)$ of a term $u \in \mathcal{T}(\mathcal{F}' \cup \{Cons\}, \mathcal{V})$ with the distinguished variable z. Let the quasi-ordering $\succsim'$ be defined on $\mathcal{T}(\mathcal{F}' \cup \{Cons\}, \mathcal{V})$ by

$$u \succsim' v \text{ if and only if } \mathcal{V}ar(v) \subseteq \mathcal{V}ar(u) \text{ and } \Omega(u) \succsim \Omega(v)$$

It is relatively simple to show that $\succsim'$ is a quasi-rewrite ordering, i.e., $\succsim'$ is closed under contexts and substitutions. The quasi-ordering $\succsim''$ defined by $\succsim'' = (\succsim' \cup \to_{\mathcal{C}_\mathcal{E}})^*$ inherits closure under contexts and substitutions and

[2]This is not true if we consider the dependency graph instead of the estimated dependency graph, as the system $f(0, 1, x) \to f(x, x, x)$ shows.

the property $u \succsim'' v \Rightarrow \mathcal{V}ar(v) \subseteq \mathcal{V}ar(u)$ from $\succsim'$ and $\to_{\mathcal{C}_\mathcal{E}}$. We claim that $\succsim''$ is a QSO on $\mathcal{T}(\mathcal{F}' \cup \{Cons\}, \mathcal{V})$. For every n-ary $f \in \mathcal{F}'$ and $1 \leq i \leq n$, we have

$$\Omega(f(x_1, \ldots, x_n)) = f(x_1, \ldots, x_n) \succsim x_i = \Omega(x_i)$$

because $\succsim$ is a QSO on $\mathcal{T}(\mathcal{F}', \mathcal{V})$. Therefore, $f(x_1, \ldots, x_n) \succsim' x_i$ and hence $f(x_1, \ldots, x_n) \succsim'' x_i$. Moreover, we have

$$Cons(x_1, x_2) \succsim'' x_i$$

because $Cons(x_1, x_2) \to_{\mathcal{C}_\mathcal{E}} x_i$, where $i \in \{1, 2\}$. Now it follows from Lemma 5.2.17 that $\succsim''$ has the subterm property. In other words, $\succsim''$ is a QSO on $\mathcal{T}(\mathcal{F}' \cup \{Cons\}, \mathcal{V})$. It is easy to verify that $\succsim''$ satisfies constraints (a)–(c) with the same AFS and $Cons(x_1, x_2) \succsim'' x_i$ holds true. We conclude that $\mathcal{R} \uplus \mathcal{C}_\mathcal{E}$ is DP quasi-simply terminating.

Lastly, DP quasi-simple termination of $\mathcal{R} \uplus \mathcal{C}_\mathcal{E}$ implies that $\mathcal{R} \uplus \mathcal{C}_\mathcal{E}$ is terminating, or equivalently, that $\mathcal{R}$ is $\mathcal{C}_\mathcal{E}$-terminating. □

It can be seen from Example 8.3.5 that $\mathcal{C}_\mathcal{E}$-termination does not imply DP quasi-simple termination.

Example 8.3.5 Let $\mathcal{R}$ consist of the rewrite rules

$$\begin{array}{rcl} f(d,e,x) & \to & f(x,g(e),e) \\ f(d,e,x) & \to & f(g(d),x,d) \\ h(g(x)) & \to & x \\ g(c) & \to & c \end{array}$$

It is not difficult to verify that $\mathcal{R}$ is nonduplicating and terminating. (In fact, it is nonself-embedding; see Lemma 6.1.41.) Therefore, it is $\mathcal{C}_\mathcal{E}$-terminating by Proposition 8.3.1. However, it is not DP quasi-simply terminating, as we will show.

The estimated dependency graph EDG($\mathcal{R}$) of $\mathcal{R}$ contains the cycle $\{\langle F(d,e,x), F(x,g(e),e)\rangle, \langle F(d,e,x), F(g(d),x,d)\rangle\}$. This yields the constraints (the case $F(d,e,x) \geq F(x,g(e),e)$ and $F(d,e,x) > F(g(d),x,d)$ is symmetric)

$$\begin{array}{rcl} F(d,e,x) & > & F(x,g(e),e) \\ F(d,e,x) & \geq & F(g(d),x,d) \\ f(d,e,x) & \geq & f(x,g(e),e) \\ f(d,e,x) & \geq & f(g(d),x,d) \\ h(g(x)) & \geq & x \\ g(c) & \geq & c \end{array}$$

Due to the fifth inequality, we can use neither the rule $h(x) \to h'$ nor the rule $g(x) \to g'$ to simplify the constraints because no QSO $\succsim$ with $u \succsim v \Rightarrow$

$\mathcal{V}ar(v) \subseteq \mathcal{V}ar(u)$ can satisfy the simplified constraints. It is not difficult to see that it is also impossible to use an F rule (independent of whether we apply $g(x) \to x$). Simplifying the constraints by the rule $g(x) \to x$ yields the inequalities $F(d,e,x) > F(x,e,e)$ and $F(d,e,x) \geq F(d,x,d)$. If there were a QSO $\succsim$ with $F(d,e,x) \succ F(x,e,e)$ and $F(d,e,x) \succsim F(d,x,d)$, then it would follow that

$$F(d,e,d) \succ F(d,e,e) \succsim F(d,e,d)$$

and thus $F(d,e,d) \succ F(d,e,d)$ by Lemma 5.4.4(7). This is clearly impossible. If we do not use an AFS at all, then we obtain a contradiction as well because

$$F(d,e,d) \succ F(d,g(e),e) \succsim F(d,e,e) \succsim F(g(d),e,d) \succsim F(d,e,d)$$

So $\mathcal{R}$ is not DP quasi-simply terminating.

8.4 Disjoint Unions

Next we give a brief overview of the basic notions of disjoint unions of TRSs. In what follows, let $(\mathcal{F}_1, \mathcal{R}_1)$ and $(\mathcal{F}_2, \mathcal{R}_2)$ be two disjoint TRSs and let $t \in \mathcal{T}(\mathcal{F}_1 \uplus \mathcal{F}_2, \mathcal{V})$. Let $t = C[t_1, \ldots, t_n]$ with $C[, \ldots,] \neq \Box$. We write $t = C[\![t_1, \ldots, t_n]\!]$ if $C[, \ldots,] \in \mathcal{T}(\mathcal{F}_d, \mathcal{V})$ and $root(t_1), \ldots root(t_n) \in \mathcal{F}_{3-d}$ for some $d \in \{1,2\}$. The t_j are the *principal* subterms (or *aliens*) of t.

For example, if $\mathcal{R}_1 = \{F(0,1,x) \to F(x,x,x)\}$ and $\mathcal{R}_2 = \{g(x,y) \to x, g(x,y) \to y\}$, then $\mathcal{R}_1$ and $\mathcal{R}_2$ are disjoint and the term $F(g(0,0),x,g(y,y))$ can be written as $C[\![g(0,0), g(y,y)]\!]$, where $C[, \ldots,] = F(\Box, x, \Box)$.

Moreover, we define for all t

$$rank(t) = \begin{cases} 1 & \text{if } t \in \mathcal{T}(\mathcal{F}_1, \mathcal{V}) \cup \mathcal{T}(\mathcal{F}_2, \mathcal{V}) \\ 1 + max\{rank(t_j) \mid 1 \leq j \leq n\} & \text{if } t = C[\![t_1, \ldots, t_n]\!] \end{cases}$$

For example, we have $rank(F(g(0,0),x,g(y,y))) = 3$.

The multiset $S(t)$ of *special* subterms of a term t is defined by $S(t) = \bigoplus_{j \geq 1} S_j(t)$, where $S_1(t) = [t]$ and

$$S_{j+1}(t) = \begin{cases} [\,] & \text{if } rank(t) = 1 \\ S_j(t_1) \oplus \cdots \oplus S_j(t_n) & \text{if } t = C[\![t_1, \ldots, t_n]\!] \end{cases}$$

Furthermore, we define for $d \in \{1,2\}$: $S^d(t) = [s \mid s \in S(t), root(s) \in \mathcal{F}_d]$. For $t = F(g(0,0),x,g(y,y))$ we have $S(t) = [t, g(0,0), g(y,y), 0, 0]$ and $S^1 = [t, 0, 0]$, for example.

The *topmost homogeneous part* of t, denoted by $top(t)$, is obtained from t by replacing all principal subterms with $\Box$, i.e.,

$$top(t) = \begin{cases} t & \text{if } rank(t) = 1 \\ C[, \ldots,] & \text{if } t = C[\![t_1, \ldots, t_n]\!] \end{cases}$$

For example, $top(F(g(0,0),x,g(y,y))) = F(\Box,x,\Box)$.

In order to enhance readability, we will call the function symbols from $\mathcal{F}_1$ *black* and those of $\mathcal{F}_2$ *white*. Variables have no color. A black (white) term does not contain white (black) function symbols (but it may contain variables). A *top black* (*top white*) term has a black (white) root symbol. In the following black function symbols are denoted by capital letters and white function symbols are printed in lowercase unless we also deal with dependency pairs. In this case both black and white function symbols will be printed in lowercase to distinguish ordinary function symbols from tuple symbols.

A reduction step $s \to_{\mathcal{R}_1 \uplus \mathcal{R}_2} t$ is called *inner*, denoted by $s \to^i_{\mathcal{R}_1 \uplus \mathcal{R}_2} t$, if the reduction takes place in one of the principal subterms of s. Otherwise, we speak of an *outer* reduction step and write $s \to^o_{\mathcal{R}_1 \uplus \mathcal{R}_2} t$.

A rewrite step $s \to_{\mathcal{R}_1 \uplus \mathcal{R}_2} t$ is *destructive at level 1* if the root symbols of s and t have different colors. A reduction step $s \to_{\mathcal{R}_1 \uplus \mathcal{R}_2} t$ is *destructive at level* $m+1$ (for some $m \geq 1$) if $s = C[\![s_1,\ldots,s_j,\ldots,s_n]\!] \to^i_{\mathcal{R}_1 \uplus \mathcal{R}_2} C[s_1,\ldots,t_j,\ldots,s_n] = t$ with $s_j \to_{\mathcal{R}_1 \uplus \mathcal{R}_2} t_j$ destructive at level m. Obviously, if a rewrite step is destructive, then the rewrite rule applied is collapsing. For example, the rewrite step $F(g(0,0),x,g(y,y)) \to F(0,x,g(y,y))$ is destructive at level 2.

Most of the following results crucially depend on the fact that $s \to_{\mathcal{R}_1 \uplus \mathcal{R}_2} t$ implies $rank(s) \geq rank(t)$ (the proof is straightforward by induction on $rank(s)$).

As in [Mid90], we introduce some special notations in order to enable a compact treatment of "degenerate" cases of $t = C[\![t_1,\ldots,t_n]\!]$. To this end, the notion of context is extended. We write $C\langle,\ldots,\rangle$ for a term containing zero or more occurrences of $\Box$ and $C\{,\ldots,\}$ for a term different from $\Box$ itself, containing zero or more occurrences of $\Box$. If $t_1,\ldots,t_n$ are the (possibly zero) principal subterms of some term t (from left to right), then we write $t = C\{\!\{t_1,\ldots,t_n\}\!\}$ provided that $t = C\{t_1,\ldots,t_n\}$. We write $t = C\langle\!\langle t_1,\ldots,t_n\rangle\!\rangle$ if $t = C\langle t_1,\ldots,t_n\rangle$ and either $C\langle,\ldots,\rangle \neq \Box$ and $t_1,\ldots,t_n$ are the principal subterms of t or $C\langle,\ldots,\rangle = \Box$ and $t \in \{t_1,\ldots,t_n\}$.

In order to code principal subterms by variables and to cope with outer rewrite steps using nonleft-linear rules the following notation is convenient. For terms $s_1,\ldots,s_n,t_1,\ldots,t_n$ we write $\langle s_1,\ldots,s_n\rangle \propto \langle t_1,\ldots,t_n\rangle$ if $s_i = s_j$ implies $t_i = t_j$ for all $1 \leq i < j \leq n$.

The following facts (their proofs are straightforward) will be heavily used in the sequel without being explicitly mentioned:

- If $s \to^o t$, then $s = C\{\!\{s_1,\ldots,s_n\}\!\}, t = C'\langle\!\langle s_{i_1},\ldots,s_{i_m}\rangle\!\rangle$ for contexts $C\{,\ldots,\}$, $C'\langle,\ldots,\rangle$, $i_1,\ldots,i_m \in \{1,\ldots,n\}$, and terms $s_1,\ldots,s_n$. If $s \to^o t$ is not destructive at level 1, then $t = C'\{\!\{s_{i_1},\ldots,s_{i_m}\}\!\}$.
- If $C\{\!\{s_1,\ldots,s_n\}\!\} \to^o C'\langle\!\langle s_{i_1},\ldots,s_{i_m}\rangle\!\rangle$, then we have $C\{t_1,\ldots,t_n\} \to^o C'\langle t_{i_1},\ldots,t_{i_m}\rangle$ by an application of the same rule whenever $t_1,\ldots,t_n$ are terms with $\langle s_1,\ldots,s_n\rangle \propto \langle t_1,\ldots,t_n\rangle$.

- If $s \to^i t$, then $s = C[\![s_1, \ldots, s_j, \ldots, s_n]\!]$ and $t = C[s_1, \ldots, s'_j, \ldots, s_n]$ for some context $C[, \ldots,]$, $j \in \{1, \ldots, n\}$, and terms $s_1, \ldots, s_n, s'_j$ with $s_j \to s'_j$. If $s \to^i t$ is not destructive at level 2, then $t = C[\![s_1, \ldots, s'_j, \ldots, s_n]\!]$.

8.4.1 $\mathcal{C}_\mathcal{E}$ and Simple Termination

This section addresses the question of sufficient conditions for the modularity of termination of TRSs. The material presented here originates from [Ohl94c]. We begin by describing a proof technique that is often applicable and that will subsequently be used in different variants. Let $\mathcal{R}_1$ and $\mathcal{R}_2$ be disjoint terminating TRSs that have the same special property (e.g. they are nonduplicating). If we want to show modularity of termination for TRSs with this special property, we have to first guarantee that $\mathcal{R} = \mathcal{R}_1 \uplus \mathcal{R}_2$ inherits the special property from its constituent TRSs (otherwise we only have a sufficient condition for the preservation of termination under disjoint union because we cannot infer the preservation of termination if more than two TRSs are combined). In order to prove that the disjoint union $\mathcal{R} = \mathcal{R}_1 \uplus \mathcal{R}_2$ is again terminating, we proceed by contradiction. Suppose that there is an infinite $\mathcal{R}$ derivation

$$D' : s'_1 \to s'_2 \to s'_3 \to \ldots$$

Because we assume that every signature contains at least one constant, we can replace every variable in D' with a constant and obtain an infinite $\mathcal{R}$ derivation $D : s_1 \to s_2 \to s_3 \to \ldots$ in which every s_j is a ground term. (In fact, this assumption is not essential; see [Ohl94c].) W.l.o.g. we may further assume that D is an infinite $\mathcal{R}$ derivation of minimal rank, where $rank(D) = rank(s_1)$. That is, any $\mathcal{R}$ derivation of smaller rank is finite. Let $rank(D) = k$. By our assumptions, it follows that for all indices j, $rank(s_j) = rank(D)$ and $root(s_j) \in \mathcal{F}_d$ for some $d \in \{1, 2\}$ (i.e., the terms all have the same rank and their root symbols have the same color). In particular, $\to$ is terminating on $\mathcal{T}^{<k} = \mathcal{T}^{<k}(\mathcal{F}_1 \uplus \mathcal{F}_2) = \{t \in \mathcal{T}(\mathcal{F}_1 \uplus \mathcal{F}_2) \mid rank(t) < k\}$. The crucial point of the proof is to find a transformation function $\Phi_d : \mathcal{T}_d^{\leq k} \to \mathcal{T}(\mathcal{F}_d)$, where

$$\mathcal{T}_d^{\leq k} = \{t \in \mathcal{T}(\mathcal{F}_1 \uplus \mathcal{F}_2) \mid rank(t) = k \text{ and } root(t) \in \mathcal{F}_d \text{ or } rank(t) < k\}$$

so that

$$\Phi_d(D) : \Phi_d(s_1) \to^*_{\mathcal{R}_d} \Phi_d(s_2) \to^*_{\mathcal{R}_d} \Phi_d(s_3) \to^*_{\mathcal{R}_d} \cdots$$

is an $\mathcal{R}_d$ derivation. If we can further ensure that $\Phi_d(D)$ is in fact infinite, i.e., infinitely many reduction steps occur therein, then we derive the contradiction we are aiming at: We assumed $\mathcal{R}_d$ was terminating.

What kind of properties does the transformation function Φ_d need to have? If all the s_j in D are top black, then every top white principal subterm occurring in D carries "black information" that may become relevant for the following rewrite steps. Pieces of that black information may come up to the top and become part of the topmost homogeneous black layer. This process may create new redexes in the top black layer which may be reduced in subsequent rewrite steps (in Example 8.2.8 the rise of the black constants 0 and 1 to the top layer was necessary to enable the infinite derivation). So the black transformation function Φ_1 has to extract the relevant black information from the top white principal subterms and store it in same fashion such that it can be selected by black rules whenever this is necessary. Thus the search for Φ_d is the creative part of the proof.

In the sequel, we use a variant of the proof technique described earlier. Parts of Φ_d, namely, the storage and selection (retrieval) of information, can be done by adding some new storing operator and associated selection rules to the TRS. This storing operator may be any binary function symbol not occurring in the signature under consideration. Denoting this symbol by $Cons$, we are able to store black information as follows: Terms $t_1, \ldots, t_n$ are listed in the term $Cons(t_1, Cons(t_2, \ldots, Cons(t_n, Nil) \ldots))$. In order to enhance readability we will write $\langle t_1, \ldots, t_n \rangle$ for this list of terms, where $\langle\ \rangle$ stands for the empty list Nil (as a matter of fact, we can use any constant from $\mathcal{F}_d$ or even a distinguished variable z instead of Nil; see [Ohl94c]). Now every term t_j can be selected from this list if we add the ("selection") rewrite rules $Cons(x, y) \to x$ and $Cons(x, y) \to y$.[3] We will show that if the disjoint union of two terminating TRSs is nonterminating, then one of the systems does not remain terminating after the addition of the rules $Cons(x, y) \to x$ and $Cons(x, y) \to y$ and the other one must contain collapsing rules. This is essentially done by giving a transformation function

$$\Phi_d : \mathcal{T}_d^{\leq k} \to \mathcal{T}(\mathcal{F}_d \uplus \{Cons, Nil\})$$

that transforms a presupposed minimal infinite $\mathcal{R}_1 \uplus \mathcal{R}_2$ derivation $D : s_1 \to s_2 \to s_3 \to \ldots$ where $rank(D) = k$ and $root(s_j) \in \mathcal{F}_d$, into an infinite $\mathcal{R}_d \uplus \mathcal{C}_\mathcal{E}$ derivation

$$\Phi_d(D) : \Phi_d(s_1) \to^*_{\mathcal{R}_d \uplus \mathcal{C}_\mathcal{E}} \Phi_d(s_2) \to^*_{\mathcal{R}_d \uplus \mathcal{C}_\mathcal{E}} \Phi_d(s_3) \to^*_{\mathcal{R}_d \uplus \mathcal{C}_\mathcal{E}} \cdots$$

where $\mathcal{C}_\mathcal{E}$ denotes $\{Cons(x, y) \to x, Cons(x, y) \to y\}$. As we shall see, this "abstract result" has interesting consequences. The "abstract result" was first shown by Gramlich [Gra94] for *finitely branching* TRSs; we will elaborate on his approach in Section 8.6.1. Because we have a tool for storing

---

[3]This idea appeared first in Kurihara and Ohuchi [KO90], but they used a varyadic operator.

and selecting information, the question is how to extract the relevant information. In [Gra94] this is done for finitely branching TRSs as follows: In the preceding situation, because $\rightarrow$ is terminating on $\mathcal{T}^{<k}(\mathcal{F}_1 \uplus \mathcal{F}_2)$, one can apply König's lemma and conclude that each term $t \in \mathcal{T}^{<k}(\mathcal{F}_1 \uplus \mathcal{F}_2)$ has only finitely many reducts w.r.t. $\rightarrow$. Let the s_j be top black. Clearly, if t is some top white principal subterm of some s_j, each top black reduct of t reveals some of the black information hidden in t. All of these are listed as suggested earlier. Moreover, because there may again be same relevant black information hidden in the top white principal subterms of the black reducts, the described process is applied recursively. Thus the black information hidden in t is pressed out of it by doing all possible reductions in advance. Needed black information is then selected only by means of the rules $Cons(x, y) \rightarrow x$ and $Cons(x, y) \rightarrow y$. Obviously, this approach fails if arbitrary (that is, not necessarily finitely branching TRSs) are involved. If we consider, e.g., the TRSs $\mathcal{R} = \{A \rightarrow B_j \mid j \in \mathbb{N}\}$, then the constant A carries the information $\{B_j \mid j \in \mathbb{N}\}$ w.r.t. $\rightarrow_{\mathcal{R}}$, which cannot be stored in a term $Cons(B_1, Cons(B_2, \dots))$ because terms are finite objects. The idea is then to retain and rearrange all the black information contained in the term s_1 (from which the presupposed infinite derivation starts) in such a way that needed black information can be selected by means of rules from both $\mathcal{R}_1$ and $\mathcal{C}_{\mathcal{E}}$. In our small example this would mean that we keep the constant A as long as we do not know to which B_j it finally rewrites.

We start the presentation of our construction by giving some needed lemmas and definitions.

Lemma 8.4.1 *Let $s \rightarrow_{\mathcal{R}} t$ be given, and let $v \in S^d(t)$ for some $d \in \{1, 2\}$. Then there is a $u \in S^d(s)$ such that $u = v$ or $u \rightarrow_{\mathcal{R}} v$.*

Proof Induction on $k = rank(s)$. The case $k = 1$ is trivial. Let us consider the inductive step $k \rightarrow k + 1$. We distinguish the following cases:

(i) If $s \rightarrow_{\mathcal{R}}^{o} t$ is nondestructive at level 1, then we may write $s = C[\![s_1, \dots, s_n]\!]$ and $t = C'\{\!\{s_{i_1}, \dots, s_{i_m}\}\!\}$ for some contexts $C[, \dots,]$, $C'\{, \dots, \}$, $i_1, \dots, i_m \in \{1, \dots, n\}$, and terms $s_1 \dots, s_n$. If $v = t$, then take $u = s$. Otherwise, there exists some s_{i_l} such that $v \in S^d(s_{i_l})$. Now the assertion follows from $S^d(s_{i_l}) \subseteq S^d(s)$, i.e., take $u = v$.

(ii) If $s \rightarrow_{\mathcal{R}}^{o} t$ is destructive at level 1, then we have $s = C[\![s_1, \dots, s_n]\!] \rightarrow_{\mathcal{R}}^{o} s_j = t$ for some $j \in \{1, \dots, n\}$. As earlier, the assertion follows immediately from $S^d(t) \subseteq S^d(s)$: again take $u = v$.

(iii) If $s \rightarrow_{\mathcal{R}}^{i} t$, then we have $s = C[\![s_1, \dots, s_j, \dots, s_n]\!]$ and $t = C[s_1, \dots, s_j', \dots, s_n]$, where $s_j \rightarrow_{\mathcal{R}} s_j'$ for some j. If $v = t$, then take $u = s$. If $v \in \bigoplus_{l \neq j} S^d(s_l)$, then $v \in S^d(s)$ and we take $u = v$. Otherwise $v \in S^d(s_j')$ and by the inductive hypothesis there is a $u \in S^d(s_j) \subseteq S^d(s)$ such that $u = v$ or $u \rightarrow_{\mathcal{R}} v$. □

Lemma 8.4.2 *Let $s \to_{\mathcal{R}}^* t$ be given. For any $v \in S^d(t)$ there is a $u \in S^d(s)$ such that $u \to_{\mathcal{R}}^* v$.*

Proof Induction on the length ℓ of the derivation $s \to_{\mathcal{R}}^{\ell} t$ using Lemma 8.4.1 proves the lemma. □

Definition 8.4.3 Let $s, t \in \mathcal{T}(\mathcal{F})$. We define

$$\psi(s,t) = min(\{rank(u) \mid u \in S(s) \text{ and } u \to_{\mathcal{R}}^* t\})$$

where $min(\emptyset) = \infty$. We will often write $\psi(t)$ instead of $\psi(s,t)$, that is, suppress the first argument whenever it is clear from the context.

The number $\psi(s,t)$ will serve as a measure of how complex the information of t is w.r.t. s and $\to_{\mathcal{R}}$. To be more precise, it gives us the minimal rank of all subterms of s that reduce to t. Evidently, $s \to^* t \Rightarrow \psi(s,t) \neq \infty$. The next lemma says that if, for example, t is top black, then in computing $\psi(s,t)$ we may focus on the top black special subterms of s.

Lemma 8.4.4 *Let $s, t \in \mathcal{T}(\mathcal{F})$, and let $root(t) \in \mathcal{F}_d$. Then*

$$\psi(t) = min(\{rank(u) \mid u \in S^d(s) \text{ and } u \to_{\mathcal{R}}^* t\})$$

Proof By definition $\psi(t) = min(\{rank(u) \mid u \in S(s) \text{ and } u \to_{\mathcal{R}}^* t\})$. If there is an $s' \in S(s)$ with $s' \to_{\mathcal{R}}^* t$, then by Lemma 8.4.2 (with $v = t$) there is also a $u \in S^d(s') \subseteq S^d(s)$ with $u \to_{\mathcal{R}}^* t$. Clearly, $rank(u) \leq rank(s')$. □

Lemma 8.4.5 *Let $s, t \in \mathcal{T}(\mathcal{F})$ such that $\psi(s,t) \neq \infty$. Then*

1. *$rank(t) \leq \psi(s,t) \leq rank(s)$*
2. *For all $t' \in \mathcal{T}(\mathcal{F})$ with $t \to_{\mathcal{R}}^* t'$ we have $\psi(t') \leq \psi(t)$.*

Proof The proof is straightforward. □

Lemma 8.4.6 *Let $s, t \in \mathcal{T}(\mathcal{F})$ such that $\psi(s,t) \neq \infty$. For every $t' \in S(t)$ with $t' \neq t$ we have $\psi(t') < \psi(t)$. (Hence $\psi(t') \leq \psi(t)$ for all $t' \in S(t)$.)*

Proof Induction on $\psi(t)$ (recall that according to Lemma 8.4.5 $rank(t) \leq \psi(t) \leq rank(s)$). $\psi(t) = 1$ implies $rank(t) = 1$, thus the lemma holds vacuously in this case. Let $\psi(t) = k > 1$ and suppose that the claim holds for any term v with $\psi(v) < k$. Let $t = C[\![t_1, \ldots, t_n]\!]$ and let $root(t) \in \mathcal{F}_d$ for some $d \in \{1,2\}$. By Lemma 8.4.4, there exists a $u \in S^d(s)$ with $rank(u) = \psi(t)$ such that $u \to_{\mathcal{R}}^* t$. Because $t' \neq t$ there is a $j \in \{1, \ldots, n\}$ such that $t' \in S(t_j)$. Then by Lemma 8.4.2 there is a $u' \in S^{3-d}(u) \subseteq S^{3-d}(s)$ such that $u' \to_{\mathcal{R}}^* t_j$ because $root(t_j) \in \mathcal{F}_{3-d}$. Clearly, $rank(u') < rank(u)$, therefore $\psi(t_j) < \psi(t)$. Now if $t' = t_j$, then the lemma follows. Otherwise, if $t' \neq t_j$, then by the inductive hypothesis $\psi(t') < \psi(t_j)$ and hence $\psi(t') < \psi(t_j) < \psi(t)$. □

Recall that $\mathcal{C}_\mathcal{E}$ denotes the TRS $\{Cons(x,y) \to x,\ Cons(x,y) \to y\}$ and that $\langle t_1,\ldots,t_n\rangle \to^+_{\mathcal{C}_\mathcal{E}} t_j$ for any index j. The following definition states how the d information contained in a term s with $root(s) \in \mathcal{F}_d$ has to be rearranged for the purpose of proving Theorem 8.4.13.

Definition 8.4.7 Let $s \in \mathcal{T}(\mathcal{F})$ with $rank(s) = k$ and $root(s) \in \mathcal{F}_d$. Let $\succ$ be some arbitrary but fixed total ordering on $\mathcal{T}(\mathcal{F} \uplus \{Cons, Nil\})$. We define

$$
\begin{aligned}
L_1^{3-d}(s) &= \langle\,\rangle \\
L_1^{d}(s) &= Sort(\{t \mid t \in S^d(s), rank(t) = 1\}) \\
L_{n+1}^{3-d}(s) &= \begin{cases} \langle L_n^d(s), L_n^{3-d}(s)\rangle & \text{if } n+1 < k \\ \langle\,\rangle & \text{otherwise} \end{cases} \\
L_{n+1}^{d}(s) &= \begin{cases} Sort(\{C[L_n^{3-d}(s),\ldots,L_n^{3-d}(s)] \mid t = C[\![t_1,\ldots,t_n]\!] \in S^d(s) \\ \text{and } rank(t) = n+1\}) \quad \text{if } n+1 \le k \\ \langle\,\rangle \quad \text{otherwise} \end{cases}
\end{aligned}
$$

where $Sort(\{t_1,\ldots,t_n\}) = \langle t_{\pi(1)},\ldots,t_{\pi(n)}\rangle$ such that $t_{\pi(j)} \succ t_{\pi(j+1)}$ for $1 \le j < n$. Note that the sets to be sorted are finite and thus the sets L_n^d and L_n^{3-d} are well-defined. As we shall see later, the sorting process is necessary in order to cope with nonleft-linear rules: The succession of the listed elements of a set has to be uniquely determined. Again, we suppress the argument s whenever it is clear from the context.

Example 8.4.8 Consider the TRSs $\mathcal{R}_1 = \{F(x,x,B_2) \to x, G(x) \to x, H(x) \to A, A \to B_j \mid j \in \mathbb{N}\}$ and $\mathcal{R}_2 = \{f(x) \to x\}$. For the term $s = F(f(G(f(B_1))), f(A), f(H(a)))$ we have (note $d = 1$)

$$
\begin{array}{rcl}
L_1^2 = & \langle\,\rangle & L_1^1 = \langle A, B_1\rangle \\
L_2^2 = & \langle L_1^1, L_1^2\rangle & L_2^1 = \langle H(L_1^2)\rangle \\
L_3^2 = & \langle L_2^1, L_2^2\rangle & L_3^1 = \langle G(L_2^2)\rangle \\
L_4^2 = & \langle L_3^1, L_3^2\rangle & L_4^1 = \langle\,\rangle \\
L_5^2 = & \langle\,\rangle & L_5^1 = \langle F(L_4^2, L_4^2, L_4^2)\rangle
\end{array}
$$

where $\succ$ is some total ordering on $\mathcal{T}(\mathcal{F} \uplus \{Cons, Nil\})$ such that $Sort(\{A, B_1\}) = \langle A, B_1\rangle$.

Lemma 8.4.9 *Let $s \in \mathcal{T}(\mathcal{F})$ with $rank(s) = k$ and $root(s) \in \mathcal{F}_d$. Then we have for all j, i with $1 \le j < i < k$:*

- $L_i^{3-d} \to^+_{\mathcal{C}_\mathcal{E}} L_j^{3-d}$

- $L_i^{3-d} \to_{\mathcal{C}_\mathcal{E}}^{+} L_j^d$

Proof The proof is straightforward. □

With the aid of Definition 8.4.7 we can define the required transformation function Φ_d.

Definition 8.4.10 Let $s \in \mathcal{T}(\mathcal{F})$ with $root(s) \in \mathcal{F}_d$.
Define $\Phi_d^s : \{t \in \mathcal{T}(\mathcal{F}_1 \uplus \mathcal{F}_2) \mid \psi(s,t) \neq \infty\} \to \mathcal{T}(\mathcal{F}_d \uplus \{Cons, Nil\})$ by

- $\Phi_d^s(t) = t$, if $t \in \mathcal{T}(\mathcal{F}_d)$
- $\Phi_d^s(t) = \langle\ \rangle$, if $t \in \mathcal{T}(\mathcal{F}_{3-d})$
- $\Phi_d^s(t) = C[\Phi_d^s(t_1), \ldots, \Phi_d^s(t_n)]$, if $root(t) \in \mathcal{F}_d$ and $t = C[\![t_1, \ldots, t_n]\!]$
- $\Phi_d^s(t) = L_{\psi(s,t)}^{3-d}(s)$, if $root(t) \in \mathcal{F}_{3-d}$ and $t = C[\![t_1, \ldots, t_n]\!]$.

Notice that Φ_d^s is well-defined (cf. Lemma 8.4.6). Again we will suppress the superscript s in Φ_d^s if it is clear from the context.

Lemma 8.4.11 *Let $s \in \mathcal{T}(\mathcal{F})$ with $root(s) \in \mathcal{F}_d$. If $u \in S^d(s)$, then $L_{rank(u)}^d \to_{\mathcal{C}_\mathcal{E}}^{+} \Phi_d(u)$.*

Proof Let $rank(u) = m$. Clearly, $m = \psi(u) \leq rank(s)$. We will show the lemma for $m > 1$, the case $m = 1$ is obtained by similar arguments. Because $m > 1$, we may write $u = C'[\![u_1, \ldots, u_n]\!]$. Clearly, $\Phi_d(u) = C'[\Phi_d(u_1), \ldots, \Phi_d(u_n)] = C'[L_{\psi(u_1)}^{3-d}, \ldots, L_{\psi(u_n)}^{3-d}]$. Moreover, $L_{rank(u)}^d = L_m^d = Sort(\{C[L_{m-1}^{3-d}, \ldots, L_{m-1}^{3-d}] \mid t = C[\![t_1, \ldots, t_n]\!] \in S^d(s), rank(t) = m\})$. Because $u \in S^d(s)$ and $rank(u) = m$, it follows that $C'[L_{m-1}^{3-d}, \ldots, L_{m-1}^{3-d}]$ occurs in L_m^d. Therefore, $L_m^d \to_{\mathcal{C}_\mathcal{E}}^{+} C'[L_{m-1}^{3-d}, \ldots, L_{m-1}^{3-d}]$. Note that $m - 1 \geq \psi(u_j)$ for all $j \in \{1, \ldots, n\}$ because $m > rank(u_j) = \psi(u_j)$. Thus $C'[L_{m-1}^{3-d}, \ldots, L_{m-1}^{3-d}] \to_{\mathcal{C}_\mathcal{E}}^{*} C'[L_{\psi(u_1)}^{3-d}, \ldots, L_{\psi(u_n)}^{3-d}]$ according to Lemma 8.4.9. All in all, $L_{rank(u)}^d \to_{\mathcal{C}_\mathcal{E}}^{+} C'[L_{m-1}^{3-d}, \ldots, L_{m-1}^{3-d}] \to_{\mathcal{C}_\mathcal{E}}^{*} C'[L_{\psi(u_1)}^{3-d}, \ldots, L_{\psi(u_n)}^{3-d}] = \Phi_d(u)$. □

Example 8.4.12 Consider the reduction sequence D

$$s = s_1 \to_{\mathcal{R}_1} s_2 \to_{\mathcal{R}_2} s_3 \to_{\mathcal{R}_1} s_4 \to_{\mathcal{R}_1} s_5 \to_{\mathcal{R}_1} s_6 \to_{\mathcal{R}_2} s_7 \to_{\mathcal{R}_1} s_8 \to_{\mathcal{R}_2} s_9$$

where s, $\mathcal{R}_1$, and $\mathcal{R}_2$ are as in Example 8.4.8 and

$$\begin{array}{ll}
s_2 = F(f(G(f(B_1))), f(A), f(A)) & s_3 = F(f(G(B_1)), f(A), f(A)) \\
s_4 = F(f(B_1), f(A), f(A)) & s_5 = F(f(B_1), f(B_1), f(A)) \\
s_6 = F(f(B_1), f(B_1), f(B_2)) & s_7 = F(f(B_1), f(B_1), B_2) \\
s_8 = f(B_1) & s_9 = B_1
\end{array}$$

Applying Φ_1 to D we obtain

$$\begin{aligned}\Phi_1(D) : \Phi_1(s) &= \Phi_1(s_1) \to^+_{\mathcal{C}_\mathcal{E}} \Phi_1(s_2) = \Phi_1(s_3) \to^+_{\mathcal{C}_\mathcal{E}} \Phi_1(s_4) = \Phi_1(s_5) \\ &= \Phi_1(s_6) \to^+_{\mathcal{R}_1 \uplus \mathcal{C}_\mathcal{E}} \Phi_1(s_7) \to_{\mathcal{R}_1} \Phi_1(s_8) \to^+_{\mathcal{R}_1 \uplus \mathcal{C}_\mathcal{E}} \Phi_1(s_9)\end{aligned}$$

where $\Phi_1(s) = F(L_4^2, L_2^2, L_3^2)$ and

$$\begin{aligned}&\Phi_1(s_2) = F(L_4^2, L_2^2, L_2^2), \quad \Phi_1(s_4) = F(L_2^2, L_2^2, L_2^2), \\ &\Phi_1(s_7) = F(L_2^2, L_2^2, B_2), \quad \Phi_1(s_8) = L_2^2, \quad \Phi_1(s_9) = B_1\end{aligned}$$

The next theorem shows that an $\mathcal{R}_1 \uplus \mathcal{R}_2$ derivation starting from some term s with $root(s) \in \mathcal{F}_d$ can always be transformed into a $\mathcal{R}_d \uplus \mathcal{C}_\mathcal{E}$ derivation starting from $\Phi_d(s)$. In fact, it expresses a more general statement.

Theorem 8.4.13 *Let s and t be terms from $\mathcal{T}(\mathcal{F})$ with $root(s) \in \mathcal{F}_d$ and $\psi(t) \neq \infty$. Then for all $t' \in \mathcal{T}(\mathcal{F})$ such that $t \to^*_{\mathcal{R}_1 \uplus \mathcal{R}_2} t'$ it follows that $\Phi_d(t) \to^*_{\mathcal{R}_d \uplus \mathcal{C}_\mathcal{E}} \Phi_d(t')$. Moreover, $t \to^o_{\mathcal{R}_d} t'$ implies $\Phi_d(t) \to_{\mathcal{R}_d} \Phi_d(t')$.*

Proof We prove the theorem by (finite) induction on $\psi(t)$, where $rank(t) \leq \psi(t) \leq rank(s)$.

The base case $\psi(t) = 1$ is straightforward because $\psi(t) = 1$ implies $rank(t) = 1$. So let $\psi(t) = k > 1$ and suppose that the theorem holds for all $v \in \mathcal{T}(\mathcal{F})$ with $\psi(v) < k$. We prove the induction step by induction on the length ℓ of the derivation $t \to^\ell_{\mathcal{R}_1 \uplus \mathcal{R}_2} t'$.

The case $\ell = 0$ is trivial, so consider $t \to^\ell_{\mathcal{R}_1 \uplus \mathcal{R}_2} t'' \to_{\mathcal{R}_1 \uplus \mathcal{R}_2} t'$. By the inner inductive hypothesis (on ℓ) $\Phi_d(t) \to^*_{\mathcal{R}_d \uplus \mathcal{C}_\mathcal{E}} \Phi_d(t'')$. It remains to be shown that $\Phi_d(t'') \to^*_{\mathcal{R}_d \uplus \mathcal{C}_\mathcal{E}} \Phi_d(t')$. The case $rank(t'') = 1$ is straightforward, so let $rank(t'') > 1$. We distinguish between the following cases:

(i) $root(t'') \in \mathcal{F}_d$: If $t'' \to^o_{\mathcal{R}_d} t'$, then $t'' = C[\![t_1, \ldots, t_n]\!]$ and $t' = C'\langle\!\langle t_{i_1}, \ldots, t_{i_m}\rangle\!\rangle$ for some contexts $C[, \ldots,]$, $C'[, \ldots,]$, $i_1, \ldots, i_m \in \{1, \ldots, n\}$, and terms $t_1, \ldots, t_n$. Applying Φ_d, we obtain $\Phi_d(t'') = C[\Phi_d(t_1), \ldots, \Phi_d(t_n)]$ and $\Phi_d(t') = C'\langle \Phi_d(t_{i_1}), \ldots, \Phi_d(t_{i_m})\rangle$. Therefore, $\Phi_d(t'') \to_{\mathcal{R}_d} \Phi_d(t')$ using the same rule as before because $\langle t_1, \ldots, t_n\rangle \propto \langle \Phi_d(t_1), \ldots, \Phi_d(t_n)\rangle$ (i.e., even nonleft-linear rules do not cause trouble). In an inner reduction step $t'' \to^i_{\mathcal{R}_1 \uplus \mathcal{R}_2} t'$, we have $t'' = C[\![t_1, \ldots, t_j, \ldots, t_n]\!]$ and $t' = C[t_1, \ldots, t'_j, \ldots, t_n]$, where $t_j \to_{\mathcal{R}_1 \uplus \mathcal{R}_2} t'_j$. Because $t_j \in S(t'')$ and $t_j \neq t''$, it follows from Lemma 8.4.6 that $\psi(t_j) < \psi(t'')$ and therefore $\psi(t_j) < \psi(t)$ (recall that $\psi(t'') \leq \psi(t)$ by Lemma 8.4.5). The outer inductive hypothesis yields $\Phi_d(t_j) \to^*_{\mathcal{R}_d \uplus \mathcal{C}_\mathcal{E}} \Phi_d(t'_j)$. Therefore, $\Phi_d(t'') = C[\Phi_d(t_1), \ldots, \Phi_d(t_j), \ldots, \Phi_d(t_n)] \to^*_{\mathcal{R}_d \uplus \mathcal{C}_\mathcal{E}} C[\Phi_d(t_1), \ldots, \Phi_d(t'_j), \ldots, \Phi_d(t_n)]$. It remains to show the equality $\Phi_d(t') = C[\Phi_d(t_1), \ldots, \Phi_d(t'_j), \ldots, \Phi_d(t_n)]$. It is easy to verify its validity if $root(t'_j) \in \mathcal{F}_{3-d}$ or $t'_j \in \mathcal{T}(\mathcal{F}_d)$. So suppose $root(t'_j) \in \mathcal{F}_d$ and $t'_j = C'[\![u_1, \ldots, u_m]\!]$.

Set $C''[,\dots,] = C[,\dots,C'[,\dots,],\dots,]$. It follows that

$$\begin{aligned}
&\Phi_d(t') \\
&= C''[\Phi_d(t_1),\dots,\Phi_d(t_{j-1}),\Phi_d(u_1),\dots,\Phi_d(u_m),\Phi_d(t_{j+1}),\dots,\Phi_d(t_n)] \\
&= C[\Phi_d(t_1),\dots,\Phi_d(t_{j-1}),C'[\Phi_d(u_1),\dots,\Phi_d(u_m)],\Phi_d(t_{j+1}),\dots,\Phi_d(t_n)] \\
&= C[\Phi_d(t_1),\dots,\Phi_d(t_j'),\dots,\Phi_d(t_n)].
\end{aligned}$$

(ii) $root(t'') \in \mathcal{F}_{3-d}$: If also $root(t') \in \mathcal{F}_{3-d}$, then by Lemma 8.4.9 $\Phi_d(t'') = L^{3-d}_{\psi(t'')}(s) \to^*_{\mathcal{C}_\mathcal{E}} L^{3-d}_{\psi(t')}(s) = \Phi_d(t')$ because $\psi(t') \le \psi(t'')$.

Otherwise, if $root(t') \in \mathcal{F}_d$, then $t'' = C[\![t_1,\dots,t_n]\!] \to_{\mathcal{R}_{3-d}} t'$ where $t' = t_j$ for some $j \in \{1,\dots,n\}$. Because $\psi(t'') \le \psi(t) \ne \infty$, there is an $s' \in S^{3-d}(s)$ with $rank(s') = \psi(t'')$ such that $s' \to^*_{\mathcal{R}_1 \uplus \mathcal{R}_2} t''$. Now $\Phi_d(s') = L^{3-d}_{rank(s')}(s) = L^{3-d}_{\psi(t'')}(s) = \Phi_d(t'')$. Hence it remains to show that $\Phi_d(s') \to^*_{\mathcal{R}_d \uplus \mathcal{C}_\mathcal{E}} \Phi_d(t')$. Because $s' \to^*_{\mathcal{R}_1 \uplus \mathcal{R}_2} t'$, $root(t') \in \mathcal{F}_d$, and $root(s') \in \mathcal{F}_{3-d}$, there exists a $u \in S^d(s') \subseteq S^d(s)$ such that $u \to^*_{\mathcal{R}_1 \uplus \mathcal{R}_2} t'$. Obviously, $\psi(u) = rank(u) < rank(s') = \psi(t'') \le \psi(t)$. Consequently it follows from the outer inductive hypothesis that $\Phi_d(u) \to^*_{\mathcal{R}_d \uplus \mathcal{C}_\mathcal{E}} \Phi_d(t')$. Eventually, we have (cf. Lemmas 8.4.9 and 8.4.11) $\Phi_d(t'') = \Phi_d(s') = L^{3-d}_{rank(s')}(s) \to^+_{\mathcal{C}_\mathcal{E}} L^d_{rank(u)}(s) \to^+_{\mathcal{C}_\mathcal{E}} \Phi_d(u) \to^*_{\mathcal{R}_d \uplus \mathcal{C}_\mathcal{E}} \Phi_d(t')$. □

Theorem 8.4.13 paves the way for our main result.

Theorem 8.4.14 *Let $\mathcal{R}_1$ and $\mathcal{R}_2$ be two disjoint terminating TRSs such that their disjoint union $\mathcal{R}_1 \uplus \mathcal{R}_2$ is nonterminating. Then $\mathcal{R}_1$ is not $\mathcal{C}_\mathcal{E}$-terminating and $\mathcal{R}_2$ is collapsing or vice versa.*

Proof Let

$$D : s = s_1 \to s_2 \to s_3 \to \dots$$

be an infinite $\mathcal{R}_1 \uplus \mathcal{R}_2$ derivation of minimal rank, i.e., any $\mathcal{R}_1 \uplus \mathcal{R}_2$ derivation of smaller rank is finite. Let $rank(D) = k$. Hence $rank(s_j) = rank(D)$ for all indices j. Let $root(s_1) \in \mathcal{F}_d$ for some $d \in \{1,2\}$. It follows that $root(s_j) \in \mathcal{F}_d$ for any j. In particular, there is no reduction step that is destructive at level 1. From the minimality assumption on $rank(D)$ we conclude that there is no index $l \in \mathbb{N}$ such that the subderivation of D beginning at s_l consists only of inner rewrite steps. Thus there must be infinitely many $\to^o_{\mathcal{R}_d}$ steps in D. W.l.o.g. we may assume that every term in D is a ground term. Now we apply the function Φ_d to D and obtain an $\mathcal{R}_d \uplus \mathcal{C}_\mathcal{E}$ rewrite derivation (note that Φ_d is well-defined on D)

$$\Phi_d(D) : \Phi_d(s) = \Phi_d(s_1) \to^*_{\mathcal{R}_d \uplus \mathcal{C}_\mathcal{E}} \Phi_d(s_2) \to^*_{\mathcal{R}_d \uplus \mathcal{C}_\mathcal{E}} \Phi_d(s_3) \to^*_{\mathcal{R}_d \uplus \mathcal{C}_\mathcal{E}} \cdots$$

By Theorem 8.4.13 it follows that a reduction step of the form $s_j \to^o_{\mathcal{R}_d} s_{j+1}$ in D corresponds to a reduction step $\Phi_d(s_j) \to_{\mathcal{R}_d} \Phi_d(s_{j+1})$ in $\Phi_d(D)$. Because there are infinitely many outer reduction steps in D, the derivation $\Phi_d(D)$ consists of infinitely many reduction steps. Hence $\mathcal{R}_d$ is not $\mathcal{C}_\mathcal{E}$-terminating.
Suppose that $\mathcal{R}_{3-d}$ is noncollapsing. Then for any $s_j \to_\mathcal{R} s_{j+1}$ we have

- $s_j \to^o_{\mathcal{R}_d} s_{j+1}$ implies $top(s_j) \to_{\mathcal{R}_d} top(s_{j+1})$, and
- $s_j \to^i_{\mathcal{R}} s_{j+1}$ implies $top(s_j) = top(s_{j+1})$.

Because there are infinitely many outer reduction steps in D, this yields an infinite $\mathcal{R}_d$ derivation, contradicting the termination of $\mathcal{R}_d$. □

Theorem 8.4.14 can be paraphrased as follows: If $\mathcal{R}_1$ and $\mathcal{R}_2$ are disjoint terminating TRSs, then their disjoint union $\mathcal{R}_1 \uplus \mathcal{R}_2$ is terminating provided one of the following conditions is satisfied:

1. Both $\mathcal{R}_1$ and $\mathcal{R}_2$ are $\mathcal{C}_\mathcal{E}$-terminating.
2. Both $\mathcal{R}_1$ and $\mathcal{R}_2$ are noncollapsing.
3. One of the systems is $\mathcal{C}_\mathcal{E}$-terminating and noncollapsing.

The combination of Theorem 8.4.14 with Propositions 8.3.1 and 8.3.2 has interesting consequences.

Theorem 8.4.15 *For disjoint TRSs, we have:*

1. *$\mathcal{C}_\mathcal{E}$-termination is modular.*
2. *Simple termination is modular.*
3. *Termination is a modular property of noncollapsing TRSs.*
4. *Termination is a modular property of nonduplicating TRSs.*
5. *Termination is a modular property of TRSs that are inconsistent w.r.t. reduction.*

Proof Let $\mathcal{R}_1$ and $\mathcal{R}_2$ be disjoint TRSs. We have to show that $\mathcal{R} = \mathcal{R}_1 \uplus \mathcal{R}_2$ has one of the properties (1)–(5) if $\mathcal{R}_1$ and $\mathcal{R}_2$ have the respective property.

(1) We know from Theorem 8.4.14 that the disjoint union of two $\mathcal{C}_\mathcal{E}$-terminating TRSs $\mathcal{R}_1$ and $\mathcal{R}_2$ is again terminating. But we have to prove that it is also $\mathcal{C}_\mathcal{E}$-terminating. That this is the case can be seen as follows: Let $Cons$ be a binary operator that does not occur in $\mathcal{F}_1 \uplus \mathcal{F}_2$. Because $\mathcal{R}_2$ is $\mathcal{C}_\mathcal{E}$-terminating, the same holds, by Lemma 8.3.3, for $\mathcal{R}_2 \uplus \{Cons(x,y) \to x, Cons(x,y) \to y\}$. Hence we may conclude by Theorem 8.4.14 that

$$\begin{aligned} &\mathcal{R}_1 \uplus (\mathcal{R}_2 \uplus \{Cons(x,y) \to x, Cons(x,y) \to y\}) \\ &= (\mathcal{R}_1 \uplus \mathcal{R}_2) \uplus \{Cons(x,y) \to x, Cons(x,y) \to y\} \end{aligned}$$

is terminating. But this amounts to $\mathcal{C}_\mathcal{E}$-termination of $\mathcal{R}_1 \uplus \mathcal{R}_2$.

(2) Because $\mathcal{R}_i$, $i \in \{1,2\}$, is simply terminating, the same holds for $\mathcal{R}_i \cup \mathcal{E}mb(\mathcal{F}_i)$. By Proposition 8.3.2, $\mathcal{R}_i \cup \mathcal{E}mb(\mathcal{F}_i)$ is $\mathcal{C}_\mathcal{E}$-terminating. The application of Theorem 8.4.14 to $\mathcal{R}_1 \cup \mathcal{E}mb(\mathcal{F}_1)$ and $\mathcal{R}_2 \cup \mathcal{E}mb(\mathcal{F}_2)$ yields

the termination of $(\mathcal{R}_1 \cup \mathcal{E}mb(\mathcal{F}_1)) \uplus (\mathcal{R}_2 \cup \mathcal{E}mb(\mathcal{F}_2))$, or equivalently, the simple termination of $\mathcal{R}_1 \uplus \mathcal{R}_2$.

(3) The combination of two noncollapsing terminating TRSs yields a noncollapsing TRS. Its termination follows from Theorem 8.4.14.

(4) Clearly, the union of two nonduplicating terminating TRSs is again nonduplicating. That it is also terminating follows from Theorem 8.4.14 in conjunction with Proposition 8.3.1.

(5) The combination of a TRS that is inconsistent w.r.t. reduction with an arbitrary TRS yields a TRS that is inconsistent w.r.t. reduction. Hence the assertion follows as in (4). □

Corollary 8.4.16 *The disjoint union of two finite DP quasi-simply terminating TRSs is $\mathcal{C}_\mathcal{E}$-terminating.*

Proof The proof is an immediate consequence of the fact that a DP quasi-simply terminating TRS is $\mathcal{C}_\mathcal{E}$-terminating (Lemma 8.3.4) in combination with Theorem 8.4.14. □

However, modularity of DP quasi-simple termination is not a direct consequence of Theorem 8.4.14. The problem is the following. If we combine two disjoint DP quasi-simply terminating TRSs $\mathcal{R}_1$ and $\mathcal{R}_2$, then their union $\mathcal{R} = \mathcal{R}_1 \uplus \mathcal{R}_2$ is terminating. Thus, by Corollary 5.4.17, for each cycle $\mathcal{P}$ in the dependency graph of $\mathcal{R}$ there is an AFS $\mathcal{A}$ and a quasi-reduction ordering $\succsim$ satisfying the usual constraints. However, this is obviously not enough to infer DP quasi-simple termination of $\mathcal{R}$ (for example, $\succsim$ must be a QSO). It will be shown in the next section that DP quasi-simple termination is indeed modular for disjoint systems.

If we combine disjoint TRSs, then it suffices to show that each constituent TRS is simply terminating, DP simply terminating, DP quasi-simply terminating, nonduplicating and terminating, inconsistent w.r.t. reduction and terminating, or $\mathcal{C}_\mathcal{E}$-terminating to infer that their combination is again terminating. Finally, the next corollary states sufficient conditions for the preservation of termination under disjoint union. The first condition is due to Middeldorp [Mid89b].

Corollary 8.4.17 *Let $\mathcal{R}_1$ and $\mathcal{R}_2$ be disjoint terminating TRSs. Their union $\mathcal{R}_1 \uplus \mathcal{R}_2$ is terminating provided that:*

- *one of the systems is nonduplicating and noncollapsing;*
- *one of the systems is simply terminating and noncollapsing;*
- *one of the systems is DP simply terminating and noncollapsing;*
- *one system is DP quasi-simply terminating and noncollapsing;*
- *one of the systems is $\mathcal{C}_\mathcal{E}$-terminating and noncollapsing.*

Proof The proof is an immediate consequence of Theorem 8.4.14 in conjunction with Propositions 8.3.1 and 8.3.2 and the implications ST $\Rightarrow$ DP-ST $\Rightarrow$ DP-QST $\Rightarrow$ $\mathcal{C}_\mathcal{E}$T. □

We have seen that, in contrast to termination, $\mathcal{C}_\mathcal{E}$ and simple termination are modular for disjoint TRSs. But does this result carry over to constructor-sharing systems? Gramlich [Gra94] proved that $\mathcal{C}_\mathcal{E}$ and simple termination are modular for finitely branching TRSs with shared constructors. The next counterexamples taken from [Ohl94c] show that this extra condition is necessary.

Example 8.4.18 Consider the TRS $\mathcal{R}_1 = \{F_j(c_j, x) \to F_{j+1}(x, x)$ $F_j(x, y) \to x, F_j(x, y) \to y \mid j \in \mathbb{N}_+\}$ and $\mathcal{R}_2 = \{a \to c_j \mid j \in \mathbb{N}_+\}$. The systems share the constructors $\{c_j \mid j \in \mathbb{N}_+\}$. $\mathcal{R}_1$ is terminating, hence simply terminating by Lemma 5.2.30 (and thus also $\mathcal{C}_\mathcal{E}$-terminating). The same is true for $\mathcal{R}_2$ but their combined system $\mathcal{R}$ is not terminating:

$$F_1(c_1, a) \to_{\mathcal{R}_1} F_2(a, a) \to_{\mathcal{R}_2} F_2(c_2, a) \to_{\mathcal{R}_1} F_3(a, a) \to_{\mathcal{R}_2} \cdots$$

In the preceding example the TRSs share infinitely many constructors. This is not essential.

Example 8.4.19 The TRSs $\mathcal{R}_1 = \{F_j(c^j(x), x) \to F_{j+1}(x, x), F_j(x, y) \to$ $x, F_j(x, y) \to y \mid j \in \mathbb{N}_+\}$ and $\mathcal{R}_2 = \{h(x) \to c^j(x) \mid j \in \mathbb{N}_+\}$ merely share the constructor c. Here $c^j(x)$ denotes the j fold application of c. $\mathcal{R}_1$ and $\mathcal{R}_2$ exhibit the same behavior as the TRSs in Example 8.4.18.

As already mentioned, Kurihara and Ohuchi [KO92] proved that the simplifying property is modular for TRSs with shared constructors. For TRSs over finite signatures, this implies that simple termination is modular for constructor-sharing systems. It may come as a surprise that $\mathcal{C}_\mathcal{E}$-termination is not modular for this class of TRSs.

Example 8.4.20 Consider the term rewriting systems $(\mathcal{F}_1, \mathcal{R}_1) =$ $(\{F, A, c\}, \{F(c^j(A), c^j(A), x) \to F(c^{j+1}(A), x, x) \mid j \in \mathbb{N}_+\})$ and $(\mathcal{F}_2, \mathcal{R}_2) = (\{h, c\}, \{h(x) \to c^j(x) \mid j \in \mathbb{N}_+\})$. Both systems are $\mathcal{C}_\mathcal{E}$-terminating but $\mathcal{R}_1$ is not simply terminating. The combined system of $\mathcal{R}_1$ and $\mathcal{R}_2$ is not terminating:

$$\begin{aligned} F(c^1(A), c^1(A), h(A)) &\to_{\mathcal{R}_1} F(c^2(A), h(A), h(A)) \\ &\to_{\mathcal{R}_2} F(c^2(A), c^2(A), h(A)) \\ &\to_{\mathcal{R}_1} \cdots \end{aligned}$$

8.4.2 DP Quasi-Simple Termination

In this section we will show that DP quasi-simple termination is modular for disjoint TRSs provided that (after normalization with an AFS $\mathcal{A}$) the constraints satisfy the following minor restriction:

- $l\downarrow_{\mathcal{A}} \notin \mathcal{V}$ or $l\downarrow_{\mathcal{A}} = r\downarrow_{\mathcal{A}}$ for every rule $l \to r$ in $\mathcal{R}$,
- $s\downarrow_{\mathcal{A}} \notin \mathcal{V}$ or $s\downarrow_{\mathcal{A}} = t\downarrow_{\mathcal{A}}$ for every dependency pair $\langle s, t\rangle$ in a cycle.

For the proof, we need the following lemma.

Lemma 8.4.21 *Let $(\mathcal{F},\mathcal{R}) = (\mathcal{F}_1 \uplus \mathcal{F}_2, \mathcal{R}_1 \uplus \mathcal{R}_2)$ be the disjoint union of the TRSs $(\mathcal{F}_1,\mathcal{R}_1)$ and $(\mathcal{F}_2,\mathcal{R}_2)$. If u, v are terms over the signature $\mathcal{F}_1$ such that $u \to_{\mathcal{R}_1} v$ and $v\sigma \to^*_{\mathcal{R}} u\sigma$ hold for a ground substitution $\sigma : \mathcal{V}ar(u) \to \mathcal{T}(\mathcal{F})$, then there is also a ground substitution $\tau : \mathcal{V}ar(u) \to \mathcal{T}(\mathcal{F}_1)$ such that $u\tau \to_{\mathcal{R}_1} v\tau \to^*_{\mathcal{R}_1 \cup \mathcal{E}mb(\mathcal{F}_1)} u\tau$.*

Proof Clearly, all terms in the cyclic derivation

$$D: \quad u\sigma \to_{\mathcal{R}_1} v\sigma \to^*_{\mathcal{R}} u\sigma$$

have the same rank. Because the root symbol of u is in $\mathcal{F}_1$, the root symbol of every term in the reduction sequence D is also in $\mathcal{F}_1$ (reduction steps that are destructive at level 1 would decrease the rank).

Suppose first that every function symbol in $\mathcal{F}_1$ has arity ≤ 1. In this case every reduction step in D that is destructive at level 2 strictly decreases the rank. Consequently, there is no reduction step of this kind in D. For every term t with $root(t) \in \mathcal{F}_1$, let $top'(t)$ be the term obtained from t by replacing all principal subterms with a constant from $\mathcal{F}_1$. Hence

$$top'(u\sigma) \to_{\mathcal{R}_1} top'(v\sigma) \to^*_{\mathcal{R}_1} top'(u\sigma)$$

is an $\mathcal{R}_1$ reduction sequence of ground terms over $\mathcal{F}_1$. Let $\mathcal{V}ar(u) = \{x_1, \ldots, x_n\}$ and note that $\mathcal{V}ar(v) \subseteq \mathcal{V}ar(u)$. We define the substitution τ by $\tau = \{x_i \mapsto top'(x_i\sigma) \mid 1 \leq i \leq n\}$ and indeed

$$u\tau = top'(u\sigma) \to_{\mathcal{R}_1} top'(v\sigma) = v\tau \to^*_{\mathcal{R}_1} top'(u\sigma) = u\tau$$

is the reduction sequence we are looking for.

Suppose otherwise that there exists a function symbol f in $\mathcal{F}_1$ with arity $m > 1$. Let $Cons$ be a binary function symbol that occurs in neither $\mathcal{F}_1$ nor $\mathcal{F}_2$ and let $\mathcal{C}_\mathcal{E} = \{Cons(x_1, x_2) \to x_1, Cons(x_1, x_2) \to x_2\}$. By Theorem 8.4.13 the reduction sequence D can be transformed by the transformation function $\Phi_1 = \Phi_1^{u\sigma}$ (defined in Definition 8.4.10) into a reduction sequence

$$\Phi_1(u\sigma) \to_{\mathcal{R}_1} \Phi_1(v\sigma) \to^*_{\mathcal{R}_1 \uplus \mathcal{C}_\mathcal{E}} \Phi_1(u\sigma)$$

of terms over $\mathcal{F}_1 \uplus \{Cons, Nil\}$. According to Definition 8.4.10, the transformation function Φ_1 satisfies $\Phi_1(t) = C[\Phi_1(t_1), \ldots, \Phi_1(t_n)]$ for every term t with $root(t) \in \mathcal{F}_1$ and $t = C[\![t_1, \ldots, t_n]\!]$. In this case, we first define $\sigma' = \{x_i \mapsto \Phi_1(x_i\sigma) \mid 1 \leq i \leq n\}$ and obtain

$$u\sigma' = \Phi_1(u\sigma) \to_{\mathcal{R}_1} \Phi_1(v\sigma) = v\sigma' \to^*_{\mathcal{R}_1 \uplus \mathcal{C}_\mathcal{E}} \Phi_1(u\sigma) = u\sigma'$$

Let $u\sigma' = u_0, u_1, \ldots, u_k = u\sigma'$ be the sequence of terms occurring in the preceding reduction sequence. In each term u_i replace every $Cons(t_1, t_2)$ with $f(t_1, t_2, c, \ldots, c)$ and every Nil with c, where c is a constant from $\mathcal{F}_1$, and denote the resulting term by $\Psi(u_i)$. The definition $\tau = \{x_i \mapsto \Psi(x_i\sigma') \mid 1 \leq i \leq n\}$ yields the desired reduction sequence

$$u\tau = \Psi(u\sigma') = \Psi(u_0) \rightarrow_{\mathcal{R}_1} \Psi(u_1) = \Psi(v\sigma') = v\tau \rightarrow^*_{\mathcal{R}_1 \cup \mathcal{E}mb(\mathcal{F}_1)} \Psi(u_k) = u\tau$$

in which $\Psi(u_i) \rightarrow_{\mathcal{R}_1 \cup \mathcal{E}mb(\mathcal{F}_1)} \Psi(u_{i+1})$ by the rule $f(x_1, \ldots, x_m) \rightarrow x_j$, $j \in \{1, 2\}$, if $u_i \rightarrow_{\mathcal{R}_1 \uplus \mathcal{C}_\mathcal{E}} u_{i+1}$ by the rule $Cons(x_1, x_2) \rightarrow x_j$. □

Now we are in a position to prove modularity of DP quasi-simple termination.

Theorem 8.4.22 *DP quasi-simple termination is modular for disjoint TRSs.*

Proof Given two disjoint DP quasi-simply terminating TRSs $(\mathcal{F}_1, \mathcal{R}_1)$ and $(\mathcal{F}_2, \mathcal{R}_2)$, we have to show that their union $(\mathcal{F}, \mathcal{R})$ is also DP quasi-simply terminating. Let $\mathcal{P}$ be a cycle in the estimated dependency graph EDG($\mathcal{R}$) of $\mathcal{R}$. Because $\mathcal{R}_1$ and $\mathcal{R}_2$ are disjoint, $\mathcal{P}$ is a cycle in EDG($\mathcal{R}_1$) or in EDG($\mathcal{R}_2$). Without loss of generality, let $\mathcal{P}$ be a cycle in EDG($\mathcal{R}_1$).

Because $\mathcal{R}_1$ is DP quasi-simply terminating, for every cycle $\mathcal{P}$ in EDG($\mathcal{R}_1$) there is an AFS $\mathcal{A}$ and a QSO $\succsim$ with $u \succsim v \Rightarrow \mathcal{V}ar(v) \subseteq \mathcal{V}ar(u)$ for all terms u and v such that

(a) $l\downarrow_\mathcal{A} \succsim r\downarrow_\mathcal{A}$ for every rule $l \rightarrow r$ in $\mathcal{R}_1$,

(b) $s\downarrow_\mathcal{A} \succsim t\downarrow_\mathcal{A}$ for every dependency pair $\langle s, t\rangle$ in $\mathcal{P}$,

(c) $s\downarrow_\mathcal{A} \succ t\downarrow_\mathcal{A}$ for at least one dependency pair $\langle s, t\rangle$ in $\mathcal{P}$.

Note that $l\downarrow_\mathcal{A} = x \in \mathcal{V}$ implies $l\downarrow_\mathcal{A} = x = r\downarrow_\mathcal{A}$ and $s\downarrow_\mathcal{A} = x \in \mathcal{V}$ implies $s\downarrow_\mathcal{A} = x = t\downarrow_\mathcal{A}$ because we assume that

- $l\downarrow_\mathcal{A} \notin \mathcal{V}$ or $l\downarrow_\mathcal{A} = r\downarrow_\mathcal{A}$ for all rules $l \rightarrow r$ in $\mathcal{R}_1$
- $s\downarrow_\mathcal{A} \notin \mathcal{V}$ or $s\downarrow_\mathcal{A} = t\downarrow_\mathcal{A}$ for all dependency pairs $\langle s, t\rangle$ in cycles.

Clearly, $x \succsim x$ is satisfied by every QSO $\succsim$.

Let $\mathcal{F}_1'$ be the set of all function symbols in the inequalities (a)–(c). Note that $\mathcal{F}_1' \cap \mathcal{F}_2 = \emptyset$. Without loss of generality, we may assume that $\mathcal{A}$ contains no rules with root symbols from $\mathcal{F}_2$. Now let

$$\begin{aligned} \mathcal{S}_1 &= \{l\downarrow_\mathcal{A} \rightarrow r\downarrow_\mathcal{A} \mid l \rightarrow r \in \mathcal{R}_1 \text{ and } l\downarrow_\mathcal{A} \neq r\downarrow_\mathcal{A}\} \\ &\cup \{s\downarrow_\mathcal{A} \rightarrow t\downarrow_\mathcal{A} \mid \langle s, t\rangle \in \mathcal{P} \text{ and } s\downarrow_\mathcal{A} \neq t\downarrow_\mathcal{A}\} \cup \mathcal{E}mb(\mathcal{F}_1') \\ \mathcal{S}_2 &= \mathcal{R}_2 \cup \mathcal{E}mb(\mathcal{F}_2) \end{aligned}$$

$\mathcal{S}_1$ is a TRS over the signature $\mathcal{F}'_1$. Hence $\mathcal{R}' = \mathcal{S}_1 \uplus \mathcal{S}_2$ is a TRS over $\mathcal{F}'_1 \uplus \mathcal{F}_2$. Note that $\rightarrow^*_{\mathcal{R}'}$ is a QSO (if $\mathcal{R}$ is a TRS over the signature $\mathcal{F}$, then $\rightarrow^*_{\mathcal{R}\cup\mathcal{E}mb(\mathcal{F})}$ is the smallest QSO containing $\rightarrow_{\mathcal{R}}$, that is, if $\succsim$ is a QSO with $\rightarrow_{\mathcal{R}}\subseteq\succsim$, then $\rightarrow^*_{\mathcal{R}\cup\mathcal{E}mb(\mathcal{F})}\subseteq\succsim$). Because the cycle $\mathcal{P}$ was chosen arbitrarily, DP quasi-simple termination follows if we can show that

(a) $l\downarrow_{\mathcal{A}}\rightarrow^*_{\mathcal{R}'} r\downarrow_{\mathcal{A}}$ for all rules $l \rightarrow r$ from $\mathcal{R}$,
(b) $s\downarrow_{\mathcal{A}}\rightarrow^*_{\mathcal{R}'} t\downarrow_{\mathcal{A}}$ for all dependency pairs $\langle s,t\rangle$ from $\mathcal{P}$,
(c) there is a dependency pair $\langle s,t\rangle$ from $\mathcal{P}$ so that $t\downarrow_{\mathcal{A}}\sigma \not\rightarrow^*_{\mathcal{R}'} s\downarrow_{\mathcal{A}}\sigma$ holds for all ground substitutions σ.

Conditions (a) and (b) are obviously satisfied because for all $l \rightarrow r \in \mathcal{R}_2$ we have $l\downarrow_{\mathcal{A}}= l$ and $r\downarrow_{\mathcal{A}}= r$. Hence we only have to show statement (c). Because $\succsim$ is the QSO used for the DP quasi-simple termination proof of $\mathcal{R}_1$, we have $\rightarrow^*_{\mathcal{S}_1}\subseteq\succsim$. Let $\langle s,t\rangle$ be a dependency pair from $\mathcal{P}$ such that $s\downarrow_{\mathcal{A}}\succ t\downarrow_{\mathcal{A}}$. Suppose that there is a ground substitution $\sigma : \mathcal{V}ar(s\downarrow_{\mathcal{A}})\rightarrow \mathcal{T}(\mathcal{F}'_1\uplus\mathcal{F}_2)$ such that $t\downarrow_{\mathcal{A}}\sigma\rightarrow^*_{\mathcal{R}'} s\downarrow_{\mathcal{A}}\sigma$. By Lemma 8.4.21, this implies the existence of a ground substitution $\tau : \mathcal{V}ar(s\downarrow_{\mathcal{A}})\rightarrow\mathcal{T}(\mathcal{F}'_1)$ such that $t\downarrow_{\mathcal{A}}\tau\rightarrow^*_{\mathcal{S}_1} s\downarrow_{\mathcal{A}}\tau$. This, however, would imply $t\downarrow_{\mathcal{A}}\tau\succsim s\downarrow_{\mathcal{A}}\tau$ and contradicts the fact that $s\downarrow_{\mathcal{A}}\succ t\downarrow_{\mathcal{A}}$. Thus, $t\downarrow_{\mathcal{A}}\sigma\not\rightarrow^*_{\mathcal{R}'} s\downarrow_{\mathcal{A}}\sigma$ holds for all ground substitutions σ. This proves statement (c). Furthermore, $\mathcal{A}$ satisfies the minor restriction. □

It may be a bit surprising that Theorem 8.4.22 cannot be extended to constructor-sharing TRSs. In other words, there are constructor-sharing TRSs $\mathcal{R}_1$ and $\mathcal{R}_2$ that are both DP quasi-simply terminating, but their union $\mathcal{R} = \mathcal{R}_1 \cup \mathcal{R}_2$ is not DP quasi-simply terminating.

Example 8.4.23 Consider the TRSs

$$\mathcal{R}_1 = \left\{ \begin{array}{lcl} f(c(x)) & \rightarrow & f(x) \\ f(b(x)) & \rightarrow & x \end{array} \right.$$

and

$$\mathcal{R}_2 = \left\{ \begin{array}{lcl} g(d(x)) & \rightarrow & g(x) \\ g(c(x)) & \rightarrow & c(g(b(c(x)))) \end{array} \right.$$

The TRS $\mathcal{R}_1$ is simply terminating and $\mathcal{R}_2$ is DP simply terminating. The latter can be shown with the AFS $\{b(x) \rightarrow b'\}$, and a recursive path ordering. However, their union $\mathcal{R}$ is not DP quasi-simply terminating, as we will show. Because $\{\langle F(c(x)), F(x)\rangle\}$ is a cycle in the estimated dependency graph of $\mathcal{R}$, there are the constraints

$$F(c(x)) \succ F(x) \tag{8.1}$$
$$f(c(x)) \succsim f(x) \tag{8.2}$$
$$f(b(x)) \succsim x \tag{8.3}$$
$$g(d(x)) \succsim g(x) \tag{8.4}$$
$$g(c(x)) \succsim c(g(b(c(x)))) \tag{8.5}$$

No QSO directly satisfies Eqs. (8.1)–(8.5) because otherwise we would have

$$\begin{array}{rcll} F(c(g(c(x)))) & \succ & F(g(c(x))) & \text{due to (8.1)} \\ & \succsim & F(c(g(b(c(x))))) & \text{due to (8.5)} \\ & \succsim & F(c(g(c(x)))) & \text{due to the subterm property} \end{array}$$

Therefore, one must apply an AFS first. By (8.1), the AFS cannot contain a c rule. If the argument of b were eliminated, then (8.3) would be transformed into $f(b') \succsim x$ and $\mathcal{V}ar(x) \not\subseteq \mathcal{V}ar(f(b'))$ yields a contradiction. The argument of g cannot be eliminated because $g' \succsim c(g')$ would contradict (8.1). Thus the only possible rules in the AFS are f and d rules and the rules $b(x) \to x$ or $g(x) \to x$. Again, we would obtain $F(c(g(c(x)))) \succ F(c(g(c(x))))$ or $F(c(c(x))) \succ F(c(c(x)))$, as earlier. Hence the TRS is indeed not DP quasi-simply terminating.

Next we will investigate the modular behavior of DP simple termination. First, the minor restriction imposed earlier is always satisfied for DP simply terminating systems. This immediately follows from Lemma 5.4.28.

Let $\mathcal{R}{\downarrow_\mathcal{A}}$ denote the TRS $\{l{\downarrow_\mathcal{A}} \to r{\downarrow_\mathcal{A}} \mid l \to r \in \mathcal{R} \text{ and } l{\downarrow_\mathcal{A}} \neq r{\downarrow_\mathcal{A}}\}$ for any TRS $\mathcal{R}$ and any AFS $\mathcal{A}$. There is the following alternative characterization of DP simple termination.

Corollary 8.4.24 *A TRS $\mathcal{R}$ is DP simply terminating if and only if for every cycle $\mathcal{P}$ in* EDG($\mathcal{R}$) *there exists an AFS $\mathcal{A}$ such that*

- $s{\downarrow_\mathcal{A}} \neq t{\downarrow_\mathcal{A}}$ *for some* $\langle s,t\rangle \in \mathcal{P}$, *and*
- $\mathcal{S}{\downarrow_\mathcal{A}}$ *is simply terminating, where*

$$\mathcal{S} = \mathcal{R} \cup \{s \to t \mid \langle s,t\rangle \in \mathcal{P}\}$$

Proof Observe that $\mathcal{S}{\downarrow_\mathcal{A}}$ is a TRS because Lemma 5.4.28 implies that

- $(\mathcal{V}ar(r\downarrow_\mathcal{A}) \subseteq \mathcal{V}ar(l\downarrow_\mathcal{A})$ and $l\downarrow_\mathcal{A} \notin \mathcal{V})$ or $l\downarrow_\mathcal{A} = r\downarrow_\mathcal{A}$ for all $l \to r$ in $\mathcal{R}$,
- $(\mathcal{V}ar(t\downarrow_\mathcal{A}) \subseteq \mathcal{V}ar(s\downarrow_\mathcal{A})$ and $s\downarrow_\mathcal{A} \notin \mathcal{V})$ or $s\downarrow_\mathcal{A} = t\downarrow_\mathcal{A}$ for all $\langle s,t\rangle$ in $\mathcal{P}$.

Furthermore, $\mathcal{S}\downarrow_\mathcal{A}$ is not empty. The corollary follows easily from this observation. □

The following counterexample shows that DP simple termination is not modular for disjoint combinations.

Example 8.4.25 Consider the simply terminating term rewriting system $\mathcal{R}_1 = \{f(s(x)) \to f(x)\}$ and the TRS $\mathcal{R}_2$ consisting of the rules

$$\begin{array}{rclcrcl} g(a) & \to & g(c(a)) & \quad & g(a) & \to & g(d(a)) \\ g(c(x)) & \to & x & & g(d(x)) & \to & x \\ g(c(a)) & \to & g(d(b)) & & g(c(b)) & \to & g(d(a)) \end{array}$$

$\mathcal{R}_2$ is DP simply terminating because there is simply no cycle in EDG($\mathcal{R}_2$). In contrast to this, in EDG($\mathcal{R}_1 \uplus \mathcal{R}_2$) there is a cycle, hence $l \downarrow_{\mathcal{A}} \succeq r \downarrow_{\mathcal{A}}$ must hold for all rules of $\mathcal{R}_2$. However, no QSO whose equivalence relation is just syntactic equality satisfies these constraints, regardless of which AFS $\mathcal{A}$ is applied.

In the preceding example, the problem is that a TRS $\mathcal{R}$ without cycles in EDG($\mathcal{R}$) is DP simply terminating, even if there is no simplification ordering $\succ$ satisfying $l \succeq r$ for all $l \to r \in \mathcal{R}$. To exclude such TRSs we will demand that the constraint (a) of Definition 5.4.20 also be satisfied for the *empty* cycle $\mathcal{P}$.

Definition 8.4.26 A TRS $\mathcal{R}$ is *restricted DP simply terminating* if and only if for every cycle $\mathcal{P}$ in EDG($\mathcal{R}$)—including the *empty* cycle—there is an AFS $\mathcal{A}$ such that

- if $\mathcal{P} \neq \emptyset$, then $s\downarrow_{\mathcal{A}} \neq t\downarrow_{\mathcal{A}}$ for some $\langle s, t\rangle \in \mathcal{P}$, and
- $\mathcal{S}\downarrow_{\mathcal{A}}$ is simply terminating, where $\mathcal{S} = \mathcal{R} \cup \{s \to t \mid \langle s, t\rangle \in \mathcal{P}\}$.

Obviously, restricted DP simple termination implies DP simple termination; cf. Corollary 8.4.24.

Theorem 8.4.27 *Restricted DP simple termination is a modular property of disjoint TRSs.*

Proof We have to show that the union $(\mathcal{F}, \mathcal{R}) = (\mathcal{F}_1 \uplus \mathcal{F}_2, \mathcal{R}_1 \uplus \mathcal{R}_2)$ of two disjoint restricted DP simply terminating TRSs $(\mathcal{F}_1, \mathcal{R}_1)$ and $(\mathcal{F}_2, \mathcal{R}_2)$ is restricted DP simply terminating as well. Let $\mathcal{P}$ be a cycle in EDG($\mathcal{R}$) (where $\mathcal{P}$ may also be empty). As in the proof of Theorem 8.4.22, we may assume that $\mathcal{P}$ is a cycle in EDG($\mathcal{R}_1$). Because $\mathcal{R}_1$ is restricted DP simply terminating, there is an AFS $\mathcal{A}_1$ such that the TRS $\mathcal{S}_1\downarrow_{\mathcal{A}_1}$ is simply terminating, where

$$\mathcal{S}_1 = \mathcal{R}_1 \cup \{s \to t \mid \langle s, t\rangle \in \mathcal{P}\}$$

and $\mathcal{S}_1\downarrow_{\mathcal{A}_1} \neq \emptyset$ if $\mathcal{P} \neq \emptyset$. Clearly, we may assume that $\mathcal{A}_1$ does not contain rules for function symbols $\notin \mathcal{F}_1 \cup Tup_{\mathcal{F}_1}$.

Moreover, because $\mathcal{R}_2$ is restricted DP simply terminating, there is an AFS $\mathcal{A}_2$ (for the empty cycle) such that the TRS $\mathcal{R}_2\downarrow_{\mathcal{A}_2}$ is simply terminating. Again, we may assume that $\mathcal{A}_2$ does not contain rules for function symbols $\notin \mathcal{F}_2$. It can readily be verified that the TRSs $\mathcal{S}_1\downarrow_{\mathcal{A}_1}$ and $\mathcal{R}_2\downarrow_{\mathcal{A}_2}$ are disjoint. Because simple termination is modular for disjoint TRSs, the combined system $\mathcal{S}_1\downarrow_{\mathcal{A}} \uplus \mathcal{R}_2\downarrow_{\mathcal{A}}$ is also simply terminating, where $\mathcal{A} = \mathcal{A}_1 \uplus \mathcal{A}_2$. Because the cycle $\mathcal{P}$ was chosen arbitrarily, the system $\mathcal{R}$ is restricted DP simply terminating. □

Example 8.4.23 also shows that restricted DP simple termination is not modular for TRSs with shared constructors. It is easy to see that both

$\mathcal{R}_1$ and $\mathcal{R}_2$ are restricted DP simply terminating. Their union, however, is not restricted DP simply terminating because it is not DP quasi-simply terminating. In essence, this is due to the fact that one cannot use the AFS rule $b(x) \to b'$ in the combined system $\mathcal{R}_1 \cup \mathcal{R}_2$ because of $f(b(x)) \to x \in \mathcal{R}_1$. Therefore, to achieve a modularity result for constructor-sharing TRSs, we have to restrict ourselves to AFSs that do not contain rules for shared symbols like b. However, this restriction is not yet sufficient for obtaining a modularity result for restricted DP simple termination of constructor-sharing systems. We will not investigate this matter any further. The reader can find sufficient conditions for the modularity of restricted DP simple termination of constructor-sharing systems in [GAO02].

8.4.3 Persistence vs. Modularity

In Section 5.5.3, persistence was defined as follows: A property $\mathcal{P}$ is persistent if, for every many-sorted TRS $\mathcal{R}$, the property $\mathcal{P}$ holds for $\mathcal{R}$ if and only if it holds for the TRS obtained from $\mathcal{R}$ by removing all type information.

The next theorem, due to Zantema [Zan94], relates the notions of persistence and modularity for disjoint (one-sorted) systems.

Definition 8.4.28 A property $\mathcal{P}$ is called *component-closed* if the following statements are equivalent for every TRS $(\mathcal{F}, \mathcal{R})$:

1. $(\mathcal{F}, \mathcal{R})$ has property $\mathcal{P}$.
2. Every component of $(\mathcal{F}, \mathcal{R})$, that is, every equivalence class of the equivalence relation $\leftrightarrow^*_{\mathcal{R}}$ on $\mathcal{T}(\mathcal{F}, \mathcal{V})$, has property $\mathcal{P}$.

Most properties of TRSs (e.g., convergence, unique normalization, confluence, local confluence, termination, and normalization) are component-closed.

Theorem 8.4.29 *Every component-closed persistent property $\mathcal{P}$ is modular for disjoint TRSs.*

Proof Let $(\mathcal{F}_1, \mathcal{R}_1)$ and $(\mathcal{F}_2, \mathcal{R}_2)$ be disjoint (one-sorted) TRSs, and let s_1 and s_2 be two distinct sorts. Define

$$\mathcal{F} = \{f :: s_1 \times \cdots \times s_1 \to s_1 \mid f \in \mathcal{F}_1\} \cup \{g :: s_2 \times \cdots \times s_2 \to s_2 \mid g \in \mathcal{F}_2\}$$

i.e., the arguments of function symbols from $\mathcal{F}_i$ must be of sort s_i, $i \in \{1, 2\}$. The TRS $\mathcal{R}$ consisting of the rules from $\mathcal{R}_1$ and $\mathcal{R}_2$ with this typing is an $\{s_1, s_2\}$ sorted TRS. The terms of sort s_i, $i \in \{1, 2\}$, correspond one to one to the terms over $\mathcal{F}_i$ and the reduction relation $\to_{\mathcal{R}}$ on terms of sort s_i corresponds one to one to $\to_{\mathcal{R}_i}$. Thus, the components of $(\mathcal{F}, \mathcal{R})$ can be viewed as the disjoint union of the components of $(\mathcal{F}_1, \mathcal{R}_1)$ and $(\mathcal{F}_2, \mathcal{R}_2)$. Because $\mathcal{P}$ is component-closed, it follows that

$$\mathcal{P}(\mathcal{R}) \Leftrightarrow \mathcal{P}(\mathcal{R}_1) \wedge \mathcal{P}(\mathcal{R}_2)$$

On the other hand, the terms over $\Theta(\mathcal{F})$ correspond one to one to the terms over $\mathcal{F}_1 \uplus \mathcal{F}_2$, and the reduction relation $\rightarrow_{\Theta(\mathcal{R})}$ corresponds one to one to $\rightarrow_{\mathcal{R}_1 \uplus \mathcal{R}_2}$. Therefore,

$$\mathcal{P}(\Theta(\mathcal{R})) \Leftrightarrow \mathcal{P}(\mathcal{R}_1 \uplus \mathcal{R}_2).$$

Because $\mathcal{P}$ is persistent, $\mathcal{P}(\mathcal{R})$ and $\mathcal{P}(\Theta(\mathcal{R}))$ are equivalent. All in all,

$$\mathcal{P}(\mathcal{R}_1 \uplus \mathcal{R}_2) \Leftrightarrow \mathcal{P}(\mathcal{R}_1) \wedge \mathcal{P}(\mathcal{R}_2)$$

and we are done. □

Therefore, persistence can be viewed as a generalization of modularity for disjoint unions. It is an open problem whether the converse of Theorem 8.4.29 is true. On the other hand, it has been shown by van de Pol [Pol92] that persistence is equivalent to the many-sorted extension of the notion of modularity for disjoint systems.

Because termination is component-closed and persistent for noncollapsing or nonduplicating TRSs (Theorem 5.5.25), we immediately obtain an alternative proof of statements (3) and (4) of Theorem 8.4.15 as a corollary to Theorem 8.4.29. This alternative proof, however, turns history upside down: First Rusinowitch [Rus87a] obtained the results and then Zantema [Zan94] proved Theorem 8.4.29.

8.5 Constructor-Sharing Systems

In this section we weaken the disjointness requirement. That is, the TRSs $(\mathcal{F}_1, \mathcal{R}_1)$ and $(\mathcal{F}_2, \mathcal{R}_2)$ are allowed to share constructors. In what follows, $(\mathcal{F}, \mathcal{R})$ denotes their union and $\rightarrow = \rightarrow_{\mathcal{R}} = \rightarrow_{\mathcal{R}_1 \cup \mathcal{R}_2}$.

We will provide a sufficient criterion for the modularity of confluence for constructor-sharing TRSs. This criterion can be extended to composable systems; see [Ohl94a]. For the sake of simplicity, however, we stick to constructor-sharing combinations. The most important consequence of our criterion is certainly the modularity of confluence for disjoint TRSs. As already mentioned, this result was first proved by Toyama [Toy87b], and therefore it is sometimes referred to as Toyama's theorem. A simplified proof of Toyama's theorem appeared in Klop et al. [KMTV94]. In fact, we will use the structure of this simplified proof. The material originally appeared in [Ohl94b].

To be able to distinguish between symbols from different sets, we use capitals $F, G, \ldots$ for function symbols from $\mathcal{D}_1$; lowercase letters $f, g, \ldots$ for those from $\mathcal{D}_2$, and small capitals $\textsc{c}, \textsc{d}, \ldots$ for shared constructors. As usual $x, y, z, x_1, y_1, z_1, \ldots$ will denote variables. To emphasize that $\mathcal{F} = \mathcal{D} \uplus \mathcal{C}$, we write $\mathcal{T}(\mathcal{D}, \mathcal{C}, \mathcal{V})$ instead of $\mathcal{T}(\mathcal{F}, \mathcal{V})$ at the appropriate places.

Definition 8.5.1 Let $s \in \mathcal{T}(\mathcal{D}, \mathcal{C}, \mathcal{V})$. Again we color each function symbol in s. Function symbols from $\mathcal{D}_1$ are colored black, those from $\mathcal{D}_2$ white, and constructors and variables are transparent. If s does not contain white (black) function symbols, we speak of a *black (white) term*. s is said to be *transparent* if it contains only constructors and variables. Consequently, a transparent term may be regarded as black or white; this is convenient for later purposes. s is called *top black (top white, top transparent)* if $root(s)$ is black (white, transparent).

Several definitions and considerations are symmetrical in the colors black and white. Therefore, we state the respective definition or consideration only for the color black (the same applies mutatis mutandis for the color white).

Definition 8.5.2 Let s be a top black term such that $s = C^b[s_1, \ldots, s_n]$ for some black context $C^b[, \ldots,] \neq \Box$ and $root(s_j) \in \mathcal{D}_2$ for $j \in \{1, \ldots, n\}$. We denote this by $s = C^b[\![s_1, \ldots, s_n]\!]$. In this case we define the multiset $S^b(s)$ of all *black principal* subterms of s to be $S^b(s) = [s]$ and the set of all *white principal* subterms of s to be $S^w(s) = [s_1, \ldots, s_n]$. The *topmost black homogeneous part* of s, denoted by $top^b(s)$, is obtained from s by replacing all white principal subterms with $\Box$. The *topmost white homogeneous part* of s is $top^w(s) = \Box$. Now let s be a top transparent term such that

$$s = \begin{cases} C^t[s_1, \ldots, s_l] & \text{where } \; C^t[, \ldots,] \in \mathcal{T}(\mathcal{C}, \mathcal{V}) \;,\; root(s_j) \in \mathcal{D}_1 \uplus \mathcal{D}_2 \\ C^b[t_1, \ldots, t_m] & \text{where } \; C^b[, \ldots,] \in \mathcal{T}(\mathcal{D}_1, \mathcal{C}, \mathcal{V}) \;,\; root(t_j) \in \mathcal{D}_2 \\ C^w[u_1, \ldots, u_n] & \text{where } \; C^w[, \ldots,] \in \mathcal{T}(\mathcal{D}_2, \mathcal{C}, \mathcal{V}) ,\; root(u_j) \in \mathcal{D}_1 \end{cases}$$

From now on this will be denoted by

$$s = \begin{cases} C^t[\![s_1, \ldots, s_l]\!] \\ C^b[\![t_1, \ldots, t_m]\!] \\ C^w[\![u_1, \ldots, u_n]\!] \end{cases}$$

In this situation, we define the multiset $S^b(s)$ ($S^w(s)$) of *black (white) principal* subterms of s to be $S^b(s) = [u_1, \ldots, u_n]$ ($S^w(s) = [t_1, \ldots, t_m]$).

The *topmost black (white) homogeneous part* of s, denoted by $top^b(s)$ ($top^w(s)$), is obtained from s by replacing all white (black) principal subterms with $\Box$.

Example 8.5.3 Let $\mathcal{D}_1 = \{F, A\}$, $\mathcal{D}_2 = \{g, b\}$, and $\mathcal{C} = \{c\}$. For $s = c(F(b), g(A))$ we have

$$s = \begin{cases} C^t[\![F(b), g(A)]\!] \text{ with } C^t[,\ldots,] = c(\square, \square) \\ C^b[\![b, g(A)]\!] \text{ with } C^b[,\ldots,] = c(F(\square), \square) \\ C^w[\![F(b), A]\!] \text{ with } C^w[,\ldots,] = c(\square, g(\square)) \end{cases}$$

as well as $S^b(s) = [F(b), A]$ and $S^w(s) = [b, g(A)]$.

Definition 8.5.4 Let s be a top black term. We define

$$rank(s) = \begin{cases} 1 & \text{if } s \in \mathcal{T}(\mathcal{D}_1, \mathcal{C}, \mathcal{V}) \\ 1 + max\{rank(s_j) \mid 1 \leq j \leq n\} & \text{if } s = C^b[\![s_1, \ldots, s_n]\!] \end{cases}$$

Now let s be a top transparent term. Then we define

$$rank(s) = \begin{cases} 0 & \text{if } s \in \mathcal{T}(\mathcal{C}, \mathcal{V}) \\ max\{rank(t_j) \mid 1 \leq j \leq m\} & \text{if } s = C^t[\![t_1, \ldots, t_m]\!] \end{cases}$$

As for disjoint unions, we have $s \rightarrow^* t \Rightarrow rank(s) \geq rank(t)$.

Definition 8.5.5 For a top black term s, the set of *special subterms* of s is defined by

$$S(s) = \begin{cases} \{s\} & \text{if } s \in \mathcal{T}(\mathcal{D}_1, \mathcal{C}, \mathcal{V}) \\ \{s\} \cup \bigoplus_{j=1}^{n} S(s_j) & \text{if } s = C^b[\![s_1, \ldots, s_n]\!] \end{cases}$$

If s is a top transparent term, then the set of special subterms of s is defined by

$$S(s) = \begin{cases} \{s\} & \text{if } s \in \mathcal{T}(\mathcal{C}, \mathcal{V}) \\ \{s\} \cup \bigoplus_{j=1}^{m} S(t_j) & \text{if } s = C^t[\![t_1, \ldots, t_m]\!] \end{cases}$$

Definition 8.5.6 Let s be a top black term. Let $s = C^b[\![s_1, \ldots, s_n]\!]$ and $s \rightarrow_{\mathcal{R}} t$ by an application of a rewrite rule from $\mathcal{R} = \mathcal{R}_1 \cup \mathcal{R}_2$. We write $s \rightarrow_{\mathcal{R}}^{i} t$ if the rule is applied in one of the s_j and we write $s \rightarrow_{\mathcal{R}}^{o} t$ otherwise. The relation $\rightarrow_{\mathcal{R}}^{i}$ is called *inner* reduction and $\rightarrow_{\mathcal{R}}^{o}$ is called *outer* reduction. Now let s be a top transparent term, i.e., $s = C^t[\![s_1, \ldots, s_n]\!]$ with $C^t[,\ldots,] \neq \square$. Let $s \rightarrow_{\mathcal{R}} t$, i.e., $t = C^t[s_1, \ldots, s_{j-1}, t_j, s_{j+1}, \ldots, s_n]$ for some $j \in \{1, \ldots, n\}$. Then we write $s \rightarrow_{\mathcal{R}}^{i} t$ if $s_j \rightarrow_{\mathcal{R}}^{i} t_j$ and $s \rightarrow_{\mathcal{R}}^{o} t$ if $s_j \rightarrow_{\mathcal{R}}^{o} t_j$. In order to identify the origin of the applied rewrite rule, we also use the notation $s \rightarrow_{\mathcal{R}_1}^{o} t$, $s \rightarrow_{\mathcal{R}_2}^{o} t$, $s \rightarrow_{\mathcal{R}_1}^{i} t$, and $s \rightarrow_{\mathcal{R}_2}^{i} t$.

Definition 8.5.7 Let s be a top black term. A rewrite step $s \rightarrow t$ is *destructive at level 1* if the root symbols of s and t have different colors, i.e., $root(t) \in \mathcal{D}_2 \cup \mathcal{C} \cup \mathcal{V}$. A rewrite step $s \rightarrow t$ is *destructive at level* $m + 1$ (for some $m \geq 1$) if $s = C^b[\![s_1, \ldots, s_j, \ldots, s_n]\!] \rightarrow^i C^b[s_1, \ldots, t_j, \ldots, s_n] = t$ with $s_j \rightarrow t_j$ destructive at level m. For a top transparent term s a rewrite step $s \rightarrow t$ is *destructive at level* m if it is of the form $s =$

$C^t[\![s_1,\ldots,s_j,\ldots,s_n]\!] \to C^t[s_1,\ldots,t_j,\ldots,s_n] = t$ with $s_j \to t_j$ destructive at level m. Note that if a rewrite step is destructive, then the applied rewrite rule is collapsing or constructor-lifting. A rule $l \to r$ is called *constructor-lifting* if $root(r)$ is a shared constructor.

Remember that we write $\langle s_1,\ldots,s_n\rangle \propto \langle t_1,\ldots,t_n\rangle$ if $t_i = t_j$ whenever $s_i = s_j$, for all $1 \le i < j \le n$. Moreover, we will use the notation $\langle s_1,\ldots,s_n\rangle \infty \langle t_1,\ldots,t_n\rangle$ if we have both $\langle s_1,\ldots,s_n\rangle \propto \langle t_1,\ldots,t_n\rangle$ and $\langle t_1,\ldots,t_n\rangle \propto \langle s_1,\ldots,s_n\rangle$.

As in the case of disjoint unions, we will tacitly use the following fact. If $s \to^o_{\mathcal{R}_1} t$, then $s = C^b\{\!\{s_1,\ldots,s_n\}\!\}$ and $t = \hat{C}^b\langle\!\langle s_{i_1},\ldots,s_{i_m}\rangle\!\rangle$ for some contexts $C^b\{,\ldots,\}$ and $\hat{C}^b\langle,\ldots,\rangle$, indices $i_1,\ldots,i_m \in \{1,\ldots,n\}$, and terms $s_1,\ldots,s_n$ with $root(s_j) \in \mathcal{D}_2$. Furthermore, for all terms $t_1,\ldots,t_n$ with $\langle s_1,\ldots,s_n\rangle \propto \langle t_1,\ldots,t_n\rangle$, we have $C^b\{t_1,\ldots,t_n\} \to \hat{C}^b\langle t_{i_1},\ldots,t_{i_m}\rangle$ by the same rewrite rule.

The special notations for "degenerate" cases of $C^b[\![s_1,\ldots,s_n]\!]$ used earlier are defined in analogy to those used for the disjoint union case.

8.5.1 Confluence

In this section, $\mathcal{R}_1$ and $\mathcal{R}_2$ denote confluent constructor-sharing TRSs. As noted in [Toy87b] and [KMTV94], the main difficulties in proving the modularity of confluence are due to the fact that the black and white layer structure of a term need not be preserved under reduction. That is, by a destructive rewrite step a, for example, black layer may disappear, thus allowing two originally distinct white layers to merge. Terms with a stable layer structure will be called *preserved.*

Definition 8.5.8 A term s is *preserved* if there is no rewrite derivation starting from s that contains a destructive rewrite step. We call s *black (white) preserved* if all its black (white) principal subterms are preserved.

Clearly, a preserved term is both black and white preserved. If a top black (top white) term is black (white) preserved, then it is preserved. Note also that the properties preserved and black (white) preserved are both conserved under reduction.

Definition 8.5.9 We write $s \to_c t$ if there exists a context $C[\,]$ and terms s_1, t_1 such that $s = C[s_1], t = C[t_1]$, s_1 is a special subterm of s, $s_1 \to^+ t_1$ and the root symbols of s_1 and t_1 have different colors. The relation $\to_c$ is called *collapsing reduction* and s_1 is a *collapsing redex.*

Note that every destructive rewrite step is a $\to_c$ step. On the other hand, every $\to_c$ step contains at least one destructive step. Furthermore, $\to_c$ is not closed under contexts in general because the notion "special subterm" depends on the surrounding context.

Lemma 8.5.10

1. *If $s \to_c t$, then $s \to^+ t$.*

2. *A term is preserved if and only if it contains no collapsing redexes.*

Proof The proof is straightforward. □

Example 8.5.11 Let $\mathcal{R}_1 = \{F(x,y) \to c(A), G(x) \to x\}$ and $\mathcal{R}_2 = \{h(x) \to c(x)\}$. We have the following collapsing reduction sequence:

$$F(A, h(G(h(A)))) \to_c F(A, h(c(A))) \to_c c(A)$$

The first step is valid because $G(h(A))$ is a special subterm of $F(A, h(G(h(A))))$, $G(h(A)) \to^+ c(A)$, and the root symbols of $G(h(A))$ and $c(A)$ have different colors.

First we show that white preserved terms are confluent w.r.t. the combined system $(\mathcal{F}, \mathcal{R})$. If $\to_c$ is normalizing, then this result can be used to show confluence of $(\mathcal{F}, \mathcal{R})$. The next proposition states that monochrome outer reduction is confluent.

Proposition 8.5.12 *The relations $\to^o_{\mathcal{R}_1}$ and $\to^o_{\mathcal{R}_2}$ are confluent.*

Proof It suffices to show the claim for $\to^o_{\mathcal{R}_1}$. Let $t_1 \; {}_{\mathcal{R}_1}\!\overset{*\,o}{\leftarrow} \; t \overset{o\,*}{\to}_{\mathcal{R}_1} t_2$. If t is an element of $\mathcal{T}(\mathcal{D}_1, \mathcal{C}, \mathcal{V})$, then the claim is true because $\mathcal{R}_1$ is confluent. Therefore, we may assume $t = C^b[\![s_1, \ldots, s_n]\!]$, $t_1 = C_1^b\langle\!\langle s_{i_1}, \ldots, s_{i_m}\rangle\!\rangle$ and $t_2 = C_2^b\langle\!\langle s_{j_1}, \ldots, s_{j_p}\rangle\!\rangle$. We choose fresh variables $x_1, \ldots, x_n$ such that $\langle s_1, \ldots, s_n\rangle \infty \langle x_1, \ldots, x_n\rangle$, and set $t' = C^b[x_1, \ldots, x_n]$, $t_1' = C_1^b[x_{i_1}, \ldots, x_{i_m}]$, and $t_2' = C_2^b[x_{j_1}, \ldots, x_{j_p}]$. Because of $\langle s_1, \ldots, s_n\rangle \propto \langle x_1, \ldots, x_n\rangle$, we obtain $t_1' \; {}_{\mathcal{R}_1}\!\overset{*}{\leftarrow} t' \to^*_{\mathcal{R}_1} t_2'$. Because this is a conversion in $(\mathcal{F}_1, \mathcal{R}_1)$, there exists a common reduct $\hat{C}^b[x_{k_1}, \ldots, x_{k_l}]$ of t_1' and t_2', that is, $t_1' \to^*_{\mathcal{R}_1} \hat{C}^b[x_{k_1}, \ldots, x_{k_l}] \; {}_{\mathcal{R}_1}\!\overset{*}{\leftarrow} t_2'$. Because of $\langle x_1, \ldots, x_n\rangle \propto \langle s_1, \ldots, s_n\rangle$, it follows that $t_1 \overset{o\,*}{\to}_{\mathcal{R}_1} \hat{C}^b\langle\!\langle s_{k_1}, \ldots, s_{k_l}\rangle\!\rangle \; {}_{\mathcal{R}_1}\!\overset{*\,o}{\leftarrow} \; t_2$. □

Definition 8.5.13 Let S be a set of confluent terms. A set $\hat{S}$ of terms *represents* S if the following two conditions are satisfied:

1. Every term s in S has a unique reduct $\hat{s}$ in $\hat{S}$, called the *representative* of s.

2. Joinable terms in S have the same representative in $\hat{S}$.

Lemma 8.5.14 *Every finite set S of confluent terms can be represented.*

Proof Because S consists of confluent terms, joinability is an equivalence relation on S. Hence we can partition S into equivalence classes $E_1, \ldots, E_n$ of joinable terms. Because these classes are finite, for every $E_j = \{s_1, \ldots, s_m\}$ there exist a common reduct t_j of $s_1, \ldots, s_m$, i.e., $s_l \to^* t_j$ for every $l \in \{1, \ldots, m\}$. Obviously, the set $\{t_1, \ldots, t_n\}$ represents S. □

Lemma 8.5.15 *Preserved terms are confluent.*

Proof We show that every preserved term t is confluent by induction on $rank(t)$. The case $rank(t) = 0$ is trivially true. Let $rank(t) = k > 0$ and suppose that the assertion holds for any term s with $rank(s) < k$. We proceed by case analysis.

Case (i): t is top black. Consider a conversion $t_1 \;{}^*{\leftarrow}\; t \to^* t_2$. Because t is preserved, each term u occurring in the conversion is top black. Let S be the set of all white principal subterms occurring in the conversion. By the inductive hypothesis, S consists of confluent terms because every element of S is preserved and has rank less than k. It follows from Lemma 8.5.14 that S can be represented by a set $\hat{S}$. We write $\tilde{u}$ for the term obtained from u by replacing each white principal subterm with its representative. Note that $u \to^* \tilde{u}$.

We claim that $\tilde{t}_1 \;{}_{\mathcal{R}_1}\!\overset{*o}{\leftarrow}\; \tilde{t} \overset{o*}{\to}_{\mathcal{R}_1} \tilde{t}_2$. Let $u_1 \to u_2$ be a step in the conversion $t_1 \;{}^*{\leftarrow}\; t \to^* t_2$. Because u_1 is top black, we may write $u_1 = C_1^b\{\!\{s_1, \ldots, s_n\}\!\}$. The claim will be proven by showing $\tilde{u}_1 \overset{o*}{\to}_{\mathcal{R}_1} \tilde{u}_2$. We distinguish the following cases:

1. If $u_1 \to^o_{\mathcal{R}_1} u_2$, then u_2 can be written as $u_2 = C_2^b\{\!\{s_{i_1}, \ldots, s_{i_m}\}\!\}$. It is a consequence of $\langle s_1, \ldots, s_n\rangle \propto \langle \hat{s}_1, \ldots, \hat{s}_n\rangle$ that $\tilde{u}_1 = C_1^b\{\hat{s}_1, \ldots, \hat{s}_n\} \to^o_{\mathcal{R}_1} C_2^b\{\hat{s}_{i_1}, \ldots, \hat{s}_{i_m}\} = \tilde{u}_2$.

2. If $u_1 \to u_2$ is not an outer $\mathcal{R}_1$ rewrite step, then, because u_1 is preserved, we may write $u_1 = C_1^b[\![s_1, \ldots, s_j, \ldots, s_n]\!] \to C_1^b[\![s_1, \ldots, s_j', \ldots, s_n]\!] = u_2$ where $s_j \to s_j'$. Because the terms s_j and s_j' are trivially joinable, we have $\hat{s}_j = \hat{s}_j'$ and therefore $\tilde{u}_1 = C_1^b[\hat{s}_1, \ldots, \hat{s}_j, \ldots, \hat{s}_n] = \tilde{u}_2$.

This shows $\tilde{t}_1 \;{}_{\mathcal{R}_1}\!\overset{*o}{\leftarrow}\; \tilde{t} \overset{o*}{\to}_{\mathcal{R}_1} \tilde{t}_2$. Because $\to^o_{\mathcal{R}_1}$ is confluent, the terms $\tilde{t}_1$ and $\tilde{t}_2$ have a common reduct, which is also a common reduct of t_1 and t_2.

Case (ii): t is top white. This case is analogous to case (i).

Case (iii): t is top transparent. Let $t = C^t[\![s_1, \ldots, s_n]\!]$ and consider a conversion $t_1 \;{}^*{\leftarrow}\; t \to^* t_2$. We may write $t_1 = C^t[u_1, \ldots, u_n]$ and $t_2 = C^t[v_1, \ldots, v_n]$ where $u_j \;{}^*{\leftarrow}\; s_j \to^* v_j$. By cases (i) and (ii), there are terms $w_1, \ldots, w_n$ such that $u_j \to^* w_j \;{}^*{\leftarrow}\; v_j$. Obviously, $C^t[w_1, \ldots, w_n]$ is a common reduct of t_1 and t_2. □

Proposition 8.5.16 *White (black) preserved terms are confluent.*

Proof We show that every white preserved term is confluent. Suppose t is a white preserved term and consider a conversion $t_1 \;{}^*{\leftarrow}\; t \to^* t_2$. It must be shown that the terms t_1 and t_2 are joinable. As in the proof of Lemma 8.5.15, let S be the set of all white principal subterms occurring in the conversion. Notice that if u is a top white term occurring in the conversion, then u itself belongs to S. By Lemma 8.5.15, S consists of confluent terms because every element of S is preserved. By Lemma 8.5.14, S can be represented by a set $\hat{S}$. Recall that $\tilde{u}$ denotes the result of replacing every white principal subterm in u with its representative.

Again we claim that $\tilde{t}_1 \ {}_{\mathcal{R}_1}\!\!\overset{*o}{\leftarrow} \ \tilde{t} \overset{o*}{\rightarrow}_{\mathcal{R}_1} \tilde{t}_2$. Let $u_1 \to u_2$ be a step in the conversion $t_1 \ {}^*\!\!\leftarrow t \to^* t_2$. The claim will be proven by distinguishing the following cases.

1. Suppose that u_1 is a top black or top transparent term, that is, $u_1 = C_1^b\{\!\{s_1, \ldots, s_n\}\!\}$. If $u_1 \to_{\mathcal{R}_1}^o u_2$, then u_2 can be written as $u_2 = C_2^b\langle\!\langle s_{i_1}, \ldots, s_{i_m}\rangle\!\rangle$ and it follows that $\tilde{u}_1 = C_1^b\{\hat{s}_1, \ldots, \hat{s}_n\} \to_{\mathcal{R}_1}^o C_2^b\langle \hat{s}_{i_1}, \ldots, \hat{s}_{i_m}\rangle = \tilde{u}_2$. Otherwise $u_1 \to u_2$ is not an outer $\mathcal{R}_1$ rewrite step. Because u_1 is white preserved, $u_1 \to u_2$ can be written as $u_1 = C_1^b[\![s_1, \ldots, s_j, \ldots, s_n]\!] \to C_1^b[\![s_1, \ldots, s_j', \ldots, s_n]\!] = u_2$ where $s_j \to s_j'$. Clearly, $\hat{s}_j = \hat{s}_j'$ and hence $\tilde{u}_1 = C_1^b[\hat{s}_1, \ldots, \hat{s}_j, \ldots, \hat{s}_n] = \tilde{u}_2$.

2. Suppose u_1 is top white. Because u_1 is preserved, u_2 must also be top white and preserved. Hence u_1 and u_2 are both in S. Of course, they must have the same representative. So $\tilde{u}_1 = \hat{u}_1 = \hat{u}_2 = \tilde{u}_2$.

This shows the claim. Because $\to_{\mathcal{R}_1}^o$ is confluent, the terms $\tilde{t}_1$ and $\tilde{t}_2$ have a common reduct $\tilde{t}_3$. We conclude that $t_1 \to^* \tilde{t}_3 \ {}^*\!\!\leftarrow t_2$. □

Lemma 8.5.17 *If $\to_c$ is normalizing, then every term t has a preserved reduct.*

Proof Because $\to_c$ is normalizing, $t \to_c^* t'$ for some $t' \in NF(\to_c)$. By Lemma 8.5.10, t' is preserved. □

The idea of the modularity proof of confluence is to project a conversion $t_1 \ {}^*\!\!\leftarrow t \to^* t_2$ to a conversion involving only white preserved terms (to use Proposition 8.5.16). The projection consists of choosing an appropriate white (black) witness, according to the following definition.

Definition 8.5.18 Let $s = C^b\langle\!\langle s_1, \ldots, s_n\rangle\!\rangle$. A *white witness* of s is a white preserved term $t = C^b\langle t_1, \ldots, t_n\rangle$ that satisfies the following two properties:

1. $s_j \to^* t_j$ for every $j \in \{1, \ldots, n\}$,

2. $\langle s_1, \ldots, s_n\rangle \propto \langle t_1, \ldots, t_n\rangle$.

Lemma 8.5.19 *If $\to_c$ is normalizing, then every term has a white (black) witness.*

Proof Let $s = C^b\langle\langle s_1, \ldots, s_n\rangle\rangle$. According to Lemma 8.5.17, every s_j has a preserved reduct t_j. Evidently, we may assume that $\langle s_1, \ldots, s_n\rangle \propto \langle t_1, \ldots, t_n\rangle$. The term $t = C^b\langle t_1, \ldots, t_n\rangle$ is white preserved. □

In the following $\dot{s}$ denotes an arbitrary white witness of s. Note that $s \to^* \dot{s}$.

Proposition 8.5.20 *Let $s \to t$. If all white principal subterms of s are confluent, then $\dot{s} \downarrow \dot{t}$.*

Proof We prove the proposition by case analysis.

Case (i): s is top black or top transparent. If $s \in \mathcal{T}(\mathcal{D}_1, \mathcal{C}, \mathcal{V})$, then $\dot{s} = s \to_{\mathcal{R}_1} t = \dot{t}$ and the assertion follows from the confluence of $\mathcal{R}_1$. Suppose $s = C^b[\![s_1, \ldots, s_n]\!]$ and $\dot{s} = C^b[t_1, \ldots, t_n]$.

1. If $s \to^o_{\mathcal{R}_1} t$, then $t = \hat{C}^b\langle\langle s_{i_1}, \ldots, s_{i_m}\rangle\rangle$. Hence $\dot{t} = \hat{C}^b\langle u_{i_1}, \ldots, u_{i_m}\rangle$ for the respective reducts $u_{i_1}, \ldots, u_{i_m}$ of $s_{i_1}, \ldots, s_{i_m}$. Because $\langle s_1, \ldots, s_n\rangle \propto \langle t_1, \ldots, t_n\rangle$, we obtain $\dot{s} \to \hat{C}^b\langle t_{i_1}, \ldots, t_{i_m}\rangle$. It follows from $t_j \;{}^*\!\leftarrow s_j \to^* u_j$ and the confluence of s_j that $t_j \downarrow u_j$ for every index $j \in \{i_1, \ldots, i_m\}$. Thus, $\dot{s} \downarrow \dot{t}$.

2. If $s \to t$ is not an outer $\mathcal{R}_1$ rewrite step, then t can be written as $t = C^b[s_1, \ldots, s'_j, \ldots, s_n]$ where $s_j \to s'_j$ for some index $j \in \{1, \ldots, n\}$. Because $C^b[, \ldots,]$ is black, we have $\dot{t} = C^b[u_1, \ldots, u_n]$ for some reducts $u_1, \ldots, u_j, \ldots, u_n$ of $s_1, \ldots, s'_j, \ldots, s_n$. The joinability of t_l and u_l for $l \in \{1, \ldots, n\}$ follows as in the previous case. Hence $\dot{s} \downarrow \dot{t}$.

Case (ii): s is top white. In this case s itself is the only white principal subterm of s. It is a consequence of $\dot{s} \;{}^*\!\leftarrow s \to t \to^* \dot{t}$ in combination with the confluence of s that $\dot{s} \downarrow \dot{t}$. □

Theorem 8.5.21 *Confluence is a modular property of constructor-sharing TRSs provided that $\to_c$ is normalizing.*

Proof By induction on $rank(t)$ we show that every term t is confluent if $\to_c$ is normalizing. If $rank(t) = 0$, then the assertion holds vacuously. Suppose $rank(t) > 0$ and consider a conversion $t_1 \;{}^*\!\leftarrow t \to^* t_2$.

Case (i): t is top black. The proof for this case is illustrated in Figure 8.3. Because $\to_c$ is normalizing, one may reduce every term in the conversion (black dots) to a white witness (white dots) by Lemma 8.5.19. Because all white principal subterms occurring in the conversion $t_1 \;{}^*\!\leftarrow t \to^* t_2$ have rank less than $rank(t)$, the inductive hypothesis implies their confluence. Repeated application of Proposition 8.5.20 yields a conversion between the white witnesses (upper gray dots). Because white witnesses are white preserved, they are confluent by Proposition 8.5.16. Hence t_1 and t_2 have a common reduct.

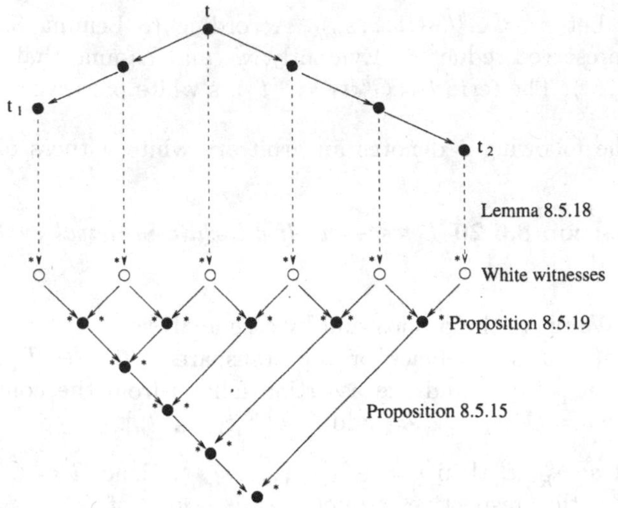

FIGURE 8.3. Proof of Theorem 8.5.21.

Case (ii): t is top white. This case is analogous to case (i) (using black witnesses).

Case (iii): t is top transparent. The assertion follows as in Lemma 8.5.15, case (iii). □

The sufficient criterion for the modularity of confluence for constructor-sharing TRSs has several interesting consequences. The most important is certainly Toyama's theorem.

Theorem 8.5.22 *Confluence is a modular property of disjoint TRSs.*

Proof Let $(\mathcal{F}_1, \mathcal{R}_1)$ and $(\mathcal{F}_2, \mathcal{R}_2)$ be disjoint TRSs. We claim that $\rightarrow_c$ is terminating. Let $(\mathbb{N}, >)$ denote the usual well-founded ordering on natural numbers and $(\mathcal{M}(\mathbb{N}), >^{mul})$ its well-founded multiset extension. We define

$$K(s) = [rank(t) \mid t \in S(s)] \in \mathcal{M}(\mathbb{N})$$

i.e., $K(s)$ denotes the multiset of the ranks of the special subterms of s. Because rewrite steps cannot increase the rank, it is not difficult to prove that $s \rightarrow_c t$ implies $K(s) >^{mul} K(t)$. Thus, $\rightarrow_c$ is terminating, hence normalizing. Now the assertion follows from Theorem 8.5.21. □

Corollary 8.5.23 *If $\mathcal{R}_1$ and $\mathcal{R}_2$ are confluent and contain neither collapsing nor constructor-lifting rules, then their combined system $\mathcal{R} = \mathcal{R}_1 \cup \mathcal{R}_2$ is confluent.*

Proof This is an immediate consequence of Theorem 8.5.21 because $\rightarrow_c$ is empty for those systems. □

In Example 8.2.1, we saw that confluence may not be modular in the presence of constructor-lifting rules. The next example (a variant of Example 8.2.1) shows why collapsing rules have to be excluded as well.

Example 8.5.24 Consider $\mathcal{R}_1 = \{F(x, c(x)) \to A, F(x, x) \to B\}$ and $\mathcal{R}_2 = \{a \to g(c(a)), g(x) \to x\}$, which share the constructor c. Both are confluent, but the term $F(a, a)$ has two normal forms A and B.

8.5.2 Unique Normalization

In this section, it will be shown that unique normalization is modular for constructor-sharing TRSs. An alternative proof of this fact can be found in [Ohl95a]. To start, we have the following result about normalization.

Proposition 8.5.25 *Normalization is a modular property of constructor-sharing TRSs.*

Proof Let $(\mathcal{F}_1, \mathcal{R}_1)$ and $(\mathcal{F}_2, \mathcal{R}_2)$ be two constructor-sharing TRSs. We have to show that their combined system $(\mathcal{F}, \mathcal{R})$ is normalizing. We will show by induction on $rank(t)$ that every term $t \in \mathcal{T}(\mathcal{F}, \mathcal{V})$ has a normal form w.r.t. $\to_{\mathcal{R}}$. If $rank(t) = 0$, then $t \in \mathcal{T}(\mathcal{C}, \mathcal{V})$ is a normal form. So let $rank(t) = k > 0$. The induction step will be proven by case analysis.

Case (i): t is top black. In this case the term t has a representation $t = C^b\{\!\{t_1, \ldots, t_n\}\!\}$. By the inductive hypothesis, every subterm t_j, $j \in \{1, \ldots, n\}$, rewrites to some $t'_j \in NF(\mathcal{F}, \mathcal{R})$. Therefore, $t \to^*_{\mathcal{R}} C^b\{t'_1, \ldots, t'_n\}$. It is clear that $C^b\{t'_1, \ldots, t'_n\} = \hat{C}^b\{\!\{s_1, \ldots, s_m\}\!\}$ for some black context $\hat{C}^b\{, \ldots, \}$ and top white normal forms $s_1, \ldots, s_m \in NF(\mathcal{F}, \mathcal{R})$. Choose fresh variables $x_1, \ldots, x_m$ satisfying $\langle s_1, \ldots, s_m\rangle \infty \langle x_1, \ldots, x_m\rangle$. Because $\hat{C}^b\{x_1, \ldots, x_m\} \in \mathcal{T}(\mathcal{F}_1, \mathcal{V})$ and the TRS $(\mathcal{F}_1, \mathcal{R}_1)$ is normalizing, it follows that $\hat{C}^b\{x_1, \ldots, x_m\} \to^*_{\mathcal{R}_1} \overline{C}^b\langle x_{i_1}, \ldots, x_{i_l}\rangle$ for some normal form $\overline{C}^b\langle x_{i_1}, \ldots, x_{i_l}\rangle \in NF(\mathcal{F}_1, \mathcal{R}_1)$. Because of $\langle x_1, \ldots, x_m\rangle \propto \langle s_1, \ldots, s_m\rangle$, we obtain $t \to^*_{\mathcal{R}} \hat{C}^b\{\!\{s_1, \ldots, s_m\}\!\} \to^*_{\mathcal{R}_1} \overline{C}^b\langle\!\langle s_{i_1}, \ldots, s_{i_l}\rangle\!\rangle = t'$. It is readily verified that $t' \in NF(\mathcal{F}, \mathcal{R})$.

Case (ii): t is top white. This case is analogous to case (i).

Case (iii): t is top transparent. Then $t = C^t[\![t_1, \ldots, t_n]\!]$ for some transparent context $C^t[, \ldots,] \neq \Box$ and top black or top white terms $t_1, \ldots, t_n$. According to cases (i) and (ii), every t_j has a normal form t'_j w.r.t. $\to_{\mathcal{R}}$. Hence $t \to^*_{\mathcal{R}} C^t[t'_1, \ldots, t'_n]$. Clearly, $C^t[t'_1, \ldots, t'_n]$ is also normal form w.r.t. $\to_{\mathcal{R}}$. □

Note that the same proof shows the modularity of innermost normalization for constructor-sharing TRSs.

Our next goal is to show that unique normalization of $\mathcal{R}_1$ and $\mathcal{R}_2$ ensures normalization of $\to_c$. According to Theorem 8.5.21, this entails that their combined system is confluent.

Definition 8.5.26 Let $C^t[,\ldots,] \in \mathcal{T}(\mathcal{C},\mathcal{V})$. Define

$$\|C^t[,\ldots,]\| = \begin{cases} 0 & \text{if } C^t[,\ldots,] = \Box \\ 1 + \sum_{i=1}^{n} \|t_i\| & \text{if } C^t[,\ldots,] = f(t_1,\ldots,t_n),\ f \neq \Box \end{cases}$$

For $s \in \mathcal{T}(\mathcal{D},\mathcal{C},\mathcal{V})$, define

$$\|s\| = \begin{cases} 0 & \text{if } s \text{ is top black or top white} \\ \|C^t[,\ldots,]\| & \text{if } s = C^t[\![s_1,\ldots,s_n]\!] \end{cases}$$

That is, $\|s\|$ denotes the number of transparent symbols occurring in the outer transparent context of s.

Lemma 8.5.27 *If $\mathcal{R}_1$ and $\mathcal{R}_2$ are uniquely normalizing, then the collapsing reduction relation $\rightarrow_c$ is terminating on $\mathcal{T}(\mathcal{D}_1,\mathcal{C},\mathcal{V}) \cup \mathcal{T}(\mathcal{D}_2,\mathcal{C},\mathcal{V})$.*

Proof W.l.o.g. it suffices to show that each $\rightarrow_c$ reduction sequence starting from some term $t \in \mathcal{T}(\mathcal{D}_1,\mathcal{C},\mathcal{V})$ is finite. We prove this by contradiction. Suppose there is an infinite reduction sequence

$$t = t_1 \rightarrow_c t_2 \rightarrow_c t_3 \rightarrow_c \ldots$$

Obviously, $t_j \notin \mathcal{T}(\mathcal{C},\mathcal{V})$ for each $j \in \mathbb{N}$ and $t_j \rightarrow_c t_{j+1}$ implies $t_j \rightarrow^+_{\mathcal{R}_1} t_{j+1}$. We first prove that $t_j \rightarrow_c t_{j+1}$ implies $\|t_j\| < \|t_{j+1}\|$, considering the following cases.

- If t_j is top black, then t_j is the only special subterm of t_j. According to the definition of $\rightarrow_c$, $t_{j+1} = C^t[\![s_1,\ldots,s_n]\!]$ for some context $C^t[,\ldots,] \neq \Box$ and top black terms $s_1,\ldots,s_n$. Consequently, $\|t_j\| = 0 < \|t_{j+1}\|$.
- If $t_j = C^t[\![s_1,\ldots,s_i,\ldots,s_n]\!]$, then the special subterms of t_j, apart from t_j itself, are the top black terms $s_1,\ldots,s_n$. According to the definition of $\rightarrow_c$, we have $t_{j+1} = C^t[s_1,\ldots,s'_i,\ldots,s_n]$, where $s_i \rightarrow^+_{\mathcal{R}_1} s'_i$ and s'_i is top transparent. Thus $\|t_j\| < \|t_{j+1}\|$.

Hence $t_j \rightarrow_c t_{j+1}$ implies $\|t_j\| < \|t_{j+1}\|$, and we obtain an infinite ascending sequence of natural numbers

$$\|t_1\| < \|t_2\| < \|t_3\| < \|t_4\| < \ldots$$

Because $\mathcal{R}_1$ is normalizing, $t \rightarrow^*_{\mathcal{R}_1} t'$ for some $t' \in NF(\rightarrow_{\mathcal{R}_1})$. Let $\|t'\| = k$. Then there is a $j \in \mathbb{N}$ such that $\|t_j\| > k$. On the other hand, because $t' \mathrel{{}^*_{\mathcal{R}_1}\!\!\leftarrow} t \rightarrow^*_{\mathcal{R}_1} t_j$, the term t' is in normal form w.r.t. $\rightarrow_{\mathcal{R}_1}$, and $\mathcal{R}_1$ is confluent, it follows that $t_j \rightarrow^*_{\mathcal{R}_1} t'$. Hence we have $t_j = C^t[\![s_1,\ldots,s_n]\!] \rightarrow^*_{\mathcal{R}_1} C^t[s'_1,\ldots,s'_n] = t'$, where $s_i \rightarrow^*_{\mathcal{R}_1} s'_i$, for every $i \in \{1,\ldots,n\}$. In conclusion, $\|t'\| \geq \|t_j\| > k$ yields a contradiction. □

In order to prove the normalization of $\rightarrow_c$ on $\mathcal{T}(\mathcal{D},\mathcal{C},\mathcal{V})$, we actually show the stronger statement that $\rightarrow_c$ is innermost normalizing.

Lemma 8.5.28 *Let s be a top white term and let $s \to_c^* s'$ be an innermost derivation such that $s' \in NF(\to_c)$. Then, for any black context $C^b[, \ldots,]$, we have $C^b[\ldots, s, \ldots] \to_c^* C^b[\ldots, s', \ldots]$*

Proof If all terms in $s \to_c^* s'$ are top white, then the lemma holds. Otherwise a top black or top transparent term u' occurs in the innermost derivation $s \to_c^* s'$. Suppose $s \to_c^* u \to_c u' \to_c^* s'$ such that u' is the first nontop-white term in the derivation. Because u is top white, the derivation is innermost, and the collapsing reduction takes place in the outer white context, it follows that $u = C^w\{\!\{u_1, \ldots, u_m\}\!\}$ where $u_1, \ldots, u_m \in NF(\to_c)$, and $u' = \hat{C}^w\langle\!\langle u_{i_1}, \ldots, u_{i_l}\rangle\!\rangle$ for some $i_1, \ldots, i_l \in \{1, \ldots, m\}$.

- If u' is top black, then $u' = u_i$ for some $i \in \{i_1, \ldots, i_l\}$. Because $u_i \in NF(\to_c)$, it follows that $s' = u'$. Clearly, the lemma is also valid in this case.
- In the remaining case u' is top transparent. Then any reduction step in the sequence $u' \to_c^* s'$ takes place in the respective outer white contexts because $u_{i_1}, \ldots, u_{i_l} \in NF(\to_c)$. Therefore, $s' = \overline{C}^w\langle\!\langle u_{j_1}, \ldots, u_{j_p}\rangle\!\rangle$ for some indices $j_1, \ldots, j_p \in \{i_1, \ldots, i_l\}$, and it follows that $C^b[\ldots, s, \ldots] \to_c^* C^b[\ldots, s', \ldots]$.

□

Proposition 8.5.29 *If $\mathcal{R}_1$ and $\mathcal{R}_2$ are uniquely normalizing, then the relation $\to_c$ is innermost normalizing on $\mathcal{T}(\mathcal{D}, \mathcal{C}, \mathcal{V})$.*

Proof It will be shown that every term t is innermost normalizing w.r.t. $\to_c$, using induction on $rank(t) = k$. The case $k = 0$ is trivially true and for $k = 1$ the assertion follows from Lemma 8.5.27 in conjunction with case (iii). So let $rank(t) = k > 1$. The following case analysis yields the result.

Case (i): t is top black. We may write $t = C^b[\![t_1, \ldots, t_n]\!]$. Because $rank(t_j) < rank(t)$, it follows from the inductive hypothesis that, for every $j \in \{1, \ldots, n\}$, there exists an innermost derivation $t_j \to_c^* t_j'$ such that $t_j' \in NF(\to_c)$. According to Lemma 8.5.28, $t = C^b[\![t_1, \ldots, t_n]\!] \to_c^* C^b[t_1', \ldots, t_n']$. Observe that this is also an innermost derivation. Moreover, because t_j' can be written as $t_j' = \hat{C}_j^b\langle\!\langle t_1^j, \ldots, t_{m_j}^j\rangle\!\rangle$, where every top white t_i^j is an element of $NF(\to_c)$, we may write $C^b[t_1', \ldots, t_n'] = \hat{C}^b\{\!\{s_1, \ldots, s_m\}\!\}$ for some black context $\hat{C}^b\{\!\{, \ldots, \}\!\}$ and top white terms $s_1, \ldots, s_m \in NF(\to_c)$. Choose fresh variables $x_1, \ldots, x_m$ satisfying the property $\langle s_1, \ldots, s_m\rangle \propto \langle x_1, \ldots, x_m\rangle$. Because $\hat{C}^b\{x_1, \ldots, x_m\} \in \mathcal{T}(\mathcal{D}_1, \mathcal{C}, \mathcal{V})$ and $\to_c$ is terminating on $\mathcal{T}(\mathcal{D}_1, \mathcal{C}, \mathcal{V})$, every innermost $\to_c$ derivation starting from $\hat{C}^b\{x_1, \ldots, x_m\}$ ends in some $\overline{C}^b\langle x_{i_1}, \ldots, x_{i_l}\rangle \in NF(\to_c)$. It follows from $\hat{C}^b\{x_1, \ldots, x_m\} \to_c^* \overline{C}^b\langle x_{i_1}, \ldots, x_{i_l}\rangle$ and $\langle x_1, \ldots, x_m\rangle \propto \langle s_1, \ldots, s_m\rangle$

that $t \to_c^* \hat{C}^b\{\!\{s_1,\ldots,s_m\}\!\} \to_c^* \overline{C}^b\langle\!\langle s_{i_1},\ldots,s_{i_l}\rangle\!\rangle = t'$. It is easy to verify that $t' \in NF(\to_c)$ and that $t \to_c^* t'$ is an innermost reduction sequence.

Case (ii): t is top white. This case is analogous to case (i).

Case (iii): t is top transparent. Let $t = C^t[\![t_1,\ldots,t_n]\!]$. According to cases (i) and (ii), every t_j reduces via innermost rewriting to some term $t'_j \in NF(\to_c)$. Clearly, $t' = C^t[t'_1,\ldots,t'_n] \in NF(\to_c)$, $t \to_c^* t'$, and the derivation is innermost. □

With the help of these preparatory results, we can now show the main result of this section.

Theorem 8.5.30 *Unique normalization is modular for constructor-sharing TRSs.*

Proof Let $\mathcal{R}_1$ and $\mathcal{R}_2$ be uniquely normalizing constructor-sharing TRSs. It must be shown that their union $\mathcal{R} = \mathcal{R}_1 \cup \mathcal{R}_2$ is also uniquely normalizing. According to Proposition 8.5.29, $\to_c$ is innermost normalizing and hence normalizing. Consequently, $\mathcal{R}$ is confluent by Theorem 8.5.21. Finally, Proposition 8.5.25 states that $\mathcal{R}$ is also normalizing. □

8.6 Hierarchical Combinations

In this section, we gather modularity results about hierarchical combinations of TRSs. Because hierarchical combinations subsume constructor-sharing systems, a property $\mathcal{P}$ can only be modular for hierarchical combinations if it is modular for constructor-sharing systems. In other words, one cannot hope to obtain a modularity result for hierarchical combinations if $\mathcal{P}$ is not modular for constructor-sharing systems. In Sections 8.6.1 and 8.6.2, we will investigate the most interesting properties in the termination hierarchy that are modular for constructor-sharing systems, viz. $\mathcal{C}_\mathcal{E}$-termination, simple termination, and innermost termination. Part of the material of Section 8.6.1 can also be found in [Ohl02]. In Section 8.6.3, we will consider local confluence, confluence for left-linear systems, and strong confluence for linear systems. Convergence will also be treated there.

8.6.1 $\mathcal{C}_\mathcal{E}$ and Simple Termination

The hierarchical combination of $\mathcal{R}_1 = \{a \to b\}$ and $\mathcal{R}_2 = \{f(b) \to f(a)\}$ from Example 8.1.2 shows that simple termination is not modular for hierarchical combinations. On the other hand, the hierarchical combination of the base system $\mathcal{R}_+$ and the extension $\mathcal{R}_*$ as introduced in Example 8.1.6

is again simply terminating:

$$\mathcal{R}_+ = \begin{cases} 0 + y & \rightarrow & y \\ s(x) + y & \rightarrow & s(x + y) \end{cases}$$

$$\mathcal{R}_* = \begin{cases} 0 * y & \rightarrow & 0 \\ s(x) * y & \rightarrow & (x * y) + y \end{cases}$$

What is the difference between these examples? That is, why is the hierarchical combination of $\mathcal{R}_+$ and $\mathcal{R}_*$ so benign and that of $\mathcal{R}_1$ and $\mathcal{R}_2$ so malignant? In essence, this is due to the fact that on the right-hand side $(x * y) + y$ of the second rule from $\mathcal{R}_*$ the function symbol $+$ from $\mathcal{D}_+$ occurs above the function symbol $*$ from $\mathcal{D}_*$, whereas on the right-hand side $f(a)$ the function symbol a from $\mathcal{D}_1$ occurs below the function symbol f from $\mathcal{D}_2$. This fact has been observed independently and contemporaneously by Dershowitz [Der95] and Krishna Rao [KR95a] and lead to the notion of proper extensions; cf. Krishna Rao [KR94, KR95a, KR95b]. In order to review the definition of proper extensions, we have to introduce the dependency relation $\trianglerighteq_d$.

Definition 8.6.1 For a TRS $(\mathcal{F}, \mathcal{R})$, the dependency relation $\trianglerighteq_d$ is the smallest quasi-ordering satisfying the condition $f \trianglerighteq_d g$ whenever there is a rewrite rule $f(\dots) \rightarrow C[g(\dots)] \in \mathcal{R}$ with $g \in \mathcal{D}$. So $f \trianglerighteq_d g$ holds if the function f depends on the definition of the function g.

Definition 8.6.2 Let $(\mathcal{F}, \mathcal{R})$ be the hierarchical combination of base system $(\mathcal{F}_1, \mathcal{R}_1)$ and extension $(\mathcal{F}_2, \mathcal{R}_2)$. The defined symbols $\mathcal{D}_2$ of $\mathcal{R}_2$ are split into two sets $\mathcal{D}_2^1$ and $\mathcal{D}_2^2$, where $\mathcal{D}_2^1$ contains all defined symbols of $\mathcal{D}_2$ that depend on a defined symbol of $\mathcal{R}_1$, i.e.,

$$\mathcal{D}_2^1 = \{f \mid f \in \mathcal{D}_2, f \trianglerighteq_d g \text{ for some } g \in \mathcal{D}_1\}$$

and $\mathcal{D}_2^2 = \mathcal{D}_2 \setminus \mathcal{D}_2^1$.

$\mathcal{R}_2$ is a *proper extension* of $\mathcal{R}_1$ if every rewrite rule $l \rightarrow r \in \mathcal{R}_2$ satisfies the following condition: If t is a subterm of r such that $root(t) \in \mathcal{D}_2^1$ and $root(t) \trianglerighteq_d root(l)$, then t does not contain a function symbol from $\mathcal{D}_1 \cup \mathcal{D}_2^1$ strictly below its root.

$\mathcal{R}_2$ is a *restricted proper extension* of $\mathcal{R}_1$ if it is a proper extension of $\mathcal{R}_1$ such that no *left-hand side* of the rewrite rules of $\mathcal{R}_2$ contains a function symbol from $\mathcal{D}_1 \cup \mathcal{D}_2^1$ strictly below its root.

Roughly speaking, in a proper extension functions depending on $\mathcal{R}_1$ are never called within a recursive call of $\mathcal{R}_2$ functions. It is easy to see that $\{f(b) \rightarrow f(a)\}$ is not a proper extension of $\{a \rightarrow b\}$, while $\mathcal{R}_*$ is a restricted proper extension of $\mathcal{R}_+$. A more complex example is the following.

Example 8.6.3 The TRS $\mathcal{R}_1$

$$\begin{array}{rcl}
0 + y & \to & y \\
s(x) + y & \to & s(x + y) \\
nil +\!\!+\, ys & \to & ys \\
xs +\!\!+\, nil & \to & xs \\
(x : xs) +\!\!+\, ys & \to & x : (xs +\!\!+\, ys) \\
sum(x : nil) & \to & x : nil \\
sum(x : y : xs) & \to & sum((x + y) : xs) \\
sum(xs +\!\!+\, (x : y : ys)) & \to & sum(xs +\!\!+\, sum(x : y : ys))
\end{array}$$

stems from [AG97a]; cf. [AG97b, example 5.1.17]. The function $sum(xs)$ computes the sum of all numbers in the list xs (e.g., sum applied to the list $[1, 2, 3]$ returns $[6]$).

The polynomial interpretation

$$\begin{array}{rclrcl}
0_{\mathbb{N}} & = & 0 & nil_{\mathbb{N}} & = & 0 \\
s_{\mathbb{N}}(x) & = & x + 1 & x :_{\mathbb{N}} xs & = & xs + 1 \\
x +_{\mathbb{N}} y & = & x + y & xs +\!\!+_{\mathbb{N}} ys & = & xs + ys + 1 \\
sum_{\mathbb{N}}(xs) & = & 1 & \mathrm{PLUS}_{\mathbb{N}}(x, y) & = & x \\
\mathrm{APP}_{\mathbb{N}}(xs, ys) & = & xs & \mathrm{SUM}_{\mathbb{N}}(xs) & = & xs \\
Cons_{\mathbb{N}}(x, y) & = & x + y & & &
\end{array}$$

shows $\mathcal{C}_{\mathcal{E}}$-termination of $\mathcal{R}_1$; see Corollary 5.4.34. ($\mathcal{R}_1$ is actually DP quasi-simply terminating.) Now we want to extend this system such that one can also compute the average of the numbers in a list. The TRS $\mathcal{R}_2$ does this:

$$\begin{array}{rcl}
0 - s(y) & \to & 0 \\
x - 0 & \to & x \\
s(x) - s(y) & \to & x - y \\
quot(0, s(y)) & \to & 0 \\
quot(s(x), s(y)) & \to & s(quot(x - y, s(y))) \\
length(nil) & \to & 0 \\
length(x : xs) & \to & s(length(xs)) \\
hd(x : xs) & \to & x \\
avg(xs) & \to & quot(hd(sum(xs)), length(xs))
\end{array}$$

By using an appropriate AFS and *rpo*, it is not difficult to show that $\mathcal{R}_2$ is DP simply terminating; see [AG00, example 9]. Therefore, $\mathcal{R}_2$ is also $\mathcal{C}_{\mathcal{E}}$-terminating. We have $\mathcal{D}_2^1 = \{avg\}$, whereas all other symbols of $\mathcal{D}_2$ belong to $\mathcal{D}_2^2$. Because avg does not occur on a right-hand side of a rewrite rule, $\mathcal{R}_2$ is a proper extension of $\mathcal{R}_1$. Furthermore, because none of the symbols $+$, $+\!\!+$, sum, and avg appears in a proper subterm of a left-hand side of the rewrite rules of $\mathcal{R}_2$, $\mathcal{R}_2$ is even a restricted proper extension of $\mathcal{R}_1$. Note that neither $\mathcal{R}_1$ nor $\mathcal{R}_2$ is simply terminating.

As hierarchical combinations with a common subsystem generalize both composable systems and hierarchical combinations, proper extension with a common subsystem extend both composable systems and proper extensions.

Definition 8.6.4 Let $(\mathcal{F}, \mathcal{R})$ be a hierarchical combination of the base system $(\mathcal{F}_1, \mathcal{R}_1)$ and the extension $(\mathcal{F}_2, \mathcal{R}_2)$ with a common subsystem $(\mathcal{F}_0, \mathcal{R}_0)$. Define $\mathcal{D}_0 = \{root(l) \mid l \to r \in \mathcal{R}_0\}$, $\mathcal{D}'_1 = \mathcal{D}_1 \setminus \mathcal{D}_0$ and $\mathcal{D}'_2 = \mathcal{D}_2 \setminus \mathcal{D}_0$. Now $\mathcal{D}'_2$ is split in two sets $\mathcal{D'}^1_2$ and $\mathcal{D'}^2_2$, where $\mathcal{D'}^1_2 = \{f | f \in \mathcal{D}'_2, f \trianglerighteq_d g \text{ for some } g \in \mathcal{D}'_1\}$ and $\mathcal{D'}^2_2 = \mathcal{D}'_2 \setminus \mathcal{D'}^1_2$. The TRS $\mathcal{R}_2$ is a called a *proper extension* of $\mathcal{R}_1$ *with a common subsystem* $\mathcal{R}_0$ if every rewrite rule of $l \to r \in \mathcal{R}_2$ satisfies the following condition: If t is a subterm of r such that $root(t) \in \mathcal{D'}^1_2$ and $root(t) \trianglerighteq_d root(l)$, then t contains no function symbol from $\mathcal{D}'_1 \cup \mathcal{D'}^1_2$ strictly below its root.

$\mathcal{R}_2$ is a *restricted proper extension* of $\mathcal{R}_1$ *with a common subsystem* $\mathcal{R}_0$ if it is a proper extension of $\mathcal{R}_1$ with a common subsystem $\mathcal{R}_0$ such that no *left-hand side* of the rewrite rules of $\mathcal{R}_2$ contains a function symbol from $\mathcal{D}'_1 \cup \mathcal{D'}^1_2$ strictly below its root.

It should be pointed out that proper extensions with a common subsystem were introduced as *generalized proper extension* in [KR95a]. As a matter of fact, Krishna Rao [KR95a] defined many more classes of extensions and it is not easy to keep track of all these different extensions. In order to keep the presentation of the material clear, we will restrict ourselves to proper extensions (with a common subsystem).

Example 8.6.5 Let $\mathcal{R}_1$ be as in Example 8.6.3 and let $\mathcal{R}_2$ consist of the rewrite rules of the second TRS in Example 8.6.3 and the rewrite rules of $\mathcal{R}_+$. Then $\mathcal{D}_0 = \{+\}$, $\mathcal{D}'_1 = \{+\!\!+, sum\}$, $\mathcal{D}'_2 = \{-, quot, length, hd, avg\}$, $\mathcal{D'}^1_2 = \{avg\}$, and $\mathcal{D'}^2_2 = \{-, quot, length, hd\}$,. It is readily verified that $\mathcal{R}_2$ is restricted proper extension of $\mathcal{R}_1$ with a common subsystem $\mathcal{R}_+$.

In the following, we will derive modularity results that allow us to conclude termination of hierarchical combinations like proper extensions. Moreover, we will develop techniques to prove termination of TRSs incrementally. These are based on the dependency pair method. We need the following refinement of Definition 5.4.8.

Definition 8.6.6 Let $(\mathcal{F}_1, \mathcal{R}_1)$ and $(\mathcal{F}_2, \mathcal{R}_2)$ be TRSs. If there is an infinite sequence $\langle s_1, t_1 \rangle \langle s_2, t_2 \rangle \ldots$ of dependency pairs from $\mathcal{R}_1$ and a substitution $\sigma : \mathcal{V} \to \mathcal{T}(\mathcal{F}_1 \cup \mathcal{F}_2, \mathcal{V})$ such that $t_j\sigma \to^*_{\mathcal{R}_1 \cup \mathcal{R}_2} s_{j+1}\sigma$ holds for all consecutive pairs $\langle s_j, t_j \rangle$ and $\langle s_{j+1}, t_{j+1} \rangle$ in the sequence, then the sequence $\langle s_1, t_1 \rangle \langle s_2, t_2 \rangle \ldots$ is called an *infinite* $\mathcal{R}_1$ *chain over* $\mathcal{R}_1 \cup \mathcal{R}_2$. Furthermore, if every (proper) subterm u of $s_j\sigma$ and $t_j\sigma$ is terminating w.r.t. $\mathcal{R}_1 \cup \mathcal{R}_2$, then the chain is called *minimal*.

In what follows, we will extend Gramlich's [Gra94] transformation—which is defined on the set $\mathcal{T}(\mathcal{F})$ of ground terms—to hierarchical combinations. To this end, we assume that every signature has at least one constant c that is not used in the rewrite rules. Then for every minimal chain that uses a substitution $\sigma : \mathcal{V} \to \mathcal{T}(\mathcal{F}, \mathcal{V})$, there is also a minimal chain that uses a *ground* substitution $\sigma' : \mathcal{V} \to \mathcal{T}(\mathcal{F})$. The substitution σ' is obtained from σ by replacing every variable in $x\sigma$ with the constant c. To assume that every signature has at least one constant c that is not used in the rewrite rules entails no loss of generality. In fact, as in [Ohl94c] one can use a distinguished variable z instead and define the transformation on the set $\mathcal{T}(\mathcal{F}, \{z\})$.

$\mathcal{C}_\mathcal{E}$-*Termination*

The results about $\mathcal{C}_\mathcal{E}$-termination until Corollary 8.6.16 are based on the ideas of Urbain [Urb01]. They are restricted to *finitely branching* TRSs. This restriction is justified by the fact that $\mathcal{C}_\mathcal{E}$-termination is not modular for nonfinitely branching constructor-sharing systems; see Examples 8.4.18–8.4.20.

To start, there is the following characterization of $\mathcal{C}_\mathcal{E}$-termination.

Lemma 8.6.7 *A TRS $\mathcal{R}$ is $\mathcal{C}_\mathcal{E}$-terminating if and only if there is no infinite $\mathcal{R}$ chain over $\mathcal{R} \uplus \mathcal{C}_\mathcal{E}$. In fact, if $\mathcal{R}$ is not $\mathcal{C}_\mathcal{E}$-terminating, then there is a minimal infinite $\mathcal{R}$ chain over $\mathcal{R} \uplus \mathcal{C}_\mathcal{E}$.*

Proof A TRS $\mathcal{R}$ is $\mathcal{C}_\mathcal{E}$-terminating if and only if $\mathcal{R} \uplus \mathcal{C}_\mathcal{E}$ is terminating. Hence the lemma follows directly from the fact that the dependency pairs of $\mathcal{R}$ and $\mathcal{R} \uplus \mathcal{C}_\mathcal{E}$ coincide (rewrite rules from $\mathcal{C}_\mathcal{E}$ do not cause dependency pairs) in conjunction with Theorem 5.4.9. □

In the following, we deal with a hierarchical combination $(\mathcal{F}, \mathcal{R})$ of the base system $(\mathcal{F}_1, \mathcal{R}_1)$ and the extension $(\mathcal{F}_2, \mathcal{R}_2)$. That is, $\mathcal{R}$ is the TRS $\mathcal{R}_1 \cup \mathcal{R}_2$ over the signature $\mathcal{F} = \mathcal{F}_1 \cup \mathcal{F}_2$ and $\mathcal{F}_1 \cap \mathcal{D}_2 = \emptyset$.

Let $s \in \mathcal{T}(\mathcal{F})$ with $root(s) \in \mathcal{F}_1$. We use the notation $s = C[\![s_1, \ldots, s_n]\!]$ if $C[, \ldots,] \in \mathcal{T}(\mathcal{F}_1)$ and $root(s_1), \ldots, root(s_n) \in \mathcal{F}_2 \backslash \mathcal{F}_1$. In this situation, a reduction step $s \to_\mathcal{R} t$ is called *inner* (denoted by $s \to^i_\mathcal{R} t$), if the reduction takes place in one of the subterms $s_1, \ldots, s_n$. Otherwise, we speak of an *outer* reduction step and write $s \to^o_\mathcal{R} t$.

Furthermore, $\mathcal{T}_{\mathrm{SN}}(\mathcal{F})$ stands for the set $\{t \in \mathcal{T}(\mathcal{F}) \mid$ every subterm t' of t with $root(t') \in \mathcal{F}_2 \setminus \mathcal{F}_1$ is terminating $\}$.

The following transformation Φ extends Gramlich's [Gra94] transformation to hierarchical combinations.

Definition 8.6.8 Define $\Phi : \mathcal{T}_{\mathrm{SN}}(\mathcal{F}) \to \mathcal{T}(\mathcal{F}_1 \uplus \{Cons, Nil\})$ by

- $\Phi(t) = t$, if $t \in \mathcal{T}(\mathcal{F}_1)$
- $\Phi(t) = C[\Phi(s_1), \ldots, \Phi(s_n)]$, if $root(t) \in \mathcal{F}_1$ and $t = C[\![t_1, \ldots, t_n]\!]$
- $\Phi(t) = Sort(\Phi^*(\Delta^*_1(t)))$, if $root(t) \in \mathcal{F}_2 \setminus \mathcal{F}_1$

with

$$\begin{aligned}
\Delta_1^*(t) &= \{u \in \mathcal{T}(\mathcal{F}) \mid t \to_{\mathcal{R}}^* u, root(u) \in \mathcal{F}_1\} \\
\Phi^*(M) &= \{\Phi(u) \mid u \in M\} \text{ for } M \subseteq \mathcal{T}_{\mathrm{SN}}(\mathcal{F}) \\
Sort(\{t_1, \ldots, t_m\}) &= \langle t_{\pi(1)}, \ldots, t_{\pi(m)} \rangle \\
&\quad \text{such that } t_{\pi(j)} \succ t_{\pi(j+1)} \text{ for } 1 \le j < m \\
\langle t_{\pi(1)}, \ldots, t_{\pi(m)} \rangle &= Cons(t_{\pi(1)}, \ldots, Cons(t_{\pi(m)}, Nil) \ldots)
\end{aligned}$$

where $\succ$ is an arbitrary but fixed total ordering on $\mathcal{T}(\mathcal{F}_1 \uplus \{Cons, Nil\})$.

Note that if $t \in \mathcal{T}_{\mathrm{SN}}(\mathcal{F})$, then $\Delta_1^*(t) \subseteq \mathcal{T}_{\mathrm{SN}}(\mathcal{F})$. Thus, Φ^* is always applied to a subset of $\mathcal{T}_{\mathrm{SN}}(\mathcal{F})$.

Example 8.6.9 Consider the two TRSs

$$\mathcal{R}_1 = \begin{cases} f(0,1,x) & \to & f(x,x,x) \\ f(x,y,z) & \to & 2 \\ 0 & \to & 2 \\ 1 & \to & 2 \end{cases}$$

$$\mathcal{R}_2 = \begin{cases} g & \to & 0 \\ g & \to & 1 \end{cases}$$

Then $\Phi(f(0,1,g)) = f(0,1,\Phi(g)) = f(0,1,Cons(0,Cons(1,Nil)))$, where $\succ$ is a total ordering on $\mathcal{T}(\mathcal{F}_1 \uplus \{Cons, Nil\})$ with $0 \succ 1$.

Lemma 8.6.10 *Let $s \in \mathcal{T}_{\mathrm{SN}}(\mathcal{F})$.*

1. *If $s \in \mathcal{T}(\mathcal{F}_1)$ and $s \to_{\mathcal{R}} t$, then $\Phi(s) \to_{\mathcal{R}_1} \Phi(t)$.*
2. *If $root(s) \in \mathcal{F}_1$ and $s = C[\![s_1, \ldots, s_n]\!]$, then*
   - *(a) $s \to_{\mathcal{R}}^{o} t$ implies $\Phi(s) \to_{\mathcal{R}_1} \Phi(t)$,*
   - *(b) $s \to_{\mathcal{R}}^{i} t$ implies $\Phi(s) \to_{\mathcal{C}_\mathcal{E}}^{*} \Phi(t)$.*
3. *If $root(s) \in \mathcal{F}_2 \setminus \mathcal{F}_1$ and $s \to_{\mathcal{R}} t$, then $\Phi(s) \to_{\mathcal{C}_\mathcal{E}}^{*} \Phi(t)$.*

Proof (1) This is trivial because $\Phi(s) = s$ and $\Phi(t) = t$.

(2a) We have either $s = C[\![s_1, \ldots, s_n]\!] \to_{\mathcal{R}}^{o} C'[\![s_{i_1}, \ldots, s_{i_m}]\!]$ with $i_1, \ldots, i_m \in \{1, \ldots, n\}$ or $s = C[\![s_1, \ldots, s_n]\!] \to_{\mathcal{R}}^{o} s_j = t$ for some $j \in \{1, \ldots, n\}$. Applying Φ, we obtain $\Phi(s) = C[\Phi(s_1), \ldots, \Phi(s_n)]$ and either $\Phi(t) = C'[\Phi(s_{i_1}), \ldots, \Phi(s_{i_m})]$ or $\Phi(t) = \Phi(s_j)$. Thus $\Phi(s) \to_{\mathcal{R}} \Phi(t)$ by the same rule because $\langle s_1, \ldots, s_n \rangle \propto \langle \Phi(s_1), \ldots, \Phi(s_n) \rangle$ (i.e., even nonleft-linear rules do not cause trouble).

(2b) Suppose $s = C[\![s_1, \ldots, s_j, \ldots s_n]\!] \to_{\mathcal{R}}^{i} C[s_1, \ldots, s_j', \ldots s_n] = t$, i.e., $s_j \to_{\mathcal{R}} s_j'$. If $root(s_j') \in \mathcal{F}_1$, then $s_j' \in \Delta_1^*(s_j)$ and hence $\Phi(s_j) \to_{\mathcal{C}_\mathcal{E}}^{+} \Phi(s_j')$. Otherwise, if $root(s_j') \in \mathcal{F}_2 \setminus \mathcal{F}_1$, then $\Delta_1^*(s_j') \subseteq \Delta_1^*(s_j)$ implies that $\Phi(s_j) \to_{\mathcal{C}_\mathcal{E}}^{*} \Phi(s_j')$.

(3) This is as in case (2b). □

Lemma 8.6.11 *If* $s \in \mathcal{T}_{SN}(\mathcal{F})$ *and* $s \to_{\mathcal{R}}^{*} t$, *then* $\Phi(s) \to_{\mathcal{R}_1 \uplus \mathcal{C}_{\mathcal{E}}}^{*} \Phi(t)$.

Proof Using Lemma 8.6.10, this follows by induction on the length of the rewrite sequence $s \to_{\mathcal{R}}^{*} t$. □

Let $\mathcal{R}_1$ and $\mathcal{R}_2$ be as in Example 8.6.9. If we apply the transformation Φ to the derivation $f(0,1,g) \to_{\mathcal{R}_1} f(g,g,g) \to_{\mathcal{R}_2} f(0,g,g) \to_{\mathcal{R}_2} f(0,1,g)$, then we obtain

$$\begin{array}{rl} & f(0,1,t) = \Phi(f(0,1,g)) \\ \to_{\mathcal{R}_1} & f(t,t,t) = \Phi(f(g,g,g)) \\ \to_{\mathcal{C}_{\mathcal{E}}} & f(0,t,t) = \Phi(f(0,g,g)) \\ \to_{\mathcal{C}_{\mathcal{E}}}^{+} & f(0,1,t) = \Phi(f(0,1,g)) \end{array}$$

where $t = \Phi(g) = Cons(0, Cons(1, Nil))$.

Lemma 8.6.12 *If there is a minimal infinite* $\mathcal{R}_1$ *chain over* $\mathcal{R}$, *then there is also an infinite* $\mathcal{R}_1$ *chain over* $\mathcal{R}_1 \uplus \mathcal{C}_{\mathcal{E}}$.

Proof Let $\langle s_1, t_1 \rangle \langle s_2, t_2 \rangle \ldots$ be a minimal infinite $\mathcal{R}_1$ chain over $\mathcal{R}$, that is, there is a substitution $\sigma : \mathcal{V} \to \mathcal{T}(\mathcal{F})$ such that $t_j\sigma \to_{\mathcal{R}}^{*} s_{j+1}\sigma$ holds for all consecutive pairs $\langle s_j, t_j \rangle$ and $\langle s_{j+1}, t_{j+1} \rangle$ in the sequence. Because the $\mathcal{R}_1$ chain is minimal, every subterm of $s_j\sigma$ and $t_j\sigma$, respectively, is an element of $\mathcal{T}_{SN}(\mathcal{F})$. Therefore, by Lemma 8.6.11, $\Phi(t_j\sigma) \to_{\mathcal{R}_1 \uplus \mathcal{C}_{\mathcal{E}}}^{*} \Phi(s_{j+1}\sigma)$ holds for all consecutive pairs $\langle s_j, t_j \rangle$ and $\langle s_{j+1}, t_{j+1} \rangle$ in the sequence. In other words, $\langle s_1, t_1 \rangle \langle s_2, t_2 \rangle \ldots$ is an $\mathcal{R}_1$ chain over $\mathcal{R}_1 \uplus \mathcal{C}_{\mathcal{E}}$. □

By means of the techniques developed so far, we can derive the following result due to Kurihara and Ohuchi [KO95a].

Proposition 8.6.13 $\mathcal{C}_{\mathcal{E}}$*-termination is a modular property of finitely branching composable TRSs.*

Proof Let $\mathcal{R}_1$ and $\mathcal{R}_2$ be $\mathcal{C}_{\mathcal{E}}$-terminating, finitely branching, and composable. Define

$$\begin{array}{rcl} \mathcal{R}_0 & = & \mathcal{R}_1 \cap \mathcal{R}_2 \\ \mathcal{R}_1' & = & \mathcal{R}_1 \setminus \mathcal{R}_0 \\ \mathcal{R}_2' & = & \mathcal{R}_2 \setminus \mathcal{R}_0 \end{array}$$

Note that $\mathcal{R}_1 \cup \mathcal{R}_2 = \mathcal{R}_1 \cup \mathcal{R}_2' = \mathcal{R}_1' \cup \mathcal{R}_2$. For a proof by contradiction, suppose that $\mathcal{R}_1 \cup \mathcal{R}_2$ is not $\mathcal{C}_{\mathcal{E}}$-terminating. According to Theorem 8.6.7, there is a minimal infinite $\mathcal{R}_1 \cup \mathcal{R}_2$ chain over $(\mathcal{R}_1 \cup \mathcal{R}_2) \uplus \mathcal{C}_{\mathcal{E}}$. If there were a minimal infinite $\mathcal{R}_1$ chain over $(\mathcal{R}_1 \cup \mathcal{R}_2) \uplus \mathcal{C}_{\mathcal{E}}$, then an application of Lemma 8.6.12 to $\mathcal{R}_1$ and $\mathcal{R}_2'$ would yield an infinite $\mathcal{R}_1$ chain over $\mathcal{R}_1 \uplus \mathcal{C}_{\mathcal{E}}'$, where $\mathcal{C}_{\mathcal{E}}' = \{Cons'(x,y) \to x,\ Cons'(x,y) \to y\}$ because we have to use a fresh function symbol $Cons'$ instead of the already-used symbol $Cons$.

This yields a contradiction to the $\mathcal{C}_\mathcal{E}$-termination of $\mathcal{R}_1$. Analogously, there cannot be a minimal infinite $\mathcal{R}_2$ chain over $(\mathcal{R}_1 \cup \mathcal{R}_2) \uplus \mathcal{C}_\mathcal{E}$. It follows that the infinite $\mathcal{R}_1 \cup \mathcal{R}_2$ chain must contain dependency pairs from both $\mathcal{R}'_1$ and $\mathcal{R}'_2$. However, it is easy to see that this is impossible. □

For example, Proposition 8.6.13 can be used to show $\mathcal{C}_\mathcal{E}$-termination of the second system in Example 8.6.5. It has already been observed that the TRS $\mathcal{R}_2$ of Example 8.6.3 is DP simply terminating, hence $\mathcal{C}_\mathcal{E}$-terminating by Lemma 8.3.4. The system $\mathcal{R}_+$ is simply terminating and thus also $\mathcal{C}_\mathcal{E}$-terminating by Proposition 8.3.2. Furthermore, $\mathcal{R}_2$ and $\mathcal{R}_+$ are constructor-sharing, hence composable. Thus, an application of Proposition 8.6.13 yields $\mathcal{C}_\mathcal{E}$-termination of their combination.

In fact, this modularity result can be generalized to restricted proper extensions (with a common subsystem). This generalization turns out to be a consequence of the following theorem, which allows incremental termination proofs.

Theorem 8.6.14 *Let $\mathcal{R}$ be the hierarchical combination of two finitely branching TRSs $\mathcal{R}_1$ and $\mathcal{R}_2$.*

1. *$\mathcal{R}$ is terminating if base system $\mathcal{R}_1$ is $\mathcal{C}_\mathcal{E}$-terminating and there is no minimal infinite $\mathcal{R}_2$ chain over $\mathcal{R}$.*
2. *$\mathcal{R}$ is terminating if $\mathcal{R}_1$ is $\mathcal{C}_\mathcal{E}$-terminating and there is a quasi-reduction ordering $\succsim$ such that*
   - *$l \succsim r$ for all rules $l \to r$ in $\mathcal{R}$ and*
   - *$s \succ t$ for all dependency pairs $\langle s, t\rangle$ of $\mathcal{R}_2$.*

Proof (1) For a proof by contradiction, suppose that $\mathcal{R} = \mathcal{R}_1 \cup \mathcal{R}_2$ is not terminating. According to Theorem 5.4.9, there is a minimal infinite $\mathcal{R}$ chain (over $\mathcal{R}$). By assumption, there is no minimal infinite $\mathcal{R}_2$ chain over $\mathcal{R}$. Therefore the minimal infinite $\mathcal{R}$ chain must contain a dependency pair from $\mathcal{R}_1$, say $\langle s_j, t_j\rangle$. Because the rewrite rules from $\mathcal{R}_1$ do not contain symbols from $\mathcal{D}_2$, every dependency pair $\langle s_i, t_i\rangle$ in the minimal infinite $\mathcal{R}$ chain with $i \geq j$ must also originate from a rewrite rule of $\mathcal{R}_1$. In other words, there is a minimal infinite $\mathcal{R}_1$ chain over $\mathcal{R}$. According to Lemma 8.6.12, there is also an infinite $\mathcal{R}_1$ chain over $\mathcal{R}_1 \uplus \mathcal{C}_\mathcal{E}$. We conclude from Lemma 8.6.7 that $\mathcal{R}_1$ is not $\mathcal{C}_\mathcal{E}$-terminating. This contradiction proves statement (1).

(2) This follows directly from (1). □

For finite TRSs, Theorem 8.6.14 can be reformulated such that it captures cycles. The next example from [Gra94] demonstrates that in Theorem 8.6.14, the presumption that "there is no infinite $\mathcal{R}_2$ chain over $\mathcal{R}_1 \cup \mathcal{R}_2$" cannot be weakened to "there is no infinite $\mathcal{R}_2$ chain over $\mathcal{R}_2$."

Example 8.6.15 Clearly, the TRS $\mathcal{R}_1 = \{a \to b\}$ is simply terminating. The system $\mathcal{R}_2 = \{h(x,x) \to h(a,b)\}$ is also simply terminating because it is obviously terminating and nonsize-increasing; see Lemma 5.2.34. According to Proposition 8.3.2 both systems are $\mathcal{C}_\mathcal{E}$-terminating, but their union is not terminating: $h(a,b) \to_{\mathcal{R}_1} h(b,b) \to_{\mathcal{R}_2} h(a,b)$.

Corollary 8.6.16 *Let $\mathcal{R}$ be the hierarchical combination of two finitely branching TRSs $\mathcal{R}_1$ and $\mathcal{R}_2$.*

1. *$\mathcal{R}$ is $\mathcal{C}_\mathcal{E}$-terminating if base system $\mathcal{R}_1$ is $\mathcal{C}_\mathcal{E}$-terminating and there is no minimal infinite $\mathcal{R}_2$ chain over $\mathcal{R} \uplus \mathcal{C}_\mathcal{E}$.*

2. *$\mathcal{R}$ is $\mathcal{C}_\mathcal{E}$-terminating if $\mathcal{R}_1$ is $\mathcal{C}_\mathcal{E}$-terminating and there is a quasi-reduction ordering $\succsim$ such that*

   - *$Cons(x,y) \succsim x$ and $Cons(x,y) \succsim y$,*
   - *$l \succsim r$ for all rules $l \to r$ in $\mathcal{R}$,*
   - *$s \succ t$ for all dependency pairs $\langle s,t \rangle$ of $\mathcal{R}_2$.*

Proof Apply Theorem 8.6.14 with $\mathcal{R}_2 \uplus \mathcal{C}_\mathcal{E}$ instead of $\mathcal{R}_2$. □

The next example is taken from [GAO02].

Example 8.6.17 Let

$$\mathcal{R}_1 = \left\{ \begin{array}{rcl} add(nil, ys) & \to & ys \\ add(0 : xs, ys) & \to & add(xs, ys) \\ add(s(n) : xs, m : ys) & \to & add(n : xs, s(m) : ys) \end{array} \right.$$

and

$$\mathcal{R}_2 = \left\{ \begin{array}{rcl} weight(n : nil) & \to & n \\ weight(n : m : xs) & \to & weight(add(n : m : xs, 0 : xs)) \end{array} \right.$$

where $n : m : x$ abbreviates $n : (m : x)$. The function *add* computes $add(n_0 : n_1 : \cdots : n_k : nil, m : ys) = (m + \sum_{i=0}^{k} n_i) : ys$ and the function *weight* computes $weight(n_0 : n_1 : \cdots : n_k : nil) = n_0 + \sum_{i=1}^{k} i \cdot n_i$. In order to show $\mathcal{C}_\mathcal{E}$-termination of the hierarchical combination of the two TRSs, will use Corollary 8.6.16. Simple termination of $\mathcal{R}_1$ can be shown by the *lpo* with the precedence $add \succ_p :$ and $add \succ_p s$. Therefore, $\mathcal{R}_1$ is $\mathcal{C}_\mathcal{E}$-terminating. We have to find a quasi-reduction ordering $\succsim$ satisfying the constraints:

$$\begin{aligned}
Cons(x,y) &\geq x\\
Cons(x,y) &\geq y\\
add(nil,ys) &\geq ys\\
add(0:xs,ys) &\geq add(xs,ys)\\
add(s(n):xs,m:ys) &\geq add(n:xs,s(m):ys)\\
weight(n:nil) &\geq n\\
weight(n:m:xs) &\geq weight(add(n:m:xs,0:xs))\\
\mathrm{WEIGHT}(n:m:xs) &> \mathrm{WEIGHT}(add(n:m:xs,0:xs))
\end{aligned}$$

Note that $\langle \mathrm{WEIGHT}(n:m:xs), \mathrm{ADD}(n:m:xs,0:xs)\rangle$ is not a dependency pair of $\mathcal{R}_2$ because $add \notin \mathcal{D}_2$. After normalization with the AFS $\mathcal{A} = \{add(x,y) \to add'(y), x:xs \to :'(xs)\}$, the inequalities are satisfied by the *lpo* based on the precedence $:' \succ_p add'$. Thus, $\mathcal{R}_1 \cup \mathcal{R}_2$ is $\mathcal{C}_\mathcal{E}$-terminating by Corollary 8.6.16.

Note that in the preceding example $\mathcal{R}_2$ is not a proper extension of $\mathcal{R}_1$. This is because $\mathcal{D}_2^1 = \{weight\}$ and $add \in \mathcal{D}_1$ occurs below *weight* on the right-hand side of the second rewrite rule of $\mathcal{R}_2$.

Now we can to extend Proposition 8.6.13 to finite restricted proper extensions. This is a very useful result, as we shall see.

Theorem 8.6.18 *Let $\mathcal{R}_1$ and $\mathcal{R}_2$ be finite $\mathcal{C}_\mathcal{E}$-terminating TRSs. If $\mathcal{R}_2$ is a restricted proper extension of $\mathcal{R}_1$, then $\mathcal{R}_1 \cup \mathcal{R}_2$ is $\mathcal{C}_\mathcal{E}$-terminating.*

Proof Let $\mathcal{R}_2^1 = \{l \to r \mid root(l) \in \mathcal{D}_2^1\}$ and $\mathcal{R}_2^2 = \{l \to r \mid root(l) \in \mathcal{D}_2^2\}$. The TRS $\mathcal{R}_2^2$ does not contain function symbols from $\mathcal{D}_1 \cup \mathcal{D}_2^1$. This is because for all $l \to r \in \mathcal{R}_2^2$ neither l (because $\mathcal{R}_2$ is a restricted proper extension of $\mathcal{R}_1$) nor r contains function symbols from $\mathcal{D}_1 \cup \mathcal{D}_2^1$ (if r would contain such a function symbol, then $root(l)$ would be an element of $\mathcal{D}_2^1$). In other words, $\mathcal{R}_1$ and $\mathcal{R}_2^2$ are constructor-sharing. Because both are $\mathcal{C}_\mathcal{E}$-terminating, so is their union by Proposition 8.6.13. In order to show $\mathcal{C}_\mathcal{E}$-termination of $\mathcal{R}_1 \cup \mathcal{R}_2 = (\mathcal{R}_1 \cup \mathcal{R}_2^2) \cup \mathcal{R}_2^1$, it suffices to show that there is no minimal infinite $\mathcal{R}_2^1$ chain over $(\mathcal{R}_1 \cup \mathcal{R}_2) \uplus \mathcal{C}_\mathcal{E}$; see Corollary 8.6.16. Suppose on the contrary that there is a minimal infinite $\mathcal{R}_2^1$ chain $\langle s_1,t_1\rangle\langle s_2,t_2\rangle\ldots$ over $(\mathcal{R}_1 \cup \mathcal{R}_2) \uplus \mathcal{C}_\mathcal{E}$, i.e., there exists a substitution $\sigma : \mathcal{V} \to \mathcal{T}(\mathcal{F} \uplus \{Cons\})$ such that $t_j\sigma \to^*_{(\mathcal{R}_1\cup\mathcal{R}_2)\uplus\mathcal{C}_\mathcal{E}} s_{j+1}\sigma$ holds for all consecutive pairs $\langle s_j,t_j\rangle$ and $\langle s_{j+1},t_{j+1}\rangle$ in the sequence. Because we consider finite TRSs, we may assume that every dependency pair in $\langle s_1,t_1\rangle\langle s_2,t_2\rangle\ldots$ belongs to a cycle $\mathcal{P}$ that consists solely of dependency pairs from $\mathcal{R}_2^1$. Let $\langle F(u_1,\ldots,u_n), G(t_1,\ldots,t_m)\rangle$ be one of the dependency pairs in $\mathcal{P}$. Suppose $\langle F(u_1,\ldots,u_n), G(v_1,\ldots,v_m)\rangle$ originates from the rewrite rule $f(u_1,\ldots,u_n) \to C[g(v_1,\ldots,v_m)]$ of $\mathcal{R}_2^1$. Clearly, we have

$f \trianglerighteq_d g$ and $g \trianglerighteq_d f$ because $\mathcal{P}$ is a cycle. Because $\mathcal{R}_2$ is a proper extension of $\mathcal{R}_1$, the terms $v_1, \ldots, v_m$ do not contain symbols from $\mathcal{D}_1 \cup \mathcal{D}_2^1$. The same is true for $u_1, \ldots, u_n$ because $\mathcal{R}_2$ is a restricted proper extension of $\mathcal{R}_1$. All in all, none of the (proper) subterms of the dependency pairs in $\mathcal{P}$ contains a symbol from $\mathcal{D}_1 \cup \mathcal{D}_2^1$.

Because $\mathcal{R}_2^2$ does not contain function symbols from $\mathcal{D}_1 \cup \mathcal{D}_2^1$, the TRS $\mathcal{R}_1 \cup \mathcal{R}_2^1 \cup \mathcal{C}_\mathcal{E}$ can be viewed as an extension of $\mathcal{R}_2^2$. Because the infinite $\mathcal{R}_2^1$ chain is minimal, (i.e., u is terminating w.r.t. $\mathcal{R}_1 \cup \mathcal{R}_2 \cup \mathcal{C}_\mathcal{E}$ for every subterm u of some $s_j\sigma$ and $t_j\sigma$), we may apply Lemma 8.6.11 to every $t_j\sigma \rightarrow^*_{\mathcal{R}_2^2 \cup (\mathcal{R}_1 \cup \mathcal{R}_2^1 \cup \mathcal{C}_\mathcal{E})} s_{j+1}\sigma$. This yields $\Phi(t_j\sigma) \rightarrow^*_{\mathcal{R}_2^2 \uplus \mathcal{C}'_\mathcal{E}} \Phi(s_{j+1}\sigma)$, where $\mathcal{C}'_\mathcal{E} = \{Cons'(x,y) \to x, Cons'(x,y) \to y\}$ because we have to use a fresh symbol $Cons'$ instead of the already used symbol $Cons$. In other words, the cycle $\mathcal{P}$ admits an infinite $\mathcal{R}_2^1$ chain over $\mathcal{R}_2^2 \uplus \mathcal{C}'_\mathcal{E}$. This contradicts $\mathcal{C}_\mathcal{E}$-termination of $\mathcal{R}_2$. □

With the aid of Theorem 8.6.18 we are able to infer $\mathcal{C}_\mathcal{E}$-termination of the hierarchical combination of the two $\mathcal{C}_\mathcal{E}$-terminating TRSs from Example 8.6.3. Because $\mathcal{R}_2$ is a restricted proper extension of $\mathcal{R}_1$, it follows from Theorem 8.6.18 that $\mathcal{R}_1 \cup \mathcal{R}_2$ is $\mathcal{C}_\mathcal{E}$-terminating. We stress that in this example none of the known modularity results is applicable. On the other hand, Theorem 8.6.18 cannot be used to infer $\mathcal{C}_\mathcal{E}$-termination of the hierarchical combination of the two TRSs from Example 8.6.17. This is because there $\mathcal{R}_2$ is a not proper extension of $\mathcal{R}_1$.

Example 8.6.15 demonstrates why a symbol from $\mathcal{D}_1 \cup \mathcal{D}_2^1$ may not occur below a $\mathcal{D}_2^1$ symbol on the right-hand side of a rewrite rule from $\mathcal{R}_2$. The requirement that function symbols from $\mathcal{D}_1 \cup \mathcal{D}_2^1$ may not occur at nonroot positions on the left-hand sides of rewrite rules from $\mathcal{R}_2$ is also necessary. This is shown by the following example.

Example 8.6.19 The term rewriting system $\mathcal{R}_1 = \{g(x,y) \to x\}$ is obviously $\mathcal{C}_\mathcal{E}$-terminating. We show that the same is true for the TRS

$$\mathcal{R}_2 = \left\{ \begin{array}{rcl} f(0,1,x) & \to & f(h(x),h(x),x) \\ h(0) & \to & 0 \\ h(g(x,y)) & \to & y \end{array} \right.$$

or equivalently that $\mathcal{R}_2 \uplus \mathcal{C}_\mathcal{E}$ is terminating. There is only one cycle in $\mathrm{EDG}(\mathcal{R}_2 \uplus \mathcal{C}_\mathcal{E})$, viz. $\{\langle F(0,1,x), F(h(x),h(x),x)\rangle\}$. After normalization with the AFS $\{f(x,y,z) \to f', h(x) \to x, g(x,y) \to y\}$ the resulting constraints are

$$\begin{array}{rcl} Cons(x,y) & \geq & x \\ Cons(x,y) & \geq & y \\ f' & \geq & f' \\ 0 & \geq & 0 \\ y & \geq & y \\ F(0,1,x) & > & F(x,x,x) \end{array}$$

We extend the algebra from Example 5.4.35 by $Cons_{\mathcal{A}}(a_1, a_2) = \lozenge$ for all $a_1, a_2 \in A$ and observe that $\succ_{\mathcal{A}}$ satisfies the constraints. Hence $\mathcal{R}_2 \uplus \mathcal{C}_{\mathcal{E}}$ is terminating by Corollary 5.4.34. But the hierarchical combination of $\mathcal{R}_1$ and $\mathcal{R}_2$ is not terminating:

$$\begin{aligned} f(0,1,g(0,1)) &\rightarrow_{\mathcal{R}_2} f(h(g(0,1)), h(g(0,1)), g(0,1)) \\ &\rightarrow_{\mathcal{R}_1} f(h(0), h(g(0,1)), g(0,1)) \\ &\rightarrow^{+}_{\mathcal{R}_2} f(0,1,g(0,1)) \end{aligned}$$

Furthermore, the next example illustrates that Theorem 8.6.18 does not remain valid if one considers finitely branching systems instead of finite systems.

Example 8.6.20 The system $\mathcal{R}_1 = \{a \rightarrow b\}$ is obviously finite and simply terminating. The TRS $\mathcal{R}_2 = \{h_j(x, x) \rightarrow h_{j+1}(a, b) \mid j \in \mathbb{N}\}$ is finitely branching and terminating, hence simply terminating because it is nonsize-increasing; see Lemma 5.2.34. According to Proposition 8.3.2. both systems are $\mathcal{C}_{\mathcal{E}}$-terminating. $\mathcal{R}_2$ is a restricted proper extension of $\mathcal{R}_1$ because $h_{j+1} \not\trianglerighteq_d h_j$ (so $a \in \mathcal{D}_1$ is allowed below $h_{j+1} \in \mathcal{D}_2^1$). However, the hierarchical combination of $\mathcal{R}_1$ and $\mathcal{R}_2$ is not terminating:

$$h_1(a,b) \rightarrow_{\mathcal{R}_1} h_1(b,b) \rightarrow_{\mathcal{R}_2} h_2(a,b) \rightarrow_{\mathcal{R}_1} h_2(b,b) \rightarrow_{\mathcal{R}_2} h_3(a,b) \rightarrow_{\mathcal{R}_1} \cdots$$

Theorem 8.6.18 can be generalized to restricted proper extensions with a common subsystem. Although the proof of Theorem 8.6.21 is very similar to that of Theorem 8.6.18, the technical details are quite involved. That is why we prefer to have two separate proofs.

Theorem 8.6.21 *Let $\mathcal{R}_1$ and $\mathcal{R}_2$ be finite $\mathcal{C}_{\mathcal{E}}$-terminating TRSs. If $\mathcal{R}_2$ is a restricted proper extension of $\mathcal{R}_1$ with a common subsystem $\mathcal{R}_0$, then $\mathcal{R}_1 \cup \mathcal{R}_2$ is $\mathcal{C}_{\mathcal{E}}$-terminating.*

Proof Let $\mathcal{R}'_1 = \{l \rightarrow r \in \mathcal{R}_1 \mid root(l) \in \mathcal{D}'_1\}$, $\mathcal{R}'^1_2 = \{l \rightarrow r \in \mathcal{R}_2 \mid root(l) \in \mathcal{D}'^1_2\}$, and $\mathcal{R}'^2_2 = \{l \rightarrow r \in \mathcal{R}_2 \mid root(l) \in \mathcal{D}'^2_2\}$. (The sets $\mathcal{D}'_1$, $\mathcal{D}'^1_2$, and $\mathcal{D}'^2_2$ are defined in Definition 8.6.4.) Thus, $\mathcal{R}_1 = \mathcal{R}_0 \cup \mathcal{R}'_1$ and $\mathcal{R}_2 = \mathcal{R}_0 \cup \mathcal{R}'^1_2 \cup \mathcal{R}'^2_2$. The TRS $\mathcal{R}'^2_2$ does not contain function symbols from $\mathcal{D}'_1 \cup \mathcal{D}'^1_2$. This is because for all $l \rightarrow r \in \mathcal{R}'^2_2$ neither l nor r contains function symbols from $\mathcal{D}'_1 \cup \mathcal{D}'^1_2$; cf. the proof of Theorem 8.6.18. In other words, $\mathcal{R}_1$ and $\mathcal{R}_0 \cup \mathcal{R}'^2_2$ are composable. Because both are $\mathcal{C}_{\mathcal{E}}$-terminating, so is their union $\mathcal{R}_1 \cup \mathcal{R}'^2_2$ by Proposition 8.6.13. In order to show $\mathcal{C}_{\mathcal{E}}$-termination of $\mathcal{R}_1 \cup \mathcal{R}_2 = (\mathcal{R}_1 \cup \mathcal{R}'^2_2) \cup \mathcal{R}'^1_2$, it suffices to show that there is no minimal infinite $\mathcal{R}'^1_2$ chain over $(\mathcal{R}_1 \cup \mathcal{R}_2) \uplus \mathcal{C}_{\mathcal{E}}$; see Corollary 8.6.16. Suppose, on the contrary, that there is a minimal infinite $\mathcal{R}'^1_2$ chain $\langle s_1, t_1\rangle\langle s_2, t_2\rangle \ldots$ over $(\mathcal{R}_1 \cup \mathcal{R}_2) \uplus \mathcal{C}_{\mathcal{E}}$, i.e., there exists a substitution $\sigma : \mathcal{V} \rightarrow \mathcal{T}(\mathcal{F} \uplus \{Cons\})$ such that $t_j\sigma \rightarrow^*_{(\mathcal{R}_1 \cup \mathcal{R}_2) \uplus \mathcal{C}_{\mathcal{E}}} s_{j+1}\sigma$ holds for all consecutive pairs $\langle s_j, t_j\rangle$ and $\langle s_{j+1}, t_{j+1}\rangle$ in the sequence. Because we consider finite TRSs, we may assume that every dependency pair in $\langle s_1, t_1\rangle\langle s_2, t_2\rangle\ldots$ belongs to a cycle $\mathcal{P}$ that consists solely of dependency pairs from $\mathcal{R'}^1_2$. As in the proof of Theorem 8.6.18, one can show that every (proper) subterm of a dependency pair in $\mathcal{P}$ does not contain a symbol from $\mathcal{D}'_1 \cup \mathcal{D'}^1_2$.

Because neither $\mathcal{R}_0$ nor $\mathcal{R'}^2_2$ contains function symbols from $\mathcal{D}'_1 \cup \mathcal{D'}^1_2$ (if $\mathcal{R}_0$ would contain a function symbol $f \in \mathcal{D}'_1$, then the rewrite rules defining f would be in $\mathcal{R}_0$, i.e., $f \in \mathcal{D}_0$), the TRS $\mathcal{R}'_1 \cup \mathcal{R'}^1_2 \cup \mathcal{C}_\mathcal{E}$ can be viewed as an extension of $\mathcal{R}_0 \cup \mathcal{R'}^2_2$. Because the infinite $\mathcal{R'}^1_2$ chain is minimal, we may apply Lemma 8.6.11 to every $t_j\sigma \rightarrow^*_{(\mathcal{R}_0 \cup \mathcal{R'}^2_2)\cup(\mathcal{R}'_1 \cup \mathcal{R'}^1_2 \cup \mathcal{C}_\mathcal{E})} s_{j+1}\sigma$. This yields $\Phi(t_j\sigma) \rightarrow^*_{(\mathcal{R}_0 \cup \mathcal{R'}^2_2)\uplus \mathcal{C}'_\mathcal{E}} \Phi(s_{j+1}\sigma)$, where $\mathcal{C}'_\mathcal{E}$ denotes the system $\{Cons'(x,y) \rightarrow x, Cons'(x,y) \rightarrow y\}$. In other words, the cycle $\mathcal{P}$ admits an infinite $\mathcal{R'}^1_2$ chain over $(\mathcal{R}_0 \cup \mathcal{R'}^2_2) \uplus \mathcal{C}'_\mathcal{E}$. Because this is an infinite $\mathcal{R}_2$ chain over $\mathcal{R}_2 \uplus \mathcal{C}'_\mathcal{E}$, we derive a contradiction to the $\mathcal{C}_\mathcal{E}$-termination of $\mathcal{R}_2$. □

By means of Theorem 8.6.21, one can, for example, infer $\mathcal{C}_\mathcal{E}$-termination of the hierarchical combination of the two TRSs from Example 8.6.5.

It follows, as in Theorem 8.4.15, that termination is modular for the following classes of hierarchical combinations.

Corollary 8.6.22

1. *Termination is modular for finite nonduplicating restricted proper extensions (with a common subsystem).*
2. *Termination is a modular property of finite restricted proper extensions (with a common subsystem) that are inconsistent w.r.t. reduction.*

Proof Clearly, the union of two nonduplicating TRSs is again nonduplicating. Furthermore, the combination of a TRS that is inconsistent w.r.t. reduction with an arbitrary TRS yields a TRS that is inconsistent w.r.t. reduction. Hence the assertions follow from Theorem 8.6.18 (Theorem 8.6.21, respectively) in conjunction with Proposition 8.3.1. □

In contrast to disjoint unions (Theorem 8.4.15), the modularity of simple termination for restricted proper extensions (with a common subsystem) does not directly follow from Theorem 8.6.18 (Theorem 8.6.21, respectively). This is because the fact that $\mathcal{R}_2$ is a proper extension of $\mathcal{R}_1$ does not imply that $\mathcal{R}_2 \cup \mathcal{E}mb(\mathcal{F}_2)$ is a proper extension of $\mathcal{R}_1 \cup \mathcal{E}mb(\mathcal{F}_1)$. Nevertheless, it will be shown that simple termination is indeed modular for restricted proper extensions (with a common subsystem).

Moreover, we immediately derive the following interesting consequences.

Corollary 8.6.23 *Let $\mathcal{R}_2$ be a restricted proper extension of $\mathcal{R}_1$ (with a common subsystem). Their hierarchical combination $\mathcal{R}_1 \cup \mathcal{R}_2$ is $\mathcal{C}_\mathcal{E}$-terminating provided that $\mathcal{R}_j$, $j \in \{1,2\}$, is finite and*

- *$\mathcal{C}_\mathcal{E}$-terminating, or*
- *DP quasi-simply terminating, or*
- *DP simply terminating, or*
- *simply terminating, or*
- *terminating and nonduplicating, or*
- *terminating and inconsistent w.r.t. reduction.*

Proof This is a consequence of Theorem 8.6.18 (Theorem 8.6.21, respectively) in combination with the fact that each of the properties implies $\mathcal{C}_\mathcal{E}$-termination; see Section 8.3. □

Simple Termination

Next we will review known results about the modularity of simple termination. We start with a lemma due to Gramlich [Gra96b].

Lemma 8.6.24 *Simple termination is a modular property of finitely branching composable TRSs.*

Proof Let $(\mathcal{F}_1, \mathcal{R}_1)$ and $(\mathcal{F}_2, \mathcal{R}_2)$ be simply terminating composable TRSs. We have to show that $(\mathcal{F}, \mathcal{R}) = (\mathcal{F}_1 \cup \mathcal{F}_2, \mathcal{R}_1 \cup \mathcal{R}_2)$ is simply terminating as well. Simple termination implies that $\mathcal{R}_1 \cup \mathcal{E}mb(\mathcal{F}_1)$ and $\mathcal{R}_2 \cup \mathcal{E}mb(\mathcal{F}_2)$ are $\mathcal{C}_\mathcal{E}$-terminating; see Proposition 8.3.2. Moreover, it is fairly easy to see that these systems are also composable. Thus, an application of Proposition 8.6.13 yields $\mathcal{C}_\mathcal{E}$-termination of $\mathcal{R} \cup \mathcal{E}mb(\mathcal{F})$. In other words, $\mathcal{R}$ is simply terminating. □

The next theorem constitutes the main result from [KR94]. As already mentioned, it cannot be obtained as a corollary to Theorem 8.6.18 because $\mathcal{R}_2$ being a proper extension of $\mathcal{R}_1$ does not imply that $\mathcal{R}_2 \cup \mathcal{E}mb(\mathcal{F}_2)$ is a proper extension of $\mathcal{R}_1 \cup \mathcal{E}mb(\mathcal{F}_1)$.

Theorem 8.6.25 *Let $(\mathcal{F}_1, \mathcal{R}_1)$ and $(\mathcal{F}_2, \mathcal{R}_2)$ be finite simply terminating TRSs. If $\mathcal{R}_2$ is a restricted proper extension of $\mathcal{R}_1$, then their hierarchical combination $(\mathcal{F}, \mathcal{R}) = (\mathcal{F}_1 \cup \mathcal{F}_2, \mathcal{R}_1 \cup \mathcal{R}_2)$ is simply terminating.*

Proof Let $\mathcal{R}_2^1 = \{l \to r \mid root(l) \in \mathcal{D}_2^1\}$ and $\mathcal{R}_2^2 = \{l \to r \mid root(l) \in \mathcal{D}_2^2\}$. Furthermore, let $\mathcal{F}_2^2 = \{f \mid f \text{ occurs in } \mathcal{R}_2^2\}$. The TRS $\mathcal{R}_2^2$ does not contain function symbols from $\mathcal{D}_1 \cup \mathcal{D}_2^1$; cf. the proof of Theorem 8.6.18. In other words, $\mathcal{R}_1$ and $\mathcal{R}_2^2$ are constructor-sharing. Because both are simply terminating, so is their union, according to Lemma 8.6.24. In order to show termination of $\mathcal{R} \cup \mathcal{E}mb(\mathcal{F})$, it is sufficient to show that there is no minimal infinite $\mathcal{R}_2^1$ chain over $\mathcal{R} \cup \mathcal{E}mb(\mathcal{F})$; see Theorem 8.6.14. Suppose, on the contrary, that there is a minimal infinite $\mathcal{R}_2^1$ chain $\langle s_1, t_1 \rangle \langle s_2, t_2 \rangle \ldots$ over $\mathcal{R} \cup \mathcal{E}mb(\mathcal{F})$, i.e., there exists a substitution $\sigma : \mathcal{V} \to \mathcal{T}(\mathcal{F})$ such that $t_j\sigma \to^*_{\mathcal{R}\cup\mathcal{E}mb(\mathcal{F})} s_{j+1}\sigma$ holds for all consecutive pairs $\langle s_j, t_j \rangle$ and $\langle s_{j+1}, t_{j+1} \rangle$ in the sequence. Because we consider finite TRSs, we may assume that every dependency pair in $\langle s_1, t_1 \rangle \langle s_2, t_2 \rangle \ldots$ belongs to a cycle $\mathcal{P}$ that consists solely of dependency pairs from $\mathcal{R}_2^1$. As in the proof of Theorem 8.6.18, one can show that none of the (proper) subterms of the dependency pairs in $\mathcal{P}$ contains a symbol from $\mathcal{D}_1 \cup \mathcal{D}_2^1$.

Let $\mathcal{F}' = (\mathcal{F}_1 \cup \mathcal{F}_2) \setminus \mathcal{F}_2^2$. Because $\mathcal{R}_2^2$ does not contain function symbols from $\mathcal{D}_1 \cup \mathcal{D}_2^1$, the TRS $\mathcal{R}_1 \cup \mathcal{R}_2^1 \cup \mathcal{E}mb(\mathcal{F}')$ can be viewed as an extension of $\mathcal{R}_2^2 \cup \mathcal{E}mb(\mathcal{F}_2^2)$. Because the infinite $\mathcal{R}_2^1$ chain is minimal, we may apply Lemma 8.6.11 to every

$$t_j\sigma \to^*_{(\mathcal{R}_2^2\cup\mathcal{E}mb(\mathcal{F}_2^2))\cup(\mathcal{R}_1\cup\mathcal{R}_2^1\cup\mathcal{E}mb(\mathcal{F}'))} s_{j+1}\sigma$$

and obtain $\Phi(t_j\sigma) \to^*_{(\mathcal{R}_2^2\cup\mathcal{E}mb(\mathcal{F}_2^2))\uplus\mathcal{C}_\mathcal{E}} \Phi(s_{j+1}\sigma)$. In other words, the cycle $\mathcal{P}$ admits an infinite $\mathcal{R}_2^1$ chain over $(\mathcal{R}_2^2 \cup \mathcal{E}mb(\mathcal{F}_2^2)) \uplus \mathcal{C}_\mathcal{E}$. Therefore, $\mathcal{R}_2 \cup \mathcal{E}mb(\mathcal{F}_2)$ is not $\mathcal{C}_\mathcal{E}$-terminating. This, however, contradicts the simple termination of $\mathcal{R}_2$; see Proposition 8.3.2. □

Theorem 8.6.25 is applicable to the hierarchical combination of $\mathcal{R}_+$ and $\mathcal{R}_*$ but to neither Example 8.6.3 (because the systems are not simply terminating) or Example 8.6.17 (because $\mathcal{R}_2$ is not a proper extension of $\mathcal{R}_1$). Krishna Rao conjectured in [KR94] that Theorem 8.6.25 can be extended to finitely branching TRSs, but Example 8.6.20 disproves his conjecture. Moreover, no example is known that shows the necessity of the condition that no left-hand side of a rewrite rule from $\mathcal{R}_2$ may contain function symbols from $\mathcal{D}_1 \cup \mathcal{D}_2^1$ strictly below its root. It should be pointed out that Example 8.6.19 shows the necessity of this condition for $\mathcal{C}_\mathcal{E}$-termination but not for simple termination (because there $\mathcal{R}_2$ is not simply terminating). Therefore, it is still an open question whether Theorem 8.6.25 is also valid for arbitrary proper extensions.

Next, we extend Theorem 8.6.25 to restricted proper extensions with a common subsystem.

Theorem 8.6.26 *Let $(\mathcal{F}_1, \mathcal{R}_1)$ and $(\mathcal{F}_2, \mathcal{R}_2)$ be finite simply terminating TRSs. If $(\mathcal{F}_2, \mathcal{R}_2)$ is a restricted proper extension of $(\mathcal{F}_1, \mathcal{R}_1)$ with a common subsystem $(\mathcal{F}_0, \mathcal{R}_0)$, then $(\mathcal{F}, \mathcal{R}) = (\mathcal{F}_1 \cup \mathcal{F}_2, \mathcal{R}_1 \cup \mathcal{R}_2)$ is also simply terminating.*

Proof Let $\mathcal{R}_1' = \{l \to r \in \mathcal{R}_1 \mid root(l) \in \mathcal{D}_1'\}$, $\mathcal{R'}_2^1 = \{l \to r \in \mathcal{R}_2 \mid root(l) \in \mathcal{D'}_2^1\}$, and $\mathcal{R'}_2^2 = \{l \to r \in \mathcal{R}_2 \mid root(l) \in \mathcal{D'}_2^2\}$. Thus, $\mathcal{R}_1 = \mathcal{R}_0 \cup \mathcal{R}_1'$ and $\mathcal{R}_2 = \mathcal{R}_0 \cup \mathcal{R'}_2^1 \cup \mathcal{R'}_2^2$. Furthermore, let $\mathcal{F'}_2^2 = \{f \mid f \text{ occurs in } \mathcal{R'}_2^2\}$. The TRS $\mathcal{R'}_2^2$ does not contain function symbols from $\mathcal{D}_1' \cup \mathcal{D'}_2^1$, hence $\mathcal{R}_1$ and

$\mathcal{R}_0 \cup \mathcal{R}'^2_2$ are composable. Because both are simply terminating, so is their union $\mathcal{R}_1 \cup \mathcal{R}'^2_2$ by Lemma 8.6.24.

To show simple termination of $\mathcal{R} = (\mathcal{R}_1 \cup \mathcal{R}'^2_2) \cup \mathcal{R}'^1_2$, it suffices to show that there is no minimal infinite $\mathcal{R}'^1_2$ chain over $\mathcal{R} \cup \mathcal{E}mb(\mathcal{F})$; see Theorem 8.6.14. Suppose, on the contrary, that there is a minimal infinite $\mathcal{R}'^1_2$ chain $\langle s_1, t_1\rangle\langle s_2, t_2\rangle \dots$ over $\mathcal{R}\cup\mathcal{E}mb(\mathcal{F})$, i.e., there exists a substitution $\sigma : \mathcal{V} \to \mathcal{T}(\mathcal{F})$ such that $t_j\sigma \to^*_{\mathcal{R}\cup\mathcal{E}mb(\mathcal{F})} s_{j+1}\sigma$ holds for all consecutive pairs $\langle s_j, t_j\rangle$ and $\langle s_{j+1}, t_{j+1}\rangle$ in the sequence. Because we consider finite TRSs, we may assume that every dependency pair in $\langle s_1, t_1\rangle\langle s_2, t_2\rangle \dots$ belongs to a cycle $\mathcal{P}$ that consists solely of dependency pairs from $\mathcal{R}'^1_2$. As in the proof of Theorem 8.6.18, one can show that none of the (proper) subterms of the dependency pairs in $\mathcal{P}$ contains a symbol from $\mathcal{D}'_1\cup\mathcal{D}'^1_2$. Let $\mathcal{F}' = \mathcal{F}\setminus(\mathcal{F}_0\cup\mathcal{F}'^2_2)$. Because neither $\mathcal{R}_0$ nor $\mathcal{R}'^2_2$ contains function symbols from $\mathcal{D}'_1\cup\mathcal{D}'^1_2$, the TRS $\mathcal{R}'_1\cup\mathcal{R}'^1_2\cup\mathcal{E}mb(\mathcal{F}')$ can be viewed as an extension of $\mathcal{R}_0\cup\mathcal{R}'^2_2\cup\mathcal{E}mb(\mathcal{F}_0\cup\mathcal{F}'^2_2)$. Because the infinite $\mathcal{R}'^1_2$ chain is minimal, we may apply Lemma 8.6.11 to every $t_j\sigma \to^*_{(\mathcal{R}_0\cup\mathcal{R}'^2_2\cup\mathcal{E}mb(\mathcal{F}_0\cup\mathcal{F}'^2_2))\cup(\mathcal{R}'_1\cup\mathcal{R}'^1_2\cup\mathcal{E}mb(\mathcal{F}'))}$ $s_{j+1}\sigma$ and obtain $\Phi(t_j\sigma) \to^*_{(\mathcal{R}_0\cup\mathcal{R}'^2_2\cup\mathcal{E}mb(\mathcal{F}_0\cup\mathcal{F}'^2_2))\uplus\mathcal{C}_\mathcal{E}} \Phi(s_{j+1}\sigma)$. In other words, the cycle $\mathcal{P}$ admits an infinite $\mathcal{R}'^1_2$ chain over $(\mathcal{R}_0 \cup \mathcal{R}'^2_2 \cup \mathcal{E}mb(\mathcal{F}_0 \cup \mathcal{F}'^2_2)) \uplus \mathcal{C}_\mathcal{E}$. Because this is an infinite $\mathcal{R}_2$ chain over $(\mathcal{R}_2 \cup \mathcal{E}mb(\mathcal{F}_2)) \uplus \mathcal{C}_\mathcal{E}$, the system $\mathcal{R}_2 \cup \mathcal{E}mb(\mathcal{F}_2)$ is not $\mathcal{C}_\mathcal{E}$-terminating. This, however, contradicts the simple termination of $\mathcal{R}_2$ according to Proposition 8.3.2. □

8.6.2 Innermost Termination

In this section we will review the main results from [GAO02]. We start with a lemma akin to Lemma 8.6.12.

Lemma 8.6.27 *Let $\mathcal{R}$ be the hierarchical combination of $\mathcal{R}_1$ and $\mathcal{R}_2$. If there is an infinite innermost $\mathcal{R}_1$ chain over $\mathcal{R}$, then there is also an infinite innermost $\mathcal{R}_1$ chain over $\mathcal{R}_1$.*

Proof Let $\langle s, t\rangle$ be a dependency pair of $\mathcal{R}_1$ and let σ be a normalized substitution (normalized w.r.t. $\mathcal{R}$). The only rules that can be used to reduce $t\sigma$ or a reduct thereof are the rules from $\mathcal{R}_1$, i.e., $\mathcal{U}_\mathcal{R}(t\sigma) \subseteq \mathcal{R}_1$. Therefore, every infinite innermost $\mathcal{R}_1$ chain over $\mathcal{R}$ is in fact an infinite innermost $\mathcal{R}_1$ chain over $\mathcal{R}_1$. □

By means of the preceding lemma we immediately get the following result from [Ohl95a].

Proposition 8.6.28 *Innermost termination is a modular property of composable TRSs.*

Proof Let $\mathcal{R}_1$ and $\mathcal{R}_2$ be innermost terminating composable TRSs. Define

$$\begin{array}{rcl}\mathcal{R}_0 & = & \mathcal{R}_1 \cap \mathcal{R}_2 \\ \mathcal{R}_1' & = & \mathcal{R}_1 \setminus \mathcal{R}_0 \\ \mathcal{R}_2' & = & \mathcal{R}_2 \setminus \mathcal{R}_0\end{array}$$

Note that $\mathcal{R}_1 \cup \mathcal{R}_2 = \mathcal{R}_1 \cup \mathcal{R}_2' = \mathcal{R}_1' \cup \mathcal{R}_2$. For a proof by contradiction, suppose that $\mathcal{R}_1 \cup \mathcal{R}_2$ is not innermost terminating. According to Theorem 5.6.12, there is an infinite innermost $\mathcal{R}_1 \cup \mathcal{R}_2$ chain (over $\mathcal{R}_1 \cup \mathcal{R}_2$). If there were an infinite innermost $\mathcal{R}_1$ chain over $\mathcal{R}_1 \cup \mathcal{R}_2'$, then there would be an infinite innermost $\mathcal{R}_1$ chain over $\mathcal{R}_1$ by Lemma 8.6.27. This, however, contradicts innermost termination of $\mathcal{R}_1$. Analogously, there cannot be an infinite innermost $\mathcal{R}_2$ chain over $\mathcal{R}_1' \cup \mathcal{R}_2$. It follows that the infinite innermost $\mathcal{R}_1 \cup \mathcal{R}_2$ chain must contain dependency pairs from both $\mathcal{R}_1'$ and $\mathcal{R}_2'$. It is not difficult to verify that this is impossible. □

The next result is the "innermost analogue" of Theorem 8.6.14. In contrast to the theorem, it is not restricted to finitely branching systems.

Theorem 8.6.29 *Let $\mathcal{R}$ be the hierarchical combination of $\mathcal{R}_1$ and $\mathcal{R}_2$.*

1. *$\mathcal{R}$ is innermost terminating if base system $\mathcal{R}_1$ is innermost terminating and there is no infinite innermost $\mathcal{R}_2$ chain over $\mathcal{R}$.*

2. *$\mathcal{R}$ is innermost terminating if $\mathcal{R}_1$ is innermost terminating and there exists a quasi-reduction ordering $\succsim$ such that for all dependency pairs $\langle s, t\rangle$ of $\mathcal{R}_2$*

   - *$l \succsim r$ for all rules $l \to r$ in $\mathcal{U}_{\mathcal{R}}(t)$ and*
   - *$s \succ t$.*

Proof (1) For a proof by contradiction, suppose that $\mathcal{R}$ is not innermost terminating. According to Theorem 5.6.12, there is an infinite innermost $\mathcal{R}$ chain (over $\mathcal{R}$). By assumption, there is no infinite innermost $\mathcal{R}_2$ chain over $\mathcal{R}$. Therefore, the infinite innermost $\mathcal{R}$ chain must contain a dependency pair from $\mathcal{R}_1$, say, $\langle s_j, t_j\rangle$. Because the rewrite rules from $\mathcal{R}_1$ do not contain symbols from $\mathcal{D}_2$, every dependency pair $\langle s_i, t_i\rangle$ in the infinite innermost $\mathcal{R}$ chain with $i \geq j$ must also originate from a rewrite rule of $\mathcal{R}_1$. So there is an infinite innermost $\mathcal{R}_1$ chain over $\mathcal{R}$. According to Lemma 8.6.27, there is also an infinite innermost $\mathcal{R}_1$ chain over $\mathcal{R}_1$. This, however, contradicts the innermost termination of $\mathcal{R}_1$.

(2) This is an immediate consequence of (1). □

For finite TRSs, Theorem 8.6.29 can, of course, be reformulated such that it captures cycles. Innermost termination of the hierarchical combination of the TRSs in Example 8.6.17 can be proven with the help of Theorem 8.6.29.

Moreover, as the system is nonoverlapping, this also proves its termination; see Theorem 5.6.10.

The following corollary to Theorem 5.6.17 shows how a finite TRS can be split into subsystems such that innermost termination of the subsystems implies innermost termination of the whole system. In what follows, $\mathcal{O}(\mathcal{P})$ denotes the *origin* of the dependency pairs in $\mathcal{P}$. That is, all dependency pairs of $\mathcal{P}$ must originate from the set of rewrite rules $\mathcal{O}(\mathcal{P})$. (If a dependency pair of $\mathcal{P}$ stems from *several* rules, then it suffices that $\mathcal{O}(\mathcal{P})$ contains just one of them.) For example, for the TRS of the example in Section 5.6.2 we have $\mathcal{O}(\{(5.18)\}) = \{f(x, c(x), c(y)) \to f(y, y, f(y, x, y))\}$ and $\mathcal{O}(\{(5.19)\}) = \{f(s(x), y, z) \to f(x, s(c(y)), c(z))\}$.

Corollary 8.6.30 *Let $\mathcal{R}$ be a finite TRS, let $\mathcal{P}_1, \ldots, \mathcal{P}_n$ be the cycles in its (estimated) innermost dependency graph, and let $\mathcal{R}_j$ be subsystems of $\mathcal{R}$ such that $\mathcal{U}_\mathcal{R}(\mathcal{P}_j) \cup \mathcal{O}(\mathcal{P}_j) \subseteq \mathcal{R}_j$ for every $j \in \{1, \ldots, n\}$. If $\mathcal{R}_1, \ldots, \mathcal{R}_n$ are innermost terminating, then $\mathcal{R}$ is also innermost terminating.*

Proof Every dependency pair from $\mathcal{P}_j$ is an $\mathcal{R}_j$ dependency pair because $\mathcal{P}_j$ is a cycle. To see this, let $\langle F(\vec{s}), G(\vec{t})\rangle$ be an $\mathcal{R}$ dependency pair in $\mathcal{P}_j$. Clearly, g is a defined symbol of $\mathcal{R}_j$ because there is also a dependency pair $\langle G(\vec{u}), H(\vec{v})\rangle$ in $\mathcal{P}_j$. Hence, because g is a defined symbol of $\mathcal{R}_j$, $\langle F(\vec{s}), G(\vec{t})\rangle$ is also an $\mathcal{R}_j$ dependency pair. Thus, every innermost $\mathcal{R}$ chain over $\mathcal{R}$ of dependency pairs from $\mathcal{P}_j$ is also an innermost $\mathcal{R}_j$ chain over $\mathcal{R}$. In fact, it is an innermost $\mathcal{R}_j$ chain over $\mathcal{R}_j$ because $\mathcal{U}_\mathcal{R}(\mathcal{P}_j) \cup \mathcal{O}(\mathcal{P}_j) \subseteq \mathcal{R}_j$. Thus, the corollary is a direct consequence of Theorem 5.6.17. □

For example, in the example in Section 5.6.2 we only have two cycles, viz. $\{(5.18)\}$ and $\{(5.19)\}$. As these dependency pairs have no defined symbols on their right-hand sides, their sets of usable rules are empty. Hence, to prove innermost termination of the whole system it suffices to prove innermost termination of the two one-rule subsystems $f(x, c(x), c(y)) \to f(y, y, f(y, x, y))$ and $f(s(x), y, z) \to f(x, s(c(y)), c(z))$; cf. Corollary 8.6.30. In fact, both subsystems are even terminating, as can easily be proven. For the first system one can use a polynomial interpretation mapping $f(x, y, z)$ to $x + y + z$ and $c(x)$ to $5x + 1$. For the second system one can use the *lpo* with the precedence $f \succ_p s$ and $f \succ_p c$. In this manner, one may use well-known reduction orderings for innermost termination proofs of non-terminating systems.

Note that the reverse direction of the corollary does not hold. Consider the TRS from Example 5.6.19. The only cycle of its innermost dependency graph is $\{\langle F(a(x), y), G(x, y)\rangle, \langle G(x, y), H(x, y)\rangle, \langle H(0, y), F(y, y)\rangle\}$. Because this cycle does not have any usable rules, Corollary 8.6.30 states that innermost termination of the subsystem consisting of the first three rules is sufficient for innermost termination of the whole TRS. However, the converse does not hold: The whole system is innermost terminating but the subsystem consisting of the first three rules is not; the term $f(a(0), a(0))$ starts an infinite innermost reduction. Conditions under which the subsystems of an innermost terminating TRS are also innermost terminating can be found in [KR00].

Krishna Rao [KR95a] also proved that innermost termination is modular for proper extensions provided that the strict part of the dependency relation $\trianglerighteq_d$ is well-founded. Example 8.6.20 shows that the latter condition cannot be dropped. Next, we will show that for finite TRSs Krishna Rao's result is a direct consequence of Corollary 8.6.30.

Theorem 8.6.31 *Let $\mathcal{R}_1$ and $\mathcal{R}_2$ be finite innermost terminating TRSs. If $\mathcal{R}_2$ is a proper extension of $\mathcal{R}_1$, then their hierarchical combination $\mathcal{R}_1 \cup \mathcal{R}_2$ is also innermost terminating.*

Proof As in the proof of Corollary 8.6.30, because $\mathcal{R}_1$ and $\mathcal{R}_2$ form a hierarchical combination, every cycle in the innermost dependency graph of $\mathcal{R}$ consists solely of $\mathcal{R}_1$ dependency pairs or $\mathcal{R}_2$ dependency pairs. If a cycle $\mathcal{P}$ consists solely of dependency pairs of $\mathcal{R}_1$, then we have $\mathcal{U}_\mathcal{R}(\mathcal{P}) \cup \mathcal{O}(\mathcal{P}) \subseteq \mathcal{R}_1$ because dependency pairs of $\mathcal{R}_1$ do not contain defined symbols of $\mathcal{R}_2$. Otherwise, the cycle $\mathcal{P}$ consists of $\mathcal{R}_2$ dependency pairs. If $\langle F(\vec{s}), G(\vec{t})\rangle$ is an $\mathcal{R}_2$ dependency pair in $\mathcal{P}$, then there is a rewrite rule $f(\vec{s}) \to C[g(\vec{t})]$ in $\mathcal{R}_2$ and $f, g \in \mathcal{D}_2$. In addition, we have $f \trianglerighteq_d g$ and $g \trianglerighteq_d f$ (because $\mathcal{P}$ is a cycle). If $g \in \mathcal{D}_2^2$, then f also belongs to $\mathcal{D}_2^2$, hence no defined symbol of $\mathcal{D}_1 \cup \mathcal{D}_2^1$ occurs in $\vec{t}$. Otherwise, if $g \in \mathcal{D}_2^1$, then by the definition of proper extensions, again all defined symbols in $\vec{t}$ are from $\mathcal{D}_2^2$. Thus, in both cases, all defined symbols of $\mathcal{U}_\mathcal{R}(G(\vec{t}))$ belong to $\mathcal{D}_2^2$. Hence, $\mathcal{U}_\mathcal{R}(G(\vec{t}))$ is a subsystem of $\mathcal{R}_2$. So for any cycle $\mathcal{P}$ of $\mathcal{R}_2$ dependency pairs, we have $\mathcal{U}_\mathcal{R}(\mathcal{P}) \cup \mathcal{O}(\mathcal{P}) \subseteq \mathcal{R}_2$. Hence, by Corollary 8.6.30, innermost termination of $\mathcal{R}_1$ and $\mathcal{R}_2$ implies innermost termination of $\mathcal{R} = \mathcal{R}_1 \cup \mathcal{R}_2$. □

By means of Theorem 8.6.31 one may infer innermost termination of the hierarchical combination of the two TRSs $\mathcal{R}_1$ and $\mathcal{R}_2$ from Example 8.6.3. However, because $\mathcal{R}_2$ is not an overlay system, Theorem 5.6.8 cannot be used to conclude that $\mathcal{R}_1 \cup \mathcal{R}_2$ terminates.

Theorem 8.6.31 can also be extended to proper extensions with a common subsystem. For the convenience of the reader, a separate proof is provided, although it is very similar to that for proper extensions.

Theorem 8.6.32 *Let $\mathcal{R}_1$ and $\mathcal{R}_2$ be finite innermost terminating TRSs. If $\mathcal{R}_2$ is a proper extension of $\mathcal{R}_1$ with a common subsystem $\mathcal{R}_0$, then their hierarchical combination $\mathcal{R}_1 \cup \mathcal{R}_2$ is also innermost terminating.*

Proof First, we observe the following fact: If $\langle F(\vec{s}), G(\vec{t})\rangle$ is a dependency pair with $f \in \mathcal{D}_1$, then $g \in \mathcal{D}_1$ because the rewrite rule $f(\vec{s}) \to C[g(\vec{t})]$ occurs in $\mathcal{R}_1$ and $\mathcal{D}'_2$ symbols are not allowed in $\mathcal{R}_1$. Moreover, $\mathcal{U}_\mathcal{R}(G(\vec{t})) \subseteq \mathcal{R}_1$ because all rules for the defined symbols in $\vec{t}$ are (also) contained in

$\mathcal{R}_1$. So for any cycle $\mathcal{P}$ of $\mathcal{R}$ containing a dependency pair $\langle F(\dots), G(\dots)\rangle$ with $f \in \mathcal{D}_1$, we obtain $\mathcal{U}_\mathcal{R}(\mathcal{P}) \cup \mathcal{O}(\mathcal{P}) \subseteq \mathcal{R}_1$. For all other dependency pairs $\langle F(\vec{s}), G(\vec{t})\rangle$ on some cycle $\mathcal{P}$ we have $f \in \mathcal{D}'_2$. Hence, there is a rule $f(\vec{s}) \to C[g(\vec{t})]$ in $\mathcal{R}_2$. Note that $g \in \mathcal{D}'_2$ as well, otherwise the dependency pair $\langle F(\dots), G(\dots)\rangle$ would not be on a cycle. As in the proof of Theorem 8.6.31 we have $f \trianglerighteq_d g \trianglerighteq_d f$. If $g \in \mathcal{D'}^2_2$, then we also have $f \in \mathcal{D'}^2_2$ and thus no symbol of $\mathcal{D}'_1 \cup \mathcal{D'}^1_2$ occurs in $\vec{t}$. Otherwise, if $g \in \mathcal{D'}^1_2$, then by the definition of proper extensions with a common subsystem, $\vec{t}$ does not contain symbols from $\mathcal{D}'_1 \cup \mathcal{D'}^1_2$ either. That is, in both cases, all defined symbols in $\vec{t}$ are from $\mathcal{D'}^2_2$. Hence, we obtain $\mathcal{U}_\mathcal{R}(\mathcal{P}) \cup \mathcal{O}(\mathcal{P}) \subseteq \mathcal{R}_2$. Therefore, innermost termination of $\mathcal{R}_1$ and $\mathcal{R}_2$ implies innermost termination of $\mathcal{R}$ according to Corollary 8.6.30. □

For example, an application of Theorem 8.6.32 yields innermost termination of the hierarchical combination of the two TRSs from Example 8.6.5.

8.6.3 Confluence

In this section, we will investigate the modular behavior of local confluence, confluence, and strong confluence. Example 8.2.1 shows that we must impose additional restrictions, like left-linearity, to obtain modularity results for confluence that go beyond disjoint unions. To begin, we define two notions that are crucial in this context.

Definition 8.6.33 Let $\mathcal{R}_1$ and $\mathcal{R}_2$ be TRSs.

1. $\mathcal{R}_1$ and $\mathcal{R}_2$ are *orthogonal to each other*, denoted by $\mathcal{R}_1 \perp \mathcal{R}_2$, if there is no overlap between a rewrite rule from $\mathcal{R}_1$ and one of $\mathcal{R}_2$.
2. $\mathcal{R}_1$ and $\mathcal{R}_2$ are *noninterfering*, if $CP(\mathcal{R}_1 \cup \mathcal{R}_2) = CP(\mathcal{R}_1) \cup CP(\mathcal{R}_2)$.

Note that neither definition excludes the existence of critical pairs. If $\mathcal{R}_1 \perp \mathcal{R}_2$, then there may be critical pairs due to overlaps between rules of $\mathcal{R}_1$ or rules of $\mathcal{R}_2$, respectively. If $\mathcal{R}_1$ and $\mathcal{R}_2$ are noninterfering, then there may even be overlaps between rules from $\mathcal{R}_1$ and rules from $\mathcal{R}_2$; however, these overlaps can only create critical pairs already contained in the set $CP(\mathcal{R}_1) \cup CP(\mathcal{R}_2)$ of all critical pairs between rules from $\mathcal{R}_1$ and between rules from $\mathcal{R}_2$. So if $\mathcal{R}_1 \perp \mathcal{R}_2$, then the systems are noninterfering but not vice versa. This subtle difference will turn out to be important. The phrase "orthogonal to each other" stems from Klop [Klo92], and the phrase "noninterfering" originates from Middeldorp [Mid90]. We point out that the notion of "noninterference" as defined in Middeldorp [Mid90] coincides with our notion of "orthogonal to each other" (so we have redefined the former).

First we will show that confluence is modular for left-linear TRSs that are orthogonal to each other.

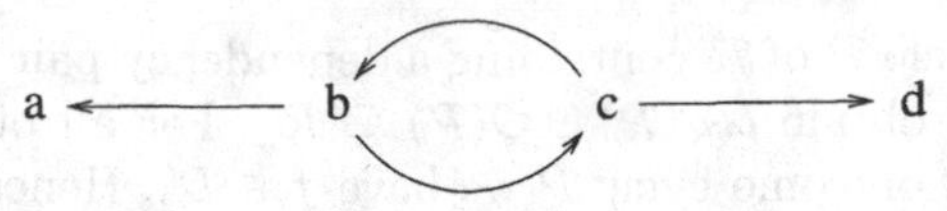

FIGURE 8.4. The combined system $\mathcal{R}_1 \cup \mathcal{R}_2$ of Example 8.6.36.

Lemma 8.6.34 *Let $\mathcal{R}_1$ and $\mathcal{R}_2$ be left-linear TRSs such that $\mathcal{R}_1 \perp \mathcal{R}_2$. If $s \mathrel{+\!\!\!+\!\!\!\!\!\rightarrow}_{\mathcal{R}_1} t_1$ and $s \mathrel{+\!\!\!+\!\!\!\!\!\rightarrow}_{\mathcal{R}_2} t_2$, then there is a term t_3 such that $t_1 \mathrel{+\!\!\!+\!\!\!\!\!\rightarrow}_{\mathcal{R}_2} t_3$ and $t_2 \mathrel{+\!\!\!+\!\!\!\!\!\rightarrow}_{\mathcal{R}_1} t_3$.*

Proof The proof is similar to that of Lemma 4.3.10; see also [BN98, theorem 9.3.11]. □

Theorem 8.6.35 *Let $\mathcal{R}_1$ and $\mathcal{R}_2$ be left-linear confluent TRSs. If $\mathcal{R}_1$ and $\mathcal{R}_2$ are orthogonal to each other, then $\mathcal{R}_1 \cup \mathcal{R}_2$ is confluent, too.*

Proof We have $\mathrel{+\!\!\!+\!\!\!\!\!\rightarrow}^*_{\mathcal{R}_1} = \rightarrow^*_{\mathcal{R}_1}$ and $\mathrel{+\!\!\!+\!\!\!\!\!\rightarrow}^*_{\mathcal{R}_2} = \rightarrow^*_{\mathcal{R}_2}$. So the relations $\mathrel{+\!\!\!+\!\!\!\!\!\rightarrow}_{\mathcal{R}_1}$ and $\mathrel{+\!\!\!+\!\!\!\!\!\rightarrow}_{\mathcal{R}_2}$ are confluent because $\mathcal{R}_1$ and $\mathcal{R}_2$ are confluent. According to Lemma 8.6.34, the relation $\mathrel{+\!\!\!+\!\!\!\!\!\rightarrow}_{\mathcal{R}_1}$ subcommutes with $\mathrel{+\!\!\!+\!\!\!\!\!\rightarrow}_{\mathcal{R}_2}$, hence it commutes with $\mathrel{+\!\!\!+\!\!\!\!\!\rightarrow}_{\mathcal{R}_2}$. It follows from Corollary 2.4.5 that the union $\mathrel{+\!\!\!+\!\!\!\!\!\rightarrow}_{\mathcal{R}_1} \cup \mathrel{+\!\!\!+\!\!\!\!\!\rightarrow}_{\mathcal{R}_2}$ is also confluent. Clearly, the reflexive transitive closure of the relation $\mathrel{+\!\!\!+\!\!\!\!\!\rightarrow}_{\mathcal{R}_1} \cup \mathrel{+\!\!\!+\!\!\!\!\!\rightarrow}_{\mathcal{R}_2}$ coincides with the relation $\rightarrow^*_{\mathcal{R}_1 \cup \mathcal{R}_2}$. Therefore, $\mathcal{R}_1 \cup \mathcal{R}_2$ is confluent. □

The TRS of Figure 8.4 can be used to show that Theorem 8.6.35 is not valid for noninterfering TRSs; see Example 8.6.36. The reader might recall that this system was used by Hindley [Hin74] to show that local confluence does not imply confluence.

Example 8.6.36 Let

$$\mathcal{R}_1 = \begin{cases} b & \rightarrow & a \\ b & \rightarrow & c \\ c & \rightarrow & b \end{cases}$$

and

$$\mathcal{R}_2 = \begin{cases} b & \rightarrow & c \\ c & \rightarrow & b \\ c & \rightarrow & d \end{cases}$$

Clearly, $\mathcal{R}_1$ and $\mathcal{R}_2$ are left-linear and confluent. Moreover, it is readily verified that the systems are noninterfering. However, their combined system $\mathcal{R}_1 \cup \mathcal{R}_2$ is obviously not confluent.

Proposition 8.6.37 *Let $\mathcal{R}$ be the hierarchical combination of base system $\mathcal{R}_1$ and extension $\mathcal{R}_2$. If no left-hand side of a rewrite rule from $\mathcal{R}_2$ contains a function symbol from $\mathcal{D}_1$, then $\mathcal{R}_1 \perp \mathcal{R}_2$.*

Proof Because $\mathcal{R}_1$ does not contain defined symbols from $\mathcal{R}_2$, a rewrite rule from $\mathcal{R}_2$ cannot overlap a rewrite rule from $\mathcal{R}_1$. If no left-hand side of a rewrite rule from $\mathcal{R}_2$ contains a function symbol from $\mathcal{D}_1$, then a rule from $\mathcal{R}_1$ cannot overlap a rule from $\mathcal{R}_2$ either. (In fact, it is sufficient to require that none of the nonvariable proper subterms of the left-hand sides of the rewrite rules from $\mathcal{R}_2$ be unifiable with a left-hand side of the rewrite rules from $\mathcal{R}_1$.) Hence $\mathcal{R}_1 \perp \mathcal{R}_2$. □

Corollary 8.6.38

1. *Confluence is modular for left-linear constructor-sharing TRSs.*
2. *Confluence is modular for left-linear restricted proper extensions.*

Proof If the TRSs $\mathcal{R}_1$ and $\mathcal{R}_2$ are constructor-sharing or if $\mathcal{R}_2$ is a restricted proper extension of $\mathcal{R}_1$, then $\mathcal{R}_1 \perp \mathcal{R}_2$ according to Proposition 8.6.37. Consequently, if both are left-linear and confluent, then so is their union by Theorem 8.6.35. □

Apparently, composable systems are not orthogonal to each other. It remains an open problem whether confluence is modular for left-linear composable TRSs.

The next proposition is in essence due to Middeldorp [Mid90]. It is the key to the modularity of local confluence for composable systems and for certain hierarchical combinations.

Lemma 8.6.39 *Let $\mathcal{R}_1$ and $\mathcal{R}_2$ be locally confluent noninterfering TRSs. Then their combined system $\mathcal{R} = \mathcal{R}_1 \cup \mathcal{R}_2$ is locally confluent.*

Proof We have $CP(\mathcal{R}) = CP(\mathcal{R}_1) \cup CP(\mathcal{R}_2)$ because $\mathcal{R}_1$ and $\mathcal{R}_2$ are noninterfering. It has to be shown that $\mathcal{R}$ is locally confluent, or equivalently, that every critical pair $\langle s, t\rangle \in CP(\mathcal{R})$ is joinable; see the critical cair lemma 4.2.3. This follows immediately from the fact that $\langle s, t\rangle \in CP(\mathcal{R}_j)$ for some $j \in \{1, 2\}$ and local confluence of $\mathcal{R}_j$. □

Proposition 8.6.40 *Let $\mathcal{R}$ be the hierarchical combination of base system $\mathcal{R}_1$ and extension $\mathcal{R}_2$ with a common subsystem $\mathcal{R}_0$. If no left-hand side of a rewrite rule from $\mathcal{R}_2$ contains a function symbol from $\mathcal{D}_1'$, then $\mathcal{R}_1$ and $\mathcal{R}_2$ are noninterfering.*

Proof The inclusion $CP(\mathcal{R}_1) \cup CP(\mathcal{R}_2) \subseteq CP(\mathcal{R})$ evidently holds, so the converse inclusion has to be shown. Let $\langle s, t\rangle \in CP(\mathcal{R})$. If the critical pair originates from an overlap of rewrite rules from $\mathcal{R}_j$ for some $j \in \{1, 2\}$, then $\langle s, t\rangle \in CP(\mathcal{R}_j)$ and we are done. So let the critical pair originate from an overlap of the rules $l_1 \to r_1 \in \mathcal{R}_1$ and $l_2 \to r_2 \in \mathcal{R}_2$. If $l_2 \to r_2$ overlaps $l_1 \to r_1$, then $l_2 \to r_2$ must also be a rule in $\mathcal{R}_1$ because $\mathcal{F}_1 \cap \mathcal{D}_2' = \emptyset$, i.e.,

$\mathcal{F}_1$ does not contain function symbols from $\mathcal{D}_2'$. Hence, $\langle s,t\rangle \in CP(\mathcal{R}_1)$. Likewise, if $l_1 \to r_1$ overlaps $l_2 \to r_2$, then $l_1 \to r_1$ must also be a rule in $\mathcal{R}_2$ because l_2 does not contain a function symbol from $\mathcal{D}_1'$. Therefore, $\langle s,t\rangle \in CP(\mathcal{R}_2)$. □

Corollary 8.6.41

1. *Local confluence is modular for composable TRSs.*

2. *Local confluence is modular for restricted proper extensions with a common subsystem.*

Proof If the TRSs $\mathcal{R}_1$ and $\mathcal{R}_2$ are composable or if $\mathcal{R}_2$ is a restricted proper extension of $\mathcal{R}_1$ with a common subsystem, then $\mathcal{R}_1$ and $\mathcal{R}_2$ are noninterfering by Proposition 8.6.40. Consequently, the claim follows from Lemma 8.6.39. □

Proposition 8.6.42 *For the class of finite TRSs we have:*

1. *Convergence is modular for $\mathcal{C}_\mathcal{E}$-terminating restricted proper extensions with a common subsystem.*

2. *Convergence is modular for restricted proper extensions with a common subsystem provided that the systems are overlay systems.*

Proof Let $\mathcal{R}_1$ and $\mathcal{R}_2$ be finite convergent TRSs such that $\mathcal{R}_2$ is a restricted proper extension of $\mathcal{R}_1$ with a common subsystem.

(1) If both systems are $\mathcal{C}_\mathcal{E}$-terminating, then the same is true for $\mathcal{R}_1 \cup \mathcal{R}_2$, according to Theorem 8.6.21. Furthermore, it is also locally confluent by Corollary 8.6.41. Hence it is convergent by Newman's lemma 2.2.5.

(2) If both systems are innermost terminating, then $\mathcal{R}_1 \cup \mathcal{R}_2$ is innermost terminating by Theorem 8.6.32. According to Corollary 8.6.41, it is also locally confluent. It is not difficult to prove that $\mathcal{R}_1 \cup \mathcal{R}_2$ is an overlay system provided that $\mathcal{R}_2$ is a *restricted* proper extension of $\mathcal{R}_1$ with a common subsystem and both systems are overlay systems. Now an application of Theorem 5.6.8, in combination with Newman's lemma 2.2.5, yields the convergence of $\mathcal{R}_1 \cup \mathcal{R}_2$. □

Corollary 8.6.43

1. *Strong confluence is modular for linear composable TRSs.*

2. *Strong confluence is modular for linear restricted proper extensions with a common subsystem.*

Proof Composable systems and restricted proper extensions with a common subsystem are noninterfering. Therefore, the claim is a consequence of Theorem 4.3.2; cf. proof of Lemma 8.6.39. □

Property	Disjoint union	Shared cons.	Composable
Confluence	Yes [Mid93]	No [KO92]	No
Local confluence	No [Mid93]	No	No
Termination	No [Toy87a]	No	No
+ layer-preservation	Yes [Mid93]	Yes [Ohl95b]	?
+ nonoverlapping	Yes [Gra96a]	Yes [Gra96a]	?
Innermost termination	No [Gra96a]	No	No
+ confluence	Yes [Gra96a]	Yes [Gra96a]	?
Innermost normalization	No [Gra96a]	No	No
+ confluence	Yes [Gra96a]	Yes [Gra96a]	?
Normalization	No [Mid93]	No	No
Unique normalization	Yes [Mid93]	Yes [Ohl95b]	?
Convergence	No [Toy87a]	No	No
+ layer-preservation	Yes [Mid93]	Yes [Ohl95b]	?
+ nonduplication	Yes [Mid93]	Yes [Ohl95b]	?
+ overlay system	Yes [Gra96a]	Yes [Gra96a]	?

TABLE 8.4. Modular properties of join 2-CTRSs.

We would like to stress that none of the modularity results presented in this section can be generalized to proper extensions. In order to see this, consider the TRSs $\mathcal{R}_1$ and $\mathcal{R}_2$ of Example 8.1.3. Obviously, $\mathcal{R}_2$ is a proper extension of $\mathcal{R}_1$. Moreover, $\mathcal{R}_1$ and $\mathcal{R}_2$ are linear, strongly confluent, and terminating overlay systems. However, their combined system $\mathcal{R}_1 \cup \mathcal{R}_2$ is not locally confluent.

8.7 Conditional Systems

In Table 8.4 we have listed a selection of known modularity results for join 2-CTRSs (systems that may have extra variables in their conditions). In general, the properties SIN, WIN, and WN are not modular for 2-CTRSs (in fact, they are not preserved under signature extensions), but they are modular for 1-CTRSs; see [Gra96a]. Moreover, there are some partial results for CTRSs without extra variables. That is, some of the question marks in Table 8.4 can be eliminated if one considers only systems without extra variables. For example, convergence is modular for composable conditional constructor systems without extra variables; see [Mid94a]. Special modularity results for join 1-CTRSs are summarized in Table 8.5. (Recall that simplifying CTRSs do not permit extra variables.)

Finally, because a left-linear normal 1-CTRS $\mathcal{R}$ is decreasing if and only if its transformed TRS $U_n(\mathcal{R})$ is terminating (Corollary 7.2.32), it follows that decreasingness is modular provided the transformed system belongs to a class of TRSs for which termination is modular; see [Mar96b]. For

Property	Disjoint union	Shared cons.	Composable
Simplifyingness	Yes [Ohl93a]	Yes [Ohl93a]	Yes [Ohl93a]
Innermost termination	Yes [Gra96a]	Yes [Gra96a]	?
Innermost normalization	Yes [Gra96a]	Yes [Gra96a]	?
Normalization	Yes [Gra96a]	Yes [Gra96a]	?
Convergence	no [Toy87a]	no	no
+ constructor system	Yes [Mid94a]	Yes [Mid94a]	Yes [Mid94a]
Unique normalization	Yes [Mid93]	Yes [Ohl95b]	?
+ constructor system	Yes [Mid93]	Yes [Ohl95b]	Yes [Mid94a]

TABLE 8.5. Modular properties of join 1-CTRSs.

example, if $\mathcal{R}_1$ and $\mathcal{R}_2$ are left-linear composable normal 1-CTRSs that are decreasing and nonoverlapping, then their combined system $\mathcal{R}_1 \cup \mathcal{R}_2$ is also decreasing for the following reasons: (i) $U_n(\mathcal{R}_1)$ and $U_n(\mathcal{R}_2)$ are terminating composable TRSs and (ii) $U_n(\mathcal{R}_1 \cup \mathcal{R}_2) = U_n(\mathcal{R}_1) \cup U_n(\mathcal{R}_2)$ is terminating because termination is modular for nonoverlapping composable TRSs.

In the rest of this section we will prove the first modularity results for *oriented* CTRSs that have extra variables on the right-hand sides of the rules. These are based on the transformations described in Section 7.2. We are aware of the fact that some of the results can be refined to demand only exactly what is required by the proof.

We have seen that simplifyingness is modular for composable 1-CTRSs. Hence it may be a bit surprising that quasi-simplifyingness is *not* modular for disjoint deterministic 3-CTRSs. The next example, taken from [Mid93, example 4.8], turns out to be a counterexample.

Example 8.7.1 Consider the normal 1-CTRS

$$\mathcal{R}_1 = \{f(x) \to f(x) \Leftarrow x \to a, x \to b\}$$

over the signature $\mathcal{F}_1 = \{f, a, b\}$. It is not difficult to show that the system $\{f(x) \to x, f(x) \to x \Leftarrow x \to a, f(x) \to f(x) \Leftarrow x \to a, x \to b\}$ is terminating because the last rule can never be applied. Hence $\mathcal{R}_1$ is quasi-simplifying by Proposition 7.2.63. The TRS

$$\mathcal{R}_2 = \left\{ \begin{array}{ll} g(x,y) & \to x \\ g(x,y) & \to y \end{array} \right.$$

is obviously quasi-simplifying, too. The combined system $\mathcal{R}_1 \cup \mathcal{R}_2$, however, is not even terminating: $f(g(a,b)) \to_{\mathcal{R}_1 \cup \mathcal{R}_2} f(g(a,b))$ is a cyclic derivation because $g(a,b) \to_{\mathcal{R}_2} a$ and $g(a,b) \to_{\mathcal{R}_2} b$.

The backward substituted system $\overline{\mathcal{R}_1}$ of $\mathcal{R}_1$ is not simplifying because no simplification ordering $\succ$ can have $f(x) \succ f(x)$. Hence Proposition 7.2.68

cannot be used to show quasi-simplifyingness of $\mathcal{R}_1$. As a matter of fact, the next proposition shows that if Proposition 7.2.68 could prove quasi-simplifyingness of $\mathcal{R}_1$, then $\mathcal{R}_1 \cup \mathcal{R}_2$ would also be quasi-simplifying.

Proposition 8.7.2 *Let $\mathcal{R}_1$ and $\mathcal{R}_2$ be composable deterministic 3-CTRSs. If both systems can be proven quasi-simplifying by Proposition 7.2.68, then their combined system $\mathcal{R} = \mathcal{R}_1 \cup \mathcal{R}_2$ can also be shown quasi-simplifying by Proposition 7.2.68.*

Proof We know that the backward substituted 1-CTRSs $\overline{\mathcal{R}_1}$ and $\overline{\mathcal{R}_2}$ are simplifying. It is easy to see that $\overline{\mathcal{R}_1}$ and $\overline{\mathcal{R}_2}$ are also composable. Their combined system $\overline{\mathcal{R}_1} \cup \overline{\mathcal{R}_2}$ is simplifying because simplifyingness is modular for composable 1-CTRSs. Because $\overline{\mathcal{R}} = \overline{\mathcal{R}_1} \cup \overline{\mathcal{R}_2}$, it follows that $\mathcal{R}$ is quasi-simplifying by Proposition 7.2.68. □

The transformed TRS $U(\mathcal{R}_1)$ of the CTRS $\mathcal{R}_1$ from Example 8.7.1 looks like this:

$$U(\mathcal{R}_1) = \left\{ \begin{array}{ll} f(x) & \to U_1(x,x) \\ U_1(a,x) & \to U_2(x,x) \\ U_2(b,x) & \to f(x) \end{array} \right.$$

It is not simply terminating as the following cyclic derivation shows:

$$\begin{aligned} f(U_1(a,b)) &\to_{U(\mathcal{R}_1)} U_1(U_1(a,b), U_1(a,b)) \to_{\mathcal{E}mb(\mathcal{F}')} U_1(a, U_1(a,b)) \\ &\to_{U(\mathcal{R}_1)} U_2(U_1(a,b), U_1(a,b)) \to_{\mathcal{E}mb(\mathcal{F}')} U_2(b, U_1(a,b)) \\ &\to_{U(\mathcal{R}_1)} f(U_1(a,b)) \end{aligned}$$

Hence Proposition 7.2.64 cannot be used to show quasi-simplifyingness of $\mathcal{R}_1$ either. This is not surprising because the combined system of two composable deterministic 3-CTRSs $\mathcal{R}_1$ and $\mathcal{R}_2$ is quasi-simplifying if both $U(\mathcal{R}_1)$ and $U(\mathcal{R}_2)$ are simply terminating. This fact is a simple consequence of the following generic proposition.

Proposition 8.7.3 *Let $\mathcal{R}_1$ and $\mathcal{R}_2$ be deterministic 3-CTRSs. Their combined system $\mathcal{R}_1 \cup \mathcal{R}_2$ is quasi-simplifying if*

1. *both $U(\mathcal{R}_1)$ and $U(\mathcal{R}_2)$ are simply terminating, and*
2. *$U(\mathcal{R}_1)$ and $U(\mathcal{R}_2)$ belong to a class of TRSs for which simple termination is modular.*

Proof Because we assume that simple termination is a modular property, the combined system $U(\mathcal{R}_1) \cup U(\mathcal{R}_2)$ is simply terminating. The proposition follows from $U(\mathcal{R}_1 \cup \mathcal{R}_2) = U(\mathcal{R}_1) \cup U(\mathcal{R}_2)$ in conjunction with Proposition 7.2.64. □

For example, consider the TRSs $\mathcal{R}_+$ and $\mathcal{R}_*$ from Example 8.1.6 and the 3-CTRS $\mathcal{R}_{fib}$ from Example 7.2.65. $\mathcal{R}_+ \cup \mathcal{R}_*$ and $\mathcal{R}_{fib}$ are obviously composable. Because both Propositions 7.2.64 and 7.2.68 can be used to show that these systems are quasi-simplifying, one can conclude by either Proposition 8.7.3 or 8.7.2 that their combined system $\mathcal{R}_+ \cup \mathcal{R}_* \cup \mathcal{R}_{fib}$ is also quasi-simplifying.

A result similar to Proposition 8.7.3 can, of course, be stated for quasi-reductivity (just replace simple termination by termination and use Proposition 7.2.50). However, better results can be obtained by taking advantage of the implications: $U(\mathcal{R})$ is terminating $\Rightarrow$ $\mathcal{R}$ is quasi-reductive $\Rightarrow$ $\mathcal{R}$ is quasi-decreasing $\Rightarrow$ $U(\mathcal{R})$ is innermost terminating (Corollary 7.2.59) and the fact that termination and innermost termination coincide for nonoverlapping TRSs (Theorem 5.6.10(1)).

Proposition 8.7.4 *Let $\mathcal{R}_1$ and $\mathcal{R}_2$ be quasi-reductive (quasi-decreasing, respectively) deterministic 3-CTRSs. Their combined system $\mathcal{R}_1 \cup \mathcal{R}_2$ is quasi-reductive if*

1. *$U(\mathcal{R}_1)$ and $U(\mathcal{R}_2)$ belong to a class of TRSs for which innermost termination is modular, and*
2. *$U(\mathcal{R}_1 \cup \mathcal{R}_2)$ is nonoverlapping.*

Proof Because $\mathcal{R}_1$ and $\mathcal{R}_2$ are quasi-decreasing, the transformed TRSs $U(\mathcal{R}_1)$ and $U(\mathcal{R}_2)$ are innermost terminating according to Corollary 7.2.59. Their combination $U(\mathcal{R}_1) \cup U(\mathcal{R}_2) = U(\mathcal{R}_1 \cup \mathcal{R}_2)$ is also innermost terminating because innermost termination is modular. Thus termination of $U(\mathcal{R}_1 \cup \mathcal{R}_2)$ is a consequence of its nonoverlappingness; cf. Theorem 5.6.10(1). The assertion follows from Proposition 7.2.50. □

A combination of Lemma 7.2.60 and Proposition 8.7.4 yields the following theorem.

Theorem 8.7.5 *Quasi-reductivity (quasi-decreasingness) is modular for nonoverlapping syntactically deterministic composable 3-CTRSs.*

Proof Let $\mathcal{R}_1$ and $\mathcal{R}_2$ be quasi-reductive nonoverlapping syntactically deterministic composable 3-CTRSs. It is relatively easy to verify that $U(\mathcal{R}_1)$ and $U(\mathcal{R}_2)$ are composable because $\mathcal{R}_1$ and $\mathcal{R}_2$ are composable (note that the U symbols U_i^ρ used in the transformation $U(\rho)$ are marked with the rule ρ). Recall that innermost termination is modular for composable TRSs; see Proposition 8.6.28. According to Lemma 7.2.60, the TRSs $U(\mathcal{R}_1)$ and $U(\mathcal{R}_2)$ are nonoverlapping. The system $U(\mathcal{R}_1 \cup \mathcal{R}_2) = U(\mathcal{R}_1) \cup U(\mathcal{R}_2)$ is also nonoverlapping because the union of two nonoverlapping composable TRSs is nonoverlapping. Hence the combined system $\mathcal{R}_1 \cup \mathcal{R}_2$ is quasi-reductive by Proposition 8.7.4. Furthermore, $\mathcal{R}_1 \cup \mathcal{R}_2$ is obviously nonoverlapping and syntactically deterministic. □

As already mentioned in Section 7.2.8, Lemma 7.2.60 can be generalized as follows: If functions are defined by distinct cases as the *quorem* function from Example 7.1.5 or the *filter* function from Example 7.4.9, then the "optimized" transformation described in Example 7.2.49 still yields a nonoverlapping transformed system $U(\mathcal{R})$. Clearly, Theorem 8.7.5 remains valid for these systems. Note that the *quorem* system and the *filter* system are syntactically deterministic composable 3-CTRSs. Both systems can be shown quasi-reductive by Proposition 7.2.50 in conjunction with the dependency pair technique. Hence we can conclude from the generalized version of Theorem 8.7.5 that their combined system is also quasi-reductive.

As another example, consider the *quot* system and the *quicksort* system from Chapter 1. A termination proof of the *quot* system can be obtained by means of the dependency pair method; cf. [AG00]. Clearly, this terminating TRS can be viewed as a quasi-reductive CTRS. Furthermore, it was shown in Example 5.4.36 that the transformed system of the *quicksort* system is terminating. Hence the *quicksort* system is also quasi-reductive. Because the systems under consideration are syntactically deterministic constructor-sharing 3-CTRSs, it follows from the generalized version of Theorem 8.7.5 that their combined system is also quasi-reductive.

In order to prove the first modularity results for hierarchical combinations of CTRSs with extra variables on the right-hand sides of the rules, we need the following definition; cf. [Mar95].

Definition 8.7.6 Let $\mathcal{R}$ be an oriented CTRS and $\mathcal{D}$ be the set of its defined symbols. The dependency relation $\trianglerighteq_d$ on $\mathcal{D}$ is the smallest quasi-order satisfying $f \trianglerighteq_d g$ whenever there is a rule $l \to r \Leftarrow s_1 \to t_1, \ldots, s_k \to t_k \in \mathcal{R}$ such that $root(l) = f$ and $g \in \mathcal{D}$ occurs in one of the terms $s_1, \ldots, s_k, r$.

If two oriented conditional systems $\mathcal{R}_1$ and $\mathcal{R}_2$ form a hierarchical combination, then the sets $\mathcal{D}_2^1$ and $\mathcal{D}_2^2$ are defined as in the unconditional case: $\mathcal{D}_2^1 = \{f \mid f \in \mathcal{D}_2, f \trianglerighteq_d g \text{ for some } g \in \mathcal{D}_1\}$ and $\mathcal{D}_2^2 = \mathcal{D} \setminus \mathcal{D}_2^1$. The combination of Lemma 7.2.60, Proposition 8.7.4, and Theorem 8.6.31 yields the following theorem.

Theorem 8.7.7 *Let $\mathcal{R}_1$ and $\mathcal{R}_2$ be quasi-reductive (quasi-decreasing, respectively) nonoverlapping syntactically deterministic 3-CTRSs. Then their hierarchical combination $\mathcal{R}_1 \cup \mathcal{R}_2$ is also a quasi-reductive nonoverlapping syntactically deterministic 3-CTRS provided every rewrite rule $l \to r \Leftarrow s_1 \to t_1, \ldots, s_k \to t_k$ in $\mathcal{R}_2$ satisfies:*

1. *Neither l nor one of the terms $t_1, \ldots, t_k$ contains a symbol from $\mathcal{D}_1$.*

If some s_j, $1 \le j \le k+1$, where $s_{k+1} = r$, contains a symbol from $\mathcal{D}_1 \cup \mathcal{D}_2^1$,

2. *then every subterm t of s_j with $root(t) \in \mathcal{D}_2^1$ and $root(t) \trianglerighteq_d root(l)$ does not contain symbols from $\mathcal{D}_1 \cup \mathcal{D}_2^1$ except at the root position, and*

3. none of the terms $s_{j+1}, \ldots, s_k, s_{k+1}$ contains a symbol $f \in \mathcal{D}_1 \cup \mathcal{D}_2^1$ with $f \trianglerighteq_d root(l)$.

Proof Obviously, $U(\mathcal{R}_1 \cup \mathcal{R}_2) = U(\mathcal{R}_1) \cup U(\mathcal{R}_2)$. The combined system $U(\mathcal{R}_1) \cup U(\mathcal{R}_2)$ is nonoverlapping because the TRSs $U(\mathcal{R}_1)$ and $U(\mathcal{R}_2)$ are nonoverlapping by Lemma 7.2.60 and every rule $l \to r \Leftarrow s_1 \to t_1, \ldots, s_k \to t_k$ in $\mathcal{R}_2$ satisfies: neither l nor one of the terms $t_1, \ldots t_k$ contains a symbol from $\mathcal{D}_1$. For the same reason, $\mathcal{R}_1 \cup \mathcal{R}_2$ is nonoverlapping and syntactically deterministic. We claim that $U(\mathcal{R}_2)$ is a proper extension of $U(\mathcal{R}_1)$. Because innermost termination is modular for proper extensions by Theorem 8.6.31, it follows from Proposition 8.7.4 that $\mathcal{R}_1 \cup \mathcal{R}_2$ is quasi-reductive.

In order to prove the claim, consider $\rho : l \to r \Leftarrow s_1 \to t_1, \ldots, s_k \to t_k \in \mathcal{R}_2$ and its transformation $U(\rho)$. If none of the terms $s_1, \ldots, s_k, s_{k+1} (= r)$ contains a symbol from $\mathcal{D}_2^1$, then every rule in $U(\rho)$ satisfies the proper extension condition. Otherwise, let j, $1 \le j \le k+1$, be the smallest index such that s_j contains a symbol from $\mathcal{D}_2^1$. Every rule $l \to U_1^\rho(s_1, \ldots)$, $U_1^\rho(t_1, \ldots) \to U_2^\rho(s_2, \ldots), \ldots, U_{j-2}^\rho(t_{j-2}, \ldots) \to U_{j-1}^\rho(s_{j-1}, \ldots)$ vacuously satisfies the proper extension condition. The rewrite rule $U_{j-1}^\rho(t_{j-1}, \ldots) \to U_j^\rho(s_j, \ldots)$ satisfies the proper extension condition by assumption (2) because for every subterm t of $U_j^\rho(s_j, \ldots)$ with $root(t) \in \mathcal{D}_2^1$ and $root(t) \trianglerighteq_d U_{j-1}^\rho$ we have $root(t) \trianglerighteq_d root(l)$. The remaining rules $U_j^\rho(t_j, \ldots) \to U_{j+1}^\rho(s_{j+1}, \ldots), \ldots, U_k^\rho(t_k, \ldots) \to r$ vacuously satisfy the proper extension condition because of assumption (3). □

For example, because the systems $\{0 + y \to y, s(x) + y \to s(x + y)\}$ and

$$\begin{array}{rcll} fib(0) & \to & \langle 0, s(0) \rangle & \\ fib(s(x)) & \to & \langle z, y + z \rangle & \Leftarrow fib(x) \to \langle y, z \rangle \end{array}$$

are quasi-reductive and meet the requirements of Theorem 8.7.7, their hierarchical combination is also quasi-reductive.

The following examples show that the assumptions of Theorem 8.7.7 are really necessary.

Example 8.7.8 Condition (1) in Theorem 8.7.7 guarantees that the combined system is also nonoverlapping and syntactically deterministic, and it is easy to find examples that show the necessity of this condition. The following example shows that condition (2) is also necessary. The quasi-reductive nonoverlapping syntactically deterministic 3-CTRSs $\mathcal{R}_1 = \{a \to b\}$ and $\mathcal{R}_2 = \{f(x, x) \to c \Leftarrow f(a, b) \to c\}$ form a hierarchical combination. If $\mathcal{R}_1 \cup \mathcal{R}_2$ were quasi-reductive w.r.t. an ordering $\succ$, then $f(b, b) \succ_{st} f(a, b) \succ f(b, b)$ would hold, but this contradicts the irreflexivity of $\succ_{st}$. Finally, we exemplify the necessity of condition (3). $\mathcal{R}_1$ and $\mathcal{R}_3 = \{c \to d \Leftarrow a \to b, c \to d\}$ form a hierarchical combination. Here $s_1 = a$ contains a symbol from $\mathcal{D}_1$ and $s_2 = c$ contains $c \in \mathcal{D}_2^1$ with $c \succeq_d root(l)$. If $\mathcal{R}_1 \cup \mathcal{R}_3$ were quasi-reductive w.r.t. an ordering $\succ$, then

$c \succ_{st} c$ would hold, but $\succ_{st}$ is irreflexive. A similar example consists of the CTRSs $\mathcal{R}_1$ and $\mathcal{R}_4 = \{c \to c \Leftarrow a \to b\}$. The function symbol $a \in \mathcal{D}_1$ occurs in $s_1 = a$ and $r = c$ contains $c \in \mathcal{D}_2^1$ with $c \succeq_d root(l)$. Thus these systems do not meet the requirements of Theorem 8.7.7. In fact, $\mathcal{R}_1 \cup \mathcal{R}_4$ is nonterminating (hence not quasi-reductive).

9
Graph Rewriting

For reasons of efficiency, term rewriting is usually implemented by graph rewriting. In term rewriting, expressions are represented as terms, whereas in graph rewriting[1] these are represented as directed graphs. In contrast to the former, the latter representation allows a sharing of common subexpressions. In graph rewriting expressions are evaluated by rule-based graph transformations. Here we will only consider directed *acyclic* graphs.

In order to illustrate the advantage of graph rewriting over term rewriting, let $\mathcal{R}$ consist of the rules

$$\begin{aligned} 0 + y &\rightarrow y \\ s(x) + y &\rightarrow s(x + y) \\ double(x) &\rightarrow x + x \end{aligned}$$

In the term rewriting step

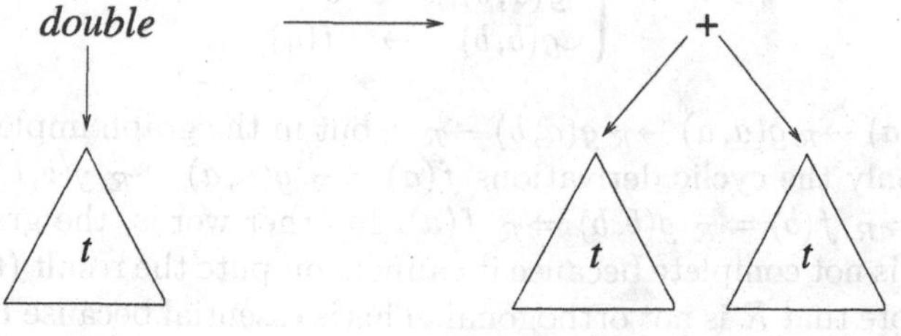

[1]Many authors use the notion *term graph rewriting* to distinguish it from other graph rewriting settings.

the subterm t is copied. If t is a large term, then this operation can be very costly in terms of space and time. Moreover, after this reduction step the value (normal form) of t has to be computed twice unless t is already in normal form. Therefore, this reduction step duplicates the work that is necessary to evaluate t. The usual way of avoiding this problem is to create two pointers to the subterm t instead of copying it.

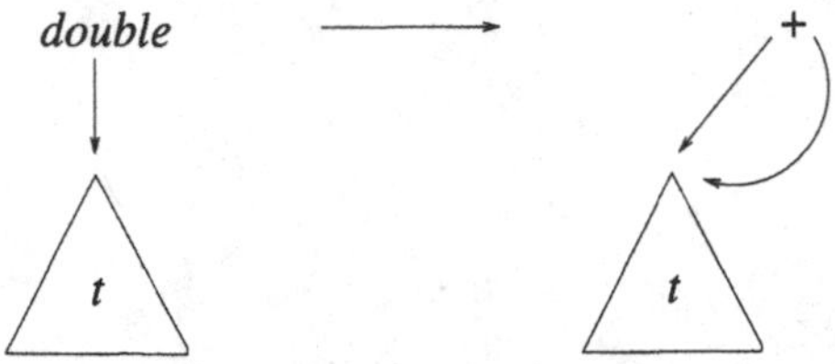

In the resulting directed acyclic graph, the subterm t is *shared*. An evaluation of t in the directed acyclic graph corresponds to a parallel evaluation of the two occurrences of t in the term $t+t$. Thus, representing expressions as graphs instead of terms saves both time and space. It has been shown by Kurihara and Ohuchi [KO95b] that directed acyclic graphs can be represented by well-marked terms; thus graph transformations can be modeled by rewriting well-marked terms. In so doing, it is possible to completely argue within the framework of term rewriting and to avoid concepts from different fields. In this chapter we will further elaborate on this viewpoint.

If one wants to implement term rewriting by graph rewriting, then one has to make sure that (1) the graph implementation cannot give incorrect results (soundness) and (2) the graph implementation gives all results (completeness). We will see later that nonleft-linear rules cause problems in this respect, but even for left-linear TRSs, graph rewriting is not complete, as the following example from Middeldorp and Hamoen [MH94] shows. In the left-linear TRS

$$\mathcal{R} = \left\{ \begin{array}{rcl} f(x) & \to & g(x,x) \\ a & \to & b \\ g(a,b) & \to & c \\ g(b,b) & \to & f(a) \end{array} \right.$$

we have $f(a) \to_{\mathcal{R}} g(a,a) \to_{\mathcal{R}} g(a,b) \to_{\mathcal{R}} c$, but in the graph implementation there are only the cyclic derivations $f(a) \Rightarrow_{\mathcal{R}} g(a,a) \Rightarrow_{\mathcal{R}} g(b,b) \Rightarrow_{\mathcal{R}} f(a)$ and $f(a) \Rightarrow_{\mathcal{R}} f(b) \Rightarrow_{\mathcal{R}} g(b,b) \Rightarrow_{\mathcal{R}} f(a)$. In other words, the graph implementation is not complete because it cannot compute the result (the normal form) c. Note that $\mathcal{R}$ is not orthogonal. This is essential because Barendregt et al. [BEG+87] have proven that graph rewriting is a sound and complete implementation of orthogonal TRSs.

Although term rewriting and graph rewriting share many common features, neither is a special case of the other. In Section 9.1 we will bridge this gap by presenting a uniform framework, called *marked rewriting.* The advantage of this new approach is that both term rewriting and graph rewriting can be viewed as instances of marked rewriting. With such an approach it is possible to prove statements in the framework of marked rewriting and to obtain results for term and graph rewriting as corollaries thereof. This will be demonstrated in Section 9.2. These results originate from [Ohl00]. Graph rewriting has been studied extensively (see Section 9.3) but to the best of our knowledge, [Ohl01a] contains the first study of conditional graph rewriting. It will be shown in Section 9.4 that conditional graph rewriting is a sound and complete implementation of almost functional CTRSs. We restrict to almost functional CTRSs because the graph rewrite relations of these systems are Church-Rosser modulo isomorphism of graphs. These results are of practical relevance because they allow the use of conditional graph rewriting for the implementation of functional CTRSs. Readers who are only interested in unconditional graph rewriting may also benefit from Section 9.4: by simply ignoring the arguments dealing with the conditions, one obtains the same results for orthogonal unconditional systems.

9.1 A Uniform Framework for Term, Graph, and Noncopying Rewriting

To start, we will introduce the concept of marked terms. Most of the following definitions stem from [KO95b].

Definition 9.1.1 Let M be a countably infinite set of objects called *marks.* Given a signature $\mathcal{F}$, let $\mathcal{F}^* = \{f^\mu \mid f \in \mathcal{F}, \mu \in M\}$ be the set of *marked function symbols.* For all $f^\mu \in \mathcal{F}^*$, the arity of f^μ coincides with that of f. Furthermore, we define $symbol(f^\mu) = f$ and $mark(f^\mu) = \mu$. Analogously, given a set of variables $\mathcal{V}$, let $\mathcal{V}^* = \{x^\mu \mid x \in \mathcal{V}, \mu \in M\}$ be the set of *marked variables*, $symbol(x^\mu) = x$, and $mark(x^\mu) = \mu$. The set of *marked terms* over $\mathcal{F}^*$ and $\mathcal{V}^*$ is defined in the usual way and is denoted by $\mathcal{T}(\mathcal{F}^*, \mathcal{V}^*)$. The set of all marks appearing in a marked term $t^* \in \mathcal{T}(\mathcal{F}^*, \mathcal{V}^*)$ is denoted by $marks(t^*)$. Two subterms t_1^* and t_2^* of a marked term t^* are *shared* in t^* if $t_1^* = t_2^*$.

We will mainly use natural numbers as marks. For example, if $\mathcal{F} = \{0, s, +, double\}$, then $0^1 +^0 (0^1 +^2 x^3)$ is a marked term in which the two occurrences of 0^1 are shared.

Definition 9.1.2 If t^* is a marked term, then $e(t^*)$ denotes the unmarked term obtained from t^* by erasing all the marks. Two marked terms s^* and

t^* are *bisimilar*[2] (denoted by $s^* \sim t^*$) if and only if $e(s^*) = e(t^*)$. Given two marked terms s^* and t^*, s^* *collapses* to t^* (denoted by $s^* \succeq t^*$) if and only if there exists a function $\Phi : marks(s^*) \to marks(t^*)$ such that $\Phi(s^*) = t^*$, where the extension of Φ to $\mathcal{T}(\mathcal{F}^*, \mathcal{V}^*)$ is defined by

$$\Phi(s^*) = \begin{cases} x^{\Phi(\mu)} & \text{if } s^* = x^\mu, \\ f^{\Phi(\mu)}(\Phi(t_1^*), \ldots, \Phi(t_n^*)) & \text{if } s^* = f^\mu(t_1^*, \ldots, t_n^*) \end{cases}$$

A collapsing step $s^* \succeq t^*$ is *proper* (denoted by $s^* \succ t^*$) if $t^* \not\succeq s^*$. The inverse relation of collapsing is called *copying* and is denoted by $\preceq$. The inverse relation $\prec$ of $\succ$ is called *proper* copying. The marked terms s^* and t^* are *isomorphic* (denoted by $s^* \cong t^*$) if and only if $s^* \succeq t^*$ and $t^* \succeq s^*$.

Lemma 9.1.3 *The marked terms s^* and t^* are isomorphic if and only if there is a bijective function $\Phi : marks(s^*) \to marks(t^*)$ with $\Phi(s^*) = t^*$.*

Proof The proof is routine. □

For example, the marked terms $0^1 +^0 0^1$ and $0^2 +^0 0^2$ are isomorphic. Because $0^1 +^0 0^2 \succ 0^1 +^0 0^1$, it follows that the marked terms $0^1 +^0 0^1$ and $0^1 +^0 0^2$ are not isomorphic. On the other hand, they are bisimilar. In fact, it is easy to see that $s^* \cong t^*$ implies $s^* \sim t^*$ but not vice versa.

The next definition uses the notion of *fresh* marks, which is defined as would be expected: The marks of a marked term s^* are called *fresh* w.r.t. another marked term t^* if $marks(s^*) \cap marks(t^*) = \emptyset$.

Definition 9.1.4 A *marked substitution* $\sigma^* : \mathcal{V}^* \to \mathcal{T}(\mathcal{F}^*, \mathcal{V}^*)$ is a substitution that satisfies $x^\mu\sigma^* \sim y^\nu\sigma^*$ for all $x^\mu, y^\nu \in \mathcal{D}om(\sigma^*)$ with $symbol(x^\mu) = symbol(y^\nu)$. Furthermore, let $marks(\sigma^*) = \bigcup_{x^\mu \in \mathcal{D}om(\sigma^*)} marks(x^\mu\sigma^*)$. Two marked substitutions σ_1^* and σ_2^* with $\mathcal{D}om(\sigma_1^*) = \mathcal{D}om(\sigma_2^*) = \{x_1^{\mu_1}, \ldots, x_n^{\mu_n}\}$ are called *isomorphic* (denoted by $\sigma_1^* \cong \sigma_2^*$) if $D^\mu(x_1^{\mu_1}\sigma_1^*, \ldots, x_n^{\mu_n}\sigma_1^*) \cong D^\mu(x_1^{\mu_1}\sigma_2^*, \ldots, x_n^{\mu_n}\sigma_2^*)$. Here D is a fresh symbol of arity n and μ is a fresh mark w.r.t. every $x_i^{\mu_i}\sigma_j^*$, where $1 \le i \le n$ and $1 \le j \le 2$. The notion *marked context* is defined in the obvious way.

For example, $\sigma_1^* = \{x_1^0 \mapsto 0^1 +^0 0^1, x_2^0 \mapsto 0^1 +^0 0^1\}$ and $\sigma_2^* = \{x_1^0 \mapsto 0^1 +^0 0^1, x_2^0 \mapsto 0^2 +^0 0^2\}$ are marked substitutions that are not isomorphic.

Our definition of marked substitution ensures that the unmarked substitution σ obtained from σ^* by erasing all marks is well-defined (i.e., σ really is a substitution). Moreover, the applications of isomorphic substitutions σ_1^* and σ_2^* to a marked term t^* with $marks(t^*) \cap marks(\sigma_1^*) = \emptyset$ and $marks(t^*) \cap marks(\sigma_2^*) = \emptyset$ yield isomorphic marked terms, i.e., $t^*\sigma_1^* \cong t^*\sigma_2^*$.

Now we are in a position to define the marked rewriting relation.

---

[2]The origin of the notion "bisimilarity" is explained in [AKP00].

Definition 9.1.5 Let $\mathcal{R}$ be a TRS over the signature $\mathcal{F}$. A rule $l^* \to r^*$ is a *marked version* of a rule $l \to r$ in $\mathcal{R}$ if $e(l^*) = l$ and $e(r^*) = r$. The *marked rewrite relation* $\rightsquigarrow_{\mathcal{R}} \subseteq \mathcal{T}(\mathcal{F}^*, \mathcal{V}^*) \times \mathcal{T}(\mathcal{F}^*, \mathcal{V}^*)$ w.r.t. $\mathcal{R}$ is defined as follows. $s^* \rightsquigarrow_{\mathcal{R}} t^*$ if there exists a marked version $l^* \to r^*$ of a rewrite rule $l \to r$ from $\mathcal{R}$, a marked substitution σ^* and a marked context $C^*[,\ldots,]$ containing at least one hole $\Box$ such that $s^* = C^*[l^*\sigma^*,\ldots,l^*\sigma^*]$, $t^* = C^*[r^*\sigma^*,\ldots,r^*\sigma^*]$, and $l^*\sigma^*$ is not a subterm of $C^*[,\ldots,]$. $l^*\sigma^*$ is called the *contracted marked redex* in s^*.

Note that in a marked rewrite step all shared subterms $l^*\sigma^*$ are replaced simultaneously with $r^*\sigma^*$. This is because marked rewriting should subsume graph rewriting. Furthermore, note that $\mathcal{V}ar(r^*) \subseteq \mathcal{V}ar(l^*)$ need not be true. For example, $double^0(0^1) \rightsquigarrow_{\mathcal{R}} 0^3 +^2 0^4$ by an application of the marked rule $double^0(x^5) \to x^6 +^2 x^7$ and the substitution $\sigma^* = \{x^5 \mapsto 0^1, x^6 \mapsto 0^3, x^7 \mapsto 0^4\}$. The next lemma states that marked rewriting is sound with respect to unmarked term rewriting.

Lemma 9.1.6 *$s^* \rightsquigarrow_{\mathcal{R}} t^*$ implies $e(s^*) \to_{\mathcal{R}}^+ e(t^*)$.*

Proof Suppose $s^* = C^*[l^*\sigma^*,\ldots,l^*\sigma^*] \rightsquigarrow_{\mathcal{R}} C^*[r^*\sigma^*,\ldots,r^*\sigma^*] = t^*$, where $C^*[,\ldots,]$ contains n holes. Define the unmarked substitution σ by $x\sigma = e(x^\mu\sigma^*)$ and let $C[,\ldots,] = e(C^*[,\ldots,])$. Then $e(s^*) = C[l\sigma,\ldots,l\sigma] \to_{\mathcal{R}}^+ C[r\sigma,\ldots,r\sigma] = e(t^*)$ in n steps. $\Box$

The set $\mathcal{T}_w(\mathcal{F}^*, \mathcal{V}^*)$ of *well-marked terms* over $\mathcal{F}^*$ and $\mathcal{V}^*$ is the subset of $\mathcal{T}(\mathcal{F}^*, \mathcal{V}^*)$ such that $t^* \in \mathcal{T}_w(\mathcal{F}^*, \mathcal{V}^*)$ if and only if, for every pair t_1^*, t_2^* of subterms of t^*, $mark(root(t_1^*)) = mark(root(t_2^*))$ implies $t_1^* = t_2^*$. For example, the term $0^1 +^0 0^1$ is well-marked but $0^1 +^1 0^1$ is not. If a term t^* is well-marked and $\mu \in marks(t^*)$, then $t^* \backslash \mu$ denotes the unique subterm s^* of t^* for which $mark(root(s^*)) = \mu$ holds. Well-marked terms correspond exactly to labeled directed acyclic graphs. In order to show this, we need a few prerequisites.

A *directed graph* $G = (V, E)$ is a set V of *vertices* together with a mapping E from V to the set of all finite sequences over V. For each vertex v, $E(v)$ is the sequence of all successors of v. Its i th successor is denoted by $E_i(v)$. If $E(v) = E_1(v), \ldots, E_n(v)$, then there is a directed edge from v to every $E_i(v)$, $1 \le i \le n$.

A *labeled directed graph* $G^* = (V, E, L)$ over a signature $\mathcal{F}$ and a set of variables $\mathcal{V}$ is a directed graph $G = (V, E)$ together with a mapping $L : V \to \mathcal{F} \cup \mathcal{V}$ such that $L(v)$ has arity n if and only if v has n successors. $L(v)$ is called the *label* of v.

Let $G^* = (V, E, L)$ be a labeled directed graph over $\mathcal{F}$ and $\mathcal{V}$ that is finite, acyclic, and rooted (i.e., it has a unique vertex v_0, called the *root*, with no incoming edge). We associate a well-marked term $term(G^*)$ with G^*, which is defined by

$$term(G^*) = subterm(v_0, G^*)$$

where $subterm(v, G^*)$ is defined inductively as

- x^v if $L(v) = x \in \mathcal{V}$,
- $f^v(t_1^*, \ldots, t_n^*)$ if $L(v) = f \in \mathcal{F}^{(n)}$ and $t_i^* = subterm(E_i(v), G^*)$.

Note that vertices are used as marks.

Conversely, with a well-marked term t^* we associate a rooted labeled directed graph $G^* = (V, E, L)$ as follows. Define $V = marks(t^*)$ and let the root be $v_0 = mark(root(t^*))$. Furthermore, for every vertex (mark) $\mu \in V$, E and L are defined by

$$L(\mu) = \begin{cases} x & \text{if } t^* \backslash \mu = x^\mu \in \mathcal{V} \\ f & \text{if } t^* \backslash \mu = f^\mu(t_1^*, \ldots, t_n^*) \end{cases}$$

$$E_j(\mu) = mark(root(t_j^*)) \text{ if } t^* \backslash \mu = f^\mu(t_1^*, \ldots, t_n^*), 1 \leq j \leq n$$

G^* is obviously finite and acyclic.

Example 9.1.7 The labeled directed acyclic graph

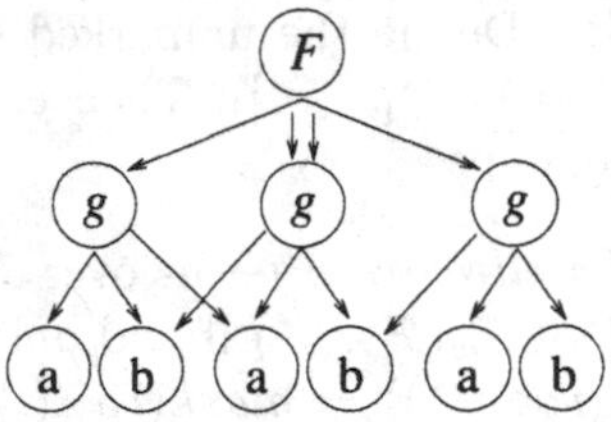

corresponds to the well-marked term

$$F^0(g^1(a^2, b^3, a^4), g^2(b^3, a^4, b^5), g^2(b^3, a^4, b^5), g^6(b^5, a^7, b^8))$$

The proofs of the following statements are rather tedious and thus omitted. If G^* is a finite, acyclic, and rooted labeled directed graph, then the labeled directed graph associated with $term(G^*)$ coincides with G^*. Conversely, if G^* is the labeled directed graph associated with a well-marked term t^*, then $t^* = term(G^*)$. In this sense, well-marked terms correspond exactly to labeled directed acyclic graphs.

A finite, acyclic, and rooted labeled directed graph and its associated well-marked term is often called a *term graph*. Next we define graph rewriting as in [Plu93, KKSV94, AK96, AKP00, Plu99].

Definition 9.1.8 The *(term) graph rewrite relation* $\Rightarrow_\mathcal{R} \subseteq \mathcal{T}_w(\mathcal{F}^*, \mathcal{V}^*) \times \mathcal{T}_w(\mathcal{F}^*, \mathcal{V}^*)$ w.r.t. $\mathcal{R}$ is defined as follows: $s^* \Rightarrow_\mathcal{R} t^*$ if $s^* \rightsquigarrow_\mathcal{R} t^*$ by a marked rule $l^* \rightarrow r^*$ such that

- for all $x^\mu, y^\nu \in \mathcal{V}ar(l^*) \cup \mathcal{V}ar(r^*)$, $symbol(x^\mu) = symbol(y^\nu)$ implies $mark(x^\mu) = mark(y^\nu)$,

- the marks on function symbols in r^* are mutually distinct and fresh w.r.t. s^*.

The first condition can be rephrased as: Every occurrence of a variable x in $l \to r$ must have the same mark in $l^* \to r^*$. This means that variables in rewrite rules are maximally shared. The last condition means that one uses a "minimal structure-sharing scheme" in graph rewriting (different structure-sharing schemes are discussed in [KO95b]).

Example 9.1.9 Consider the system $\mathcal{R}$ from the beginning of this chapter and the $\Rightarrow_{\mathcal{R}}$ reduction sequence:

$$\begin{array}{lll} double^0(0^1 +^2 s^3(0^4)) & \Rightarrow_{\mathcal{R}} & (0^1 +^2 s^3(0^4)) +^5 (0^1 +^2 s^3(0^4)) \\ & \Rightarrow_{\mathcal{R}} & s^3(0^4) +^5 s^3(0^4) \end{array}$$

In the last $\Rightarrow_{\mathcal{R}}$ step the shared subterms $(0^1 +^2 s^3(0^4))$ are replaced simultaneously with $s^3(0^4)$, whereas in term rewriting two steps would be necessary to obtain the same effect. If we view the well-marked terms as term graphs, then the reduction sequence looks like this:

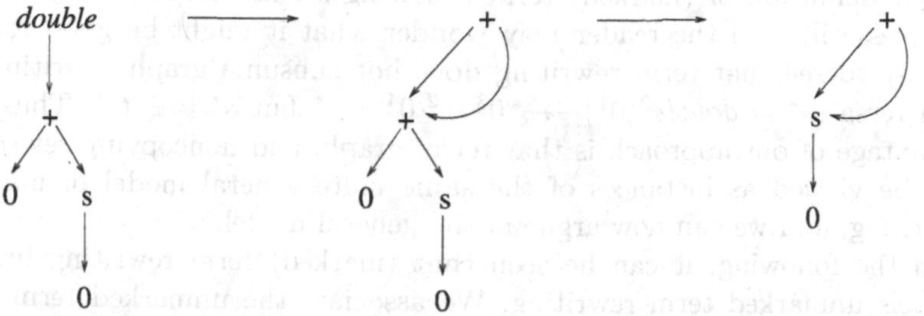

The noncopying rewrite relation introduced by Kurihara and Ohuchi [KO95b] differs slightly from the graph rewrite relation.

Definition 9.1.10 The *noncopying rewrite relation* $\Rightarrow^{nc}_{\mathcal{R}} \subseteq \mathcal{T}_w(\mathcal{F}^*, \mathcal{V}^*) \times \mathcal{T}_w(\mathcal{F}^*, \mathcal{V}^*)$ w.r.t. $\mathcal{R}$ is defined as follows: $s^* \Rightarrow^{nc}_{\mathcal{R}} t^*$ if $s^* \leadsto_{\mathcal{R}} t^*$ by a marked rule $l^* \to r^*$ such that every marked variable in r^* also appears in l^*.

Both the graph rewrite relation, as defined in [Plu93, KKSV94, AK96, AKP00, Plu99], and the noncopying rewrite relation as defined in [KO95b] can be viewed as a special case of marked rewriting.

Note that the definition of marked rewriting (Definition 9.1.5) is heavily inspired by the definition of noncopying rewriting. The sole difference is that $\mathcal{V}ar(r^*) \subseteq \mathcal{V}ar(l^*)$ is not required in marked rewriting.

In contrast to graph rewriting, the definition of noncopying rewriting does not specify how the right-hand side r should be marked. It is only necessary that a reduct of a well-marked term is again a well-marked term. This is the case if one uses, for example, the minimal structure-sharing scheme as in graph rewriting. As a matter of fact, the inclusion $\Rightarrow_{\mathcal{R}} \subseteq \Rightarrow_{\mathcal{R}}^{nc}$ holds true, because the first condition of Definition 9.1.8 implies $\mathcal{V}ar(r^*) \subseteq \mathcal{V}ar(l^*)$. If one uses the minimal structure-sharing scheme and the system $\mathcal{R}$ is left-linear, then the converse implication also holds because in left-linear systems variables are automatically maximally shared [BEG+87, Ohl01a]. However, the converse implication does not hold in general, as the following example shows. Let $\mathcal{R} = \{eq(x,x) \to true\}$. Because the same variable on the left-hand side of a marked rule may have different marks in noncopying rewriting, $s^* = eq^0(eq^1(0^2,0^3), eq^1(0^2,0^3)) \Rightarrow_{\mathcal{R}}^{nc} eq^0(true^6, true^6) = t^*$ by using the rule $eq^1(x^4,x^5) \to true^6$. In contrast to this, $s^* \not\Rightarrow_{\mathcal{R}} t^*$ because a marked version of the rule $eq(x,x) \to true$ in which the two occurrences of x have the same mark cannot match the (shared) subterm $eq^1(0^2,0^3)$.

In contrast to graph rewriting and noncopying rewriting, subterms are never shared in term rewriting. Formally, the set $\mathcal{T}_t(\mathcal{F}^*,\mathcal{V}^*)$ of *terms* over $\mathcal{F}^*$ and $\mathcal{V}^*$ is the subset of $\mathcal{T}(\mathcal{F}^*,\mathcal{V}^*)$ such that $s^* \in \mathcal{T}_t(\mathcal{F}^*,\mathcal{V}^*)$ if and only if every mark in s^* appears only once. Furthermore, the *(marked) term rewrite relation* $\to_{\mathcal{R}} \subseteq \mathcal{T}_t(\mathcal{F}^*,\mathcal{V}^*) \times \mathcal{T}_t(\mathcal{F}^*,\mathcal{V}^*)$ is just the restriction of the marked rewrite relation $\rightsquigarrow_{\mathcal{R}}$ to $\mathcal{T}_t(\mathcal{F}^*,\mathcal{V}^*)$.

Our definition of (marked) term rewriting seems to complicate things unnecessarily and the reader may wonder what it might be good for. It is easy to see that term rewriting does not subsume graph rewriting or vice versa ($s^* = double^0(0^1) \to_{\mathcal{R}} 0^3 +^2 0^4 = t^*$ but $s^* \not\Rightarrow_{\mathcal{R}} t^*$). Thus the advantage of our approach is that term, graph, and noncopying rewriting can be viewed as instances of the same more general model of marked rewriting, and we can now argue in the general model.

In the following, it can be seen that (marked) term rewriting indeed models unmarked term rewriting. We associate the unmarked term $s = e(s^*)$ with every term $s^* \in \mathcal{T}_t(\mathcal{F}^*,\mathcal{V}^*)$. Conversely, with every unmarked term s we associate a term $s^* \in \mathcal{T}_t(\mathcal{F}^*,\mathcal{V}^*)$ by marking the function symbols and variables in s with marks that are pairwise distinct. Clearly, s^* is unique up to isomorphism.

Lemma 9.1.11 *The following statements hold:*

1. $s^* \to_{\mathcal{R}} t^*$ *implies* $e(s^*) \to_{\mathcal{R}} e(t^*)$.

2. *Let s and t be unmarked terms such that $s \to_{\mathcal{R}} t$ and let s^*, t^* be associated terms. Then there is a marked term u^* such that $s^* \to_{\mathcal{R}} u^* \cong t^*$.*

Proof (1) Because every mark appears only once in s^*, there is at most one occurrence of a subterm $l^*\sigma^*$ in s^*. Thus the claim follows from Lemma 9.1.6.

(2) Suppose $s = C[l\sigma] \to_{\mathcal{R}} C[r\sigma] = t$. Mark every variable in $\mathcal{V}ar(l)$ with pairwise distinct marks that are fresh w.r.t. s^*. Then let l^*, σ^*, and

$C^*[\,]$ be the marked versions of l, σ, and $C[\,]$ such that $s^* = C^*[l^*\sigma^*]$. Furthermore, we mark r with pairwise distinct marks that are fresh w.r.t. s^* and $\mathcal{V}ar(l^*)$. For every $x_i^{\mu_i}$ in $\mathcal{V}ar(r^*) = \{x_1^{\mu_1}, \ldots, x_n^{\mu_n}\}$ let v_i^* be a term associated with $symbol(x_i^{\mu_i})\sigma$ such that all marks in v_i^* are fresh w.r.t. s^* and v_j^*, where $1 \le j \le n$ and $j \ne i$. Finally, we extend σ^* from $\mathcal{V}ar(l^*)$ to $\mathcal{V}ar(l^*) \cup \mathcal{V}ar(r^*)$ by defining $x_i^{\mu_i}\sigma^* = v_i^*$ for all $1 \le i \le n$. We infer $s^* = C^*[l^*\sigma^*] \to_{\mathcal{R}} C^*[r^*\sigma^*]$. Moreover, by construction $C^*[r^*\sigma^*] \in \mathcal{T}_t(\mathcal{F}^*, \mathcal{V}^*)$ and $C^*[r^*\sigma^*] \sim t^*$. Hence $C^*[r^*\sigma^*] \cong t^*$. □

9.2 An Application of the Framework

We saw that termination is not modular for disjoint TRSs. In Toyama's counterexample [Toy87a], the combination of the terminating rewrite systems $\mathcal{R}_1 = \{F(0,1,x) \to F(x,x,x)\}$ and $\mathcal{R}_2 = \{g(x,y) \to x, g(x,y) \to y\}$ admits the following cyclic derivation

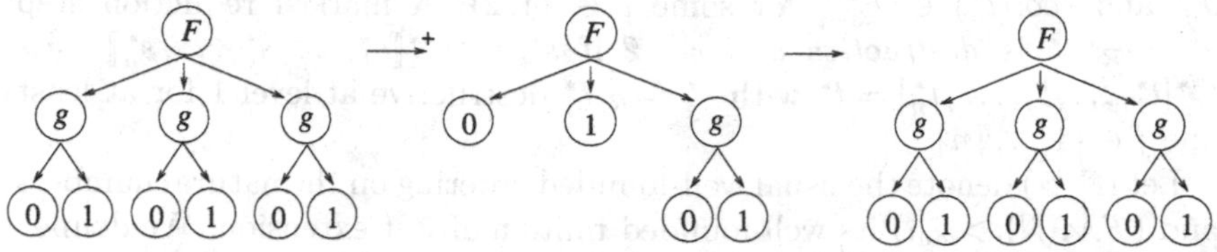

In the context of graph and noncopying rewriting, however, this counterexample vanishes:

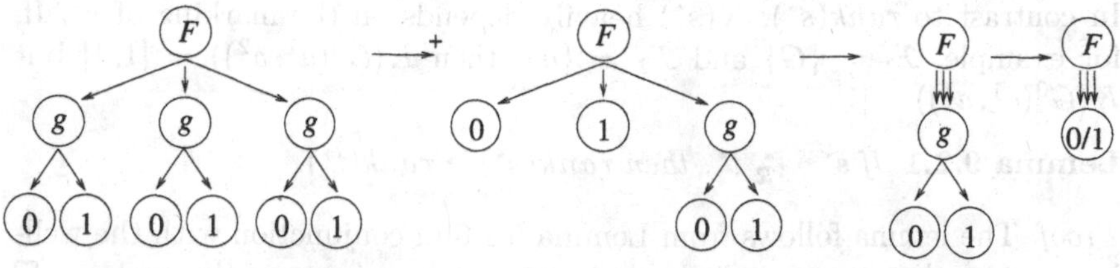

Modularity of termination for graph rewriting was first proven by Plump [Plu91] in the context of jungle evaluation. Kurihara and Ohuchi [KO95b] obtained the same result for noncopying rewriting. A simpler proof for both results was presented in [Ohl98b]. The simple proof uses essentially the same ideas as that of [Ohl93b], and it shows that there is a very close relationship between nonduplicating term rewriting and graph rewriting. We will take this one step further. In the uniform framework of term, graph, and noncopying rewriting, it is possible to give one proof for the three modularity results from different fields.

Throughout the rest of this section, let $\mathcal{R}_1$ and $\mathcal{R}_2$ be TRSs over the disjoint signatures $\mathcal{F}_1$ and $\mathcal{F}_2$ and let $\mathcal{R} = \mathcal{R}_1 \uplus \mathcal{R}_2$ be their combined system over the signature $\mathcal{F} = \mathcal{F}_1 \uplus \mathcal{F}_2$.

We start with a brief overview of the basic notions of disjoint unions of marked rewrite relations. These notions are very similar to those of Section 8.4. Let $t^* \in \mathcal{T}(\mathcal{F}^*, \mathcal{V}^*)$. Suppose $t^* = C^*[t_1^*, \ldots, t_n^*]$ with $C^*[, \ldots,] \neq \square$. We write $t^* = C^*[\![t_1^*, \ldots, t_n^*]\!]$ if $C^*[, \ldots,] \in \mathcal{T}(\mathcal{F}_i^*, \mathcal{V}^*)$ and $root(t_1^*), \ldots, root(t_n^*) \in \mathcal{F}_{3-i}^*$ for some $i \in \{1, 2\}$. In this case we define the *set* $S(t^*)$ of all marked *principal* subterms of t^* to be $S(t^*) = \{t_1^*, \ldots, t_n^*\}$. Moreover, let

$$rank(t^*) = \begin{cases} 1, \text{ if } t^* \in \mathcal{T}(\mathcal{F}_1^*, \mathcal{V}^*) \cup \mathcal{T}(\mathcal{F}_2^*, \mathcal{V}^*) \\ 1 + max\{rank(t_j^*) \mid 1 \leq j \leq n\}, \text{ if } t^* = C^*[\![t_1^*, \ldots, t_n^*]\!] \end{cases}$$

Note that $rank(t^*) = rank(e(t^*))$, that is, the rank of a term is independent of its marking. The *topmost homogeneous part* of t^*, denoted by $top(t^*)$, is obtained from t^* by replacing all principal subterms with $\square$, i.e.,

$$top(t^*) = \begin{cases} t^* & \text{if } \; rank(t^*) = 1 \\ C^*[, \ldots,] & \text{if } \; t^* = C^*[\![t_1^*, \ldots, t_n^*]\!] \end{cases}$$

A marked rewrite step $s^* \rightsquigarrow_{\mathcal{R}} t^*$ is *destructive at level 1* if $root(s^*) \in \mathcal{F}_i^*$ and $root(t^*) \in \mathcal{F}_{3-i}^*$ for some $i \in \{1, 2\}$. A marked reduction step $s^* \rightsquigarrow_{\mathcal{R}} t^*$ is *destructive at level 2* if $s^* = C^*[\![s_1^*, \ldots, s_j^*, \ldots, s_n^*]\!] \rightsquigarrow_{\mathcal{R}} C^*[t_1^*, \ldots, t_j^*, \ldots, t_n^*] = t^*$ with $s_j^* \rightsquigarrow_{\mathcal{R}} t_j^*$ destructive at level 1 for at least one $j \in \{1, \ldots, n\}$.

Let $(\mathbb{N}, >)$ denote the usual well-founded ordering on the natural numbers and $(\mathcal{FM}(\mathbb{N}), >_{mul})$ its well-founded finite multiset extension. We define

$$K(s^*) = [rank(t^*) \mid t^* \in S(s^*)] \in \mathcal{FM}(\mathbb{N})$$

i.e., $K(s^*)$ denotes the multiset of the ranks of the terms in the set $S(s^*)$. In contrast to $rank(s^*)$, $K(s^*)$ heavily depends on the marking of s^*. If, for example, $\mathcal{F}_1 = \{G\}$ and $\mathcal{F}_2 = \{a\}$, then $K(G^0(a^1, a^2)) = [1, 1]$ but $K(G^0(a^1, a^1)) = [1]$.

Lemma 9.2.1 *If $s^* \rightsquigarrow_{\mathcal{R}}^* t^*$, then $rank(s^*) \geq rank(t^*)$.*

Proof The lemma follows from Lemma 9.1.6 in conjunction with the well-known fact that an unmarked rewrite step cannot increase the rank. $\square$

Lemma 9.2.2 *If $s^* \rightsquigarrow_{\mathcal{R}} t^*$ is destructive at level 1 or 2, then $K(s^*) >^{mul} K(t^*)$.*

Proof If $s^* \rightsquigarrow_{\mathcal{R}} t^*$ is destructive at level 1, then the lemma immediately follows. Suppose $s^* \rightsquigarrow_{\mathcal{R}} t^*$ is destructive at level 2. We have $s^* = C^*[\![s_1^*, \ldots, s_n^*]\!] \rightsquigarrow_{\mathcal{R}} C^*[t_1^*, \ldots, t_n^*] = t^*$, where either $s_j^* = t_j^*$ or $s_j^* \rightsquigarrow_{\mathcal{R}} t_j^*$ for $1 \leq j \leq n$. Note that the outer context C^* is not affected by the marked reduction step. Moreover, there is at least one index k such that $s_k^* \rightsquigarrow_{\mathcal{R}} t_k^*$ is destructive at level 1. Apparently, $[rank(s_k^*)] >^{mul} K(t_k^*)$. It is not difficult to see that $K(s^*) >^{mul} K(t^*)$ follows as a consequence because $s_i^* = s_j^*$ implies $t_i^* = t_j^*$. $\square$

Definition 9.2.3 For every marked rewrite derivation $D : s_1^* \rightsquigarrow_{\mathcal{R}} s_2^* \rightsquigarrow_{\mathcal{R}} \ldots$ we define the *rank* of D by $rank(D) = rank(s_1^*)$.

Theorem 9.2.4 *Let both $\rightsquigarrow_{\mathcal{R}_1}$ and $\rightsquigarrow_{\mathcal{R}_2}$ be marked, term, graph, or non-copying rewrite relations. If $\rightsquigarrow_{\mathcal{R}_1}$ and $\rightsquigarrow_{\mathcal{R}_2}$ are terminating, then $\rightsquigarrow_{\mathcal{R}} \subseteq \rightsquigarrow_{\mathcal{R}}$ is also terminating provided the following condition holds: For every rewrite step $s^* \rightsquigarrow_{\mathcal{R}} t^*$ that is not destructive at level 1 or 2, we have $K(s^*) \geq_{mul} K(t^*)$ and $top(s^*) \rightsquigarrow_{\mathcal{R}}^* top(t^*)$.*

Proof For an indirect proof, suppose that there is an infinite $\rightsquigarrow_{\mathcal{R}}$ derivation

$$D : s_1^* \rightsquigarrow_{\mathcal{R}} s_2^* \rightsquigarrow_{\mathcal{R}} s_3^* \rightsquigarrow_{\mathcal{R}} \cdots$$

Without loss of generality, we may assume that $rank(D)$ is minimal, i.e., any $\rightsquigarrow_{\mathcal{R}}$ derivation of smaller rank is finite.

First, notice that D can be viewed as a $\rightsquigarrow_{\mathcal{R}}$ derivation because $\rightsquigarrow_{\mathcal{R}} \subseteq \rightsquigarrow_{\mathcal{R}}$. Furthermore, we have $rank(s_j^*) = rank(D)$ for all indices j. In particular, there is no step that is destructive at level 1. Finally, without loss of generality we may assume that $root(s_1^*) \in \mathcal{F}_1^*$ and hence $root(s_j^*) \in \mathcal{F}_1^*$ for all $j \geq 1$.

There is only a finite number of steps in D that are destructive at level 2 because $>_{mul}$ is well-founded and

- $s_j^* \rightsquigarrow_{\mathcal{R}} s_{j+1}^*$ destructive at level 2 implies $K(s_j^*) >_{mul} K(s_{j+1}^*)$ by Lemma 9.2.2,
- $s_j^* \rightsquigarrow_{\mathcal{R}} s_{j+1}^*$ nondestructive at level 2 yields $K(s_j^*) \geq_{mul} K(s_{j+1}^*)$.

Thus, without loss of generality, we may further assume that there is no step in D that is destructive at level 2. According to the premise, we then have $top(s_j^*) \rightsquigarrow_{\mathcal{R}_1}^* top(s_{j+1}^*)$ for every step $s_j^* \rightsquigarrow_{\mathcal{R}} s_{j+1}^*$ in D. Because $\rightsquigarrow_{\mathcal{R}_1}$ is terminating, there can only be a finite number of steps with $top(s_j^*) \rightsquigarrow_{\mathcal{R}_1}^+ top(s_{j+1}^*)$ in D. So we may assume that D contains none of these steps, or in other words, $top(s_j^*) = top(s_{j+1}^*)$ for all $j \geq 1$. Hence if $s_1^* = C[\![t_1^*, \ldots, t_n^*]\!]$, then there must be an infinite $\rightsquigarrow_{\mathcal{R}}$ derivation starting from some $t_k^* \in S(s_1^*)$. This, however, contradicts the fact that $rank(D)$ is minimal because $rank(t_k^*) < rank(s_1^*)$. □

The next lemma shows that the last condition in Theorem 9.2.4 is satisfied by every relation under consideration.

Lemma 9.2.5 *Let $\rightsquigarrow_{\mathcal{R}}$ be $\rightsquigarrow_{\mathcal{R}}$, $\Rightarrow_{\mathcal{R}}$, $\Rightarrow_{\mathcal{R}}^{nc}$, or $\rightarrow_{\mathcal{R}}$. If $s^* \rightsquigarrow_{\mathcal{R}} t^*$ is not destructive at level 1 or 2, then $top(s^*) \rightsquigarrow_{\mathcal{R}} top(t^*)$ or $top(s^*) = top(t^*)$.*

Proof The proof is routine. □

Because the other condition is also fulfilled by the noncopying rewrite relation, it is an immediate consequence of Theorem 9.2.4 that termination is modular for noncopying rewriting and for graph rewriting.

Lemma 9.2.6 *If $s^* \Rightarrow_{\mathcal{R}}^{nc} t^*$ is nondestructive at level 1 or 2, then the inequality $K(s^*) \geq_{mul} K(t^*)$ holds true.*

Proof Suppose $root(s^*) \in \mathcal{F}_1^*$ and $s^* = C^*[\![s_1^*, \ldots, s_n^*]\!] \Rightarrow_{\mathcal{R}}^{nc} t^*$. We have $t^* = \overline{C}^*[\![t_1^*, \ldots, t_m^*]\!]$, where either $C^* \Rightarrow_{\mathcal{R}}^{nc} \overline{C}^*$ or $C^* = \overline{C}^*$ and for every $k \in \{1, \ldots, m\}$, there is a $j_k \in \{1, \ldots, n\}$ such that either $s_{j_k}^* = t_k^*$ or $s_{j_k}^* \Rightarrow_{\mathcal{R}}^{nc} t_k^*$. Hence $K(s^*) \geq^{mul} K(t^*)$ follows from $rank(s_{j_k}^*) \geq rank(t_k^*)$. □

Because $\Rightarrow_{\mathcal{R}} \subseteq \Rightarrow_{\mathcal{R}}^{nc}$, the preceding lemma remains valid if we replace the noncopying rewrite relation $\Rightarrow_{\mathcal{R}}^{nc}$ with the graph rewrite relation $\Rightarrow_{\mathcal{R}}$. The same is true for the next corollary.

Corollary 9.2.7 *Termination is modular for noncopying rewriting, i.e., $\Rightarrow_{\mathcal{R}}^{nc}$ is terminating if both $\Rightarrow_{\mathcal{R}_1}^{nc}$ and $\Rightarrow_{\mathcal{R}_2}^{nc}$ are terminating.*

Proof This follows directly from Theorem 9.2.4 in combination with Lemmas 9.2.5 and 9.2.6. □

However, if a (marked) term rewriting step $s^* \to_{\mathcal{R}} t^*$ is not destructive at level 2, then $K(s^*) \geq_{mul} K(t^*)$ can only be concluded if the applied rewrite rule is nonduplicating. It is not surprising that Toyama's example constitutes a counterexample for duplicating systems. In the rewrite step

$$\begin{array}{rcl} s^* & = & F^0(0^1, 1^2, g^3(0^4, 1^5)) \\ & \to_{\mathcal{R}} & F^6(g^7(0^8, 1^9), g^{10}(0^{11}, 1^{12}), g^{13}(0^{14}, 1^{15})) = t^* \end{array}$$

we have $K(s^*) = [2]$ and $K(t^*) = [2, 2, 2]$.

Lemma 9.2.8 *If $s^* \to_{\mathcal{R}} t^*$ is nondestructive at level 1 or 2 and the applied rewrite rule is nonduplicating, then $K(s^*) \geq_{mul} K(t^*)$.*

Proof Suppose $root(s^*) \in \mathcal{F}_1^*$ and $s^* = C^*[\![s_1^*, \ldots, s_n^*]\!] \to_{\mathcal{R}} t^*$. The reduction step takes place either in the outer context (so $C^*[, \ldots,] \to_{\mathcal{R}} \overline{C}^*[, \ldots,]$) or in one of the principal subterms. In the former case, we have $t^* = \overline{C}^*[\![t_1^*, \ldots, t_m^*]\!]$. Fix some $k \in \{1, \ldots, m\}$. There is at least one index $j_k \in \{1, \ldots, n\}$ such that $e(s_{j_k}^*) = e(t_k^*)$. Moreover, the number of terms in $S(t^*) = \{t_1^*, \ldots, t_m^*\}$ with $e(t_i^*) = e(t_k^*)$ is smaller than or equal to the number of terms in $S(s^*) = \{s_1^*, \ldots, s_n^*\}$ with $e(s_j^*) = e(t_k^*)$ because the rule applied in the reduction step is nonduplicating. Therefore,

$$\begin{array}{rcl} K(s^*) & = & [rank(s_1^*), \ldots, rank(s_n^*)] \\ & = & [rank(e(s_1^*)), \ldots, rank(e(s_n^*))] \\ & \geq_{mul} & [rank(e(t_1^*)), \ldots, rank(e(t_m^*))] \\ & = & [rank(t_1^*), \ldots, rank(t_m^*)] \\ & = & K(t^*) \end{array}$$

If the contracted redex is a subterm of one of the principal subterms of s^*, then we have $s_j^* \to_{\mathcal{R}} t_j^*$ for some index j, $1 \leq j \leq n$, and hence $t^* = C^*[\![s_1^*, \ldots, s_{j-1}^*, t_j^*, s_{j+1}^*, \ldots, s_n^*]\!]$. In this case

$$\begin{array}{ll} & K(s^*) \\ = & [rank(s_1^*), \ldots, rank(s_{j-1}^*), rank(s_j^*), rank(s_{j+1}^*), \ldots, rank(s_n^*)] \\ \geq_{mul} & [rank(s_1^*), \ldots, rank(s_{j-1}^*), rank(t_j^*), rank(s_{j+1}^*), \ldots, rank(s_n^*)] \\ = & K(t^*) \end{array}$$

because $rank(s_j^*) \geq rank(t_j^*)$. □

It follows immediately from Theorem 9.2.4 in conjunction with Lemmas 9.2.5 and 9.2.8 that termination is a modular property of nonduplicating disjoint TRSs. This is an alternative proof of Theorem 8.4.15(4).

9.3 Further Topics

We have seen that in plain graph rewriting $eq^0(eq^1(0^2, 0^3), eq^1(0^2, 0^3))$ does not reduce to $eq^0(true^6, true^6)$ because 0^2 and 0^3 are not shared and thus the rule $eq^1(x^4, x^4) \to true^6$ cannot be applied. In order to cope with this phenomenon, one can use intermediate *collapsing* steps $\succ$; see [Plu93, Plu99]. For example, after the collapsing step

$$eq^0(eq^1(0^2, 0^3), eq^1(0^2, 0^3)) \succ eq^0(eq^1(0^3, 0^3), eq^1(0^3, 0^3))$$

the rule $eq^1(x^4, x^4) \to true^6$ is applicable, so that

$$eq^0(eq^1(0^3, 0^3), eq^1(0^3, 0^3)) \Rightarrow_{\mathcal{R}} eq^0(true^6, true^6)$$

Termination of graph rewriting is also modular in the presence of intermediate collapsing steps. To be precise, termination of the relation $\Rightarrow_{\mathcal{R}}^{coll} = \Rightarrow_{\mathcal{R}} \cup \succ$ is also modular for disjoint TRSs. This follows from Theorem 9.2.4 and the fact that $s^* \succ t^*$ implies $K(s^*) \geq_{mul} K(t^*)$ and $top(s^*) \succeq top(t^*)$.

The preceding modularity results for graph and noncopying rewriting have been generalized in several respects. Kurihara and Ohuchi [KO95b] showed that noncopying rewriting is also modular for constructor-sharing systems. Their main conclusion covers *crosswise disjoint* unions as well. This kind of combination was introduced by Plump [Plu91].

Definition 9.3.1 The TRSs $\mathcal{R}_1$ and $\mathcal{R}_2$ are *crosswise disjoint* if the function symbols occurring on the left-hand sides of the rules in $\mathcal{R}_i$ do not occur on the right-hand sides of the rules in $\mathcal{R}_{3-i}$ for $i \in \{1, 2\}$.

Plump [Plu91] first proved that termination of $\Rightarrow_{\mathcal{R}}^{coll}$ is modular for *crosswise disjoint* unions. To conclude, Krishna Rao [KR98] showed that termination of $\Rightarrow_{\mathcal{R}}^{coll}$ is even modular for certain hierarchical combinations.

It is interesting to note that confluence of $\Rightarrow_{\mathcal{R}}^{coll}$ and $\Rightarrow_{\mathcal{R}}^{nc}$ is not modular for disjoint TRSs; see [Plu93] and cf. [KO95b]. On the other hand, convergence of $\Rightarrow_{\mathcal{R}}^{coll}$ is modular for disjoint TRSs; see [Plu93]. The same is true for noncopying rewriting, provided one uses the minimal structure-sharing scheme; see [KO95b]. In summary, for disjoint unions, the major properties termination, confluence, and convergence show a totally different modular behavior w.r.t. term rewriting and graph rewriting.

Modular?	Term rewriting	Graph rewriting
Termination	No	Yes
Confluence	Yes	No
Convergence	No	Yes

In graph rewriting one encounters the same problems as in term rewriting; for example:

- Under which conditions is $\Rightarrow_{\mathcal{R}}$ confluent?
- Under which conditions is $\Rightarrow_{\mathcal{R}}$ terminating?

Moreover, the same questions arise if one studies $\Rightarrow_{\mathcal{R}}^{nc}$ or one of the relations

$$\begin{aligned}\Rightarrow_{\mathcal{R}}^{coll} &= \Rightarrow_{\mathcal{R}} \cup \succ\\ \Rightarrow_{\mathcal{R}}^{copy} &= \Rightarrow_{\mathcal{R}} \cup \prec\\ \Rightarrow_{\mathcal{R}}^{bi} &= \Rightarrow_{\mathcal{R}} \cup \succ \cup \prec\end{aligned}$$

instead of the plain graph rewrite relation $\Rightarrow_{\mathcal{R}}$. Plump's comprehensive overview article [Plu99] addresses all these problems for unconditional term graph rewriting (in a different terminology though); thus we will refrain from repeating the results he surveyed. It should be pointed out that there is an abundance of articles dedicated to graph rewriting, and references to the literature can be found in [Plu99].

9.4 Conditional Graph Rewriting

In this section we will consider conditional (term) graph rewriting w.r.t. *almost functional* CTRSs. Recall that a 3-CTRS $\mathcal{R}$ with strict equality is called almost functional if it is orthogonal and every conditional rewrite rule $l \to r \Leftarrow s_1 == t_1, \ldots, s_k == t_k$ in $\mathcal{R}$ satisfies:

1. If $\mathcal{V}ar(r) \not\subseteq \mathcal{V}ar(l)$, then $\mathcal{V}ar(s_i) \subseteq \mathcal{V}ar(l) \cup \bigcup_{j=1}^{i-1} \mathcal{V}ar(t_j)$ for every i, $1 \le i \le k$.
2. Every t_j, $1 \le j \le k$, is a constructor term.

It will be shown that graph rewriting is adequate for simulating term rewriting in almost functional CTRSs. In particular, conditional graph rewriting is a sound and complete implementation (w.r.t. the computation of normal forms) of these systems. Furthermore, we have seen that every almost functional CTRS is level-confluent, and it will be shown that a similar result holds for its graph implementation. All these results can be extended to *almost orthogonal* systems except for the last one.

In the rest of the section, $\mathcal{R}$ denotes an almost functional CTRS unless stated otherwise. Moreover, we solely consider well-marked terms.

Definition 9.4.1 A rewrite rule $l^* \to r^* \Leftarrow c^*$ is a *marked version* of a rewrite rule $l \to r \Leftarrow c$ in $\mathcal{R}$ if $e(l^*) = l$, $e(r^*) = r$, $e(c^*) = c$, and for all $x^\mu, y^\nu \in \mathcal{V}ar(l^* \to r^* \Leftarrow c^*)$, $symbol(x^\mu) = symbol(y^\nu)$ if and only if $mark(x^\mu) = mark(y^\nu)$.

So every marked occurrence of a variable $x \in \mathcal{V}ar(l \to r \Leftarrow c)$ must have the same mark in $l^* \to r^* \Leftarrow c^*$. For the sake of simplicity, marks on variables in marked rewrite rules will be omitted in the following because these marks are unique anyway. Hence variables in rewrite rules are maximally shared. On the other hand, by using fresh and mutually distinct marks for the right-hand side and the conditional part of a rewrite rule, we adopt the "minimal structure-sharing scheme."

Definition 9.4.2 Let $\mathcal{R}$ and the marked terms s^* and t^* be given. Set $\Rightarrow_{\mathcal{R}_0} = \emptyset$ and for $n > 0$ define $s^* \Rightarrow_{\mathcal{R}_n} t^*$ if there exists a marked version $l^* \to r^* \Leftarrow s_1^* == t_1^*, \ldots, s_k^* == t_k^*$ of a conditional rewrite rule $\rho : l \to r \Leftarrow s_1 == t_1, \ldots, s_k == t_k$ from $\mathcal{R}$, a marked substitution σ^* and a marked context $C^*[,\ldots,]$ such that

- $s^* = C^*[l^*\sigma^*, \ldots, l^*\sigma^*]$ and $t^* = C^*[r^*\sigma^*, \ldots, r^*\sigma^*]$,
- $l^*\sigma^*$ is not a subterm of $C^*[,\ldots,]$,
- for every $1 \le i \le k$, there are marked ground constructor terms u_i^* and v_i^* such that $s_i^*\sigma^* \Rightarrow_{\mathcal{R}_{n-1}}^* u_i^*$, $t_i^*\sigma^* \Rightarrow_{\mathcal{R}_{n-1}}^* v_i^*$, and[3] $u_i^* \sim v_i^*$,
- all marks on function symbols in r^*, s_i^*, t_i^*, and $x\sigma^*$ (for every variable $x \in \mathcal{EV}ar(\rho)$) are mutually distinct and fresh w.r.t. s^*.

We call $\Rightarrow_{\mathcal{R}} = \bigcup_{n \ge 0} \Rightarrow_{\mathcal{R}_n}$ *(term) graph rewrite relation* w.r.t. $\mathcal{R}$.

$l^*\sigma^*$ is called the *contracted marked redex* in s^*. We use the notation $s^* \Rightarrow_{\mathcal{R}_n}^{l^*\sigma^*} t^*$ to specify the contracted marked redex. Note that all shared subterms $l^*\sigma^*$ are replaced simultaneously by $r^*\sigma^*$.

Definition 9.4.3 The *deterministic* graph rewrite relation $\Rightarrow_{\mathcal{R}^d}$ is defined analogously to $\Rightarrow_{\mathcal{R}}$, but in a $\Rightarrow_{\mathcal{R}^d}$ rewrite step it is additionally required that $x\sigma^*$ is a marked ground constructor term for every extra variable x in $l \to r \Leftarrow c$.

[3]Note that $u_i^* \cong v_i^*$ is not required.

To illustrate how conditional graph rewriting works, let $\mathcal{R}$ be the CTRS $\mathcal{R}_{fib}$ from Example 7.2.65 augmented by the rules $double(x) \to x + x$ and $snd(\langle x, y\rangle) \to y$. There is the $\Rightarrow_{\mathcal{R}}$ (in fact, $\Rightarrow_{\mathcal{R}^d}$) reduction sequence:

$$\begin{array}{ll} & double^0(snd^1(fib^2(s^3(0^4)))) \\ \Rightarrow_{\mathcal{R}} & snd^1(fib^2(s^3(0^4))) +^5 snd^1(fib^2(s^3(0^4))) \\ \Rightarrow_{\mathcal{R}} & snd^1(t^*) +^5 snd^1(t^*) \\ \Rightarrow_{\mathcal{R}} & (0^8 +^{12} s^9(0^{10})) +^5 (0^8 +^{12} s^9(0^{10})) \\ \Rightarrow_{\mathcal{R}} & s^9(0^{10}) +^5 s^9(0^{10}) \end{array}$$

because $fib^6(0^4) \Rightarrow_{\mathcal{R}} \langle 0^8, s^9(0^{10})\rangle^7$. In the derivation, t^* denotes the marked term $\langle s^9(0^{10}), 0^8 +^{12} s^9(0^{10})\rangle^{11}$.

9.4.1 Adequacy

Next we will show that the mapping e that erases all marks from a well-marked term is adequate in the sense of Kennaway et al. [KKSV94]. That is, it is surjective, it preserves normal forms, it preserves reductions, and it is cofinal. Surjectivity ensures that every term can be represented as a directed acyclic graph (well-marked term). The normal form condition ensures that a graph is a final result of a computation if the term that it represents is, and vice versa. Preservation of reduction ensures that every graph reduction sequence represents some term reduction sequence. Cofinality ensures that for every term rewriting computation, there is a graph rewriting computation that can be mapped, not necessarily to that term rewriting computation, but to some extension of it.

Theorem 9.4.4 *For all $n \in \mathbb{N}$, $\Rightarrow_{\mathcal{R}^d_n}$ is an adequate implementation of $\to_{\mathcal{R}^d_n}$, that is,*

1. *e is surjective,*
2. *$\forall t^* \in \mathcal{T}_w(\mathcal{F}^*, \mathcal{V}^*)$: $t^* \in NF(\Rightarrow_{\mathcal{R}^d_n})$ if and only if $e(t^*) \in NF(\to_{\mathcal{R}^d_n})$,*
3. *$\forall s^* \in \mathcal{T}_w(\mathcal{F}^*, \mathcal{V}^*)$: if $s^* \Rightarrow^*_{\mathcal{R}^d_n} t^*$, then $e(s^*) \to^*_{\mathcal{R}^d_n} e(t^*)$,*
4. *$\forall s^* \in \mathcal{T}_w(\mathcal{F}^*, \mathcal{V}^*)$: if $e(s^*) \to^*_{\mathcal{R}^d_n} u$, then there is a $t^* \in \mathcal{T}_w(\mathcal{F}^*, \mathcal{V}^*)$ such that $s^* \Rightarrow^*_{\mathcal{R}^d_n} t^*$ and $u \to^*_{\mathcal{R}^d_n} e(t^*)$.*

Proof We use induction on n.

(1) Surjectivity is obvious.

(2) The if direction is easily shown. For an indirect proof of the only-if direction, suppose $e(t^*) \notin NF(\to_{\mathcal{R}^d_n})$, i.e., $e(t^*) = C[l\sigma] \to_{\mathcal{R}^d_n} C[r\sigma]$ by using the rule $\rho : l \to r \Leftarrow s_1 == t_1, \ldots, s_k == t_k$ at position p. So, for every $s_i == t_i$, there is a ground constructor term u_i such that $s_i\sigma \to^*_{\mathcal{R}^d_{n-1}} u_i$ and $t_i\sigma \to^*_{\mathcal{R}^d_{n-1}} u_i$. Let l^* and σ^* be marked versions of

l and σ such that $t^*|_p = l^*\sigma^*$. Let $l^* \to r^* \Leftarrow s_1^* == t_1^*, \ldots, s_k^* == t_k^*$ be a marked version of ρ such that all marks on r^*, s_i^*, and t_i^* are fresh w.r.t. t^* and mutually distinct. Furthermore, σ^* is extended to $\mathcal{EV}ar(\rho)$ in the usual way: For all $z \in \mathcal{EV}ar(\rho)$ let $z\sigma^*$ be a marked version of $z\sigma$ such that all marks are mutually distinct and fresh w.r.t. t^*, r^*, s_i^*, and t_i^*. Let $C^*[,\ldots,]$ be the marked context such that $t^* = C^*[l^*\sigma^*,\ldots,l^*\sigma^*]$ and $l^*\sigma^*$ is not a subterm of $C^*[,\ldots,]$. Because $e(s_i^*\sigma^*) = s_i\sigma \to^*_{\mathcal{R}^d_{n-1}} u_i$, $e(t_i^*\sigma^*) = t_i\sigma \to^*_{\mathcal{R}^d_{n-1}} u_i$, and u_i is a ground constructor term, it follows from the inductive hypothesis that there exist marked terms v_i^* and w_i^* such that $s_i^*\sigma^* \Rightarrow^*_{\mathcal{R}^d_{n-1}} v_i^*$, $t_i^*\sigma^* \Rightarrow^*_{\mathcal{R}^d_{n-1}} w_i^*$, and $e(v_i^*) = u_i = e(w_i^*)$. The latter particularly implies that v_i^* and w_i^* are ground constructor terms and $v_i^* \sim w_i^*$. Therefore, $t^* \Rightarrow_{\mathcal{R}^d_n} C^*[r^*\sigma^*,\ldots,r^*\sigma^*]$, which contradicts $t^* \in NF(\Rightarrow_{\mathcal{R}^d_n})$.

(3) We proceed by induction on the length ℓ of $s^* \Rightarrow^*_{\mathcal{R}^d_n} t^*$. The base case $\ell = 0$ clearly holds. Thus consider $s^* \Rightarrow^{l^*\sigma^*}_{\mathcal{R}^d_n} u^* \Rightarrow^{\ell}_{\mathcal{R}_d} t^*$. According to the inductive hypothesis on ℓ, $e(u^*) \to^*_{\mathcal{R}^d_n} e(t^*)$. Because $s^* \Rightarrow^{l^*\sigma^*}_{\mathcal{R}^d_n} u^*$, we have $s^* = C^*[l^*\sigma^*,\ldots,l^*\sigma^*]$, $l^*\sigma^*$ is not a subterm of $C^*[,\ldots,]$, $u^* = C^*[r^*\sigma^*,\ldots,r^*\sigma^*]$, and, for every $s_i^* == t_i^*$, there are marked ground constructor terms u_i^* and v_i^* such that $s_i^*\sigma^* \Rightarrow^*_{\mathcal{R}^d_{n-1}} u_i^*$, $t_i^*\sigma^* \Rightarrow^*_{\mathcal{R}^d_{n-1}} v_i^*$, and $u_i^* \sim v_i^*$. Let $\sigma = e(\sigma^*)$, i.e., $x\sigma = e(x\sigma^*)$ for all $x \in \mathcal{D}om(\sigma^*)$. By the inductive hypothesis on n, $e(s_i^*)\sigma \to^*_{\mathcal{R}^d_{n-1}} e(u_i^*) = e(v_i^*) \,{}^*_{\mathcal{R}^d_{n-1}}\!\leftarrow e(t_i^*)\sigma$. Hence $l\sigma \to_{\mathcal{R}^d_n} r\sigma$ and $e(s^*) \to^+_{\mathcal{R}^d_n} e(t^*)$.

(4) We use induction on the length ℓ of $e(s^*) \to^*_{\mathcal{R}^d} u$. The proof is illustrated in Figure 9.1. The case $\ell = 0$ holds. Consider $e(s^*) \to^{\ell}_{\mathcal{R}^d_n} \overline{u} \to_{\mathcal{R}^d_n} u$. By the inductive hypothesis on ℓ, there exists a $\overline{t}^* \in \mathcal{T}_w(\mathcal{F}^*, \mathcal{V}^*)$ such that $s^* \Rightarrow^*_{\mathcal{R}^d_n} \overline{t}^*$ and $\overline{u} \to^*_{\mathcal{R}^d_n} e(\overline{t}^*)$. Let $\overline{t} = e(\overline{t}^*)$. Suppose $\overline{u} = C[l\sigma] \to_{\mathcal{R}^d_n} C[r\sigma] = u$ by using the rule $\rho : l \to r \Leftarrow s_1 == t_1, \ldots, s_k == t_k$ at the position p, i.e., $C[l\sigma]|_p = l\sigma$. By the parallel moves Lemma 7.4.19 for $\to_{\mathcal{R}^d_n}$, there is a $v \in \mathcal{T}(\mathcal{F}, \mathcal{V})$ such that $u \mathrel{+\!\!\!\!\!\!\;+\!\!\!\!\!\!\rightarrow}^*_{\mathcal{R}^d_n} v$ and $\overline{t} \mathrel{+\!\!\!\!\!\!\;+\!\!\!\!\!\!\rightarrow}_{\mathcal{R}^d_n} v$. As a matter of fact, if one extends the notion of descendant from Definition 4.3.6 to the conditional case, then the parallel moves Lemma 7.4.19 can be formulated as the parallel moves Lemma 4.3.10 for orthogonal unconditional TRSs; see [Ohl01a] for details. In particular, the redexes contracted in the step $\overline{t} \mathrel{+\!\!\!\!\!\!\;+\!\!\!\!\!\!\rightarrow}_{\mathcal{R}^d_n} v$ are the descendants $p\backslash(\overline{u} \to^*_{\mathcal{R}^d_n} \overline{t})$ of p in $\overline{t}$. Let $Q = p\backslash(\overline{u} \to^*_{\mathcal{R}^d_n} \overline{t})$. Note that $Q \subseteq \mathcal{P}os(\overline{t})$ consists of pairwise independent positions. For every $q \in Q$, $\overline{t}^*|_q$ can be written as $\overline{t}^*|_q = l_q^*\tau_q^*$, where l_q^* is a marked version of l and τ_q^* is a marked substitution. As in the proof of (2), one can show that $l_q^*\tau_q^* \Rightarrow_{\mathcal{R}^d_n} r^*\tau_q^*$. Let

$$Q' = \{q' \in \mathcal{P}os(\overline{t}^*) \mid \overline{t}^*|_{q'} = l_q^*\tau_q^* \text{ for some } q \in Q\}$$

$$
\begin{array}{ccccccc}
e(s^*) & \longrightarrow^{\ell}_{\mathcal{R}_n^d} & \overline{u} & \longrightarrow_{\mathcal{R}_n^d} & u & & \\
 & & {\scriptstyle *}\downarrow{\scriptstyle \mathcal{R}_n^d} & & {\scriptstyle *}\downarrow{\scriptstyle \mathcal{R}_n^d} & & \\
 & & e(\overline{t}^*) & \longrightarrow^*_{\mathcal{R}_n^d} & v & \longrightarrow^*_{\mathcal{R}_n^d} & e(t^*) \\
 & & & & & & \\
s^* & \Longrightarrow^*_{\mathcal{R}_n^d} & \overline{t}^* & \Longrightarrow^*_{\mathcal{R}_n^d} & & & t^*
\end{array}
$$

FIGURE 9.1. Proof of Theorem 9.4.4.

Note that $Q \subseteq Q'$. It is not difficult to prove that Q' consists of pairwise independent positions. Let t^* be the marked term obtained from $\overline{t}^*$ by contracting all the redexes $l_q^*\tau_q^*$. Let $\tau_q = e(\tau_q^*)$. Because $\overline{t} \twoheadrightarrow\!\!\!\!\!\!\!\shortparallel_{\mathcal{R}_n^d} v$ by contracting the redexes in Q and $\overline{t} \twoheadrightarrow\!\!\!\!\!\!\!\shortparallel_{\mathcal{R}_n^d} e(t^*)$ by contracting the redexes in Q', it follows that $v \twoheadrightarrow\!\!\!\!\!\!\!\shortparallel_{\mathcal{R}_n^d} e(t^*)$ by contracting the redexes in $Q' \setminus Q$. All in all, $s^* \Rightarrow^*_{\mathcal{R}_n^d} t^*$ and $u \rightarrow^*_{\mathcal{R}_n^d} e(t^*)$. □

Corollary 9.4.5 $\forall n \in \mathbb{N}:$ $\Rightarrow_{\mathcal{R}_n}$ *is an adequate implementation of* $\rightarrow_{\mathcal{R}_n}$.

Proof One can prove statements (1)–(3) as in Theorem 9.4.4. Statement (4) remains to be shown: For $s^* \in \mathcal{T}_w(\mathcal{F}^*, \mathcal{V}^*)$ and $u \in \mathcal{T}(\mathcal{F}, \mathcal{V})$ with $e(s^*) \rightarrow^*_{\mathcal{R}_n} u$, there must be a $t^* \in \mathcal{T}_w(\mathcal{F}^*, \mathcal{V}^*)$ such that $s^* \Rightarrow^*_{\mathcal{R}_n} t^*$ and $u \rightarrow^*_{\mathcal{R}_n} e(t^*)$.

By Proposition 7.4.21, there is a term v such that $e(s^*) \rightarrow^*_{\mathcal{R}_n^d} v \;{}^*_{\mathcal{R}_n^d}\!\leftarrow u$. By Theorem 9.4.4, there is a marked term t^* such that $s^* \Rightarrow^*_{\mathcal{R}_n^d} t^*$ and $v \rightarrow^*_{\mathcal{R}_n^d} e(t^*)$. In fact, this t^* does the job because $\Rightarrow_{\mathcal{R}_n^d} \subseteq \Rightarrow_{\mathcal{R}_n}$, $u \rightarrow^*_{\mathcal{R}_n^d} v \rightarrow^*_{\mathcal{R}_n^d} e(t^*)$, and $\rightarrow_{\mathcal{R}_n^d} \subseteq \rightarrow_{\mathcal{R}_n}$. □

Corollary 9.4.6 $\Rightarrow_{\mathcal{R}}$ *is an adequate implementation of* $\rightarrow_{\mathcal{R}}$.

Proof The proof follows immediately from Corollary 9.4.5. □

It is a direct consequence of the preceding results that $\Rightarrow_{\mathcal{R}}$ is a sound and complete implementation of $\rightarrow_{\mathcal{R}}$ in the sense of Barendregt et al. [BEG+87]. Recall that soundness ensures that the graph implementation of a CTRS cannot give incorrect results, while completeness ensures that graph rewriting gives all results.

Corollary 9.4.7 $\Rightarrow_{\mathcal{R}}$ *is a sound and complete implementation of* $\rightarrow_{\mathcal{R}}$, *i.e.,*

1. $s^* \Rightarrow^*_{\mathcal{R}} t^* \in NF(\Rightarrow_{\mathcal{R}})$ *implies* $e(s^*) \rightarrow^*_{\mathcal{R}} e(t^*) \in NF(\rightarrow_{\mathcal{R}})$ *(soundness),*

2. $\forall s^* \in \mathcal{T}_w(\mathcal{F}^*, \mathcal{V}^*)$: *if* $e(s^*) \rightarrow^*_{\mathcal{R}} u \in NF(\rightarrow_{\mathcal{R}})$, *then there is a marked term* t^* *such that* $s^* \Rightarrow^*_{\mathcal{R}} t^* \in NF(\Rightarrow_{\mathcal{R}})$ *and* $e(t^*) = u$ *(completeness).*

Proof The proof follows directly from Corollary 9.4.6. □

Note that in the entire section, there is only one place where we made use of the fact that $\mathcal{R}$ is orthogonal: Theorem 9.4.4(4) crucially depends on the fact that the parallel moves lemma holds for $\rightarrow_{\mathcal{R}_n^d}$. Because the parallel moves lemma remains valid if $\mathcal{R}$ is almost orthogonal, so do all of the preceding results if we replace orthogonality with almost orthogonality.

We conclude this section by showing why one has to impose certain restrictions. We have already seen that orthogonality is necessary for completeness. The other two conditions in the definition of almost functional 3-CTRSs are also necessary, as the following example shows.

Example 9.4.8 Let $\mathcal{R}$ consist of the rules

$$\begin{array}{rcll} a & \rightarrow & x & \Leftarrow g(x) == e \\ g(b) & \rightarrow & e & \\ g(c) & \rightarrow & e & \\ h(x) & \rightarrow & f(x,x) & \\ f(b,c) & \rightarrow & d & \end{array}$$

Because $a \rightarrow_{\mathcal{R}} b$ and $a \rightarrow_{\mathcal{R}} c$ (consequently, the system is not confluent), it follows that $h(a) \rightarrow_{\mathcal{R}} f(a,a) \rightarrow_{\mathcal{R}}^* f(b,c) \rightarrow_{\mathcal{R}} d$. In the corresponding graph rewrite relation, however, $f(a,a)$ does not reduce to $f(b,c)$, and hence it does not reduce to the normal form d. That is, the graph implementation is not complete.

In fact, $\mathcal{R}$ is not almost functional because the variable x in $g(x)$ does not occur on the left-hand side a of the first rule. If we replace the condition $g(x) == e$ with $e == g(x)$, then the resulting 3-CTRS is also not almost functional because $g(x)$ is not a constructor term.

The next example shows why we need $u_i^* \sim v_i^*$ but not $u_i^* \cong v_i^*$ in Definition 9.4.2.

Example 9.4.9 In the CTRS

$$\mathcal{R} = \left\{ \begin{array}{lll} g(x) & \rightarrow c(x,x) & \\ f(x) & \rightarrow x & \Leftarrow g(x) \rightarrow c(d,d) \end{array} \right.$$

$f^0(d^1)$ rewrites to d^1 because $g^2(d^1) \Rightarrow_{\mathcal{R}} c^3(d^1,d^1)$ and $e(c^3(d^1,d^1)) = c(d,d) = e(c^4(d^5,d^6))$. If $c^3(d^1,d^1) \cong c^4(d^5,d^6)$ were required, then $f^0(d^1)$ would be a normal form w.r.t. $\Rightarrow_{\mathcal{R}}$ and graph rewriting would not be an adequate implementation of conditional term rewriting because $f(d)$ is not a normal form w.r.t. $\rightarrow_{\mathcal{R}}$.

9.4.2 Confluence

In this section it will be shown that orthogonal conditional rules give rise to a subcommutative deterministic graph rewrite relation (up to isomorphism). This implies that the graph rewrite relation is Church-Rosser modulo $\cong$. Similar results for unconditional systems were achieved by Staples [Sta80] and Barendregt et al. [BEG$^+$87]. In order to prove the preceding statement, the following auxiliary result is useful.

Lemma 9.4.10 *Let $\Rightarrow_n$ denote $\Rightarrow_{\mathcal{R}_n^d}$ or $\Rightarrow_{\mathcal{R}_n}$. If $s^* \cong t^* \Rightarrow_n^\ell u^*$ (so the reduction of t^* to u^* consists of ℓ graph rewrite steps), then there is a marked term v^* such that $s^* \Rightarrow_n^\ell v^* \cong u^*$.*

Proof Because $s^* \cong t^*$, there is bijective function $\Phi : marks(t^*) \to marks(s^*)$ with $\Phi(t^*) = s^*$. We show that Φ can be extended to a bijective function $marks(t^*) \cup marks(u^*) \to marks(s^*) \cup marks(\Phi(u^*))$ such that $\Phi(t^*) = s^* \Rightarrow_n^\ell \Phi(u^*) \cong u^*$.

The claim obviously holds for $\ell = 0$. We show the lemma for $\ell = 1$, the whole claim then follows by induction on the length of the reduction sequence. We proceed further by induction on the depth n. Suppose $t^* \Rightarrow_n^{l^*\sigma^*} u^*$, where a marked version of the rule $\rho : l \to r \Leftarrow s_1 == t_1, \ldots, s_k == t_k$ is used. Then for every $1 \le i \le k$, there are marked ground constructor terms u_i^* and v_i^* such that $s_i^*\sigma^* \Rightarrow_{n-1}^* u_i^*$, $t_i^*\sigma^* \Rightarrow_{n-1}^* v_i^*$, and $u_i^* \sim v_i^*$. Let M_1 be the set of all fresh marks used in r_1^* and in the sequences $s_i^*\sigma^* \Rightarrow_{n-1}^* u_i^*$ and $t_i^*\sigma^* \Rightarrow_{n-1}^* v_i^*$, $1 \le i \le k$. Moreover, let M_2 be a set of (fresh) marks with $M_2 \cap (M_1 \cup marks(s^*) \cup marks(t^*)) = \emptyset$ and $card(M_2) = card(M_1)$, where $card(M_i)$ denotes the cardinality of M_i. Let $\Phi' : M_1 \to M_2$ be an arbitrary bijective function. Now we extend Φ from $marks(t^*)$ to $M_1 \cup marks(t^*)$ by

$$\Phi(\mu) = \Phi'(\mu) \text{ if } \mu \in M_1$$

Clearly, $\Phi : M_1 \cup marks(t^*) \to M_2 \cup marks(s^*)$ is bijective. By the inductive hypothesis on n, we have $\Phi(s_i^*\sigma^*) \Rightarrow_{n-1}^* \Phi(u_i^*) \cong u_i^*$ and $\Phi(t_i^*\sigma^*) \Rightarrow_{n-1}^* \Phi(v_i^*) \cong v_i^*$ for all $1 \le i \le k$. Because $e(\Phi(u_i^*)) = e(u_i^*) = e(v_i^*) = e(\Phi(v_i^*))$, we infer $s^* = \Phi(t^*) \Rightarrow_n \Phi(u^*)$. Finally, $\Phi(u^*) \cong u^*$ because the restriction of Φ to $marks(u^*) \to marks(\Phi(u^*))$ is bijective. □

The next lemma shows that the deterministic graph rewrite relation is subcommutative modulo $\cong$.

Lemma 9.4.11 *For all $m, n \in \mathbb{N}$, the following statements hold:*

1. *If $s^* = l_1^*\sigma_1^* \Rightarrow_{\mathcal{R}_m^d} r_1^*\sigma_1^*$ and $s^* = l_2^*\sigma_2^* \Rightarrow_{\mathcal{R}_n^d} r_2^*\sigma_2^*$, then $r_1^*\sigma_1^* \cong r_2^*\sigma_2^*$.*

2. *If $s^* \Rightarrow_{\mathcal{R}_m^d}^{l_1^*\sigma_1^*} \overline{s}^*$, $t^* \Rightarrow_{\mathcal{R}_n^d}^{l_2^*\sigma_2^*} \overline{t}^*$, and $s^* \cong t^*$, then there are marked terms $\tilde{s}^*$ and $\tilde{t}^*$ such that (i) $\overline{s}^* \Rightarrow_{\mathcal{R}_n^d}^{l_2^*\sigma_2^*} \tilde{s}^*$ or $\overline{s}^* = \tilde{s}^*$, (ii) $\overline{t}^* \Rightarrow_{\mathcal{R}_m^d}^{l_1^*\sigma_1^*} \tilde{t}^*$ or $\overline{t}^* = \tilde{t}^*$, and (iii) $\tilde{s}^* \cong \tilde{t}^*$.*

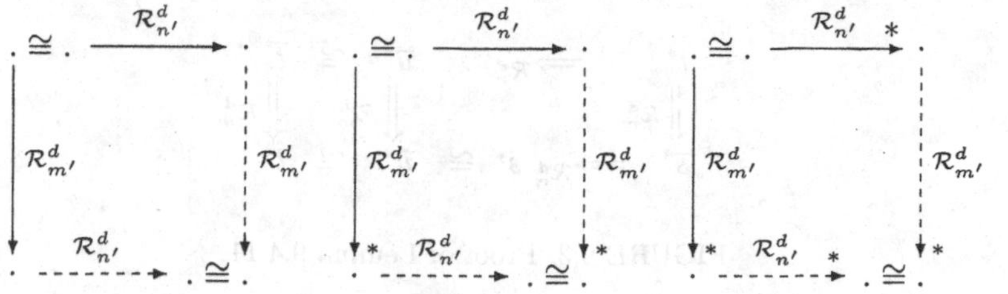

FIGURE 9.2. The inductive hypothesis of Lemma 9.4.11.

Proof We proceed by induction on $m+n$. The base case $m+n=0$ holds vacuously. Suppose the lemma holds for all m' and n' with $m'+n'<\ell$. In the induction step, we have to prove that the lemma holds for all m and n with $m+n=\ell$. By using Lemma 9.4.10, it is not difficult to prove that the inductive hypothesis implies the validity of the diagrams in Figure 9.2, where $m'+n'<\ell$ and $\rightarrow$ stands for $\Rightarrow$.

(1) Let $s^* = l_1^*\sigma_1^* \Rightarrow_{\mathcal{R}_m^d} r_1^*\sigma_1^*$ and $s^* = l_2^*\sigma_2^* \Rightarrow_{\mathcal{R}_n^d} r_2^*\sigma_2^*$. Clearly, $l_1^* \rightarrow r_1^* \Leftarrow c_1^*$ and $l_2^* \rightarrow r_2^* \Leftarrow c_2^*$ are marked versions of the same rewrite rule $\rho : l \rightarrow r \Leftarrow c \in \mathcal{R}$ because $\mathcal{R}$ is orthogonal. Apparently, the restrictions of σ_1^* and σ_2^* to $\mathcal{V}ar(l)$ coincide. So if $\mathcal{V}ar(r) \subseteq \mathcal{V}ar(l)$, then $r_1^*\sigma_1^* \cong r_2^*\sigma_2^*$ because r_1^* and r_2^* are freshly marked. Suppose otherwise that $\mathcal{V}ar(r) \not\subseteq \mathcal{V}ar(l)$. In this case we show that $\sigma_1^* \cong \sigma_2^*$ holds. Because $\sigma_1^* = \sigma_2^*\ [\mathcal{V}ar(l)]$, it remains to be shown that $\sigma_1^* \cong \sigma_2^*\ [\mathcal{EV}ar(\rho)]$. We show by induction on i that $\sigma_1^* \cong \sigma_2^*\ [\mathcal{V}ar(l) \cup \bigcup_{j=1}^{i} \mathcal{V}ar(t_j)]$. If $i=0$, then $\sigma_1^* = \sigma_2^*\ [\mathcal{V}ar(l)]$. So let $i>0$. According to the inductive hypothesis, $\sigma_1^* \cong \sigma_2^*\ [\mathcal{V}ar(l) \cup \bigcup_{j=1}^{i-1} \mathcal{V}ar(t_j)]$. Because $\mathcal{V}ar(s_i) \subseteq \mathcal{V}ar(l) \cup \bigcup_{j=1}^{i-1} \mathcal{V}ar(t_j)$, it is sufficient to show $\sigma_1^* \cong \sigma_2^*\ [\mathcal{V}ar(t_i)]$. There are marked ground constructor terms $u_1^*, u_2^*, v_1^*, v_2^*$ such that $s_i^*\sigma_1^* \Rightarrow^*_{\mathcal{R}_{m-1}^d} u_1^*$, $t_i^*\sigma_1^* \Rightarrow^*_{\mathcal{R}_{m-1}^d} u_2^*$, where $u_1^* \sim u_2^*$, and $s_i^*\sigma_2^* \Rightarrow^*_{\mathcal{R}_{n-1}^d} v_1^*$, $t_i^*\sigma_2^* \Rightarrow^*_{\mathcal{R}_{n-1}^d} v_2^*$, where $v_1^* \sim v_2^*$. It now follows from the inductive hypothesis on ℓ in combination with $s_i^*\sigma_1^* \cong s_i^*\sigma_2^*$ that $u_1^* \cong v_1^*$. Thus $u_2^* \sim u_1^* \sim v_1^* \sim v_2^*$. As in the proof of Lemma 7.4.19, for every extra variable x, there are marked ground constructor terms u_x^* and v_x^* such that $x\sigma_1^* = u_x^*$, $x\sigma_2^* = v_x^*$, and $u_x^* \sim v_x^*$. Because the marks on instantiated extra variables are fresh and mutually distinct, we finally derive $\sigma_1^* \cong \sigma_2^*\ [\mathcal{V}ar(t_i)]$.

(2) By Lemma 9.4.10, it is sufficient to prove that if $t^* \Rightarrow_{\mathcal{R}_m^d}^{l_1^*\sigma_1^*} \overline{s}^*$ and $t^* \Rightarrow_{\mathcal{R}_n^d}^{l_2^*\sigma_2^*} \overline{t}^*$, then (i) $\overline{s}^* \Rightarrow_{\mathcal{R}_n^d}^{l_2^*\sigma_2^*} \tilde{s}^*$ or $\overline{s}^* = \tilde{s}^*$, (ii) $\overline{t}^* \Rightarrow_{\mathcal{R}_m^d}^{l_1^*\sigma_1^*} \tilde{t}^*$ or $\overline{t}^* = \tilde{t}^*$, and (iii) $\tilde{s}^* \cong \tilde{t}^*$ for some marked terms $\tilde{s}^*$ and $\tilde{t}^*$. We distinguish three cases:

(a) $l_1^*\sigma_1^* = l_2^*\sigma_2^*$,
(b) $l_1^*\sigma_1^*$ is neither a subterm of $l_2^*\sigma_2^*$ nor conversely,
(c) $l_1^*\sigma_1^*$ is a proper subterm of $l_2^*\sigma_2^*$.

(a) With the aid of (1), this follows easily.

$$
\begin{array}{ccccccc}
t^* & \Longrightarrow_{\mathcal{R}_n^d} & & & \overline{u}^* & \cong & \overline{t}^* \\
\Big\Downarrow \mathcal{R}_m^d & & & & \Big\Downarrow \mathcal{R}_m^d & & \Big\Downarrow \mathcal{R}_m^d \\
\overline{s}^* & \Longrightarrow_{\mathcal{R}_n^d} & \tilde{s}^* & \cong & \tilde{u}^* & \cong & \tilde{t}^*
\end{array}
$$

FIGURE 9.3. Proof of Lemma 9.4.11.

(b) The proof is analogous to proposition 3.19(1), case 1 in [KO95b]. We may write $t^* = C^*[l^*_{i_1}\sigma^*_{i_1}, \ldots, l^*_{i_p}\sigma^*_{i_p}]$, where $i_j \in \{1,2\}$ for every index $j \in \{1,\ldots,p\}$. Without loss of generality, we may assume that $1 = i_1 \leq i_2 \leq \cdots \leq i_p = 2$. That is, $t^* = C^*[l^*_1\sigma^*_1, \ldots, l^*_2\sigma^*_2]$. Then $\overline{s}^* = C^*[r^*_1\sigma^*_1, \ldots, l^*_2\sigma^*_2]$ and $\overline{t}^* = C^*[l^*_1\sigma^*_1, \ldots, r^*_2\sigma^*_2]$. According to Lemma 9.4.10, we may assume that all marks on function symbols in r^*_1, r^*_2, $x\sigma^*_1$ and $y\sigma^*_2$ (for every variable $x \in \mathcal{EV}ar(l_1 \to r_1 \Leftarrow c_1)$ and $y \in \mathcal{EV}ar(l_2 \to r_2 \Leftarrow c_2)$) are pairwise distinct and fresh w.r.t. t^*. (If $(marks(r^*_1) \cup marks(\sigma^*_1)) \cap (marks(r^*_2) \cup marks(\sigma^*_2)) \neq \emptyset$, then we take marked versions $\overline{r}^*_2$ and $\overline{\sigma}^*_2$ with $(marks(r^*_1) \cup marks(\sigma^*_1)) \cap (marks(\overline{r}^*_2) \cup marks(\overline{\sigma}^*_2)) = \emptyset$, observe that $t^* \Rightarrow^{l^*_2\overline{\sigma}^*_2}_{\mathcal{R}^d_n} C^*[l^*_1\sigma^*_1, \ldots, \overline{r}^*_2\overline{\sigma}^*_2] = \overline{u}^*$, and apply Lemma 9.4.10; see Figure 9.3.) Now if we contract the redex $l^*_2\sigma^*_2$ in $\overline{s}^*$ to $r^*_2\sigma^*_2$, then we obtain $\tilde{s}^* = C^*[r^*_1\sigma^*_1, \ldots, r^*_2\sigma^*_2]$. Analogously, contracting $l^*_1\sigma^*_1$ in $\overline{t}^*$ yields $\tilde{t}^* = C^*[r^*_1\sigma^*_1, \ldots, r^*_2\sigma^*_2]$.

(c) We proceed in analogy to proposition 3.19(1), case 2 in [KO95b]. As in (b), we may write t^* as

$$t^* = C^*[l^*_1\sigma^*_1, \ldots, l^*_2\sigma^*_2] = C^*[l^*_1\sigma^*_1, \ldots, \overline{C}^*[l^*_1\sigma^*_1, \ldots, l^*_1\sigma^*_1]]$$

where $l^*_2\sigma^*_2 = \overline{C}^*[l^*_1\sigma^*_1, \ldots, l^*_1\sigma^*_1]$, and $l^*_1\sigma^*_1$ is neither a subterm of $C^*[,\ldots,]$ nor of $\overline{C}^*[,\ldots,]$. Hence

$$\overline{s}^* = C^*[r^*_1\sigma^*_1, \ldots, \overline{C}^*[r^*_1\sigma^*_1, \ldots, r^*_1\sigma^*_1]]$$

$$\overline{t}^* = C^*[l^*_1\sigma^*_1, \ldots, r^*_2\sigma^*_2] = C^*[l^*_1\sigma^*_1, \ldots, \tilde{C}^*[l^*_1\sigma^*_1, \ldots, l^*_1\sigma^*_1]$$

for some context $\tilde{C}^*[,\ldots,]$ that does not contain $l^*_1\sigma^*_1$. Again, by Lemma 9.4.10 we may assume that the marks on function symbols in r^*_1, r^*_2, $x\sigma^*_1$ and $y\sigma^*_2$ (for all extra variables x and y) are pairwise distinct and fresh w.r.t. t^*. Observe that no occurrence of $\overline{C}^*[r^*_1\sigma^*_1, \ldots, r^*_1\sigma^*_1]$ can be found in $\overline{s}^*$ aside from those obtained by contracting the marked redex $l^*_1\sigma^*_1$ because we use fresh marks. For the same reason, $C^*[,\ldots,\tilde{C}^*[,\ldots,]]$ does not contain $l^*_1\sigma^*_1$. Now if $l^*_1\sigma^*_1$ is not a subterm of $\overline{t}^*$, then let $\tilde{t}^* = \overline{t}^*$. Otherwise define

$$\tilde{t}^* = C^*[r^*_1\sigma^*_1, \ldots, \tilde{C}^*[r^*_1\sigma^*_1, \ldots, r^*_1\sigma^*_1]]$$

and observe that $\overline{t}^* \Rightarrow^{l^*_1\sigma^*_1}_{\mathcal{R}} \tilde{t}^*$. The situation is depicted in Figure 9.4,

$$\begin{array}{ccc} t^* & \Longrightarrow_{l_2^*\sigma_2^*} & \overline{t}^* \\ \Big\Downarrow l_1^*\sigma_1^* & & \Big\Downarrow l_1^*\sigma_1^* \\ \overline{s}^* & & \tilde{t}^* \end{array}$$

FIGURE 9.4. Proof of Lemma 9.4.11.

where $l_2^*\sigma_2^* = \overline{C}^*[l_1^*\sigma_1^*, \ldots, l_1^*\sigma_1^*] \Rightarrow_{\mathcal{R}} \tilde{C}^*[l_1^*\sigma_1^*, \ldots, l_1^*\sigma_1^*] = r_2^*\sigma_2^*$. Next we will show that $\overline{C}^*[r_1^*\sigma_1^*, \ldots, r_1^*\sigma_1^*] \Rightarrow_{\mathcal{R}_n^d} \tilde{C}^*[r_1^*\sigma_1^*, \ldots, r_1^*\sigma_1^*]$. To this end, recall that $l_2^*\sigma_2^* = \overline{C}^*[l_1^*\sigma_1^*, \ldots, l_1^*\sigma_1^*] \Rightarrow_{\mathcal{R}_n^d} r_2^*\sigma_2^*$. Thus, for every $s_i^* == t_i^*$ in c_2^*, there exist marked ground constructor terms u_i^* and v_i^* such that $s_i^*\sigma_2^* \Rightarrow^*_{\mathcal{R}_{n-1}^d} u_i^*$, $t_i^*\sigma_2^* \Rightarrow^*_{\mathcal{R}_{n-1}^d} v_i^*$, and $u_i^* \sim v_i^*$. Because $\mathcal{R}$ is orthogonal, for every occurrence of $l_1^*\sigma_1^*$, there is a variable $x \in \mathcal{V}ar(l_2)$ such that $x\sigma_2^* = C_x^*[l_1^*\sigma_1^*, \ldots, l_1^*\sigma_1^*]$ contains this particular occurrence. Define $\overline{\sigma}_2^*$ by $x\overline{\sigma}_2^* = C_x^*[r_1^*\sigma_1^*, \ldots, r_1^*\sigma_1^*]$ for all those variables x and $y\overline{\sigma}_2^* = y\sigma_2^*$ otherwise. Now $l_2^*\overline{\sigma}_2^* \Rightarrow_{\mathcal{R}_n^d} r_2^*\overline{\sigma}_2^* = \tilde{C}^*[r_1^*\sigma_1^*, \ldots, r_1^*\sigma_1^*]$. In order to see this, use the inductive hypothesis on ℓ in conjunction with $s_i^*\sigma_2^* \Rightarrow^*_{\mathcal{R}_{n-1}^d} u_i^*$ and $s_i^*\sigma_2^* \Rightarrow_{\mathcal{R}_m^d} s_i^*\overline{\sigma}_2^*$ to infer that there is a marked ground constructor term $\overline{u}_i^*$ such that $s_i^*\overline{\sigma}_2^* \Rightarrow^*_{\mathcal{R}_{n-1}^d} \overline{u}_i^*$ and $u_i^* \cong \overline{u}_i^*$. Analogously, there is a marked ground constructor term $\overline{v}_i^*$ such that $t_i^*\overline{\sigma}_2^* \Rightarrow^*_{\mathcal{R}_{n-1}^d} \overline{v}_i^*$, and $v_i^* \cong \overline{v}_i^*$. Hence the claim follows from $\overline{u}_i^* \sim u_i^* \sim v_i^* \sim \overline{v}_i^*$. □

Corollary 9.4.12 $\forall n \in \mathbb{N}$: *$\Rightarrow_{\mathcal{R}_n^d}$ is almost Church-Rosser modulo $\cong$.*

Proof The proof is an immediate consequence of Lemma 9.4.11. □

In order to show that $\Rightarrow_{\mathcal{R}}$ is Church-Rosser modulo $\cong$, we need one more proposition.

Proposition 9.4.13 *If $s^* \Rightarrow^*_{\mathcal{R}_n} t^*$, then there are marked terms u^* and v^* such that $s^* \Rightarrow^*_{\mathcal{R}_n^d} u^*, t^* \Rightarrow^*_{\mathcal{R}_n^d} v^*$, and $u^* \cong v^*$.*

Proof We proceed by induction on the depth n of $s^* \Rightarrow^*_{\mathcal{R}_n} t^*$. The proposition holds vacuously for $n = 0$. So let $n > 0$. We proceed further by induction on the length ℓ of the reduction sequence $s^* \Rightarrow^*_{\mathcal{R}_n} t^*$. The case $\ell = 0$ holds vacuously. Suppose the claim is true for ℓ. In order to show it for $\ell+1$, we consider $s^* = C^*[l^*\sigma^*, \ldots, l^*\sigma^*] \Rightarrow^{l^*\sigma^*}_{\mathcal{R}_n} C^*[r^*\sigma^*, \ldots, r^*\sigma^*] = \overline{t}^* \Rightarrow^{\ell}_{\mathcal{R}_n} t^*$, where $s^* \Rightarrow_{\mathcal{R}_n} \overline{t}^*$ by a marked version of the rule $\rho : l \to r \Leftarrow s_1 == t_1, \ldots, s_k == t_k$. We will show that there are marked terms $\overline{u}^*$ and $\overline{v}^*$ such that $s^* \Rightarrow_{\mathcal{R}_n^d} \overline{u}^*$, $\overline{t}^* \Rightarrow_{\mathcal{R}_n^d} \overline{v}^*$, and $\overline{u}^* \cong \overline{v}^*$. The whole claim then follows from the inductive hypothesis on ℓ in combination with Corollary 9.4.12 and Lemma 9.4.10. Because $s^* \Rightarrow_{\mathcal{R}_n} \overline{t}^*$, there are marked ground constructor terms u_i^* and v_i^* such that $s_i^*\sigma^* \Rightarrow^*_{\mathcal{R}_{n-1}} u_i^*$, $t_i^*\sigma^* \Rightarrow^*_{\mathcal{R}_{n-1}} v_i^*$, and $u_i^* \sim v_i^*$. By the inductive hypothesis on n and the fact that u_i^* is a normal form, we conclude that there are marked terms $\overline{u}_i^*$ and $\overline{v}_i^*$ such that $s_i^*\sigma^* \Rightarrow^*_{\mathcal{R}^d_{n-1}} \overline{u}_i^* \cong u_i^*$ and $t_i^*\sigma^* \Rightarrow^*_{\mathcal{R}^d_{n-1}} \overline{v}_i^* \cong v_i^*$. Note that $\overline{u}_i^* \sim u_i^* \sim v_i^* \sim \overline{v}_i^*$. So if $\mathcal{V}ar(r) \subseteq \mathcal{V}ar(l)$, then $s^* \Rightarrow_{\mathcal{R}^d_n} \overline{t}^*$ and the claim follows. Suppose otherwise that $\mathcal{V}ar(r) \not\subseteq \mathcal{V}ar(l)$ and let $x \in \mathcal{EV}ar(\rho)$. Then $x \in \mathcal{V}ar(t_j)$ for some $s_j^* == t_j^*$. Because $t_j^*\sigma^* \Rightarrow^*_{\mathcal{R}^d_{n-1}} \overline{v}_j^* \cong v_j^*$, t_j^* is a marked constructor term, and $\overline{v}_j^*$ is a marked ground constructor term, it follows that $x\sigma^* \Rightarrow^*_{\mathcal{R}^d_{n-1}} \overline{v}_x^*$ for some ground constructor subterm $\overline{v}_x^*$ of $\overline{v}_j^*$. Note that even if x occurs more than once in t_j^*, every occurrence of $x\sigma^*$ in $t_j^*\sigma^*$ is reduced to $\overline{v}_x^*$ because redexes with identical marks are shared and are thus reduced simultaneously by $\Rightarrow_{\mathcal{R}^d_{n-1}}$. Define $\overline{\sigma}^*$ by $x\overline{\sigma}^* = \overline{v}_x^*$ for every $x \in \mathcal{EV}ar(\rho)$ and $y\overline{\sigma}^* = y\sigma^*$ for every $y \in \mathcal{V}ar(l)$. Let $\overline{v}^* = C^*[r^*\overline{\sigma}^*, \ldots, r^*\overline{\sigma}^*]$. Because $z\sigma^* = z\overline{\sigma}^*$ for every $z \in \mathcal{V}ar(l)$ and $z\sigma^* \Rightarrow^*_{\mathcal{R}^d_{n-1}} z\overline{\sigma}^*$ for every $z \in \mathcal{EV}ar(\rho)$ we derive $\overline{t}^* \Rightarrow^*_{\mathcal{R}^d_{n-1}} \overline{v}^*$ (taking into account that $z\sigma^*$ gets fresh marks for every $z \in \mathcal{EV}ar(\rho)$). We also claim that $s^* \Rightarrow_{\mathcal{R}^d_n} \overline{v}^*$. This is because for every i, $1 \le i \le k$, we can conclude $s_i^*\overline{\sigma}^* \Rightarrow^*_{\mathcal{R}^d_{n-1}} \tilde{u}_i^* \cong \overline{u}_i^*$ (for some $\tilde{u}_i^*$) from $s_i^*\sigma^* \Rightarrow^*_{\mathcal{R}^d_{n-1}} \overline{u}_i^*$, $s_i^*\sigma^* \Rightarrow^*_{\mathcal{R}^d_{n-1}} s_i^*\overline{\sigma}^*$, and the fact that $\Rightarrow_{\mathcal{R}^d_{n-1}}$ is almost Church-Rosser modulo $\cong$. Analogously, $t_i^*\overline{\sigma}^* \Rightarrow^*_{\mathcal{R}^d_{n-1}} \tilde{v}_i^* \cong \overline{v}_i^*$. It then follows from $\tilde{u}_i^* \sim \overline{u}_i^* \sim \overline{v}_i^* \sim \tilde{v}_i^*$ that $l^*\sigma^* = l^*\overline{\sigma}^* \Rightarrow_{\mathcal{R}^d_n} r^*\overline{\sigma}^*$. Hence $s^* = C^*[l^*\overline{\sigma}^*, \ldots, l^*\overline{\sigma}^*] \Rightarrow^{l^*\sigma^*}_{\mathcal{R}^d_n} C^*[r^*\overline{\sigma}^*, \ldots, r^*\overline{\sigma}^*] = \overline{v}^*$. □

Theorem 9.4.14 *For every $n \in \mathbb{N}$, $\Rightarrow_{\mathcal{R}_n}$ is Church-Rosser modulo $\cong$.*

Proof $\Rightarrow_{\mathcal{R}_n}$ is a refinement of $\Rightarrow_{\mathcal{R}^d_n}$ because $\Rightarrow_{\mathcal{R}^d_n} \subseteq \Rightarrow_{\mathcal{R}_n}$. According to Proposition 9.4.13, it is even a compatible refinement of $\Rightarrow_{\mathcal{R}^d_n}$ modulo $\cong$. Because $\Rightarrow_{\mathcal{R}^d_n}$ is confluent modulo $\cong$ by Corollary 9.4.12 and $\Rightarrow_{\mathcal{R}_n}$ is compatible with $\cong$ by Lemma 9.4.10, we can conclude from Corollary 2.6.9 that $\Rightarrow_{\mathcal{R}_n}$ is Church-Rosser modulo $\cong$. □

In contrast to the preceding section, the results in this section do *not* extend to almost orthogonal systems. This can be seen in the following example taken from [Plu99].

Example 9.4.15 In the almost orthogonal TRS

$$\mathcal{R} = \left\{ \begin{array}{lcl} f(x) & \to & g(x,x) \\ f(a) & \to & g(a,a) \end{array} \right.$$

we have $f^0(a^1) \Rightarrow_{\mathcal{R}} g^2(a^1, a^1)$ and $f^0(a^1) \Rightarrow_{\mathcal{R}} g^2(a^3, a^4)$ but $g^2(a^1, a^1) \not\cong g^2(a^3, a^4)$.

We conclude this chapter with the observation that $\Rightarrow_{\mathcal{R}_n}$ and $\Rightarrow_{\mathcal{R}^d_n}$ have the same normal forms.

Corollary 9.4.16 *For every* $n \in \mathbb{N}$, *the sets* $NF(\Rightarrow_{\mathcal{R}_n})$ *and* $NF(\Rightarrow_{\mathcal{R}_n^d})$ *coincide.*

Proof The proof follows from Theorem 9.4.4(2), Corollary 9.4.5(2), and Lemma 7.4.23. □

10 Proving Termination of Logic Programs

Proving correctness of a program consists in showing partial correctness (that is, the program meets its specification) and termination (that is, the program cannot run forever). Methods for deciding termination of programs cannot exist because termination is in general undecidable. This motivates the search for sufficient conditions that guarantee termination of a program. If such a technique is successful, it will return the answer: "Yes, the program is terminating." In all other cases, it might not be able to determine whether the program terminates. In the last decade, the problem of (automatically) proving termination of logic programs has been receiving increasing attention. Many methods have been proposed to prove termination of logic programs; we will not attempt to review all of them here. Instead, we refer to the overview article of De Schreye and Decorte [SD94]; more recent techniques are discussed in Krishna Rao et al. [KRKS98].

There are several different approaches to proving termination of logic programs: The most prominent is the *norm-based* approach; see [SD94] for details. In the *transformational approach*, one transforms a logic program into a (conditional) term rewriting system. If the transformation is *sound*, i.e., termination of the rewrite system implies termination of the logic program, then termination techniques for rewrite systems can be employed to show termination of logic programs. This approach is confined to a certain subclass of logic programs because of the following important difference between logic programming and term rewriting. Term rewriting (and functional programming) is directed in the sense that the instantiated left-hand side of a rule is replaced with the corresponding right-hand side. In logic programming, however, there is no notion of input or output and thus the flow of information is not necessarily directed. Because predicates are relations rather than functions, it is a priori not clear which argument positions of a predicate are input positions and which are output positions. This generality complicates the analysis of logic programs considerably. On the other hand, in most cases the programmer intends the predicate to be used as a function anyway. In these cases, modes can be used to declare which argument positions are input positions and which are output positions. If a logic program is *well-moded*, that is, if it fulfills a certain restriction concerning the flow of information, then the transformational approach is (potentially) applicable.

To our knowledge, the first termination proof technique for well-moded logic programs that uses a transformation into unconditional term rewriting systems was described by Krishna Rao et al. [KRKS98]. Subsequently, Ganzinger and Waldmann [GW93] devised a transformation of well-moded logic programs into deterministic conditional term rewriting systems. If the transformed system $R_{\mathcal{P}}$ is quasi-reductive, then the logic program $\mathcal{P}$ is terminating for every well-moded goal. Ganzinger and Waldmann's method is not only conceptually easier; it is also able to prove termination of logic programs for which the method in [KRKS98] fails. Ganzinger and Waldmann's method, as any other method discussed herein is only applicable if Prolog's left-most selection rule is used, that is, in SLD derivations it is always the left-most literal of a goal selected for the next resolution step (such SLD derivations are called LD derivations in the following). The drawback of their method, however, is the lack of techniques to show quasi-reductivity of CTRSs automatically; see [GW93].

In an unpublished manuscript, Chtourou and Rusinowitch [CR93] stated a second transformation that transforms the conditional system $R_{\mathcal{P}}$ into an *unconditional* TRS such that termination of the transformed TRS implies termination of the logic program $\mathcal{P}$. It turns out that the transformed TRS coincides with the TRS $U(R_{\mathcal{P}})$ obtained by applying the transformation from Definition 7.2.48 to $R_{\mathcal{P}}$. By means of the resulting two-stage transformation, termination of the logic program can be shown by proving termination of a TRS.

Independently, Aguzzi and Modigliani [AM93] described a method that takes a logic program and a goal and transforms them into a TRS and a starting term. In contrast to the other techniques, their method does not require any prior information about modes of predicates because these are computed during the transformation according to a given goal. This complicates a comparison of their approach with the other approaches. For a given well-moded logic program and goal, however, their technique yields a TRS akin to the one obtained by the two-stage transformation of Chtourou and Rusinowitch.

Similar to Aguzzi and Modigliani's approach, Arts and Zantema [AZ95, AZ96] designed an imperative procedure that directly transforms a well-moded logic program $\mathcal{P}$ into an *unconditional* TRS. This TRS is essentially

Method	Requirement
Ganzinger and Waldmann	Quasi-reductivity of $R_\mathcal{P}$
Chtourou and Rusinowitch	Termination of $U(R_\mathcal{P})$
Arts and Zantema	Single-redex termination of $U(R_\mathcal{P})$

TABLE 10.1. Transformational approaches.

the same as $U(R_\mathcal{P})$. They showed that *single-redex* termination (hence *innermost* termination) of $U(R_\mathcal{P})$ suffices to prove termination of $\mathcal{P}$. Consequently, it is remarked in [AZ95] that the suggested method "is applicable to a wider class of logic programs" and hence it is "stronger than the other results."

The results are summarized in Table 10.1. Aguzzi and Modigliani's method is not listed in the table because it cannot be directly compared with the others. For the same reason, two other transformational approaches [Mar94, Raa97] will be discussed at the end of the chapter. In this chapter it will be shown that all three methods from Table 10.1 are equally powerful. That is, a well-moded logic program can be shown to be terminating by any of the methods if one of the methods can successfully be applied. Nevertheless, the two-stage transformation has a certain advantage over the direct transformation of [AZ95]. A well-moded logic program $\mathcal{P}$ is called *uniquely* terminating if every LD derivation starting from a well-moded goal is terminating and computes the same answer substitution. Avenhaus and Loría-Sáenz [ALS94] proved that *unique* termination of a well-moded logic program $\mathcal{P}$ follows from quasi-reductivity of $R_\mathcal{P}$ and the joinability of all conditional critical pairs in $R_\mathcal{P}$. If one is interested in unique termination, then one should not directly transform a logic program $\mathcal{P}$ into $U(R_\mathcal{P})$ because a similar criterion on the level of the TRS $U(R_\mathcal{P})$ is rarely applicable.

It has already been shown by Ganzinger and Waldmann [GW93] that their method is not *complete.* That is, termination of the logic program $\mathcal{P}$ generally does not imply quasi-reductivity $R_\mathcal{P}$. Because the three methods described earlier have equal power, neither of them is complete (in fact, the same counterexample shows this). The same is true for Aguzzi and Modigliani's technique. None of these four papers characterize classes of well-moded logic programs for which the respective transformational approach is complete. In [AM93] it is shown that the transformation applied to an input-driven logic program and goal yields a TRS and a starting term whose reduction tree is finite if and only if the corresponding LD tree is finite. However, we would like to stress that this does *not* imply that the method is complete for the class of input-driven logic programs. Completeness means that termination of the logic program implies termination of the TRS obtained by the transformation and a TRS is terminating if every reduction sequence is finite. Aguzzi and Modigliani's result, however, guarantees only that every reduction sequence starting from the starting term is finite. It does not say anything about the termination behavior of other terms. In this chapter it will be shown that the two-stage transformation is complete for the class of *simply moded* and well-moded logic programs.

The previously mentioned results constitute the theoretical part of this chapter, but the two-stage transformation is also of practical relevance. This is because powerful methods for automatically proving termination of TRSs exist. For example, simplification orders like the recursive path order (cf. Definition 5.2.21) are amenable to automation and can thus be used for automatic termination proofs of TRSs. However, it has already been observed in [CR93] that the two-stage transformation in combination with recursive path orders works only for simplistic logic programs (due to the fact that the TRS obtained from a logic program is quite complex). This rather unsatisfactory situation changes drastically if one uses the newer dependency pair technique instead of simplification orders; see Section 5.4. In our implementation [OCM00], we use the dependency pair technique in combination with polynomial interpretations. More precisely, we use a prerelease of the CiME 2 system, which is available from [CiM]; see also [CM96]. Marché et al. are still improving the CiME 2 system, but the current prototype is already able to automatically prove termination of most logic programs in the test suites of [Plü90, AP94a, SD94].

The material presented in this chapter stems from [Ohl01b].

10.1 Logic Programs

We assume that the reader is familiar with logic programming and SLD derivations; see Apt [Apt97] and Lloyd [Llo87], for example. Here we will only review the following basic notions. If p is an n-ary predicate symbol and $t_1, \ldots, t_n$ are terms, then $p(t_1, \ldots, t_n)$ is an *atom*. A *Horn clause* is a formula of the form $A \leftarrow B_1, \ldots, B_m$ where $m \geq 0$ and A, B_i are atoms. A *logic program* $\mathcal{P}$ is a finite set of Horn clauses. A *goal* is a formula of the form $\leftarrow B_1, \ldots, B_m$ where $m \geq 1$ and B_i are atoms. Here only left-to-right SLD derivations (called *LD derivations* in what follows; see [AP94a]) will be considered. In these derivations it is always the left-most literal of a goal that is selected for the next resolution step. Moreover, we will restrict our attention to well-moded programs, a concept due to Dembinski and Maluszynski [DM85]. Let us review the notions needed in this context. A *mode* for an n-ary predicate symbol p is a function $m_p : \{1, \ldots, n\} \to \{in, out\}$. If $m_p(i) = in$ ($m_p(i) = out$) then position i is called an *input position (output position)* of p. This definition assumes one mode per relation in a logic program. Multiple modes can be obtained by renaming the relations; see, e.g., [AZ96, example 2.8]. A clause or a logic program is *moded* if all its predicate symbols are moded. As in [AE93, Raa97] we will use the following conventions that enable an elegant definition of well-modedness. If p is a predicate symbol, then we assume without loss of generality that the input positions precede the output positions. Furthermore, the notation $p(\vec{s}, \vec{t})$ used for an atom means that $\vec{s}$ is a sequence of terms filling the input positions of p and $\vec{t}$ is a sequence of terms filling the output positions of p.

Definition 10.1.1

1. A goal $\leftarrow p_1(\vec{s}_1, \vec{t}_1), \ldots, p_m(\vec{s}_m, \vec{t}_m)$ is called *well-moded* if $\mathcal{V}ar(\vec{s}_i) \subseteq \bigcup_{j=1}^{i-1} \mathcal{V}ar(\vec{t}_j)$ for every $i \in \{1, \ldots, m\}$.

2. A clause $p_0(\vec{t}_0, \vec{s}_{m+1}) \leftarrow p_1(\vec{s}_1, \vec{t}_1), \ldots, p_m(\vec{s}_m, \vec{t}_m)$ is said to be *well-moded* if $\mathcal{V}ar(\vec{s}_i) \subseteq \bigcup_{j=0}^{i-1} \mathcal{V}ar(\vec{t}_j)$ for every $i \in \{1, \ldots, m+1\}$.

3. A logic program $\mathcal{P}$ is *well-moded* if every clause in $\mathcal{P}$ is well-moded.

According to this definition, if $\leftarrow B_1, \ldots, B_m$ is a well-moded goal and $B_1 = p(t_1, \ldots, t_n)$, then t_i is a ground term for every input position i of B_1. The following lemma stems from [GW93].

Lemma 10.1.2 *Let $\mathcal{P}$ be a well-moded logic program and $G_0, G_1, \ldots$ an LD derivation starting with a well-moded goal G_0. Then all goals G_i are well-moded, and the first atom of every nonempty G_i is ground on all its input positions.*

Proof It can be proven by induction on i. □

Definition 10.1.3 A well-moded logic program $\mathcal{P}$ is (*uniquely*) *terminating* if every LD derivation starting from an arbitrary well-moded goal is terminating (and every LD refutation computes the same answer substitution).

10.2 The Transformation

We will transform every moded logic program $\mathcal{P}$ into a CTRS $R_{\mathcal{P}}$ as in [GW93, ALS94]. For every predicate symbol p there are two new function symbols p_{in} and p_{out} and for every atom $A = p(\vec{s}, \vec{t})$, we define $\rho_{in}(A) = p_{in}(\vec{s})$, $\rho_{out}(A) = p_{out}(\vec{t})$, and $\rho(A) = \rho_{in}(A) \to \rho_{out}(A)$. The transformation $\rho(C)$ of a moded clause $C = A \leftarrow B_1, \ldots, B_m$ is defined to be the rule

$$\rho(A) \Leftarrow \rho(B_1), \ldots, \rho(B_m)$$

and with every moded logic program $\mathcal{P}$ we associate the CTRS $R_{\mathcal{P}} = \{\rho(C) \mid C \text{ in } \mathcal{P}\}$ over the signature $F_{\mathcal{P}} = F_{\mathcal{P}}^{p} \cup F_{\mathcal{P}}^{T}$, where $F_{\mathcal{P}}^{p} = \{p_{in}, p_{out} \mid p$ is a predicate in $\mathcal{P}\}$ and $F_{\mathcal{P}}^{T} = \{f \mid f$ occurs in a term of an atom in $\mathcal{P}\}$.

Lemma 10.2.1 *A moded logic program $\mathcal{P}$ is well-moded if and only if $R_\mathcal{P}$ is a deterministic 3-CTRS.*

Proof In order to prove the only-if direction, let $C = p^0(\vec{t_0}, \vec{s}_{k+1}) \leftarrow p^1(\vec{s_1}, \vec{t_1}), \ldots, p^k(\vec{s_k}, \vec{t_k})$ be a well-moded clause in $\mathcal{P}$, that is, $\mathcal{V}ar(\vec{s_i}) \subseteq \bigcup_{j=0}^{i-1} \mathcal{V}ar(\vec{t_j})$ holds for every $i \in \{1, \ldots, k+1\}$. Clearly, $\mathcal{V}ar(\vec{s}_{k+1}) \subseteq \bigcup_{j=0}^{k} \mathcal{V}ar(\vec{t_j})$ implies $\mathcal{V}ar(p^0_{out}(\vec{s}_{k+1})) \subseteq \mathcal{V}ar(p^0_{in}(\vec{t_0})) \cup \bigcup_{j=1}^{k} \mathcal{V}ar(p^j_{out}(\vec{t_j}))$. That is, the transformed conditional rewrite rule $\rho(C)$ is of type 3 (it may have extra variables on its right-hand side but all of these also occur on its left-hand side or in the conditions). Furthermore, $\mathcal{V}ar(\vec{s_i}) \subseteq \bigcup_{j=0}^{i-1} \mathcal{V}ar(\vec{t_j})$ for every $i \in \{1, \ldots, k\}$ implies that $\rho(C)$ is deterministic. Because this holds for every well-moded clause in $\mathcal{P}$, $R_\mathcal{P}$ is a deterministic 3-CTRS. The if direction follows similarly. □

Example 10.2.2 Consider the logic program $\mathcal{P}$ that implements the *quicksort* algorithm:

$$\begin{aligned}
&qsort([\,],[\,]) \leftarrow\\
&qsort(x:l,s) \leftarrow split(l,x,l_1,l_2), qsort(l_1,s_1),\\
&\qquad\qquad\qquad\qquad qsort(l_2,s_2), app(s_1,x:s_2,s)
\end{aligned}$$

$$\begin{aligned}
&split([\,],y,[\,],[\,]) \leftarrow\\
&split(x:l,y,x:l_1,l_2) \leftarrow less(x,y), split(l,y,l_1,l_2)\\
&split(x:l,y,l_1,x:l_2) \leftarrow geq(x,y), split(l,y,l_1,l_2)
\end{aligned}$$

$$\begin{aligned}
&app([\,],l,l) \leftarrow\\
&app(x:l_1,l_2,x:l_3) \leftarrow app(l_1,l_2,l_3)
\end{aligned}$$

$$\begin{aligned}
&less(0,s(x)) \leftarrow\\
&less(s(x),s(y)) \leftarrow less(x,y)
\end{aligned}$$

$$\begin{aligned}
&geq(x,x) \leftarrow\\
&geq(s(x),0) \leftarrow\\
&geq(s(x),s(y)) \leftarrow geq(x,y)
\end{aligned}$$

with input positions $m_{qsort}(1) = m_{split}(1) = m_{split}(2) = m_{app}(1) = m_{app}(2) = m_{less}(1) = m_{less}(2) = m_{geq}(1) = m_{geq}(2) = in$ and output positions $m_{qsort}(2) = m_{split}(3) = m_{split}(4) = m_{app}(3) = out$. The transformation applied to the clauses of the *qsort* predicate yields the conditional rewrite rules

$$\begin{aligned}
qsort_{in}([\,]) &\rightarrow qsort_{out}([\,])\\
qsort_{in}(x:l) &\rightarrow qsort_{out}(s) \Leftarrow split_{in}(l,x) \rightarrow split_{out}(l_1,l_2),\\
&\qquad qsort_{in}(l_1) \rightarrow qsort_{out}(s_1),\\
&\qquad qsort_{in}(l_2) \rightarrow qsort_{out}(s_2),\\
&\qquad app_{in}(s_1,x:s_2) \rightarrow app_{out}(s)
\end{aligned}$$

$$\begin{array}{rcll}
split_{in}([\,], y) & \to & split_{out}([\,], [\,]) & \\
split_{in}(x : l, y) & \to & split_{out}(x : l_1, l_2) & \Leftarrow less_{in}(x, y) \to less_{out}, \\
 & & & \quad split_{in}(l, y) \to split_{out}(l_1, l_2) \\
split_{in}(x : l, y) & \to & split_{out}(l_1, x : l_2) & \Leftarrow geq_{in}(x, y) \to geq_{out}, \\
 & & & \quad split_{in}(l, y) \to split_{out}(l_1, l_2)
\end{array}$$

$$\begin{array}{rcll}
app_{in}([\,], l) & \to & app_{out}(l) & \\
app_{in}(x : l_1, l_2) & \to & app_{out}(x : l_3) & \Leftarrow app_{in}(l_1, l_2) \to app_{out}(l_3)
\end{array}$$

$$\begin{array}{rcll}
less_{in}(0, s(x)) & \to & less_{out} & \\
less_{in}(s(x), s(y)) & \to & less_{out} & \Leftarrow less_{in}(x, y) \to less_{out}
\end{array}$$

$$\begin{array}{rcll}
geq_{in}(x, x) & \to & geq_{out} & \\
geq_{in}(s(x), 0) & \to & geq_{out} & \\
geq_{in}(s(x), s(y)) & \to & geq_{out} & \Leftarrow geq_{in}(x, y) \to geq_{out}
\end{array}$$

From a term rewriting point of view, the system $R_{\mathcal{P}}$ has a very restricted syntactic structure. This fact will be exploited later.

Lemma 10.2.3 *If $\mathcal{P}$ denotes a well-moded logic program, then every conditional rewrite rule $l \to r \Leftarrow s_1 \to t_1, \ldots, s_k \to t_k \in R_{\mathcal{P}}$ has the form*

$$p^0_{in}(\vec{s}_0) \to p^0_{out}(\vec{t}_0) \Leftarrow p^1_{in}(\vec{s}_1) \to p^1_{out}(\vec{t}_1), \ldots, p^k_{in}(\vec{s}_k) \to p^k_{out}(\vec{t}_k)$$

where $\vec{s}_i$ and $\vec{t}_i$ are sequences of terms from $\mathcal{T}(F^T_{\mathcal{P}}, \mathcal{V})$ for every $0 \le i \le k$. In particular it satisfies:

1. *The root symbol is the only defined symbol in l and s_i.*

2. *r and t_i are constructor terms (they do not contain defined symbols).*

Proof The proof is obvious. □

In particular, if $\mathcal{P}$ is a well-moded logic program, then $R_{\mathcal{P}}$ is a strongly deterministic 3-CTRS; cf. Definition 7.2.35. $R_{\mathcal{P}}$ is always terminating, but this is not enough to show termination of $\mathcal{P}$.

Theorem 10.2.4 *If $\mathcal{P}$ is a well-moded logic program such that $R_{\mathcal{P}}$ is quasi-reductive, then $\mathcal{P}$ is terminating. If additionally every conditional critical pair in $R_{\mathcal{P}}$ is joinable, then $\mathcal{P}$ is uniquely terminating.*

Proof In view of Corollary 10.3.4 and Theorem 10.2.7, we refrain from giving a rigorous proof. We just sketch the proof.

Ganzinger and Waldmann [GW93, lemma 13] proved the following fact (cf. Lemma 10.2.6): If $\mathcal{P}$ is a well-moded program, $\leftarrow p(\vec{u}, \vec{v})$ is a well-moded goal, and there is an LD refutation of $\leftarrow p(\vec{u}, \vec{v})$ with computed answer σ, then there is an $R_{\mathcal{P}}$ derivation $p_{in}(\vec{u}) \to^+_{R_{\mathcal{P}}} p_{out}(\vec{v}\sigma)$.

From this fact, it follows (similarly to the proof of Theorem 10.2.7) that quasi-reductivity of $R_{\mathcal{P}}$ implies termination of $\mathcal{P}$; see [GW93, theorem 14].

Moreover, if $R_{\mathcal{P}}$ is quasi-reductive and every conditional critical pair in $R_{\mathcal{P}}$ is joinable, then $R_{\mathcal{P}}$ is confluent by Theorem 7.3.2. Unique termination of $\mathcal{P}$ is a consequence of the confluence of $R_{\mathcal{P}}$ and the preceding fact. This result is due to Avenhaus and Loría-Sáenz [ALS94, theorem 5.1]. □

As already mentioned, the major drawback of Ganzinger and Waldmann's method is the lack of techniques for showing quasi-reductivity of CTRSs automatically. In order to overcome this obstacle, we use the transformation of Definition 7.2.48 to further transform the deterministic 3-CTRS $R_{\mathcal{P}}$ into an unconditional TRS $U(R_{\mathcal{P}})$.

Example 10.2.5 The TRS $U(R_{\mathcal{P}})$ of the 3-CTRS $R_{\mathcal{P}}$ from Example 10.2.2 consists of the rules

$$
\begin{array}{rcl}
qsort_{in}([\,]) & \rightarrow & qsort_{out}([\,]) \\
qsort_{in}(x:l) & \rightarrow & U_1^1(split_{in}(l,x),x,l) \\
U_1^1(split_{out}(l_1,l_2),x,l) & \rightarrow & U_2^1(qsort_{in}(l_1),x,l,l_1,l_2) \\
U_2^1(qsort_{out}(s_1),x,l,l_1,l_2) & \rightarrow & U_3^1(qsort_{in}(l_2),x,l,l_1,l_2,s_1) \\
U_3^1(qsort_{out}(s_2),x,l,l_1,l_2,s_1) & \rightarrow & U_4^1(app_{in}(s_1,x:s_2),x,l,l_1,l_2,s_1,s_2) \\
U_4^1(app_{out}(s),x,l,l_1,l_2,s_1,s_2) & \rightarrow & qsort_{out}(s)
\end{array}
$$

$$
\begin{array}{rcl}
split_{in}([\,],y) & \rightarrow & split_{out}([\,],[\,]) \\
split_{in}(x:l,y) & \rightarrow & U_1^2(less_{in}(x,y),x,y,l) \\
U_1^2(less_{out},x,y,l) & \rightarrow & U_2^2(split_{in}(l,y),x,y,l) \\
U_2^2(split_{out}(l_1,l_2),x,y,l) & \rightarrow & split_{out}(x:l_1,l_2) \\
split_{in}(x:l,y) & \rightarrow & U_1^3(geq_{in}(x,y),x,y,l) \\
U_1^3(geq_{out},x,y,l) & \rightarrow & U_2^3(split_{in}(l,y),x,y,l) \\
U_2^3(split_{out}(l_1,l_2),x,y,l) & \rightarrow & split_{out}(l_1,x:l_2)
\end{array}
$$

$$
\begin{array}{rcl}
app_{in}([\,],l) & \rightarrow & app_{out}(l) \\
app_{in}(x:l_1,l_2) & \rightarrow & U_1^4(app_{in}(l_1,l_2),x,l_1,l_2) \\
U_1^4(app_{out}(l_3),x,l_1,l_2) & \rightarrow & app_{out}(x:l_3)
\end{array}
$$

$$
\begin{array}{rcl}
less_{in}(0,s(x)) & \rightarrow & less_{out} \\
less_{in}(s(x),s(y)) & \rightarrow & U_1^5(less_{in}(x,y),x,y) \\
U_1^5(less_{out},x,y) & \rightarrow & less_{out}
\end{array}
$$

$$
\begin{array}{rcl}
geq_{in}(x,x) & \rightarrow & geq_{out} \\
geq_{in}(s(x),0) & \rightarrow & geq_{out} \\
geq_{in}(s(x),s(y)) & \rightarrow & U_1^6(geq_{in}(x,y),x,y) \\
U_1^6(geq_{out},x,y) & \rightarrow & geq_{out}
\end{array}
$$

It has already been mentioned that in an unpublished manuscript [CR93], Chtourou and Rusinowitch state a similar transformation for the particular case of transforming a logic program $\mathcal{P}$ into a TRS. The TRS obtained by their transformation coincides with $U(R_\mathcal{P})$. In order to show that termination of $U(R_\mathcal{P})$ implies termination of $\mathcal{P}$, we need the following lemma.

Lemma 10.2.6 *Let $\mathcal{P}$ be a well-moded program and $\leftarrow p(\vec{u},\vec{v})$ be a well-moded goal. If there is an LD refutation of $\leftarrow p(\vec{u},\vec{v})$ with computed answer σ, then there is an $U(R_\mathcal{P})$ derivation $p_{in}(\vec{u}) \to^+_{U(R_\mathcal{P})} p_{out}(\vec{v}\sigma)$.*

Proof We proceed by induction on the length ℓ of the LD refutation. If $\ell = 1$, then $\leftarrow p(\vec{u},\vec{v}) \vdash \Box$. Consequently, $\mathcal{P}$ contains a clause $C = p(\vec{s},\vec{t}) \leftarrow$ such that $p(\vec{u},\vec{v})$ and $p(\vec{s},\vec{t})$ are unifiable with most general unifier σ. That is, $\vec{u}\sigma = \vec{s}\sigma$ and $\vec{v}\sigma = \vec{t}\sigma$. The rewrite rule corresponding to $p(\vec{s},\vec{t}) \leftarrow$ is $p_{in}(\vec{s}) \to p_{out}(\vec{t})$. Because the goal $\leftarrow p(\vec{u},\vec{v})$ is well-moded, $\vec{u}$ consists of ground terms and hence $p_{in}(\vec{u}) = p_{in}(\vec{s}\sigma)$. Therefore, $p_{in}(\vec{u}) \to_{U(R_\mathcal{P})} p_{out}(\vec{t}\sigma) = p_{out}(\vec{v}\sigma)$ proves the base case. Suppose $\ell > 1$. Let $C = p(\vec{s},\vec{t}) \leftarrow p^1(\vec{s_1},\vec{t_1}),\ldots,p^k(\vec{s_k},\vec{t_k})$ be the clause used in the first resolution step and σ_0 a most general unifier of $p(\vec{u},\vec{v})$ and $p(\vec{s},\vec{t})$. The LD refutation must have the form

$$\begin{array}{lll} p(\vec{u},\vec{v}) & \vdash & p^1(\vec{s}_1,\vec{t}_1)\sigma_0,\ldots,p^k(\vec{s}_k,\vec{t}_k)\sigma_0 \quad \vdash \ldots \\ & \vdash & p^2(\vec{s}_2,\vec{t}_2)\sigma_0\sigma_1,\ldots,p^k(\vec{s}_k,\vec{t}_k)\sigma_0\sigma_1 \quad \vdash \ldots \\ & \vdots & \\ & \vdash & p^k(\vec{s}_k,\vec{t}_k)\sigma_0\sigma_1\ldots\sigma_{k-1} \quad \vdash \ldots \\ & \vdash & \Box \end{array}$$

where σ_i is the computed answer to $\leftarrow p^i(\vec{s},\vec{t})\sigma_0,\ldots,\sigma_{i-1}$. The rewrite rules $\rho(C)$ of the transformation of C are

$$\begin{array}{rcl} p_{in}(\vec{s}) & \to & U_1(p^1_{in}(\vec{s}_1),\mathcal{V}ar(\vec{s})) \\ U_1(p^1_{out}(\vec{t}_1),\mathcal{V}ar(\vec{s})) & \to & U_2(p^2_{in}(\vec{s}_2),\mathcal{V}ar(\vec{s}),\mathcal{EV}ar(\vec{t}_1)) \\ & \vdots & \\ U_k(p^k_{out}(\vec{t}_k),\mathcal{V}ar(\vec{s}),\mathcal{EV}ar(\vec{t}_{1,k-1})) & \to & p_{out}(\vec{t}) \end{array}$$

where $\mathcal{EV}ar(\vec{t}_{1,i})$ denotes the sequence $\mathcal{EV}ar(\vec{t}_1),\mathcal{EV}ar(\vec{t}_2),\ldots,\mathcal{EV}ar(\vec{t}_i)$.

We show by induction on i that

$$p_{in}(\vec{u}) \to^+_{U(R_\mathcal{P})} U_i(p^i_{in}(\vec{s}_i),\mathcal{V}ar(\vec{s}),\mathcal{EV}ar(\vec{t}_{1,i-1}))\sigma_0\ldots\sigma_{i-1}$$

for all $1 \le i \le k$. The equality $\vec{u}\sigma_0 = \vec{s}\sigma_0$ holds because σ_0 is a unifier of the goal and the head of the clause. Because the goal is well-moded, $\vec{u}$ consists of ground terms and hence $p_{in}(\vec{u}) = p_{in}(\vec{s}\sigma)$. An application of the first rule in $\rho(C)$ proves the base case $i = 1$ because

$$p_{in}(\vec{u}) \to_{U(R_\mathcal{P})} U_1(p^1_{in}(\vec{s}_1),\mathcal{V}ar(\vec{s}))\sigma_0$$

Let $i > 1$. Because $\leftarrow p^{i-1}(\vec{s}_{i-1}, \vec{t}_{i-1})\sigma_0 \dots \sigma_{i-2}$ has an LD refutation of length $< \ell$ with computed answer σ_{i-1}, we may apply the inductive hypothesis on ℓ and obtain

$$p_{in}^{i-1}(\vec{s}_{i-1})\sigma_0 \dots \sigma_{i-2} \rightarrow^+_{U(R_\mathcal{P})} p_{out}^{i-1}(\vec{t}_{i-1})\sigma_0 \dots \sigma_{i-2}\sigma_{i-1}$$

Because $p_{in}(\vec{u}) \rightarrow^+_{U(R_\mathcal{P})} U_{i-1}(p_{in}^{i-1}(\vec{s}_{i-1}), \mathcal{V}ar(\vec{s}), \mathcal{E}\mathcal{V}ar(\vec{t}_{1,i-2}))\sigma_0 \dots \sigma_{i-2}$ by the inductive hypothesis on i, and $\vec{u}$ consists of ground terms, it follows that $x\sigma_0 \dots \sigma_{i-2}$ is a ground term for every $x \in \mathcal{V}ar(\vec{s}) \cup \bigcup_{j=1}^{i-2} \mathcal{E}\mathcal{V}ar(\vec{t}_j)$. As a consequence,

$$\begin{aligned} &U_{i-1}(p_{in}^{i-1}(\vec{s}_{i-1}), \mathcal{V}ar(\vec{s}), \mathcal{E}\mathcal{V}ar(\vec{t}_{1,i-2}))\sigma_0 \dots \sigma_{i-2} \\ &\rightarrow^+_{U(R_\mathcal{P})} U_{i-1}(p_{out}^{i-1}(\vec{t}_{i-1}), \mathcal{V}ar(\vec{s}), \mathcal{E}\mathcal{V}ar(\vec{t}_{1,i-2}))\sigma_0 \dots \sigma_{i-1} \end{aligned}$$

Furthermore,

$$\begin{aligned} &U_{i-1}(p_{out}^{i-1}(\vec{t}_{i-1}), \mathcal{V}ar(\vec{s}), \mathcal{E}\mathcal{V}ar(\vec{t}_{1,i-2}))\sigma_0 \dots \sigma_{i-1} \\ &\rightarrow_{U(R_\mathcal{P})} U_i(p_{in}^{i}(\vec{s}_i), \mathcal{E}\mathcal{V}ar(\vec{t}_{1,i-1}))\sigma_0 \dots \sigma_{i-1} \end{aligned}$$

This proves $p_{in}(\vec{u}) \rightarrow^+_{U(R_\mathcal{P})} U_i(p_{in}^{i}(\vec{s}_i), \mathcal{V}ar(\vec{s}), \mathcal{E}\mathcal{V}ar(\vec{t}_{1,i-1}))\sigma_0 \dots \sigma_{i-1}$, for all $1 \leq i \leq k$. In particular, if $i = k$, then

$$p_{in}(\vec{u}) \rightarrow^+_{U(R_\mathcal{P})} U_k(p_{in}^{k}(\vec{s}_k), \mathcal{V}ar(\vec{s}), \mathcal{E}\mathcal{V}ar(\vec{t}_{1,k-1}))\sigma_0 \dots \sigma_{k-1}$$

A renewed application of the inductive hypothesis on ℓ yields

$$\begin{aligned} &U_k(p_{in}^{k}(\vec{s}_k), \mathcal{V}ar(\vec{s}), \mathcal{E}\mathcal{V}ar(\vec{t}_{1,k-1}))\sigma_0 \dots \sigma_{k-1} \\ &\rightarrow^+_{U(R_\mathcal{P})} U_k(p_{out}^{k}(\vec{t}_k), \mathcal{V}ar(\vec{s}), \mathcal{E}\mathcal{V}ar(\vec{t}_{1,k-1}))\sigma_0 \dots \sigma_k \end{aligned}$$

and hence

$$U_k(p_{out}^{k}(\vec{t}_k), \mathcal{V}ar(\vec{s}), \mathcal{E}\mathcal{V}ar(\vec{t}_{1,k-1}))\sigma_0 \dots \sigma_k \rightarrow_{U(R_\mathcal{P})} p_{out}(\vec{t})\sigma_0 \dots \sigma_k$$

The computed answer σ is the restriction of the substitution $\sigma_k \circ \dots \circ \sigma_0$ to the variables of $\vec{u}$ and $\vec{v}$. Because $\vec{t}\sigma_0 = \vec{v}\sigma_0$, it follows $\vec{t}\sigma = \vec{t}\sigma_0 \dots \sigma_k = \vec{v}\sigma_0 \dots \sigma_k = \vec{v}\sigma$ and therefore $p_{in}(\vec{u}) \rightarrow^+_{U(R_\mathcal{P})} p_{out}(\vec{v}\sigma)$. □

Chtourou and Rusinowitch [CR93, theorem 3] proved that simple termination of $U(R_\mathcal{P})$ implies termination of $\mathcal{P}$. The following theorem generalizes their result.

Theorem 10.2.7 *Let $\mathcal{P}$ be a well-moded program. If the TRS $U(\mathcal{R}_\mathcal{P})$ terminates, then $\mathcal{P}$ terminates as well. If additionally $U(\mathcal{R}_\mathcal{P})$ is confluent, then $\mathcal{P}$ is uniquely terminating.*

Proof To show the first statement, we have to show that every LD derivation starting from an arbitrary well-moded goal is terminating. First, we define a partial ordering as follows:

$$p(\vec{u},\vec{v}) \succ q(\vec{s},\vec{t}) \quad \text{if} \quad p_{in}(\vec{u}) \; (\rightarrow_{U(R_\mathcal{P})} \cup \rhd)^+ \; q_{in}(\vec{s})$$

According to Lemma 7.2.4, $\succ = (\rightarrow_{U(R_\mathcal{P})} \cup \rhd)^+$ is well-founded because $\rightarrow_{U(R_\mathcal{P})}$ is well-founded and closed under contexts. We show by induction on $\succ$ that every LD derivation starting from a well-moded goal $\leftarrow p(\vec{u},\vec{v})$ is finite. If the goal is not unifiable with the head of a clause from $\mathcal{P}$, then it admits no LD derivation at all. If the goal is solely unifiable with heads of clauses of the form $p(\vec{s},\vec{t}) \leftarrow$, then clearly every LD derivation starting from $\leftarrow p(\vec{u},\vec{v})$ terminates. Suppose otherwise that $\leftarrow p(\vec{u},\vec{v})$ and the head of the clause

$$C = p(\vec{s},\vec{t}) \leftarrow p^1(\vec{s_1},\vec{t_1}),\ldots,p^k(\vec{s_k},\vec{t_k})$$

are unifiable with most general unifier σ_0. Then we have

$$\leftarrow p(\vec{u},\vec{v}) \vdash \leftarrow p^1(\vec{s_1},\vec{t_1})\sigma_0,\ldots,p^k(\vec{s_k},\vec{t_k})\sigma_0$$

and consequently $p_{in}(\vec{u}) \rightarrow_{U(R_\mathcal{P})} U_1(p^1_{in}(\vec{s_1}), \mathcal{V}ar(\vec{s}))\sigma_0$. The latter implies that $p(\vec{u},\vec{v}) \succ p^1(\vec{s_1},\vec{t_1})\sigma_0$ and, according to the inductive hypothesis, every LD derivation starting from $\leftarrow p^1(\vec{s_1},\vec{t_1})\sigma_0$ is finite. Now if there is no LD refutation of $\leftarrow p^1(\vec{s_1},\vec{t_1})\sigma_0$, then the whole LD derivation is finite and we are done. Otherwise there is an LD refutation of $\leftarrow p^1(\vec{s_1},\vec{t_1})\sigma_0$ with computed answer σ_1, and Lemma 10.2.6 yields a derivation

$$p^1_{in}(\vec{s_1})\sigma_0 \rightarrow^+_{U(R_\mathcal{P})} p^1_{out}(\vec{t_1})\sigma_0\sigma_1$$

In this case,

$$p_{in}(\vec{u}) \rightarrow_{U(R_\mathcal{P})} U_1(p^1_{in}(\vec{s_1}), \mathcal{V}ar(\vec{s}))\sigma_0 \rightarrow^+_{U(R_\mathcal{P})} U_1(p^1_{out}(\vec{t_1}), \mathcal{V}ar(\vec{s}))\sigma_0\sigma_1$$

$U_1(p^1_{out}(\vec{t_1}), \mathcal{V}ar(\vec{s}))\sigma_0\sigma_1 \rightarrow_{U(R_\mathcal{P})} U_2(p^2_{in}(\vec{s_2}), \mathcal{V}ar(\vec{s}), \mathcal{EV}ar(\vec{t_1}))\sigma_0\sigma_1$ in combination with the preceding derivation implies that $p(\vec{u},\vec{v}) \succ p^2(\vec{s_2},\vec{t_2})\sigma_0\sigma_1$. Hence the inductive hypothesis is applicable again. By continuing with this reasoning, we infer that the whole LD derivation is finite.

Let us turn to the second statement of the theorem. If $U(\mathcal{R}_\mathcal{P})$ is convergent, then it follows from Lemma 10.2.6 that $\mathcal{P}$ is uniquely terminating. □

By means of Theorem 10.2.7, proving termination of a well-moded logic program $\mathcal{P}$ boils down to proving termination of the TRS $U(R_\mathcal{P})$. The advantage over Theorem 10.2.4 consists of the fact that there are sophisticated methods for automatically showing termination of TRSs. For example, termination of the *quicksort* program from Example 10.2.2 can automatically be shown by using Theorem 10.2.7 in combination with the dependency pair method.

We stress that unique termination of $\mathcal{P}$ can only seldom be proven by means of Theorem 10.2.7. This is because the transformed system $U(\mathcal{R}_\mathcal{P})$ is usually not confluent. For example, the critical pair $\langle U_1^2(less_{in}(x,y),x,y,l), U_1^3(geq_{in}(x,y),x,y,l)\rangle$ in Example 10.2.5 is not joinable, thus the TRS is not locally confluent.

10.3 Comparison of the Different Methods

Arts and Zantema [AZ95, AZ96] designed an imperative procedure[1] that directly transforms a logic program $\mathcal{P}$ into an *unconditional* TRS. This TRS[2] is essentially the same as $U(R_\mathcal{P})$. They showed that single-redex termination of $U(R_\mathcal{P})$ suffices to prove termination of $\mathcal{P}$.

Definition 10.3.1 Let $\mathcal{R}$ be a TRS. A reduction step $s \to_\mathcal{R} t$ is called a *single-redex* reduction step if s contains exactly one redex. If a term does not have exactly one redex, then it is in *single-redex normal form.* A *single-redex derivation* is a reduction sequence consisting solely of single-redex reduction steps. $\mathcal{R}$ is called *single-redex terminating* if all single-redex derivations are finite.

Note that innermost termination implies single-redex termination.

Theorem 10.3.2 *If $\mathcal{P}$ is a well-moded logic program such that $U(R_\mathcal{P})$ is single-redex terminating, then $\mathcal{P}$ is terminating.*

Proof In view of Corollary 10.3.4 and Theorem 10.2.7, the proof is omitted. It can be found in [AZ95, theorem 4.8] and [Art97, theorem 8.2.9]. □

The following hierarchy

	$U(R_\mathcal{P})$ is terminating	
$\Rightarrow$	$R_\mathcal{P}$ is quasi-reductive	(Proposition 7.2.50)
$\Rightarrow$	$U(R_\mathcal{P})$ is innermost terminating	(Corollary 7.2.59)
$\Rightarrow$	$U(R_\mathcal{P})$ is single-redex terminating	(obvious)
$\Rightarrow$	$\mathcal{P}$ is terminating	(Theorem 10.3.2)

suggests that Arts and Zantema's method is more powerful than Ganzinger and Waldmann's, which in turn seems to be more powerful than Chtourou and Rusinowitch's technique: There might be a logic program $\mathcal{P}$ such that $U(R_\mathcal{P})$ is single-redex terminating but $R_\mathcal{P}$ is not quasi-reductive or there

[1] There is a flaw in the procedure, which was corrected in [Art97, def. 8.2.2].

[2] More precisely, the TRS obtained by the imperative procedure in [Art97, def. 8.2.2].

might be a logic program $\mathcal{P}$ such that $R_\mathcal{P}$ is quasi-reductive but $U(R_\mathcal{P})$ is not terminating. Theorem 10.3.3, however, implies that all three methods are equally powerful.

Theorem 10.3.3 *If $U(R_\mathcal{P})$ is single-redex terminating, then it is terminating.*

Proof To prove the theorem, we use type introduction; see Theorem 5.5.25. This is possible because $U(R_\mathcal{P})$ lacks collapsing rules. Hence we may assume that the function symbols come from a many-sorted signature such that the left- and right-hand sides of every rewrite rule are well-typed and of the same type. We use two sorts 1 and 2. Every $p_{in}, p_{out} \in \mathcal{F}^p_\mathcal{P}$ has type $1 \times \cdots \times 1 \to 2$; every $f \in \mathcal{F}^T_\mathcal{P}$ has type $1 \times \cdots \times 1 \to 1$; and every U symbol U^ρ_i has type $2 \times 1 \times \cdots \times 1 \to 2$. According to Theorem 5.5.25, termination of $U(R_\mathcal{P})$ follows from termination of the typed (many-sorted) version of $U(R_\mathcal{P})$.

Next we show that every well-typed term u contains at most one redex. To this end, we proceed by case analysis:

(a) If u is of type 1, then it is term over the signature $\mathcal{F}^T_\mathcal{P}$ and hence a normal form.

(b) If $u = p_{out}(v_1, \ldots, v_m)$, then u is a normal form because every v_j is a term of type 1 and p_{out} is a constructor.

(c) If $u = p_{in}(v_1, \ldots, v_m)$, then again every v_j is a term of type 1 and hence in normal form. In other words, u itself is the only potential redex in u.

(d) In the last possible case, $root(u)$ is a U symbol. Because u is well-typed, it must have the form $U^{\rho_1}_{i_1}(U^{\rho_2}_{i_2}(\ldots, U^{\rho_k}_{i_k}(q(w_1, \ldots, w_n), \ldots) \ldots))$, where either $q = q_{in}$ or $q = q_{out}$ and every subterm different from $U^{\rho_\ell}_{i_\ell}(\ldots)$ and $q(w_1, \ldots, w_n)$ is a term of type 1 and hence in normal form. If $q = q_{in}$, then $q_{in}(w_1, \ldots, w_n)$ is the only potential redex in u because every $U^{\rho_\ell}_{i_\ell}(\ldots)$ subterm is obviously not a redex. Similarly, if $q = q_{out}$, then $U^{\rho_k}_{i_k}(q_{out}(w_1, \ldots, w_n), \ldots)$ is the only potential redex.

Because every well-typed term u contains at most one redex, every well-typed $U(R_\mathcal{P})$ derivation is a single-redex derivation. All these derivations are finite because $U(R_\mathcal{P})$ is single-redex terminating. □

Corollary 10.3.4 *If $\mathcal{P}$ is a well-moded logic program, then*

$$
\begin{aligned}
& U(R_\mathcal{P}) \text{ is terminating} \\
\Leftrightarrow\ & R_\mathcal{P} \text{ is quasi-reductive} \\
\Leftrightarrow\ & U(R_\mathcal{P}) \text{ is innermost terminating} \\
\Leftrightarrow\ & U(R_\mathcal{P}) \text{ is single-redex terminating} \\
\Rightarrow\ & \mathcal{P} \text{ is terminating}
\end{aligned}
$$

Proof Combine the preceding results to prove the corollary. □

In the next section we will investigate under which conditions the last implication is an equivalence.

10.4 Completeness

It should be pointed out that the methods under consideration do not yield a complete criterion for proving termination of well-moded logic programs. The following example taken from [GW93] demonstrates this.

Example 10.4.1 Consider the logic program $\mathcal{P}$

$$p(x, g(x)) \leftarrow$$
$$p(x, f(y)) \leftarrow p(x, g(y))$$

with the modes $m_p(1) = in$ and $m_p(2) = out$. Clearly, $\mathcal{P}$ is a well-moded logic program.

Transforming $\mathcal{P}$ into a deterministic 3-CTRS $R_{\mathcal{P}}$ gives

$$\begin{array}{lll} p_{in}(x) & \to & p_{out}(g(x)) \\ p_{in}(x) & \to & p_{out}(f(y)) \quad \Leftarrow p_{in}(x) \to p_{out}(g(y)) \end{array}$$

The second transformation of $R_{\mathcal{P}}$ into $U(R_{\mathcal{P}})$ yields

$$\begin{array}{rcl} p_{in}(x) & \to & p_{out}(g(x)) \\ p_{in}(x) & \to & U(p_{in}(x), x) \\ U(p_{out}(g(y)), x) & \to & p_{out}(f(y)) \end{array}$$

This TRS is obviously not (single-redex) terminating. Hence all three methods fail in proving termination of $\mathcal{P}$. The point is that the input argument remains constant during the recursive call of p. However, it is easy to see that $\mathcal{P}$ terminates for every well-moded goal because $p(x, f(y))$ is not unifiable with $p(x', g(y'))$.

The preceding example also reveals another major difference between logic programming and term rewriting: LD resolution steps are based on unification whereas rewrite steps are based on matching.

Next we will show that the two-stage transformation is complete for the class of simply moded and well-moded logic programs. In essence, this is due to the fact that simply moded and well-moded logic programs are *unification free*, that is, unification can be replaced with iterated matching; see [AE93]. The next definition stems from [AE93]. As in Definition 10.1.1, it is assumed that every predicate symbol is moded.

Definition 10.4.2

1. A goal $\leftarrow p_1(\vec{s}_1, \vec{t}_1), \ldots, p_m(\vec{s}_m, \vec{t}_m)$ is called *simply moded* if

(a) $\vec{t}_1, \ldots, \vec{t}_m$ is a sequence of pairwise distinct variables, and

(b) $\mathcal{V}ar(\vec{s}_i) \cap \bigcup_{j=i}^{m} \mathcal{V}ar(\vec{t}_j) = \emptyset$ for every $i \in \{1, \ldots, m\}$.

2. A clause $p_0(\vec{s}_0, \vec{t}_0) \leftarrow p_1(\vec{s}_1, \vec{t}_1), \ldots, p_m(\vec{s}_m, \vec{t}_m)$ is said to be *simply moded* if

   (a) $\leftarrow p_1(\vec{s}_1, \vec{t}_1), \ldots, p_m(\vec{s}_m, \vec{t}_m)$ is simply moded and

   (b) $\mathcal{V}ar(\vec{s}_0) \cap \bigcup_{j=1}^{m} \mathcal{V}ar(\vec{t}_j) = \emptyset$.

3. A logic program $\mathcal{P}$ is *simply moded* if every clause in $\mathcal{P}$ is simply moded.

For example, the *quicksort* program from Example 10.2.2 is simply moded. Apt and Etalle [AE93] showed the following lemma, which is similar to Lemma 10.1.2.

Lemma 10.4.3 *An LD resolvent of a simply moded goal and a simply moded clause that have no variables in common is again simply moded.*

Proof For the proof see [AE93, lemma 27]. □

In order to show completeness of the two-stage transformation, we have to show that termination of a simply moded and well-moded logic program $\mathcal{P}$ implies termination of $U(R_\mathcal{P})$, or equivalently, that nontermination of $U(R_\mathcal{P})$ implies nontermination of $\mathcal{P}$. We need some auxiliary results. In the following, if C is a clause in $\mathcal{P}$ and $\rho(C)$ is its transformed rule in $R_\mathcal{P}$, then we abbreviate the symbol $U_i^{\rho(C)}$ in $U(R_\mathcal{P})$ to U_i^C. The first preparatory lemma actually does not require that the logic program is simply moded.

Lemma 10.4.4 *Let* $C : p^0(\vec{s}_0, \vec{t}_0) \leftarrow p^1(\vec{s}_1, \vec{t}_1), \ldots, p^k(\vec{s}_k, \vec{t}_k)$ *be a clause in a well-moded logic program* $\mathcal{P}$ *and let* $1 \leq \ell \leq k$. *For every derivation* $D : p^0_{in}(u_1, \ldots, u_m) \to^*_{U(R_\mathcal{P})} U^C_\ell(v_1, \ldots, v_n)$ *with* $u_j \in \mathcal{T}(F^\mathcal{T}_\mathcal{P})$, $1 \leq j \leq m$, *there is a ground substitution* σ *such that* D *can be written as*

$$
\begin{array}{ll}
p^0_{in}(\vec{s}_0)\sigma & \to_{U(R_\mathcal{P})} \; U^C_1(p^1_{in}(\vec{s}_1), \mathcal{V}ar(\vec{s}_0))\sigma \\
& \to^+_{U(R_\mathcal{P})} \; U^C_1(p^1_{out}(\vec{t}_1), \mathcal{V}ar(\vec{s}_0))\sigma \\
& \to^*_{U(R_\mathcal{P})} \; \ldots \\
& \to_{U(R_\mathcal{P})} \; U^C_\ell(p^\ell_{in}(\vec{s}_\ell), \mathcal{V}ar(\vec{s}_0), \mathcal{EV}ar(\vec{t}_{1,\ell-1}))\sigma \\
& \to^*_{U(R_\mathcal{P})} \; U^C_\ell(v_1, \ldots, v_n)
\end{array}
$$

Proof We proceed by induction on ℓ. If $\ell = 1$, then there must be a ground substitution σ such that $p^0_{in}(u_1, \ldots, u_m) = p^0_{in}(\vec{s}_0)\sigma \to_{U(R_\mathcal{P})} U^C_1(p^1_{in}(\vec{s}_1), \mathcal{V}ar(\vec{s}_0))\sigma$ (otherwise $p^0_{in}(u_1, \ldots, u_m) \to^*_{U(R_\mathcal{P})} U^C_1(v_1, \ldots, v_n)$ would be impossible). It follows that $p^1_{in}(\vec{s}_1) \to^*_{U(R_\mathcal{P})} v_1$ and $\mathcal{V}ar(\vec{s}_0)\sigma =$

$v_2, \ldots, v_n$. Suppose $p^0_{in}(u_1, \ldots, u_m) \rightarrow^*_{U(R_\mathcal{P})} U^C_{\ell+1}(v_1, \ldots, v_n)$ for $1 \leq \ell < k$. Clearly, there is a (matching) substitution σ such that

$$\begin{array}{lll} p^0_{in}(u_1, \ldots, u_m) & \rightarrow^*_{U(R_\mathcal{P})} & U^C_\ell(p^\ell_{out}(\vec{t}_\ell), \mathcal{V}ar(\vec{s}_0), \mathcal{EV}ar(\vec{t}_{1,\ell-1}))\sigma \\ & \rightarrow_{U(R_\mathcal{P})} & U^C_{\ell+1}(p^{\ell+1}_{in}(\vec{s}_{\ell+1}), \mathcal{V}ar(\vec{s}_0), \mathcal{EV}ar(\vec{t}_{1,\ell-1}))\sigma \\ & \rightarrow^*_{U(R_\mathcal{P})} & U^C_{\ell+1}(v_1, \ldots, v_n) \end{array}$$

An application of the inductive hypothesis to the rewrite sequence $p^0_{in}(u_1, \ldots, u_m) \rightarrow^*_{U(R_\mathcal{P})} U^C_\ell(p^\ell_{out}(\vec{t}_\ell), \mathcal{V}ar(\vec{s}_0), \mathcal{EV}ar(\vec{t}_{1,\ell-1}))\sigma$ yields a substitution τ such that

$$\begin{array}{lll} p^0_{in}(\vec{s}_0)\tau & \rightarrow^*_{U(R_\mathcal{P})} & U^C_\ell(p^\ell_{in}(\vec{s}_\ell), \mathcal{V}ar(\vec{s}_0), \mathcal{EV}ar(\vec{t}_{1,\ell-1}))\tau \\ & \rightarrow^*_{U(R_\mathcal{P})} & U^C_\ell(p^\ell_{out}(\vec{t}_\ell), \mathcal{V}ar(\vec{s}_0), \mathcal{EV}ar(\vec{t}_{1,\ell-1}))\sigma \\ & \rightarrow_{U(R_\mathcal{P})} & U^C_{\ell+1}(p^{\ell+1}_{in}(\vec{s}_{\ell+1}), \mathcal{V}ar(\vec{s}_0), \mathcal{EV}ar(\vec{t}_{1,\ell}))\sigma \\ & \rightarrow^*_{U(R_\mathcal{P})} & U^C_{\ell+1}(v_1, \ldots, v_n) \end{array}$$

Let $x \in \mathcal{V}ar(\vec{s}_0) \cup \bigcup_{j=1}^{\ell-1} \mathcal{EV}ar(\vec{t}_j)$. $x\tau$ is a ground normal form because it is a term in $\mathcal{T}(F^T_\mathcal{P})$. Hence $x\tau = x\sigma$, and it follows that

$$\begin{array}{lll} p^0_{in}(\vec{s}_0)\sigma & \rightarrow^*_{U(R_\mathcal{P})} & U^C_{\ell+1}(p^{\ell+1}_{in}(\vec{s}_{\ell+1}), \mathcal{V}ar(\vec{s}_0), \mathcal{EV}ar(\vec{t}_{1,\ell}))\sigma \\ & \rightarrow^*_{U(R_\mathcal{P})} & U^C_{\ell+1}(v_1, \ldots, v_n) \end{array}$$

□

Observe that as in the proof of Lemma 10.4.4 it can be shown that for every rewrite derivation $D : p^0_{in}(u_1, \ldots, u_m) \rightarrow^*_{U(R_\mathcal{P})} p^0_{out}(v_1, \ldots, v_n)$ with $u_j \in \mathcal{T}(F^T_\mathcal{P})$, $1 \leq j \leq m$, there is a substitution σ such that D can be written as $p^0_{in}(\vec{s}_0)\sigma \rightarrow^+_{U(R_\mathcal{P})} p^0_{out}(\vec{t}_0)\sigma$.

Proposition 10.4.5 *Let* $C : p^0(\vec{s}_0, \vec{t}_0) \leftarrow p^1(\vec{s}_1, \vec{t}_1), \ldots, p^k(\vec{s}_k, \vec{t}_k)$ *be a clause in a simply moded and well-moded logic program* $\mathcal{P}$. *If there is derivation*

$$\begin{array}{lll} p^0_{in}(\vec{s}_0)\sigma & \rightarrow_{U(R_\mathcal{P})} & U^C_1(p^1_{in}(\vec{s}_1), \mathcal{V}ar(\vec{s}_0))\sigma \\ & \rightarrow^+_{U(R_\mathcal{P})} & \cdots \\ & \rightarrow_{U(R_\mathcal{P})} & U^C_k(p^k_{out}(\vec{t}_k), \mathcal{V}ar(\vec{s}_0), \mathcal{EV}ar(\vec{t}_{1,k-1}))\sigma \\ & \rightarrow_{U(R_\mathcal{P})} & p^0_{out}(\vec{t}_0)\sigma \end{array}$$

such that $p^0_{in}(\vec{s}_0)\sigma$ *is ground (and hence* σ *is a ground substitution), then there is an LD derivation*

$$\leftarrow p^0(\vec{s}_0\sigma, \vec{x}) \vdash \cdots \vdash \square$$

with computed answer substitution τ such that $\vec{x}\tau = \vec{t_0}\sigma$, provided that $p^0(\vec{s_0}\sigma, \vec{x})$ is a simply moded and well-moded goal (in other words, $\vec{x}$ is a sequence of pairwise distinct variables).

Proof We proceed by induction on the length ℓ of the derivation. In the base case $\ell = 1$, we have $p^0_{in}(\vec{s_0})\sigma \to_{U(R_\mathcal{P})} p^0_{out}(\vec{t_0})\sigma$. This implies that $p^0(\vec{s_0}, \vec{t_0})$ is a fact in the logic program $\mathcal{P}$. Let $p^0(\vec{s'_0}, \vec{t'_0})$ be a variant (i.e., a variable renamed version) of $p^0(\vec{s_0}, \vec{t_0})$ such that $p^0(\vec{s_0}, \vec{t_0})$, $p^0(\vec{s'_0}, \vec{t'_0})$, and $\vec{x}$ have no variables in common. In order to unify $p^0(\vec{s_0}\sigma, \vec{x})$ and $p^0(\vec{s'_0}, \vec{t'_0})$, let τ'_0 be defined on $\mathcal{V}ar(\vec{s'_0})$ by $\vec{s'_0}\tau'_0 = \vec{s_0}\sigma$ and let τ''_0 be defined on $\mathcal{V}ar(\vec{x})$ by $\vec{x}\tau''_0 = \vec{t'_0}\tau'_0$. Then $\tau_0 = \tau'_0 \cup \tau''_0$ is a most general unifier of $p^0(\vec{s_0}\sigma, \vec{x})$ and $p^0(\vec{s'_0}, \vec{t'_0})$. Hence $\leftarrow p^0(\vec{s_0}\sigma, \vec{x}) \vdash \Box$ with computed answer substitution τ_0 and $\vec{x}\tau_0 = \vec{t'_0}\tau'_0 = \vec{t_0}\sigma$. The last equality follows from the fact that $\mathcal{V}ar(\vec{t_0}) \subseteq \mathcal{V}ar(\vec{s_0})$ and $\mathcal{V}ar(\vec{t'_0}) \subseteq \mathcal{V}ar(\vec{s'_0})$ because $\mathcal{P}$ is well-moded.

Suppose $\ell > 1$. Then $p^0_{in}(\vec{s_0})\sigma \to_{U(R_\mathcal{P})} U^C_1(p^1_{in}(\vec{s_1}), \mathcal{V}ar(\vec{s_0}))\sigma$, where C is a clause $p_0(\vec{s_0}, \vec{t_0}) \leftarrow p_1(\vec{s_1}, \vec{t_1}), \dots, p_m(\vec{s_m}, \vec{t_m})$. Let $C' = p_0(\vec{s'_0}, \vec{t'_0}) \leftarrow p_1(\vec{s'_1}, \vec{t'_1}), \dots, p_m(\vec{s'_m}, \vec{t'_m})$ be a variant of C such that C, C', and $\vec{x}$ have no variables in common. As in the base case, $\tau_0 = \tau'_0 \cup \tau''_0$ is a most general unifier of $p^0(\vec{s_0}\sigma, \vec{x})$ and $p^0(\vec{s'_0}, \vec{t'_0})$, where τ'_0 is defined on $\mathcal{V}ar(\vec{s'_0})$ by $\vec{s'_0}\tau'_0 = \vec{s_0}\sigma$ and τ''_0 is defined on $\mathcal{V}ar(\vec{x})$ by $\vec{x}\tau''_0 = \vec{t'_0}\tau'_0$. This yields (note that $\vec{t'_j}\tau_0 = \vec{t'_j}$ because $\mathcal{P}$ is simply moded)

$$\leftarrow p^0(\vec{s_0}\sigma, \vec{x}) \vdash \leftarrow p^1(\vec{s'_1}\tau_0, \vec{t'_1}), \dots, p^k(\vec{s'_k}\tau_0, \vec{t'_k})$$

$\vec{s'_1}\tau_0 = \vec{s_1}\sigma$ is a consequence of $\mathcal{V}ar(\vec{s_1}) \subseteq \mathcal{V}ar(\vec{s_0})$ and $\mathcal{V}ar(\vec{s'_1}) \subseteq \mathcal{V}ar(\vec{s'_0})$ (the program $\mathcal{P}$ is well-moded). Hence $\vec{s'_1}\tau_0$ is a sequence of ground terms. According to Lemmas 10.1.2 and 10.4.3, the goal $\leftarrow p^1(\vec{s'_1}\tau_0, \vec{t'_1}), \dots, p^k(\vec{s'_k}\tau_0, \vec{t'_k})$ is again well-moded and simply moded (in particular, $\vec{t'_1}$ is a sequence of pairwise distinct variables). Therefore, an application of the inductive hypothesis to the derivation $p^1_{in}(\vec{s_1})\sigma \to^+_{U(R_\mathcal{P})} p^1_{out}(\vec{t_1})\sigma$ yields an LD derivation

$$\leftarrow p^1(\vec{s_1}\sigma, \vec{t'_1}) = \leftarrow p^1(\vec{s'_1}\tau_0, \vec{t'_1}) \vdash \dots \vdash \Box$$

with computed answer substitution τ_1 such that $\vec{t'_1}\tau_1 = \vec{t_1}\sigma$. Without loss of generality, we may assume that the preceding LD derivation did not use variables from $\bigcup_{j=2}^k \mathcal{V}ar(\vec{t'_j})$ and hence $\mathcal{D}om(\tau_1) \cap \bigcup_{j=2}^k \mathcal{V}ar(\vec{t'_j}) = \emptyset$. Consequently,

$$\begin{aligned} \leftarrow p^0(\vec{s_0}\sigma, \vec{x}) &\vdash \leftarrow p^1(\vec{s'_1}\tau_0, \vec{t'_1}), \dots, p^k(\vec{s'_k}\tau_0, \vec{t'_k}) \\ &\vdash \dots \\ &\vdash \leftarrow p^2(\vec{s'_2}\tau_0\tau_1, \vec{t'_2}), \dots, p^k(\vec{s'_k}\tau_0\tau_1, \vec{t'_k}) \end{aligned}$$

Notice that $\vec{s_2'}\tau_0\tau_1 = \vec{s_2}\sigma$ because $\mathcal{V}ar(\vec{s_2}) \subseteq \mathcal{V}ar(\vec{s_0}) \cup \mathcal{V}ar(\vec{t_1})$. Moreover, the last goal is again simply moded and well-moded. Thus the inductive hypothesis is applicable, as earlier. Continuing with this reasoning, we obtain LD derivations

$$\leftarrow p^j(\vec{s_j}\sigma, \vec{t_j'}) = \leftarrow p^j(\vec{s_j'}\tau_0 \ldots \tau_{j-1}, \vec{t_j'}) \vdash \cdots \vdash \Box$$

with computed answer substitutions τ_j such that $\vec{t_j'}\tau_j = \vec{t_j}\sigma$. These can be combined into an LD derivation

$$\leftarrow p^0(\vec{s_0}\sigma, \vec{x}) \vdash \cdots \vdash \Box$$

with computed answer substitution $\tau = \tau_0\tau_1 \cdots \tau_k$. Because $\mathcal{V}ar(\vec{t_0}) \subseteq \mathcal{V}ar(\vec{s_0}) \cup \bigcup_{j=1}^{k} \mathcal{V}ar(\vec{t_j})$ and $\vec{t_j'}\tau = \vec{t_j'}\tau_j = \vec{t_j}\sigma$ for every $1 \leq j \leq k$, it follows that $\vec{x}\tau = \vec{t_0'}\tau_0\tau_1 \cdots \tau_k = \vec{t_0}\sigma$. This proves the proposition. $\Box$

Corollary 10.4.6 *Let $C : p^0(\vec{s_0}, \vec{t_0}) \leftarrow p^1(\vec{s_1}, \vec{t_1}), \ldots, p^k(\vec{s_k}, \vec{t_k})$ be a clause in a simply moded and well-moded logic program $\mathcal{P}$. If there exists a derivation $p^0_{in}(\vec{s_0})\sigma \rightarrow^+_{U(R_\mathcal{P})} U^C_{\ell+1}(p^{\ell+1}_{in}(\vec{s}_{\ell+1}), \mathcal{V}ar(\vec{s_0}), \mathcal{EV}ar(\vec{t}_{1,\ell}))\sigma$ for some $1 \leq \ell < k$ in which $\vec{s_0}\sigma$ is a sequence of ground terms, then there is an LD derivation*

$$\leftarrow p^0(\vec{s_0}\sigma, \vec{x}) \vdash \cdots \vdash \leftarrow p^\ell(\vec{s_\ell}\tau_0 \cdots \tau_{\ell-1}, \vec{t_\ell}), \ldots, p^k(\vec{s_k}\tau_0 \cdots \tau_{\ell-1}, \vec{t_k})$$

Proof This is a special case of the proof of Proposition 10.4.5. $\Box$

Theorem 10.4.7 *Let $\mathcal{P}$ be a simply moded and well-moded logic program. If $\mathcal{P}$ is terminating, then $U(R_\mathcal{P})$ is terminating as well.*

Proof For a proof by contradiction, suppose that $U(R_\mathcal{P})$ is not terminating. Then there must be an infinite $U(R_\mathcal{P})$ derivation starting from a term $p^0_{in}(u_1', \ldots, u_m')$ with $u_j' \in \mathcal{T}(F^T_\mathcal{P}, \mathcal{V})$, $1 \leq j \leq m$; cf. Theorem 10.3.3. If we instantiate every variable in u_j', $1 \leq j \leq m$, by a ground term from $\mathcal{T}(F^T_\mathcal{P})$, then we obtain an infinite $U(R_\mathcal{P})$ derivation D starting from a ground term $p^0_{in}(u_1, \ldots, u_m)$ with $u_j \in \mathcal{T}(F^T_\mathcal{P})$, $1 \leq j \leq m$. Let $p^0_{in}(u_1, \ldots, u_m) = p^0_{in}(\vec{s_0})\sigma \rightarrow_{U(R_\mathcal{P})} U^C_1(p^1_{in}(\vec{s_1}), \mathcal{V}ar(\vec{s_0}))\sigma$ be the first rewrite step in D and let $C : p^0(\vec{s_0}, \vec{t_0}) \leftarrow p^1(\vec{s_1}, \vec{t_1}), \ldots, p^k(\vec{s_k}, \vec{t_k})$ be the corresponding clause in $\mathcal{P}$. Our goal is to construct an infinite LD derivation from D. There must be an index ℓ such that D can be written as $p^0_{in}(u_1, \ldots, u_m) \rightarrow^+_{U(R_\mathcal{P})} U^C_\ell(v_1, \ldots, v_n) \rightarrow_{U(R_\mathcal{P})} \cdots$ and after $U^C_\ell(v_1, \ldots, v_n)$ every term in D has root symbol U^C_ℓ. This is because D is infinite and hence a normal form

$p^0_{out}(\ldots)$ cannot occur in D. According to Lemma 10.4.4, D has the form

$$\begin{array}{ll} p^0_{in}(\vec{s}_0)\sigma & \to_{U(R_\mathcal{P})} \; U^C_1(p^1_{in}(\vec{s}_1), \mathcal{V}ar(\vec{s}_0))\sigma \\ & \to^*_{U(R_\mathcal{P})} \; \ldots \\ & \to_{U(R_\mathcal{P})} \; U^C_\ell(p^\ell_{in}(\vec{s}_\ell), \mathcal{V}ar(\vec{s}_0), \mathcal{EV}ar(\vec{t}_{1,\ell-1}))\sigma \\ & \to^*_{U(R_\mathcal{P})} \; U^C_\ell(v_1, \ldots, v_n) \\ & \to_{U(R_\mathcal{P})} \; \ldots \end{array}$$

By Corollary 10.4.6, there is an LD derivation

$$\leftarrow p^0(\vec{s}_0\sigma, \vec{x}) \vdash \cdots \vdash \leftarrow p^\ell(\vec{s}_\ell\tau_0 \cdots \tau_{\ell-1}, \vec{t}_\ell), \ldots, p^k(\vec{s}_k\tau_0 \cdots \tau_{\ell-1}, \vec{t}_k)$$

Because D is infinite, it must contain an infinite subderivation starting from $p^\ell_{in}(\vec{s}_\ell)\sigma$ (the other arguments of U^C_ℓ are normal forms). Now we repeat the same process with $p^\ell_{in}(\vec{s}_\ell)\sigma$ instead of $p^0_{in}(\vec{s}_0)\sigma$ and find an LD derivation

$$\leftarrow p^\ell(\vec{s}_\ell\tau_0 \cdots \tau_{\ell-1}, \vec{t}_\ell) \vdash \cdots \vdash \leftarrow A_{\ell'}\tau', \ldots, A_{k'}\tau'$$

A combination of these LD derivations yields

$$\begin{array}{l} \leftarrow p^0(\vec{s}_0\sigma, \vec{x}) \vdash \cdots \vdash \\ \leftarrow p^\ell(\vec{s}_\ell\tau_0 \cdots \tau_{\ell-1}, \vec{t}_\ell), \ldots, p^k(\vec{s}_k\tau_0 \cdots \tau_{\ell-1}, \vec{t}_k) \vdash \\ \leftarrow A_{\ell'}\tau', \ldots, A_{k'}\tau', p^{\ell+1}(\vec{s}_{\ell+1}\tau_0 \cdots \tau_{\ell-1}, \vec{t}_{\ell+1})\tau', \ldots, p^k(\vec{s}_k\tau_0 \cdots \tau_{\ell-1}, \vec{t}_k)\tau' \end{array}$$

By continuing with this reasoning, we can construct an infinite LD derivation from D. □

In summary, the transformational methods for proving termination of well-moded logic programs are complete for the class of simply moded logic programs but they are not complete in general. As a matter of fact, Example 10.4.1 shows that they already lack completeness for the class of nicely moded logic programs (which differ from simply moded logic programs in that they allow constructors in the $\vec{t}_j$; see [AP94b]).

10.5 Proving Termination Automatically

In the two-stage transformational approach, proving termination of a well-moded logic program boils down to proving (innermost) termination of the TRS obtained by the two transformations. In practice, one is interested in a software tool that can do the termination test automatically. Polynomial interpretations and recursive path orders are methods for automatically proving termination of rewrite systems, in the sense that these orders can automatically be generated. However, the two-stage transformation in combination with polynomial interpretations or recursive path orders works only for rather simplistic logic programs (due to the fact that the TRS obtained from a logic program is quite complex). The newer dependency pair method as described in Section 5.4 remedies this situation. We exemplify this by considering the TRS from Example 10.2.5. There are the following cycles in its estimated dependency graph:

$$\{\langle \mathrm{GEQ}_{in}(s(x),s(y)),\mathrm{GEQ}_{in}(x,y)\rangle\}$$
$$\{\langle \mathrm{LESS}_{in}(s(x),s(y)),\mathrm{LESS}_{in}(x,y)\rangle\}$$
$$\{\langle \mathrm{APP}_{in}(x:l_1,l_2),\mathrm{APP}_{in}(l_1,l_2)\rangle\}$$
$$\{\langle \mathrm{SPLIT}_{in}(x:l,y),\mathrm{U}_1^2(less_{in}(x,y),x,y,l)\rangle, \langle \mathrm{U}_1^2(less_{out},x,y,l),\mathrm{SPLIT}_{in}(l,y)\rangle\}$$
$$\{\langle \mathrm{SPLIT}_{in}(x:l,y),\mathrm{U}_1^3(geq_{in}(x,y),x,y,l)\rangle, \langle \mathrm{U}_1^3(geq_{out},x,y,l),\mathrm{SPLIT}_{in}(l,y)\rangle\}$$
$$\{\langle \mathrm{QSORT}_{in}(x:l),\mathrm{U}_1^1(split_{in}(l,x),x,l)\rangle, \langle \mathrm{U}_1^1(split_{out}(l_1,l_2),x,l),\mathrm{QSORT}_{in}(l_1)\rangle\}$$
$$\text{and } \{\langle \mathrm{QSORT}_{in}(x:l),\mathrm{U}_1^1(split_{in}(l,x),x,l)\rangle, \langle \mathrm{U}_1^1(split_{out}(l_1,l_2),x,l),\mathrm{U}_2^1(qsort_{in}(l_1),x,l,l_1,l_2)\rangle, \langle \mathrm{U}_2^1(qsort_{out}(s_1),x,l,l_1,l_2),\mathrm{QSORT}_{in}(l_2)\rangle\}$$

Termination of the TRS in Example 10.2.5 can be shown automatically by using the dependency pair technique in combination with polynomial quasi-orders. The polynomial quasi-order induced by the following polynomial interpretation simultaneously satisfies the inequalities of every cycle in the estimated dependency graph:

$$\begin{array}{rclrcl}
split_{in\mathbb{N}}(l,y) &=& l+1 & [\,]_{\mathbb{N}} &=& 0\\
split_{out\mathbb{N}}(l_1,l_2) &=& l_1+l_2+1 & x :_{\mathbb{N}} l &=& l+1\\
U^1_{1\,\mathbb{N}}(z,x,l) &=& z & qsort_{in\mathbb{N}}(l) &=& l\\
U^1_{2\,\mathbb{N}}(z,x,l,l_1,l_2) &=& l_2+1 & qsort_{out\mathbb{N}}(l) &=& 0\\
U^1_{3\,\mathbb{N}}(z,x,l,l_1,l_2,s_1) &=& 0 & app_{in\mathbb{N}}(l_1,l_2) &=& 0\\
U^1_{4\,\mathbb{N}}(z,x,l,l_1,l_2,s_1,s_2) &=& 0 & app_{out\mathbb{N}}(l) &=& 0\\
U^2_{1\,\mathbb{N}}(z,x,y,l) &=& l+2 & 0_{\mathbb{N}} &=& 0\\
U^2_{2\,\mathbb{N}}(z,x,y,l) &=& z+1 & s_{\mathbb{N}}(x) &=& x+1\\
U^3_{1\,\mathbb{N}}(z,x,y,l) &=& l+2 & less_{in\mathbb{N}}(x,y) &=& 0\\
U^3_{2\,\mathbb{N}}(z,x,y,l) &=& z+1 & less_{out\mathbb{N}} &=& 0\\
U^4_{1\,\mathbb{N}}(z,x,l_1,l_2) &=& 0 & geq_{in\mathbb{N}}(x,y) &=& 0\\
U^5_{1\,\mathbb{N}}(z,x,y) &=& 0 & geq_{out\mathbb{N}} &=& 0\\
U^6_{1\,\mathbb{N}}(z,x,y) &=& 0 & \mathrm{QSORT}_{in\mathbb{N}}(l) &=& l\\
\mathrm{U}^1_{1\mathbb{N}}(z,x,l) &=& z & \mathrm{SPLIT}_{in\mathbb{N}}(l,y) &=& l\\
\mathrm{U}^1_{2\mathbb{N}}(z,x,y,l_1,l_2) &=& l_2+1 & \mathrm{APP}_{in\mathbb{N}}(l_1,l_2) &=& l_1\\
\mathrm{U}^2_{1\mathbb{N}}(z,x,y,l) &=& l & \mathrm{LESS}_{in\mathbb{N}}(x,y) &=& x\\
\mathrm{U}^3_{1\mathbb{N}}(z,x,y,l) &=& l & \mathrm{GEQ}_{in\mathbb{N}}(x,y) &=& x
\end{array}$$

Thus the *quicksort* program from Example 10.2.2 is terminating. Because every conditional critical pair in $\mathcal{R}_{\mathcal{P}}$ is infeasible (hence vacuously joinable), the logic program is also uniquely terminating according to Theorem 10.2.4.

It is interesting to note that we did not find a termination proof of the *quicksort* program that uses the dependency pair method in combination with argument filtering systems and recursive path orderings; see Section 5.4 for details of this technique.

10.6 Empirical Results

Our implementation of the transformational technique consists of two parts. Given a well-moded logic program, the logic program is first transformed into an unconditional TRS, as described in Section 10.2. This unconditional TRS is further simplified by eliminating superfluous variables as follows. If $\rho : l \to r \Leftarrow s_1 \to t_1, \ldots, s_k \to t_k$ is a rule in the CTRS and $U(\rho)$ is the set of unconditional rules obtained from ρ, then every variable x in the sequence $\mathcal{V}ar(l), \mathcal{EV}ar(t_1), \ldots, \mathcal{EV}ar(t_{\ell-1})$ is dropped from the right-hand side $U_\ell^\rho(s_\ell, \mathcal{V}ar(l), \mathcal{EV}ar(t_1), \ldots, \mathcal{EV}ar(t_{\ell-1}))$ of a rule from $U(\rho)$ and in subsequent rules if it does not occur in one of the terms $t_\ell, \ldots, t_k, s_{\ell+1}, \ldots, s_k, r$. For example, the elimination of superfluous variables from the *qsort* rules of the TRS from Example 10.2.5 yields the rules

$$\begin{array}{rcl} qsort_{in}([\,]) & \to & qsort_{out}([\,]) \\ qsort_{in}(x : l) & \to & U_1^1(split_{in}(l, x), x) \\ U_1^1(split_{out}(l_1, l_2), x) & \to & U_2^1(qsort_{in}(l_1), x, l_2) \\ U_2^1(qsort_{out}(s_1), x, l_2) & \to & U_3^1(qsort_{in}(l_2), x, s_1) \\ U_3^1(qsort_{out}(s_2), x, s_1) & \to & U_4^1(app_{in}(s_1, x : s_2)) \\ U_4^1(app_{out}(s)) & \to & qsort_{out}(s) \end{array}$$

A careful inspection of the relevant proofs shows that this simplification of the TRS does not affect the soundness and completeness results for our transformational method.

The second part of the implementation consists of a prerelease of the CiME 2 system, which is available from [CiM]; see also [CM96]. The CiME 2 system provides a prototype implementation of the dependency pair technique in combination with polynomial interpretations as described in Section 5.4. (Alternatively, one could use Arts's [Art00] implementation of the dependency pair technique, which uses argument filtering systems in combination with lexicographic path orderings.) To be precise, CiME performs the following steps:

1. It computes the estimated dependency graph of the rewrite system.

2. From the cycles in that graph, it computes a set of constraints of the form $t_1 > t_2$ or $t_1 \geq t_2$ that have to be satisfied by a quasi-reduction ordering.

The next goal is to find such an ordering, which is done as follows:

Program	Goal (mode)	LP TRS	TALP	others	Ref.
permute	`permute(i,o)`	+ +	+	+ + +	1.2
reverse	`reverse(i,o,i)`	+ +	+	+ + +	4.2
duplicate	`duplicate(i,o)`	+ +	+	+ + +	4.7
sum	`sum(i,i,o)`	+ +	+	+ + +	4.8
dis-con	`dis(i), con(i)`	+ +	+	+ + +	4.11

TABLE 10.2. De Schreye and Decorte [SD94]

3. With each function symbol f in the signature, say of arity n, it associates a parametric polynomial interpretation of the simple linear form $P_f(x_1, \dots, x_n) = a_1 x_1 + \cdots + a_n x_n + c$.
4. Every constraint is translated into constraints on polynomials and then into nonlinear Diophantine constraints over the a_i and c, by means of some (incomplete) positiveness criteria [HJ98].
5. The Diophantine constraints are solved for variables in the interval $[0; B]$, where B is a bound for coefficients given by the user, by using finite domain constraint solving techniques [BC93].

These two parts (the front-end and the back-end CiME) have been integrated into one system named TALP [OCM00]. TALP is an acronym for termination analysis of logic programs.

In order to compare the practical usefulness of the two-stage transformational method with other approaches to proving termination of logic programs, we tested the TALP system on three well-known test suites, which are collected in [LS97]. We compared the success behavior of our system with those systems for which test data w.r.t. the three test suites is available, viz. [DSV99, LS97, SSS97]. All of these are norm-based approaches. A fourth norm-based system, due to Codish and Taboch [CT99], shows a similar success behavior for several programs from the test suites. Because the authors did not provide results for every program in the test suites, we did not include their system in Tables 10.2–10.4. However, their system is taken into account in Table 10.5.

Before describing the outcome of this comparison, let us first comment on the differences between our method and the norm-based methods. In our method, a termination proof actually shows that the well-moded logic program is terminating for *every* well-moded goal. In contrast, the norm-based approaches (similar to Aguzzi and Modigliani's [AM93] technique) take a logic program *and* an abstract goal (given as an abstract atom where the argument positions are abstracted as **b** and **f** for input (bound) and output (free) argument positions) as input and try to prove termination of the logic program w.r.t. that goal. On the one hand, our approach has the advantage that it proves termination for *all* well-moded goals (even those

Program	Goal (mode)	LP	TRS	TALP	others		
list	`list(i)`	+	+	+	+	+	+
fold	`fold(i,i,o)`	+	+	+	+	+	+
lte	`goal`	+	+	+	+	+	+
map	`map(i,o)`	+	+	+	+	+	+
member	`member(o,i)`	+	+	+	+	+	+
mergesort_ap	`mergesort(i,o)`	+	+	+	+	+	+
naive_rev	`reverse(i,o)`	+	+	+	+	+	+
ordered	`ordered(i)`	+	+	+	+	+	+
overlap	`overlap(i,i)`	+	+	+	+	+	+
select	`select(o,i,o)`	+	+	+	+	+	+
subset	`subset(i,i)`	+	+	+	+	+	+
subset	`subset(o,i)`	–	–	–	–	–	–
sum	`sum(o,o,i)`	+	+	+	+	+	+

TABLE 10.3. Apt and Pedreschi [AP94a]

that are different from the abstract goal). On the other hand, it has the disadvantage that it cannot handle logic programs that are not well-moded or terminate for a given (abstract) goal but not for all goals.

In order to test the TALP system on the benchmarks, we proceeded as follows. Given a logic program and a goal, we first checked whether modes can be assigned to the predicates such that both the logic program and the goal are well-moded. If so, then the two-stage transformation was applied to the well-moded logic program.

The results of the tests are shown in Tables 10.2–10.4. Those programs that belong to more than one test suite are listed in Table 10.4. The first two columns specify the program from the test suite and how it was queried. A "+" in the LP column means that the logic program is terminating for the given goal (w.r.t. Prolog's selection rule), while "–" stands for nontermination. In the goal, **i** and **o** denote the input and output positions, respectively. A "+" in the TRS column means that the TRS $U(R_{\mathcal{P}})$ obtained from the logic program $\mathcal{P}$ is terminating, while "–" stands for nontermination. The next four columns display success or failure of the TALP system and the systems [DSV99, LS97, SSS97] (from left to right). A "+" indicates that the system is able to prove termination, while "–" stands for failure. The results in [SSS97] were obtained after transforming the programs to Mercury (which sometimes changes the termination behavior of the program); see [SSS97, DSV99] for details. Furthermore, the technique in [DSV99] can only handle directly recursive programs, and thus mutually recursive programs are first transformed into directly recursive program. Note that mutual recursion is no problem in our approach. The last column contains a reference to the examples in the respective paper. The tables show that the TALP system can compete with the sophisticated norm-based systems:

Program	Goal (mode)	LP	TRS	TALP	others	Ref.
append	`append(i,i,o)`	+	+	+	+ + +	1.1
append	`append(o,o,i)`	+	+	+	+ + +	1.1
permutation	`perm(i,o)`	+	+	+	+ − +	1.2
transitivity	`p(i,o)`	+	+	+	− − −	2.3.1
single element list	`p(o)`	−	−	−	− − −	3.5.6
single element list	`p(o)`	+[3]	−	−	+ + −	3.5.6a
append3	`append3(i,i,i,o)`	+	+	+	+ + +	4.0.1
merge	`merge(i,i,o)`	+	+	+	+ + +	4.4.3
prim. rec. 'perm'	`perm(i,o)`	+	+	+	+ + +	4.4.6a
simplification	`s(i,o)`	−	−	−	− − −	4.5.2
loops	`p(i)`	−	−	−	− − −	4.5.3a
turing machine	`turing(i,i,i,o)`	−	−	−	− − −	5.2.2
quicksort	`qsort(i,o)`	+	+	+	+ + +	6.1.1
mult	`mult(i,i,o)`	+	+	+	+ + +	7.2.9
reachability	`reach(i,i,i)`	−	−	−	− − −	7.6.2a
reachability	`reach(i,i,i,i)`	−	−	−	− − −	7.6.2b
reachability	`reach(i,i,i,i)`	+	+	+	+ + +	7.6.2c
mergesort	`mergesort(i,o)`	+	+	−	− − −	8.2.1
mergesort	`mergesort(i,o)`	+	+	+	+ + +	8.2.1a
minsort	`minsort(i,o)`	+	+	−	− − −	8.3.1
minsort	`minsort(i,o)`	+	+	+	+ + +	8.3.1a
even, odd	`even(i), odd(i)`	+	+	+	+ + +	8.4.1
parser for expr.	`e(i,o)`	+	+	+	+ + +	8.4.2

TABLE 10.4. Plümer [Plü90]

The systems under consideration show almost the same success behavior on the test suites.

During our experiments we made the following observations. For all those examples for which the back-end CiME was able to find a termination proof, it was also able to generate a suitable linear polynomial interpretation with coefficients in the interval [0; 2].

Next we briefly comment on the differences in the success behavior of the systems. Program 3.5.6a in Table 10.4 cannot be handled by our method because the program is nonterminating (hence the same is true for the transformed TRS) but it terminates for goals `p(o)`. In contrast to that, the TALP system can prove termination of the transitivity program in Table 10.4. According to [DSV99, LS97, SSS97], the other systems cannot prove termination of this program, which contains the following clauses:

$$p(x, z) \leftarrow q(x, y), p(y, z)$$
$$p(x, x) \leftarrow$$
$$q(a, b) \leftarrow$$

[3] The program terminates for goals `p(o)` but is nonterminating for other goals.

Program	Goal (mode)	LP	TRS	TALP	Others				Ref.
minsort	`minsort(i,o)`	+	+	−	−	−	−	−	[Plü90]
permutation	`perm(i,o)`	+	+	+	+	−	+	+	[Plü90]
transitivity	`p(i,o)`	+	+	+	−	−	−	⊟	[Plü90]
mergesort	`mergesort(i,o)`	+	+	−	−	−	−	+	[Plü90]
mergesort_t	`mergesort(i,o)`	+	+	+	−	+	−	⊞	[LS97]
flat	`flat(i,o)`	+	+	+	⊕	⊟	⊟	⊟	[AZ96]

TABLE 10.5. Interesting examples

It is interesting to note that the transformational method of [KRKS98] also fails in this case. Note that this logic program is terminating w.r.t. Prolog's selection rule, but infinite SLD derivations exist if a different selection rule is used; cf. [Plü90, example 2.3.1].

The four most interesting examples from Plümer's [Plü90] test suite and two other interesting examples are collected in Table 10.5. This time, the results from [CT99] are included in the penultimate column (i.e., columns 6–9 contain the results from [DSV99, LS97, SSS97, CT99]). The results ⊞ and ⊟ were obtained by our own experiments with the respective systems because these results were not included in the papers. The ⊕ entry in Table 10.5 will be explained.

None of the systems under consideration can provide a termination proof of the minsort program. Termination proofs of this program obtained by a termination prover coupled with an induction prover are known; see, e.g., [Wal94, Gie95b]. The permutation program can be handled by every system, except for the one from [LS97]. The transitivity program can solely be proven terminating by our system, while the other systems fail. On the other hand, only the system from [CT99] is able to prove termination of the *mergesort* program. Our system could prove termination of this program as well, if it were able to detect that an answer substitution σ to the goal $split([e, f|u], w, y)$ must satisfy $w\sigma = [e|\ldots]$ and $y\sigma = [f|\ldots]$. On the level of the resulting TRS, this corresponds to the fact that $split_{in}(cons(e, cons(f, u)))\sigma \to_{U(R_{\mathcal{P}})} split_{out}(w, y)\sigma$ implies $w\sigma = cons(e, \ldots)$ and $y\sigma = cons(f, \ldots)$. It should be worthwhile to investigate whether partial evaluation techniques can be applied to TRSs to infer such facts automatically. The technique of instantiating dependency pairs [GA01, theorem 12] could make use of such knowledge. In contrast to the *mergesort* program, the TALP system is able to show termination of the *mergesort_t* program. Note that the systems from [DSV99] and [SSS97] are not able to handle this program. Lastly, we have tested the systems under consideration on the flat program from [AZ96]. Our system has no problems with this program, while the other systems—except for [DSV99]—were not able to prove termination. Unfortunately, the prototype of [DSV99] does not currently work so that we cannot say whether this system is able to show termination of the flat program. However, according to De Schreye (personal communication), a "decent implementation" of the method should be able to do so; hence the $\oplus$ entry.

10.7 Summary and Related Work

We have shown that the transformational approaches of Ganzinger and Waldmann [GW93], Chtourou and Rusinowitch [CR93], and Arts and Zantema [AZ95, AZ96] are equally powerful. The two-stage transformation consisting of the phases (i) translation of a logic program $\mathcal{P}$ into a deterministic 3-CTRS $R_{\mathcal{P}}$ [GW93] and (ii) translation of $R_{\mathcal{P}}$ into an unconditional TRS $U(R_{\mathcal{P}})$ [CR93] is much easier to grasp than a direct transformation via an imperative procedure [AZ95, AZ96]. Because unique termination of $\mathcal{P}$ can more often be proven on the level of $R_{\mathcal{P}}$ than on the level of $U(R_{\mathcal{P}})$, the two-stage transformation has another advantage over the direct transformation.

A very similar fourth method due to Aguzzi and Modigliani [AM93] takes a logic program and a goal and transforms these into a TRS and a starting term. In their method, the modes of predicates are computed during the transformation according to the given goal. This prevents a direct comparison with the other three methods. We conjecture, however, that their method has the same power as the other techniques. All four methods are more powerful than the very first transformational method developed by Krishna Rao et al. [KRKS98]; see [GW93, AM93].

None of the four papers discussed earlier characterizes classes of well-moded logic programs for which the respective transformational technique is complete. In this chapter, it was shown that the methods of Ganzinger and Waldmann, Chtourou and Rusinowitch, and Arts and Zantema are complete for the class of simply moded and well-moded logic programs. Krishna Rao et al. [KRKS98] also showed that their method is complete for subclasses of the class of well-moded logic programs. However, these subclasses are quite small.

Marchiori [Mar94] devised two transformations, which he called `Tswm` and `Tfwm`. In stark contrast to the two-stage transformation described in this article, his transformations are not easy to understand. It is stated in [Mar94] that `Tswm` is sound and complete for simply moded and well-moded logic programs. However, we expect that the immense complexity of the TRS obtained by `Tswm` will be a drawback in practical applications. Of course, only experiments can support this supposition but we do not have an implementation of the transformation to experiment with. Furthermore, it is stated in [Mar94] that `Tfwm` is sound and complete for the class of flatly well-moded logic programs. This is interesting because the logic program from Example 10.4.1 is flatly well-moded. In other words, `Tfwm` can handle logic programs for which the two-stage transformation fails.

Another translation of logic programs into conditional rewrite systems has been given by van Raamsdonk [Raa97]. Her approach is restricted to the class of simply moded and well-moded logic programs (so in contrast to the methods described in this chapter, it cannot handle logic programs that are not simply moded). The main result of [Raa97] states that one resolution step using a clause C corresponds to a rewrite sequence consisting of at least one step using the translation of C. Hence termination of a logic program is implied by termination of its transformed CTRS. As another consequence, the translation can be used as a basis for an alternative implementation of simply moded and well-moded logic programs via functional programs.

To summarize, we have seen that the two-stage transformational approach to proving termination of a well-moded logic program $\mathcal{P}$ boils down to proving (innermost) termination of the unconditional TRS $U(R_{\mathcal{P}})$. Our implementation, the TALP system, uses the dependency pair technique in combination with polynomial interpretations to automatically prove termination of the resulting rewrite system. The empirical results show that the TALP system can compete with sophisticated norm-based systems. For some of the examples from the test suites, it even has a better success behavior than the other systems.

Appendix A
Kruskal's Theorem

The proof of the following fact is based on Kruskal's theorem [Kru60]: Every simplification ordering that is defined on a set of terms over a finite signature is well-founded. A beautiful simplified proof of Kruskal's theorem was presented by Nash-Williams [NW63]. In order to give this proof, we need some notions and results from the theory of partial well-orderings, the partial order variant of well-quasi-orderings. Our presentation was originally inspired by Rosenstein's book on linear orderings [Ros82]; see [Ohl92]. The term rewriting literature, e.g. [DJ90, Gal91, MZ97], also deals with this topic. We especially recommend Middeldorp and Zantema's article [MZ97]. Some historical remarks and further references can also be found in [Ros82] and [MZ97].

A.1 Partial Well-Orderings

Definition A.1.1 Let $(A, \succ)$ be a partial ordering and let $a_1, a_2, a_3, \ldots$ be a sequence of elements from A. The sequence is called *good* if there are indices $j < k$ such that $a_j \preceq a_k$; otherwise it is called *bad*. The sequence is called an *antichain* if its elements are pairwise *incomparable*, i.e., for all $j < k$ neither $a_j \preceq a_k$ nor $a_k \preceq a_j$ holds.

Definition A.1.2 A partial ordering $(A, \succ)$ is called a *partial well-ordering* (PWO), if every infinite sequence $a_1, a_2, a_3, \ldots$ over A is good.

Lemma A.1.3 *For every partial ordering $(A, \succ)$, the following statements are equivalent:*

1. *$(A, \succ)$ is a PWO.*

2. *Any infinite sequence $a_1, a_2, a_3, \ldots$ of elements of A contains an infinite subsequence $a_{i_1}, a_{i_2}, a_{i_3}, \ldots$ such that $i_j < i_k$ implies $a_{i_j} \preceq a_{i_k}$.*

3. *$(A, \succ)$ is well-founded and has no infinite antichain.*

Proof (1) $\Rightarrow$ (2): Let $a_1, a_2, a_3, \ldots$ be an infinite sequence over A. We call an index $m \in \mathbb{N}_+$ *terminal* if there is no $n > m$ such that $a_m \preceq a_n$. Let $a_{m_1}, a_{m_2}, a_{m_3}, \ldots$ be the subsequence of $a_1, a_2, a_3, \ldots$ consisting of all elements a_{m_j} for which m_j is a terminal index. If this subsequence is infinite, then it is bad. However, in a PWO every infinite sequence is good. Hence it is finite, and thus there is an index $i_1 \in \mathbb{N}_+$ such that all indices $m_j \geq i_1$ are not terminal. We define the desired subsequence inductively. Assume that $i_1 < i_2 < \cdots < i_k$ with $a_{i_1} \preceq a_{i_2} \preceq \cdots \preceq a_{i_k}$ are already defined. Now there is an index $i_{k+1} > i_k$ with $a_{i_k} \preceq a_{i_{k+1}}$ because $i_k \geq i_1$ is not terminal.

(2) $\Rightarrow$ (3): If $\succ$ is not well-founded, then there exists an infinite sequence $a_1 \succ a_2 \succ a_3 \succ \ldots$. Because $a_j \preceq a_k$ does not hold for any $j < k$, this sequence cannot have an infinite subsequence $a_{i_1}, a_{i_2}, a_{i_3}, \ldots$ with $a_{i_j} \preceq a_{i_k}$ for $i_j < i_k$. If $\succ$ admits an infinite antichain, then we obtain a contradiction in the same way.

(3) $\Rightarrow$ (1): For an indirect proof, suppose that $a_1, a_2, a_3, \ldots$ is a bad sequence. Because $\succ$ is well-founded, this sequence contains an element a_j such that $a_j \succ a_k$ is false for all $k > j$. In fact, $a_1, a_2, a_3, \ldots$ contains infinitely many such elements, say $a_{i_1}, a_{i_2}, a_{i_3}, \ldots$ with $i_1 < i_2 < i_3 \ldots$. Let $i_j < i_k$. By construction, $a_{i_j} \succ a_{i_k}$ is impossible. Clearly, $a_{i_j} \preceq a_{i_k}$ is also impossible because the sequence $a_{i_1}, a_{i_2}, a_{i_3}, \ldots$ is bad. Therefore, $a_{i_1}, a_{i_2}, a_{i_3}, \ldots$ is an antichain. This contradicts (3). □

Definition A.1.4 Let $(A, \succ)$ be a partial ordering. We define a relation $\succ^*$ on A^* as follows: If $w_1 = a_1 a_2 \cdots a_m$ and $w_2 = b_1 b_2 \cdots b_n$ are elements from A^*, then $w_1 \succ^* w_2$ if $w_1 \neq w_2$ and either $w_2 = \varepsilon$ or $m \geq n \geq 1$ and there are indices $1 \leq i_1 < i_2 < \cdots < i_n \leq m$ such that $a_{i_j} \succeq b_j$ for every j, $1 \leq j \leq n$.

In the following, the inverse of $\succ^*$ and $\succeq^*$ will be denoted by $\prec^*$ and $\preceq^*$, respectively. The next lemma was first proven by Higman [Hig52] and is thus referred to as Higman's lemma. The elegant proof that follows originates from Nash-Williams [NW63].

Lemma A.1.5 *If $(A, \succ)$ is a PWO, then so is $(A^*, \succ^*)$.*

Proof It is not difficult to show that $\succ^*$ is a partial ordering. In order to show that every infinite sequence over A is good, suppose, on the contrary, that there are bad sequences of elements from A^*. We will develop a bad sequence $w_1, w_2, w_3, \ldots$ with strong minimality properties and derive a contradiction.

Choose $w_1 \in A^*$ such that there is a bad sequence starting with w_1 but there is no bad sequence starting with a shorter string. Proceeding inductively, suppose that $w_1, w_2, \ldots, w_i$ have already been selected and choose w_{i+1} to be the shortest string such that there is a bad sequence starting with $w_1, w_2, \ldots, w_{i+1}$.

Clearly, ε cannot occur in a bad sequence because $w \succeq^* \varepsilon$ for any $w \in A^*$. Thus, $w_i \neq \varepsilon$ for every index i and we may write $w_i = a_i v_i$. According to Lemma A.1.3, the infinite sequence $a_1, a_2, a_3, \ldots$ contains an infinite subsequence $a_{i_1}, a_{i_2}, a_{i_3}, \ldots$ such that $i_j < i_k$ implies $a_{i_j} \preceq a_{i_k}$. Because v_{i_1} is shorter than w_{i_1}, the sequence $w_1, w_2, \ldots, w_{i_1-1}, v_{i_1}, v_{i_2}, v_{i_3}, \ldots$ must be good. If $w_\ell \preceq^* v_{i_j}$ were true for some $1 \leq \ell \leq i_1 - 1$ and $j \geq 1$, then $v_{i_j} \preceq^* w_{i_j}$ would imply $w_\ell \preceq^* w_{i_j}$. This, however, contradicts the fact that $w_1, w_2, w_3, \ldots$ is bad. Because (1) $w_1, w_2, w_3, \ldots$ is bad, (2) $w_\ell \preceq^* v_{i_j}$ does not hold for all $1 \leq \ell \leq i_1 - 1$ and $j \geq 1$, and (3) $w_1, w_2, \ldots, w_{i_1-1}, v_{i_1}, v_{i_2}, v_{i_3}, \ldots$ is good, it follows that there must be indices $i_j < i_k$ with $v_{i_j} \preceq v_{i_k}$. Combining this with $a_{i_j} \preceq a_{i_k}$ yields $w_{i_j} \preceq w_{i_k}$. This contradicts the badness of $w_1, w_2, w_3, \ldots$, and we are done. □

A.2 A Proof of Kruskal's Theorem

For a proof of Kruskal's theorem, we need to define the *homeomorphic* embedding relation that generalizes embedding.

Definition A.2.1 Let $\succ$ be a partial ordering on a signature $\mathcal{F}$. The TRS $\mathcal{E}mb(\mathcal{F}, \succ)$ contains the embedding rules, i.e., all rules from $\mathcal{E}mb(\mathcal{F})$, and for every $f \in \mathcal{F}^{(n)}$, $g \in \mathcal{F}^{(m)}$ with $n \geq m \geq 0$ and $f \succ g$ the rewrite rules

$$f(x_1, \ldots, x_n) \to g(x_{i_1}, \ldots, x_{i_m})$$

where the variables $x_1, \ldots, x_n$ are pairwise distinct and $1 \leq i_1 < \cdots < i_m \leq n$ whenever $m > 0$. We abbreviate $\to^+_{\mathcal{E}mb(\mathcal{F},\succ)}$ to $\succ_{\text{emb}}$. The relation $\preceq_{\text{emb}}$ is called *homeomorphic embedding.*

Observe that if $\succ$ is the empty partial ordering $\emptyset$ on $\mathcal{F}$, then $\mathcal{E}mb(\mathcal{F}, \emptyset) = \mathcal{E}mb(\mathcal{F})$ and hence $\succ_{\text{emb}} = \rhd_{\text{emb}}$.

Now we are able to prove the general version of Kruskal's theorem. As already mentioned, we will follow the proof given by Nash-Williams [NW63]. The structure of the proof is similar to that of Higman's lemma A.1.5.

Theorem A.2.2 *If* $(\mathcal{F}, \succ)$ *is a PWO, then so is* $(\mathcal{T}(\mathcal{F}), \succ_{\text{emb}})$.

Proof For an indirect proof, assume that there exist bad sequences of terms. As in Higman's lemma, we will develop a bad sequence that has strong minimality properties and derive a contradiction.

Choose $t_1 \in \mathcal{T}(\mathcal{F})$ such that there is a bad sequence starting with t_1 but there is no bad sequence starting with a term s where $|s| < |t_1|$. Proceeding inductively, suppose that $t_1, t_2, t_3, \ldots, t_j$ have all been carefully selected and choose t_{j+1} such that there exists a bad sequence starting with $t_1, t_2, t_3, \ldots, t_j, t_{j+1}$ but there is no bad sequence beginning with $t_1, t_2, t_3, \ldots, t_j, s$ where $|s| < |t_{j+1}|$.

For all terms t_j occurring in the constructed sequence let f_j denote the root of t_j, and define

$$S_j = \begin{cases} \emptyset & \text{if } t_j \in \mathcal{F}, \\ \{s_1^j, \ldots, s_{n_j}^j\} & \text{if } t_j = f_j(s_1^j, \ldots, s_{n_j}^j) \end{cases}$$

$$w_j = \begin{cases} \varepsilon & \text{if } t_j \in \mathcal{F}, \\ s_1^j, \ldots, s_{n_j}^j & \text{if } t_j = f_j(s_1^j, \ldots, s_{n_j}^j) \end{cases}$$

S_j denotes the set of all immediate proper subterms of t_j, and w_j denotes the finite sequence of the immediate proper subterms of t_j.

We claim that $(S, \succ_{\text{emb}})$ is a PWO, where $S = \bigcup_{j \geq 1} S_j$. To prove the claim, suppose that $(S, \succ_{\text{emb}})$ is not a PWO, i.e., there is a bad sequence of elements from S, say, $s_1, s_2, s_3, \ldots$. Because $s_1 \in S$, there exists a (smallest) $j_1 \in \mathbb{N}_+$ such that $s_1 \in S_{j_1}$, that is, s_1 is an immediate proper subterm of some t_{j_1} occurring in the constructed bad sequence. There are only finitely many s_i, $i > 1$, where s_i is an immediate proper subterm of some t_{j_i} such that $j_1 \geq j_i$ (otherwise $s_1, s_2, s_3, \ldots$ would contain an infinite bad subsequence of elements from the finite set $S' = \bigcup_{\ell=1}^{j_1} S_\ell$). Therefore, we may assume w.l.o.g. (deleting all such s_i) that $s_1, s_2, s_3, \ldots$ is a bad sequence of elements from S where s_k, $k > 1$, is an immediate proper subterm of some t_{j_k} such that $j_1 < j_k$. Because $t_i \preceq_{\text{emb}} t_k$ cannot hold (by construction, where $1 \leq i < k \leq j_1 - 1$) and $t_i \preceq_{\text{emb}} s_k$ cannot be true either (otherwise $t_i \preceq_{\text{emb}} t_{j_k}$ because $s_k \preceq_{\text{emb}} t_{j_k}$, where $i < j_1 \leq j_k$), it follows that $t_1, t_2, t_3, \ldots, t_{j_1-1}, s_1, s_2, s_3, \ldots$ is a bad sequence of elements from $\mathcal{T}(\mathcal{F})$, contradicting the minimality property of the constructed bad sequence $t_1, t_2, t_3, \ldots$. This proves the claim.

According to Higman's Lemma A.1.5, $(S^*, \succ_{\text{emb}}^*)$ is a PWO as well. Note that $w_j \in S^*$ for all $j \in \mathbb{N}_+$.

Now consider the infinite sequence $f_1, f_2, f_3, \ldots$ of elements in $\mathcal{F}$, where $f_j = root(t_j)$. Because $(\mathcal{F}, \succ)$ is a PWO, $f_1, f_2, f_3, \ldots$ contains an infinite subsequence $f_{i_1}, f_{i_2}, f_{i_3}, \ldots$ such that $i_j < i_k$ implies $f_{i_j} \preceq f_{i_k}$; cf. Lemma A.1.3. If any of these f_{i_j} is a constant (i.e., $f_{i_j} = t_{i_j}$), then $f_{i_j} \preceq_{\text{emb}} t_{i_k}$ yields a contradiction to the badness of $t_1, t_2, t_3, \ldots$. Hence $w_{i_j} \neq \varepsilon$ for all $j \in \mathbb{N}_+$.

Let the indices $i_1, i_2, i_3, \ldots$ be as earlier and consider the infinite sequence $w_{i_1}, w_{i_2}, w_{i_3}, \ldots$ of elements of S^*. Because $(S^*, \succ^*_{\text{emb}})$ is a PWO, there are indices $i_j < i_k$ such that $w_{i_j} \preceq^*_{\text{emb}} w_{i_k}$. Let $f_{i_j} \in \mathcal{F}^{(n)}$ and $f_{i_k} \in \mathcal{F}^{(m)}$, that is, $t_{i_j} = f_{i_j}(s_1^{i_j}, \ldots, s_n^{i_j})$ and $t_{i_k} = f_{i_k}(s_1^{i_k}, \ldots, s_m^{i_k})$. Because $w_{i_j} = s_1^{i_j}, \ldots, s_n^{i_j} \neq \varepsilon \neq w_{i_k} = s_1^{i_k}, \ldots, s_m^{i_k}$, we have $n \geq 1$ and $m \geq 1$. Now $w_{i_k} \succeq^*_{\text{emb}} w_{i_j}$ means that there are indices $1 \leq l_1 < l_2 < \cdots < l_n \leq m$ such that $s_{l_q}^{i_k} \succeq_{\text{emb}} s_q^{i_j}$ for each $q \in \{1, \ldots, n\}$. This, however, implies (the first step follows from $f_{i_k} \succeq f_{i_j}$)

$$t_{i_k} = f_{i_k}(s_1^{i_k}, \ldots, s_m^{i_k}) \succeq_{\text{emb}} f_{i_j}(s_{l_1}^{i_k}, \ldots, s_{l_n}^{i_k}) \succeq_{\text{emb}} f_{i_j}(s_1^{i_j}, \ldots, s_n^{i_j}) = t_{i_j}$$

All in all, $t_{i_k} \succeq_{\text{emb}} t_{i_j}$ contradicts the fact that $t_1, t_2, t_3, \ldots$ is a bad sequence. □

Theorem 5.2.19, the finite version of Kruskal's theorem, is a corollary to Theorem A.2.2: If $\mathcal{F}$ is finite, then the empty relation $\emptyset$ is a PWO on $\mathcal{F}$. Because $\mathcal{E}mb(\mathcal{F}, \emptyset) = \mathcal{E}mb(\mathcal{F})$, it follows that $\succ_{\text{emb}} = \rhd_{\text{emb}}$ is a PWO over $\mathcal{T}(\mathcal{F})$.

We conclude this appendix by mentioning that Kruskal's theorem has been generalized by Puel [Pue89].

References

[AE93] K.R. Apt and S. Etalle. On the unification free Prolog programs. In *Proceedings of the 18th International Symposium on Mathematical Foundations of Computer Science*, volume 711 of *Lecture Notes in Computer Science*, pages 1–19, Springer-Verlag, Berlin, 1993.

[AEH94] S. Antoy, R. Echahed, and M. Hanus. A needed narrowing strategy. In *Proceedings of the 21st ACM Symposium on Principles of Programming Languages*, pages 268–79, 1994.

[AG97a] T. Arts and J. Giesl. Automatically proving termination where simplification orderings fail. In *Theory and Practice of Software Development (Proceedings of the 22nd International Colloquium on Trees in Algebra and Programming)*, volume 1214 of *Lecture Notes in Computer Science*, pages 261–72, Springer-Verlag, Berlin, 1997.

[AG97b] T. Arts and J. Giesl. Termination of term rewriting using dependency pairs. *Technical Report IBN 97/46*, Darmstadt University of Technology, 1997.

[AG00] T. Arts and J. Giesl. Termination of term rewriting using dependency pairs. *Theoretical Computer Science*, 236:133–78, 2000.

[AK96] Z.M. Ariola and J.W. Klop. Equational term graph rewriting. *Fundamenta Informaticae*, 26:207–40, 1996.

[AKP00] Z.M. Ariola, J.W. Klop, and D. Plump. Bisimilarity in term graph rewriting. *Information and Computation*, 156:2–24, 2000.

[ALS93] J. Avenhaus and C. Loría-Sáenz. Canonical conditional rewrite systems containing extra variables. *SEKI-Report SR-93-03*, University of Kaiserslautern, 1993.

[ALS94] J. Avenhaus and C. Loría-Sáenz. On conditional rewrite systems with extra variables and deterministic logic programs. In *Proceedings of the 5th International Conference on Logic Programming and Automated Reasoning*, volume 822 of *Lecture Notes in Artificial Intelligence*, pages 215–29, Springer-Verlag, Berlin, 1994.

[AM93] G. Aguzzi and U. Modigliani. Proving termination of logic programs by transforming them into equivalent term rewriting systems. In *Proceedings of the 13th Conference on the Foundations of Software Technology and Theoretical Computer Science*, volume 761 of *Lecture Notes in Computer Science*, pages 114–24, Springer-Verlag, Berlin, 1993.

[Aot98] T. Aoto. Solution to the problem of Zantema on a persistent property of term rewriting systems. In *Principles in Declarative Programming (Proceedings of the 7th International Conference on Algebraic and Logic Programming)*, volume 1490 of *Lecture Notes in Computer Science*, pages 250–65, Springer-Verlag, Berlin, 1998.

[AP94a] K.R. Apt and D.H. Pedreschi. Modular termination proofs for logic and pure Prolog programs. In *Advances in Logic Programing*, pages 183–229, Oxford University Press, 1994.

[AP94b] K.R. Apt and A. Pellegrini. On the occur-check free Prolog programs. *ACM Transactions on Programming Languages and Systems*, 16(3):687–726, 1994.

[Apt97] K.R. Apt. *From Logic Programming to Prolog.* Prentice-Hall, 1997.

[Art97] T. Arts. *Automatically Proving Termination and Innermost Normalisation of Term Rewriting Systems.* Ph.D. thesis, Utrecht University, 1997.

[Art00] T. Arts. System description: The dependency pair method. In *Proceedings of the 11th International Conference on Rewriting Techniques and Applications*, volume 1833 of *Lecture Notes in Computer Science*, pages 261–4, Springer-Verlag, Berlin, 2000.

[AT97a] T. Aoto and Y. Toyama. On composable properties of term rewriting systems. In *Proceedings of the 6th International Conference on Algebraic and Logic Programming*, volume 1298 of *Lecture Notes in Computer Science*, pages 114–28, Springer-Verlag, Berlin, 1997.

[AT97b] T. Aoto and Y. Toyama. Persistency of confluence. *Journal of Universal Computer Science*, 3(11):1134–47, 1997.

[Ave95] J. Avenhaus. *Reduktionssysteme.* Springer-Verlag, 1995.

[AZ95] T. Arts and H. Zantema. Termination of logic programs via labelled term rewrite systems. In *Proceedings of Computing Science in the Netherlands*, pages 22–34, 1995.

[AZ96] T. Arts and H. Zantema. Termination of logic programs using semantic unification. In *Proceedings of the 5th International Workshop on Logic Program Synthesis and Transformation*, volume 1048 of *Lecture Notes in Computer Science*, pages 219–33, Springer-Verlag, Berlin, 1996.

[Bar84] H.P. Barendregt. *The Lambda Calculus: Its Syntax and Semantics*, 2nd edition. Studies in Logic and the Foundations of Mathematics. North-Holland, 1984.

[BC93] F. Benhamou and A. Colmerauer, editors. *Constraint Logic Programming: Selected Research.* MIT Press, 1993.

[BCL87] A. Ben-Charifa and P. Lescanne. Termination of rewrite systems by polynomial interpretations and its implementation. *Science of Computer Programming*, 9(2):137–59, 1987.

[BEG+87] H.P. Barendregt, M.C.J.D. van Eekelen, J.R.W. Glauert, J.R. Kennaway, M.J. Plasmeijer, and M.R. Sleep. Term graph rewriting. In *Proceedings of Parallel Architectures and Languages Europe*, volume 259 of *Lecture Notes in Computer Science*, pages 141–58, Springer-Verlag, Berlin, 1987.

[BG89] H. Bertling and H. Ganzinger. Completion-time optimization of rewrite-time goal solving. In *Proceedings of the 3rd International Conference on Rewriting Techniques and Applications*, volume 355 of *Lecture Notes in Computer Science*, pages 45–58, Springer-Verlag, Berlin, 1989.

[BK86] J.A. Bergstra and J.W. Klop. Conditional rewrite rules: Confluence and termination. *Journal of Computer and System Sciences*, 32(3):323–62, 1986.

[BKM89] J.A. Bergstra, J.W. Klop, and A. Middeldorp. *Termherschrijfsystemen.* Kluwer Bedrijfswetenschappen, Deventer, 1989.

[BM84] J.A. Bergstra and J.-J.Ch. Meyer. On specifying sets of integers. *Elektronische Informationsverarbeitung und Kybernetik*, 20(10/11):531–41, 1984.

[BN98] F. Baader and T. Nipkow. *Term Rewriting and All That.* Cambridge University Press, 1998.

[BO93] R.V. Book and F. Otto. *String-Rewriting Systems.* Springer-Verlag, 1993.

[Bün98] R. Bündgen. *Termersetzungssysteme: Theorie, Implementierung, Anwendung.* Verlag Vieweg, 1998.

[Car91] A.-C. Caron. Linear bounded automata and rewrite systems: Influence of initial configurations on decision properties. In *Proceedings of the 16th Colloquium on Trees in Algebra and Programming*, volume 493 of *Lecture Notes in Computer Science*, pages 74–89, Springer-Verlag, Berlin, 1991.

[CF58] H.B. Curry and R. Feys. *Combinatory Logic*, volume 1. North-Holland, 1958.

[CHR92] P.-L. Curien, T. Hardin, and A. Ríos. Strong normalization of substitutions. In *Proceedings of the 17th International Symposium on Mathematical Foundations of Computer Science*, volume 629 of *Lecture Notes in Computer Science*, pages 209–17, Springer-Verlag, Berlin, 1992.

[Chu41] A. Church. *The Calculi of Lambda Conversion.* Princeton University Press, 1941.

[CiM] CiME 2. Prerelease available at `http://www.lri.fr/~marche/cime.html`.

[CM96] E. Contejean and C. Marché. CiME: Completion Modulo *E*. In *Proceedings of the 7th International Conference on Rewriting Techniques and Applications*, volume 1103 of *Lecture Notes in Computer Science*, pages 416–19, Springer-Verlag, Berlin, 1996.

[Cou90] B. Courcelle. Recursive applicative program schemes. In L. van Leeuwen, editor, *Formal Models and Semantics*, volume B of *Handbook of Theoretical Computer Science*, chapter 9, pages 459–92. Elsevier–The MIT Press, 1990.

[CR93] M. Chtourou and M. Rusinowitch. Méthode transformationnelle pour la preuve de terminaison des programmes logiques. Unpublished manuscript in French, Centre de Recherche en Informatique de Nancy, 1993.

[CT99] M. Codish and C. Taboch. A semantic basis for the termination analysis of logic programs. *The Journal of Logic Programming*, 41:103–23, 1999.

[Dau92] M. Dauchet. Simulation of Turing machines by a regular rewrite rule. *Theoretical Computer Science*, 103(2):409–20, 1992.

[Der79] N. Dershowitz. A note on simplification orderings. *Information Processing Letters*, 9(5):212–15, 1979.

[Der81] N. Dershowitz. Termination of linear rewriting systems (preliminary version). In *Proceedings of the 8th International Colloquium on Automata, Languages and Programming*, volume 115 of *Lecture Notes in Computer Science*, pages 448–58, Springer-Verlag, Berlin, 1981.

[Der82] N. Dershowitz. Orderings for term-rewriting systems. *Theoretical Computer Science*, 17(3):279–301, 1982.

[Der87] N. Dershowitz. Termination of rewriting. *Journal of Symbolic Computation*, 3(1):69–116, 1987.

[Der95] N. Dershowitz. Hierarchical termination. In *Proceedings of the 4th International Workshop on Conditional and Typed Rewriting Systems*, volume 968 of *Lecture Notes in Computer Science*, pages 89–105, Springer-Verlag, Berlin, 1995.

[Der97] N. Dershowitz. Innocuous combinations. In *Proceedings of the 8th International Conference on Rewriting Techniques and Applications*, volume 1232 of *Lecture Notes in Computer Science*, pages 202–16, Springer-Verlag, Berlin, 1997.

[DH95] N. Dershowitz and C. Hoot. Natural termination. *Theoretical Computer Science*, 142(2):179–207, 1995.

[DJ90] N. Dershowitz and J.-P. Jouannaud. Rewrite systems. In J. van Leeuwen, editor, *Formal Models and Semantics*, volume B of *Handbook of Theoretical Computer Science*, chapter 6, pages 243–320. Elsevier—The MIT Press, 1990.

[DJK95] N. Dershowitz, J.-P. Jouannaud, and J.W. Klop. Problems in rewriting III. In *Proceedings of the 6th International*

Conference on Rewriting Techniques and Applications, volume 914 of *Lecture Notes in Computer Science*, pages 457–71, Springer-Verlag, Berlin, 1995.

[DKM90] J. Dick, J. Kalmus, and U. Martin. Automating the Knuth-Bendix ordering. *Acta Informatica*, 28:95–119, 1990.

[DM79] N. Dershowitz and Z. Manna. Proving termination with multiset orderings. *Communications of the ACM*, 22(8):465–76, 1979.

[DM85] P. Dembinski and J. Maluszynski. AND-parallelism with intelligent backtracking for annotated logic programs. In *Proceedings of the 2nd IEEE Symposium on Logic Programming*, pages 29–38, 1985.

[DO90] N. Dershowitz and M. Okada. A rationale for conditional equational programming. *Theoretical Computer Science*, 75:111–38, 1990.

[DOS88] N. Dershowitz, M. Okada, and G. Sivakumar. Canonical conditional rewrite systems. In *Proceedings of the 9th Conference on Automated Deduction*, volume 310 of *Lecture Notes in Computer Science*, pages 538–49, Springer-Verlag, Berlin, 1988.

[Dro89] K. Drosten. *Termersetzungssysteme*, volume 210 of *Informatik-Fachberichte*. Springer-Verlag, 1989.

[DSV99] S. Decorte, D. De Schreye, and H. Vandecasteele. Constraint-based termination analysis of logic programs. *ACM Transactions on Programming Languages and Systems*, 21:1137–95, 1999.

[EM85] H. Ehrig and B. Mahr. *Fundamentals of Algebraic Specifications I: Equations and Initial Semantics*. Springer-Verlag, 1985.

[Fer95] M. Ferreira. *Termination of Term Rewriting: Well-Foundedness, Totality, and Transformations*. Ph.D. thesis, University of Utrecht, 1995.

[FJ95] M. Fernández and J.-P. Jouannaud. Modular termination of term rewriting systems revisited. In *Recent Trends in Data Type Specification (Proceedings of the 10th Workshop on Specification of Abstract Data Types)*, volume 906 of *Lecture Notes in Computer Science*, pages 255–72, Springer-Verlag, Berlin, 1995.

[FZ94] M.C.F. Ferreira and H. Zantema. Syntactic analysis of total termination. In *Proceedings of the 4th International Conference on Algebraic and Logic Programming*, volume 850 of *Lecture Notes in Computer Science*, pages 204–22, Springer-Verlag, Berlin, 1994.

[FZ96] M. Ferreira and H. Zantema. Total termination of term rewriting. *Applicable Algebra in Engineering, Communication and Computing*, 7(2):133–62, 1996.

[GA01] J. Giesl and T. Arts. Verification of Erlang processes by dependency pairs. *Applicable Algebra in Engineering, Communication and Computing*, 12:39–72, 2001.

[Gal91] J. Gallier. What's so special about Kruskal's theorem and the ordinal γ_0? A survey of some results in proof theory. *Annals of Pure and Applied Logic*, 53:199–260, 1991.

[Gan91] H. Ganzinger. Order-sorted completion: The many-sorted way. *Theoretical Computer Science*, 89:3–32, 1991.

[GAO02] J. Giesl, T. Arts, and E. Ohlebusch. Modular termination proofs for rewriting using dependency pairs. *Journal of Symbolic Computation*, 2002, to appear.

[Ges97] A. Geser. Omega-termination is undecidable for totally terminating term rewriting systems. *Journal of Symbolic Computation*, 23:399–411, 1997.

[Ges00] A. Geser. On normalizing, non-terminating one-rule string rewriting systems. *Theoretical Computer Science*, 243:489–98, 2000.

[Gie95a] J. Giesl. Generating polynomial orderings for termination proofs. In *Proceedings of the 6th International Conference on Rewriting Techniques and Applications*, volume 914 of *Lecture Notes in Computer Science*, pages 426–31, Springer-Verlag, Berlin, 1995.

[Gie95b] J. Giesl. Termination analysis for functional programs using term orderings. In *Proceedings of the International Symposium on Static Analysis*, volume 983 of *Lecture Notes in Computer Science*, pages 154–71, Springer-Verlag, Berlin, 1995.

[GM86] E. Giovannetti and C. Moiso. A completeness result for E-unification algorithms based on conditional narrowing. In *Foundations of Logic and Functional Programming*, volume

306 of *Lecture Notes in Computer Science*, pages 157–67, Springer-Verlag, Berlin, 1986.

[GM87] E. Giovannetti and C. Moiso. Notes on the elimination of conditions. In *Proceedings of the 1st International Workshop on Conditional Term Rewriting Systems*, volume 308 of *Lecture Notes in Computer Science*, pages 91–7, Springer-Verlag, Berlin, 1987.

[GMHGRA92] J.C. González-Moreno, M.T. Hortalá-González, and M. Rodríguez-Artalejo. Denotational versus declarative semantics for functional programming. In *Proceedings of the 5th Workshop on Computer Science Logic*, volume 626 of *Lecture Notes in Computer Science*, pages 134–48, Springer-Verlag, Berlin, 1992.

[GMOZ97] A. Geser, A. Middeldorp, E. Ohlebusch, and H. Zantema. Relative undecidability in term rewriting. In *Proceedings of the 10th International Workshop on Computer Science Logic*, volume 1258 of *Lecture Notes in Computer Science*, pages 150–66, Springer-Verlag, Berlin, 1997.

[GMOZ02a] A. Geser, A. Middeldorp, E. Ohlebusch, and H. Zantema. Relative undecidability in term rewriting, part 1: The termination hierarchy. *Information and Computation*, 2002, to appear.

[GMOZ02b] A. Geser, A. Middeldorp, E. Ohlebusch, and H. Zantema. Relative undecidability in term rewriting, part 2: The confluence hierarchy. *Information and Computation*, 2002, to appear.

[Gra94] B. Gramlich. Generalized sufficient conditions for modular termination of rewriting. *Applicable Algebra in Engineering, Communication and Computing*, 5:131–58, 1994.

[Gra95] B. Gramlich. Abstract relations between restricted termination and confluence properties of rewrite systems. *Fundamenta Informaticae*, 24:3–23, 1995.

[Gra96a] B. Gramlich. On termination and confluence properties of disjoint and constructor-sharing conditional rewrite systems. *Theoretical Computer Science*, 165(1):97–131, 1996.

[Gra96b] B. Gramlich. *Termination and Confluence Properties of Structured Rewrite Systems*. Ph.D. thesis, Universität Kaiserslautern, 1996.

[GW93] H. Ganzinger and U. Waldmann. Termination proofs of well-moded logic programs via conditional rewrite systems. In *Proceedings of the 3rd International Workshop on Conditional Term Rewriting Systems*, volume 656 of *Lecture Notes in Computer Science*, pages 113–27, Springer-Verlag, Berlin, 1993.

[Han94] M. Hanus. The integration of functions into logic programming: From theory to practice. *The Journal of Logic Programming*, 19&20:583–628, 1994.

[Hig52] G. Higman. Ordering by divisibility in abstract algebras. *Proceedings of the London Mathematical Society*, 2:326–36, 1952.

[Hin64] R. Hindley. *The Church-Rosser Property and a Result in Combinatory Logic*. Ph.D. thesis, University of Newcastle-upon-Tyne, 1964.

[Hin74] R. Hindley. An abstract Church-Rosser theorem, part II: Applications. *Journal of Symbolic Logic*, 39:1–21, 1974.

[HJ98] H. Hong and D. Jakus. Testing positiveness of polynomials. *Journal of Automated Reasoning*, 21:23–38, 1998.

[HL78] G. Huet and D.S. Lankford. On the uniform halting problem for term rewriting systems. *Rapport laboria 283*, IRIA, 1978.

[HL86] T. Hardin and A. Laville. Proof of termination of the rewriting system SUBST on CCL. *Theoretical Computer Science*, 46:305–12, 1986.

[HO80] G. Huet and D.C. Oppen. Equations and rewrite rules: A survey. In *Formal Language Theory: Perspectives and Open Problems*, pages 349–405. Academic Press, 1980.

[Hoa62] C.A.R. Hoare. Quicksort. *Computer Journal*, 5(1):10–15, 1962.

[Hof92] D. Hofbauer. Termination proofs by multiset path orderings imply primitive recursive derivation length. *Theoretical Computer Science*, 105:129–40, 1992.

[Hue80] G. Huet. Confluent reductions: Abstract properties and applications to term rewriting systems. *Journal of the ACM*, 27(4):797–821, 1980.

[Jan88] M. Jantzen. *Confluent String Rewriting and Congruences*, volume 14 of *EATCS Monographs on Theoretical Computer Science*. Springer-Verlag, Berlin, 1988.

[JM84] J.-P. Jouannaud and M. Munoz. Termination of a set of rules modulo a set of equations. In *7th International Conference on Automated Deduction*, volume 170 of *Lecture Notes in Computer Science*, pages 175–93, Springer-Verlag, Berlin, 1984.

[JW86] J.-P. Jouannaud and B. Waldmann. Reductive conditional term rewriting systems. In *Proceedings of the 3rd IFIP Working Conference on Formal Description of Programming Concepts*, pages 223–44, 1986.

[Kap84] S. Kaplan. Conditional rewrite rules. *Theoretical Computer Science*, 33(2):175–93, 1984.

[Kap87] S. Kaplan. Simplifying conditional term rewriting systems: Unification, termination and confluence. *Journal of Symbolic Computation*, 4(3):295–334, 1987.

[KB70] D.E. Knuth and P. Bendix. Simple word problems in universal algebra. In J. Leech, editor, *Computational Problems in Abstract Algebra*, pages 263–97. Pergamon Press, 1970.

[KK90] M. Kurihara and I. Kaji. Modular term rewriting systems and the termination. *Information Processing Letters*, 34:1–4, 1990.

[KKSV94] J.R. Kennaway, J.W. Klop, M.R. Sleep, and F.-J. de Vries. On the adequacy of term graph rewriting for simulating term rewriting. *ACM Transactions on Programming Languages and Systems*, 16:493–523, 1994.

[KL80] S. Kamin and J.-J. Lévy. Attempts for generalizing the recursive path ordering. Unpublished note, Dept. of Computer Science, University of Illinois, 1980.

[Klo92] J.W. Klop. Term rewriting systems. In S. Abramsky, D. Gabbay, and T. Maibaum, editors, *Handbook of Logic in Computer Science*, volume 2, pages 1–116. Oxford University Press, 1992.

[KM68] K. Kuratowski and A. Mostowski. *Set Theory*. North-Holland Publishing Company, 1968.

[KMTV94] J.W. Klop, A. Middeldorp, Y. Toyama, and R. de Vrijer. Modularity of confluence: A simplified proof. *Information Processing Letters*, 49(2):101–9, 1994.

[KN85] M.S. Krishnamoorthy and P. Narendran. On recursive path ordering. *Theoretical Computer Science*, 40:323–8, 1985.

[KNO80] D. Kapur, P. Narendran, and F. Otto. On ground-confluence of term rewriting systems. *Information and Computation*, 86(1):14–31, 1980.

[KNT99] K. Kusakari, M. Nakamura, and Y. Toyama. Argument filtering transformation. In *Principles and Practice of Declarative Programming (Proceedings of the 1st International Conference)*, volume 1702 of *Lecture Notes in Computer Science*, pages 47–61, Springer-Verlag, Berlin, 1999.

[KO90] M. Kurihara and A. Ohuchi. Modularity of simple termination of term rewriting systems. *Journal of IPS Japan*, 31(5):633–42, 1990.

[KO92] M. Kurihara and A. Ohuchi. Modularity of simple termination of term rewriting systems with shared constructors. *Theoretical Computer Science*, 103:273–82, 1992.

[KO95a] M. Kurihara and A. Ohuchi. Decomposable termination of composable term rewriting systems. *IEICE*, E78-D(4):314–20, 1995.

[KO95b] M. Kurihara and A. Ohuchi. Modularity in noncopying term rewriting. *Theoretical Computer Science*, 152:139–69, 1995.

[KR94] M.R.K. Krishna Rao. Simple termination of hierarchical combinations of term rewriting systems. In *Proceedings of the 2nd International Symposium on Theoretical Aspects of Computer Software*, volume 789 of *Lecture Notes in Computer Science*, pages 203–23, Springer-Verlag, Berlin, 1994.

[KR95a] M.R.K. Krishna Rao. Modular proofs for completeness of hierarchical term rewriting systems. *Theoretical Computer Science*, 151:487–512, 1995.

[KR95b] M.R.K. Krishna Rao. Semi-completeness of hierarchical and super-hierarchical combinations of term rewriting systems. In *TAPSOFT'95: Theory and Practice of Software Development (Proceedings of the 20th Colloquium on Trees in Algebra and Programming)*, volume 915 of *Lecture*

Notes in Computer Science, pages 379–93, Springer-Verlag, Berlin, 1995.

[KR98] M.R.K. Krishna Rao. Modular aspects of term graph rewriting. *Theoretical Computer Science*, 208:59–86, 1998.

[KR00] M.R.K. Krishna Rao. Some characteristics of strong innermost normalization. *Theoretical Computer Science*, 239:141–64, 2000.

[KRKS92] M.R.K. Krishna Rao, D. Kapur, and R.K. Shyamasundar. A transformational methodology for proving termination of logic programs. In *Proceedings of the 5th Workshop on Computer Science Logic*, volume 626 of *Lecture Notes in Computer Science*, pages 213–26, Springer-Verlag, Berlin, 1992.

[KRKS98] M.R.K. Krishna Rao, D. Kapur, and R.K. Shyamasundar. Transformational methodology for proving termination of logic programs. *The Journal of Logic Programming*, 34(1):1–42, 1998. (A preliminary version appeared in [KRKS92].)

[Kru60] J. Kruskal. Well-quasi-ordering, the tree theorem, and Vazsonyi's conjecture. *Transactions of the American Mathematical Society*, 95:210–25, 1960.

[KV90] J.W. Klop and R. de Vrijer. Extended term rewriting systems. In *Proceedings of the 2nd International Workshop on Conditional and Typed Rewriting Systems*, volume 516 of *Lecture Notes in Computer Science*, pages 26–50, Springer-Verlag, Berlin, 1990.

[Lan75] D.S. Lankford. Canonical algebraic simplification in computational logic. *Technical Report ATP-25*, University of Texas, Austin, 1975.

[Lan79] D.S. Lankford. On proving term rewriting systems are Noetherian. *Technical Report MTP-3*, Lousiana Technical University, Ruston, 1979.

[Les94] P. Lescanne. On termination of one rule rewrite systems. *Theoretical Computer Science*, 132:395–401, 1994.

[Llo87] J. Lloyd. *Foundations of Logic Programming.* Springer-Verlag, 1987.

[LS97] N. Lindenstrauss and Y. Sagiv. Automatic termination analysis of logic programs (with detailed experimental results). Technical report, Hebrew University, Jerusalem, 1997. Test suites at `http://www.cs.huji.ac.il/~naomil/` and system available from `http://www.cs.huji.ac.il/~talre/form.html`.

[Mar94] M. Marchiori. Logic programs as term rewriting systems. In *Proceedings of the 4th International Conference on Algebraic and Logic Programming*, volume 850 of *Lecture Notes in Computer Science*, pages 223–41, Springer-Verlag, Berlin, 1994.

[Mar95] M. Marchiori. Unravelings and ultra-properties. *Technical Report 8*, Dept. of Pure and Applied Mathematics, University of Padova, Italy, 1995.

[Mar96a] M. Marchiori. On the modularity of normal forms in rewriting. *Journal of Symbolic Computation*, 22(2):143–54, 1996.

[Mar96b] M. Marchiori. Unravelings and ultra-properties. In *Proceedings of the 5th International Conference on Algebraic and Logic Programming*, volume 1139 of *Lecture Notes in Computer Science*, pages 107–21, Springer-Verlag, Berlin, 1996.

[Mar97a] M. Marchiori. On deterministic conditional rewriting. Computation Structures Group, Memo 405, MIT Laboratory for Computer Science, 1997.

[Mar97b] M. Marchiori. On the expressive power of rewriting. In *Proceedings of the 17th International Conference on the Foundations of Software Technology and Theoretical Computer Science*, volume 1346 of *Lecture Notes in Computer Science*, pages 88–102, Springer-Verlag, Berlin, 1997.

[Mar98] M. Marchiori. Bubbles in modularity. *Theoretical Computer Science*, 192(1):31–54, 1998.

[MG95] A. Middeldorp and B. Gramlich. Simple termination is difficult. *Applicable Algebra in Engineering, Communication and Computing*, 6(2):115–28, 1995.

[MH94] A. Middeldorp and E. Hamoen. Completeness results for basic narrowing. *Applicable Algebra in Engineering, Communication and Computing*, 5:213–53, 1994.

[Mid89a] A. Middeldorp. Modular aspects of properties of term rewriting systems related to normal forms. In *Proceedings of the 3rd International Conference on Rewriting Techniques and Applications*, volume 355 of *Lecture Notes in Computer Science*, pages 263–77, Springer-Verlag, Berlin, 1989.

[Mid89b] A. Middeldorp. A sufficient condition for the termination of the direct sum of term rewriting systems. In *Proceedings of the 4th IEEE Symposium on Logic in Computer Science*, pages 396–401, 1989.

[Mid90] A. Middeldorp. *Modular Properties of Term Rewriting Systems.* Ph.D. thesis, Vrije Universiteit te Amsterdam, 1990.

[Mid93] A. Middeldorp. Modular properties of conditional term rewriting systems. *Information and Computation*, 104(1):110–58, 1993.

[Mid94a] A. Middeldorp. Completeness of combinations of conditional constructor systems. *Journal of Symbolic Computation*, 17:3–21, 1994.

[Mid94b] A. Middeldorp. A simple proof to a result of Bernhard Gramlich, 1994. Presented at the 5th Japanese Term Rewriting Meeting, Tsukuba, February 3–4.

[MM82] A. Martelli and U. Montanari. An efficient unification algorithm. *Transactions on Programming Languages and Systems*, 4(2):258–82, 1982.

[MN70] Z. Manna and S. Ness. On the termination of Markov algorithms. In *Proceedings of the 3rd Hawaii International Conference on System Science*, pages 789–92, 1970.

[MO00] A. Middeldorp and H. Ohsaki. Type introduction for equational rewriting. *Acta Informatica*, 36(12):1007–29, 2000.

[MOZ96] A. Middeldorp, H. Ohsaki, and H. Zantema. Transforming termination by self-labelling. In *Proceedings of the 13th International Conference on Automated Deduction*, volume 1104 of *Lecture Notes in Artificial Intelligence*, pages 373–87, Springer-Verlag, Berlin, 1996.

[MS96] Y. Matiyasevich and G. Senizergues. Decision problems for semi-Thue systems with a few rules. In *Proceedings of the 11th IEEE Annual Symposium on Logic in Computer Science*, pages 523–31, 1996.

[MT93] A. Middeldorp and Y. Toyama. Completeness of combinations of constructor systems. *Journal of Symbolic Computation*, 15(3):331–48, 1993.

[MZ97] A. Middeldorp and H. Zantema. Simple termination of rewrite systems. *Theoretical Computer Science*, 175(1):127–58, 1997.

[New42] M.H.A. Newman. On theories with a combinatorial definition of equivalence. *Annals of Mathematics*, 43(2):223–43, 1942.

[NT99] T. Nagaya and Y. Toyama. Decidability for left-linear growing term rewriting systems. In *Proceedings of the 10th International Conference on Rewriting Techniques and Applications*, volume 1631 of *Lecture Notes in Computer Science*, pages 256–70, Springer-Verlag, Berlin, 1999.

[NW63] C.St.J.A. Nash-Williams. On well-quasi-ordering finite trees. *Proceedings of the Cambridge Philosophical Society*, 59:833–5, 1963.

[OCM00] E. Ohlebusch, C. Claves, and C. Marché. TALP: A tool for the termination analysis of logic programs. In *Proceedings of the 11th International Conference on Rewriting Techniques and Applications*, volume 1833 of *Lecture Notes in Computer Science*, pages 270–3, Springer-Verlag, Berlin, 2000. System available at `http://bibiserv.techfak.uni-bielefeld.de/talp/`.

[O'D77] M.J. O'Donnell. *Computing in Systems Described by Equations*, volume 58 of *Lecture Notes in Computer Science*. Springer-Verlag, Berlin, 1977.

[Ohl92] E. Ohlebusch. A note on simple termination of infinite term rewriting systems. *Report Nr. 7*, Technische Fakultät, Universität Bielefeld, 1992.

[Ohl93a] E. Ohlebusch. Combinations of simplifying conditional term rewriting systems. In *Proceedings of the 3rd International Workshop on Conditional Term Rewriting Systems*, volume 656 of *Lecture Notes in Computer Science*, pages 113–27, Springer-Verlag, Berlin, 1993.

[Ohl93b] E. Ohlebusch. A simple proof of sufficient conditions for the termination of the disjoint union of term rewriting systems. *Bulletin of the European Association for Theoretical Computer Science*, 49:178–83, 1993.

[Ohl94a] E. Ohlebusch. *Modular Properties of Composable Term Rewriting Systems.* Ph.D. thesis, Universität Bielefeld, 1994.

[Ohl94b] E. Ohlebusch. On the modularity of confluence of constructor-sharing term rewriting systems. In *Proceedings of the 19th Colloquium on Trees in Algebra and Programming*, volume 787 of *Lecture Notes in Computer Science*, pages 261–75, Springer-Verlag, Berlin, 1994.

[Ohl94c] E. Ohlebusch. On the modularity of termination of term rewriting systems. *Theoretical Computer Science*, 136:333–60, 1994.

[Ohl95a] E. Ohlebusch. Modular properties of composable term rewriting systems. *Journal of Symbolic Computation*, 20:1–41, 1995.

[Ohl95b] E. Ohlebusch. Modular properties of constructor-sharing conditional term rewriting systems. In *Proceedings of the 4th International Workshop on Conditional and Typed Rewriting Systems*, volume 968 of *Lecture Notes in Computer Science*, pages 296–315, Springer-Verlag, Berlin, 1995.

[Ohl95c] E. Ohlebusch. Termination is not modular for confluent variable-preserving term rewriting systems. *Information Processing Letters*, 53:223–8, 1995.

[Ohl98a] E. Ohlebusch. Church-Rosser theorems for abstract reduction modulo an equivalence relation. In *Proceedings of the 9th International Conference on Rewriting Techniques and Applications*, volume 1379 of *Lecture Notes in Computer Science*, pages 17–31, Springer-Verlag, Berlin, 1998.

[Ohl98b] E. Ohlebusch. Modularity of termination for disjoint term graph rewrite systems: A simple proof. *Bulletin of the European Association for Theoretical Computer Science*, 66:171–7, 1998.

[Ohl99a] E. Ohlebusch. On quasi-reductive and quasi-simplifying deterministic conditional rewrite systems. In *Proceedings of the 4th International Symposium on Functional and Logic Programming*, volume 1722 of *Lecture Notes in Computer Science*, pages 179–93, Springer-Verlag, Berlin, 1999.

[Ohl99b] E. Ohlebusch. Transforming conditional rewrite systems with extra variables into unconditional systems. In *Proceedings of the 6th International Conference on Logic for Pro-*

gramming and Automated Reasoning, volume 1705 of *Lecture Notes in Artificial Intelligence*, pages 111–30, Springer-Verlag, Berlin, 1999.

[Ohl00] E. Ohlebusch. A uniform framework for term and graph rewriting applied to combined systems. *Information Processing Letters*, 73:53–9, 2000.

[Ohl01a] E. Ohlebusch. Implementing conditional term rewriting by graph rewriting. *Theoretical Computer Science*, 262:311–31, 2001.

[Ohl01b] E. Ohlebusch. Termination of logic programs: Transformational methods revisited. *Applicable Algebra in Engineering, Communication and Computing*, 12:73–116, 2001.

[Ohl02] E. Ohlebusch. Hierarchical termination revisited. *Information Processing Letters*, 2002, to appear.

[Oos94] V. van Oostrom. Confluence by decreasing diagrams. *Theoretical Computer Science*, 126(2):259–80, 1994.

[PJ87] S.L. Peyton Jones. *The Implementation of Functional Programming Languages*. Prentice Hall, 1987.

[Pla85] D. Plaisted. The undecidability of self-embedding for term rewriting systems. *Information Processing Letters*, 20:61–4, 1985.

[Pla93] D. Plaisted. Equational reasoning and term rewriting systems. In D.M. Gabbay, C.J. Hogger, and J.A. Robinson, editors, *Handbook of Logic in Artificial Intelligence and Logic Programming*, volume 1, pages 274–367. Oxford University Press, 1993.

[Plü90] L. Plümer. *Termination Proofs for Logic Programs*, volume 446 of *Lecture Notes in Artificial Intelligence*. Springer-Verlag, Berlin, 1990.

[Plu91] D. Plump. Implementing term rewriting by graph reduction: Termination of combined systems. In *Proceedings of the 2nd International Workshop on Conditional and Typed Rewriting Systems*, volume 516 of *Lecture Notes in Computer Science*, pages 307–17, Springer-Verlag, Berlin, 1991.

[Plu93] D. Plump. Collapsed tree rewriting: Completeness, confluence, and modularity. In *Proceedings of the 3rd International Workshop on Conditional Term Rewriting Systems*, volume 656 of *Lecture Notes in Computer Science*, pages 97–112, Springer-Verlag, Berlin, 1993.

[Plu99] D. Plump. Term graph rewriting. In H. Ehrig, G. Engels, H.-J. Kreowski, and G. Rozenberg, editors, *Handbook of Graph Grammars and Computing by Graph Transformation*, World Scientific, 1999, volume 2, chapter 1, pages 3–61.

[Pol92] J. van de Pol. Modularity in many-sorted term rewriting systems. Master's thesis, Utrecht University, 1992.

[Pos46] E. Post. A variant of a recursively unsolvable problem. *Bulletin of the American Mathematical Society*, 52:264–68, 1946.

[PPE94] R. Pino Pérez and Ch. Even. An abstract property of confluence applied to the study of the lazy partial lambda calculus. In *Proceedings of the 3rd International Symposium on Logical Foundations of Computer Science*, volume 813 of *Lecture Notes in Computer Science*, pages 278–90, Springer-Verlag, Berlin, 1994.

[Pre94] Ch. Prehofer. On modularity in term rewriting and narrowing. In *Proceedings of the 1st International Workshop on Constraints in Computational Logics*, volume 845 of *Lecture Notes in Computer Science*, pages 253–68, Springer-Verlag, Berlin, 1994.

[Pue89] L. Puel. Using unavoidable sets of trees to generalize Kruskal's theorem. *Journal of Symbolic Computation*, 8:335–82, 1989.

[Raa97] F. van Raamsdonk. Translating logic programs into conditional rewriting systems. In *Proceedings of the 14th International Conference on Logic Programming*, pages 168–82. MIT Press, 1997.

[Rob65] J.A. Robinson. A machine-oriented logic based on the resolution principle. *Journal of the ACM*, 12(1):23–41, 1965.

[Ros73] B.K. Rosen. Tree-manipulating systems and Church-Rosser theorems. *Journal of the ACM*, 20(1):160–87, 1973.

[Ros82] J. Rosenstein. *Linear Orderings*. Academic Press, 1982.

[Rub95] A. Rubio. Extension orderings. In *Proceedings of the 22nd International Colloquium on Automata, Languages and Programming*, volume 944 of *Lecture Notes in Computer Science*, pages 511–22, Springer-Verlag, Berlin, 1995.

[Rus87a] M. Rusinowitch. On termination of the direct sum of term rewriting systems. *Information Processing Letters*, 26:65–70, 1987.

[Rus87b] M. Rusinowitch. Path of subterms ordering and recursive decomposition ordering revisited. *Journal of Symbolic Computation*, 3:117–31, 1987.

[RV80] J.-C. Raoult and J. Vuillemin. Operational and semantic equivalence between recursive programs. *Journal of the ACM*, 27(4):772–96, 1980.

[Sal91] K. Salomaa. Decidability of confluence and termination of monadic term rewriting systems. In *Proceedings of the 4th International Conference on Rewriting Techniques and Applications*, volume 488 of *Lecture Notes in Computer Science*, pages 264–74, Springer-Verlag, Berlin, 1991.

[Sch24] M. Schönfinkel. Über die Bausteine der mathematischen Logik. *Mathematische Annalen*, 92:305–16, 1924.

[Sch97] U. Schöning. *Theoretische Informatik—kurzgefaßt*, 3rd edition, Spektrum Akademischer Verlag, 1997.

[SD94] D. De Schreye and S. Decorte. Termination of logic programs: The never-ending story. *The Journal of Logic Programming*, 19&20:199–260, 1994.

[SMI95] T. Suzuki, A. Middeldorp, and T. Ida. Level-confluence of conditional rewrite systems with extra variables in right-hand sides. In *Proceedings of the 6th International Conference on Rewriting Techniques and Applications*, volume 914 of *Lecture Notes in Computer Science*, pages 179–93, Springer-Verlag, Berlin, 1995.

[SS89] M. Schmidt-Schauß. Unification in a combination of arbitrary disjoint equational theories. *Journal of Symbolic Computation*, 8:51–99, 1989.

[SSMP95] M. Schmidt-Schauß, M. Marchiori, and S.-E. Panitz. Modular termination of r-consistent and left-linear term rewriting systems. *Theoretical Computer Science*, 149(2):361–74, 1995.

[SSS97] C. Speirs, Z. Somogyi, and H. Søndergaard. Termination analysis for Mercury. In *Proceedings of the 4th International Symposium on Static Analysis*, volume 1302 of *Lecture Notes in Computer Science*, pages 157–71, Springer-Verlag, Berlin, 1997. The Mercury system is available from `http://www.cs.mu.oz.au/research/mercury`.

[Sta75] J. Staples. Church-Rosser theorems for replacement systems. In J. Crosley, editor, *Algebra and Logic*, volume 450 of *Lecture Notes in Mathematics*, pages 291–307. Springer-Verlag, Berlin, 1975.

[Sta80] J. Staples. Computation on graph-like expressions. *Theoretical Computer Science*, 10:171–85, 1980.

[Ste95] J. Steinbach. Simplification orderings: History of results. *Fundamenta Informaticae*, 24:47–88, 1995.

[TKB89] Y. Toyama, J.W. Klop, and H.P. Barendregt. Termination for the direct sum of left-linear term rewriting systems. In *Proceedings of the 3rd International Conference on Rewriting Techniques and Applications*, volume 355 of *Lecture Notes in Computer Science*, pages 477–91, Springer-Verlag, Berlin, 1989.

[TKB95] Y. Toyama, J.W. Klop, and H.P. Barendregt. Termination for direct sums of left-linear complete term rewriting systems. *Journal of the ACM*, 42(6):1275–1304, 1995. A preliminary version appeared in [TKB89].

[Toy87a] Y. Toyama. Counterexamples to termination for the direct sum of term rewriting systems. *Information Processing Letters*, 25:141–3, 1987.

[Toy87b] Y. Toyama. On the Church-Rosser property for the direct sum of term rewriting systems. *Journal of the ACM*, 34(1):128–43, 1987.

[Tur79] D.A. Turner. A new implementation technique for applicative languages. *Software Practice and Experience*, 9:31–49, 1979.

[Urb01] X. Urbain. Automated incremental termination proofs for hierarchically defined term rewriting systems. In *Proceedings of the International Joint Conference on Automated Reasoning*, volume 2083 of *Lecture Notes in Artificial Intelligence*, pages 485–99, Springer-Verlag, Berlin, 2001.

[Wal94] C. Walther. On proving the termination of algorithms by machine. *Artificial Intelligence*, 71:101–57, 1994.

[Yam01] T. Yamada. Confluence and termination of simply typed term rewriting systems. In *Proceedings of the 12th International Conference on Rewriting Techniques and Applications*, volume 2051 of *Lecture Notes in Computer Science*, pages 338–52, Springer-Verlag, Berlin, 2001.

[Zan94] H. Zantema. Termination of term rewriting: Interpretation and type elimination. *Journal of Symbolic Computation*, 17:23–50, 1994.

[Zan95a] H. Zantema. Termination of term rewriting by semantic labelling. *Fundamenta Informaticae*, 24:89–105, 1995.

[Zan95b] H. Zantema. Total termination of term rewriting is undecidable. *Journal of Symbolic Computation*, 20:43–60, 1995.

[Zan00] H. Zantema. Termination of term rewriting. *Report UU-CS-2000-04*, Utrecht University, 2000.

[Zan01] H. Zantema. The termination hierarchy for term rewriting. *Applicable Algebra in Engineering, Communication and Computing*, 12:3–19, 2001.

[ZG96] H. Zantema and A. Geser. Non-looping rewriting. *Technical Report UU-CS-1996-03*, Utrecht University, 1996.

Index